Praise for Walter Stahr's *Sewa*  S0-AYU-697

Winner of the William H. Seward Book Award
Winner of the Henry Adams Prize
History News Network's Best Books of 2012
Seattle Times Best Books of 2012

"[A] masterly new biography . . . [of] one of the most influential and polarizing American politicians of the nineteenth century."

—*The New Yorker*

"This magnificent biography finally provides what William Henry Seward so justly deserves—a full, terrific and complex portrait of his endlessly fascinating life."

—Doris Kearns Goodwin, author of *Team of Rivals*

"Walter Stahr's new biography offers an overdue reminder of the much broader scope of [Seward's] work."

—*The Economist*

"This highly readable biography, based on thorough research in original sources, effectively shows that Seward deserves more fame as a patriot-statesman than he has traditionally enjoyed."

—Michael Burlingame, *The Wall Street Journal*

"Writing like [this] makes history come alive: a researcher digging into the mines of the past and quarrying new insight on an old story. *Seward: Lincoln's Indispensable Man* is filled with . . . stories powerfully told by a historian who has provided a great book worthy of a great man."

—*The Dallas Morning News*

"In this fine volume, Walter Stahr has rendered a signal service by resurrecting the life of the often neglected William Henry Seward. His sweeping portrait of the long-standing secretary of state is always lucid, engaging, scrupulously fair-minded, and deeply researched. This biography stands as a valuable addition to the rich literature of American politics in the mid-nineteenth century."

—Ron Chernow, author of *Washington: A Life*

"Stahr gives Seward his due in this intelligent and illuminating biography of one of the most important political figures of the 19th century. . . . He wasn't just Lincoln's indispensable man; throughout his career Seward was an indispensable man to the nation as well."

Huffington Post

"In this first major biography of Seward in more than 40 years, Stahr dutifully chronicles his rise from young provincial lawyer to chief diplomat of a rended nation."

—The New York Times Book Review

"An intriguing featured character in Lincoln lore and biography, William H. Seward has long needed an updated, authoritative biography—and Walter Stahr has at last produced the life story Seward deserves. Mining neglected sources and bringing analytical wisdom and literary craft to Seward's complicated life, Stahr reveals the principled humanity within a political giant too long considered merely a crafty, frustrated office-seeker. Seward emerges from these pages as a major influence—not only on Abraham Lincoln, but on the transformation of 19th-century America."

—Harold Holzer, author of *Lincoln at Cooper Union* and
Lincoln President-Elect

"After a rocky start during which Seward crossed swords with Lincoln in the issue of Fort Sumter and other matters, the secretary of state did indeed become the president's most indispensable ally. Politician, diplomat, raconteur, a figure of controversy and power, Seward has finally found a biographer equal to his importance."

—James M. McPherson, author of *Battle Cry of Freedom: The Civil War Era*

"A close acquaintance of Seward once said that he was 'kind, genial, approachable and humorous—full of good points, diplomatic to a fault.' So too is this biography."

—Washington Independent Review of Books

"This formidable figure has finally gained the biographer he's long deserved . . . a first-rate biography."

—Publishers Weekly, starred review

"Walter Stahr's highly readable account, the first in over 40 years, shows why Seward is ranked by most historians, along with John Quincy Adams, as America's greatest and most influential secretary of state."

—David Roll, *The Wall Street Journal*

"Walter Stahr sets the record straight in his compelling *Seward: Lincoln's Indispensable Man*, arguing convincingly that 'other than presidents, Seward was the foremost American statesman of the nineteenth century.' . . . Stahr presents a detailed but crisp narrative."

—USA Today

"*Seward* is a fascinating biography about one of the most elusive men in history. Seward once claimed that he was an enigma even to himself; fortunately, he is not an enigma to Walter Stahr, who has succeeded admirably in capturing the full complexity of President Lincoln's right hand man. Stahr has written an important and necessary book."

—Amanda Foreman, author of *World on Fire: Britain's Crucial Role in the American Civil War*

"A beautifully told, carefully researched narrative of William H. Seward's momentous career, from his days as a rising young antislavery politician to his role as Lincoln's right-hand man during the Civil War, culminating in his achievements as architect of American empire. Walter Stahr has delivered a biography worthy of one of America's greatest statesmen."

—Daniel Walker Howe, author of *What Hath God Wrought: The Transformation of America, 1815–1848*

"This monumental biography of Lincoln's secretary of state is impeccably researched and written in an engaging manner that keeps the pages turning easily."

—*Seattle Times*

"*Seward* is the first full biography of William Seward in more than 40 years and is packed with fresh insight into Lincoln's secretary of state and closest Civil War adviser."

—*The Oregonian*

"A complex man, often engulfed in controversy before, during and after the Civil War, William H. Seward is one of those rare American politicians who made a significant difference in the history of his time. Walter Stahr has reminded us of his importance in this superbly written book."

—Thomas Fleming, author of *The Intimate Lives of the Founding Fathers*

"A worthy tribute to one of the most important political figures of the nineteenth century."

—*Booklist*

"A thorough, refreshing biography by an independent-minded historian."

—*Kirkus Reviews*

"Stahr completes Seward's life and demonstrates his enormous impact on American history before, during, and long after the 1860's."

Library Journal

ALSO BY WALTER STAHR

John Jay: Founding Father

SEWARD

LINCOLN'S INDISPENSABLE MAN

WALTER STAHR

SIMON & SCHUSTER PAPERBACKS
New York   London   Toronto   Sydney   New Delhi

For Masami

Simon & Schuster Paperbacks
A Division of Simon & Schuster, Inc.
1230 Avenue of the Americas
New York, NY 10020

Copyright © 2012 by Walter Stahr

All rights reserved, including the right to reproduce this book or
portions thereof in any form whatsoever. For information address
Simon & Schuster Subsidiary Rights Department,
1230 Avenue of the Americas, New York, NY 10020.

First Simon & Schuster paperback edition September 2013

SIMON & SCHUSTER PAPERBACKS and colophon are
registered trademarks of Simon & Schuster, Inc.

For information about special discounts for bulk purchases,
please contact Simon & Schuster Special Sales at
1-866-506-1949 or business@simonandschuster.com.

The Simon & Schuster Speakers Bureau can bring authors
to your live event. For more information or to book an event,
contact the Simon & Schuster Speakers Bureau at
1-866-248-3049 or visit our website at www.simonspeakers.com.

Designed by Joy O'Meara

Manufactured in the United States of America

10   9   8   7   6   5   4   3   2   1

The Library of Congress has cataloged the hardcover edition as follows:

Stahr, Walter.
    Seward : Lincoln's indispensable man / by Walter Stahr. —
1st Simon & Schuster hardcover ed.
        p.   cm.
    Includes bibliographical references and index.
1. Seward, William Henry, 1801–1872.   2. Cabinet officers—United States—
Biography.   3. Statesmen—United States—Biography.   4. United States.
Dept. of State—Biography.   5. United States—Foreign relations—1861–1865.
6. United States—Politics and government—1861–1865.   I. Title.
    E415.9.S4S73 2012
    973.7092—dc23
    [B]   2011052984

ISBN 978-1-4391-2116-0
ISBN 978-1-4391-2118-4 (pbk)
ISBN 978-1-4391-2794-0 (ebook)

CONTENTS

MAP LIST AND
ILLUSTRATION CREDITS

All illustrations are from the Library of Congress except illustration 1, National Archives; and illustrations 2, 3, 4, 24, 28, 29, 30, 32, 33, and 36, Seward House, Auburn.

SEWARD

INTRODUCTION

Outside the Lafayette Square home of Secretary of State William Henry Seward, in the shadows of an early spring evening in Washington, two assassins watched and waited, their horses and weapons at hand. Lewis Powell and David Herold knew from the local papers that the aged secretary was confined to his bed by severe injuries he had suffered a few days earlier in a driving accident. So they realized that although Powell, the tall, strong southern veteran set to enter the house and kill the secretary, might have some difficulties in finding and reaching his victim, once he found him, Seward would not fight back. Herold and Powell were part of the team assembled by the actor John Wilkes Booth in order to kill, on one night and at one time, President Abraham Lincoln, Vice President Andrew Johnson, and Secretary Seward. Booth himself was a few blocks away at Ford's Theater, about to enter Lincoln's box to shoot and kill the president.[1]

At around ten o'clock, Powell handed Herold his reins, ascended the steps, and knocked on Seward's door. Powell explained to the young black servant, William Bell, that he was a messenger from Seward's doctor bringing medicine for Seward; he pointed to a small package that Booth had provided him as a prop. Bell offered to take the package, but Powell refused, saying the doctor had asked Powell to bring the medicine to Seward himself. Powell and Bell bickered for a minute or two, and then Powell started upstairs, with Bell behind, urging him not to make so much noise.[2]

At the top of the stairs Powell met Seward's son Frederick, and there was a similar conversation, with Frederick saying he would accept the package and Powell insisting he had to deliver it personally. Seward's daughter Fanny, who along with a male nurse, George Robinson, was with Seward in his room, thought that someone, perhaps even the president, had come to see her father. She opened the door and whispered to her brother that their father was awake. Fred scowled; Fanny recalled that "something in Fred's manner led me at once to think that he did not wish me to say so, and that I had better not have opened the door." Powell asked her abruptly: "Is the Secretary asleep?" She glanced back into the room and replied: "Almost." Frederick or Fanny closed the door, but now Powell knew where to find his victim.

After a few more words with Frederick, Powell pretended to give up and turned to go down the stairs. Then, as Frederick later wrote, Powell turned again, "sprang up and forward, having drawn a navy revolver, which he levelled, with a muttered oath, at my head, and pulled the trigger." The gun misfired, but Powell used it as a club to hit Frederick savagely on the head, breaking the gun and nearly killing Frederick.

Fanny, hearing the noise in the hall, and thinking that the servants might be chasing a rat, asked Robinson to go to the door and check. She went to the door as well. As soon as Robinson opened the door, Powell charged into the bedroom, pistol in one hand, Bowie knife in the other. Robinson grabbed at him, but Powell slashed Robinson with the knife and shoved him to the floor. Fanny screamed and her father woke with a start. Seward later said that he "knew the man sought his life, [but] still he feared for Fanny and, with great effort, rose up in his bed to interpose his shattered frame as a protection." Powell was upon Seward in an instant, pressing him down into the bed with one arm, raising the knife with the other, and stabbing down with all his force. Perhaps because of the dim light, perhaps because Seward was on the far side of the bed to protect his broken arm, Powell's first blow missed. But he stabbed again and again, cutting Seward's face and neck with long bloody slashes.

George Robinson now tackled Powell from behind; this may have pushed Seward off the bed, or he may have rolled to escape the assassin's knife blows. Fanny's screams brought her brother Augustus, who had been asleep in a nearby room, and he joined Robinson in the struggle. The two wrestled Powell away from Seward's bed and into the hall, both suffering severe cuts. In the hall, Powell, who had been silent throughout this fight, looked into Augustus's eyes and said, "I'm mad, I'm mad." With that, he fled down the stairs and out of the house. Fanny rushed back to her father's bed but he was not there. At the side of the bed she saw what she first thought was "a pile of bed clothes." Then she realized that this bloody mess was her father, and she ran to his side, screaming, "Oh my God! Father's dead!"[3]

———

Who was William Henry Seward? Why was he a target for Booth and other assassins? Born in rural New York in 1801, educated as a lawyer, Seward served four years in the state senate and four years as governor of New York. As governor, Seward was known for his progressive policies: improving the state's transportation system, extending public education to the children of immigrants, and defending the rights of slaves and free blacks. After he was elected to the U.S. Senate in 1849, he established himself as the leading opponent of the extension of slavery, declaring that a "higher law than the Constitution" dedicated the national territories to freedom. Seward was not an abolitionist—he favored a gradual and voluntary end of slavery rather than immediate abolition—but he was prepared to take risks for freedom, such as sheltering fugitive slaves in his Auburn home.

Seward was an early member of the Republican Party and almost received the party's first presidential nomination. In late 1859 and early 1860, it seemed all but certain that he would be the Republican nominee and likely that he would be elected president. But after the surprising nomination of Lincoln, he mastered his disappointment and campaigned for his rival throughout the North, doing more to secure Lincoln's election than any other man. Soon after the election, Lincoln offered and Seward accepted the most prominent and powerful position in the cabinet: secretary of state. Seward was the central figure in the drama of the so-called secession winter, working with men from all sections toward an elusive compromise. Once the Civil War started, he skillfully managed the nation's foreign affairs, avoiding the foreign intervention that would have ensured that the Confederacy would become a separate nation. Seward's role was not limited to foreign policy: he was involved in almost every aspect of the war, an indispensable friend and adviser to Lincoln, who more than once refused to part with his controversial secretary.

Many viewed Seward as the real power in the administration. During the first months of the war, he was responsible for domestic security, and he was quoted as boasting that he could arrange any man's arrest just by ringing a little bell. In late 1862, when almost all the Republican senators urged Lincoln to remove Seward, one of their main charges was that he rather than the president set policy. William Lloyd Garrison, the abolitionist editor, argued in his paper that if voters gave Lincoln a second term, they would just be electing "Seward to be again acting president." John Wilkes Booth, who disagreed with Garrison on almost every issue, agreed with him about Seward, telling his sister Asia Booth Clark that "other brains [than Lincoln] rule the country."[4]

Booth was a Shakespearean actor, the black sheep in a famous family of actors, and one of the plays he knew best was *Julius Caesar*. Booth viewed Lincoln as a tyrant like Caesar, and saw Seward as a co-tyrant like Marc Antony. Brutus killed Caesar, but failed in his attempt to restore the republic, because he failed to kill Antony. Booth was determined that his version of the play would have a different ending: that he would kill both tyrants, Lincoln and Seward.[5]

Seward survived Powell's knife, and the death of his friend and leader Lincoln, and the death soon thereafter of his own wife, who was shocked by the murderous attacks and drained by the family's nursing efforts. Seward not only lived; he continued to serve as America's secretary of state for another four years, negotiating the purchase of Alaska and securing its approval by a reluctant Congress, the accomplishment for which he is best known, and of which he was justifiably most proud. It was also during this period that Seward laid the foundation for the United States to become not merely a continental power but an international empire, working to acquire critical territory such as Panama and Hawaii. After his retirement, and in spite of his weak physical condition, he traveled to Alaska and around the world, before his death in late 1872.

William Henry Seward was a major figure in American history, generally ranked as the second greatest secretary of state, behind only his friend and mentor John Quincy Adams. Another way to measure his stature is to note that, among the northern civilian leaders in the Civil War, Seward was more influential than any man other than Lincoln. Many nineteenth-century presidents are nearly forgotten, and rightly so, because they did little during their time in office. Seward can never be forgotten, because of the mark he made on the shape of the nation, in Alaska and in other respects.

Seward was not only important: he was fascinating. He was a well-educated and sophisticated diplomat; but his hair was unruly, his clothes untidy, and his manner casual. Charles Francis Adams, Jr., who knew him well, once described him as "small, rusty in aspect, dressed in a coat and trousers apparently made twenty years ago, and by a bad tailor at that." More than most men, Seward was capable of contradiction. During the 1840s, he argued in a famous murder trial that the white jurors should view the black defendant as their brother, and treat him as if he were white, for he was like them made in "the image of our Maker." And yet after the war, as southern whites were persecuting and even murdering southern blacks, Seward reportedly said that "the North has nothing to do with the [southern] Negroes," that he himself had "no more concern for them than I have for the Hottentots." He was a famous host, gathering diplomats, soldiers, politicians, actors, and their wives around his Washington table for fine food and wine. But he was also very private, rarely revealing his inner views. With Seward, in the words of Henry Adams, who also knew him well, "the political had become personal," so that "no one could tell which was the mask and which the features."[6]

Most Americans know Seward's name and that Alaska was "Seward's folly," but they do not know much else about him. It has been a long time, more than forty years, since there was a serious full-length biography of the man. This book has a simple aim: to bring to life for a new generation one of the great Americans of the Civil War generation.

CHAPTER 1

"Elements of a Statesman":

1801–1830

William Henry Seward was born on May 16, 1801, in rural New York, about sixty miles northwest of New York City. His father, Samuel Swezy Seward, was the leading man of the village of Florida: physician, merchant, farmer, financier, church trustee, legislator, and judge. In politics, Samuel Seward supported the Jeffersonian Republicans, and Jefferson rewarded him by appointing him village postmaster, a position he held, while pursuing his other careers, for thirty years. Even through the generous light of his son's memoir, it is clear that Samuel was a harsh father. Seward recalled how his father "placed me on the counter of the store, and directed me to recite a poetical address, which I had committed to memory, before an audience of admiring neighbors." As the applause died down, someone asked the boy which of his father's many callings he would pursue. When he answered that he would like to be a magistrate, his father rebuked him for his presumption: magistrates were chosen by the people, not by themselves. Perhaps because her husband was harsh, Mary Jennings Seward was kind; Seward recalled his mother as a "model of hospitality, charity, and self-forgetfulness." Seward remembered his maternal grandmother, Margaret Jackson Jennings, as being "of Irish descent," but with a strong "antipathy toward the Roman Catholic religion." Recent research suggests that Seward had no Irish ancestry, but he *believed* that he did, and this belief would color his attitudes toward the Irish and the Catholics for life.[1]

When Seward was born in 1801, he was the third child in the family, with two older brothers, Benjamin Jennings and Edwin Polydore. The boys were known by their middle names: Jennings, Polydore, and Henry. Two more children would follow: Louisa Cornelia and George Washington. In addition to the parents and children, the household included slaves, seven at the time of the 1820 census. Seward remembered that he spent much of his boyhood with the slaves, who "were vivacious and loquacious." The family was not unusual in owning slaves; the state legislature had passed a law in 1799 to end slavery over time, but the law did not affect the status of slaves born before that date. The Sewards were unusual, however, in their attitude toward their slaves. Seward's father was the only man in the village who allowed the children of his slaves to attend school, and Seward recalled that his parents "never uttered an expression that could tend to make me think that the negro was inferior to the white person."[2]

The house in which Seward was born was a modest one, with five rooms on the main floor and a few more upstairs. At some point in his youth, the family moved across the street to a somewhat larger house, known as the Seward mansion. The village as Seward remembered it had "not more than a dozen dwellings," set in a "sweet little valley." The only substantial building in town was the Presbyterian church, of which Henry's father was a trustee, and which the family presumably attended regularly. Although Samuel Seward served in the New York legislature for only a few years, he was always involved in local and state politics, and Henry Seward must have heard many political debates around the kitchen table. Seward recalled that in addition to his schoolwork he had many chores, including driving cattle to distant pastures and chopping wood for the parlor fire.[3]

The village in which Seward grew up was in many ways typical of the United States of this period. Almost all Americans lived in rural settings, for there were only thirty-three towns in 1800 with more than 2,500 people. The population of the county in which Florida was located, Orange County, was growing rapidly, like most counties of the nation. The region had an agricultural economy, but one that was increasingly tied with the broader commercial and manufacturing economy. Steamboat service started on the Hudson River in 1807, and Newburgh, about twenty miles east of Florida, prospered as a steamboat stop. New York City itself was only a two-day ride south of the village, so the residents could and did travel to the city for services.[4]

Henry Seward was a bright young boy, eager for school and books. Indeed, in later years one of the former slaves would tell visitors that "unlike most little boys of the village, instead of running away from school to go home, Henry would frequently run away from home to go to school." Seward recalled how he started at the bottom of the spelling class, which included many older students, and soon worked his way to the top. Henry was apparently the sort of precocious boy who annoys other children. He was also somewhat superstitious. He was not yet five when he was at the schoolhouse on the date of the 1806 solar eclipse. The boy recalled that the schoolroom became suddenly dark, and he expected to see ghosts emerge and "make short work of us all." He fled for home, crying loudly.[5]

At the age of nine, Henry was sent to Farmers' Hall Academy, a boarding school in nearby Goshen. The boy initially found the work hard—his rural school had not prepared him well in Latin—but he soon prospered. When a new and better school was formed in Florida, he returned home for two years, then went back to Goshen for a few months of final preparation for college. One of his notebooks from this period survives, complete with his fine illustrations of trigonometry problems, in one of which he added a man on top of the courthouse, proudly waving an American flag.[6]

————

In September 1816, at the age of fifteen, Henry Seward left home to attend Union College, the only member of his family to have the honor and responsibility of college. Seward still recalled fifty years later the Hudson River steamboat—"a prodigy of power"—on which he traveled the hundred miles from Newburgh to Albany, and his first sight of the state capital—"so vast, so splendid, so imposing." When he arrived in Schenectady, a town of about 3,000 inhabitants not far northwest

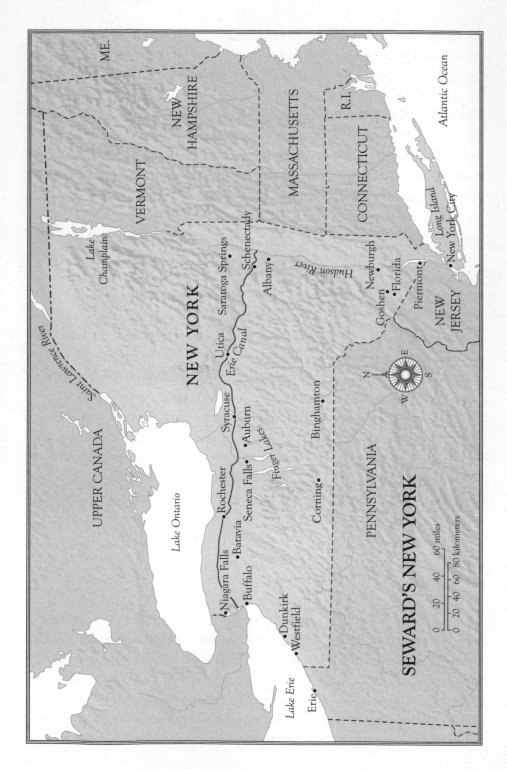

SEWARD'S NEW YORK

of Albany, he "climbed the College Hill with a reluctant and embarrassed step," for he feared he might not pass the entrance examination. Professor Thomas McAuley "asked me what books I had studied and examined me, gave me the name of an excellent scholar." McAuley introduced Seward to the Reverend Eliphalet Nott, the college president, who spoke with him "like a parent," and "finally settled me in the sophomore [class] in as good standing as any of the students." He described these details in letters to his own "revered parent," which he signed "your ever dutiful son."[7]

Seward's letters from college show that he worked hard yet also enjoyed himself. He studied the usual subjects—classics, mathematics, and science—but he devoted himself especially to the debates of the Adelphic Society. There were no women, fraternities, or organized athletics at colleges at this time, so student life centered on such literary societies. Even before he arrived on campus, Seward was getting advice as to which of the two rival societies he should join; he recalled the society's debates as the "part of my college education [from which] I derived the greatest advantage." Although Union College was large for the time, with more than two hundred students, it was not so large that the students did not get to know President Nott personally. In one letter to his father, Seward described Nott as a "very able smart good old man Great Orator clever but strict"; in another, he wrote that "I suppose that never was a President of a College more loved and respected than Dr. Nott." In letters to his friends, much less frequent than to his father, Seward related how students attempted to burn down one of the outhouses and exulted in the theft of the bell clapper. He later recalled an incident in which he tried to hide a set of playing cards in his hat but was caught when the hat fell off and cards fell out in the presence of a teacher.[8]

Like that of many students, Seward's attitude toward school was ambivalent. On the one hand, he was ambitious: he wanted to distinguish himself. After a successful first term, Seward asked Nott whether he could move from the sophomore to the junior class. Dr. Nott explained that to change classes now, midway through his college career, would be "contrary both to law and custom." A few months later, when a chapter of Phi Beta Kappa was established at Union College—only the fifth such chapter in the nation—Seward was determined to become one of its early members. He recalled in his memoir that he and his roommate intensified their efforts, rising to study at three in the morning; and in June 1818, at the end of his junior year, Seward was one of a dozen students elected to Phi Beta Kappa. But although he was ambitious, he was also proud and difficult. He wrote his father that "I am resolved never to purchase popularity with the faculty by any cringing, which is very common here. As far as my duty extends I will do, and further I do not esteem the honor of the faculty as worthy of having." The instructors generally called on students in a predictable pattern, but one day Francis Wayland varied this pattern and called upon Seward, who was not prepared. Seward, insisting that Wayland should have given notice of his intent to change the system, stopped attending classes. Dr. Nott summoned him and demanded to know why he was not at school. Seward explained and insisted that Wayland apologize. The president cleverly apologized on Wayland's behalf, and Seward in turn apologized and returned to school.[9]

Seward was apparently quite content when he returned to college in the fall of 1818 to start his senior year. His letters suggest that he was popular with the other students, and that he enjoyed his courses, especially one on criticism from Nott, in which he guided the young men in how to think and argue more carefully and critically. Seward wrote to his father that the Reverend Nott "has introduced us to a new sphere and every observation that drops from his lips confirms his greatness." Seward was getting good grades: he informed his father that he would in all likelihood have the honor of being one of the speakers at commencement at the end of the school year.[10]

While he was at home in December for winter break, however, Seward and his father quarreled about money. The father required his son to account for every penny he spent, and provided him with a meager allowance, so that Seward would often have to write to request a few extra dollars to allow him to travel home. During this particular vacation, before Seward could even suggest an increased allowance, his father anticipated the issue and charged him with "prodigality." Seward returned to college as planned in early January 1819, but later in the month, without notice to his father or the college, he left with a classmate, Alvah Wilson, bound for rural Georgia.[11]

Seward and this friend Wilson first traveled by stage to New York City, then by boat to Savannah, from where Seward wrote a long letter to his father, explaining and justifying his decision to start a new life in a new part of the country. From Savannah, the two young men went on by stage to Augusta, where Wilson found a position as the rector of the Richmond Academy, leaving Seward to continue on his own to Eatonton, a small town in the interior of Georgia, on the frontier of the expanding cotton economy. Arriving there on foot with almost no money left, Seward chanced to meet Dr. Iddo Ellis, a physician, formerly from Auburn, and one of the trustees of a new school, Union Academy. The next day, the trustees met and examined Seward, concluded that he was more than qualified, and hired him, not only as a teacher but as the rector, with duties to start in a few weeks, upon the opening of the school.[12]

In early March 1819, an advertisement appeared for several weeks in one of the main papers of Georgia, announcing that Union Academy would open in Putnam County in April. The rector of the new school would be William H. Seward, "late from Union College, New-York, from which institution he comes highly recommended." Seward would teach "the Latin and Greek languages, theoretical and practical mathematics, logic, rhetoric, natural and moral philosophy, chemistry, geography, English grammar and such other branches as are usually taught in the northern colleges." There were various details regarding tuition and boarding, as well as a note that there would be a "female teacher" to "conduct the female department."[13]

In letters to his family, Seward assured them that he was not (as they feared) living in unhealthy swamps but in the healthy higher lands of the state. Since their letters suggested that his mother and sister were "frantic and despairing," Seward said that he would return to New York. He could not do so immediately, he explained, because his name had been advertised, and he was thus duty-bound to the new school. But he had worked out an arrangement with the trustees: he would write to friends at Union College, find a substitute, and after the substitute was in place he would return to New York. Indeed, he hoped to return in time to take his examinations at Union College and graduate with his class there. Seward signed himself "your regretting and undutiful son."[14]

The Eatonton school opened as scheduled in April. Seward wrote home that there were about seventy scholars, half of whom were girls, under the instruction of the female teacher. He was boarding with Major William Alexander, "a man of respectability [who] contributes every-thing in his power to my ease and happiness." It is possible that Seward, while staying with Alexander, may have slept with one of the slaves. Years later, in early 1866, he received a letter from one Rosetta Alexan-der, who claimed that she had always heard, both from her mother and her former owner Major Alexander, that Seward was her father. Now that slavery was over, she wrote, she was struggling to raise her family, and she asked for Seward's help. If he responded, his response has not survived; nor is there other evidence on this issue.[15]

Seward's substitute arrived in Georgia and satisfied the trustees, so he was able in June to take "leave of my spirited and generous patrons, and affectionate scholars." It proved impossible for him to graduate with his Union College class as he had planned, so he decided to stay in Orange County for six months and return to college in January 1820, to graduate with the next class. He spent the latter part of the year study-ing law with a local attorney and mingling in local society. At least one person was sorry to see him leave: Jane Westcott of Goshen wrote him a long letter after his departure about the "sorrows of my bosom."[16]

———

When Seward returned to Schenectady in January 1820, he settled into his class work, but he also started to pay attention to politics. There were two main factions in New York at this time: the Bucktails, headed by Martin Van Buren, and the Clintonians, headed by Governor DeWitt Clinton, under whose leadership the Erie Canal was under construc-tion. Seward was a Bucktail, and like other Bucktails he opposed Clinton's canal as expensive and impracticable. In a letter to his father, Seward wrote that "the Big Ditch has made so many proselytes here to the Clintonian Creed that it were almost heresy to declare oneself a Madisonian"—a supporter of Madison and Van Buren. In a college de-bate, Seward argued that the Erie Canal "was an impossibility," and that "even if it should be successfully constructed, it would financially ruin the State." It is ironic that Seward, who would become one of the great advocates of canals and other internal improvements, started his political life as an opponent of such projects.[17]

Seward's graduation from college took place in the midst of an intense national debate about the future of the Union. The issue had ignited in early 1819, when James Tallmadge, an upstate New York congressman, insisted that Congress should not admit Missouri as a state unless it passed a law to end slavery there. Southern representatives immediately attacked Tallmadge and his proposal, arguing that it was an improper attempt to limit a legitimate institution and could lead to a sectional division of the Union. Tallmadge responded that "if a dissolution of the Union must take place, let it be so! If civil war, which gentlemen so much threaten, must come, I can only say, let it come!" The House approved Tallmadge's proposal—with almost all northerners voting in favor and almost all southerners voting against—but the Senate did not, and so there was no resolution. Public meetings throughout the North took place over the summer and fall, with speakers arguing against the extension of slavery, and urging their representatives to stand fast against southern threats. In the spring of 1820, in the Missouri Compromise, Congress admitted Missouri as a slave state and Maine as a free state. But for many in the North this compromise did not resolve the issue; they urged Congress to reject the Missouri constitution and to prohibit any extension of slavery.[18]

This national debate had its parallel on the campus of the college. In early 1819, the southern students at Union College seceded from the two long-standing societies and formed their own new society. This may have exacerbated the sectional tension on campus; Seward reported home in early 1820 that "the southern gentlemen are still carrying on their opposition but fortunately our party is united and strong." At the commencement, he later recalled, the graduates from the North and the South sat on opposite sides of the platform, glaring at one another.[19]

On the basis of his class rank, Seward was one of several students selected to speak at commencement, and he worked hard on his remarks. In June, he wrote his father that his draft oration had "received one flattering commendation, from Dr. Nott, having passed through the mill of his criticism without receiving one single alteration." Seward added that he intended to "give it another draft." On the morning of commencement, the students and faculty of the college moved in procession downhill and into town for the services, which by tradition were held at the Dutch Reformed church. Seward argued in his short address that the "American Union will probably be permanent." He admitted that most earlier republics, including Athens and Switzerland, had relatively short lives. The United States, however, was blessed with resources far greater than any of these, including an extensive territory and enterprising people. "A thousand sails" would carry to every corner of the earth "the productions of our garden." [20]

In later life, Seward claimed that he had always been an opponent of slavery, always concerned about a potential division of the Union. There is not a word about these issues in his early speeches or letters, however, except in this commencement address, in which he said that both northern and southern states should work toward "gradual emancipation" of the slaves. Although most northern slaves were now free, the North shared the South's guilt, Seward said, for the North had "assisted oh! too industriously assisted to impose on the Negro Spirit those mountains of oppression under which he now labors." Perhaps thinking of his own time in the South, Seward predicted that internal migration would reduce sectional identities and tensions, so that Americans would soon "worship the same God and revere the same laws whether on the banks of the Hudson or the Mobile or the Missouri." He concluded by saying that Americans were happy, "thrice happy," because "your destiny is in your own hands." The destiny of the nation would indeed often rest in the hands of this young man. [21]

———

After graduation Seward returned to Goshen, where he studied for a year in a local law office. In the fall of 1821, he moved to New York City, where he continued his legal studies and spent much of his time with David Berdan, a fellow graduate of Union College and colleague in the law office. Berdan was not much interested in the law; he wrote to Seward that he longed for a "literary life" that would allow him to "range through the whole garden of knowledge." Together, the two young men explored the city and shared their love of literature and theater. In the spring of 1822, Seward returned to Goshen and joined the law office of Ogden Hoffman, later a member of Congress. Although Seward was not yet a member of the bar, Hoffman allowed him to keep the fees he earned in arguing cases before justices of the peace, and shared with him the fees from their office work. Seward passed the bar examination handily in the fall, missing only one question.[22]

Seward could have remained in Goshen and practiced with Hoffman, but he disliked the place. He later wrote his father that "I have a loathing towards that same Goshen, a disgust which is too violent to be suppressed; a low mean and grovcling race are most of its inhabitants, and it is questionable which is most desired, their love or hate." So he traveled north and west, visiting several towns before deciding upon Auburn, and joining the law practice there of Elijah Miller, a retired judge. Years later, Seward advised a young man that it was best "to settle in a county town, in the county, not in the great cities, and better to settle in a *new* county than in an old one." This explains well why he himself selected Auburn. Both Auburn and Cayuga County, of which it was the county seat, were relatively new and rapidly growing. Auburn was about 150 miles west of Albany, on the turnpike between Albany and the booming western part of the state. Auburn was not on the route of the Erie Canal, which was under construction along an east-west line about fifteen miles to the north. But Seward was not yet a canal enthusiast, so this probably did not matter much to him. Far more important were the many small businesses in and about Auburn, including sawmills, carpenter shops, cabinet makers, flour mills, and cloth factories. Auburn was an eager, expanding, entrepreneurial town, just the place for a young lawyer to start life.[23]

Seward recalled that younger lawyers of this era generally confined themselves to the office and allowed their senior partners to argue in court. He, on the other hand, immediately started to argue his own cases and to have success in court. Like most lawyers of the time, Seward was a generalist; he handled criminal and civil cases, including real estate and commercial matters. The cases may have been small, but as he noted in one letter, they were often "full of very intricate and unheard points." One of his major early cases was the liquidation of

Grover & Gunn, a leading mercantile firm in Auburn. He wrote to his father that the liquidation process was "perplexing and overwhelming. It calls for my attention North, South, East and West. There are so many doubtful debts; so much depends upon care and attention in such cases."[24]

Seward devoted much of his energy in this period to the pursuit and praise of women. In 1822, while he was still in Goshen, his friend Berdan wrote to ask him about the girls he had mentioned: "After the compliments you have paid them in your epistle of last week, are you still inclined to launch into encomiums on their wit beauty and accomplishments? Have you as yet discerned nothing earthly in their composition?" In early 1823, when Seward was just settling into Auburn, Berdan wrote that he was confused by all the women Seward mentioned; he seemed to "have as many deities as people in the good old days had devils."[25]

One reason that Seward chose Auburn was that he knew Frances Miller, the young daughter of Judge Miller. Frances and Seward's sister Cornelia had both attended the nation's most advanced school for women, the Troy Female Seminary, run by Miss Emma Willard, and Cornelia had invited Frances to visit her at home. But during his first few months in Auburn, Seward's main romantic interest was not Frances Miller, but Mary Ann Kellogg, daughter of Daniel Kellogg, a prosperous lawyer in nearby Skaneateles. He wrote home in June 1823 that although he enjoyed the "correspondence of young Kellogg and the extreme politeness of Father and Mother," he was not inclined to propose to her, because her coolness had wounded his pride. The "public report" was that he would marry Frances Miller; but he had "too much regard for her good sense to think of making overtures to her under present circumstances," in which he found himself "reduced to my last shilling and in debt." He proudly claimed to his father that "I have learnt at least one thing—that I will never ask nor demand the hand of any woman until I am ahead of this world as much as I am now behind it."[26]

Within a few weeks, Seward disregarded his own advice and asked Frances Miller to marry him, writing happily to his father that she satisfied his three prerequisites for marriage: a strong attachment, a proper respect, and financial prospects. Elijah Miller was not quite as wealthy as Daniel Kellogg, Seward noted, but he was a widower, with only two daughters, whereas Kellogg had seven children. There was only one problem: Seward had not yet sought the consent of Judge Miller. He arranged for Frances to visit an out-of-town cousin, so that she would not be present for what might prove a difficult discussion. But soon Seward reported to his father that "the question is proposed and answered in the affirmative," and that he was keen to see his father in Auburn and introduce him to "your daughter Frances."[27]

William Henry Seward and Frances Adeline Miller were married in St. Peter's Episcopal Church in Auburn in October 1824. The slim, black-haired Frances stood about an inch or two taller than her slight, red-haired husband, who was only about five feet six. Frances was well educated, in some respects an early feminist, and yet she deeply respected and loved her husband. The most curious aspect of the marriage was that, at Judge Miller's insistence, the young couple moved into the Miller house, where they would remain for decades. It was a large house, set on four beautiful acres, but it was far from empty: it included the judge, his elderly mother, and his sister Clara. Soon the household would include the Sewards' first children: Augustus, born in 1826, and Frederick, born in 1830. Three-generation families were not unusual at the time, but it *was* unusual for a successful young lawyer to live in a household headed by his father-in-law. As one perceptive author has noted, the arrangement allowed Henry to travel for weeks and months, without worrying too much about his wife in her "comfortable house, with the care of servants and the companionship of father, grandmother and aunt." As for Frances, she "made no sharp break from her girlhood to accompany her husband or to adjust to new and different responsibilities." As time passed, Frances would often be ill, confined to her room by headaches and bouts of depression.[28]

Seward remained close to David Berdan, "always writing to me," Berdan wrote to a mutual friend in early 1825, "about the fine women of his acquaintance and exciting my imagining by the glowing pictures of female worth and delicacy that have come under his observation." When Berdan arrived in Auburn a few months later, the two men enjoyed what Berdan described as a "long delightful ride" along the shores of Cayuga Lake, and then Berdan "took a most melancholy leave." It would prove a final leave, for two years later Berdan died. Seward was crushed by Berdan's early death, describing him in a letter to their college literary society as "amongst my earliest and always my truest most loving and confidential friend." Several months later, Seward wrote Berdan's brother that he felt "as if I should not wish to survive the greenness of my affections." [29]

———

Almost from the day he arrived in Auburn, Seward was active in politics. As he put it in his memoir, "politics was the important and engrossing business of the country." Many observers agreed. Alexis de Tocqueville, the Frenchman who toured the United States in the early 1830s, observed that it was hard to overstate the importance of politics for Americans: "If an American were condemned to confine his activity to his own affairs, he would be robbed of one half of his existence; he would feel an immense void in the life which he is accustomed to lead, and his wretchedness would be unbearable." [30]

Political parties were new and still slightly suspect, and some people disliked their constant conflict. One of the Auburn papers lamented, after the close of a campaign, that "politics are the only species of warfare that admits of no cessation of hostilities. There is reason to fear that the frequency of elections in this country, connected with the bitterness and asperity with which they are conducted, have produced a belligerent state of feeling." Elections were indeed frequent in New York: every spring there were town elections, every fall there were state elections, and every other fall there were federal elections. Parties were starting to select their candidates through conventions, so there would be a town convention to select delegates for a county convention, at which local nominees were selected along with delegates for a state convention. Almost every week, the Auburn papers would report on the meeting or convention of one party or another. [31]

To complicate matters, there were many parties and factions in New York and the cast of parties was constantly changing. As an Auburn paper observed in 1827, "perhaps a time never existed when there was such a total subversion of old party lines, and when such a variety of new interests and new party names were brought into action: Masonic and Anti-Masonic, Republican, Bucktail, and Clintonian, Adamites, Jacksonians, and Federalists, People's Men, Van Burenites, etc. etc." One way to summarize the situation is to note that there was always, during this period in New York history, the party headed by Martin Van Buren and at least one opposition party. Van Buren held a succession of senior positions: senator from New York, governor of New York for a brief period, secretary of state, minister to England, vice president, and finally president. His supporters called themselves the Republicans or the Democrats; more informally they were known first as "the Bucktails" and then as "the Regency," because they governed in New York while Van Buren was away. The inner circle of the Regency was a small group of capable, diligent, and forceful men; their "official organ" was the *Albany Argus.* The *Argus* was echoed in dozens of newspapers around the state, just as Van Buren was supported by hundreds of local political leaders. The Regency's opponents in New York were, in rough succession, the Clintonians, the People's men, the National Republicans, the Workingmen, the Antimasons, and then the Whigs, formed in 1834. In general, these opposition parties were less organized and less successful than the Regency, which controlled the legislature in almost every session from 1820 through 1837.[32]

Politics shaded into and blended with the civic life of Auburn. As Seward wrote in his memoir: "I took my pew and paid my assessments in the church, attended the municipal, political, and social meetings and caucuses, acting generally as secretary. I enrolled myself in the militia, and wore my musket on parade. I paid my contributions, and, when required, managed dancing assemblies, although, for want of skill, I never have danced myself. And so I rendered, to my neighbors and acquaintances, such good offices as my training and position made convenient." The church in which Seward took a pew was not the Presbyterian church of his youth but the Episcopal church of his father-in-law and wife. He became a member of the vestry in Auburn in 1827, although he was not yet a communicant. During this period he appeared almost weekly in the local newspapers: one week in his role as the colonel of the local militia regiment, another as secretary of a private company to construct a canal to Lake Owasco, and another as the anonymous opponent of "the attempt by the Presbyterian Clergy to gain an ascendancy in matters of state by means of Sabbath keeping societies, temperance societies etc."[33]

When Seward arrived in Auburn in late 1822, he was, according to a later report, "a thorough-going Bucktail—dealing out unmeasured censure upon all who deviated from that faith." But soon he started to have doubts about the Bucktail's leader Van Buren. In late 1823, Seward wrote his father that "with all his sins Clinton has talents great and expanded" while "Van Buren's genius has sunk into cunning and chicanery." One of the main issues in New York at this time was whether federal presidential electors should be selected by the state legislature (which meant that Van Buren and his party could control the process) or selected by direct popular vote (a system that would give other parties more voice). The "People's men" favored popular elections, and in early 1824 Seward joined this group. He wrote to his father that "circumstances have rendered it necessary that I should abandon" Van Buren "and I have done it." He would "sink or swim hereafter with the People. So I held myself in common honesty bound to do. I have suffered some vilification in consequence of it but it is past now."[34]

After Seward switched sides, he threw himself into the 1824 election with energy. In early July, he attended a meeting of the young men of Auburn and was appointed to a committee to draw up resolutions opposing Van Buren and supporting popular elections. In October, he attended a larger convention in Auburn and drafted its address. In his memoir, Seward wrote that he supported DeWitt Clinton for governor and John Quincy Adams for president in 1824 because they supported internal improvements, but Seward's address did not favor anyone or anything; it was a rather simplistic attack on Van Buren and the Regency. Seward was pleased with the results of the election: Clinton was elected as governor and the new assembly was largely anti-Regency. No presidential candidate had a majority in the electoral college, so the election was decided by the House of Representatives, which selected Adams as the nation's sixth president.[35]

Seward was not very active in politics during 1825, but he was a leader in the two main events in Auburn of that summer, the reception of Lafayette and the Fourth of July. The marquis de Lafayette, now sixty-seven years old, one of the last living leaders of the revolutionary generation, was nearing the end of a triumphal yearlong tour of the United States when Seward and a few others greeted him as he entered Cayuga County. They escorted Lafayette on horseback to Auburn, where (according to the local paper) the "ear was almost deafened" by the estimated crowd of 8,000 people. A small group, including Seward, later sat down with the general for an "elegant dinner," after which there were the customary toasts. At around eleven, the great guest left for Syracuse, again accompanied by Seward and others. It was one in the morning when they reached Skaneateles, but they found the streets thronged with people, and there were similar receptions at other towns along the route. One wonders how the aged general survived more than a year of such travel and such enthusiasm.[36]

On the Fourth of July, as the keynote speaker at the Auburn celebration, Seward returned to the theme of his graduation speech: the American Union. He noted that "prophets of evil" had often predicted that the Union would split into northern and southern halves, but there had been no separation; he believed there never would be. The people of the North would "not willingly give up the power they now have in the national councils, of gradually completing a work in which, whether united or separate, from proximity of territory, we shall ever be interested—the emancipation of the slaves." And southern leaders, he said, would "never, in a moment of resentment, expose themselves to a war with the North, while they have such a great domestic population of slaves, ready to embrace any opportunity to assert their freedom and inflict their revenge." Seward was speaking in the Presbyterian church and he sounded like a preacher. The Union was the "ark of safety in which are deposited the hopes of the world" and preserving it would "bring down blessings upon us and our posterity."[37]

By 1826, the People's movement had essentially disappeared; the main parties in New York both called themselves Republicans, so they are perhaps more easily termed the Van Buren and the Clinton factions. Clinton was once again a candidate for governor, and Seward's father-in-law Elijah Miller was a Clintonian candidate for Congress. An Auburn paper claimed that "if there is in this community one man whose reputation for strong mind, and incorruptible morality is established beyond question, that man is Elijah Miller." Seward recalled making similar arguments for his father-in-law with friends and neighbors. But Miller's character was not enough to carry him to Congress against the strong Van Buren tide; he lost by a large margin.[38]

A new political movement was getting underway at this time: Antimasonry. Almost every American city and town had a Masonic lodge and many of New York State's leaders were Masons. In the late summer of 1826, William Morgan, a lapsed Mason, threatened to publish a book revealing the secrets of the Masons; Morgan was arrested on weak charges, then kidnapped and apparently killed near Niagara Falls. If the Morgan murder and related crimes had been promptly investigated, and if Masons had cooperated in the investigation, there never would have been an Antimasonic movement. But it soon became clear to most New Yorkers that the Masons were impeding the investigation and prosecution, and it was this obstruction that outraged non-Masons and launched the new movement. During the summer and fall of 1827, groups met in many counties in the western part of the state to nominate Antimasonic candidates for the legislature, of whom fifteen were elected in November. Seward was friendly with the local Antimasons, although it does not appear that he attended any of their initial meetings. In the spring of 1828, however, he wrote his father that "we are all becoming anti-masonick, and in this region of the county the delusion which has blinded the people of all conditions on the subject of freemasonry has passed away forever."[39]

It was at about this same time—in late 1827 or early 1828—that Seward tried and failed to secure appointment as Cayuga County surrogate. In his memoir, he described how a friend resigned the position and recommended Seward as his successor, and how he traveled to Albany to meet with Governor Clinton, who received him "kindly and cordially" and nominated him for the position. Then, according to the memoir, "a political secret was divulged which at once convulsed and astounded the state," namely, that Clinton "had become reconciled with" Van Buren and would support Andrew Jackson for president in 1828. When Seward himself failed to support Jackson—indeed, attended an Albany meeting supporting Adams—the state senate rejected Seward's nomination as surrogate.[40]

One difficulty with Seward's version of this episode is that Clinton's support of Jackson was not a "secret" that "astounded" anyone. On the contrary, Jabez Hammond, a politician and historian of the period, recalled that "from the year 1824, down to the time of his death, Mr. Clinton declared openly and frankly, his preference of General Jackson." Another difficulty is a letter from Seward to his father in December 1827, reporting on a visit to Albany, but with no mention of either his nomination or rejection. A third difficulty is that the *Cayuga Patriot*, not long after these events, reported that Seward had promised to support Jackson in order to secure the surrogate post. "Did you," the paper asked Seward, "offer yourself for sale to the opponents of President Adams, promising to follow where they should lead; and was your price the office of Surrogate of Cayuga county? And on their refusal to *purchase* you, did you join in calumniating General Jackson?" Even if the *Patriot* overstated its case, its version seems closer to the truth than the memoir; Seward indicated he would support Jackson if he was confirmed as surrogate, and only after his nomination was rejected did Seward emerge as an ardent Adams man.[41]

As in 1824, Seward was an active participant in the 1828 presidential campaign. He probably drafted a letter that appeared in the local papers in May, describing Adams as a man "whose talents, learning and experience in the affairs of government have long since rendered him the most conspicuous among living American statesmen." Jackson on the other hand was a man whose "private character is a record of immoralities, broils and bloodshed." Seward was one of more than three hundred young men who attended an Adams convention in August in Utica. On the eve of the convention, strong differences emerged among the delegates about who should preside, with those from New York City insisting that because they were most numerous, one of them should have the honor. Seward pleaded for unanimity behind whoever received the most votes, and he was surprised to learn, the next day, that he himself was the person so selected. According to later reports, young Seward handled himself well, making the convention one which it was "an honor to participate in, and a pleasure to remember."[42]

A few weeks later, in late September 1828, while Seward was out of town on business, an Auburn Antimasonic convention nominated him to represent in Congress the district whose boundaries coincided with those of Cayuga County. In his memoir, Seward explained that he had to decline this nomination because the convention had used, in its praise of Seward, language he himself had drafted to describe another possible nominee. A review of the local papers, however, shows that Seward's memoir was again wrong. Seward had hoped, when nominated by the Antimasons, that he would also be nominated by the Adams Party. In this way he could combine the strength of the two anti-Jackson parties and perhaps defeat the Jackson candidate for Congress. When the local Adams Party, however, refused to follow the lead of the Antimasonic Party, Seward wrote a public letter withdrawing his name. The local Jackson paper claimed that this proved that Seward was merely a politician, without real principles, willing to attempt to straddle the two parties in his effort to get to Congress. Perhaps even with both nominations, Seward would not have won: the local Jackson candidate received more than 60 percent of the vote and in the national election Jackson handily prevailed.[43]

The Adams Party faded quickly in New York State after this, and Seward devoted his political time to the Antimasonic Party. In February 1829, he was one of the delegates at an Antimasonic state convention in Albany, and in March he organized a town convention to nominate an Antimasonic slate of town officers. He wrote his father in August that "we are finally in the political campaign, but my business prevents me being much more than a spectator. My friends were anxious to put me in nomination for the assembly but I declined." One reason he declined is that he did not think an Antimason could yet win a state assembly seat in Cayuga County. He was right; the Regency candidates carried Cayuga by comfortable margins that year. But Seward was not easily discouraged; he simply looked forward to the next election.[44]

———

On the first day of 1830, Seward and the other Antimasons of Cayuga County gathered at an Auburn hotel. The address Seward drafted for this small group, instead of detailing the evils of Masonry, attempted to appeal to the Workingmen, another new party, one focused on the rights of "farmers, mechanics and workingmen." The Auburn convention chose

Seward as one of the county's representatives to a state Antimasonic convention, held in Albany in late February. This state convention in turn selected a slate of delegates, again including Seward, to attend a national Antimasonic convention, scheduled for Philadelphia in September. Those attending the Albany convention also decided that their movement needed a state newspaper, and within a month they had launched the *Albany Evening Journal* with Thurlow Weed as its editor.[45]

Seward knew Weed only slightly at this time, as a leader of the state Antimasonic movement, and a clever and combative newspaper editor. The two had first met in Rochester in 1823 or 1824, when Weed helped Seward get his carriage out of the mud; they met thereafter from time to time at political meetings and conventions. In promotional materials for the new newspaper, Weed promised that the *Journal* would work for "the cause, the whole cause, and nothing but the cause of Antimasonry." The cause of Antimasonry was not just to limit the power of the Masons; it was to promote "domestic manufactures, internal improvements, the abolition of the imprisonment for debt, reform of our militia system, and all other measures calculated to secure and promote the general interest and welfare of the people." Seward and Weed were determined to make Antimasonry a political party that could win elections, not merely close down Masonic lodges.[46]

Even in the first months of 1830, local newspapers had a sense that Seward would be a candidate in the fall. The *Cayuga Patriot*, the main Jackson paper of the county, argued that Seward and a friend were "like the stick which was so crooked it couldn't be still. What do they want? To abolish masonry? They had much rather it would exist, if it could be made the means of excitement, and minister to their personal ambition." On the other side, the *Onondaga Republican* included Seward among a list of Antimasonic leaders and argued that "the destinies of this state may safely be confided" to such men.[47]

There were two celebrations of the Fourth in Auburn that year: a general one organized by the town and an Antimasonic one organized by Seward. The Antimasonic orator, Henry Dana Ward, wrote to Seward pleading with him to make this a temperate celebration. "Let the wine flow, if it please, but burn the brandy and rum." Seward must have been nervous when Dana did not arrive until ten o'clock on the morning of the event. But show up he did, and spoke eloquently not only about the Masons but also about internal improvements, attacking Jackson in Washington and the Regency in Albany for frustrating necessary public projects.[48]

During August, Seward attended first a county convention in Auburn and then a state Antimasonic convention in Utica. He had two tasks at Utica, as he later recalled: to prepare the resolutions, and to convince the convention to nominate Samuel Stevens for lieutenant governor. Stevens was not really an Antimason—he was a Workingman from New York City—but his nomination was viewed as essential in uniting the two anti-Regency movements. For governor, the convention nominated Francis Granger, a lawyer from Canandaigua, previously a National Republican candidate for governor, now an Antimasonic member of the state assembly. Regency newspapers claimed that the nomination of men such as Granger and Stevens, men with no Antimasonic credentials, proved that Seward and his friends were not really interested in attacking Masonry; they were just interested in achieving political power.[49]

In early September, Seward left Auburn for Philadelphia to attend the first national political convention in American history, the Antimasonic Convention of 1830. The date of the convention was no accident: September 11 was the fourth anniversary of the abduction of William Morgan. Seward was one of the youngest delegates but also one of the most active, drafting resolutions, giving speeches, and meeting others from around the country. The key question facing the convention was whether and when to make a presidential nomination. Some wanted to make an immediate nomination, others to make no nomination, and others, especially the New Yorkers, to postpone the question for a year. The New Yorkers prevailed on this point, which enabled them to avoid having presidential politics complicate their gubernatorial election. As the convention ended, after a full week of discussion, Seward was proud of his minor role in what he viewed as a major national event.[50]

Seward was also proud to learn, when he reached New York City on his way home, that he had been nominated as the Antimasonic candidate for the seventh state senate district.[51] New York State was divided into eight senate districts, each represented by four senators, with one senator elected annually by each district for a four-year term.

The seventh district consisted of Cayuga, Onondaga, Ontario, Seneca, Wayne, and Yates counties. The Antimasons had never elected a senator from this district, falling short in the most recent election by about 3,000 votes. There was a clear east-west division in the district's voting pattern, with the Antimasons strong in the three western counties and weak in the three eastern counties. So the task for the seventh district Antimasons in 1830 was to maintain their strength in the west and gain strength in the east, in counties like Cayuga.[52]

Seward was almost the perfect nominee for these purposes. Not only was he from Cayuga, but he was familiar in all six counties through his legal and political work. He was known as an Adams man, an advocate of canals and other improvements, and could thus appeal to those more interested in practical policies than theoretical Antimasonry. The small convention which had nominated Seward argued in its address to the voters that his "distinguished talents and irreproachable character have already affixed a sufficient index to his name to direct the people to his future usefulness as a statesman." The address also appealed to farmers and mechanics, saying they had too much "virtue and intelligence" to be led by the Regency "like lambs to the slaughter."[53]

The local newspapers praised or panned the Seward nomination according to their politics. One claimed that he was "well known as a sound lawyer, an eloquent advocate and a ripe scholar." Another argued that "a better selection could not have been made," for Seward was "a firm, undeviating Anti-Mason, and a democrat of the old Jeffersonian stock." A third reported that "there is no man more feared by the [Regency] than Mr. Seward: his talents, his fair and upright dealing, secure to him too much of the public confidence, not to call down their persecuting enmity." On the other side, a Regency paper accused Seward of political inconsistency, favoring first one party and then another. Another Jackson paper, alluding to his background in an area known as Federalist territory, argued that "his present boyhood is alone distinguished for his rancorous hostility to the republican party, so hopefully cherished in his early education."[54]

The most interesting comments about Seward and his opponent David McNeil appeared in a nominally neutral paper, the *Onondaga Register & Syracuse Gazette*. This paper disliked the Antimasonic obsession with the Masons, but it also disliked the Regency. Reviewing the candidates for various offices, it noted of Seward that he was opposed to the Regency: "that's good." Moreover, the editors heard that he was "a high-minded honorable man, and a right down clever fellow; and withal, the smartest lawyer in Cayuga County, and if elected, he will be on the people's side—that he will be opposed to high salaries and direct taxes." As to McNeil, he was a "common sort of country merchant, not very intelligent, and was fond of horse-racing, and all that sort of thing." The allusion to alcohol was picked up in a few other papers, showing that temperance was already an important issue for some voters.[55]

Seward himself, in a letter to his father, was pleased and hopeful. "Present appearances indicate that I shall be elected. My opponents almost concede it." Consistent with the practices of the day, Seward did not campaign through visits or speeches. Indeed, the local papers do not report many speeches or rallies; it seems the campaign was conducted through the papers and face-to-face discussions among voters.[56]

Voting was spread over the first three days in November. Even before all the votes were counted, Seward knew from informal tallies that he had won. He estimated for his father that his majority would be about 1,500. In a letter to Thurlow Weed on November 8—the first letter of hundreds between the two men—he made a similar prediction. In the end, Seward won by about 2,000 votes out of the 30,000 cast in the district. In the state as a whole, however, the Regency prevailed. The Antimasons carried almost every western county, but the Regency carried almost every eastern county, including the ever more populous New York City. In a second letter to Weed, in late November, Seward called Granger's loss a "cruel disappointment" but predicted that "one more battle and the struggle is won." Seward also asked Weed where he should room while in Albany.[57]

When he left Auburn for Albany in late December 1830, Seward was still a young man, not yet thirty. But he was not a neophyte. He had participated in campaigns, attended state and national conventions, drafted complex legal documents, argued difficult court cases. Weed later recalled that when he first got to know Seward, he was impressed by his "stern integrity, earnest patriotism, and unswerving fidelity. I also saw in him a rare capacity for intellectual labor, with an industry which never tired and required no relaxation." Seward's political philosophy was not yet formed, but many of the characteristics which made him a political leader—his intelligence, diligence, eloquence, sociability, likability—were already in place. As the Cayuga convention had claimed, Seward already had about him the "elements of a statesman."[58]

CHAPTER 2

"Who Is William H. Seward?":

1831–1838

A fter leaving his wife and boys at home in Auburn, and traveling four long days by stage coach, Seward arrived in Albany on the first day of 1831. He settled into his room at the Eagle Tavern, took his seat in the senate chamber of the Capitol, and began to learn about legislative life. He soon realized that as the youngest member of a small minority—there were only seven Antimasons among the thirty-two members of the senate—he was not going to have much effect on legislation. He also learned, however, that the Antimasons were not without power, especially on issues on which the majority Democrats were divided. Seward and the Antimasons, for example, persuaded enough Democrats to join them to pass in this session a bill to abolish the practice of imprisonment for debt.[1]

Seward spent his free time with other Antimasonic legislators, especially Albert Haller Tracy of Buffalo. Tracy, eight years older than Seward, was a lawyer with six years of experience in Washington as a member of Congress. Seward wrote to Frances that Tracy was "a man of original genius, of great and varied literary acquirements, of refined tastes, and high and honorable principles." While Tracy was away from Albany for a few days, he wrote Seward that "it shames my manhood that I am so attached to you. . . . Every day and almost every hour since [leaving] I have suffered a womanish longing to see you." Seward wrote back of his "rapturous joy" in learning that Tracy reciprocated the "feelings which I had become half ashamed for their effeminacy to confess I possessed." A modern reader of these letters might assume that there was a homosexual relationship between the two men, but that seems unlikely, since they were both happily married. Theirs was one of the close, almost romantic, relationships among otherwise straight young men that were more common in those days than in ours.[2]

Other legislators with whom Seward spent time that winter included Millard Fillmore, Trumbull Cary, Francis Granger, and John Spencer. All these men would play roles in Seward's later life, but none more important than Thurlow Weed, who although not in the legislature was a key member of this small set. Weed was older than Seward, taller, heavier, and stronger. Unlike Seward, who had a college degree, and whose family had some wealth, Weed came from a poor home and had almost no formal education. But he had learned how to run a press, and how to write and edit a newspaper, and he was editor of the state's leading Antimasonic paper, the *Albany Evening Journal*. Seward told his wife that "Weed is very much with me, and I enjoy his warmth of feeling. A politician skilful in design and persevering in execution, whose exciting principle is personal friendship or opposition, and not self-interest—that is just Thurlow Weed."[3]

Seward wrote Frances from Albany almost every day, long letters filled with vivid details. In one, he related how he met Aaron Burr, now residing in "one of the fourth rate houses of this city" and making his way as a somewhat disreputable lawyer. "Do I actually grasp the hand which directed only too successfully the fatal ball which laid low Alexander Hamilton?" In another, he complained about the constant press of visitors. "My room is a thoroughfare, and I have less time for study than is at all compatible with my duty to my constituents or myself." In letter after letter, Seward assured his wife of his love. As a busy week ended, he noted that he "could remember no good I had done but that of writing to you daily. I could remember no pleasure I had enjoyed but that derived from recollections of, and reflections upon, home. I smoked a cigar [and] wished for Gus and Fred to play in the smoke of it."[4]

However much Seward loved his home and family, he did not spend much time in Auburn. The legislative session of 1831 finished in late

April, and he was home for a few weeks in May and June. He traveled to Syracuse to deliver the Fourth of July oration, then spent a week in western New York, visiting with various political leaders. In late August, he returned to Albany, covering the last few miles on an early horse-drawn railroad. "Only think," he wrote Frances, "of riding from Schenectady to Albany without jolting, jarring, or bouncing!" In September, he journeyed to New England to meet Antimasonic leaders. The highlight of this trip was a three-hour visit with John Quincy Adams at the family home in Massachusetts. Seward respected Adams but found him, on this first visit, quite cold. In early October, he left for Baltimore, for the Antimasonic national convention.[5]

Seward brought his wife and children to Albany for the last weeks of 1831 and first few months of 1832. In her letters home, Frances described the social and political life of the capital. She related how much she admired the speaking style of one senior senator—"he makes no gestures stands perfectly still"—and how she fled down the stairs rather than allow others to watch her reactions as her own husband spoke. She praised many men, but especially Tracy. His conversation "reminds me of a book of synonyms—he hardly ever makes use of the same words to express ideas that have a shade of difference"; she maintained that he could "convince me a chameleon was blue, green, or black just as he should choose." When away, Tracy wrote Seward about Frances. "Give my most sincere love to her, and ask her to kiss the little boys many times, in my behalf especially." And Seward wrote Tracy of his wife Harriet: "It is soothing it is even delightful to withdraw from the busy field of political controversy to the society of women we love."[6]

Seward's first major policy speech was about the Second Bank of the United States. The Bank had important federal roles, such as receiving tax payments and selling federal debt, but it was a private institution, headed by its aristocratic president Nicholas Biddle. President Jackson disliked banks in general and Biddle's bank in particular. In early 1832, Congress passed a bill to extend the Bank's charter, but Jackson, with one of the most famous and forceful veto messages in American history, killed the bill. Seward, in his speech, defended the Bank and attacked the Democrats for their blind loyalty to Jackson. The president was a great man, Seward said, "honored, loved, revered," but he was less important than the American people. "Let their interest, not his glory, their welfare and prosperity, not his success in an election, determine our votes on this measure." Weed printed the speech and called it an "effort of genius and patriotism." Seward also drafted the end-of-session address for the Antimasons, emphasizing the economic issues they hoped would succeed in the fall elections.[7]

As a member of the state senate, Seward was also a member of the state's highest court, the Court for the Trial of Impeachments and the Correction of Errors. Like most states at this time, New York had two court systems: one for actions at law (cases in which the plaintiff sought money damages), headed by the state supreme court; and one for actions in equity (cases in which the plaintiff sought an injunction or other order), headed by the chancellor. The Court of Errors, as it was known, was a curious institution, for it heard appeals from decisions of both the chancellor and the supreme court, and its members included the chancellor, the members of the supreme court, and the members of the state senate. Because the senators far outnumbered their judicial colleagues, they served as a commonsense check on the lower courts. But the decisions of the Court of Errors were not made (or at least not visibly made) on political grounds; they were careful judicial decisions, written by the lawyers on the court, based on prior precedents.[8]

Seward wrote several opinions for the Court of Errors, two of which are interesting because they relate to larger questions. In the first case, the U.S. Supreme Court had reversed a prior decision of the Court of Errors, sending the case back for further proceedings consistent with its decision. The chancellor suggested a clever order, which dismissed the case while defending the state court's prior decision on technical grounds. Seward would have none of this evasion; for him the only question was how to comply fully with the decision of the Supreme Court. Up to the time of the *Dred Scott* decision in 1857, Seward consistently deferred to the Supreme Court; after that, as we shall see, he changed his approach.[9]

The second case involved a settler in western New York who, like many others, had signed a contract to acquire his land by improving the property and making payments over time. The settler made the payments and improvements, but lost the land due to a third-party lawsuit against the seller from whom he had purchased. Seward was outraged that the settler could lose the land over which he had labored because of an unknown lawsuit against the seller. It made little sense, he wrote, to expect "the humble tenant, located in the woods in the extreme western part of the state, to search the office of the register or assistant register of chancery, at Albany or New York, every time an installment becomes due on his contract, to see if peradventure a bill may not have been filed by some creditor." When the time came for decision, the chancellor read his opinion against the settler, Seward read his opinion in favor of the settler, and Seward prevailed by a vote of 20 to 1. Seward, who was already alive to the concerns of the western settlers, would become more so in his years as land agent, governor, and senator.[10]

Seward did not attend the Antimasonic state convention in the fall of 1832—he was attending a special session of the legislature—but he was pleased with the results. The Antimasons again nominated Seward's friend Francis Granger for governor, and they secured support from the National Republicans (the former supporters of Adams) for their nominations. Seward wrote to his wife that "the fair prospect is that we shall combine in support of our ticket the whole opposition, and many entertain confident hopes of the election of Granger." There was some talk among national Antimasonic leaders about sending Seward to Ohio to campaign there, but he did not go. Instead, he was active on the local level, drafting the address of the town convention and leading the country committee. In the end, state and local issues did not matter much. This was an election about Jackson: was he "King Andrew the First," because of his vetoes of the bank and other bills, or was he the people's man in Washington? A slight majority of the voters in New York, about 52 percent, sided with Jackson, and this was sufficient to give Jackson and his running mate Van Buren all of the state's electoral votes, to elect William Marcy as governor, and to return Jackson majorities to the state legislature. Seward wrote to Frances that "our opponents have achieved so destructive a victory that in common decency they are compelled, when in our presence, to suppress the expression of their exultation."[11]

Not long after the election, South Carolina declared the recent federal tariff laws unconstitutional and threatened to secede from the

Union if the tariffs were not repealed or modified. More ominously, the state started to raise a substantial armed militia to defend itself against the federal government. Jackson responded that nullification and secession were both contrary to the Constitution. "Do not be deceived by names," Jackson declared, "disunion by armed force is *treason.*" Van Buren, not yet vice president but already thinking about his presidential prospects, tried to weave his way between North and South, drafting a report for the state legislature that opposed secession but also praised the doctrine of states' rights. Seward opposed Van Buren and supported Jackson, insisting in a speech that the Union must be preserved and the Constitution upheld.[12]

The Nullification crisis was the most important national issue of the winter, but the state legislature also considered local issues, of which the most interesting for Seward's future was the Chenango Canal. The proposed canal, connecting the Erie Canal at Utica with the Susquehanna River at Binghamton, had been under discussion for several years. To those who lived along the route, it was obvious that the canal was necessary; to others, including the state canal commissioners, it seemed unlikely that the project would ever pay for itself. Seward had voted in favor of the canal twice before, but this winter he voted against, because the bill authorized an unlimited expenditure for construction.[13]

———

In the spring of 1833, Seward's father asked his son to join him for a European summer tour. Seward persuaded himself that it was his duty to accompany his father—"it is not proper that you should go alone or look beyond your family for a traveling companion"—and prepared for the journey with his customary energy, gathering books and soliciting letters of introduction. One of the last letters he wrote before leaving was a warm letter to Tracy. Now that the journey was imminent, Seward regretted the decision to leave his wife and children; he predicted an "absence long and cheerless and perplexing from those whose smiles and caresses have made me certainly the happiest of men." He would also miss Tracy; "whether I again set my foot or not upon my native land I shall carry with me the remembrance of no friendship more gratifying." Weed urged Seward to write letters not only for his family but also for the public. "By this means the chain between your constituents and yourself will remain unbroken." [14]

On the first day of June, Seward and his father departed from New York City by one of the weekly packet ships; they arrived at Liverpool in eighteen days, a short passage by the standards of the presteam era. Seward enjoyed Europe immensely. He attended debates in the House of Commons, traveled by canal boat through Holland, climbed mountains in Switzerland, and visited with the elderly Lafayette outside Paris. His letters home, as Weed suggested, were frequent and detailed. In a library in Liverpool, he was amused to find journals from the period of the American Revolution, castigating Samuel Adams and John Hancock. On the ferry to Ireland, all the passengers enjoyed a glass of whiskey, and "the maxims of the temperance society notwithstanding, I could not decline the invitation to join them over their favorite beverage." He admitted that the people of Ireland were not well educated, but he nevertheless favored Irish independence, for he had "seen enough to convince me that until the [separation from England] shall take place, the people will never be enlightened and educated." In France, talking with Lafayette, he was impressed by the general's "paternal" feelings for America. "His solicitude is for the whole nation," Seward wrote, "and in the exercise of that feeling he overlooks the bickerings and controversies which disturb our domestic peace." [15]

Travels in Europe gave Seward a new perspective on the United States. Thinking back to the Nullification crisis and similar incidents, he wrote home that he now realized "the fearful responsibility of the American people to the nations of the whole earth, to carry successfully through the experiment which . . . is to prove that men are capable of self-government." If some misguided American should imagine that "a northern or a southern, an eastern or a western confederacy, or the independence of [one state] would still be enough to accomplish this great purpose of proving the capability of man for self-government, he would find that it is only as a whole, one great, flourishing, united, happy people, that the United States command respect abroad." If the Union were dissolved, its separate states would "sink below the level of the South American states." [16]

Seward and his father sailed from Le Havre for home in early October. Their voyage was long, rough, and difficult, and it was not until early November that the *Albany Evening Journal* could report that they had arrived safely in New York City. A few days later Frances happily wrote to her sister that her beloved Henry was home at last. "We have had so many things to talk over that for the last two nights slumber has not visited my eyelids until past two o'clock."[17]

Not long after Seward returned, Weed started to press him to revise his European letters for publication. Seward complied and the letters appeared in the *Albany Evening Journal* during the spring and summer of 1834. Although Weed did not print Seward's name with the letters, there were probably few readers who did not know the author's identity. The letters allowed people to see a different side of Seward, not merely the partisan politician but the impartial, inquisitive American abroad. Even some of Seward's political opponents wrote him to commend the letters.[18]

One of Seward's first visitors after his return from Europe was Albert Tracy, on his way from Buffalo to Albany for a session of the Court of Errors. "I was very glad to see him," Frances wrote to her sister, "as I love him very much." In late December 1833, when Seward returned to Albany for the four-month legislative session, he brought along Frances and the two boys. Frederick, who was not quite four at the time, later recalled that three men were especially frequent visitors to their hotel suite in early 1834: his "uncles" Albert Tracy, Thurlow Weed, and Trumbull Cary, another state senator. There is no hint in the memoirs, but it is clear from later letters that at some point during this winter Tracy crossed the line between friendly familiarity and inappropriate intimacy with Frances. Exactly what happened cannot be reconstructed—it seems unlikely that there was any physical relationship—but one day Frances came to her husband in tears, handed him a set of letters from Tracy, and asked him to decide whether she had acted improperly. Seward burned the letters without reading them, wrapped his wife in his arms, and assured her that he loved and trusted her. For some reason he did not confront Tracy—that would not come for several months—and indeed he continued in the interim to write Tracy friendly letters.[19]

The economic outlook in New York in early 1834 was grim. Philip Hone, the New York City diarist, recorded that "public confidence is shaken, personal property has no fixed value and *sauve qui peut* is the maxim of the day." The *New York Commercial Advertiser* reported that it had "never seen so deep a cloud of gloom hanging over the [stock] exchange." Different parties had different explanations for the economic situation. According to Seward and his friends, the recession was caused by President Jackson, who had removed millions of dollars of federal deposits from the Bank of the United States and placed these funds in various local banks, termed "pet banks" by his critics. Jackson's opponents insisted that his course was ill-advised and illegal, contrary to a statute which prohibited removal of the deposits from the Bank unless the secretary of the Treasury made a determination that the deposits were unsafe. According to Jackson's defenders, the economic problem was caused not by Jackson but by Biddle and the way in which he managed the Bank. Jackson, when visited at the White House by a group of distressed merchants, urged them to "go to Nicholas Biddle. We have no money here, gentlemen. Nicholas Biddle has all the money." [20]

In the New York legislature, the Democratic majority introduced resolutions to approve Jackson's course. The Democrats hoped the resolutions would pass without comment, but Seward, as he reported to his father, could not "permit the resolutions to go forth with the appearance that there was not one man in the legislature who had the moral courage to expose their impropriety and show their disastrous tendency." He opposed the resolutions in a two-day speech in late January 1834, arguing that the president had acted unwisely, illegally, and indeed unconstitutionally. Seward claimed that Jackson was behaving not like a president, limited by federal statutes, but instead as if he were a dictator or emperor. [21]

New York's Democratic governor William Marcy proposed to ease the financial distress by having the state borrow $6 million, loaning $4 million to New York City banks and $2 million to individuals in other counties. For Seward, Weed, and their friends, this was another improper Jacksonian scheme: an immense state slush fund, directed to favored state banks and individuals in the same way that Jackson was directing federal funds to his pet banks. Seward argued in an April speech that Marcy wanted to use the "money of the people" in order to "corrupt the people themselves." It was especially outrageous that the state would mortgage all its lands as security for the proposed loan. The time had come, Seward maintained in the end-of-session address, for the people to turn out of office those who had "impoverished our treasury, mortgaged our soil, and degraded the character of the state."[22]

Seward and Weed were among the first members of a new party forming at this time: the Whig Party. The early Whig Party was bound together not just by hatred of Andrew Jackson but also by principles: that power should rest with elected legislatures, governing through laws, not with an imperial president, governing through decrees. The name "Whig" was chosen to link the current struggle against "King" Andrew Jackson with the revolutionary struggle against King George III. Antimasons readily joined the new party, seeing it as a logical continuation of their crusade for government by laws and not by men. In the spring municipal elections in New York City, the new party elected several councilmen and nearly elected its candidate as mayor. Seward and other Whigs viewed this as a strong showing for a new party and looked forward eagerly to the fall state election.[23]

In early May, Seward wrote to his father that his Whig friends were inclined toward Jesse Buel as the nominee for governor and "a certain wild and thoughtless son of yours" for lieutenant governor. Tracy wrote Seward to argue that the "office of senator is ten times more important to yourself and to the party" than that of lieutenant governor, but Seward politely disagreed, telling Tracy he saw no reason why he should not at least seek the nomination. Weed was worried that Seward's vote against the Chenango Canal might pose a problem in the valley through which the canal would run. Seward explained that he had been concerned about the excessive cost of the project. "If this offend the brethren of the valley so much that the nomination will lose us votes let us cast about in search of a less offending candidate."[24]

The choice of state candidates was complicated by the factions within the new Whig Party: Antimasons would not accept a Mason; easterners were suspicious of western candidates. Weed wrote Seward in July that, as name after name was eliminated, Seward might emerge as the final choice for governor. Seward was flattered but not especially eager, writing Weed that he was not "intoxicated by the exhilarating gas." He was busy with legal work that summer around the state. Wherever he went, there was talk about who should be the Whig candidate for governor, and his own name kept coming up. He apparently did not ask for the nomination, but he certainly did not discourage it either. Writing to his wife from Albany in late August, Seward reported that Weed was "quite zealous" for his nomination, but "it is not rational." [25]

The Whigs gathered at Utica in early September 1834 for their first state convention. Seward was at home in Auburn, but Weed was at the convention, working for and reporting to his friend. Weed was not yet what he would later become, the dictator of the New York Whig Party, but he already had friends throughout the state, and he was especially skilled at the backroom politics of conventions. On the evening of the 10th, Weed could write to Seward that "the prospect is that you will be nominated." Weed's only concern was the "railroad question," by which he meant Seward's vote, earlier that year, against state funding for the New York & Erie Railroad company. The next day, the 11th, Weed reported to Seward that "all ends well," that Seward was the nominee for governor. Weed cautioned that the railroad was still an issue; to secure votes Weed had assured people that Seward was "entirely friendly" to the project, but had merely "voted against the *principle* of giving the public money for the benefit of an *incorporated company*." A grateful Seward wrote back to Weed that he was "astonished at your success." [26]

The campaign now moved into a more public phase, with the Whig papers praising and the Democratic papers criticizing Seward. In his *Albany Evening Journal*, Weed proclaimed Seward "a sound and enlightened statesman, and abundantly qualified for the wise administration of government." The *New York Evening Star* reported that he had "the most amiable manners—frank, social, and republican." Many of the Democratic papers harped on Seward's youth, but the Whigs responded that Seward's youth and honesty were just what the state needed. The *Auburn Journal* reminded its readers that it was the incumbent governor, Marcy, who had coined the infamous phrase "to the victor belong the spoils." The *New York Spectator*, in a long article headed "Who Is William H. Seward?," recounted in glowing terms some of his early exploits, including his success at college and skillful management of the 1828 convention. As to his four-year legislative career, "it would perhaps be a sufficient description and eulogy . . . to state that he has strenuously opposed every leading measure of the Van Buren party, since his advent to the Senate."[27]

The campaign was not only about Seward's youth and Marcy's experience; it was about issues. The main issue for the *Albany Evening Journal* was Marcy's proposal to mortgage the state's assets in support of a substantial new state debt. For the *Albany Argus*, the issue was equally simple: Seward was the candidate of the Bank of the United States and Marcy was the candidate of the people. Thus did each party strive to show that it represented the people against the entrenched power of the other side. To follow through on Weed's convention promises Seward drafted a public letter explaining that he not only favored the Erie Railroad but more generally believed in internal improvements. "I regard it as one of the most important duties of government, as fast as its rapidly developing resources will allow, to prosecute such a system of improvements of that description as will enable all the different sections of the country to enjoy, as equally as possible, the advantages of a speedy communication with the great commercial metropolis of the state."[28]

In late September, after their convention in Syracuse, a large number of young Whigs marched the thirty miles to Auburn to honor their candidate for governor. Frances enthused to her sister Lazette that "they rode past the house and saluted Henry (who stood in the front door) by bowing and waving their banners of which there were a great number. I could not refrain from tears when I saw one so honored whom I love so much and whom I know to be so deserving." It is hard to imagine that Seward did not address this throng, but if he did, his remarks have not survived. In keeping with the custom of the day, he maintained a low profile in the campaign. But he was busy behind the scenes, meeting leaders and answering letters. In one case, he drafted a long letter in the third person, to defend "Mr. Seward" on the railroad question, and sent it to a friendly editor for publication.[29]

Weed traveled in the western part of the state in the weeks leading up to the election, talking with supporters and distributing campaign funds. Upon his return to Albany on the eve of the election, he wrote Seward that, although his information pointed towards success, "I cannot conceal from you an inexplicable, but settled, apprehension, that we are to be beaten." Weed's fears were well founded, for Seward was beaten, by about 12,000 votes. He was strong in the west, the traditional home of the Antimasons; he carried the western senate district by more than 10,000 votes. But he was weak almost everywhere else. He lost his own Cayuga County by almost 1,000 votes, and he lost in New York City by more than 2,000 votes.[30]

Seward's initial reaction to his defeat was calm; "my cheerfulness is beyond the reach of this calamity," he wrote to Weed. His second reaction was concern, and he asked friends around the state whether the Whigs could and should continue as a party. His friends offered different explanations for the defeat, but they were uniform in their view of the Whig Party: it should remain together as the anti-Jackson, anti-Van Buren party of the state. The real explanation for Seward's defeat seems to be that economic conditions were better in the fall than they had been in the spring. A visiting Frenchman commented that "the re-establishment of industrial affairs has turned to the disadvantage of the opposition"—the Whigs. Horace Greeley, an editor who would soon become Seward's friend, had a similar explanation in his memoir: "Money was abundant, every one had employment who wanted [and so] we were badly defeated."[31]

Because he was a candidate for governor, Seward was not a candidate for re-election to the state senate, and so his defeat meant that, instead of being governor, he would have no political position at all in the new year. Seward returned to Albany for a few weeks in late 1834, for a session of the Court of Errors, and was soon writing long, emotional letters to his wife. "What a demon is this ambition," he noted, leading him "away in thought, purpose, communion and sympathy from the only being who purely loves me." He apologized for the way in which he had neglected her. "I banished you from my heart. I made it so desolate, so destitute of sympathy for you, that you could no longer dwell in it, and when the wretched T [Tracy] took advantage of my *madness* and offered sympathies, and feelings and love such as I had sworn, and your expelled heart was half won by his falsehoods, I still did not know and see that *I* was the criminal. God be praised for the escape of both of us from that fearful peril." A few days later, he reported a long conversation he had had with Tracy about little Fred Seward, who was at this time ill at home in Auburn. Tracy could still profess to care for Frances and the children, Seward noted, but he himself could not care for Tracy as he once had, in light of "his base conduct towards us last winter." These vague letters, unfortunately, are the most precise description we have of Tracy's "base conduct" toward Frances in early 1834: Tracy offered her the "feelings and love" which Seward should have offered her as her husband, and Frances was "half won by his falsehoods." Seward now wrote Frances that he wanted to "adopt some system of life which will enable me to be what I have never I fear been, a partner in your thoughts and cares and feelings; to have my place at the fireside in the evenings and devote the time to employments and thoughts and conversation congenial to your taste."[32]

Frances wrote back to reassure her husband. "You reproach yourself, dear Henry, with too much severity." She pressed him to strengthen his religious faith, something about which he was unsure. "Heaven only knows whether I can become a Christian," he wrote her. As the end of the year approached, Seward received a warm letter from Tracy, regretting that they were no longer as close as they had been when they first met. "Commend me to your dear wife," Tracy wrote on December 29, for "she knows the strength and purity of my love and will not doubt its constancy." This was too much for Seward, who wrote back on the same day to accuse Tracy of "pursuing towards the one being nearest and dearest to me a course which, but for the strength of her virtue, would have destroyed my peace and hers, if not my honor." He noted that he had intended to speak to Tracy about his misconduct many months ago, but because Tracy had been tending to an ailing mutual friend, had put off confrontation. Now Seward could not remain silent. He claimed that he had forgiven Tracy for his offense, but not forgotten it, and that they would part as mere friends, nothing more. He asked Tracy to return his letter, so that "no record remains of this violation of my friendship, or which may in any event preserve the connection of the name of the being I love most on earth with the cause of our separation." Tracy apparently complied, for the letter is among Seward's papers, along with a detailed summary of both letters that Henry sent to Frances the next day.[33]

—

Seward went home to Auburn in early 1835, but he did not remain long by his fireside. He wrote frequent letters to Thurlow Weed, seeking news from Albany and commenting on events. In February, after an assassination attempt against President Jackson, Seward wrote that he was thankful the assassin failed, but did not regret the attempt against the man he viewed as a tyrant. In April, he predicted that it would be impossible to prevent Vice President Van Buren from winning the 1836 presidential election. "The people are for him," he wrote, "not so much for *him* as for the principle they suppose he represents. That principle is democracy." Seward was busy with his law practice, writing to his father that he was at the office until ten or later each night. And he was planning a southern summer trip, convinced that it was the only way to improve his wife's fragile health. Exactly what ailed Frances is not clear: Seward wrote his father that she was generally confined to the house and often to her room, but he did not describe her symptoms. Frances was not eager to leave Auburn, but she allowed herself to be persuaded by her husband.[34]

Years later, Frederick would write that his father's "favorite form of recreation was travel. Activity and motion seemed to accord with his temperament . . . [and] an hour's ride, a day's excursion, or a month's journey . . . always seemed to have an animating and even exhilarating effect upon him." In late May, Seward, Frances, Frederick (age five), and a servant set out from Auburn by carriage, headed south toward Virginia. Seward enjoyed the trip from the outset: appreciating the mountain scenery of southern New York and northern Pennsylvania and fishing in the streams and rivers. Frances did not: she regretted leaving their older son Augustus, now nine, behind; she fretted when she did not hear from Auburn; she suffered from the rough roads and rude inns. Seward admitted to his father that his wife was so weak that the "utmost she is able to walk is ten or twelve rods," about sixty yards. To allow her to rest, they stopped several days at Harrisburg, where a local paper reported that Seward's "plain and unassuming deportment" and "fine colloquial powers" favorably impressed those he met.[35]

From Harrisburg, the Sewards continued to Harpers Ferry, Virginia.

Seward had seen the South before, during his time in Georgia, but this visit seemed to impress upon him much more what he described in a letter to Tracy as "the curse of slavery." He wrote that of "all the countries I have seen, France only, whose energies have for forty years been expended in war and whose population has been more than decimated by the sword, is as much decayed as Virginia." Seward's letters generally focused on the economic and political costs of slavery, while his wife lamented the human misery, exclaiming to her sister that "disguise thyself as thou wilt, still, slavery, thou art a bitter draught."[36]

The Sewards hated slavery, but they did not, as some accounts suggest, leave Virginia hastily. They spent two weeks there, entering the caverns, marveling at the Natural Bridge and visiting the great houses. They were unable to enter the house at Monticello—"we found every door closed"—but they strolled around the immense gardens and visited Jefferson's grave—"in a very rough, dilapidated condition." Seward was much impressed by the University of Virginia: "the plan and system of education in this institution are superior to those adopted in any other American college with which I am acquainted." At Mount Vernon, they toured the house under the guide of a mulatto maid, and even Frances conceded in her journal that it was "a beautiful place."[37]

From Virginia, the Sewards crossed to Washington, the nation's unfinished capital. At the insistence of a political friend, they called upon President Jackson, and Seward was forced to admit to Weed that the president received them in "the most obliging and gentlemanly manner." In Philadelphia, they toured Independence Hall and Frances consulted a famous doctor. On his advice they spent two weeks at New Jersey's seashore, to see whether daily saltwater bathing would improve her health. On one rainy day, as Frances reported to her sister, her husband occupied himself by reading *Don Quixote* and smoking poor cigars. After a visit to Henry's parents in Orange County, the family finally reached Auburn in early September.[38]

———

Seward was soon busy again in his law practice. "My office was never better patronized than it now is," he wrote his father, "and its labor, care and responsibility never greater." He was as always involved in politics, speaking at the cornerstone ceremony for the Auburn & Owasco Canal, and ensuring that the speech was printed in pamphlet form. And he was busy with real estate, selling his peripheral lands around the county in order to invest in a new set of four-story stone buildings in the center of Auburn. "The rise of real estate here," he told his father, "has indemnified me for my heavy expenditures and loss of business during the summer." [39]

In early 1836, Seward received an offer to participate in a much larger land venture. The Holland Land Company had purchased, forty years earlier, millions of acres of western New York, roughly the area that is now the seven western counties of the state. In late 1835, two of Seward's friends, Trumbull Cary and George Lay, acquired all the company's lands and contracts in Chautauqua County, the westernmost county. When Cary and Lay proposed new terms to the tenants, they revolted, destroying the land office in the county seat of Mayville and threatening the life of the land agent. Cary and Lay were thus in the market not only for additional investors to share the risks of this venture but also for a new land agent to handle the business of collecting rents and negotiating terms. Cary approached Seward, who agreed to serve as agent and to join the partnership. Although Seward had never been to Chautauqua, he was already popular there; in the election of 1834 he had received more than two thirds of the votes cast in the county. When his new role was announced, one paper described him as "a distinguished citizen, whose character is a sufficient guarantee to the settlers, that their rights and interests will be scrupulously respected." [40]

In a long letter to his father, written soon after he started work in the new venture, Seward justified his decision to leave Auburn and his legal practice there. He was doing well as a lawyer, he wrote, but he did not enjoy the work. "It is and for years has been irksome to me to labor for hire in other men's quarrels when my temper seeks and desires peace and repose." In his new role as land agent, he was entitled to a share of the partnership profits and a salary of $25,000 per year, plus expenses. So even if the land business failed, Seward claimed, he would be compensated through his salary. He did not mention to his father that he was also joining the partnership's debts, that he would sign a note in which he and his partners promised to pay $170,000 to the Holland Land Company. But with land values increasing rapidly, the partners anticipated that they would easily repay or refinance this note.[41]

Seward spent the summer and fall of 1836 shuttling back and forth between his home in Auburn and his land office in Westfield, a village in remote Chautauqua County. The distance was only two hundred miles, but the journey took two or three days, given the transport system of the day. In the warmer months one could travel part of the way by the Erie Canal, to its western end near Niagara, but from that point the roads west and south to Westfield were, in Seward's word, simply "horrible." He was in Westfield in July, in Auburn in August for the birth of his third child Cornelia, in Westfield in September and early October, in New York City and Philadelphia in late October, in Auburn in November, and back in Westfield in early December. While in New York City, on the eve of the election, Seward attended a Whig meeting, at which he reportedly called Martin Van Buren, the Democratic presidential candidate, a "crawling reptile, whose only claim was that he had inveigled the confidence of a credulous, blind dotard" (Jackson). Van Buren prevailed in the election, but Seward was not dismayed, writing Weed that he was "ready and willing to renew the contest, and I will never yield an inch of ground." As the year-end deadline for payment approached, Seward worked in Westfield from eight in the morning till eight and later in the evening, meeting with tenants, negotiating and revising agreements, and accepting payments from dozens of tenants. He was busy and happy.[42]

In early January 1837, a letter from Frances arrived, alerting Seward that their infant daughter was ill in Auburn with smallpox. Traveling as fast as he could, Seward reached Auburn in less than two days, arriving only in time to see what he described as the last hours of her "unspeakable suffering." Seward buried Cornelia, he wrote to Weed, with "only the consolation that her spirit is fairer and purer than ever saint or prophet presented himself at the judgment of God." After a brief period with his grieving wife in Auburn, he returned to work in Westfield, but he naturally reflected on the meaning of these events. Seward had attended the Episcopal church for many years—he was even a member of the vestry in Auburn—but had never been baptized or taken communion. On Easter Sunday, in the small Episcopal church in Westfield, he presented himself for baptism and participated for the first time in communion. He wrote Frances that throughout the service he thought continually of "you and my boys, and our child-angel, 'that left her errand with my heart and straight returned to heaven.' " He told Weed that he did not claim to "have experienced any miraculous change of heart or to have in any way gone through that ordeal of despair so commonly supposed to be the entrance and the only entrance upon Christian life." He had resolved, however, "to live more in the fear of and under the influence of love and gratitude to God," and he hoped this would "gradually elevate and refine my motives of action."[43]

Not long after the Sewards' personal tragedy, there was a national tragedy, the Panic of 1837. There was at this time no national paper currency; people used the paper notes of various banks, backed by each bank's promise to redeem its own notes for specie, or metal coins. On May 10, 1837, after the failure of several major firms, all the banks in the city of New York suspended their specie payments. Banks in other cities soon suspended their own payments; stock prices declined; factories closed; thousands lost their jobs. Seward commented to his father in May, with misplaced optimism, that "there is no other consolation other than that things are now at the worst and any change must be for the better." While he was in Philadelphia on land office business in June, he wrote home that "no adequate conception can be formed of the pressure in New York. It is sweeping like a pestilence, and poverty and suffering follow in its train." Back in Auburn, he wrote Weed that there had been no failures there as yet, but a "gloom still hangs over the country, heavier and blacker than ever." People believed, rightly in Seward's view, that "the calamities which have fallen upon the country have resulted from the erroneous policy of the Government." He predicted that anger at the governing Democrats would lead to Whig victories in the fall state elections.[44]

Seward and Weed blamed the crisis not just on the national government but also on the state government, where the Democrats refused to pass legislation to allow banks to issue bills in small denominations.

Weed wrote Seward in late May that "people are demanding small notes, and they must know *who* refused them and *how* it was done." Weed believed that "we have the Regency on the hip and must keep them there." Although Seward was busy with the land office, he did what he could to help the Whig campaign. In July 1837, he gave an extended address in Chautauqua on education: he argued for improving the overall educational system, and in particular for better education of girls and young women, since they were "equally qualified with the other sex for the study of the magnificent creation around us." In early October, he spoke to the Whig county convention in Auburn, arguing that the disastrous economic conditions were due to the Democrats and their policies. Later in October, he addressed a railroad convention in Elmira, presenting a broad argument in favor of internal improvements. These were only two of his many speeches in the last weeks of the campaign; he wrote his father after the election that he had "devoted four weeks to assiduous duty in traversing the county and addressing my old neighbors and friends." [45]

Seward's friends in Cayuga had tried to persuade him during the late summer to run for assembly or for state senate. He declined, in part because of his land office work, in part because he knew that, given the voter outrage against the Democrats, his name was not necessary to secure the seat for the Whigs. The Whigs indeed won a landslide victory in November 1837. In the state assembly, where previously they held only about one fourth of the seats, the Whigs would control four fifths of the body. The state senate would remain in Democratic control, but only because of the staggered voting system; Whigs were elected to six out of the eight seats available, including the seat in Seward's home district. After he voted in Auburn, Seward left for Westfield and met with Whig celebrations in every village and town through which he passed. "The overthrow of the administration is complete," he wrote to Weed, "and I am grateful for it, for the country's sake." Seward joined in these celebrations, and hosted one himself in Westfield, where he "threw open the land office" one evening. [46]

———

The smashing Whig success in 1837 complicated Seward's own plans for 1838. As he explained to his father, before the election the consensus among New York Whigs had been that their next candidate for governor would be "the candidate whom your parental affection commends to your favor." This consensus arose from the view that "the contest next year was to be, as all the recent elections had been, one of doubtful result." After the "recent revolution in the state," however, there was a strong prospect of success in 1838, so the Whig party leaders were no longer prepared to concede the nomination to Seward. He claimed to his father that this did not distress him, that he would "not lift a finger for my own advancement." [47]

Yet, even as he wrote this, Seward was working to secure his nomination. One of his key steps was to bring in his brother, Benjamin Jennings Seward, as his successor in the Westfield land office. Jennings, as he was known, although almost eight years older than Henry, was very much the junior partner in this venture: Henry kept a close eye on him and sent frequent letters of instruction. Seward was well aware, as Weed wrote him in April, that it was critical for him to "preserve amiable relations in that quarter," with the Chautauqua settlers. [48]

A second way in which Seward advanced his candidacy was by frequent visits around the state. He was in New York City in January 1838, in Albany in February, in New York again in April and May, and in Troy in late June. He traveled in part for business—he was working to renegotiate the loans for the Chautauqua venture—but also for politics. He wrote Frances from New York that he dined out every evening, and sometimes twice, in order to accept all his invitations. Writing Weed from Troy, where he addressed the Young Men's Association, Seward commented that he was "surprised and gratified" by the large audience and warm reception. [49]

A third way in which Seward improved his chances was through a new paper, the *Jeffersonian*, edited by Horace Greeley. Greeley was in some ways like Weed; he had worked his way up from poverty and learned the trades of printer and editor. But Greeley was more interested in abstract ideas than political power, and not at all suited to the face-to-face politics in which Weed excelled. Weed provided Greeley with office space in Albany; Seward and others secured subscriptions;

and the first issue of the paper appeared in February. The *Jeffersonian* did not (overtly at least) side with one party or the other, but claimed to present "the views of public men on both sides of the great political questions of the day." By avoiding squabbles and adopting a more balanced and elevated tone, Greeley was able to reach voters who would never listen to the partisan Whig press. Seward was delighted with the *Jeffersonian*, writing Weed that he "liked every word of it right well," and that as soon as time permitted he would "put a shoulder to the wheel once more" to solicit additional subscriptions.[50]

The leading Whig candidates for governor were Seward, Francis Granger, and Luther Bradish, speaker of the assembly. There were no real differences among them in terms of policy, so the competition turned on personal and regional popularity. The *Buffalo Commercial Advertiser* argued that Granger, whom it considered a western man, should be the candidate because the western counties had always voted Whig. Weed was neutral in the pages of his *Evening Journal*, but behind the scenes he worked tirelessly for Seward, whom he believed was just the man to beat the incumbent Democratic governor William Marcy. Weed wrote to Seward in August that "the battle is to be fought at the convention, and there I shall make a determined effort to save our cause." Seward found it difficult to wait quietly in Auburn, but that was what he had to do in late August and early September. Weed must have been pleased to receive a report from a mutual friend who visited Auburn and found the candidate "*tongue tied* and *handcuffed* and *shackled* besides, as he should be about these days."[51]

The Whig state convention opened on September 12 in Utica. Weed was there, twisting arms for Seward, but at least as far as the surviving letters show, he did not send him daily progress reports. It is thus possible that Seward did not know much about the progress of the convention until he learned on September 15 that he was the nominee for governor and his rival Bradish the nominee for lieutenant governor. In his letter reporting their success, Weed wrote that they were "again embarked on a sea of difficulties, and must go earnestly to work." The newspapers reacted to Seward's nomination as one might have predicted from their politics. The local *Auburn Journal* said he was "a gentleman, a scholar, and a person of indefatigable labor." The *New*

York Daily Whig commented that "he is the very man we would have wished; the first choice of nine-tenths of the Whigs of the Commercial Emporium." The *Morning Courier* argued that Seward was "a man with the capacity to mark out great enterprises, and the energy to execute them—a man with the spirit and soul of a Clinton," a governor under whom "our state will soon recover from the influence of the pygmy dynasty, and with a great tread resume her onward march."[52]

Greeley in the *Jeffersonian* adopted a more subtle course; he praised both Seward and his Democratic rival Marcy, saying they were "men of undoubted capacity, energy, industry, and unspotted private character." The key issue, according to Greeley, was the sub-Treasury scheme, Van Buren's proposal to require the U.S. government to keep its funds in the Treasury building and regional subtreasuries, rather than in private banks. Under the proposal, the government would not accept private bank notes as payment; it would only accept specie, that is, coins. The *Jeffersonian* explained, in simple but persuasive terms, why this would be a disaster for the American economy. It imagined the plight of a settler, seeking to make a payment to the government for his land, and unable to do so because he could not find, in his remote region, a sufficient quantity of coins. By electing Seward the voters of Van Buren's own state would be rejecting this pernicious proposal.[53]

A similar issue involved the state's Small Bill Law. While under Democratic control, the state legislature had passed in 1835 a law prohibiting banks from issuing small bills, defined as those for five dollars or less. This law had complicated commerce by forcing people to use notes issued by individuals and merchants instead. One of the first acts of the Whig assembly in early 1838 had been to repeal the Small Bill Law, but the senate, still dominated by Democrats, refused to go along; it instead suspended the law for two years. The Whigs argued that the right course was to repeal the Small Bill Law entirely so that it did not, in Seward's words, "disgrace the statute book" and threaten to disrupt commerce when suspension ended. As a Baltimore newspaper noted wittily, since both candidates were named William, and the larger Marcy favored larger bills, the question came down to whether you were "for big Bill Marcy or little Bill Seward."[54]

The Democrats, for their part, tried to link Seward with banks and elites. The *Albany Argus* argued that Seward as land agent was effectively the agent of Nicholas Biddle and the Bank; fortunately the *Argus* did not have Seward's correspondence with Biddle about refinancing the Chautauqua loans. In early October, the *Argus* printed a letter from unnamed "settlers" claiming that Seward had charged them interest at 7 percent on their mortgages, and raised money in Philadelphia at a mere 5 percent, pocketing the difference for himself. Seward responded in a long public letter, describing and defending his work as land agent.[55]

All of these issues related to the larger debate between Whigs and Democrats over the proper scale and role of government. The Democrats of the late 1830s and early 1840s favored small government with a limited role. The *United States Democratic Review* declared itself in favor of "as little government as possible; that little emanating from, and controlled by, the people; and uniform in its application to all." The Whigs, in the words of the leading historian of their party, "believed government must promote prosperity. Especially in hard times, the government must take positive action to stimulate economic recovery." Whigs favored a national bank and state support for internal improvement projects, such as roads and canals, that would not only provide jobs but also lay the groundwork for future growth. These ideas appealed not only to Whigs but also to conservative Democrats, and a group of "Bank Democrats" convened in early October in Syracuse and resolved to support Seward rather than Marcy.[56]

Nineteenth-century elections were played by rough rules. George Templeton Strong, at the time a young law student, described in his diary how Democrats were creating citizens by questionable naturalizations at New York City Hall. "It was enough to turn a man's stomach . . . to see the way they were naturalizing this morning at the Hall. Wretched, filthy, bestial-looking Italians and Irish . . . in short the very scum and dregs of human nature filled the . . . office so completely that I was almost afraid of being poisoned by going in." This was the same election in which Weed allegedly dispatched agents to Philadelphia, hired "floaters" there for thirty dollars each, and brought them back to New York, where they voted repeatedly and illegally for the Whigs. There is some evidence that Seward was aware of the techniques being used on his behalf. In late

September, a Whig leader wrote to Seward's friend Christopher Morgan, claiming that "if we can raise $5000 we can carry the doubtful counties," and seeking "large aid from your friend." Morgan forwarded the letter to Seward, who responded through Weed. "All I possess," he wrote, "is open to the draught of reasonable and discreet friends," but it is "insulting to me and wrong to propose that I should pay for illegal purposes." Seward seemed to suggest that he did not oppose improper techniques in general, only that he himself did not want to be involved in them.[57]

The abolitionist movement in the late 1830s was only a fringe movement, but one that could sway some voters. In early October, Seward received an unwelcome letter from two New York abolitionist leaders, William Jay and Gerrit Smith. They posed three questions: whether Seward favored a jury trial for those claimed as fugitive slaves; whether he favored ending the distinctions in the state constitution based on "complexion"; and whether he supported repealing the law that allowed slaveowners to bring slaves into the state for a limited period. Jay and Smith sent the same questions to all the other candidates for state office. Seward instantly realized that however he answered these questions he would lose some voters, either abolitionists or conservatives. He sought advice from Weed and delayed his answers as long as he could. He might not have responded at all, but his hand was forced by Luther Bradish, the Whig candidate for lieutenant governor, who responded in a way that delighted the abolitionists.[58]

Seward's answers, when they finally appeared, were cautious and equivocal. On the first question, he favored a jury trial for those claimed as fugitive slaves. On the second issue, he argued that the provision in the New York Constitution that imposed a stiff property qualification on black voters, but none on white voters, was not really a "distinction founded solely on complexion, but should rather be considered a test to discriminate between those of that race who possess the requisite intelligence and capacity to discharge the responsibilities of freemen, and those who do not." On the third point, he questioned whether it would be wise "to declare to our fellow-citizens of the southern and southwestern states, that if they travel to or from, or pass through, the state of New York, they shall not bring with them the attendants whom custom or education or habit may have rendered necessary to them."[59]

Seward's answers were not at all acceptable to the abolitionists. At an angry meeting in New York City, the merchant and abolitionist Lewis Tappan argued to the blacks in the crowd that "Bradish takes you cordially by the hand—Seward, my colored brethren and sisters, shoves you off with a ten foot pole." Abolitionist papers urged their readers to vote for Bradish but against Seward. Weed and Seward were concerned that, in a close election, the loss of a few thousand votes could tip the balance. On the eve of the election, they wrote letters to one another in which each predicted that, because of the abolition issue, Seward would lose. Seward was "satisfied that the abolition question defeat us." [60]

In the end, Seward won by a margin of about 10,000 votes. The abolition issue was far less important than the economy: voters wanted to punish the Democrats for what they viewed as their role in the economic crisis. Turnout was immense: almost 400,000 men voted, in contrast with about 300,000 two years earlier. As expected, Seward was especially strong in the western counties, the traditional home of Antimasonry. But he was strong almost everywhere in the state. There was no telegraph yet, so it took several days for him to learn the results in Auburn as newspapers arrived from distant counties. A friend recalled that one evening, as they stood in the news office reading the reports, Seward exclaimed: "God bless Thurlow Weed! I owe this result to him." [61]

Seward now had only six weeks in which to wind up his affairs in Auburn and Westfield and prepare to take office in Albany. He was suddenly anxious, writing Weed that it was a "fearful post I have coveted. I shudder at my own temerity." He wrote to his brother Jennings in Westfield, first assuring him that he would visit, then apologizing for not visiting and instructing him on how to continue the land agency. Letters poured in upon Seward from every corner of the state, generally seeking state offices. He initially intended to answer them all, explaining to Weed that "the kindness and attention thus manifested will be useful," but soon realized this would be impossible. [62]

One of the issues he could not avoid was where to live in Albany. Under Governor Marcy, the state had purchased a "governor's mansion," but Weed had mercilessly attacked the purchase in his paper as wasteful, so Seward could not possibly live there. After some discussion with

Weed, he rented the Kane Mansion, a large yellow-brick house within walking distance of the Capitol building. There was a spacious main hall, about fifty feet by twenty, suitable for entertainments on a grand scale, and four acres of lovely wooded grounds. The only disadvantage was that renting, furnishing, and staffing the house would cost twice as much as the governor's annual salary; but Seward was determined to live in the proper style for his position.[63]

His main task in these weeks was preparing his first message to the legislature. He knew that this document would answer, for the people of New York and the nation, the question one paper had posed four years earlier: "Who is William Henry Seward?" Up to this point in his career, Seward had been defined largely by what he opposed, the policies of Van Buren and the Democrats. Now he had to declare what he supported. After soliciting input from experts on various issues, he worked and revised day by day, finishing a first draft before he left Auburn. He continued the process of seeking comments and making changes when he reached Albany. In late December, Seward wrote to Frances that when she read the final message in the papers, she would "scarcely recognize a paragraph of the draft I read to you at Auburn," but he assured her that "there is not a sentence in it which is not my own handiwork." Frances remained behind with their younger son Frederick, in part because she was three months pregnant, in part because she could not face the prospect of hosting 5,000 guests at an inaugural reception.[64]

CHAPTER 3

"A Higher Standard of Social Perfection":

1839–1842

A t about ten o'clock on the morning of January 1, 1839, on a landing in the state Capitol building in Albany, surrounded by legislators and spectators, William Henry Seward took the oath of office and became governor of the state of New York. It was a simple ceremony, without a speech or music, because Seward did not want what he called "ostentatious display." The young governor—he was just thirty-seven—paused in the executive office after the ceremony, penned a brief note to his wife in Auburn, then walked back to his rented Albany residence. Even a Democratic paper praised his simplicity, noting that while other Whigs paraded like peacocks in all their finery, Seward was dressed "as Thomas Jefferson used to be, in a plain, unpretending suit of black."[1]

Seward's servants had rolled up the carpets, set out long tables, and filled them with food and drink. According to one paper, the feast included "turkeys, geese, fowls by the hundreds" and the local hotel provided "the choicest and richest wines." Returning a bit late from the Capitol, and finding he could not get in the front door, Seward's son Augustus "went around the house two or three times trying to get in the house but after a while I got in the kitchen window." Augustus reported home that the guests "crowded in so fast that they upset one of the tables." A Democratic paper claimed that some of Seward's guests "broke his chandeliers, demolished his mirrors, smashed his decanters on the floor and against the walls [and] broke his tables to pieces." Thurlow Weed, in the *Albany Evening Journal*, responded that "there were no excesses, nor any intentional disorder; nothing was wantonly broken or destroyed."[2]

While Seward was preparing for and attending this reception, clerks were reading his message to the legislators, and copies were being printed in the papers. Annual messages of this era were usually dull documents, and Seward's first message had its share of statistics, but it also brimmed with his youth, energy, ambition, and optimism. In one passage he proclaimed that this was a new age in which "the light of the human intellect increases in brilliancy and reveals new mysteries to man's persevering investigation." Americans would be "froward indeed," he said, if they failed to see that "our race is ordained to reach, on this continent, a higher standard of social perfection than it has ever yet attained, and that hence will proceed the spirit that shall renovate the world." Seward is not known as an early advocate of "manifest destiny," but perhaps he should be. This section of his message was echoed several months later, in an article often cited as the first statement of manifest destiny, which said that the United States was "destined" to expand and that no "earthly power" could "set limits to our onward march."[3]

One of his main themes in this first message was education. Without better and wider education, he said, the United States could not reach its great goals. Education "banishes the distinctions, old as time, of rich and poor, master and slave. It banishes ignorance and lays axe to the root of crime." Seward recommended the creation of a state board of education to replace the indolent local school inspectors. Noting that blacks were overrepresented in the prisons and underserved by the schools, he asked whether "a solicitous regard for the public welfare, justice to an injured race, and the dictates of an enlightened humanity, do not require us to provide more effectually for their education." And he recommended that the state provide schools for immigrant children in which they could "enjoy advantages of education equal to our own, with free toleration of their peculiar creeds and instructions."[4]

Immigrants were a second major focus of Seward's message. New

York was home to thousands of recent immigrants, mainly Irish but also German, Italian, and other. Many Whigs were anti-immigrant and anti-Catholic, and many intellectual leaders, such as the inventor Samuel Morse, published strong and in some cases outrageous anti-Catholic articles and pamphets. Governor Seward, in his message, took a brave stand against the views of many in his own party, making it clear that he would welcome immigrants and oppose religious discrimination. New York, he said, should greet immigrants "with all the sympathy which their misfortunes at home, their condition as strangers here, and their devotion to liberty, ought to excite." And if the immigrants remained for a sufficient period, New York should "extend to them the right of citizenship, with all its inestimable franchises."[5]

Internal improvements were a third major theme. Seward pressed the legislators to complete the ongoing expansion of the Erie Canal and to start several other canal projects. Rather than trying to decide upon one single east-west rail route, the state should build three major railroads west from the Hudson: one along the southern border of the state; one along the Erie Canal; and one on a northern route. Although he included a perfunctory warning against waste, Seward's emphasis was on the benefits of transport projects. "We are required," he proclaimed, "to carry forward the policy of internal improvements, by the abounding experience of its benefits already enjoyed; by its incalculable benefits yet to be realized, and by all our obligations to promote the happiness of the people, to multiply and raise their social enjoyments, to maintain the fame of the state [and] to preserve the integrity of the Union." These were not the words of a man inclined to count every penny.[6]

Another part of the message advised the legislature to reform the state's judicial and administrative systems. Seward raised questions about the Court of Chancery and its head the chancellor, arguing that the court's powers were "too vast, and its patronage too great, to be vested in a single individual." He recommended that judges should not have any powers of appointment, for this involved them in politics. As to other offices, he proposed that state officials should be compensated through fixed salaries rather than through perquisites such as the fees charged by various clerks, commissioners, and inspectors. The state, in

Seward's view, should pay its employees "the amount necessary to secure the requisite skill, industry, and ability"—and nothing more.[7]

Seward's message was printed not just in every newspaper in New York but in many other papers around the country. Reactions varied. Weed, who had seen the message several times in draft form, now commended it in his *Evening Journal* as "earnest, energetic—clear, and strong." The state's leading Democratic paper, the *Albany Argus*, derided it as "the effusion rather of the sophomore than of the statesman." The *Daily National Intelligencer* in Washington called it a "sensible and manly document," with "liberal and enlarged views." Seward himself wrote that he was satisfied the message "disgraces neither me nor my friends."[8]

Seward's next task was to select state officials. There were a handful of positions that he could fill on his own, such as his personal secretary. There were also cabinet positions, such as secretary of state, appointed by the combined vote of the assembly and senate; because of their majority in the more numerous assembly, the Whigs could fill these posts without Democratic interference. Seward let Weed make the cabinet decisions, explaining to a friend that he believed it was his duty "to receive, not to make, a cabinet." There was a vast third group of positions, however, to be nominated by the governor and confirmed by the state senate. This category included hundreds of mayors, county clerks, judges, and inspectors for various products.[9]

It was initially unclear how the senate, still under the control of the Democrats, would handle nominations from Seward. Each eager Whig candidate for office assumed that—however the senate might treat any other candidate—his own nomination would be approved, so they besieged Seward with requests. He reviewed hundreds of applications and made nominations, but the senate by and large ignored them. Weed complained in the *Albany Evening Journal* that the senate was rejecting even neutral or Democratic nominations, but the senate persisted. Relatively few Whigs were confirmed during Seward's first year in office, leading many to look forward to the fall election because they hoped to be appointed to state offices in the new year. One paper described these Whigs as being "as badly off as [the mythological] thirsty Tantalus, up to his chin in the water" but unable to drink.[10]

The main debate in the legislature in 1839 was over Seward's internal improvement proposals. The Democratic papers believed that his plan to extend canals and roads "through every valley and over every hill" would lead to a debt of tens of millions of dollars and ultimately to "oppressive taxation." The Whig assembly passed several improvement bills, but they were all "strangled" (in Weed's word) in the Democratic senate. Weed argued in the *Evening Journal* that this set up a clear issue for voters in the fall elections: if they wanted further internal improvements, they needed to vote for Whigs. More generally, if voters wanted to give Seward a chance to implement his vision of a strong, progressive state government, they needed to give the Whigs control of both houses of the legislature.[11]

Although Seward did not explicitly campaign, he traveled extensively and spoke frequently in this critical political year. In May, at the annual meeting of the American Bible Society, he remarked that "the existing government of this country could never have had its existence but for the Bible." After a few weeks in Auburn, during which his third son, William, was born, Seward was back in New York City, where he addressed thousands of Sunday School teachers and students, wishing them "God speed in your benevolent and patriotic labors." Both speeches were widely reprinted in evangelical newspapers. But evangelicals were not the only religious voters whom Seward courted; he also wrote a letter to the sheriff of Lewis County, directing him to allow a Catholic priest to visit a condemned Catholic prisoner. *Niles' National Register*, the leading national paper, printed the letter and commended the governor for avoiding the anti-Catholic bigotry so common among Whigs.[12]

Seward spent two weeks in August touring northern New York, explaining that he did so in order "to learn the resources, the interests, and the exigencies of this portion of the state." After only a few days in Auburn, he was off for another long trip, this time to the western part of the state. He was received with so much enthusiasm at Buffalo, including five hundred men in a torchlight parade, that he wrote to Weed it "flattered my vanity exceedingly." After checking on the land office in Chautauqua, he returned to Auburn by way of the southern tier of counties. In late October, on the eve of the election, he hosted a large reception in Albany. Frances, who was in Albany on one of her rare visits, complained to her sister that their house was filled with people "who came here to drink Champagne and cover the carpet with mud tobacco spit and lamp oil." These, she said, were the "beauties of Democracy." [13]

There is a story about Seward's travels during this period, probably apocryphal, but so appropriate that he would later tell it on himself. He was traveling by stagecoach, sitting on the box and talking with the driver, who did not recognize him and could not guess his occupation. Seward told him that he was the governor. The driver would not believe it; it was impossible that one so young, so unpretentious, should be governor. Seward suggested that they ask the innkeeper at the next stop, but there the innkeeper said that the driver was right, that the passenger was not the governor. "Well then who," Seward demanded, "*is* the governor?" "Why," came the response, "Thurlow Weed." The popular image of Seward as a puppet of Weed was not in fact correct. The two men worked together closely, with Weed taking the lead on questions of patronage and Seward on policy questions. Both recognized, however, that in the end Seward was governor and Weed just a friend and adviser. They occasionally disagreed, but on the whole it is remarkable how well they worked together during Seward's years as governor. [14]

Seward was not the only politician traveling New York for political purposes in the summer of 1839. President Martin Van Buren, hoping to retain Democratic control of the state senate, and looking forward to his own re-election campaign the following year, spent much of the summer in his home state. Seward was invited to a dinner to honor the president, but declined in a long letter, reprinted in the newspapers, explaining that although he honored the office of the presidency, he disagreed with all the policies of its current incumbent. Henry Clay, the Whig senator from Kentucky, was running again for president and spent several weeks touring New York that summer. When Seward and Clay met by chance on a ferryboat on Lake Champlain, Seward tried to hint at the difficulties Clay would face in New York among evangelical Whigs. Clay ignored the warning and pressed Seward to visit him in Saratoga Springs, but Seward declined, anxious to remain neutral among the various Whig presidential candidates. [15]

One would never have guessed, from the way in which Seward had responded to the abolitionist campaign questions, or from his passing mention of blacks in his first message, that Governor Seward would become an advocate for New York's black citizens. Yet in the summer of 1839, he took the first steps in this direction. In late July, the governor received an official request from Virginia to hand over three free black seamen who had helped a slave escape from Norfolk. Seward did not grant the request, responding informally through his secretary that he thought the three men, who were in jail in New York City, should have a chance to be heard in court. A month later, after city officials had released all three, Seward received another letter from Virginia, asking him for an official answer. Seward cited the technical defects in the Virginia papers, and also argued that "there is no law of this State which recognizes slavery, no statute which admits that one man can be the property of another, or that one man can be stolen from another." This elicited an angry attack from Virginia, which led to another letter from Seward, in which he defended his state's right to make its own decisions on extradition requests. But although he wrote these letters during the election campaign, he did not publish them, because he did not want to anger southern sympathizers in New York. The letters did not emerge until after election day, when they were published in Virginia.[16]

Both parties were prepared to use questionable tactics in this election. On the Sunday before election day, several of Seward's friends in New York City raised funds, chartered a steamboat, traveled upriver to Albany, and handed Weed a handkerchief containing $8,000. Weed later recalled that he did not use all of this cash, but did distribute it generously, especially in the crucial senate district in and around Albany. Weed's account strongly suggests that Seward was aware of these events, and there is also a letter from Seward's friend, the New York lawyer and financier Richard Blatchford, just after the election, pressing Seward to do a political favor for one of those who had helped raise the funds. It took a while for the votes to be counted—Frances reported home that nothing was discussed in Albany for a week other than election results—but by mid-November it was clear that the Whigs would have majorities in both houses of the next legislature.[17]

Before the new legislature met, however, Seward faced a tenant crisis in the region around Albany, somewhat like the tenant crisis he had faced as land agent in Chautauqua. The roots of the crisis were in the feudal agreements between the Van Rensselaer landlords and their tenants, under which the tenants were required to make annual rent payments, to provide the landlord with services, and also to pay a substantial fee upon any sale of their land. Any breach of any covenant in these agreements would entitle the landlord to repossess not only the land but also any improvements attached to the land—houses, barns, and crops. In the fall of 1839, tenants made it difficult to enforce the leases by obstructing sheriffs as they tried to serve court writs. In early December the sheriff of Albany County, accompanied by a crowd of several hundred serving as his "deputies," encountered an even larger crowd of tenants who refused to let the sheriff pass or to serve his writs. The sheriff asked Seward for military force. Seward was reluctant—he did not want to anger those who had just voted for the Whigs—but when an armed posse met similar resistance a few days later, his hand was forced. After an all-night cabinet meeting, Seward summoned troops and declared that anyone who resisted would be severely punished. Informally, the governor suggested that he would find a way, with the new legislature, to weaken the tenant agreements. Seward's actions pacified the tenants for a while, but in the end he was not able to solve the complex problems created by these ancient leases.[18]

———

While Seward was busy in Albany with this tenant rebellion, Weed was busy in Harrisburg, Pennsylvania, at the first national convention of the Whig Party. As the convention gathered in December, there were three leading candidates for the presidential nomination: Henry Clay, the great Kentucky senator; General Winfield Scott, originally from Virginia but now known nationwide for his military service, first in the War of 1812 and later in Indian wars; and William Henry Harrison, hero of the battle against the Indians at Tippecanoe and more recently senator from Ohio. Seward was neutral among the candidates, not wanting to alienate the friends of any of them as he looked forward to his own 1840 re-election campaign. Weed, however, was far from neutral, strongly favoring Scott and then, when it became clear that Scott could not prevail, throwing his support and that of the New York delegation behind Harrison. The convention nominated Harrison for president and John Tyler of Virginia for vice president, leading to the slogan "Tippecanoe and Tyler too." Clay and his supporters were understandably upset; a friend reported to Seward that Clay was "fully satisfied that he has been driven off by a few individuals in New York." The hostility of the Clay men against Seward may have been unfair, since it was Weed, not Seward, who was at the convention. But fair or unfair, their anger was intense and persistent. As one Clay partisan wrote seven years later, he was determined to see the "punishment of Seward & Co. for defrauding the country of Mr. Clay in 1840."[19]

Once again, in the latter part of December, Seward devoted every waking hour to the preparation of his message, due at the outset of the legislative session in early January 1840. Frances reported to Henry's father that "there were ten nights that [Seward] never went to bed. All the sleep he had was obtained by throwing himself upon the sofa in the room where he wrote." Seward was well aware of the importance of this message, not just for the state but for the nation. Harrison and Tyler would form a strong Whig ticket, but Van Buren, known with reason as the "Little Magician," would run a strong race for the Democrats. The election in New York would be close and crucial, since the state had about one out of every six electoral votes for president. So Seward in his message had to think not just about New York and his own re-election but the nation, and the election of the first Whig president.[20]

Although he did not mention Harrison or Van Buren by name in his message, Seward did include strong criticism of the Van Buren administration, calling its economic policies "impracticable," "unjust," and "unmitigated evil." He also attacked the way in which, first under Jackson and now Van Buren, "the power and influence of the executive department of the federal government are greatly increased," and he suggested that the federal Constitution be amended to "limit the tenure of the presidential office to a single term." He did not need to say that the simplest way to limit Van Buren to one term would be to elect Harrison.[21]

It was more difficult this year to argue for an aggressive internal improvement program because the estimated costs of some projects had proved far too low, and because economic conditions made it difficult and expensive to borrow. Indeed, several American states were on the verge of default, making investors doubtful about any state debt. Seward was not discouraged. The revolutionary generation, he said in his message, had obtained independence "not for one generation only, nor for a narrow cycle of years, nor for any period, but for all generations, and for all time." The current generation should proceed in the same spirit, for internal improvements would be "everywhere salutary in encouraging emigration and the settlement and improvement of new lands, in augmenting national wealth, in promoting agriculture, commerce, manufactures, and the diffusion of knowledge, and in strengthening the bonds of our national Union." Democrats scoffed that Seward was simply proposing more spending in order to buy votes in the upcoming election. But the Whig legislators agreed with him and voted to expand the Erie Canal and undertake several other key projects.[22]

For many New York City Whigs, the most urgent issue for the state legislature was electoral reform; they wanted to keep Democrats from stealing elections through the use of illegal voters, generally those of immigrants who were not yet citizens. Seward agreed, up to a point. "It is of vital importance to the security of our institutions," he said in this message, "not only that our elections should be conducted with impartiality . . . but that there should be entire and universal confidence in their purity." He made it clear, however, that he was not willing to use electoral reform as an excuse to render it more difficult for immigrants to become citizens or for those who were citizens to vote.[23]

Seward also returned, in this message, to the related topic of the education of the children of immigrants, especially the thousands of Irish Catholics in New York City. At this time the "public" schools in the city were run by a Protestant group, the Public School Society (PSS), and used the King James Bible and other Protestant texts. Very few Catholic children attended PSS schools, and although there were a handful of Catholic schools, their resources were far from adequate. Seward recommended "the establishment of schools in which [immigrant children] may be instructed by teachers speaking the same language with themselves and professing the same faith." What he was really suggesting was that the Catholic schools should receive a share of public school funding, as religious schools in the city had done until 1825 and as such schools elsewhere still did.[24]

The legislature ignored the governor's education proposals but passed a voter registration law. The law applied only to New York City and required every voter there to register with three commissioners, vesting almost unchecked powers in these commissioners. Seward, who viewed the law as unwise and unconstitutional, drafted a veto message. The text of his draft was not made public, but the fact that he was drafting a veto was reported, and many Whigs were outraged that their governor was questioning a measure they viewed as so vital. One legislator reportedly told Seward that "the party would not permit such an indignity as a refusal," and that if he persisted, the legislature would adjourn, without passing any necessary bills. Seward finally yielded and signed the registry bill. He wrote to a friend that he did so "against every sentiment of his heart."[25]

The status of slaves was another issue in this legislative year. Although Seward's message did not include any formal proposals, he worked informally with Whig legislators who were keen to do something about the "diabolical man-catchers" employed to capture alleged fugitive slaves in New York. One law passed in 1840 implemented Seward's position that any person accused of being a fugitive slave should have the right to a jury trial. This law also required the state's district attorneys to intervene on behalf of anyone accused of being a fugitive, an important protection for blacks who often did not have the funds to pay for private lawyers. A second law, passed and signed soon thereafter, authorized the governor to appoint agents to go to slave states to negotiate the rescue of free blacks captured and sold into slavery.[26]

After he presented his message, Seward devoted many weeks to appointments. He heard from hundreds of applicants and their friends, from people as diverse as Washington Irving (who hoped to find a position for a nephew) and General Winfield Scott (who did not want to trouble Seward but then *did* trouble him with three separate requests). The governor read letters and interviewed candidates from morning till night; he later estimated that he "conversed with fifty persons every day." Seward was well aware that patronage was a double-edged sword, that in rewarding some he was disappointing others, and in many cases exacerbating local political tensions. After this wave of appointments was over, he wrote a friend that "if the Whig party is not ruined by the results of the appointments it is because, as I believe in fact, it is incapable of ruin. I have already appointed 1,200 persons and disappointed *five* times that number." To another friend he wrote that he made only one claim about his appointments: "that no interest, passion, prejudice, or partiality of my own has controlled any decision I have made." There were inevitably some mistakes, but historians generally agree that Seward made good appointments.[27]

He gained one important ally in his education efforts in July, when the Catholic leader and bishop John Hughes returned to New York City after a year in Europe. Hughes immediately threw himself into the struggle against the Public School Society and its monopoly on public school funding in the city. In August 1840, he forwarded to Seward a copy of one of his speeches, with a letter commending the governor's "high, liberal, and *true* American views" on education. Seward responded with equal warmth: "I need not assure you of my sympathy in regard to the ultimate object of your efforts, the education of the poor. I content myself therefore with saying that it will afford me great pleasure to consult with you freely on the subject." The two would become fast friends.[28]

That same August, the Whig state convention wholeheartedly nominated Seward to serve a second term. His Democratic opponent was William Bouck, a former state legislator. In keeping with the custom, Seward did not campaign, but he still managed to get his views before the voters. On the Fourth of July, for example, in a speech in Otsego County, he declared that republican government could "only be maintained in a community where education is universally enjoyed, and where internal improvements bind together the various portions of a country in a community of interest and affection." In August, in a letter declining an invitation to speak, he commented on the "glorious spectacle" of the current campaign, saying he expected the people would correct the error they had made in electing Van Buren. In another such letter, Seward praised the log cabin, the symbol of the Harrison-Tyler campaign, saying that he had always found a warmer welcome among the log cabins of the poor than the marble palaces of the rich. All of these letters were printed in various newspapers, including the *Log Cabin*, the highly successful Whig campaign paper edited by Seward's friend Horace Greeley.[29]

Seward knew how to get himself into the newspapers, but he also knew how to stay out of them. Throughout the summer of 1840, the governor of Virginia, Thomas Gilmer, pressed Seward to respond to his renewed request for the three men who had helped the Virginia slave escape. Seward kept putting Gilmer off with excuses. He did not send Gilmer his answer, in which he reiterated and expanded his position, until a few days after the election, thus ensuring that the Virginia correspondence was not an issue in the New York campaign.[30]

Other aspects of his work as governor, however, were issues in the state campaign. The Democrats charged that Seward was spending and borrowing carelessly, which would ultimately lead to higher taxes; that he had needlessly called out the militia from Albany during the anti-rent crisis; that he was still a land agent for the Holland Land Company, and thus a puppet of the banks rather than a servant of the people; and that he had used the pardon power for political purposes. Seward responded to this last allegation in a long public letter, listing and explaining every pardon he had given to date, and showing with statistics that he was granting fewer pardons than his predecessors. At the end of the campaign, the Democratic papers printed charges that James Glentworth, a Whig operative, had imported illegal voters from Philadelphia to New York in 1838. The papers could not prove that Seward himself was involved in this operation, but they showed that his close friends were, and that after the election Seward had rewarded Glentworth with the prime position of inspector of tobacco for New York City. The Whig papers parried these Democratic attacks as best they could.[31]

In November, after the campaign was over and the votes were counted, William Henry Harrison was elected president and Seward was re-elected governor. Harrison prevailed in New York over Van Buren by a comfortable margin of about 14,000 votes. Seward, on the other hand, had only a narrow margin of 5,000 votes over his opponent Bouck. Many observers believed that the difference was primarily due to what one paper called Seward's "attempts to conciliate the Catholics," and some friends pressed him to reverse what they viewed as his pro-Catholic policies. Seward angrily refused. "This right hand drops off," he wrote to Benjamin Silliman, a Whig supporter in New York City, "before I do one act with the Whig or any other party in opposition to any portion of my fellow citizens, on the ground of the difference of their nativity or of their religion." Seward also rejected as "untrue" and "unworthy" the charge that "Bishop Hughes and his clergy have excited the Catholics against us." Seward shared this correspondence with Hughes, who wrote back to thank him and to lament how his "poor people" seemed to be "at the disposition of reckless and unprincipled leaders." [32]

With the election of Harrison as president, Whigs could begin to hand out among themselves thousands of federal patronage positions. Seward's consistent response to requests for help in this process was that he would "refrain from interfering in any way with the dispensation of federal patronage." In reality, he would interfere in some cases. The most important federal office in New York, because it controlled hundreds of other offices, was the customs collector of the port of New York. Seward wanted this post for Edward Curtis, a Union College man now serving in Congress. With the help of Christopher Morgan, another Whig in Congress, Seward and Weed secured this lucrative appointment for Curtis. Seward also interested himself in various other federal positions, such as postmaster of New York City, which he sought without success for his friend James Watson Webb, editor of the *Morning Courier & New-York Enquirer*.[33]

William Henry Harrison's tenure as president was brief; after less than a month in office he sickened and died. Seward was saddened by Harrison's death, but he thought that the change might help the Whigs. "President Harrison's obsequies," he wrote to his friend Francis Granger, "are a vindication of Whiggism that will sanctify it forever." President Tyler, Seward also believed, was making a good start: his inaugural was "exactly what was wanting."[34]

Seward was sometimes so sure that he was right that he failed to see how others could disagree. Such was the case with his school policy.

He wrote to an editor in 1840 that "if there was one policy in which I supposed all Republican and Christian citizens would concur in, it was this. I found however to my surprise that the proposition encountered unkind reception. . . . My surprise was followed by deep mortification when I found that a considerable portion of the political party to which I belong adopted the same perversion and condemned the policy recommended." He returned to the issue in his third annual message, delivered at the outset of 1841, in which he noted with regret that the recent census had found that many New Yorkers were illiterate. "When the census of 1850 shall be taken, I trust it will show that within the borders of the state of New York, there is no child of sufficient years who is unable to read and write." To achieve this ambitious goal, it was essential to extend education more widely in New York City. Seward insisted that "no system is perfect that does not accomplish what it proposes; that our system is, therefore, deficient in comprehensiveness, in the exact proportion of the children that it leaves uneducated." He stressed that he sought to educate these children "less from sympathy, than because the welfare of the state demands it, and can not dispense with it." He did not repeat the suggestion he had earlier made about instruction in foreign languages: what he wanted now was "the education of the entire rising generation in all the elements of knowledge we possess, and in that tongue which is the universal language of our countrymen."[35]

Catholic citizens in New York City, reading this message and knowing they would have the governor's support, promptly petitioned the legislature to change the law so that their schools could obtain a share of the public school fund. The petition was referred to the secretary of state, Seward's friend John Spencer, who served *ex officio* as the state school superintendent. Spencer's report in April 1841 confirmed and amplified the arguments Seward had been making; he estimated that less than half of the school-age children in New York City were attending school. The problem, in Spencer's view, was that the Public School Society schools ignored the wishes of parents, especially parents who disagreed with the version of Christianity taught in those schools. Spencer proposed to divide the city into smaller school districts and to allow all schools that were educating poor children to share in the public school fund.[36]

Seward fully supported Spencer's recommendations, and the two visited New York City to recruit allies. In early May, the assembly passed by a large margin a bill implementing the Spencer plan. The debate in the senate proved more difficult. Hiram Ketchum, a lawyer whom Seward had recently nominated for a judicial position, submitted to the senate a point-by-point critique of the Spencer report. The *Journal of Commerce* attacked the Catholics in a venomous article, a copy of which was provided to each senator. After several days of debate, the senate voted in late May, by a margin of only one vote, to postpone consideration of the issue until January of the following year. Seward could not do anything against the senators, but he could reach Ketchum, and he did so by withdrawing his nomination.[37]

In general, the legislative session of 1841 was a disappointment for Seward; several key measures failed at the end of the session when absences gave Democrats control of the assembly. In one respect, however, he was pleased, for the legislature supported him in his ongoing debate with Virginia. The stakes were higher this year, for Virginia had passed a law requiring that ships bound for New York be inspected for fugitives. This law would impose a substantial burden on trade between the two states, and was thus a serious concern for merchants in New York City. The Virginia law would take effect in May 1842 unless, prior to that time, New York delivered the three fugitives and repealed its Fugitive Slave Law. Seward urged the legislators not to yield to this pressure and they did not; they left the Fugitive Slave Law untouched. Moreover, the legislature reversed the state's prior policy of allowing slaveholders to keep slaves during temporary residences in the state. Seward's stance elicited praise even from Lewis Tappan, the abolitionist leader who had attacked him so mercilessly in the 1838 election. As Seward explained in a letter to two Canadian blacks, his main concern was not fairness to blacks but "the security and prosperity of my country. It is not alone the degraded race which suffers. Slavery has brought a thousand evils which affect the whole American community and will long survive the cause which produced them."[38]

In early June, a letter from Seward appeared, announcing that he would not be a candidate for reelection in November of the following year. In a long private letter to his friend Christopher Morgan, Seward explained some of the reasons for his decision. First, he did not want to lose the election: "Defeat after holding such a place four years is disgrace and ruin." Second, he was frustrated with the Whigs and their failure to follow him on such key issues as the voter registry law. "My principles are too liberal, too philanthropic, if it be not vain to say so, for my party." Third, he hoped that if he was not a candidate, he could carry the school legislation. "That measure I can carry by disconnecting it from the supposed interest I now have in advocating it." A fourth factor, which he did not mention to Morgan, was financial; he was spending far more than his income, and he needed to get back to his law practice.[39]

Seward watched with dismay in the summer of 1841 as tensions between President Tyler and congressional Whigs escalated into open warfare. In early September, all of the members of Tyler's cabinet except Secretary of State Daniel Webster resigned in protest. Equally dismaying for Seward was the financial condition of the state government. Canal and other revenues were lower than in earlier years, due to the economic slowdown; expenses were higher, due to construction on canals and roads. Conditions for borrowing were very difficult, as several states defaulted on their debts and others threatened to do so. New York's finance officials found it impossible to place long-term bonds as they had planned.[40]

At Seward's insistence, state officers went to New York City to negotiate short-term high-interest loans. This solved the immediate problem, but not the problem of how to pay these debts the next year. In November, Seward wrote to a friend in Tyler's cabinet to press the federal government to aid the struggling states: "The Union has no interests separate from those of the states, and their prosperity is the object of the federal as well as the state institutions." The debts of the states, he claimed, were mainly incurred building roads and canals that were of use to the federal government. Would it not make sense for the federal government to purchase from the states the perpetual right to enjoy these various state improvements? President Tyler was not at all interested in such a scheme, informing Congress that he could not accept "the slightest approach to an assumption by this [federal] government of the debts of the states." The states alone, Tyler said, were responsible for their debts.[41]

The fighting between Tyler and Congress, along with the continued economic difficulties, meant that Whigs lost in almost every state in the fall of 1841. New York was no exception: Democrats secured a massive majority in the assembly and a slight majority in the state senate. In a letter to John Quincy Adams, Seward tried to be philosophical: "The country demands the existence of parties, and those parties must alternate in the public councils." With his friend Spencer, however, he was more candid: "my heart is sick." There was only one silver lining in the cloud; Bishop Hughes was able to show, by endorsing some candidates and withholding endorsement from others, that he controlled a critical bloc of votes in New York City. Hughes was charged with practicing politics and serving Whig interests, but he laughed off the charges. "I was chafed and jealous when you *alone* were getting all the abuse," he wrote Seward, "but now that I am classed with you in it, I am revenged and happy."[42]

———

It is sometimes said that Seward, before he became secretary of state in 1861, had no foreign policy experience. This ignores not only his foreign travel, and his service on the Senate Foreign Relations Committee in the late 1850s, but also his central role in the major foreign policy crisis of the early 1840s, the McLeod crisis.[43]

Starting in 1836, some residents of Canada rebelled against British colonial rule. A group of these Patriots, as they called themselves, along with some American supporters, established a base on an island on the New York side of the Niagara River using an American supply ship, the *Caroline*. Late in 1837 a British-Canadian force crossed the river, attacked the *Caroline*, killed one of the crew members, and pushed the flaming vessel into the river, where it went over the Falls. Americans and especially New Yorkers were incensed, but Seward said nothing about the *Caroline* incident in public, and the excitement gradually subsided. In late 1840, however, New York authorities arrested Alexander McLeod, a Canadian officer who had foolishly boasted in an upstate tavern that he was a leader of the *Caroline* raid. Now Governor Seward could no longer avoid the issue.[44]

The British minister in Washington, Henry Fox, demanded that the United States release McLeod immediately, arguing that the *Caroline* raid was a "public act of persons in her Majesty's service," for which no one individual could properly be held responsible. Secretary of State John Forsyth responded that the federal government could not interfere in the state's prosecution of McLeod. Forsyth forwarded the correspondence to Seward, who wrote back that New Yorkers viewed the *Caroline* raid as "an unjustifiable invasion in time of peace of a portion of the territory of the United States, by a band of armed men, resulting in the destruction of American property, and the murder of one or more citizens of this State." The raiders had committed state crimes and the state authorities would prosecute those crimes. Seward admitted there was some "popular excitement" against McLeod in New York, but he claimed it would not affect the fairness of his trial.[45]

By this time there was indeed considerable popular excitement about McLeod on both sides of the Atlantic. For the *Philadelphia Public Ledger,* the British demand for his release was an insult and British demands should be met with "resistance to the last." *The Times* of London declared that if the Americans committed an act so "atrocious and disgusting" as the execution of McLeod, every Englishman would insist upon war. Lord Palmerston, the British foreign minister, agreed, warning Fox in Washington that "McLeod's execution would produce war, war immediate and frightful in its character, because it would be a war of retaliation and vengeance."[46]

In early March 1841, there was a change of cast in this drama, when Harrison became president and Webster secretary of state. Webster was determined to avoid an unnecessary war with Britain, and he sent John Crittenden, the new U.S. attorney general, to New York with instructions to speak with Seward and ensure that McLeod had "eminent counsel" for his defense. Webster also wrote to Seward himself, saying that he had heard that the governor intended to terminate the prosecution of McLeod, and thanking him for an action that would help avoid "dangers of collision with a foreign power." When Crittenden arrived in New York, he learned that Webster was mistaken about Seward's plans, that the governor had no intention of terminating the state's prosecution. Seward emphasized to Crittenden the outcry that an early dismissal of the case would cause in New York and elsewhere. Such a dismissal would "be certain and utter ruin to him [Seward] and the whole Whig party of this state." Seward also hinted to Crittenden that, in the unlikely event that McLeod was convicted, Seward would use his pardon power to prevent execution. This hint somehow did not make its way back to Webster in Washington.[47]

In late March and early April, there were two further changes in the McLeod cast. The first was momentous for the nation: Harrison died and Tyler became president. The second was far more modest: an upstate lawyer, Joshua Spencer, joined the McLeod defense team. A few weeks later, when he learned that Tyler had appointed Spencer as the federal district attorney, Seward immediately suspected what is now clear from the archives: that Webster arranged both of Spencer's appointments so that he could direct McLeod's defense from Washington. Seward dashed off a short letter to the president, suggesting that he consider whether it was wise to have the federal district attorney appear in opposition to the state government in such a high-profile case.[48]

Tyler replied that Spencer was representing McLeod merely as a private lawyer and not in an official capacity; at this time it was normal for a government lawyer to continue to have a private practice. The federal government's only role, Tyler claimed, was to provide McLeod's counsel with copies of official correspondence. The president may not have known it, but this was not true; within days of Tyler's letter, Webster was in New York, meeting quietly with Spencer to plan McLeod's defense. Seward wrote back to Tyler to argue that, given the intense interest in New York in the McLeod case, it was unwise and improper to allow a federal official to serve as his counsel. Tyler, in a long letter probably drafted by Webster, responded that they would not "deprive a man placed upon trial for his life, of the services of his retained counsel merely because that counsel holds a commission from this government." Seward responded in an even longer letter. "The State of New York," he insisted, "cannot without dishonor, especially under what must be construed as a menace by Great Britain, retire from the prosecution in which she is vindicating the property and lives of her citizens."[49]

While Seward and Tyler wrote back and forth, McLeod's motion to dismiss was heard by the state supreme court. As Webster directed,

Spencer contended that the case should be dismissed because the British government had acknowledged the raid as an official act. As Seward suggested, state Attorney General Willis Hall argued that McLeod could not be immunized from his personal criminal responsibility by some after-the-fact comments from British diplomats. The state court sided with Seward, ruling that the case could proceed to trial. Webster disagreed with the court's opinion and was displeased with Seward, calling him "a contemptible fellow." Seward was aware of Webster's wrath if not his precise words, writing that "Daniel Webster has the most powerful intellect in the land; and yet one possessed of much less wisdom might have been expected to consult so important a party as New York."[50]

Alexander McLeod was by this time in a jail near Utica, the neutral venue to which his trial had been moved. Rumors reached Seward, both from sources in New York and from Webster in Washington, that some Patriots intended to attack the jail, kill McLeod, and thereby start a war between the United States and Britain. Here was an issue on which Seward and Webster could agree; it would be, in Seward's words, "an outrage upon all law and justice" if the prisoner was attacked or harmed while in state custody. The governor immediately posted additional guards; he traveled to Utica himself to inspect the arrangements; and he reported to Webster on these steps, assuring him that the people around Utica were prosperous and settled, not at all likely to support a lawless attack upon a county jail.[51]

In early October, in a packed courtroom in Utica, the trial of McLeod on murder and arson charges finally started. Attorney General Hall, in his opening for the state, described how the Canadians had attacked the *Caroline* and murdered the innocent sailor. Hall then presented various state witnesses, but those who were on the *Caroline* on the night of the attack were not sure that they had seen McLeod, and those who heard him boast of the attack were not very reliable. Spencer presented as the key defense witness a retired British Army officer, who testified that McLeod had spent the night in question at his home. When the defense tried to impeach the officer by showing that McLeod was engaged in an adulterous relationship with the officer's daughter, the judge ruled the questions out of order. After a week's trial, the jury decided that McLeod was not guilty. Willis Hall, understandably upset, wrote Seward that "I have saved you the trouble of pardoning McLeod." Seward was not surprised; his private secretary Samuel Blatchford had reported from Utica that it appeared McLeod had a solid defense. And the governor was not displeased, for he had achieved his main goal: a state trial, free from federal or foreign interference.[52]

———

In his fourth and final annual message to the legislature, presented in January 1842, Seward renewed his call for education legislation. The Public School Society, "after a fair and sufficient trial," had failed to secure the confidence of thousands of parents in New York City. The PSS trustees seemed to believe that "society must conform itself to the public schools, instead of the public schools adapting themselves to the exigencies of society." The critical point for Seward was to give the citizens of the city of New York proper control over the education of their children. He was less concerned with the details of how this was done than to see that it was done.[53]

As a result of the 1841 election, the Democrats led the legislature to which the governor presented this message, but many Democratic leaders were also keen to take action on the school issue, for they did not want to see Bishop Hughes influence the spring city election in the same way he had influenced the fall elections. The Democrats appointed as chairman of the relevant assembly committee William Maclay, a New York City Democrat who was acceptable to both the PSS and the Catholic leaders. After consultations with Seward and others, Maclay's committee issued a bill to treat each ward of the city as a separate school district, electing its own school trustees and inspectors. By implication these trustees would be free to provide some school funds to Catholic schools. The bill passed the assembly by a substantial margin in late March.[54]

Hughes wrote to Seward on the day after the bill passed the assembly to "congratulate you with my whole heart on the triumph which you have gained over false friends and ferocious enemies." Bishop Hughes was concerned, however, about the fate of the bill in the senate. "I know not how far the suggestion may be a violation of propriety—but if it be, I throw myself on your indulgence—that you and Mr. Weed . . . should use your influence to bring out friends of justice and equal rights on the Whig side as well as the other [side] of the senate." He closed by asking Seward "to destroy this [letter] as soon as read"—a suggestion Seward disregarded, for the letter is still among his papers.[55]

Exactly what Seward did over the next weeks to secure Whig support for the Maclay bill in the senate is not known. It would appear that he did not succeed, for when the bill passed the senate in April, every Whig present (a few were absent) voted against it. Perhaps the Whig legislators agreed with Horace Greeley, who criticized the last version of the bill as a "barefaced [Democratic] party measure" designed only to influence the city election, which was already in progress. Perhaps the Whig legislators knew that there would be enough Democratic votes to pass the bill, and voted no to please their constituents. Seward complained to a friend that the education issue was a "fiery trial" through which his party forced him to pass alone. Even though the final Maclay bill was not exactly what they would have wished, Seward and Hughes chose to regard it as a success. Seward wrote Hughes that the bill was "an acknowledgement of the vices of the old system and its unequal operation." He thought that the very flaws in the bill would perhaps prove useful, for they would force continued public attention to the issue, and perhaps lead to better legislation in the near future.[56]

Many of the questions Seward faced in 1842 were over whether to veto bills passed by the Democrats. In general, he agreed with his friend Greeley, now editor of the *New York Tribune,* who wrote to remind him that Whigs believed "the legislature is chosen to make and alter laws, not the governor." But Seward sometimes encountered difficulties in following this advice. In one instance, when he signed a law and added an explanation of why he disagreed with its policy, the senate voted to remove his explanation from its journal.[57]

In some cases, Seward achieved success simply because the legislators could not agree among themselves. South Carolina had now joined Virginia in passing a law to require rigorous inspection of ships bound for New York. Like the Virginia law, the South Carolina law was set to take effect on May 1, 1842, unless on or before that date New York repealed its Fugitive Slave Law. Seward relayed the South Carolina law to the state legislators, making it clear that he continued to support the Fugitive Slave Law and oppose the proposed repeal. There was some debate in the legislature, but the repeal bill died; all the legislature could manage was a non-binding resolution declaring that stealing a slave was in its view a crime under the federal Constitution.[58]

The governor and the state faced once again, in early 1842, the inter-related issues of internal improvements and state finances. Seward was determined to continue work on improvements, and contended that stopping work would cost more, in terms of damages on contracts, than carrying the work forward. He saw no reason to believe that the cost of the current projects would surpass the state's resources, either in the form of canal revenues or taxes. Michael Hoffman, a leading Democrat in the state assembly, contended in response that Seward's reckless spending had increased the state debt from about $11 million to more than $27 million in only three years. In early March, Hoffman's com-mittee reported a "stop and tax" bill, proposing to stop the ongoing public works and tax property in order to reduce debt. Ironically, on almost the same day, Seward and many of the legislators traveled by rail to Springfield, Massachusetts, where there was a joint session of the legislatures of the two states to celebrate the new rail connection between them. This grand event, at which the governor was one of the principal speakers, did not dissuade the New York legislature from its determination—at the end of the month the legislators passed and Seward reluctantly signed the stop and tax bill into law.[59]

During the summer of 1842, while the legislators were back at their homes, Seward remained in Albany, working on the book he entitled *Notes on the State of New York*. He hoped to survey all aspects of New York—ranging from history to politics to agriculture—as Thomas Jef-ferson had done in his *Notes on the State of Virginia*. But Seward al-lowed himself too little time for this project and relied too heavily on the contributions of outside experts. By the end of the process he was heartily sick of it, writing to Frances that he was "in the hands of the printers, who so slowly drag along that they chain me here, I know not how long." Much of the final product was forgettable, but there were passages of pure Seward. The section on political history, for ex-ample, lauded John Jay's early efforts against slavery and denounced the provision in the 1821 state constitution that set a prohibitive property requirement for black voters. In the section on public libraries, Seward said they were now "distributed so as to bring a library within the reach of every family" in the state, and that given the state's role in the world, "it is perhaps not presumptuous to suppose that the ripened fruits of the plan are to be developed in the intellectual, moral, and social improvement of the whole human family."[60]

Seward played almost no role in the election of 1842 other than to serve as a target for Democratic attacks. The Democratic candidate for governor prevailed by 20,000 votes; the Democrats also won an overwhelming majority in the assembly and strengthened their majority in the senate. As Weed conceded in the *Albany Evening Journal,* "we are beaten, not by the 'meagre' majority anticipated, but by an avalanche! It is a regular out-and-out Waterloo affair."[61]

Seward had little time to comment on the election because he was busy considering a contentious pardon request from John Colt, brother of the inventor Samuel Colt. Many of the facts were clear: there had been a quarrel between Colt and another man, which escalated into a fight, during which Colt killed the man with a hatchet. Colt confessed to the killing, but claimed that he had acted in self-defense, as his opponent had almost choked him to death. Colt was convicted and after some unsuccessful appeals sentenced to death. Seward devoted many long days to "hearing every form of application for pardon to Colt," to "studying the voluminous papers submitted," and then to writing his explanation for why he refused the pardon. Even after this explanation, there were many last-minute pleas to Seward to spare Colt from execution. Colt in the end managed to avoid the hangman; an hour before his appointed execution he was found dead in his cell, having committed suicide with a smuggled dagger.[62]

The excitement over Colt had scarcely subsided when Seward was presented with another controversial pardon case, that of his friend the editor James Watson Webb. Webb's newspaper had mercilessly attacked the members of Congress opposed to a national bankruptcy law, and one of these members challenged Webb to a duel. Webb traveled to Delaware for the confrontation, during which he was slightly wounded. Not long after his return, Webb was accused of violating the law against leaving the state for purposes of a duel. He admitted the facts, was convicted, and sentenced to two years in prison. Seward granted the pardon, noting that although dueling was both immoral and illegal, Webb was one of very few ever charged or convicted under New York's laws against dueling, and that none of these had served prison time. Seward's pardon included some unusual conditions: he prohibited Webb from dueling and from publishing "any justification or defense of the practice of dueling."[63]

On the last day of 1842, as his term as governor came to a close, Seward wrote to his friend Weed: "My public career is honorably closed, and I am yet young enough, if a reasonable age is allotted to me, to repair all the waste of private fortune it has cost. Gratitude to God, and gratitude and affection towards my friends, and most of all to you, my first and most efficient and most devoted friend, oppresses me, until tears like such as woman sheds flow whenever I am alone." Seward was puzzled as to why Weed and others had helped him so generously. "I am a mystery to myself. What am I? What is there belongs to me that has entitled me or secured to me, without a claim, such friendship and affection?" He knew that without Weed, he could not have become or survived as governor. "Without your aid how hopeless would have been my prospect of reaching the elevation from which I am descending; how could I have sustained myself there; how could I have avoided the assaults to which I have been exposed; how could I have secured the joyous reflections of this hour?"[64]

The first day of 1843 was a Sunday, and Seward spent it attending church and visiting friends. On Monday, he attended the inauguration of his rival and successor, after which he stepped forward, shook the new governor by the hand, and congratulated him in a few words. This had never happened before; people "stood in open-mouthed surprise" at the sight of a Whig governor speaking with his Democratic successor. After a few more days, Seward left Albany by train, taking with him (in the words of the *Evening Journal*) "the unfeigned and heartfelt wishes of thousands of our citizens for his happiness and prosperity." There were no thousands at the other end of the journey in Auburn. Indeed, because he arrived a bit ahead of schedule, there was no one to meet him at all. As he reported in a letter to Weed, he walked from the train station to his home "solitary and alone, through the dark streets wet with plashy snow and ice."[65]

In many ways, Seward's four years as governor were not successful. The Maclay bill did not measurably increase the proportion of children attending school in New York City. The enlargement of the Erie Canal was stalled for several years by the Stop and Tax Act, and then progressed so slowly that it was not finished for two decades. Immigrants did not receive the warm welcome Seward advocated; indeed, they would soon be subjected to even stronger attacks. Blacks received some limited protections under the laws passed while Seward was governor, but they remained an oppressed minority. Yet in other ways Seward was a great governor. He established the principle that the public schools of New York City had to be run by public officials. He proclaimed the ideals of universal public education and universal literacy. He bravely opposed religious prejudice. He persuaded people that internal improvements were not just about transportation; they were about extending prosperity more widely and knitting the nation together more closely. As a mainstream political leader, Governor Seward highlighted and legitimized concerns about slavery and former slaves in a way that the abolitionists, perceived as mere extremists, never could. He set out an agenda for legal and administrative reform that would be implemented over time, starting with the New York state constitution of 1846, which abolished the Court of Chancery and the Court of Errors. In all these ways, Seward showed that the Whig Party was not just a party of the past, committed to protecting privilege; the Whig Party could be a party of the future, looking to extend political rights and economic prosperity to the people of the state and the nation.

CHAPTER 4

"You and I Can and Must Do It":

1843–1849

W hen Seward returned to Auburn in early 1843, he was in his early forties but he was still, in his wife's words, "the most indefatigable of men." Frances wrote to her sister Lazette that he had spent a spring day with the servants, moving shrubs and trees into the yard, working in shirtsleeves until well after dark. His son Frederick recalled this same vigor: "He liked a large house, and plenty of people in it; a good fire, and a large family-circle round it; a full table, strong coffee, and the dishes 'hot and sweet and nice.' He preferred long rides, long and fatiguing walks, bathing in cold water or strong surf, working steadily for hours, and even taking recreation with determination and perseverance. No one ever saw him listless, or complaining of ennui."[1]

Seward would need this energy in order to deal with his debts: at the end of his second term as governor he owed various creditors at least $200,000 and perhaps as much as $400,000. In part this debt was the result of his generous lifestyle. Frederick later claimed that the family did not live extravagantly, but the claim is belied by receipts in the Seward House files for silver from Galt's and glassware from Tiffany's, not to mention champagne, oysters, and Cuban cigars. The largest part of the debt, however, was the bond Seward had given to secure his share of the Chautauqua lands, which were not yet paying rents equal to the interest. Seward was understandably concerned about his ability to repay these immense sums.[2]

He had no law firm to which he could return; the two men who had been his Auburn law partners before he became governor were now engaged in other pursuits. So Seward started over, opening a one-man office and advertising that he would attend to any legal work given to him. At first he had none. He wrote that "thus far my neighbors, astonished by the discovery that a Governor can descend to the bar, favor me with congratulations but not with fees." By May, however, he could report that "my professional business steadily increases and with length of life I may redeem even the hopes of a statesman." He estimated that he would earn $5,000 in his first year, perhaps more thereafter.[3]

The household Seward was supporting at this time included himself, his wife Frances, her father Judge Miller, her aunt Clara Miller, and four children, soon to be five. There were a few servants, although Frances often complained to her sister about their incompetence. And there were frequent guests, including Seward's parents, who arrived in May 1843, occupied two prime rooms, and (Frances told her sister) did not give any indication that they intended to depart.[4]

Other visitors in the summer of 1843 were two artists, Chester Harding and Henry Inman. There was a tradition that after a governor's retirement, his portrait would be painted for the collection of New York City Hall. Because Seward and his friends could not agree on which artist should paint the portrait, each of the two artists spent a week or so at the house, painting and enjoying the hospitality. Harding reported home that "Madam is also very beautiful; black eyes; dark hair; and a fine figure. She is very modest, and very intelligent; has read a great deal, and talks politics almost as well as her husband—not from choice, but only when the others choose to give the conversation a political turn." Seward wrote to Weed that Inman's portrait was "admitted on all hands to be a strong likeness; but it is generally said that it is not a pleasing one." When both pictures were finished and presented, the city's committee of experts could not decide which to prefer, and Inman and Harding agreed that they would "toss up." Inman won the coin toss, so his portrait of Seward is now part of the collection at New York's City Hall. Seward loaned the Harding portrait to the state when he left for Washington in 1849, and it is still in the state collection in Albany today.[5]

In late July, former President John Quincy Adams, on a tour of New York, and accompanied by several family members, arrived at Seward's house. Frances, who was not expecting company, barely had time to take off her slippers and light some candles. Adams made a few remarks from the steps of the house, but Frances could not hear much because her aunt was complaining about "the devastation made by men and boys upon the shrubbery." There was predictable confusion about where the Adams family members should sleep. The next morning, Seward and Adams arose at five to tour the town's most famous institution, the state prison, returned for breakfast, and then went out again for a municipal welcome ceremony. One benefit of this visit for Frances was that it roused her father-in-law out of his room "for the first time in weeks, looking very much like a dead man."[6]

The summer of 1843 was also when Seward's oldest son Augustus enrolled at West Point. Frances had hoped that her son would attend a standard college, not the military academy, but Augustus realized that he was not a scholar, and he pleaded with his father to secure him an Army commission. Seward forwarded his son's letter to his congressional friend Christopher Morgan, with a note saying that "I am willing to do almost anything rather than my boy should be disappointed." After Augustus started at West Point, his mother, whose aversion to war made her almost a pacifist, fretted that he did not have proper food and complained that he was given demerits for trivial offenses. Every time Augustus returned home, Frances pressed him to reconsider and resign. "One suggestion from Henry I think would change the whole matter," she wrote to her sister, but her husband supported Augustus, and "with his father's influence on that side mine will weigh but little." In another letter Frances said that her son would "never know—(*men* never *do* know half the suffering they cause)—how many sleepless nights and sad days he will bring his mother." Augustus managed to graduate in the summer of 1847, ranked thirty-fourth in his class of thirty-eight men.[7]

The next child in order of age in the household was Clarence, adopted by Seward after the death of his brother Jennings. Clarence enrolled at Hobart College, in nearby Geneva, New York, in 1844, and upon graduation joined Seward's law office. Frederick, slight of build but very bright, started at Union College at the age of fifteen in 1845. A few months later Seward received a stiff letter from Dr. Nott, still college president, informing him that Frederick was attending a local dancing school, with "citizens of both sexes," without the permission of the college. Seward admonished Frederick to adhere to the rules of the college, although (as Frances wrote her sister) "we do not consider dancing in itself reprehensible." William Seward, Jr., usually known as Willie, was an active boy with weak eyes that kept him from doing much schoolwork. But he was a favorite of his father's, as evidenced by an undated note, addressed to "Master William Seward, in the Nursery," in which his father accepted "with much pleasure Master Willie's polite invitation for this evening; but as the weather is inclement hopes that the giver of the party will send a sleigh and horses for his guests—with plenty of buffalo skins."[8]

Like many men of middle age, Seward was sometimes caught between the older and younger generations. In December 1844 he received a letter from his father, summoning him to Florida, New York, where his mother was dying. Seward responded that although he wanted to be with "the best of women and of mothers" as she "passed from mortality into immortality," he could not leave his wife, who was expecting any day to deliver a child. Seward's daughter Fanny was born on December 9; his mother died on December 11. As soon as his wife and baby were out of danger, Seward departed for his parents' home, about four hundred miles over difficult winter roads. As he was returning by coach, sitting on the bench with the driver enjoying a cigar, the axle broke, and Seward was thrown to the icy ground. He remained several days near Hudson with a broken arm and bruised body, but was soon back in Auburn and at his office. Frances complained that her husband would recover faster if he could "restrain his impatience sufficiently to continue at home a week or two longer."[9]

The cigar which was, in some sense, the cause of Seward's injuries was a key part of his daily life—the "inevitable cigar," his son later wrote. Some people disapproved. One summer Sunday afternoon, when Seward called at the home of his friend David Wright, both Wright and his wife were away. As the servant showed him into the parlor, Seward asked if he could smoke. The girl hesitated, so Seward said that he would sit on the window ledge and keep his cigar outside. Mrs. Wright found him in this awkward position, but Seward told her that it was quite all right, "that they were very strict with him at home." Cigars were not his only vice; he also enjoyed a drink. On another occasion, after an evening concert, the Wrights were guests at the Seward home and were distressed to see champagne. "There was a time," Mrs. Wright wrote to her sister, "while Mr. S. was governor, that he professed to be a 'cold water man,' but I perceive he now places wine before his guests." Mrs. Wright was alluding to reports in early 1842 that Seward had served lemonade at his annual reception, which led to erroneous claims that he had "signed the total abstinence pledge." Seward never signed such a pledge, nor could he have, given how much he enjoyed wine with and after dinner.[10]

Seward was away from Auburn more than he was home in the 1840s, writing his wife often, assuring her that he loved her and the children. On the first day of 1846, for example, writing from Washington, he addressed her as the one "whose joys and sorrows are mine own, who cannot be happy without making me glad, who cannot be grieved without making me disconsolate." Henry surely loved Frances and the children, but he was not content to remain in Auburn, and she was not content to follow him in his travels around the state and around the country. They worked out an arrangement which, while not ideal, was satisfactory; Frances stayed at home in Auburn and Henry traveled more or less as he wanted or needed.[11]

In the first two years after his governorship, Seward's trips were mainly in New York and mainly for legal work. In the summer of 1845, however, he traveled in the Northwest for a month with two friends, reaching remote parts of Lake Superior. In the spring of 1846, he spent two months on a western and southern tour, visiting Cincinnati, St. Louis, and New Orleans, and stopping on the way home for a few days in Eatonton, Georgia, the home of his old school, Union Academy. Seward's letters home were long, frequent, and interesting. Observing the bustling commerce at Pittsburgh, he "could not but smile at the miserable fears of the disunion of the Republic. No political ties bring it together, and no political convulsion can shake it to pieces. The union is the handiwork of Nature." New Orleans should, by virtue of its place at the mouth of the Mississippi, be the commercial capital of the United States, he wrote in another letter, but it was comparatively unimportant. Why? Partly because of the difficulties of navigation, partly because the site was "unhealthy," but above all because power "can never permanently reside, on this continent, in a community where slavery exists."[12]

Although most of Seward's legal work in the early part of this period was commercial litigation in state courts, he did have some interesting political cases. Horace Greeley as editor of the *New York Tribune* hired Seward to defend him against libel charges filed by James Fenimore Cooper, not only a famous author but an ardent Democrat. Seward attempted to establish, through the case, a more press-friendly libel law. "The conductors of the press," he argued, "have legitimate functions to perform, and if they perform them honestly, fairly, and faithfully, they ought to be upheld, favored and protected, rather than discouraged, embarrassed, and oppressed." Another of his early clients was James Bowen, head of the New York & Erie Railroad, for whom Seward wrote an opinion letter arguing that the proposed railroad was a proper recipient of state aid. Greeley printed both these arguments in the *Tribune*.[13]

Such cases, although they advanced Seward's political goals, did not do much to reduce his debts. He probably would never have achieved the financial success necessary to allow him to return to political office without the aid of one client: James G. Wilson. Frederick later recounted how Wilson, happening to hear Seward argue a case in Albany court, immediately asked him to handle a patent case. "Seward explained that he was not familiar with that class of cases, and that the sciences of mechanics and mathematics had never been among his favorite studies, so that he doubted his ability." Wilson responded that he would take that risk if Seward would argue his cases as well as those he had just heard. Seward agreed and accepted a retainer of $200.[14]

Wilson is often described as the owner of a patent on a wood-planing machine, but this far understates his role. The machine in question, originally patented by William Woodworth in 1828, revolutionized the woodworking industry, allowing a machine rather than men to do the difficult work of preparing smooth, straight planks. Wilson acquired the patent rights from Woodworth's son and then enforced them vigorously against a host of similar machines. By the end of the 1840s, according to *Scientific American,* the Woodworth patent was known "to almost every child in the land by the amount of litigation arising therefrom." Indeed, *Scientific American* waged a minor war against Wilson, arguing that he was using the patent improperly to discourage other inventors. In modern terms, Wilson was what is known as a "patent troll," skilled in patent litigation rather than mechanical invention, and Seward was one of Wilson's principal lawyers in this controversial effort.[15]

Seward's first argument for Wilson took place in late 1845 in the federal court in Albany; when the case was appealed to the U.S. Supreme Court, Seward was part of what he called a "grand array of counsel" that included Daniel Webster. Seward billed Wilson $5,000 for his first few months of work, but this was just the start. He traveled to Cincinnati, Philadelphia, Baltimore, and Charleston, South Carolina, to argue Wilson cases in lower federal courts, and in 1850 he argued two separate Wilson cases in the Supreme Court. All of these were patent cases in some sense, but the key issues were often contractual, procedural, or constitutional. In South Carolina, for example, Seward successfully defeated two leading local lawyers in their attempt, on constitutional grounds, to force Wilson's patent claims to be decided by a jury. The *Charleston Mercury* protested against what it viewed as an outrageous decision—an abrogation of the sacred right to trial by jury—but it protested in vain.[16]

Seward's success for Wilson brought him other patent work. His clients included Jethro Wood, inventor of the modern iron plow; Erastus Corning, manufacturer of rails and railroad spikes, and founder of the town of the same name in New York; George Corliss, who developed the Corliss steam engine; and Samuel Morse, inventor of the telegraph. Seward generally represented the inventor's side, so he came to appreciate and applaud the role of inventions. "No citizen of the United States has conferred greater economical benefits on his country than Jethro Wood," he once said, and "none of her benefactors have been more inadequately rewarded." He himself, however, was amply rewarded for his patent work. Frederick wrote that patent litigation proved so lucrative that it enabled his father to "escape from the sea of debts."[17]

Seward often complained about his legal work. "I fear, abhor, detest, despise and loathe litigation," he once wrote to his wife. In another letter he told her that "we have a bright morning, which it seems almost a sacrilege to devote to this vile litigation." But these complaints must be balanced against the energy, intelligence, and passion that he brought to his legal work. One of his clerks from this period recalled that Seward did much of his work in the evening, after dinner, and the young men would arrive in the morning to find the floor "covered with manuscript" in Seward's unique hand. A man who could work in this way did not detest or despise the law; he merely had the ambivalence many lawyers feel toward their profession. Seward's legal work took him all over the country, letting him make and cement friendships, and giving him a more thorough understanding of the whole nation than almost any other politician of his generation.[18]

———

Before the end of his first month at home in Auburn, former Governor Seward was writing a political friend to lament how the Democrats, now in power in Albany, were reversing all his policies, down to trivial items such as the survey of the state's geology. In frequent letters to Weed, Seward kept in close touch with the man he affectionately addressed as the "late Dictator." In June, for example, when the Bunker Hill Monument was dedicated outside Boston, Seward joked to Weed that "the holy shrine of Mecca never witnessed more ardent worship." In September, he reported a "pleasant interview" with Millard Fillmore, at the time merely a former Whig member of Congress from Buffalo, in which each man urged the other to be the vice-presidential nominee. In October, Seward noted that his name was frequently being mentioned for vice president or governor, but told Weed that he had ended these efforts by sending a letter to a New York City newspaper declining to be a candidate in the 1844 elections.[19]

Seward's relationship with Weed during his years out of power was different than it was during the years when he was governor. Weed was still, as Seward put it, "my first last and best of friends." The two men wrote one another often and saw one another often, in Auburn, Albany, or New York City. Their families were close, and Weed's daughter Harriet was almost another daughter to Frances. With Seward out of office, however, and busy with his legal work, the two were not in daily touch as they were while Seward was governor. There were occasional disagreements. But both men knew that Seward's political career was not over, and that Weed would manage his next campaign, whether for governor or senator or some day for president. One of Seward's cabinet colleagues would later recall him declaring that "Seward is Weed and Weed is Seward. What I do, Weed approves. What he says, I endorse. We are one." Even if these were not his precise words, there is no question that for much of their political lives Seward and Weed were close to one.[20]

In September 1843, Seward attended the Whig convention for Cayuga County, and the crowd demanded that he make a short speech. He noted that he was now busy with domestic duties but that such duties were not exclusive. "If I can be of service among you," he said, "let the call come; it will never be unseasonable. It will find me willing with all my ancient zeal, stimulated and increased by enduring gratitude." It does not seem, however, that Seward did much in the fall state election, which resulted in another victory for the Democrats, in part because abolitionists deserted the Whigs.[21]

As the year of the presidential election started, observers expected that the candidates would be Henry Clay for the Whigs and Martin Van Buren for the Democrats. Most Whigs were confident that Clay would prevail, but Seward was more cautious. To win this election, he commented, the Whig Party "would need the fervor, the popular enthusiasms of 1840 to carry us through." The sources of fervor in 1840—the enthusiasm about Harrison's log cabin background and his Indian victories—would not be present in 1844. What, Seward asked, would take their place? He was also troubled by the prospect of losing yet more Whig votes to the third, abolition party.[22]

In late February 1844, in spite of the miserable weather and roads, there was an informal gathering of Whigs at Auburn. Seward started his speech with praise of Henry Clay, whom he called the certain candidate of the Whigs. He predicted that just as national gratitude had made Washington the first Whig president, so gratitude would make Clay the next Whig president. There was intense applause, and Seward tried to sit down, but the crowd insisted that he continue. "Thus far I have spoken of men," he responded, "but the principles of our cause are more important." The principles of the Whigs were not developed in the past ten years, or even past fifty years, he said; they dated back hundreds of years, to those in England, Scotland, and Ireland who resisted the tyranny of kings. The "pure Whig creed," according to Seward, was simple: "equal popular representative government, jealousy of executive power, the education of children, and the worship of God." A Whig vote was thus not merely for a particular set of men; it was for a set of eternal and essential principles.[23]

One of Seward's strengths was his flexibility, his ability to address different issues for different audiences. Later in the year, before academic audiences at Amherst and Schenectady, he made a less political argument, drawing on his own travels around the nation. Anyone who doubted the "stability of the Union" should spend a day near Niagara, where the river "gathers within its narrow banks the floods of the Lakes Erie, Huron, Michigan, Superior and the Woods." The doubter should count the ships in the locks there, bearing the products of all the interior regions toward the Atlantic, and bearing the products from the eastern states toward all "the communities which cluster and ripen on the western lakes and rivers." Or the doubter could stand at the confluence of the Ohio and Mississippi rivers, watching the "ever-passing, ever-swelling tides of inland trade, and then ask himself, are these fit stations for custom houses and walls and castellated towns and frontier armies?" The doubtful man would soon realize, Seward concluded, that the "Union exists, because it is inevitable, and must endure, because it is indispensable."[24]

———

In April 1844, President Tyler presented to the U.S. Senate a signed treaty between the United States and the independent Republic of Texas under which Texas would be annexed to the United States. Many southerners favored annexation as a way to acquire a huge new area for cotton and for slavery; they also argued that annexation was necessary to keep Texas out of Britain's hands. Many northerners, including Seward, opposed annexation because it would extend slavery and would lead to war with Mexico, which had never recognized Texan independence and still claimed Texas as Mexican territory. Seward wrote to Weed that Whigs must take care to "place our opposition to annexation solely on the ground of opposition to slavery" and to "give no occasion to charge us with pusillanimity or favor toward Great Britain or Mexico."[25]

Initially it seemed that Texas would not be much of an issue in the presidential campaign because Clay, nominated by the Whigs in early May, and Van Buren, the leading candidate for the Democratic nomination, were both against annexing Texas. Then there was a deadlock in the Democratic Convention, and the delegates settled on a dark horse, nominating James K. Polk for president. Polk, a protégé of Andrew Jackson, was known to favor the annexation of Texas, and the Democratic Convention underlined this point by adopting a platform seeking annexation of both Texas and Oregon, at the time jointly controlled by the United States and Great Britain. Suddenly Texas—and the extension of slavery into Texas—was the main issue in the ongoing campaign in New York. Seward reported happily to Weed in June about a mass Whig meeting at which "one of the banners, and the most popular one, was a white sheet, on which was Polk dragging a negro in chains after him." Seward was confident that the Whigs' stance on Texas would make them "safe and right" in New York in the fall.[26]

In a campaign speech at Syracuse in early July, before one of the largest crowds that had ever gathered in that part of the state, Seward argued that the Democratic desire to acquire Texas would lead to "a war with Mexico—an unjust war—a war to extend the slave-trade and the slave-piracy." The only benefit of the proposed acquisition—additional territory—was no benefit at all. "Land! Have we not a thousand millions of uncultivated acres already?" Like most Whigs at this time, Seward was skeptical of, even opposed to, territorial expansion. A few weeks later, in another address, he predicted that the United States would obtain territory, if at all, by consent and not by conquest, and that America would have "no distant colonies."[27]

Seward's ideas about Texas were close to those of his wife, which were in turn close to those of her friends. One of her best friends was Martha Coffin Wright, an Auburn neighbor and sister of the famous Lucretia Coffin Mott, herself a frequent visitor to Auburn. The Coffin sisters were already active in the abolition movement and the nascent women's movement. Four years later, in 1848, they would help organize the first women's rights convention, held at Seneca Falls, only fifteen miles from Auburn. The world-changing ideas these women would proclaim at Seneca Falls—that all men *and women* are created equal, and that women should have the same rights as men—did not appear overnight. Indeed, as early as 1841, Frances and her sister Lazette were part of a spirited teatime debate with Martha and her husband David Wright about the rights of married women. At one of his speeches in the 1844 campaign, Seward noted the presence of many women, and that Democrats "insist that women have no place in political assemblies." Seward disagreed, saying that women already had a role in politics: "By their teachings of the young, and by their persuasions addressed to all, [women] influence the decree of the ballot-box." Women understood that a war with Texas would "cost the blood, the lives, of your fellow-men," and they would not advise their men "to go out to battle, when the battle is not in defense of [their] country's flag, but for the extension of human slavery." [28]

As the summer progressed, two public letters from Henry Clay clouded the Texas issue. In the first, Clay explained that his opposition to annexation was not designed to please northern abolitionists but rather to preserve the Union. In the second and more damaging letter, Clay said that he had no personal objection to annexation if it could be achieved without war, and that slavery had nothing to do with the issue. Democrats seized on these letters to argue that there was little difference between Clay and Polk on Texas. Seward reported to Weed that he "met that letter" everywhere he went, and that "everybody droops, despairs." The letter "jeopards, perhaps loses this state." [29]

Another unexpected issue in the election was opposition to immigration and especially Catholic immigrants. Nativism was not new to American politics, but in 1844, for the first time, it affected a presidential election. The nativists showed their strength first in April, winning the mayoral election in New York City. In May and again in July, they showed their strength in a different way, in ugly anti-Catholic riots in Philadelphia. Although some Whigs favored an alliance with the nativists, Seward spoke out against the riots and (implicitly) against any such alliance. In a speech at Utica, he lamented that "men, women and children were compelled by American citizens to flee from burning dwellings in the night-time." Their only offense, he said, "was that they or their ancestors were born in Ireland, and that they worshipped God according to the creed and ritual of the Roman Catholic Church." Writing to his wife, Seward boasted that he had "asserted my opinions concerning the Philadelphia riots in a way that will for long put me out of favor with a portion of my countrymen."[30]

During the course of the 1844 campaign, Seward spoke in almost every corner of New York State, in more than twenty of the sixty counties. In addition to his speeches, Seward was meeting with local Whig leaders, shaking hands with voters, sharing tables with men and women in taverns. With only one exception, he declined invitations to speak outside of the state. Even that one exception, his late July address in Amherst, Massachusetts, had a political flavor; it was reported in one Vermont newspaper just under its banner of "Henry Clay for President." It would appear that Seward was concentrating on New York, rebuilding his political base, granting favors to local Whigs upon whom he might soon call.[31]

Seward was so busy campaigning that he was unsure how the campaign would come out. He wrote Clay in late October that he would "not undertake to give you an opinion of the probable result of the election in this state, upon which is suspended the whole question and of course the fate of the country. I think however the election will not prove as close a one as many suppose, and the present setting of the current is clearly and strongly flowing rapidly enough to give us success." Seward's cautious optimism about New York would prove incorrect. If Clay had received only 5,000 additional votes in New York, out of the almost half a million cast, he would have carried New York and become president. Some have suggested that the election of Clay would have prevented the Civil War; Clay would not have gone to war with Mexico, and thus not acquired the territory whose status, slave or free, divided the nation into North and South. As it was, however, in one of the closest and most critical presidential elections in American history, James Polk eked out a victory.[32]

Seward, like other observers, was left to wonder how the Whigs had lost. In a long letter to Clay, he explained that Whig efforts against the abolitionists would have sufficed "but for the entrance of another and very ruinous element into the canvass," namely, the nativists and their Whig allies. Seward had tried to "check the tendency to Native Americanism," as anti-immigrants termed the movement at the time, but "the aid it promised was too seductive to our friends already imbued with its spirit." He believed that "the Native Americans gave us one vote only for two of which they deprived us, and the result is our defeat in the state." For Seward, cooperation with the nativists was not only wrong as a moral matter; it was wrong as a practical matter, for it lost more votes than it gained.[33]

———

Seward handled many important cases over the course of a long legal career, during which he argued in the highest courts in New York and Washington. His most famous case, however, was a comparatively simple local murder trial: the trial of William Freeman in the summer of 1846. To understand the Freeman trial one must start with another case Seward handled at the same time, that of Henry Wyatt.

While serving time in Auburn state prison, Wyatt had stabbed and killed another inmate. A few days before his murder trial was to start, Wyatt sent word to Seward, who visited him in his prison cell and agreed to undertake his defense. There was no question that Wyatt had killed the man, but there were indications that Wyatt was not sane, and Seward arranged for experts to examine him and testify at the trial. Seward also presented evidence that Wyatt had been "flogged and tortured with an inhuman instrument of torture" while in prison. Seward's daylong closing argument for Wyatt, one paper reported, was "an extremely eloquent and ingenious effort." After a day of deliberation, the jurors informed the judge that they were hopelessly divided, and the judge discharged them, sending Wyatt back to prison to await a second trial.[34]

Only three weeks after the end of the first Wyatt trial, William Freeman, a young black man recently released from the same prison, entered a home about four miles outside Auburn and stabbed to death John Van Nest, his pregnant wife Sarah, Van Nest's elderly mother-in-law, and his two-year-old daughter. Freeman was captured and almost killed by an angry mob even before he reached prison. Frances wrote to her husband, who was in Albany at the time, that "there was a terrible commotion in the village as [Freeman] was carried through; it is a matter of wonder to me now that, in that excited state of popular feeling, the creature was not murdered on the spot. Fortunately, the law triumphed; and he is in prison awaiting his trial, condemnation and execution."[35]

People and papers soon began linking the two murders, saying that Seward's strong defense of Wyatt had somehow encouraged Freeman. The *New York Tribune* printed a letter from Auburn describing the "horrible murder" and reporting that many were "boldly and loudly asserting that a failure to convict Wyatt settled all doubt in Freeman's mind as to his premeditated act." The *Albany Argus* complained about the "mistaken and false humanity of the anti-capital punishment advocates, who sometimes creep upon juries, [so] that even in the most undoubted cases of murder the wretch . . . is as likely to escape as to suffer the just punishment of his dreadful deeds of blood."[36]

Seward claimed that the anger was merely political. He wrote his brother-in-law Alvah Worden that "the Loco Focos [the derogatory term for Democrats] here are playing on the prejudices of the Whigs against Negro Suffrage, now roused by the late tragedy in which a Negro murdered a white family as a sacrifice to hellish revenge. It will not amount to much." A few days later, he wrote to Weed that "the world is all mad with me here because I defended Wyatt too faithfully. God help them to a better morality. The Loco Focos have put us in jeopardy. Their prejudice against the Negroes by reason of the Van Nest murders is an auxiliary of Loco Focoism also." It was not merely the Loco Focos who were outraged, however; people of all political persuasions joined in the condemnation of Freeman and the suspicion of Seward.[37]

Many assumed that Seward would immediately undertake the defense of Freeman, but instead, he went away for several weeks, partly to handle some patent work, partly for pleasure. When he returned in late May, the second trial of Wyatt and the trial of Freeman were both imminent. Seward wrote Weed that "there is a busy war around me, to drive me from defending and securing a fair trial for the negro Freeman." Nobody other than Seward's friend John Austin, the local Universalist minister, had even visited Freeman in jail. "He is deaf, deserted, ignorant," Seward wrote, "and his conduct is unexplainable on any principle of *sanity*. It is natural that he trusts me to defend him. If he does, I shall do so." Weed's letters to Seward for these months are missing from the files, but it seems that Weed advised against defending Freeman, and that Seward disregarded his advice and instead listened to his wife and Austin.[38]

On Monday, June 1, 1846, the Auburn courthouse was densely packed with an eager crowd. Judge Bowen Whiting opened court, the shackled defendant Freeman was brought in, and District Attorney Luman Sherwood arraigned him on the four murder charges. Seward argued that Freeman could not be tried because he was not competent, not sane, and that a jury should determine this question of sanity. Sherwood disagreed, saying that the judge could decide the issue himself, without a jury. Judge Whiting was not ready to rule on this issue immediately, and so the Freeman trial was suspended.[39]

The next day, at the outset of the second Wyatt trial, Seward moved that the trial be postponed or moved to another county. Almost everyone in Cayuga County, he said, "eagerly believed and thoughtlessly published that [Wyatt's] partial escape from justice has excited Freeman to commit his crimes." Judge Whiting denied the motion, saying that he would not presume that an attempt to find an impartial jury in Auburn would fail. The attempt almost did fail: it took two weeks, and the examination of almost two hundred potential jurors, before an apparently impartial jury was in place. After that, the second trial of Wyatt moved quickly, and the jury took less than two hours to render a verdict of guilty. On June 24, Judge Whiting sentenced Wyatt to death. Frances reported to Lazette that "the village is said to be full of joy in anticipation of Wyatt's execution—poor human nature." Frances noted that almost all of Henry's friends were urging him not to defend Freeman—even her father urged him to "abandon the nigger"—but Henry "will do what is right. He will not close his eyes and know that a great wrong is perpetrated."[40]

The trial of Freeman resumed later on this same day. Judge Whiting granted Seward's request to have a jury trial on the question of sanity, but denied him the right to challenge the jurors. As a result, in Seward's words, "many of the jurors entered the panel with settled opinions that the prisoner was not only guilty of the homicide, but sane." Seward presented medical evidence, notably from Dr. Amariah Brigham, at the time America's foremost expert on insanity, who testified that on the basis of his own examination of the prisoner, and the evidence of others at the trial, he had concluded that the prisoner was insane. There were also lay witnesses who recounted bizarre conversations with Freeman in prison, including one in which he claimed to "read" the Bible in a nonsense mixture of religious words. And Seward introduced evidence that Freeman had been beaten so severely in prison that he had lost his hearing; these beatings could well have caused him to lose his sanity as well.[41]

Seward started his closing argument in this preliminary trial at about two o'clock in the afternoon of the Fourth. Outside that evening there were fireworks and a festive mood; inside the dim courtroom, in the words of Austin, "a lone voice was pleading with all the energies of one of the mightiest minds of the age in behalf of a poor friendless demented African." Seward closed by telling the jurors that some day "my remains will rest here in your midst, with those of my kindred and neighbors. It is very possible that they may be unhonored, neglected, spurned! But perhaps, years hence, when the passion and excitement which now agitate this community shall have passed away, some wandering stranger, some lone exile, some Indian, some Negro, may erect over them a humble stone, and thereon this epitaph, 'He was faithful.' "[42]

On the next day, a Sunday, the jury deliberated all day and finally returned a compromise verdict: "We find the prisoner sufficiently sane in mind and memory to distinguish between right and wrong." Seward objected and asked the court to instruct the jury to render a verdict on the proper legal question of whether Freeman was sane or insane. But Judge Whiting declined, finding that the jury's verdict was "equivalent to a verdict of sanity, under the rule laid down in his charge."[43]

Freeman was arraigned again on Monday morning, in a scene Austin found "sufficient to melt the heart of a stone." When District Attorney Sherwood asked Freeman to respond to the indictment, he answered, "Ha!" Sherwood asked Freeman how he would plead: "I don't know." After Freeman gave several similar responses to similar questions, "Gov. Seward could no longer restrain himself. He buried his face in his hands, and burst into tears—and finally seized his hat and rushed from the courtroom." Seward's co-counsel David Wright then "declared that he could not consent longer to take part in a cause which had so much the appearance of a *terrible farce.*" Seward had by this time returned to the courtroom, and when the judge asked whether anyone would represent Freeman, he "sprang to his feet and exclaimed '*I shall remain counsel for the prisoner until his death!*' " Wright also agreed to continue to serve.[44]

The main Freeman trial was similar to the preliminary trial; Seward and Wright again brought experts to testify that Freeman was insane. In his closing, Seward skillfully showed the jury that he too was grieved by the murders: "A whole family, just, gentle, and pure, were thus, in their own house, in the night time, without any provocation, without one moment's warning, sent by the murderer to join the assembly of the just." He argued, however, that it would be as wrong for the jury to convict Freeman, if he was indeed insane, as it had been for Freeman to kill the Van Nest family. The prosecution had suggested that Freeman was a barbarian black, with perhaps some savage Indian ancestors as well. Seward responded that "the color of the prisoner's skin, and the form of his features, are not impressed upon the spiritual, immortal mind which works beneath." Freeman was "still your brother, and mine, and bears equally with us the proudest inheritance of our race—the image of our Maker. Hold him then to be a man. Exact of him all the responsibilities which should be exacted under like circumstances if he belonged to the Anglo-Saxon race, and make for him all the allowances . . . which, under the circumstances, you would expect for yourselves." Seward's eloquence had no effect: The jury convicted Freeman after only two hours of deliberation, and Judge Whiting sentenced him to hang in two months' time.[45]

Seward attempted to delay Wyatt's execution, but it was carried out as scheduled in August. He also tried to persuade the governor to pardon Freeman, but was rebuffed. In early September, however, just days before the date set for Freeman's execution, the state supreme court granted a stay. In November, Seward traveled to Rochester, where he successfully argued Freeman's appeal before that court, which decided that the trial judge had improperly accepted the compromise verdict on sanity and erroneously excluded evidence of insanity from the main trial. After this decision, Seward and his co-counsel Wright faced the prospect of a second Freeman trial, which Seward hoped to move to another county. Wright's wife Martha said to Seward that he must "dread going all over it again," to which he responded, "not at all, he was fresh and ready for a new start." But there was no second trial, for prison officials determined that Freeman was not competent for trial. When he died in jail a few months later, Frances wrote to her husband that Freeman had at last gone to God, "whose benevolence is not chilled by the color of the skin of his children."[46]

Seward's work for Freeman led to a third case, that of John Van Zandt. Salmon Chase, at the time a lawyer in Ohio and leader of the Liberty Party there, after reading about the Freeman trial, invited Seward to join him in representing Van Zandt in the U.S. Supreme Court. Seward readily agreed. The case arose out of the assistance that Van Zandt, a poor white farmer from southern Ohio, had provided to a group of slaves escaping from nearby Kentucky. The owner of one of the slaves sued for damages and prevailed in the lower court. Seward's brief was a mixture of narrow technical points and grand philosophical arguments. He and Chase admitted that the precedents were against them but urged that these precedents be reconsidered. "We humbly supplicate, that Slavery, with its odious form and revolting features . . . may not receive in this great Tribunal, now, sanction and countenance, denied to it by a Convention of the American States more than half a century ago." As they expected, Seward and Chase lost in the Supreme

Court, but their real audience was public opinion, which they engaged through the printed version of their argument and summaries in the newspapers.[47]

In August 1846, after Wyatt's execution and Freeman's conviction, Seward wrote to Weed that he was "exhausted in mind and body, covered with public reproach, and stunned with duns and protests." Moreover, he had gone against Weed's advice, so that "the telegraphic sympathy between myself and you, my first last and best of friends, was disturbed and deranged." But in this case Seward's instincts were surer than those of Weed. Through these trials, he had established himself as a defender of the defenseless, a reputation that would prove a vital political asset.[48]

———

Seward devoted relatively little time to formal politics in 1846 and 1847, but he did keep a close eye on the coming presidential election. As early as January 1846, while in Washington, D.C., to argue a patent case, he reported to his wife that General Winfield Scott was "in full chase of the presidency," and added in jest that Scott's nomination by the Whigs was "quite as near as the publication of his memoirs." Some Scott supporters invited Seward to join them in announcing "in some authoritative way, the general as the chosen candidate," but Seward declined.[49]

He was in New Orleans in May 1846 when news arrived of the fighting with Mexico that would soon lead to the Mexican War. "You wake to the music of the fife and drum," Seward wrote to Frances, "and are put to rest at midnight by the undying notes of the same clamorous instruments." Seward opposed the Mexican War, but at least initially he did not speak out against it. He wrote to Weed that he did not expect Whigs to succeed if they were "found apologizing for our adversaries. I cannot go with such friends, for my sense of patriotism forbids, even more than policy." The war was personal for the Seward family, for Augustus was about to graduate from West Point, and when he did, he departed immediately for duty in Mexico. "This event has plunged his mother into inconsolable affliction," Seward wrote Weed, "which is attended by a relapse of her recent illness. I pray God she may have fortitude to carry her through so severe a trial."[50]

By January 1847, when Seward returned to Washington to argue another case, other candidates for the Whig presidential nomination had come forward, including Supreme Court Justice John McLean. Seward met several times with McLean and described him to Weed as "quite happy. Last winter he was alone. Now he is manifestly the head of a party, and is visited, consulted and flattered as such." Seward also spent much time with the Adams family. The aged John Quincy Adams, still serving as a member of Congress, pressed upon his protégé an uncomfortable charge: "You made General Harrison President; you can make the next President. Will you give us a man who is not for slavery? Tell me that. Assure me of that, and I shall be prepared to make my testament."[51]

Winfield Scott was by this time no longer a serious candidate. Though the portly general was leading troops in Mexico, in a war that was popular in most parts of the country, people were laughing over some of his letters, especially one in which he described his supper as being just "a hasty plate of soup." Part of Scott's problem was that he was not Zachary Taylor, the previously obscure officer whose recent Mexican victories made him an instant American hero. Americans loved not only Taylor's success: they loved his simplicity, exemplified by the story of how a visitor mistook him for a servant and asked him to shine his boots. Seward admitted Taylor's strengths, noting that he "fights well, and writes better than he fights." It seemed to some that "his nomination and election scarcely admit of doubt," but Seward's tone made it clear that he was not a Taylor supporter. One of his concerns was that Taylor was a southern slaveowner, not at all the kind of man whom Adams and like-minded men would favor.[52]

For many Whigs, the only sensible candidate was Henry Clay. He was already seventy years old, older than any president to date, but Clay was still strong, both physically and politically. "What man lives," Greeley asked the *Tribune*'s readers, "except Henry Clay whom any great proportion of the people really desire to see President?" From Washington, Seward wrote to his wife about how "matrons save the gloves [Clay] has pressed for relics" and "young ladies insist on kissing him in public assemblies." He also found it "amusing to mark the respect shown to Colonel Taylor," brother of the famous General Taylor. But Seward continued to have doubts about the general, writing to Weed from Auburn that the Mexican War was, in that part of the state, viewed as "so odious" that people were not "thinking about Genl. Taylor as an available candidate."[53]

As the presidential year began, Seward had in mind three political possibilities for himself. The first was that the Whig Convention would deadlock, like the Democratic Convention of 1844, and would settle upon a dark horse, nominating Seward for president. Seward's close friend George W. Patterson, a Whig leader in western New York, wrote to Weed in January 1848 that neither Clay nor Taylor would work as presidential candidates, that the "true course is to take a known Whig of the North, one who has not been mixed up with the war question, and his election would be quite sure." According to Patterson, their mutual friend Seward was just the man. Weed did not endorse any of the leading candidates in his *Albany Evening Journal*, suggesting that he also thought that Seward had some chance for the presidential nomination.[54]

The second, more likely possibility was that Seward would be nominated as vice president. Writing home to his wife from Albany after a long evening with Weed, Seward reported that the "sum of his speculations" was that Clay would be nominated as president and "a friend of yours" as vice president. Others were thinking along similar lines. Clay wrote to Greeley that he was considering Seward as his vice-presidential partner. "He would bring much Irish and Catholic support to the Whig ticket. Of that I am sure. Would that counterbalance the opposition to him (I regret to learn) from Whigs in New York and Whigs at the South? That is the question." Greeley responded that the name of Seward would "bring votes to any ticket it is on in every state where there are Catholics or Irishmen." But he added that "it may be best to take another man," for there were many who disliked Seward.[55]

The third possibility for Seward in 1848 was election to the U.S. Senate. Federal senators at this time were selected by state legislatures, and one of the two senators from New York was a Democrat whose term would expire in March 1849. The Whigs had achieved in late 1847 what Seward termed an "astounding" victory, electing majorities in both the state senate and assembly. Since the state senators would remain in place for two years, all the Whigs needed to do was retain their majority in the assembly in the fall election, and they would be in position to elect another Whig senator. Seward, the most prominent Whig in New York, was the obvious candidate. Greeley assured a friend that Seward would not be interested in a cabinet position in a possible Whig administration. "We are making a fight to place him in the Senate, and we do not entertain a doubt of success."[56]

In February 1848, while Seward was in Albany to argue an appeal, news arrived of two dramatic events: the treaty ending the Mexican War, and the death of John Quincy Adams. The treaty provided for Mexico to cede to the United States an immense area—essentially what are now the states of California, Nevada, Arizona, and New Mexico—in return for payment of $15 million. Adams had consistently opposed the Mexican War, and it is likely that if he had lived, he would have opposed the treaty. Seward, however, agreed with Weed, who wrote in the *Evening Journal* that "though the treaty is not what we would wish, let it not, we entreat and implore, be rejected by Whig votes." The treaty was soon approved by the Senate, including most Whigs.[57]

Two days after the death of Adams, Seward gave a brief eulogy in court in Albany, saying that humanity had lost "her most eloquent, persevering, and indomitable advocate," and that he personally had lost "a patron, a guide, a counselor and a friend." A few weeks later, before an audience of hundreds in an Albany church, he delivered a more formal and provocative speech. He started with a long set of questions about Mexico, the questions he said were under discussion at the time of Adams's death: "Shall we be content with the humiliation of the foe? Or shall we complete his subjugation? Would that severity be magnanimous, or even just? Nay, is the war itself just?" He continued: "Where shall we trace the ever-advancing line of our empire? Shall it be drawn on the banks of the Rio Grande, or on the summit of the Sierra Madre? . . . Will these conquests extend [freedom's] domain, or will they be usurped by ever-grasping slavery?" Seward's questions indicate his own continuing doubts about the Mexican War and Mexican territory. The remainder of his eulogy was more traditional, a celebration of the career of his friend and mentor. Some criticized Seward for mixing politics and praise, but the feisty old Adams would probably have approved.[58]

———

As the Whig Convention approached, Seward debated with himself whether he really wanted the vice-presidential nomination. In March, he indicated to Weed that he was not interested; by late May, he was apparently interested again. Seward was concerned that his in-state rival Millard Fillmore would become vice president and use the position to direct federal patronage away from Seward's supporters. In addition to Seward and Fillmore, the other serious contenders for the nomination were Abbott Lawrence, a wealthy merchant from Massachusetts, and Thomas Ewing, a political leader from Ohio. It appears that Weed pressed for presidential candidates other than General Taylor in part because he thought that Taylor had already committed himself to Lawrence as the vice-presidential nominee. Once Taylor secured the nomination, Weed bargained with Taylor's brother to secure for Seward the position of secretary of state. The convention as a whole, however, nominated Fillmore for vice president, which would mean that Seward (as another New Yorker) could not plausibly be secretary of state. One of Fillmore's supporters exulted that "Weed was never more surprised. He was sure of Taylor & Lawrence & Seward for Secretary of State. He was *foiled*."[59]

Seward, as was his custom, was not at the June convention; he remained in Auburn while Weed was on the ground in Philadelphia. When Seward learned that the convention had nominated Taylor and Fillmore, he wrote to Weed that it was "altogether fortunate that our ambition did not lead that way," that is, toward the vice presidency. But he lamented that so many Whigs were "quite willing to gather the harvest we so diligently sowed. If this ticket shall be elected it seems to me that for the next four or even eight years we shall be in the unpleasant category of a faction, apparently opposed to the New York leader [Fillmore] in the general council of the Whigs of the Union." It seems that, despite his protests, Seward had indeed wanted the vice-presidential nomination.[60]

Seward was thus not at first inclined to campaign for Taylor and Fillmore. He was a loyal Whig, however, and firmly believed that the nation would be better off under a Whig administration. He soon had invitations to speak around New York and throughout the nation. As he thought about his own situation, Seward knew that if he wanted the U.S. Senate seat he could not ignore these invitations. He started campaigning in early September, with speeches in upstate New York, and he kept traveling and speaking right through election day.[61]

In late September, Seward spoke at Tremont Temple in Boston before what he described to his wife as "a most intelligent and respectable body of men." He argued in favor of basic Whig principles: for a protective tariff, for education, against the extension of slavery, and against foreign wars. Although the Mexican War was over, Seward continued to press the point, saying that the Democrats had "plunged us into war" and favored "swallowing the whole of Mexico," while Whigs "want peace" and are "opposed to the occupation of any part" of Mexico. He was followed by a speaker from Illinois, a young congressman who spoke in what one paper called a "humorous strain of Western eloquence." When Abraham Lincoln finished, the audience "gave three hearty cheers for 'Old Zack,' three more for Governor Seward, three more for Mr. Lincoln, and then adjourned."[62]

More than twenty years later, after Lincoln's death, Seward recalled for the artist Francis Carpenter that this 1848 campaign event in Boston was his first meeting with Lincoln. According to Carpenter, Seward told him that "the following night we passed together in Worcester, occupying the same lodging room at the hotel." On that second night, wrote Carpenter, Seward "insist[ed] that the time had come for sharp definition of opinion and boldness of utterance" on the slavery issue. Lincoln "admitted that I was right in my anti-slavery position and principles." Carpenter's account of Seward and Lincoln sharing a room has become a standard part of Lincoln and Seward biographies.[63]

There are two problems with this anecdote. The first is that Seward and Lincoln were not in Worcester on the evening after their joint appearance in Boston. Seward was in Springfield, Massachusetts, where he addressed a large meeting of Whigs that evening. Lincoln was on his way home by train to Illinois; if he took the morning train (as reported in a Boston newspaper), he likely reached Albany by that evening. The other difficulty with the story is that the comments Carpenter attributed to Lincoln do not much sound like him. Lincoln's views and speeches on slavery at this time were close to those of Seward, so Lincoln would not have "admitted" that Seward was "right" and thereby implied that he had been wrong. In short, it seems that the incident never occurred. Whether it was an invention by Carpenter, or by Seward, or perhaps a misunderstanding by Carpenter of Seward's comments, we do not know.[64]

From Massachusetts, Seward traveled on to Pennsylvania, a critical state for the Whigs this year. In his speech at Pottsville, a coal-mining town, he said that the Whigs were advancing the cause of "universal freedom," while under the Democrats "the cause of Slavery has been advanced by war, the acquisition of useless territory by conquest, [and] the extension of ·Slavery [into] such territory." He also emphasized, in a state and region worried about imports, that the Whigs favored protective tariffs. Linking the two issues, Seward argued that under Democratic policies, "the free white laborers of the North are to be superseded by the Slave-labor of the South," and that "iron, cutlery, and fabricated goods . . . instead of being manufactured at home, and thereby giving employment to thousands of our people, are [to be] obtained from Europe."[65]

Making use of the rails in a way that would not have been possible five or ten years earlier, Seward was in New York City a few days later, addressing a huge crowd, mainly of workers. He noted that some Whigs were disappointed that neither of the great Whigs of their generation, Clay and Webster, was the presidential nominee. But Seward (in words that would apply to his own career) argued that greatness did not depend on office. "Was Aristides, was Cato, was Cicero, more fortunate? Is it not by popular injustice that greatness is burnished? What is the Presidency of the United States compared with the fame of a patriot-statesman, who triumphs over popular injustice and establishes his country on the sure foundations of freedom and empire?" He returned to Pennsylvania, speaking both in the suburbs and in the center of

Philadelphia, then traveled to Washington and Delaware, where he had the odd task of persuading voters in that slaveholding state that they should vote for Taylor to prevent the expansion of slavery. After a few days at home in Auburn, he was off again by rail, this time to Ohio, where he spoke in at least ten different places, writing home that he had "large and attentive audiences."[66]

At Cleveland, Seward declared that there were two opposing elements in American society: "freedom and slavery." Each of these elements, he argued, was represented by one of the great parties: the Whig Party for freedom, and the Democratic Party for slavery. The "party of slavery patronizes labor which produces only exports to commercial nations abroad—tobacco, cotton and sugar." The party of freedom, on the other hand, sought to build up the nation through the "ingenuity, skill, and labor" of the "free minds and willing hands of our own people." Seward noted that slavery was an issue not just in the slave states but also in free states; New York imposed an onerous property requirement on blacks who wanted to vote, and Ohio had "a system of black-laws, still more aristocratic and odious." The ultimate problem, he said, was not in laws but in public opinion. The task was therefore both simple and difficult: to change public opinion throughout the United States so that it would no longer support slavery. "Slavery can be limited to its present bounds, it can be ameliorated, it can be and must be abolished, and you and I can and must do it." He stressed, however, that he and his listeners should proceed peacefully, "in the spirit of moderation and benevolence, not of retaliation and fanaticism."[67]

Seward did not reach home until the eve of election day. Although he had occasionally complained in his letters about the intense pace of the campaign, it is also clear that he loved the excitement of the campaign trail. He loved meeting new people, seeing new places, traveling by train and stagecoach and steamship, and speaking to large and small crowds. In keeping with the unwritten rules, he had not done much traveling or speaking in his own campaigns, first in 1830 for state senate and then in 1834 and 1838 for governor. It was only in 1844, and even more so in 1848, that Seward proved that he was one of the most effective and enthusiastic political campaigners of his generation.[68]

In November 1848, for the first time in American history, all of the voters went to the polls on the same day, rather than on different days, to
select their next president. Zachary Taylor and Millard Fillmore prevailed
nationally, and the Whigs generally won in the states where Seward had
been most active: New York, Massachusetts, and Pennsylvania. The only
exception was Ohio, but Seward had known that would be the case; he
had written to Weed in late October that none of the Ohio Whigs with
whom he spoke expected to prevail there. In New York, Seward's friend
and protégé Hamilton Fish was elected governor and Whigs would
dominate in the next assembly. The way thus seemed clear for Seward
to become New York's next federal senator. Seward's rivals within the
Whig Party, however, were not prepared to grant him the Senate seat
without a struggle. Seward and Fillmore did not disagree much on policy, but they had different political friends, and their respective friends
coveted the same patronage posts. The Fillmore faction pressed its own
candidate for Senate, John Collier, a former state comptroller, and attacked Seward in newspapers such as the *Rochester Daily American*.[69]

The campaign against Seward started with a purported letter from
Seward to Seth Hawley, a lawyer and leader in Buffalo, printed in the
papers in December 1848, in which Seward allegedly argued that Collier must be defeated. Seward denied that he had ever written such a
letter, and Hawley denied that he had ever received such a letter, but
these public denials did not end the matter, and the newspapers devoted column after column to the controversy. Only later did Seward's
opponents mention their true concern: that Seward was more of an
abolitionist than a Whig, too much of a radical to represent New York
in Washington. A pamphlet published in January 1849 quoted at length
from Seward's Cleveland speech, and argued that "with him, it is not a
Whig Party at all, it is a Liberty Party, an Anti-Slavery Party, an Abolition Party." At about this same time, Seward's main opponent in the
state senate wrote to Representative Frederick Tallmadge in Washington to urge him and other moderates to write letters against the radical
Seward. Instead, Tallmadge responded that he favored Seward, and

he recalled how kindly Governor Seward had treated Tallmadge when he was just a young man. Somehow Weed obtained both of these letters and printed them in the *Albany Evening Journal* on the eve of the voting.[70]

Tallmadge's letter points to one of Seward's strengths in this election: he was known and respected among the Whigs of New York. Through his constant travels he had met hundreds, perhaps thousands of Whigs. He probably knew every one of the Whig legislators, and if he did not know them, Weed did. The Whig legislators favored Seward not only because they knew him but also because they agreed with him, especially on slavery. As one Saratoga newspaper put it, "New York needs its earliest and most eloquent defender of *freedom*" in the Senate. Another of Seward's strengths was Weed's network of Whig editors throughout the state; indeed, one of the Fillmore papers contended that these papers wrote editorials supporting Seward merely because they were ordered to do so by Weed.[71]

By tradition, the legislators of the majority party, from both the assembly and the senate, would hold a joint caucus to select their candidate for senator, and then ratify their choice in separate, formal votes in their respective houses. Fillmore's men knew that they did not have the votes to defeat Seward in such a joint caucus, so for a brief period they delayed the caucus by refusing to join it. This was too much even for some Fillmore papers; they insisted that the Whigs had to meet and agree upon a candidate. Seward's friend James Watson Webb, editor of the *Morning Courier,* told Seward that he could end all Whig opposition with a letter that proved he was not a radical abolitionist, that he would work to represent the whole state and whole party. Both Webb and Weed sketched such a letter for Seward, and Seward polished and extended their remarks into a final letter to Webb. Seward committed to support the Whig administration and Whig Party, "to which I sustain the most lasting obligations." As to slavery, Seward wrote that although he favored "circumscribing slavery within its present bounds" and would work for its gradual "removal," he strongly believed that this process must be "constitutional, lawful, and peaceful."[72]

Seward handed the letter to Webb in New York City, who published a brief summary of it in the *Courier* and called upon Weed to publish the full letter in the *Evening Journal*. When Weed saw the article, and the letter itself, he exploded in a letter to Seward: Webb had expressly agreed that the Seward letter was not to be published, and now Webb had made it as good as public. Weed also suggested that Seward had been drinking when he wrote: "the last paragraph looks as if it was composed under the Astor House table." Weed's explosion probably reflected the tension of the election as much as any substantive difference over the letter, and was especially curious because, by the date of Weed's missive, the Whig caucus had already voted in favor of Seward by an overwhelming majority. In the words of one of Seward's friends in the assembly, the Seward Whigs had achieved victory after "one of the most desperate political sieges ever known," a struggle in which "no means were deemed too low or disreputable against you."[73]

Seward's friends rejoiced in, and his enemies regretted, his election to the Senate. Horace Greeley claimed in the *New York Tribune* that "probably no man ever yet appeared for the first time in Congress so widely known and so warmly appreciated as William H. Seward." Bishop John Hughes wrote to Seward that "I hope I shall yet have the pleasure of congratulating you on your appointment to a still more elevated station in the Republic." Reverend Eliphalet Nott, Seward's former headmaster and lifelong friend, wrote him that "it is by the defense of true principles—of Irish rights, of Negro rights, of Catholic rights, of the poor man's rights—that you have become politically what you are. Your future rise or fall must depend on your adherence to your principles, and the rise or fall of those principles."[74]

Not everyone was excited to see Seward go to Washington. The *New York Evening Post* regretted "the presence near the president of such a man, trained as he has been, to politics, from his youth upwards, not over scrupulous in his means, nor very lofty in his aims." And the Washington correspondent for the *Mississippi Free Trader & Natchez Gazette* noted that "if there be one man in the whole Empire State more obnoxious to the people of the South than ex-Gov. Seward, I have yet to hear of his name and whereabouts. An abolitionist of the deepest dye, a notorious intriguer, and an avowed enemy to everything Southern, his appearance in the United States Senate at this particular juncture is much to be deplored by all lovers of our glorious Union."[75]

CHAPTER 5

"A Higher Law Than the Constitution":

1849–1854

L eaving his wife and children behind in Auburn, Seward departed for Washington by way of Albany, where Weed hosted a dinner with his rival Fillmore. Weed recalled that over dinner "everything was pleasantly arranged. The Vice-President [Fillmore] and Senator [Seward] were to consult from time to time, as should become necessary, and agree upon the important appointments to be made in our State." When Seward arrived in Washington in late February 1849, he was disappointed to learn that Zachary Taylor's advisers had already formed the cabinet, but gratified by Taylor's kind inquiries about Augustus, now on Army duty in remote Indian Territory. Seward was soon spending time almost daily with Taylor, writing home that the general was "sensible and sagacious," with "far higher intellectual merit and acquirements than we have supposed." Seward was also meeting with Fillmore, but they talked only of generalities, not specific appointments.[1]

On March 5, under a "gloomy, snow-spitting sky," Seward made his way through the muddy streets to the Capitol. The Senate chamber was an ornate but not immense room, described in one account as "graceful in proportions, with its dark marble columns and crimson hangings." Much of the floor space was taken up by sixty-two small wooden desks, one for each senator, arranged in a semicircular pattern, facing the raised desk of the presiding officer. There were two second-floor galleries, and the ladies' gallery was so crowded this day that three women fainted. The floor was equally jammed, with members of Congress, foreign diplomats, and other distinguished guests. After the presiding officer called the Senate into session, Seward and the other new senators went forward one by one to take the oath of office. Many of the greatest men ever to serve were senators at this time: Henry Clay, John Calhoun, Daniel Webster, Thomas Hart Benton, Samuel Houston, Jefferson Davis, and Stephen Douglas. Now Seward was one of them.[2]

At about eleven thirty, the current vice president, George Dallas, and the new vice president, Millard Fillmore, entered the Senate chamber arm-in-arm. After Fillmore took the oath and gave a brief address, the crowd waited eagerly for Taylor, who finally made his appearance around twelve thirty, arm-in-arm with his predecessor Polk. Then all the officials, including Seward, processed out to the east portico, from which they could see the crowd of about 10,000 people. Seward wrote Weed that Taylor's brief address was "well enough" since "the people want short speeches and generalities." There were three balls that evening, and Seward attended two of them, not getting home until after two in the morning. He wrote to Frances that among the ladies with whom he conversed were Mrs. Wilson, wife of his client, and Mrs. Wood, daughter of the president.[3]

The custom at this time was for the whole Congress to gather each year in December, and for the Senate alone to meet for about a month at the outset of each new presidential term, to consider appointments. Seward's first days in the Senate were in this short special session, starting the day after Taylor's inauguration. In one of his frequent letters home, Seward commented on the speaking styles of various senators. Daniel Webster, he thought, "always speaks well." John Calhoun, the great senator from South Carolina, "speaks seldom more than once, and that always on important occasions." Thomas Hart Benton of Missouri followed Calhoun's pattern. Seward thought that John Parker Hale, a Free Soiler from New Hampshire, spoke "too often and too impulsively," and that Stephen Douglas of Illinois also spoke "quite too much."[4]

Seward's main focus in these weeks was patronage. It is hard for us, in an age when important federal positions remain empty for many months, to understand why nineteenth-century politicians cared so strongly about federal offices. One reason was that many federal positions paid well. The naval officers in the major ports, for example, were paid $5,000 per year, while federal senators received only $8 per day for their services. The grateful recipients of such positions were not only expected to vote for those who secured them their offices; they were expected to contribute to campaigns and obtain contributions from all those who worked under them. Moreover, certain federal officials played important political roles. In 1850, each federal marshal would be in charge of the federal census in his district and appoint deputies to assist in this effort. One of Fillmore's friends warned him that if Seward's candidate became marshal, "every county in the district will have a deputy to take the canvass thoroughly committed to do Seward's bidding." Postmasters, in some cases, would not deliver newspapers or campaign material for the rival political party. So obtaining federal positions for one's friends was not only a way of rewarding them and securing their support; it was also a way of avoiding the damage that opponents could do in these positions.[5]

Given the intense interest in patronage, it is not surprising that the Albany arrangement among Weed, Seward, and Fillmore soon collapsed. A few days after the inaugural, Seward reported to his wife that "I have attempted to agree with [Fillmore], but he agrees on nothing that does not prefer one of his small band to a place due to the Whigs of the state who have stood by me." He complained to Weed that "you can get nothing, *nothing, nothing* by Mr. Fillmore's consent." Seward suggested that Weed obtain a letter from the New York governor and lieutenant governor, his friends Hamilton Fish and George Washington Patterson, confirming that "I am the exponent of the policy and principles of the Albany Administration of New York." Weed was able to obtain a letter along these lines, and the combination of the letter and Seward's personal relations with Taylor gave Seward control over most New York federal patronage. "Where is Fillmore?" an Albany paper asked. "The recent appointments in New York and Albany answer this question in the most significant manner. He is nowhere." But Seward did not win all the patronage battles. The most important post in New York, perhaps the most important position in the nation other than those in the cabinet, was that of customs collector in New York City. Seward and Fillmore each pressed their candidate for the post, and Taylor appointed a nominally neutral third man, who would later became an ally of Fillmore.[6]

Those who sought Seward's patronage help were not only friends in New York. Daniel Webster, who had called Seward "contemptible" during the McLeod dispute, now sought Seward's support for his son Fletcher, whom Webster hoped to make the federal district attorney for Massachusetts. Seward pressed the president to appoint young Webster, but he also lamented to his wife that the great Webster "would destroy all his mighty influence by being enslaved to selfish ends" and in particular to "nepotism." Abraham Lincoln, who as best we know had only met Seward once, during the 1848 campaign, also sought Seward's aid in early 1849. Lincoln wrote Seward from Springfield, Illinois, asking for his support in becoming head of the federal land office. It appears that Seward did not assist Lincoln, did not even answer his letter, not surprising given how many similar requests he was receiving at the time.[7]

After the special session was over in late March, Seward returned to Auburn and to his legal work. His cases took him to small towns, such as Canandaigua and Troy in New York, and major cities, including Philadelphia and Charleston. He wrote his wife from Charleston that many viewed him as an abolitionist, and so received him coolly, "excepting the people who stand behind the chairs at dinner." Some Whig leaders were prepared to welcome him, however; he was invited to dinner almost every day, and one local paper commended his courtroom argument as "lucid and logical, replete with happy illustrations, and interspersed with . . . refined humor."[8]

In August, Seward was called home to Florida, New York, by the death of his father. Samuel Seward's will appointed Seward and George Grier, a second cousin of Seward, as trustees; they were charged with running the Samuel Seward Institute, a secondary school that Samuel Seward had established in Florida, and with administering the estate for the benefit of his children and grandchildren. Seward would spend much time over many years dealing with the complex issues of his father's substantial estate. Perhaps the most difficult issues were those raised by the beneficiaries of the estate; some of Seward's nephews criticized him for selling the assets and distributing the proceeds too slowly, and years later some descendants would sue him for what they alleged was an improper division of the assets. Seward would still be dealing with his father's estate during his own retirement years.[9]

———

Seward arrived back in Washington in December 1849, this time with his wife and three younger children. Frederick, just graduated from college, would serve as his father's private secretary. William, at age ten, was not especially happy in Washington, "homesick because he has no horse and no playmates," his mother noted. Fanny, only five, was already serious and bookish, attending William's lessons. The family rented a house on F Street that Frederick recalled as a "respectable, unpretending, red brick structure" close to the shops and not far from the Capitol. One evening the Sewards dined at the White House and Frances had the honor of sitting next to the president. When Taylor apologized to her for his "slight knowledge of etiquette," she said that in her view the social rules in Washington were far too complex and too obscure. "They should have a book like the Army regulation," she said, "and reduce such matters to a system that might be studied." The president laughed and agreed.[10]

Not long before the congressional session started, news arrived that California had adopted a constitution and petitioned for admission as a state. For many northerners, including Seward, the first priority for the new Congress was to admit California as the next free state in the Union. For them it was an easy issue: California already had a large population, rapidly growing because of the gold rush, and would form a vital link to the Pacific. Moreover, by admitting California as a state, rather than forming it first as a territory, Congress could avoid the controversial issue of whether it should allow slavery in the territorial stage. Although Taylor was a southern slaveowner, he believed, as one paper reported, that California "should be received as she presents herself and no questions asked."[11]

For other southerners, the issue was far more complex. If California was admitted as a free state, the Senate would have, for the first time, a free state majority. This majority would likely increase as other free states, such as Oregon and New Mexico, were admitted. The New Mexico issue involved not just the possible creation of a new free state but the reduction of the area committed to slavery, because there was a dispute about the boundary between the slave state of Texas and the free territory of New Mexico, a dispute in which Texas was claiming most of what we now call New Mexico. If this disputed area became part of a new free state, it would represent the first step in what southerners feared would be the gradual elimination of slavery. Already there were reports that Texans were preparing to use military force to defend "their" part of New Mexico.[12]

Southerners therefore insisted that, if California was admitted, it had to be as part of a compromise, perhaps one that organized New Mexico as a slave territory, or that divided Texas into several slave states. Seward reported to Weed that "the malcontents of the South mean to be factious and they expect to compel compromise." Some went beyond demands for compromise and threatened secession. Representative Robert Toombs of Georgia declared that "if, by your legislation, you seek to drive us from the territories of California and New Mexico, purchased by the common blood and treasure of the whole people . . . *I am for disunion.*"[13] Seward was to some extent the cause of these threats, for southerners saw Seward as having an undue and pernicious influence on Taylor. The president had given "the entire patronage of the North [into] the hands of Seward and his party," Toombs wrote, which forced "the whole Northern Whig party into the extreme anti-slavery position of Seward." For the southern-sympathizing *New York Herald,* Seward's "red republicanism" made him the "originator" of the crisis. With "his agents in the cabinet, his organs among the newspapers, [and] his clique in Congress," Seward was "the head and font of the free soil party."[14]

Taylor released his annual message in late December, urging as expected that Congress should admit California promptly as a state. Taylor also hinted that when New Mexico applied for statehood he would favor the same approach. As Seward had predicted to Weed, several senators now sought the "honors and rewards of compromise." Foremost among them was Henry Clay, the aged but still ambitious senator from Kentucky, famed for his roles in the resolution of earlier sectional crises, and eager to cement his role in history with one more compromise.

The president, however, did not intend to compromise. "I think the P. as willing to try conclusions with them," Seward told Weed, "as General Jackson was with the Nullifiers." Just as Seward had supported Jackson in the Nullification crisis, he now intended to support Taylor in the current crisis.[15]

In late January 1850, Clay outlined for the Senate what he described as his "comprehensive scheme" for the "amicable arrangement of all questions in controversy between the free and slave states." Clay sketched eight points, including admitting California as a free state, leaving open the question of slavery in the remaining western territory, and strengthening the Fugitive Slave Law. A few days later, the Senate chamber was crowded with those eager to hear Clay explain his proposals in more detail. Frances was part of the "brilliant and fashionable throng of fair and lovely women." Clay was interrupted often by applause, but Frances was not impressed. She wrote to her sister that Clay seemed to think "that all the differences of opinion between the North and South were to be settled and forever by his persuasion." [16]

Five weeks later, in early March, there was another dramatic set speech in the Senate, by John Calhoun. The senator from South Carolina was dying of tuberculosis, too weak to stand or speak, so another senator read his remarks for him. Calhoun argued that the current danger to the Union stemmed from northern aggression, which was destroying the voluntary association among the states. Calhoun pleaded with his northern colleagues to compromise: to offer the South its fair share of the western territory, to ensure that southerners could recapture fugitive slaves, and to amend the Constitution to give the South the power to protect itself in the national government.[17]

Daniel Webster, the third member of the "great triumvirate"—as Clay, Calhoun, and Webster were already known—spoke on March 7. Frances was sitting in her husband's seat on the Senate floor, with Seward standing nearby, as Webster argued that to preserve the Union both sides had to compromise. The North had to recognize that under the "laws of nature" slavery could not prosper in the arid Southwest, and so it should not insist upon explicit legal prohibitions against slavery in that region. With respect to fugitive slaves, Webster believed the Constitution entitled the South to stronger protections, and announced that he would

support a new fugitive slave law, to ensure that southerners could recover their "property" when slaves fled to the North. "Peaceable secession," Webster warned, was an impossibility; any attempt at secession
would lead to civil war, "such a war as I will not describe."[18]

Once again, Frances was unimpressed. She wrote her sister that
Webster "is much less eloquent than Henry Clay because his heart is
decidedly colder—people must have feeling themselves to touch others." She was not surprised by Webster's concessions. "A man who has
been so long here without being impelled to raise his voice on behalf
of the oppressed, would not be very likely to do it now when all the
country were seeking of him a compromise." Even the word "compromise," Frances wrote, "is becoming hateful to me." Many joined her in
condemning Webster. The *Boston Atlas*, previously favorable to Webster,
declared now that "his sentiments are not our sentiments." The *New
York Tribune* commented that his speech was "unequal to the occasion
and unworthy of its author."[19]

On the afternoon of March 11, Seward rose in the Senate to give
what would prove to be the most important speech of his life. A reporter noted that the Senate "galleries were very full," but there were
not as many "fashionable ladies" present as there had been a few days
before to hear Webster. Among those absent was Frances; as she explained to her sister the day before, "the interest I feel is too deep to
make it pleasant to be there."[20]

Seward started with a detailed argument for the immediate admission of California. He noted that the region was already more populous
than many states, with extensive agricultural, mineral, and commercial
resources. California and Oregon would complete the national territory,
from the Atlantic to the Pacific, and there would be "no seat of empire
so magnificent as this." In an offhand and ill-advised remark, Seward
said that he was so determined to attach California to the Union that
he would admit it as a slave state, if that is what its people wanted. He
rejected the argument that Taylor had somehow acted improperly in
encouraging California to form a constitution and apply for statehood.
On the contrary, the "present eminent chief magistrate" had acted quite
correctly in seeking to establish "civil institutions, regulated by law, in
distant provinces."[21]

Seward turned to an examination of the key parts of the Clay compromise. As to the proposed fugitive slave law, the people of the North could not "in our judgment, be either true Christians or real freemen, if we impose on another a chain that we defy all human power to fasten on ourselves." (At this point, according to a reporter, "you might almost have heard a pin drop.") The people of the South "believe and think otherwise, and doubtless with equal sincerity." But since a fugitive slave law would have to be enforced in the North, and could not be enforced there consistent with northern views, it would prove ineffective and inflammatory. As to the proposed boundary between Texas and New Mexico—effectively a boundary between slavery and freedom—Seward suggested that it was premature to attempt to settle this issue.[22]

Seward disagreed fundamentally with Calhoun's argument that the Constitution was a compact among the states. Such an approach would reduce the United States to a mere corporation, formed for private gain. Extension of slavery into the western territories was, he said, utterly inconsistent with the "sublime" purposes of the United States, as set out in the preamble to the Constitution. "It is true indeed," he declared, "that the national domain is ours; it is true it was acquired by the valor and with the wealth of the whole nation; but we hold, nevertheless, no arbitrary power over it." The Constitution, he continued, "regulates our stewardship; the Constitution devotes the domain to union, to justice, to defense, to welfare, and to liberty." And, he added, "there is a higher law than the Constitution, which regulates our authority over the domain, and devotes it to the same noble purposes. The territory is a part—no inconsiderable part—of the common heritage of mankind, bestowed upon them by the Creator of the universe. We are his stewards, and must so discharge our trust as to secure, in the highest attainable degree, their happiness."[23]

Seward turned at the end of his speech to Webster's argument that the Union was in danger, that it could only be saved by compromise. The current threats of disunion were, in Seward's view, mere words, whereas the Union was perpetual. The Union was far stronger than when it was created: stronger in territory and in population; stronger in the canals and railroads that linked the states; and above all stronger in the "habits of veneration and affection for institutions so stupendous and so useful." As to slavery, which some argued would divide the Union, Seward disagreed with the extremists on both sides. The abolitionists were absurd to think that any power, other than the southern people themselves, could abolish slavery in the southern states. It was equally absurd for slavery's most ardent defenders to insist that it was ordained by God. Seward believed that "slavery must give way, and will give way, to the salutary instructions of economy, and to the ripening influences of humanity," and that Congress should assist the states in this gradual, peaceful process.[24]

During the first part of his speech, on California, a reporter observed that Seward hesitated somewhat. But when he came to this second part, in which he "denounce[d] compromises between slavery and freedom," the senator "warmed up and became truly eloquent and excited." Calhoun, according to this report, was initially restless, but was soon riveted in his seat, "eyeing his new and formidable opponent." Webster "kept looking at Mr. Seward very earnestly." And Clay, who at first stood at a distance, then took his seat "next to Seward and looked at him."[25]

Seward spoke for more than three hours. He spent much of the remainder of the month of March editing and printing and distributing his speech. By the end of the month he could boast to Weed that more than 100,000 copies had been sent out from Washington, "nearly half of them under my own frank," that is, with his own signature on the envelope. And hundreds of thousands of people read the speech in the newspapers, many of which printed extended excerpts.[26]

Reactions started on the day of the speech and flooded in over the next weeks. A New Yorker who was in the crowded gallery wrote Seward that evening that it was a "great speech," one that "would have done credit to any living orator." Horace Greeley declared in the *New York Tribune* that "Governor Seward's speech will live longer, be read with a more hearty admiration, and exert a more potential and pervading influence on the national mind and character than any other speech of the session." The *Brattleboro Semi-Weekly Eagle* said that Seward had expressed "clearly, boldly, and eloquently the prevailing sentiment of the Free States." There were some who noticed the inconsistency between Seward's strong defense of freedom and his remark that he would if necessary admit California as a slave state. One was Salmon

Chase, now an antislavery senator from Ohio, who wrote that anyone who would admit a slave state was not "with us" on the slavery issue.[27]

Even though Seward had argued against immediate abolition, southern papers and their northern allies called him an abolitionist. The *New York Herald* wrote that the senator "declares himself in favor of the extreme measures of the abolitionists, running not only to the utter extirpation of slavery in the South, but to the ultimate amalgamation of the races, and the deterioration of the white race." Seward viewed the Constitution and the higher law as consistent, but many interpreted him as suggesting that he would disregard the Constitution in favor of some higher law. The *New Orleans Picayune* charged that the senator "now proclaims himself ready to set [the] Constitution at naught, merely for the sake of developing a moral principle." And the *Washington Union* castigated him for saying "that when he believed the will of God was in opposition to a provision of the Constitution, he would violate the latter before he would disobey the former."[28]

President Taylor, according to a much later memoir, was so upset by Seward's speech that he tripped over his words as he instructed Alexander Bullitt, editor of the *Washington Republic*, a newspaper that often spoke for the administration, on how to respond. "The speech must be disclaimed at once, authoritatively and decidedly," Taylor reportedly told Bullitt, for "the Constitution is not worth one straw if every man is to be his own interpreter." The *Washington Republic* did attack the speech, and many viewed the attack as evidence of a rift between Taylor and Seward. Whether there was ever such a conversation between Taylor and Bullitt, or such a rift between Taylor and Seward, is doubtful. Frances wrote her sister only days after the Bullitt article that "the Administration had nothing to do with the article in the *Republic*." Taylor and Seward continued their friendly relations; as Frances put it, the president was "honest and true as we have ever thought him."[29]

Perhaps most distressing to Seward was that his friend and mentor Weed disliked the speech. Weed wrote to Seward that he did not believe Seward would really vote for the admission of California as a slave state; if that was the case, he should have omitted this remark. More generally Weed believed Seward should have followed more closely the line set out by Taylor, and should have praised "the good and faithful and fearless man who has incurred the hostility of the South by his devotion to the North." The most worrisome aspect of the speech for Weed was that Seward was starting to sound like a presidential candidate himself. That *"is one of the dangers,"* Weed stressed. A few weeks earlier, he had argued strenuously that Seward should not assist in preparing a book about his life. "It is about as much as you can do to stand up against reproach and obloquy while no great cause for either is found in your conduct; but if, after the manner of Presidential aspirants, you are advertised, in a Book, the whole pack will be let loose." Seward yielded for a while on the book, but not much on the speech. Weed's questions and concerns, Seward wrote to his friend, "have given me much pain." But, he continued, "I *know* that I have spoken words that will tell when I am dead, and even while I am living, for the blessing and benefit of mankind, and for myself that is consolation enough."[30]

——

The Senate debate on California and compromise lasted all spring and all summer. In May, a committee chaired by Clay reported several bills, including one that became known as the Omnibus because it contained several key elements of the compromise. Seward opposed the Omnibus bill, arguing that Congress should act immediately on California and later on the Texas–New Mexico border. Clay responded that it was Seward and others like him who were trying "to postpone, to delay, to impede, to procrastinate." Senator Henry Foote of Mississippi alleged that Seward desired "to procure a bloody adjustment of the question of the boundary," that he "has put himself in such an attitude as to be recognized everywhere as a counselor to bloodshed and violence." Seward ignored Foote's attacks and responded to Clay. The "regular and customary mode of legislation," he said, was to do "one thing at one time and on one occasion." The proponents of this "multifarious" compromise were the real cause of the delay. "If we cannot break the bill down by a common opposition, I am willing to take it to pieces joint by joint, limb by limb."[31]

Seward's second major speech on the compromise took place in early July, in a chamber which was not especially crowded; indeed, some southern senators rudely walked out as he started to speak. This time Seward heeded Weed's advice and specifically supported Taylor. Seward said that he agreed with the president's plan for immediate, unconditional admission of California, because he "honor[ed] [Taylor's] patriotism and confide[d] fully in his wisdom." Seward predicted that the compromise under consideration would not, as many hoped, settle the question of slavery in the territories. "That question cannot be settled by this bill. Slavery and freedom are conflicting systems, brought together by the union of the states, not neutralized, nor even harmonized. Their antagonism is radical, and therefore perpetual." [32]

Some papers criticized Seward's speech; the editors of the *Albany Morning Express* did not share his confidence "that there is no danger of disunion," saying they would "not be at all surprised if a civil war broke out . . . before the first of September." But the editors of the *Boston Atlas* read the speech with "unmixed delight and gratification." Thurlow Weed, in the *Albany Evening Journal*, commented that the speech would "find in this state, at least, more readers, and a warmer approval, than that of any other statesman." In private, Weed was even stronger, writing to Frances that "I would not change or spare a word. All is perfect." [33]

The Fourth of July was an "intensely warm day" in Washington, the *New York Tribune* reported, so hot that the traditional parade was canceled. The celebration at the Washington Monument construction site, however, was not canceled. President Taylor was dutifully present, but almost no senators or representatives, because the speaker was the bombastic Senator Foote. After the event Taylor slaked his thirst with water and his hunger with cherries. Seward wrote home on July 8 that Taylor was suffering from a "bilious attack" and by the next day Seward had "dreadful apprehensions" about his friend. His fears were realized when "the sad tolling of the bells at midnight" on July 9 announced the death of the president "in whom all trusted and whom all loved." [34]

Seward visited with the new president, Millard Fillmore, several times over the next few days and "tendered what counsel and aid I could render." He advised Fillmore to keep the current cabinet and to continue Taylor's policies; but as he feared and expected, Fillmore intended to be his own president. Fillmore appointed a new cabinet, headed by Webster as secretary of state, and let it be known that he would support the Omnibus compromise. Seward surely reflected that, if the Whigs had only nominated him rather than Fillmore for vice president, he would now be the president.[35]

In late July, Seward was at the center of an ugly incident in the Senate. Hoping to secure a day of delay to allow some opponents of the Omnibus to return to Washington, Seward offered an amendment that he knew would fail: to admit New Mexico immediately as a free state. Senator Thomas Pratt of Maryland, "much excited" and perhaps intoxicated, argued that the proposal was unconstitutional because it was not clear that New Mexico had a republican constitution. Such an "extraordinary" proposal, Pratt continued, could only come from Seward, who had already "declared that there is a higher law overruling the Constitution, and which he would obey, even though in violation of his oath to maintain the Constitution." Seward instantly denied that he had made any such declaration. Pratt insisted that he had, and called for Seward to be expelled from the Senate. Senator William Dayton of New Jersey, trying to save Seward, suggested that he be allowed to withdraw his amendment by unanimous consent. Clay, eager to see Seward suffer somewhat, opposed the suggestion. Seward said that he "had no intention of responding to Mr. Pratt's personal remarks" and would if necessary defend himself against expulsion by quoting the precise language of his speeches. He was not expelled, but the peremptory rejection of his amendment showed how alone he was in the Senate.[36]

On the last day of July, in what one reporter called "a room as hot as an oven," the Senate dismantled the Omnibus "joint by joint," as Seward had suggested several weeks earlier. The opponents of different elements of the bill, northern and southern, stripped out everything other than the section establishing a Utah territory, then passed the bill in that form. The *New York Tribune* exulted that "the Omnibus is smashed—wheels, axles, and body." At day's end, the *New York Express* reported, Senator Clay was sitting "as melancholy as Caius Marius over the ruins of Carthage" while Seward was "dancing about like a little top." Yet Seward soon realized that the debate was not over; he wrote to Weed two days later that Fillmore now hoped to pass the Texas border and territorial bills separately, "thus effecting the 'Compromise' in another way."[37]

One of those who voted against the Omnibus at the end of July was Thomas Rusk, a Democratic senator from Texas. In a letter to a friend, he explained that he had done so because of conversations with Seward, in which Seward advised that Texas could obtain a better boundary, and more generous compensation, through a separate bill rather than the Omnibus. Seward advised Rusk to draw up a bill for these purposes, and promised to introduce the bill himself, or have it introduced and supported in the House by his friends there. Rusk drafted the bill and provided it to Seward, but the latter merely filed it in his desk drawer.[38]

As Seward feared, the death of the Omnibus was not the death of the compromise. The Senate started in early August to debate and pass separate bills relating to California, Texas, and New Mexico. Some senators, including Clay, left Washington for cooler climates, but Seward stayed, complaining to his wife about senators who were "absent from the city, at such a time!" After the Senate passed a bill devised by Senator James Pearce of Maryland, setting the New Mexico boundary and providing federal compensation to Texas, Seward started to work to prevent passage of the Pearce bill in the House. When he learned of this, Rusk lost all patience; he called upon Seward and threatened to reveal how Seward had reneged on his promise. Rusk may have even threatened a duel. Seward offered only weak excuses and agreed to leave Washington for a while. Rusk did not denounce Seward on the Senate floor, but he did talk with colleagues, who in turn talked with reporters. The *Baltimore Clipper* soon summarized the conversations and circumstances of Seward's departure. The *New Orleans Picayune* commented that the senator "left Washington under some apprehension of a personal attack from Senator Rusk of Texas, in regard to which he was unable to make the slightest defense. The New York demagogue was caught in a *double entendre* (called a falsehood in Saxon) and had to make tracks to avoid personal indignities."[39]

Although Seward was out of Washington for the last two weeks of August, he was back in early September, working the House floor and the lobbies to rally opposition against the Pearce bill. President Fillmore made it clear to House Whigs that if they wanted any federal patronage, they would have to support Pearce's bill. After a complex and contentious series of votes, the House passed the Pearce bill by a narrow margin. In the lobby outside the House, Seward, grim in defeat, remarked that he supposed the country was now safe, to which a pro-compromise representative responded: "yes, in spite of you." Most people, North and South, cheered the compromise. In Washington, there were fireworks, illuminations, and marching bands. In New York, George Templeton Strong wrote in his diary that Congress had "blighted the hopes of Billy Seward and his gang of incendiaries, who wanted to set the country on fire that they might fill themselves with place and profit in the confusion." Strong was a Whig, and a personal friend of Seward's, yet on this issue, he and many other Whigs opposed Seward.[40]

As the Senate wrapped up its work on the several bills comprising the compromise, Seward offered an amendment to abolish slavery in the District of Columbia, subject to a referendum of the district's voters. His motion was debated for three days. Responding to the suggestion that it was not yet time to consider this divisive issue, Seward asked sarcastically: "Will gentlemen oblige me and the country by telling us how far down in the future the right time lies? When will it be discreet to bring before Congress and the people the abolition of slavery in the District of Columbia?" The motion was defeated, without even a record of the vote. A few days later Fillmore signed into law the last piece of what we now call the Compromise of 1850.[41]

————

Fillmore and Seward did not agree on the compromise, but they did agree on the importance of party unity in the fall elections in New York. Just before the Whig state convention gathered in Syracuse in late September, Fillmore wrote to Daniel Ullman, one of his key supporters, to urge that they not offend the Seward men. Seward likewise wrote to Weed to urge moderation: "Mr. Fillmore hopes that there will be no approval of my course by the state committee. . . . I cordially agree with him in deprecating an indorsement at such a time and under such circumstances." But neither Seward nor Fillmore had control over their supporters. A Seward delegate offered a resolution to the convention praising Seward for the way in which he had defended freedom in the recent Senate debates. When the resolution passed, the Fillmore men angrily marched out of the convention hall. The seceding Whigs were led by Seward's old friend Francis Granger, whose gray hair gave the group its name, the Silver Grays.[42]

Seward lamented this schism, agreeing with his friend Hamilton Fish, who wrote him that "some of our professing Whig friends are becoming tired of belonging to a party in power." When Seward returned to Washington in December 1850, he made a point of visiting Fillmore, and soon the papers were reporting that "a truce has been confirmed between the administration and the Seward Whigs, and Mr. Seward is often seen at the White House." One element of the truce was that Seward would not agitate on slavery, and indeed he did not mention slavery at all during this congressional session. He spoke instead on other issues, such as reducing postage rates and improving inland harbors and rivers. The common theme of his speeches was commerce, which he called "the chief agent of [American] advancement in civilization and enlargement of empire." Not long after the end of the session, Fillmore broke the implicit truce by removing many Seward men from federal positions. Seward's friends were predictably outraged, and Seward himself now published a letter decrying the Fugitive Slave Law as an attempt "to extend the economy of the slave states throughout states which repudiate slavery as a moral, social, and political evil."[43]

Although relations between Seward and the president were strained, the two men were part of a large group that celebrated the completion in May 1851 of the New York & Erie Railroad. (Seward explained to Frances that he had a "better right than most to exult" in the railroad, "having periled more for it than any other public man.") The party traveled by train, with many stops for feasts and speeches, all the way from Piermont, on the Hudson just north of New York City, to Dunkirk, on the shores of Lake Erie. Speaking from the train platform on his way home, Seward said he had been to a wedding, "the great wedding in which the retired water of Lake Erie was the bride and the old salt sea was the groom. The hoary Alleghenies gave away the bride, the Susquehanna, the Delaware . . . and others were the bridesmaids. The ring was the gift of the merchants of New York, an iron ring woven in two strands." To see the ring, he said, his listeners merely had to look down at the iron rails.[44]

Seward devoted the summer of 1851 to the trial of forty-four men accused of conspiring to burn down the Detroit rail depot. The state charged that the defendants, most of whom were from the western part of the state, and not even in Detroit on the night of the fire, were part of a vast conspiracy to destroy the entire railroad. The prosecution lawyers were leading members of the local bar, amply funded by the railroad. The defense lawyers, "neither able nor distinguished," begged Seward to join their team. His first step was to ask that several defendants be released, but the court set bail at an exorbitant level, with the result that the defendants were (in Seward's words) "held fast in a cage of iron" through the long, hot summer. Several sickened and two died, including the key defendant Abel Fitch. By August, Seward was complaining to his wife that "this everlasting trial, like revolution, seems to have almost banished Sundays." In his closing argument, presented in a large hall "thronged to suffocation," Seward showed that there was no credible evidence to prove that the remaining defendants had conspired to burn the depot; he suggested that the prosecution itself was a conspiracy against the defendants, an attempt to punish them for their protests. Seward reminded the jurors how Fitch died protesting his innocence. "If he was innocent, then there is not one of these, his associates in life, who can be guilty." It seems today that Seward was right, that the state had not proved its case against the defendants, but the jury was only partially persuaded, and it convicted twelve of the men.[45]

Seward was deeply involved in the presidential campaign of 1852, both in the Whig nomination and the general election. There were three main Whig candidates: Fillmore, Webster, and General Winfield Scott. Seward's relationship with the general dated back to the late 1830s, when Seward was governor and Scott in charge of the defense of the northern frontier. Although Scott was fifteen years older than Seward, the general always deferred to the governor on political matters. As Scott wrote Seward in 1839, "I certainly cannot have a more able, judicious and disinterested counselor than yourself." Indeed, one of Scott's main problems, especially in the South, was his connection with Seward. The *Savannah Republican* argued in early 1851 that Scott, if nominated, would not carry a single southern state. "The fact that he comes forward under the auspices of Mr. Seward of New York . . . is

enough to damn him to utter defeat in this section of the confederacy."
The few southerners who were willing to support Scott wanted him to
issue a letter confirming that he accepted the Compromise of 1850 as
a final settlement. Seward opposed any such letter, which he predicted
to Weed would "ruin" Scott in states like New York and Pennsylvania.[46]

Immigrants promised to play a larger role in 1852 than in any earlier
presidential election. Hundreds of thousands were arriving each year,
mainly but not only from Ireland and Germany. Once they could vote—
generally after five years—immigrants usually voted for Democrats. But
Seward and other progressive Whigs hoped that at least some of these
new citizens could be persuaded to vote Whig. An opportunity to appeal to this large and growing group appeared in December 1851, in
the person of Louis Kossuth, Hungarian revolutionary and refugee. Kossuth's attempt to establish an independent Hungary had ended badly
in August 1849, when Russian troops arrived to help the Austrians in
restoring their rule over Hungary. When he landed in New York City, he
was hailed as a hero, a Hungarian version of George Washington. Politicians rushed to embrace him, both literally and figuratively. "Each party,
each clique of each party," observed one paper, "would appropriate the
great Magyar as an electioneering machine for the next Presidency."[47]

Nobody embraced Kossuth more closely than Seward. In part this
was a matter of politics; he knew how Kossuth's cause would appeal to
many foreign-born citizens. In part it was a matter of principle; Seward
had always welcomed immigrants, especially those fighting for freedom
in their native lands. Within a few days of Kossuth's arrival, Seward
proposed a resolution of welcome in the Senate. The resolution was opposed by several southern senators, who noticed that Kossuth had spoken out against slavery, and who disliked in general the idea of freedom
fighters. Many northerners were also concerned once they learned that
Kossuth wanted to secure official support, perhaps military support,
from the United States for the Hungarian cause. And one large group of
immigrants, the Irish Catholics, were opposed to Kossuth, seeing him as
a Protestant rebel against a legitimate Catholic regime. The newspaper
most closely associated with Seward's friend John Hughes, now an archbishop, denounced Kossuth as a "humbug."[48]

In spite of all this, Seward persisted. In early December, during the debate on his resolution, which did not pass, he dismissed the argument that a vote for the resolution would offend Austria and Russia, saying the United States would always be "a living offence to . . . despotic powers everywhere." After Kossuth arrived in Washington in late December, Seward visited him daily and organized a grand congressional dinner in his honor. He introduced a second Kossuth resolution in January 1852, to condemn the armed intervention of Russia in Hungary as "wanton and tyrannical," and to warn that America would not be "indifferent to similar acts of national injustice, oppression, and usurpation." This second resolution never came to a vote, for most Americans were coming to view Kossuth as a dangerous troublemaker. Seward remained his friend and supporter, however, and when Kossuth returned to Washington in April, almost ignored, Seward and Frances took a day to travel with Kossuth and his wife to Mount Vernon.[49]

Frances spent the first four months of 1852 in Washington, one of her longest stays in the capital. She wrote her sister that "visiting and receiving visits constantly is certainly not the kind of life adapted to my taste, feelings or constitution"; she had hoped that, with better health, "these duties might be less tiresome," but was "compelled to admit that I am peculiarly, and considering my position, unfortunately constituted." One visitor was welcome to her: Charles Sumner, who had recently joined the Senate as a Free Soil Democrat from Massachusetts. Many found Sumner peculiar, vain and difficult, but Frances liked and admired him: "It is certainly agreeable to hear a man talk who has such clear moral perceptions." Sumner's moral perceptions often led him to disregard mere politics. Even though he knew the measure was doomed to defeat, he insisted on forcing the Senate to vote on a bill to repeal the Fugitive Slave Law. Seward, with an eye on the imminent election, did not vote one way or the other. But Frances wrote Sumner that she had "read with great pleasure your eloquent and convincing argument against the fugitive slave bill."[50]

Seward generally avoided in this election year any mention of slavery, focusing instead on commerce. In January, in the Supreme Court, he argued that the federal courts should have the right to decide cases arising out of events on the Great Lakes. The prior law, based on English precedents, was that federal admiralty jurisdiction extended only to places affected by the ebb and flow of the tide. But the Court now agreed with Seward, and extended federal jurisdiction to the Great Lakes, since they "are in truth inland seas." In April, in the course of a speech advocating a subsidy for a steamship line, Seward confidently predicted that the United States, with its extensive territory, growing population, ingenious inventors, and enterprising merchants, would become the leading commercial nation in the world. And in July, he gave an extended speech on the whaling industry, advocating a naval survey of the seas around the Bering Strait to facilitate whaling. The ships involved in the survey, during the months when they could not be in the Arctic, should explore and chart Asian waters, especially the approaches to China and Japan. Trade and migration between Asia and the United States, he believed, would some day be as important as between Europe and the eastern United States, and it was the duty of the government to facilitate this "reunion of two civilizations."[51]

The Whigs were set to gather in mid-June in Baltimore, and as the national convention approached, Seward's home in Washington become the informal Scott headquarters. He reported to Frances that "the southern men all demand a platform of finality of the Compromise, and the northern men are preparing to go for it to avoid a breakup of the Convention. If I advise against it, I am denounced as a Dictator. If I listen and refer the subject to the Convention, lo! I have agreed on a platform." Seward did not attend the convention but kept in close touch with events through friends. As he hoped, the convention in the end nominated Scott, and as he feared, the convention's platform endorsed the Compromise of 1850. Seward wrote home that the "wretched platform, contrived to defeat General Scott . . . comes to him like an order of a superior power, and he is incapable of understanding that it is not obligatory on him to execute it." Much against Seward's wishes, Scott soon declared that he would campaign on the platform as adopted by the convention.[52]

The Scott campaign did not start well. The platform was unpopular in the North: "we defy it, execrate it, spit upon it," wrote Greeley in the *New York Tribune*. The candidate was unpopular in the South: nine southern Whig leaders announced that they would not support Scott because he was ambivalent about the Compromise of 1850 and too close to Seward. Many northerners agreed. Daniel Webster refused to endorse Scott, telling friends that as president he "would be a mere tool in the hands of the New York Whig regency, headed by William H. Seward." In a vain attempt to address such concerns, Seward issued a letter saying that he would not accept "any public station or preferment" from Scott as president.[53]

After the congressional session was over, Seward and his wife toured for a while in New York and Vermont. It was thus that Seward found himself in Rutland, where he spoke to thousands at the state fair on an "oppressively sultry" afternoon. He started by praising American agriculture, saying he regretted that there was no department of agriculture within the federal government, only a "subordinate clerk in the basement of the Patent Office." In the second part of his speech, on American expansion, Seward both predicted that the United States would expand and voiced his concerns. Alluding to recent southern efforts to mount private attacks on Cuba, he asked: "What [do] these ill-suppressed and desperate expeditions from Louisiana and Florida against Cuba [show] but covetousness of the sugar-plantations and coffee-grounds of that beautiful island?" The United States should be patient: "I would not seize with haste and force the fruit, which ripening in time, will fall of itself into our hands." Seward did not mention Scott or the Whigs by name, but he clearly intended to contrast the peaceful Whig approach with the aggressive Democratic way.[54]

Throughout the summer and the fall, Seward received frequent and generally positive reports on the progress of the Whig campaign. He also received periodic requests from Whig leaders, such as a letter from Schuyler Colfax, an Indiana editor, asking him to persuade John Parker Hale, the antislavery senator from New Hampshire, not to run as the Free Soil candidate. "If you can't influence Hale, I don't know who in our party can." Apparently even Seward could not influence Hale, for he accepted the Free Soil nomination. In September, in an effort to secure Catholic votes, Elihu Washburne, a Whig leader in Illinois, suggested that Seward obtain an endorsement from his friend Archbishop Hughes. "I am quite sure," Seward responded, "that Arch Bishop Hughes has never done any such thing as to write a letter of the nature you suppose possible, and that he would not feel at liberty to do so."[55]

At about this same time, General Scott was on a western tour, nominally for the purpose of inspecting military facilities, but obviously for political purposes as well. During a speech in Cleveland, when Scott heard a voice in the crowd with an Irish accent, he said, "I love that Irish brogue—I have heard it before on many battle fields, and I wish to hear it many times more." This transparent attempt to appeal to Catholics angered some Whig leaders, one of whom wrote Seward: "For God's sake, Seward, keep Scott at home. One more Cleveland speech and we are ruined. . . . Write him some speeches and forward as soon as possible. Don't trust him a single minute alone." But it does not appear that Seward tried to rein Scott in or help him with speeches. Perhaps he feared that any such attempt would become public, and would simply reinforce the Democratic charges that Scott was a puppet of Seward. Perhaps Seward failed Scott, however, by first securing his nomination, and then not giving Scott the advice and assistance he needed to be an effective candidate. Even when Scott stopped in Seward's hometown and the Auburn crowd demanded that Seward give a speech, Seward declined, offering only a few bland words of praise.[56]

General Scott carried only four states in November, and lost to Franklin Pierce in twenty-seven others, including traditional Whig strongholds. In New York, the Democrats not only secured the state's 35 electoral votes for Pierce; they also elected Horatio Seymour as governor and achieved a two-to-one majority in the assembly. Seward wrote Weed that "the play is played out for this time, and played out practically for us perhaps forever." Many believed that the Whig Party, as a national party, was now dead. Sumner wrote Seward that "now is the time for a new organization. Out of the chaos the party of freedom must arise." Seward disagreed; he responded that "no new party will arise, nor will any old one fail." To his friend Henry Raymond, formerly an editor under Greeley of the *New York Tribune*, and now the editor of his own paper, the *New York Times*, Seward wrote at more length: "I trust that you mistake in supposing that the Whig party will not come up as such. The Whig party cannot indeed come up again now, nor could any other come up now, nor at any time until occasion calls for one to rise. Can't we sleep in the meantime with our old flag wrapped around us as well as if we should tear it to pieces? It will be easier to recall the scattered to its folds than to another. Pray think on this."[57]

———

After the debacle of the 1852 election, Seward returned to Washington for the short, final session of the thirty-second Congress. A number of his speeches related to railroads. Seward was in favor of the "speediest possible construction" of a railroad to the west coast. Unlike others, he was not too concerned about the choice of route, believing that commercial considerations would ensure that New York and San Francisco were the de facto end points. He opposed an effort to force Mexico to grant territory for an American railroad across the Tehuantepec isthmus, in part because he saw this as an attempt to start a second Mexican war, and in part because he was confident there would soon be a more direct rail route to the Pacific. He also opposed an effort to eliminate the tariff on imported iron rails, saying it would be a disgrace to "bring iron from abroad to make roads over our own iron ore beds."[58]

Seward argued several important cases before the U.S. Supreme Court during this winter. One was a complex case involving rival claims to a property in Mobile, Alabama. The New York Times found it "a little singular that a client in Alabama should wander all the way up to Mr. Seward's latitude in search of a safe counsel." A few weeks later, he was before the Court again, this time representing several New York clients in a patent dispute over railroad spikes. In a third case, he represented a Wisconsin creditor challenging the procedures used in the lower courts. Political opponents sometimes questioned Seward's legal skills, but as the Times noted, he seemed to handle more than his fair share of "exceedingly intricate" cases.[59]

Later in the year, Seward spoke at the dedication of a new university in Ohio. He predicted a great future for the United States: that its borders would "be extended so that it shall greet the sun when he touches the tropic, and when he sends his glancing rays toward the polar circle"; that its population "now counted by tens of millions, shall ultimately be reckoned by hundreds of million"; and that "mankind shall come to recognize in us a successor of the few great states which have alternately borne commanding sway in the world." He cautioned, however, that history would not count the United States as truly great unless it also achieved intellectual and moral distinction. "It is well that we can rejoice in the renown of a Cooper, an Irving, and a Bancroft; but we have yet to give birth to a Shakespeare, a Milton, and a Bacon." Colleges "must imbue the national mind with correct convictions of the greatness and excellence to which it ought to aspire."[60]

Seward also worked closely in 1853 with his young friend George Baker on the preparation and publication of three volumes of Seward's works. In this endeavor, Seward for the first time framed the narrative of his own life. He highlighted the William Freeman trial; the volumes included long quotes from the transcript and reprinted an adulatory article by John Austin. He downplayed his work as a patent lawyer; the name of his key client, James G. Wilson, was not even mentioned. Seward released a number of papers that had not previously been made public, items Weed would no doubt have omitted. The registry law veto message that he had drafted but then discarded in early 1840 was now published, for example. He also published his letters to Benjamin Silliman, including the one in which he proclaimed that his right hand would drop off before he took any action against fellow citizens on the basis of their birth or their religion. In short Seward, perhaps too eager to provide a full picture of his life, provided ammunition for his enemies. Weed's views are suggested by a letter from Baker to Weed, pleading with him not to view the books with "entire disapprobation" or as "wholly unpardonable."[61]

Baker's three volumes received extended reviews. The *New York Times* praised especially how Seward had taken principled but unpopular positions: "Standing upon the rock of his own personal convictions, he has withstood private persuasion, public pressure and the clamor of expediency. Let his positions on the registry law, upon the McLeod question, concerning the pardon of Watson Webb, regarding the trial of William Freeman, in respect to the discussion of the school question, relative to the demands of Virginia, and to the finality of the compromises, be the few out of many instances to attest our argument." Even the *New York Herald*, which hated Seward, conceded that his writings "have generally been able, popular, and admirably adapted for their several purposes." Seward himself remarked to Baker that "these will be good volumes to die on. The heresies are all in."[62]

———

In early January 1854, Senator Stephen Douglas of Illinois, as chairman of the Committee on Territories, reported a bill to organize the territory of Nebraska. The territory in question was immense: much of what is now Kansas, Nebraska, South and North Dakota, Colorado, Wyoming, and Montana. All of this area was well north of the Missouri Compromise line, and thus should have been free territory under the terms of the compromise. But the Douglas bill did not prohibit slavery; all it said on the issue was that states formed from the Nebraska territory would "be received into the Union, with or without slavery, as their constitution[s] may prescribe at the time of their admission." Seward immediately recognized that Douglas's language could extend slavery into this immense and fertile territory. He wrote home that Douglas was attempting, as best he could, to abolish the key provision of the compromise, and he promised his wife that "I shall do my duty in this matter."[63]

Seward set out to defeat what he termed "this infamous Nebraska bill." He reported to Weed that he hoped that "we may get up a division in the South on the subject, and perhaps draw [John] Clayton [of Delaware] out to lead an opposition to 'the repeal of the Missouri Compromise.'" It appears that Seward worked to "get up a division in the South" by suggesting to Senator Archibald Dixon, a Kentucky Whig, that the bill was ambiguous on the question of slavery during the territorial stage of government. Dixon agreed, and announced that he would offer an amendment to provide that the Missouri Compromise would not prohibit slavery in the territory, and that slaveowners could (regardless of territorial laws) take their slaves into all parts of the territory. Southern Democrats, eager to avoid seeing a southern Whig lead on this issue, developed a new version of the bill, which stated that the Missouri Compromise had been "superseded" by the Compromise of 1850. Seward was pleased with the way the bill was evolving, believing that there would be opposition in both North and South to any explicit repeal of the Missouri Compromise.[64]

The Senate was not especially crowded when Seward delivered his first Nebraska speech, but a friend noted that many senators "listened attentively," while a few, notably Douglas, "bustled about or left the Chamber." Seward started with an extended historical discussion. He pointed out that Thomas Jefferson, as early as 1784, had advocated the language banning slavery in the Northwest Territory that later became part of the Northwest Ordinance of 1787. He described at length the Compromise of 1820, how the northern states had conceded that slave states could be organized south of the agreed line, and the southern states conceded that the territory north of the line would be "forever free." Now, Seward charged, the southern states wanted to abrogate only one part of the compromise, the part that dedicated the northern territory to freedom, while keeping the southern slave states, including Missouri and Arkansas, that had come into the Union under the compromise.[65]

Seward gained strength as he reached the end of his speech; an observer recalled that "never was he in finer trim." Those who favored the compromise believed that it would "secure permanent peace and harmony on the subject of slavery," but Seward derided such hopes as vain. "I tell you now, as I told you in 1850, that it is an error, an unnecessary error, to suppose that because you exclude slavery from these halls today, that it will not revisit them tomorrow." The reason was that, as long as there were slave states and free states, their interests would clash, and these clashes would come to Congress. The struggle could not be suppressed, any more than Congress could "compel the sea to suppress its upheavings, and the round earth to extinguish its internal fires." In closing, he reminded the senators of the higher issues involved: "You may legislate, and abrogate, and abnegate as you will; but there is a superior Power that overrules all your actions, and all your refusals to act; and I fondly hope and trust overrules them to the advancement of the greatness and glory of our country [and] to the distant but inevitable result of the equal and universal liberty of men."[66]

Seward's speech was quickly printed in the newspapers, and in pamphlet form, and warmly received by many. The Washington correspondent for the *New York Times* reported that "many Northern and Southern Senators speak of it in terms of highest praise." The *New York*

Herald criticized the speech but nevertheless predicted that he would be the northern presidential candidate in 1856, "upon anti-slavery principles, and sustained by a powerful northern party." One of many letters of praise came from William Herndon in Illinois, reporting that his law partner and "your friend" Abraham Lincoln "thinks your speech most excellent." (Herndon exaggerated in saying that Lincoln was Seward's friend—they had met only the one time—but such is the way of political friendship.) Neither Seward's speech, however, nor the continued public outcry against the Nebraska bill in the North had much effect on the outcome in the Senate. After an intense all-night debate in early March, in which Seward played a major part, the Senate passed the Kansas-Nebraska bill by a vote of 37 to 14. Almost all southern Whigs voted with the Democrats in favor of the bill. It was, in Seward's words, "sad" and "humiliating."[67]

The House, after its own long discussion, passed the bill in late May in slightly different form. When the House bill returned to the Senate for final passage, Seward argued in a late-night speech that slavery and freedom were irreconcilable. Freedom would triumph, he predicted, "in a constitutional way, without any violent shock to society, or to any of its great interests." He lamented the passage of the Kansas-Nebraska bill but hoped that slavery would extend at most to the Kansas territory established in the bill, that the far larger Nebraska territory would remain free because its climate was not suited to cotton and other slave crops. "Through all the darkness and gloom of the present hour, bright stars are breaking that inspire me with hope and excite me to perseverance. They show me that the day of compromises has passed away forever, and that henceforward all great questions between freedom and slavery shall be decided, as they ought to be, on their merits." At about one o'clock in the morning, amid a roar of celebratory cannon, the Senate passed the Kansas-Nebraska bill, and a few days later President Pierce signed it into law.[68]

CHAPTER 6

"Foremost Statesman of the Whole North":

1854–1856

I n retrospect, history often seems simple: northern outrage over the Kansas-Nebraska Act led to the formation of the Republican Party; that party's success in the election of 1860 led the southern states to secede. For those living through history, however, it is never simple, and few periods of American political history were more complex than the middle years of the 1850s.[1]

The defection of so many southern Whigs to support the Kansas-Nebraska Act led to an intense debate among northern Whigs about whether they should form a new, separate antislavery party. Henry Wilson, a Whig senator from Massachusetts, wrote to Seward that "the time has come to dissolve the infamous union of Whigs of the North and South." Wilson said that he would support Seward for president in 1856, but not as part of a national Whig party, for Wilson was determined "to combine in one great party all the friends of freedom." Horace Greeley declared in the *New York Tribune* that "the passage of this Nebraska bill will arouse and consolidate the most gigantic, determined and overwhelming party for freedom that the world ever saw." Seward's friend Henry Raymond, in the *New York Times*, disagreed with the approach advocated by his former editor Greeley. "Under existing circumstances the policy in question is very much like that of disbanding a strong, disciplined, and well-organized army, on the eve of an engagement, in the hope of raising a better one by calling for volunteers." Weed, in the *Albany Evening Journal*, agreed with Raymond. "Having found the Whig party of the North, on all occasions, and in every emergency, the most efficient and reliable organization both to resist the aggressions of slavery and to uphold the cause of Freedom, we concur . . . that it is best, now and ever, for the Whig party to stand by its colors." [2]

Seward himself was decidedly against the idea of a new northern party in 1854. He wrote to Weed from Washington in late May that "the Free Soilers here are engaged in schemes for nominating [Senator Thomas Hart] Benton and dissolving the Whig Party." Seward dismissed such schemes as "absurdities." In a letter to Theodore Parker, the Boston abolitionist minister, who was urging him to attend a national anti-Nebraska convention, he wrote that "we are not ready yet for a great national convention at Buffalo, or elsewhere. It would bring together only the old veterans. The states are the places for activity, just now. They have elections for Senators and Congressmen coming off in the autumn." Seward's position angered the "new party" men in New York and Washington; one of them wrote in disgust that "Seward hangs fire." [3]

In many states new parties formed in 1854 under various names: anti-Nebraska, anti-administration, and Republican. In New York, however, although there was an anti-Nebraska convention, there was no new party, largely because of Seward. For Weed and Seward, the first priority was Seward's own reelection to the Senate in early 1855, which would depend upon the election of a strong Whig assembly. And looking ahead to the presidential election of 1856, Seward still believed that a national Whig party was more likely to prevail than a northern anti-slavery party. The *National Era* reported regretfully that Seward hoped to maintain a national Whig organization with support from the border states and Louisiana, states where many Whigs opposed or questioned the repeal of the Missouri Compromise. [4]

Several other issues promised to complicate the 1854 election in New York. One was the division in the state's Democratic Party into two factions, known as the "Hard Shells" and the "Soft Shells." If the Hards and the Softs nominated separate candidates for assembly seats, as they had in the last election, these candidates would split the Democratic vote and allow more Whigs to be elected. But there was also the possibility that the Hard Democrats and Fillmore Whigs, whose conservative views were similar, would merge into one party, leaving the Seward Whigs as a small minority. One of Fillmore's friends, urging just such a merger, wrote Fillmore that he was "morally convinced that there is no national success for us *unless we can clear our skirts of Sewardism*, which will ruin us at the South."[5]

Temperance was another complication. The state legislature had passed in the spring of 1853 a bill, modeled on a recent Maine law, to prohibit the manufacture and sale of hard liquor. Governor Horatio Seymour, a Soft Democrat, vetoed the bill. Temperance men were thus determined to nominate and elect a governor who would sign a Maine bill into law. Many of these "Maine law men" were otherwise Seward Whigs: hardworking, plain-living, God-fearing people. They distrusted Seward on this issue, for he was known as a convivial host, and indeed he was sometimes alleged to drink to excess. Seward's friends Weed and George Patterson thought about running Seward for governor in 1854, but quickly abandoned this idea; as Weed explained to Patterson, "the Maine law question would be fatal to Seward as a candidate for governor."[6]

Still another issue, more important than the others, was the rapid rise of the Know Nothings. The Know Nothings were not a political party, at least not at first; they were a loosely connected set of secret lodges, united by their anti-immigrant, anti-Catholic, antiparty views. The Know Nothings railed against the increasing numbers and increasing political power of immigrants, and they despised the Catholic Church, and especially its influence on American politics. Know Nothings were generally disgusted with the existing political parties, both Democrat and Whig. Gideon Welles, at the time a Connecticut newspaper editor, observed that "there is a general feeling to throw off both the old organizations and their intrigues and machinery."[7]

In New York, many of the Know Nothings were strongly opposed to Seward. A friend warned Weed in August that "secretly the K.N. are pledged against you and Seward and *Abolitionism*—so much for their hostility to the Pope!" A few weeks later, Greeley wrote to a friend that "in this state Know-Nothingism is notoriously a conspiracy to overthrow Seward, Weed and Greeley, and particularly to defeat Gov. Seward's re-election to the Senate." Seward himself recognized the threat but at first dismissed it. During a Senate debate on a bill to make it easier for farmers to acquire western homesteads, in which he argued against an anti-immigrant provision, Seward read aloud from a Boston nativist newspaper. Another senator asked him whether these were the principles of the Know Nothings. "I know nothing of the Know Nothings," Seward responded, to laughter. A few weeks later, commenting on the upcoming New York election, he wrote to a friend that "the 'Know-Nothing' bubble is the only occasion of alarm, and that alarm threatens only *me*. To that I am indifferent."[8]

In July 1854, several New York leaders published a call for a state anti-Nebraska convention, to meet in the fashionable resort town of Saratoga in August. Greeley was not only planning to attend this convention; he hoped that the convention would declare itself a new political party and nominate him for governor. With some difficulty, Weed persuaded Greeley that he should *not* be a candidate, that it would create too much division among Whigs, and thus put at risk Seward's election as senator. Seward was in Saratoga at the time of the convention, working on a legal case, and it seems likely that he collaborated with Weed and Greeley in their successful effort to prevent the convention from making nominations or adopting incendiary resolutions. The Saratoga delegates did agree that they would meet again at the end of September, and thus preserved the threat that they would make their own nominations at that time, if the Whig nominees or platform were unacceptable.[9]

In late September, just before the state Whig convention was set to assemble in Syracuse, Weed admitted in a letter to a friend that he did not "see how we are to get through the convention safely." Both the temperance advocates and the Know Nothings would be present in force, and both groups were insisting that one of their own should be the nominee for governor. After some intense maneuvers, the Whig convention nominated Myron Clark, a state senator, for governor, and Henry Raymond for lieutenant governor. Clark was a Seward Whig, but he was also a temperance man, and even had Know Nothing credentials, of a sort; some friends in his hometown had created a lodge and inducted him as a member. Seward believed that the convention had "done wisely" in dealing with the many conflicting factions, but many Whigs did not.[10]

The adjourned Saratoga convention resumed in Auburn in late September. Seward was not a delegate, but he was at home in Auburn, and worked with Weed to prevent the convention from nominating its own candidates, and to secure an endorsement of the Whig candidates. This Auburn convention also adopted resolutions condemning the Fugitive Slave Act and calling for a national convention of the various state groups forming at this time under the name "Republican." Seward may not have played much of a role in drafting or adopting these resolutions, but given that the convention was in his hometown, and given that the resolutions echoed his views on slavery, people naturally assumed that these were "Seward" resolutions. The Fillmore Whigs were outraged: one of them wrote to Fillmore that the resolutions were "a declaration of perpetual warfare against the South"; another commented that "the Whig candidates have all gone over to a sectional Seward abolition movement."[11]

It was in part in reaction to the Auburn convention that a fourth convention was held, a "grand council" of Know Nothings that met behind closed doors in New York City in early October. This gathering nominated Daniel Ullman, a lawyer and Fillmore Whig whom Seward had known for many years, for governor. There were thus four serious candidates for governor: Horatio Seymour, the incumbent Democratic governor; Greene Bronson, the Hard Democratic nominee; Myron Clark, with nominations from the Whig and anti-Nebraska and Temperance parties; and Ullman as the Know Nothing candidate with Fillmore support.[12]

The parallel races for assembly seats were even more confused than the race for governor. As local Whig conventions were held around the state in September and October, Know Nothings attended and nominated their members as Whig candidates for assembly. Weed attempted to ensure that those nominated were pledged that, if elected, they would vote for Seward. But the Know Nothings also attempted to ensure that nominees were pledged to vote *against* Seward. Because these pledges were given in secret, and because most of the assembly candidates were political novices, there was really no way to know who were the Seward Whigs and who were the anti-Seward Know Nothings.[13]

In one sense, Seward played little role in the 1854 fall campaign. He spent much of September and October in Saratoga, involved in another phase of the patent dispute over railroad spikes. The U.S. Supreme Court had ruled against Seward's clients and named the former chancellor of New York, Reuben Walworth, as special master to determine the damages. Walworth's inquiry became legendary for its duration, complexity, and cost. At one point Walworth's wife asked Seward to explain to her "what this everlasting spike suit is about; I don't understand it." Seward responded with a smile that he "should be very much ashamed if you did. I have been engaged in it for several years, and I don't understand it yet." Seward ultimately won a victory of sorts; the damages awarded against his clients were minimal compared with the legal expenses his opponents incurred. In late October, he was busy in court again, representing Cyrus McCormick, inventor of the reaper, in a patent appeal in Albany.[14]

In another sense, however, Seward and his views were central to the campaign. Whig newspapers argued that slavery was the main issue. The *New York Times*, for example, claimed that southern leaders were determined to extend the region in which slavery was permitted, "to assume control of the federal government, and to convert this Republic into the grandest and most powerful slaveholding empire the world has ever seen." The only way for New Yorkers to check these schemes was to vote Whig. Democratic papers claimed that a vote for the Whigs was a vote for the radical, anti-southern, anti-Union views of Seward and his followers. The *New York Herald* argued that the paramount issue was "the preservation of the Union," and that the "defeat of Seward will be the triumph of law and order between the two sections, over the elements of agitation and disruption." The *Albany Evening Journal,* reprinting part of the *Herald*'s article, commented that this determination to defeat Seward was for the Democrats "the great work of the canvass."[15]

It took several days after the election for the votes to be counted. Clark, with only about a third of the votes, narrowly edged Seymour to become governor. Far more impressive to most observers was that Daniel Ullman received about one quarter of all the votes for governor. "Who could have believed," exclaimed George Baker in a letter to Seward, "that K.N. fanatacism was so extensive and so well organized?" [16]

The new state assembly would have at least seventy Whigs, with the remaining fifty-eight seats divided among the two factions of Democrats and a few independents. With such a strong Whig majority, some newspapers quickly predicted that Seward would win reelection to his Senate seat. But the presence of the Know Nothings, mixed in amongst the Whigs, made predictions dangerous. The *Rochester Daily American*, one of the few Know Nothing newspapers, claimed that there "are at least sixty-nine men in the Assembly opposed to Mr. Seward and half the Senate is like-minded. If these men honestly represent the sentiments of the state, they will dispose of Mr. Seward's claims, by selecting some other gentleman for the important post in question." Day after day the *Daily American* reminded readers of the reasons to vote against Seward. He was "the bosom friend and collaborator of Arch Bishop Hughes." He had nearly vetoed the registry law—the law so necessary to prevent illegal voting by immigrants. He had tried to secure public funding for Catholic schools "for the purpose of teaching Popery and High Dutch." [17]

While this anti-Seward campaign was getting started, Seward received an extraordinary letter from Horace Greeley, in which he announced the "dissolution of the political firm of Seward, Weed & Greeley," to take effect after the senatorial election was complete. This did not come as a complete shock to Seward; a few weeks earlier he had received a letter from Greeley complaining that "Weed likes me and always did—I don't think he ever had a dog about his house he liked better—but he thinks I know nothing about politics." But now Greeley went on for several strident pages about how he had helped Seward over many years, then watched as Seward and Weed gave lucrative positions to other men, while Greeley struggled in poverty. [18]

Perhaps because this letter caused such a stir when it was released six years later—perhaps because it is so quotable—historians have tended to make much of it. But at the time, and in context, the letter did not change much in the relations between Seward and Greeley. There was no "political firm" of Seward, Weed, and Greeley to dissolve; the three men often disagreed on issues, such as temperance, of which Greeley was an ardent advocate and on which Seward and Weed were agnostics. Seward visited Greeley in New York City not long after receiving the November 11 letter, and Seward continued to visit and correspond with Greeley thereafter. So relations among the three men remained close, although perhaps not as close, after this outburst.[19]

As the state legislative session started in January 1855, the campaigns for and against Seward grew more intense. Through letters, personal interviews, and their newspapers, the Know Nothing leaders pressed their legislators to vote against Seward. A key theme in their campaign was that the Know Nothing members had "taken an oath" to do so. On the other side, Weed (in the words of one of his opponents) "whipped or coaxed" the legislators "like sorry hounds." The Seward leaders promised temperance legislators that if they voted for Seward, they would secure votes in favor of temperance legislation. Governor Clark delayed making appointments so that legislators would know that they would only secure patronage by supporting Seward. As one Seward man wrote to another at the end of January, "never were such efforts made to secure a political object of this description. The state creeps all over, like an old cheese, and swarms of maggots are out."[20]

In early February, as the assembly debated the senatorial question over the course of several days, the members explained why they would vote for or against Seward. Some Know Nothings declared they would never vote for a man who had favored foreigners and Catholics. Some Whig members supported Seward for his positions on internal improvements, on education, and on slavery. The most interesting comments, however, came from men who were *both* Whigs and Know Nothings. One of these quoted from letters he had received ordering him to vote against Seward, and asked indignantly whether he was "to be told by these American Jesuits that I shall not, but at the hazard of their displeasure and proscription, answer my conscience and my God as a legislator?" Another argued that the paramount question was slavery. "What are personal considerations—what is personal popularity—when

weighed in the scale against justice and freedom?" Yet another explained that "true Americanism" must oppose "tyranny, and every
tendency towards slavery, in every form in which it can be presented.
It can no more love or tolerate slavery in the negro than in the white,
under the southern planter than under the Pope." [21]

When the debate was over and the vote taken, Seward prevailed
easily. He received 69 votes in the assembly, with the remaining 58 scattered among a dozen other candidates. In the Senate he received 18 out
of 32 votes, with the others scattered. How many of those who voted
for Seward were Know Nothings can never be known with certainty,
but it was probably at least two dozen, the number denounced as "traitors" not long after the election in the *Know Nothing Almanac*. After
the two houses voted separately, they joined together in the crowded
assembly chamber, and Seward's friend, the new Lieutenant Governor
Raymond, proudly announced the result. Raymond's announcement
was greeted (one paper reported) with "long continued cheers from
the galleries and lobbies—by waving of handkerchiefs from the ladies'
gallery—and by applause on the floor of the house—renewed when, on
a temporary lull, a few hisses were heard in the crowd." A friend wrote
to Seward from Albany that evening that "we really cannot see the town
here tonight with all the bonfires in every direction throughout the city,
guns firing, cannons roaring, music playing, people dancing, soldiers
marching." [22]

Seward was not in Albany for the vote and the celebration; he was
at his desk in the Senate when he learned the news by telegram. As
friends came up to congratulate him, a reporter observed that the senator seemed calm: "the only demonstration he made was to take an extra
pinch of snuff and turn his sandy, close shaven head round in his high
starched collar," as if to say, "it is all right, just as I expected." That evening, Seward's house in Washington was "thronged with visitors" and
he "received a serenade from a brass band," hardly expected given the
southern sympathies of Washington. Seward's first impulse was to thank
his friends. He wrote Raymond to praise "the manliness and boldness
as well as firmness with which you in common with so many and such
noble friends carried me through the most perilous crisis of my public

life." And he wrote Weed "to express not so much my deep and deep-
ening gratitude to you as my amazement at the magnitude and complexity of the dangers through which you have conducted our shattered
bark and the wonderful sagacity and skill with which you have saved us
all from so imminent a wreck." Seward was not on the battleground, but
he knew how close he had come to defeat.[23]

Seward's reelection was major news not just in New York but
throughout the United States. The *Richmond Whig* lamented that
Seward was "a more dangerous enemy to the Union than Aaron Burr."
The *Springfield* [*Massachusetts*] *Republican* praised Seward as "the foremost statesman of the whole North, and one of the most influential and
able men in the government of the nation." The *Newark* [*New Jersey*]
Mercury commented that Seward's "devotion to the cause of freedom,
his stern and unwavering attachment to the purest political principles,
his commanding intellect and personal integrity, have endeared him
to the whole people of the North, who rejoice in his triumph as they
would have mourned in his defeat." The *Albany Evening Journal* announced Seward's victory with its full-page image of the soaring American eagle, the image it reserved for "great victories of freedom." Fanny
Seward, now ten years old, at home with her mother and brother in
Auburn, clipped this page, turned it into a flag, and paraded around
the house. Even Frances was pleased, although her pleasure was muted
because she knew this meant her husband would spend at least another
six years away from Auburn.[24]

———

For contemporary observers, Seward's victory in the early 1855 Senate
election was a preview of his strength for the presidential contest in the
fall of 1856. The *New York Times* declared that Seward was now "recognized throughout the Union, by all parties and all sections, as embody-
ing more distinctly than any other living man the anti-slavery sentiment
of the northern states." The *Washington Daily Union*, a Democratic
paper, agreed in its own way, calling him "the head and font of the abolition party." The Boston minister Theodore Parker wrote to Seward that

he hoped he "would do noble deeds for your country, and win shortly the highest honors the nation can bestow."[25]

Seward's most notable Senate speech in this session of Congress was on the Fugitive Slave Act, which he denounced as "unnecessary, unwise, inhuman, and derogatory from the Constitution." As to emancipation, Seward said that he did not believe the federal government had constitutional authority to abolish slavery in the southern states, but that if he were a southerner, he would favor state legislation to emancipate slaves with compensation for their owners, and that as a federal legislator he would favor federal compensation to any states which passed such legislation. In an aside, he said that he was not and never could be a Know Nothing. Weed advised Seward to avoid such remarks: he should stick to "practical measures."[26]

Weed would have disapproved even more strongly of the measures Seward was taking to help former and fugitive slaves. The most famous former slave in the United States, Frederick Douglass, wrote Seward to thank him for financial support for his controversial newspaper. Seward's friend and neighbor John Austin, the Universalist minister, recorded in his diary an instance in which Seward suggested that he should collect money to "help forward a poor fugitive slave from the South to Canada." Austin did so, then "went over to the Governor's and gave it to the poor fugitive," who was hiding there. In another instance, while Seward was at home in Auburn and Frances away, he reported to her that "the underground railroad works wonderfully. Two passengers came here last night." Seward sold a small house in Auburn to Harriet Tubman, a fugitive slave active in helping other slaves escape. He offered Tubman very easy terms—only $25 down and $10 per quarter thereafter—and he did not object when she failed to make even these payments. Some have suggested that Seward helped Tubman and other fugitives for political reasons, to strengthen his position among abolitionists. It seems far more likely that he helped fugitives in spite of the legal and political risks, especially among moderate and border state voters. It was one thing to argue on the Senate floor that the Fugitive Slave Law should be repealed; it was quite another thing to commit a federal crime by sheltering fugitives in one's own home.[27]

Seward's comments about the Know Nothings, and his actions with fugitives, suggest a man indifferent to his political fate. In early 1855, when his protégé George Baker wrote him eagerly about the chances that Seward would secure the Republican nomination and become president, Seward wrote back to discourage him. "I wish that we could rest, retire, withdraw, and leave it to work out," Seward told Baker. "I do so for two reasons. First, because henceforth we can do nothing, but what will be set down to the account of an ambition we do not feel. Secondly, that I think it is by no means certain, and even hardly probable, that it is to work out completely and safely next year. . . . I do not want that you and I should bear the responsibility of such a disaster."[28]

Other actions, however, suggest that Seward was an eager candidate. He worked with Baker to edit his life and works down into a single volume, priced at only one dollar. Almost every time he made a speech, Seward arranged for it to be printed and distributed in pamphlet form; more than thirty such pamphlets were published from 1850 through early 1856. He also kept up political correspondences with editors and others throughout the North and even to some extent in the South. These were not the actions of a man without ambition.[29]

In July 1855, the *Albany Evening Journal* announced that two conventions, one Whig and one Republican, would be held on the same day in Syracuse in September. When a friend asked Seward which to attend, he responded that it did not matter: the delegates would enter through two doors, but they would exit through only one. As Seward predicted, the Whig delegates assembled first, and then Weed led them into the adjoining hall, where the Republicans greeted them with intense applause. The two groups largely melded into one, the Republican Party of New York, although a few recalcitrant Whigs, including Seward's friend Hamilton Fish, refused to go along.[30]

To cement his place as a national Republican leader, Seward now had to speak out as a Republican. His first speech of the 1855 state campaign, delivered in Albany in early October, started with a brilliant review of how the "privileged class"—a few thousand southern slaveholders—had dominated American politics from the very outset, and managed still to control all three branches of the federal government. Seward then asked which of the political parties could best resist the efforts of this privileged class to extend and consolidate slavery.

The Know Nothings? They tried to support slavery in the South and to oppose it in the North, an impossible contradiction. The Democrats? They were mere doughfaces, the northern allies of the slaveholders. The Whigs? The party had done noble work for two decades, but it had almost disappeared. "Let, then, the Whig party pass," he intoned. Only the new Republican Party, with its sound and liberal platform, with the strength of former Whigs and former Democrats, was strong enough to combat the privileged class of slaveholders. "Its banner is untorn in former battles, and unsullied by past errors. That is the party for us."[31]

One former Democrat with whom Seward was now joined in the Republican Party was Charles Sumner. "I am so happy," he wrote to Seward after the Albany speech, "that we are at last on the same platform and in the same political pew." Relations between the two men were not always easy. Seward had tried in 1854 to persuade Sumner to vote for a transport bill. Henry Adams, to whom Seward later told the story, wrote that after "exhausting all other arguments, [Seward] tried to act on his feelings and urged him to vote for it in order to aid his re-election. Sumner replied that he wasn't sent to the Senate to get Mr. Seward's re-election. On which the Governor, losing his philosophical self-command, said 'Sumner you're a damned fool,' and they didn't speak again for six months." Thurlow Weed, learning of the quarrel, brought the two men back together, and when Sumner stayed with the Sewards in Auburn for a few days in the spring of 1855, he was "welcomed hospitably and kindly." Relations between Frances Seward and Charles Sumner were always warmer than those between the two men. She addressed him in letters as "dear Charles Sumner," and signed herself "yours affectionately." This was not the youthful enthusiasm Frances had felt for Albert Tracy; it was the mature respect of one antislavery activist for another.[32]

Seward's second major speech of the 1855 campaign was in Buffalo, where he answered the Democratic charge that the Republican Party, because its stance alienated the South, was disloyal to the Union. "Are loyalty and patriotism peculiar virtues of slaveholders only? Are sedition and treason natural vices of men who, fearing God and loving liberty for themselves, would therefore extend its blessings to all mankind?" Southern slaveholders, an "insidious aristocracy," threatened not merely their slaves, but northerners and their freedoms. The Fugitive Slave Act forced every northerner, on pain of federal prison, to aid southerners in recovering alleged fugitives. Republican papers praised and Democratic papers attacked these speeches; the *Raleigh Register* charged that the Albany speech "breathed nothing but treason to the Constitution and the Union."[33]

Stirring speeches, however, were not enough to carry New York for the Republicans in 1855. The highest office at issue, secretary of state, was won by the Know Nothing or American candidate, who received 12,000 more votes than his Republican rival, with the Democratic vote split among two candidates. Republicans also fell short in other states. In Pennsylvania, a Fusion candidate for governor, drawing mainly on Know Nothing and Whig support, trounced the other candidates. As the results were coming in, Seward wrote that some friends were "panic struck about the future," but for himself, "my philosophy is not disturbed." The Know Nothings, he predicted, would "inevitably disappear in the heat of the great national contest."[34]

Seward's prediction may have had a tactical as well as philosophical basis. Since the Republican Party did not really exist in the South, the Republican presidential candidate, in order to win, would have to carry almost all of the northern states. Such a northern sweep would be difficult given the Know Nothing strength in several states. The Republican leaders most worried about the Know Nothings naturally viewed Seward as an impossible candidate. As the *New York Times* noted, Seward would "undoubtedly" be the first choice of the Republicans but for his "fixed hostility to the principles and policy of the American party." Conversely, Republican leaders who were not especially concerned about the Know Nothings—those most interested in slavery and Kansas—favored Seward. Gamaliel Bailey, editor of the *National Era*, argued that "Seward is by all odds the strongest man we could run." By downplaying the nativist threat, Seward was supporting those like Bailey who supported his own candidacy.[35]

In late December 1855, the senior statesman Francis Preston Blair invited Senators Seward, Chase, and Sumner and a few others to a dinner at his home in Silver Spring, Maryland. The guest list was unusual not only because it included two of the leading candidates for the

Republican nomination—Seward and Chase—but also because Blair was working for a third candidate, John Frémont, the former explorer and senator. Seward declined Blair's invitation, pleading a "rule which prohibits me from taking part personally in plans or schemes for political action." His real concern, he explained to Weed, was that he feared the group intended to pursue a mixed strategy, "half Republican and half Know Nothing." Seward refused to help in the "profanation of a good cause" by working with the Know Nothings. Weed was much less of a purist; he wrote Seward that he should have attended the meeting, and he wrote Blair that he would support the Republican candidate, whoever it might be.[36]

———

Starting in the late 1840s, American merchants imported dried seabird dung, known as guano, for use as a fertilizer. But the growth of the industry was hampered by the difficulties of dealing with Peru, Ecuador, and other nations that claimed the remote guano islands. To encourage the industry, and perhaps incidentally to expand the American empire, Seward introduced in early 1856 a bill to authorize the United States to take possession of any guano islands outside the jurisdiction of foreign nations. Seward was a patent lawyer, and he saw the guano bill as a kind of patent law for the industry. "The world has never been injured," he argued, "by excessive liberality on the part of nations to discoverers and to inventors. On the other hand, I think the progress of society has been injured by the exercise of too great jealousy, by nations and monarchs, in restricting and embarassing discovery."[37]

Seward minimized the territorial implications of his bill, arguing that it was "framed so as to embrace only those more ragged rocks, which are covered with this deposit in the ocean, which are fit for no dominion, or for anything else, except for the guano which is found upon them." He claimed the bill could not be used for "the establishment of colonies or any other form of permanent occupation" because by its terms "whenever the guano should be exhausted, or cease to be found on the islands, they should revert and relapse out of the jurisdiction of the United States." His claim was a bit misleading; what his bill provided was that the United States was not *obliged* to retain islands after the guano was exhausted.[38]

With relatively little debate, the guano bill passed Congress and became law. Seward's modest bill proved far more important than even he imagined. As he hoped, Americans quickly claimed dozens of small guano islands in the Caribbean and the Pacific. These islands did not provide much guano—other fertilizers soon emerged to supplant it—but the guano islands tended to remain American for a long time. During World War II, several islands first claimed under the guano island law, including Johnston and Midway, were important military bases. Even today, the guano island law remains in effect, and the United States retains a dozen islands first claimed under Seward's law.[39]

The main issue facing Congress in 1856 was Kansas. During the first territorial election, held in early 1855, thousands of Missourians had entered Kansas temporarily and elected a proslavery legislature. This legislature, meeting in a schoolroom only three miles west of the Missouri border, passed a set of stringent proslavery laws. The antislavery settlers, excluded from this legislature, assembled later in Topeka and adopted their own constitution. Thus by the end of the year, there were two rival governments in Kansas, both heavily armed. A fragile peace held over the winter, mainly because of bitterly cold weather.[40]

President Franklin Pierce, in a message in January 1856, denounced the Topeka constitution and legislature as "revolutionary" and "treasonable." Senator Stephen Douglas proposed that Kansas be admitted as a state only after its population reached and exceeded 90,000. Effectively, Pierce and Douglas were proposing to leave the territory for several years in the control of the governor appointed by Pierce and the Lecompton legislature elected by the proslavery Missouri interlopers. Seward countered with a bill to admit Kansas immediately under the Topeka constitution. He argued, in a slashing Senate speech, that Pierce was treating Kansas in the same infamous way that George III had treated the American colonies.[41]

Both the motivation behind and the reaction to Seward's speech were political. The Know Nothings, at a convention in February, had nominated Millard Fillmore for president, and many Republicans were looking for ways to appease and attract Know Nothings. Seward would go the other way; as he wrote to Weed, he would make a "bold effort" for Kansas, one "which may present an issue on which we can rally the party." The *Washington Daily Union* commented that Seward's speech "was evidently made for the presidential campaign," because Seward hoped "to rally to his own standard the anti-Nebraska men of all shades." Republican papers praised the speech, but many suggested Seward was not the right candidate. The *New York Times* insisted the party would have to take up a new candidate, "one not identified with the political struggles and animosities of the past." The leading new candidate was Frémont of California, supported by Blair and others. Seward reported regretfully in early April to Weed that "the consultations about organization have ripened here [in Washington] into the general impression that it will be expedient to nominate the California candidate."[42]

Weed counseled Seward that this was not the year for his nomination, that it would be necessary to nominate someone acceptable to the nativists. At the same time, he insisted that Seward not withdraw his name from consideration before the convention; Weed wanted to keep his options open. Seward wrote back that it seemed "unnecessarily hard" for his friends to make him "stand in the way of the candidates they want to nominate." Although Seward told Weed that he was prepared to yield to his judgment, he told another friend that he was sure that, if nominated, he could carry Pennsylvania. Weed remained more cautious, telling this same friend that "we do not want [Seward] nominated *for fun*."[43]

———

As both the Democrats and the Republicans prepared to hold their conventions, Charles Sumner visited the Sewards' house in Washington to read to Seward and Frances from a draft speech on Kansas. Both husband and wife expressed doubts, and Frances wrote Sumner to explain: "I would on no account have you suppose that I objected to the general tone of all that you read. Neither my heart nor my conscience would allow me to say that any words were too strong spoken in favor of a wronged and suffering people or against their oppressors. I objected only to the cutting personal sarcasm, which seldom amends, and is less frequently forgiven." Sumner did not heed their advice, for the speech he gave in the Senate on May 19 and 20 was filled with personal insults. Senator Andrew Butler of South Carolina, according to Sumner, was like Don Quixote, a chivalrous knight pledged to a mistress. In Butler's case, the mistress, "though polluted in the sight of the world, is chaste in his sight—I mean the harlot Slavery." As for Senator Stephen Douglas, he was "the squire of Slavery, its very Sancho Panza, ready to do all its humiliating offices."[44]

Many people, upon hearing Sumner's Kansas speech, shared the fears that Frances Seward had expressed. Douglas remarked to another senator that "this damn fool," Sumner, "is going to get himself shot by some other damn fool." Two days later, Representative Preston Brooks of South Carolina, a nephew of Butler, waited in the Senate chamber until the session ended and the galleries emptied. Brooks then approached Sumner, who was still sitting at his desk, and accused him of an unfair personal attack. Before Sumner could respond, Brooks started to beat him about the head and shoulders with a thick cane. By the time someone finally pulled Brooks away, Sumner was lying on the Senate floor, bloody, unconscious, near death.[45]

Seward was not in the Senate chamber at the time of the attack, but he visited Sumner at his home soon thereafter.[46] Frances wrote to the Seward children that Sumner was "covered with blood when your father arrived at the house. Sumner was on the bed, recovered from the bewilderment of his faculties and much in hopes that some benefit to the anti-slavery cause might accrue from the affair." That evening, the Republican senators gathered at Seward's house to discuss their response; they agreed that he should take the lead in pressing for an investigation. The Senate investigation, however, was useless; it simply referred the issue to the House, which also did nothing to punish Brooks.[47]

Northern newspapers unanimously condemned the attack. The normally calm *New York Evening Post* asked whether northerners had reached the point where "we must speak with bated breath in the presence of our southern masters? . . . Are we to be chastised as they chastise their slaves?" Southern newspapers were almost as unanimous in praise of the attack. The *Richmond Enquirer* declared the "act good in conception, better in execution, and best of all in consequences. The vulgar abolitionists in the Senate are getting above themselves. . . . They must be lashed into submission." The *Richmond Whig* "rejoiced" at the assault and hoped that "the ball may be kept in motion and Seward and others may catch it next." The *Petersburg Intelligencer* agreed that "if thrashing is the only remedy by which the foul conduct of the abolitionist can be controlled, that it will be very well to give Seward a double dose at least every other day until it operates freely on his political bowels." [48]

The news of the assault on Sumner arrived almost at the same time as news of an armed assault by eight hundred proslavery men on the antislavery town of Lawrence, Kansas. The initial reports in the Republican newspapers were even more lurid than the actual events. The *New York Tribune* reported that Lawrence had been "devastated and burned to ashes," leaving only "a few bare and tottering chimneys." The two events were quickly linked. "Violence has now found its way into the Senate chamber," lamented the *New York Evening Post,* and "violence overhangs [Kansas] like a storm-cloud charged with hail and lightning." [49]

These press reports were still appearing as the Democratic Convention assembled in Cincinnati on June 2. The Democrats realized that they could not run President Pierce or Senator Douglas, both of whom were, fairly or unfairly, associated with the crisis in Kansas. So they turned instead to James Buchanan, an experienced leader from Pennsylvania, who had only recently returned to the States after serving three years as America's minister in London. Republicans sensed that the attacks on Sumner and Lawrence had dramatically increased their chances of winning the presidency. One of Seward's friends wrote to him that "I have never before seen anything like the present state of deep, determined and desperate feelings of hatred and hostility to the further extension of slavery and its political power." Seward realized that, as the candidate most firmly on record on Kansas, his own chance of securing the nomination had improved. Many Republican leaders, as they traveled to their convention in Philadelphia, stopped to see him in Washington and press him to be their candidate. At least one of these friends, James Watson Webb, editor of the *Morning Courier,* inferred from Seward's remarks that he was willing to run. [50]

At some point on June 17, the first day of the Republican Convention, Seward received two letters from Philadelphia. "One word from you will give the country its candidate," Webb wrote. "I tell you again, you can succeed." If Seward did not want the nomination himself, "*you* can say *who* shall be nominated." The other message was from Seward's close friend John Schoolcraft, saying that he and Weed believed "nomination now would be unwise and unsafe, on the ground that the election would be impossible." Seward wrote to Webb and Schoolcraft, yielding to Weed's pressure. Seward told his wife that he had declined the nomination because "the Republican convention was not prepared to adopt all my principles and policy" and that "I would not modify *them* to secure the presidency." Seward's claim was not quite right: he had no indication the convention would not adopt his policies, but he believed he had no choice other than to follow Weed's advice.[51]

It appears that Seward's letters did not reach Philadelphia for a day or two, or that Seward's letter to Schoolcraft was not as "peremptory" as he claimed in his letter to his wife. It is in any case clear that it was not Seward's letters that caused the 1856 Republican Convention to pass over him; it was the actions of his closest political colleagues. In brief remarks on June 18, George Patterson explained to the convention that although "nothing would have given the state of New York more pleasure than to do honor to her favorite son," he "had been requested to withdraw his name." Webb interrupted Patterson to say that the request had not come from Seward. Patterson conceded that his authority was not from Seward but rather from "the delegation." According to a letter from Thomas Miller, an ardent Seward supporter, the convention was ready to nominate Seward and would have nominated him but for the actions of Weed. Schoolcraft told Miller that Weed "did not think anybody could be elected, and that it was better that Frémont should be sacrificed than Seward." Miller disagreed; he argued with Schoolcraft that "we could carry the election on the Kansas issue, that Mr. Seward was the embodiment of that issue." Schoolcraft replied that Seward would "lose the Know Nothing Vote while Frémont could carry it."[52]

With New York's delegation behind him, Frémont easily secured the nomination. After the convention was over, Seward endorsed Frémont and the party's platform, but then for many months he was silent, playing no role in the campaign. In part this was because he was busy in Washington; Congress did not finish work until the end of August. In part the issue may have been Seward's health; he claimed in early September that he was too ill to be of use to himself or to his friends. But no doubt the main reason for Seward's silence was that he was angered by the way he had been treated by Weed and other close friends. He probably agreed with Frances, who wrote that Weed's "abandonment seems to have been a matter of very cool calculation. . . . A magnanimous friendship might suggest a more elevated course and even reconcile one to struggling against the current."[53]

The Frémont presidential campaign did not go well. Some of the problems were those Weed had expected, the problems of organizing a new political party. Others were unexpected, such as the revelations that Frémont and his wife were married by a Catholic priest and their daughters attended a Catholic school. Seward wrote with a smile to Frances that "Frémont, who was preferred over me because I was not a bigoted Protestant, is nearly convicted of being a Catholic." Some Republicans noticed Seward's silence and Weed, concerned, wrote to press him to make a few speeches. Seward reluctantly agreed.[54]

Seward's speeches were given late in the campaign and did not receive much press coverage. Perhaps this was because, by the middle of October 1856, after the Democrats won state elections in Indiana and Pennsylvania, it was clear that Buchanan would win.[55] In the end, Buchanan carried every southern state except Maryland, and he also prevailed in several key northern states. New York Republicans, although disappointed by the national results, were pleased that they had elected a governor and assembly. Many believed that the defeat of Fillmore and other Know Nothings spelled the end of that party; a friend wrote to Seward that "the Know Nothing party, the meanest, paltriest of all mean and paltry parties has been killed dead, dead forever, never to rise again." If the Know Nothing Party was indeed dead, Seward's chances in the presidential election of 1860 were much improved. He told his friend and neighbor David Wright that he "never went to Washington in better spirits."[56]

CHAPTER 7

"An Irrepressible Conflict":

1857–1859

T he first few months of 1857 were pleasant ones for the Seward family. Frances spent most of that winter with her husband in Washington, and although she did not go out much, at least he had her company at home. The Sewards had secured an appointment for Augustus with the coast survey in Florida, close enough that he could visit his parents from time to time while on home leave. Frederick was married and working in Albany for the *Evening Journal*, and William was making his start as a clerk in Auburn. Fanny, now twelve, was with her parents in Washington, a serious, bookish child. When someone told Frances that it must be hard educating and marrying off a daughter, Frances responded that she was educating Fanny "not to be married." The family also had the company this winter of Mary Grier, a lively cousin, about twenty years old. Frances reported to Augustus in December that "your father and Mary Grier have the fashionable world to attend to at present; they have already attended two evening parties and made countless calls." Mary's letters home were filled with details of the dresses she wore, the young women and men she met, the parties she attended, and the grand style of entertainment at the Sewards' house.[1]

Seward's main legislative effort in early 1857 was to secure federal support for the transatlantic telegraph project of Cyrus West Field. The proposed underwater cable would run from Ireland to Newfoundland; other lines from these points would enable communication between London and New York. Seward was the author and floor manager of the bill and worked closely with Field, who spent much of the winter in Washington. Field's brother later noted that these weeks in Washington, among the politicians, "were worse than among the icebergs off the coast of Newfoundland." To those who argued that the project was impractical, Seward recalled how in his youth people had derided the Erie Canal as "visionary and impracticable." After what he described as a "severe contest," he secured passage of the bill in late February.[2]

By early March, Washington was packed with thousands who came for the inauguration of James Buchanan. Seward had campaigned against Buchanan, but he hoped, like the *New York Times,* that Buchanan would prove an "independent" and "statesmanlike" president. In his inaugural address, Buchanan said that the people of Kansas and each other territory should decide for themselves whether to allow or to ban slavery. There was a question about when settlers could make this decision: whether they could do so when they formed a territorial government, or only later when forming a state constitution. Fortunately, Buchanan said, this was a judicial question, that would be resolved soon by the U.S. Supreme Court. "To their decision, in common with all good citizens, I shall cheefully submit."[3]

Everyone understood that Buchanan was referring to the *Dred Scott* case pending before the Court. The immediate issue was whether the slave Scott had been rendered free by spending time in free states and territories, but it was understood that the Court would also address whether and when territories could prohibit slavery. Two days after the inauguration, while Seward was upstairs in the Senate chamber, a crowd gathered in the courtroom on the ground floor of the Capitol, eager to hear the opinion. Starting at eleven that morning, and continuing for two hours in an almost inaudible voice, the aging Chief Justice Roger Taney read out his opinion. Although Taney would not issue his written opinion for several months, the key points were clear enough: that blacks, whether slave or free, were not citizens of the United States; that slaves could not acquire freedom by entering a free territory; and that the Constitution did not allow a prohibition against a slaveowner taking his property (his slaves) into any territory of the United States. In effect, the Supreme Court ruled that Congress had no constitutional power to prohibit slavery in the territories, no authority to implement the key plank of the platform of the Republican Party.[4]

Although informed observers had predicted that the Court would rule in roughly this way, Republican newspapers reacted to the *Dred Scott* decision with outrage. The *Chicago Tribune* could scarcely find words to "express our detestation of its inhuman dicta, or to fathom the wicked consequences which may flow from it." The *New York Tribune* argued that, given the southern slant of the Supreme Court, the decision was "entitled to just so much moral weight as would be the judgment of a majority of those congregated in any Washington bar-room." The New York legislature, filled with Seward Republicans, resolved that because of their "sectional and aggressive" decision, the justices had "lost the confidence and respect of the people of this state." Seward himself did not comment immediately.[5]

In the summer, after the congressional session was over, Seward set out on a long Canadian vacation. He was accompanied on the first part of the trip, which included a week of fishing in the Thousand Island region, by several political friends, including Francis Preston Blair. On the second part of the trip, Seward, Frederick, and Frederick's wife Anna chartered a small boat and traveled out to Labrador. The weather was cold and wet, the winds often absent or adverse, and the fishing poor. But Seward was exhilarated. He described in a detailed journal the people they met, the dramatic scenery, and the varied wildlife. When they left the ship, still dressed in "Labrador clothes," Seward was shunned in the first-class section of the train, so he settled into second class, where "by virtue of my liberality, sharing fruit and cigars with my fellow passengers, I got on well."[6]

Seward not only observed the sights of Canada while on this trip; he reconsidered the relations among Canada, Britain, and the United States. In one of his letters, soon published in the *Albany Evening Journal*, he admitted that like most Americans he had believed that Canada would soon separate from Britain and become part of the United States. He now realized that Canada was itself an immense country, with its own "vigorous, hardy [and] energetic" people, and that it could not be conquered by the United States or permanently held by Britain. Canada would be a great independent nation, he wrote, and might one day pose a threat to the United States, if the United States allowed itself to be weakened by the continued control of the slave states.[7]

He arrived back in Auburn in early September, in time to read the first reports of what we now know as the Panic of 1857. Seward was not too worried until October, when the Illinois Central Railroad, in whose bonds he had heavily invested, defaulted and sought bankruptcy protection. This occurred more or less at the same time as the suspension by all the banks in New York City, and then all the banks in the country, of their customary practice of redeeming their notes for specie. Seward was so concerned that he made what he called a "hurried trip to Chicago," to meet with bank and railroad officials. He also met with Senator Stephen Douglas, political patron of the railroad. By November Seward was in serious financial difficulty. "For the first time in twenty years," he wrote, "I have been told by my banker that my account is overdrawn." Frances wrote that "so many girls have been dismissed from their places that we have constant application to hire." These poor girls in Auburn were a tiny sliver of the thousands around the country—but especially in the cities—who were without work that winter.[8]

The main issue facing Congress in late 1857 was again Kansas. A few months before Congress convened, proslavery settlers had gathered at Lecompton and drafted a new state constitution. Instead of putting the entire constitution to a vote, the Lecompton delegates arranged a vote on only one provision, the one that authorized slavery. This was far from the only controversial provision in the constitution: another protected the rights of existing slaveholders; yet another prohibited foreign-born citizens from holding state office. Buchanan, in his December message, argued that the Lecompton convention was legitimate and that the limited approval procedure was adequate. On the day after Buchanan's message was presented, Douglas rose in the Senate to attack, in a three-hour speech that many considered one of his finest, the Lecompton convention and especially the approval process: "If this constitution is to be forced down our throats, in violation of the fundamental principles of free government, under a mode of submission that is a mockery and an insult, I will resist it to the last." The split among the Democrats, which Seward had predicted for some months, had now emerged, and he was ecstatic. He reported to Frances that he and Douglas talked at length right after the speech, and Seward was convinced that the "Administration and the slave power are now broken."[9]

Another territory, Utah, was also the subject of debate at this time. The Mormon territory was in a state of near rebellion against the federal government, forcing Buchanan to send troops and to ask Congress for an increase in the size of the Army. When the resulting bill came to the Senate floor, almost all Republicans other than Seward opposed it. Some Republicans hated the idea of a standing army; Greeley wrote to Seward that the Army was an "absurd business, unworthy of the nineteenth century." Others focused on the way in which the administration was using the Army to support the proslavery government in Kansas. Seward opposed the administration's policy in Kansas, but he was also troubled by reports of the dangers facing the federal soldiers near Utah. In one speech he described them as "that small band of men who are now representing the United States, and hemmed in in winter quarters, distant from every part of our civilized country, in danger and wasting by disease." In part, his motivation for supporting the Army bill was political—he later said that "one fundamental principle of politics is to be always on the side of your country in a war"—and in part his motivation was personal—he knew that it was only by chance that his son Augustus was not serving in Utah himself.[10]

Seward's position on the Army bill surprised and displeased Republicans. The *New York Evening Post* argued that he supported the Army bill because he gave, "to pretty much every measure contemplating the expenditure of money, a systematic support." Seward's spendthrift ways, the *Post* continued, gave him influence that he sometimes used for New York's benefit, but in this case his position was just wrong. Senator John Parker Hale of New Hampshire lamented in a Senate speech that Seward, like Daniel Webster in 1850, was effectively supporting the extension of slavery, and thus falling from party leadership. Seward rose immediately to respond. He was not, he said, at all influenced by the suggestion that he was being untrue to the Republican Party. "I know nothing, I care nothing—I never did, I never shall, for party." He had a proper regard for the "honored friends with whom I cooperate in public life," but insisted that he placed the interests of the nation ahead of those of mere party. The minor issue of the size of the Army should not obscure the larger issue of freedom in the new states. "This battle," Seward declared, was "already fought; it is over." He did not explain what he meant by the "battle" or in what sense it was over.[11]

Seward's Senate remarks about the party and the antislavery struggle caused, as George Baker reported to him, "the most intense excitement among your friends." Greeley wrote in the *New York Tribune* that it was unclear to what "battle" Seward was referring, "but if it be the battle between slavery and freedom, we do not share the sanguine anticipations of our Senator. On the contrary, we consider this battle so far from being 'over' that it is barely begun." Seward responded to Greeley indirectly, through their mutual friend Richard Blatchford, in a long letter in which he accused the Republican Party of being like a "hedgehog," with "nothing but bristles, bristles on all sides, bristles always raised against everybody." As for himself, Seward claimed that he had "given up all aspirations and seek now nothing more than to close my term here" and return to private life.[12]

After Blatchford shared Seward's letter with Weed, there was a heated exchange between the senator and his oldest friend. "I don't think your vote on the Army Bill was half so bad," Weed wrote, "as saying that you care nothing for party, and that the battle has been fought. There are not fifty men in the entire North who know what the latter expression means, or who comprehend the sense in which it is true." Seward replied: "I feel deeply that you are unjust and harsh to me." Weed, sensing that Seward was upset not just about recent events, wrote that his "reflections must now be embittered by the knowledge that you feel that I was, in 1856, unfaithful to a purpose which, for twenty years, engrossed my thoughts and controlled my actions." Seward agreed: "your severity towards me in 1856 determined me to abstain from seeking your counsels and to follow my own." (Indeed, from late 1856 through early 1858, there were very few letters between

Weed and Seward, and these were more formal than personal.) "I there-fore appeal to you," Seward continued, "to withdraw in my name and behalf all my supposed or imagined claims for continuance in public life in any sphere, and to let me know when I can go to the rest I de-sire." Seward thus returned to the point he had made to Blatchford: he would not be a presidential candidate in 1860. But this Weed could not allow; he had, as he noted, spent twenty years working to make Seward president, and 1860 promised to be the year in which they would achieve their common goal. Somehow, over the next few weeks, Weed, Blatchford, and others persuaded Seward to change his mind, to continue his quest for the presidency. Or perhaps they did not need to change his mind; perhaps these letters were merely Seward's way of insisting that Weed consult him more closely in 1860 than he had in 1856. In any case, by the summer of 1858, Seward was back on the presidential trail.[13]

————

Meanwhile, the Kansas debate continued in Congress. In early March 1858, as part of his major Senate speech on the issue, Seward de-nounced the *Dred Scott* decision, especially the "coalition between the executive and judicial departments to undermine the national legislature and the liberties of the people." Those who attended the Buchanan inauguration, Seward said, including himself, were "unaware of the im-port of the whisperings carried on between the President and the Chief Justice." The Court, in making a political rather than a judicial decision, "forgot its own dignity"; the justices "forgot that judicial usurpation is more odious and intolerable than any other among the manifold prac-tices of tyranny." The Court's decision, Seward continued, "attempts to command the people of the United States to accept the principle that one man can own other men." But the people of the United States "never can, and they never will, accept principles so unconstitutional and so abhorrent. Never, never." The Court could reverse its decision— or the unnecessary portion of its decision that purported to invalidate the Missouri Compromise—more easily than the American people could accept the decision. Or Congress could "reorganize the Court, and thus reform its political sentiments and practices, and bring them into harmony with the Constitution and the laws of nature."[14]

Buchanan was reportedly so outraged by this section of Seward's speech that he denied him access to the White House. Chief Justice Taney later told a friend that if Seward instead of Lincoln had been elected president in 1860, he would "have refused to administer the oath to him." Historians have determined, however, that there were serious discussions between certain justices and Buchanan before the *Dred Scott* decision. Did Seward know about these discussions? Or did he merely guess and, as one author put it, "hit uncomfortably close to the mark"? Seward probably had some inside information from his friend Samuel Nelson, formerly a judge in upstate New York and now a justice of the Supreme Court.[15] Seward's specific proposal for Court reform was that the states should be represented among the justices "more nearly on the basis of their federal population" and that "the administration of justice made more speedy and efficient." The *New York Times*, often Seward's voice, argued that "what is required is to put the Court into correspondence with the great interests and sentiments of the people, so that every portion of the confederacy may have its due weight through judges from its own territory." For a modern reader, this sounds similar to the proposal made in 1937 by President Franklin Roosevelt, to expand the number of justices and otherwise "reform" the federal court system. Seward's plan died more quietly than that of Roosevelt, but it shows that he was not afraid to take on even the Supreme Court in his quest for freedom.[16]

Turning to Kansas itself, Seward argued in his March speech that it was pointless for Congress to try to force the proslavery Lecompton constitution upon the antislavery Kansas settlers. A better approach would be to follow the lead of the "eminent senator from Illinois," Stephen Douglas, and allow the settlers to decide for themselves whether to accept or reject the draft constitution. Kansas, Seward predicted, would be just the first of many victories for freedom. The free labor system had "driven back" slave labor in California and Kansas; "it will invade you soon in Delaware, Maryland, Virginia, Missouri and Texas." This "invasion," Seward claimed, would be peaceful and even "beneficent" to the slave states "if you yield seasonably to its just and moderated demands." Freedom would prevail not only through changes within the slave states but also through the admission of new free states. The inexorable expansion of the American empire would "go on until the ends of the continent are the borders of our Union." Unlike Buchanan, who wanted to be done with the Kansas question, Seward was pleased to be part of this process, "for I know that heaven cannot grant, nor man desire, a more favorable occasion to acquire fame, than he enjoys who is engaged in laying the foundations of a great empire."[17]

Seward's eloquence had little effect on the Senate, which soon passed a bill to admit Kansas under the Lecompton constitution. The House rejected the bill, however, and a conference committee from both houses, including Seward, was appointed to work out a compromise. The result was the English bill, known after Representative William English, to admit Kansas immediately as a slave state if the Kansas voters would accept the Lecompton constitution, or to delay its admission for several years if they rejected it. Seward dissented from the committee's report and explained his reasons in a speech in late April. The bill presented Kansans with a false choice, he argued: they could either become a state immediately, under an odious constitution, or wait to apply for statehood, but face likely rejection, if they again sought to come in as a free state. His eloquence was again in vain; about an hour after his speech the Senate passed the English bill. As he predicted, though, the voters in Kansas rejected the Lecompton constitution, by a margin of more than six to one. Kansas would remain a territory for the next few years.[18]

Seward's comments on slavery were often harsh, but his relations with individual southerners were often warm. In early 1857, Seward and Senator Thomas Rusk of Texas, who had evidently long since forgotten their dispute, discussed the possibility that they would travel together around the world. A few months later, when Seward learned that Rusk had killed himself, he lamented in a letter to Frances that it was "a public misfortune" and a "personal disaster." Later in that year, Seward was the guest of John Pendleton, former congressman from Virginia, at his estate near Culpeper Court House. Seward commented to his wife that the slaves were "treated with kindness, and they appear clean, tidy, and comfortable." In early 1858, when Senator Jefferson Davis of Mississippi was suffering from a severe eye illness and confined to his darkened room for seven weeks, Seward visited him every day and spent an hour amusing the invalid with stories. A few weeks later, when Senator Davis quarreled with Senator Zachariah Chandler of Michigan, and it appeared that a duel was imminent, it was to Seward that the two senators turned as arbiter.[19]

Seward received many invitations to give political speeches in the summer and fall of 1858, but he declined almost all of them, except for an invitation to speak at Rochester in October. The Republican candidate for governor was Seward's friend Edwin Morgan, and many saw the election as a referendum on Seward, especially his policies on slavery. A young man in the audience later recalled that when Seward stepped onto the stage, he was greeted with intense applause, which he received in "the least elegant of postures, spreading wide his parenthetical legs and thrusting his hands deep into the pockets of his pantaloons." After the applause died down, he asked: "Are you in earnest?" There was silence, so he asked again: "Are you in earnest?" This time he was answered with intense applause. "So am I," Seward responded. Thus did Seward, even before his speech, connect with his audience.[20]

Seward argued in his Rochester speech that the United States now had "two radically different political systems; the one resting on the basis of servile or slave labor, the other on the basis of voluntary labor of freemen." Although they had co-existed for many years, "these antagonistic systems are continually coming into closer contact, and collision results. Shall I tell you what this collision means? They who think it is accidental, unnecessary, the work of interested, or fanatical agitators, and therefore ephemeral, mistake the case altogether. It is an irrepressible conflict between opposing and enduring forces, and it means that the United States must and will, sooner or later, become entirely either a slave-holding nation, or entirely a free-labor nation." Seward did not explain how slavery would end, other than to say he expected it would be "through the action of the several states cooperating with the federal government, and all acting in strict conformity with their respective constitutions."[21]

The young observer, who later became a professor of rhetoric, recalled that Seward's manner of delivery at Rochester "was effective in defiance of every rhetorical rule." He "slowly paced to and fro along the ample rostrum, his hands in his pockets or locked behind him, and ejaculated his speech piecemeal as he succeeded in recalling it"; it seemed "as if a self-absorbed man, in a tense state of moral and mental excitement, had got a couple thousand of us closeted alone with him, and was thinking aloud to us." The effect was "electric."[22]

Seward's Rochester speech, and especially the phrase "irrepressible conflict," attracted instant attention. The *New York Tribune* called the speech "clear, calm, sagacious, profound and impregnable." The *New York Times* also praised it, but wished that Seward had described by what means he thought the United States would "become a land of universal freedom." The *Times* could not "help thinking that he would allay a good deal of very natural alarm in one quarter, and solve a good many disturbances and perplexing doubts in others, by being somewhat more explicit upon a point of such vital interest and importance." There were some, however, even in Republican ranks, who disapproved. Gideon Welles, the Connecticut editor, argued in the *New York Evening Post* that the speech showed Seward was "an imperialist rather than a republican statesman. He would not confine his views to a confederated republic of separate and distinct states, possessing only limited and specified powers, but would give us instead, a splendid empire, and a government with omnipotent authority." According to the *New York Herald*, Seward was now "a more repulsive abolitionist" than even ministers like Theodore Parker. Seward himself told Parker that he did not view the speech as especially new or novel and that he was amused by the outcry against it.[23]

William Herndon, Lincoln's law partner, wrote Seward to note the similarities in recent speeches of Seward and Lincoln, especially the speech in which Lincoln argued that "a house divided against itself cannot stand." Lincoln's speech, however, was little noticed outside of

Illinois, where he failed to win his 1858 campaign for the Senate seat held by Douglas. Seward responded to Herndon from Washington: "No one can regret more than I do the failure of Mr. Lincoln's election. He is just the man we need here, and Illinois just the state for which such a man is wanted." During the Illinois senate campaign, there had been some suspicion that Seward supported Douglas because of their cooperation on Kansas. Herndon, although he was one of those who had complained about eastern interference, now assured Seward that Illinois would support him if he was the presidential nominee. "We will fight to the bitter end our common enemy."[24] Herndon's letters to Seward show the relative positions of Seward and Lincoln at the time—one the front-runner and the other a very dark horse—as does a late 1858 letter to Seward from one of his New York supporters: "I assume that you will be nominated by the Republican Party for President in 1860. I think this will be, if it is not voiced, generally conceded. The question of Vice President is one of almost equal importance. He should come from a state which would be likely to go against us if he were not nominated but which would be quite sure to go for us if he were. Is Illinois that state, and Lincoln that man?"[25]

———

The Seward house in Washington was crowded in late 1858 and early 1859: Frances was there, although often confined to her room by unexplained illness, as were William and Fanny, and Frederick and his wife Anna, who generally served as hostess. This was the winter when Fanny turned fourteen and started her detailed diary. In a long description of Christmas, she noted that she could not understand "the southern custom of firing guns, pistols, crackers etc. on the day of all others sacred to peace and good will toward men." The Sewards spent much time that winter with two diplomatic families: Lord and Lady Napier of Britain and their four children, and the Count and Countess Sartiges of France and their two children. The Napiers were preparing to return to Britain, and Seward was one of the organizers of the elaborate ball and banquet held in their honor at Willard's Hotel. A few weeks later, Lady Napier remarked to Fanny that she "loved my father and mother better than any one else in America." On another occasion, after the Sewards dined *en famille* with the Sartiges in Georgetown Heights, Fanny noted the wonderful food and the family's "perfect simplicity." [26]

Cuba was one of the main issues in Congress in early 1859. Buchanan proposed that the United States should acquire Cuba from Spain, and southern senators, eager to acquire more slave territory, urged an appropriation of $30 million. Seward, now a member of the Senate Foreign Relations Committee, opposed the proposal. Like most Americans of this era, he firmly believed that Cuba would ultimately be part of the United States. But he argued against the bill on financial grounds (the United States did not have sufficient funds to complete the purchase) and on constitutional grounds (the bill would give the president too much discretion over how much to pay for Cuba and how to organize it once purchased). Homestead legislation was another major issue; the House passed legislation to make it easier for settlers to acquire western land, but the bill stalled in the Senate. Near the end of the session, Seward charged that the Senate was wasting its time on the president's "impracticable" scheme of acquiring Cuba "to fortify and extend slavery in the United States" rather than "opening the public lands to settlement by the inhabitants and citizens of the United States." This prompted an instant and angry reaction from Senator Robert Toombs of Georgia, who called Seward a coward for avoiding the "great question" of Cuba and a demagogue for prattling about "land for the landless." Neither bill passed the Senate, but the debate showed that both southern fears of northern oppression, and northern fears of southern expansionism, were growing. [27]

In early April 1859, Seward wrote to his friend George Patterson that "all our discreet friends unite in sending me out of the country to spend the recess of Congress." These friends hoped to keep Seward from saying or doing anything that would prejudice his chances in 1860. Patterson agreed: "you had better be absent a few months—no need to go before June unless you prefer it." He added that "everything looks well now for 1860, and as no mistake will be made next winter, I feel as if the thing was pretty much finished." At almost this same moment, Seward endorsed a controversial recent book, Hinton Helper's *Impending Crisis of the South*. Helper, a southerner, argued that the North was prospering and the South languishing because of their different labor systems. Most of Helper's book was a dull statistical argument, but there were a few passages in which he seemed to suggest the use of violence to overthrow the southern political order. Seward, who probably only skimmed the work, called it one "of great merit, rich yet accurate in statistical information, and logical in analysis."[28]

Seward spent much of April planning his trip to Europe, gathering letters of introduction and dealing with personal and political issues. He made one important side trip during this period, to Harrisburg, to visit the influential Senator Simon Cameron of Pennsylvania. Seward reported to Weed that Cameron "took me to his home, told me all was right. He was for me, and Pennsylvania would be. It might want to cast a first ballot for him—or might not—but he was not in. He brought the whole legislature of both parties to see me—feasted them gloriously and they were in the main so free, so generous as to embarrass me." The *New York Herald* confirmed that Cameron had pledged Pennsylvania for Seward, but added that many of Cameron's supporters hated Seward, and questioned how they would vote when the time came to nominate the Republican presidential candidate.[29]

In May 1859, as Seward departed for Europe, he was fêted and hailed as if he were already the next president. Two different chartered boats, one from New York City and one from Brooklyn, both filled with friends and supporters, accompanied Seward out to the *Ariel*, his oceangoing steamship. According to the newspapers, the senator was in "excellent spirits" and "amused his friends greatly by his playful humor and anecdotes." Pressed for a speech, Seward stepped up on a bench and said that "no one but a beneficent Providence" knew whether he would return. "If it be my lot not to return among you, I trust I shall be remembered as one who . . . died far away from his native land without a regretful remembrance—without an enemy to be recalled, and with the conviction that he had tried to deserve the good opinion which his friends had cherished concerning him." When the Brooklyn boat approached, he went aboard, and at the insistence of that group, gave them a speech as well. After he finally boarded the *Ariel*, the three vessels, joined by a fourth, steamed out into the ocean with "guns firing, bells ringing, handkerchiefs waving, flags flying, and people cheering." Seward mounted to the bridge, where he "continued to wave his hat and handkerchief until he was lost to view." [30]

Less than two weeks later, he was in London, staying at Fenton's Hotel and dining daily with the elite of British society. Among others, Seward met Lord Palmerston (who formed his first government while Seward was in London), Lord John Russell (foreign secretary in the new government), William Gladstone (the new chancellor of the exchequer), and John Bright (the leading Radical member of Parliament). The secretary at the American Embassy, Benjamin Moran, perhaps annoyed that a mere visitor should receive such attention, complained in his diary that Queen Victoria received Seward kindly both at a concert and then at her annual spring ball. "No American in my time," Moran wrote, "has been received so well by all classes in England as Governor Seward." There are some indications that some Britons disliked Seward: Lord Palmerston wrote in 1861 that he was "vapouring, blustering, ignorant," and Thurlow Weed, when he visited London later that year, heard stories about how Seward had insulted the British by calling their books "absurdly expensive" and by "laughing at the enormous sums paid for paintings." These comments, however, were written after Seward became secretary of state, and after tensions flared between Britain and America. It seems unlikely that he would have been entertained so widely and handsomely in 1859 if he had been as unpleasant as he was described in 1861.[31]

Seward spent two months in Britain, seeing not only London but also the northern manufacturing regions and Scotland. From Britain, his travels took him to Paris, Lyons, Marseilles, Rome, Naples, Sicily, Malta, Alexandria, Cairo, Jaffa, Jerusalem, Trieste, Vienna, Venice, Milan, Turin, the Hague, Amsterdam, Brussels, and back to Paris. He was impressed with the public spaces of Paris, and was granted interviews with Napoleon III and his foreign minister, but his letters home described the regime as a dictatorship. (Perhaps because Seward feared the consequences of such comments, this time Weed did not print his travel letters in the *Albany Evening Journal*.) Pope Pius the IX, with whom Seward had an extended interview, thanked him for his aid to American

Catholics and (as Seward reported in a letter home) "playfully" referred to the possibility of his "higher advancement." While in northern Italy, he met with both Victor Emmanuel (future king of Italy) and Cavour (future prime minister), and walked over the battlefield at Solferino, only six weeks after the combat there between the French, Italians, and Austrians.[32]

It was in November, while Seward was in Paris, that news arrived that the crazed abolitionist John Brown had attacked Harpers Ferry, Virginia, hoping and failing to incite the local slaves to slaughter their masters. The scholar John Bigelow, who was with Seward in Paris at the time, wrote a friend that Seward was "not disturbed in the least about the Harper's Ferry incident." He was also "not disturbed" by the commentary in the *New York Herald*, which termed Seward "the arch agitator who is responsible for this insurrection." Seward might have been more troubled by a letter from Hugh Forbes, an English accomplice of Brown, that appeared in some American papers not long after the Brown attack. Forbes described his efforts to dissuade Brown from his violent plans and a meeting with Seward in Washington in May 1858, at which "I went fully into the whole matter in all its bearings." Exactly what Forbes said to Seward is unclear, but the Forbes letter forced the *New York Times* and others to defend Seward, arguing that there was no proof that Seward knew what Brown intended.[33]

Seward boarded the *Arago* in Le Havre in mid-December. The voyage was rough, so rough that on Christmas Day "we could not keep our feet to sing and recite the Christmas service." When he arrived home in Auburn in bitter cold weather in late December, he was greeted at the train station by 10,000 people. The crowd demanded a speech and Seward obliged, telling them that although he had traveled for eight months and through four continents, "it is not until now that I have found the place which, above all others, I admire the most, love the best." He loved Auburn, he said, more than the town in which he was born, or the one in which he was educated, or the state capital, or even the national capital. He loved Auburn because here he was "simply a citizen—a man—your equal and your like." The crowd escorted him from the station to his house, through streets decorated with banners and arches. When he reached the path to his front door, Seward found that all the clergymen of the town had gathered there to greet him, including his old friend Reverend John Austin. Seward shook each by the hand, overcome with emotion—according to Austin, he "could not speak a syllable"—but when he reached the door, he turned and exclaimed: "God bless you all, my friends!"[34]

CHAPTER 8

"Lincoln Nominated Third Ballot":

1860

T he Washington to which Seward returned in January 1860 was on the surface the same city he had left in March 1859: James Buchanan was still president, the Capitol building was still under construction, and the streets were still a muddy mess. But the mood of Washington was more violent. Virginia had recently executed John Brown, but his influence lived on in the form of northern praise and southern revulsion. Many southerners saw a connection between the antislavery *rhetoric* of Seward and the antislavery *violence* of Brown. In December, Senator James Chesnut of South Carolina denounced Seward's Senate speech about the "invasion" of the South, saying it had stimulated "much of the violence we have seen in this country." In the House, Representative Martin Crawford of Georgia attacked Seward for endorsing Helper's book, claiming it urged "the slaves of the South to sacrifice the lives of their owners." Representative Otho Singleton of Mississippi declared that, if the North elected Seward or another Republican as president, the South would unite to resist, and Reuben Davis of Mississippi added that, in this scenario, "we of the South will tear this Constitution to pieces, and look to our guns for justice and right against aggression and wrong."[1]

Seward realized that, to secure the Republican presidential nomination, he had to show that he was not a fire-breathing radical, and he informed the press he would make a major speech in late February. His young daughter Fanny was among those in the crowded galleries as Seward told his southern colleagues that the Republicans did not intend to interfere with slavery in their states: "You are sovereign on the subject of slavery within your own borders, as we are on the same subject within our borders." The Republican policy was simply to save "the territories of the United States, if possible, by constitutional and lawful means, from being homes for slavery and polygamy." Republicans did not support John Brown; on the contrary, Seward denounced Brown's invasion of Virginia as treason and pronounced his execution to be "necessary and just." In an attempt to shift the focus of the debate, Seward said that the Republican Party was not just concerned with slavery: it was in favor of "freedom of speech and of the press," would "favor the speedy improvement of the public domain by homestead laws," and would support "needful connections between the Atlantic and Pacific states."[2]

In closing, Seward argued that those who were predicting disunion did not understand or appreciate the strength of the Union. "He strangely, blindly misunderstands the anatomy of this great system who thinks that its only bonds, or even its strongest ligaments, are the written compact or even the multiplied and thoroughly ramified roads and thoroughfares of trade, commerce and social intercourse." These bonds were indeed strong, but the bonds which rendered the Union "inseparable and indivisible" were the "millions of fibers of millions of contented, happy human hearts, binding by their affections, their ambitions and their best hopes" all Americans to their government. Americans were "perpetually forgetting this subtle and complex, yet obvious and natural mechanism of our Constitution; and because we do forget it, we are continually wondering how it is that a Confederacy of thirty or more States, covering regions so vast, and regulating interests so various of so many millions of men, constituted and conditioned so diversely, works right on." But the "wonderful machine" of the Union kept on working, and Seward predicted that it would do so until men feared its failure no more than they feared that "the sun will cease to hold his eternal place in the heavens." The crowd violated the rules several times to interrupt with applause, and afterward, Fanny noted, her father was "surrounded by friends."[3]

As he hoped, his speech was printed and praised in all the major Republican newspapers. The *New York Times* declared that Seward's tone was "eminently dispassionate and moderate, and indicates a desire to allay agitation and remove unfounded prejudice." The *New York Evening Post* commented that the speech was "distinguished for its insight, its ability, its manliness [and] its comprehensive and statesmanlike views." The *New York Journal of Commerce*, a Democratic paper, "conceded as a settled fact" that Seward would be the Republican nominee. Seward did not have the newspaper pages all to himself, however. Abraham Lincoln had spoken at Cooper Union in New York City two days before him, and Lincoln's speech was also widely printed. Indeed, many readers saw the two speeches in the same issue or successive issues of their papers.[4]

Seward's speech set out the grand themes of his campaign for the nomination, but he also focused on small details. In early March, he wrote to Weed that their friend James Watson Webb, editor of the *Morning Courier & New-York Enquirer*, wanted to be one of the official delegates from New York. "You will do what is wise," Seward wrote, and Weed wisely decided against giving Webb any official status. Seward reminded Weed several times that Simon Cameron of Pennsylvania wanted to see him, but Weed avoided Cameron, probably because he did not want to get into a conversation about whether Cameron would have a place in a Seward cabinet. In late April, Seward asked Weed whether Henry Winter Davis, a Maryland Know Nothing, but one who leaned toward the Republicans, would make a good vice-presidential nominee. Given Seward's consistent opposition to the Know Nothings, his question about Davis shows just how serious he and Weed were about winning this election.[5]

Although there were no primaries in 1860, and thus no certainty about how delegates would vote once the Republican Convention met in May in Chicago, almost everyone expected that Seward would receive the nomination. *Harper's* magazine, in its portrait gallery of the leading candidates published on the eve of the convention, made Seward's portrait larger than any of the others, and gave him the central position, almost as if he already had the nomination. The *Washington Evening Star* reported that Seward would win because he was the "great representative man" of the Republican Party, and managed "to render himself popular as a gentleman" even to those with whom he disagreed. The *Providence Post* said simply that "the nomination belongs to him." Experts expected Seward would receive all 70 votes from the New York delegation and almost all the votes from the six New England states. He was also (according to a letter in the *New York Times*) "beyond all question, the first choice of the masses of western Republicans," and would likely receive the votes of the delegates from Michigan, Wisconsin, Minnesota, and California. These eleven state delegations together had 178 votes. If Seward could (as expected) pick up votes from Pennsylvania and elsewhere, he would obtain the 233 votes necessary to prevail at the convention.[6]

One complicating factor in this calculus was the presence of favorite sons. The Pennsylvania delegation intended to vote, at least on the first ballot, for Simon Cameron. New Jersey intended to give its initial vote to former Senator William Dayton, and Vermont's delegates to vote for current Senator Jacob Collamer. After one or two ballots, these and other states would probably abandon their favorite sons and vote for one of the leading candidates, but nobody knew which candidate would secure these later votes. Another complication was that the Republicans did not know whom the Democrats would nominate. The Democratic Convention, meeting in Charleston, South Carolina, in late April and early May, could not agree on a nomination: northern delegates favored Senator Stephen Douglas, and southern delegates, many of whom had seceded to form a separate convention, insisted upon a southern rights man. The Democrats planned to reconvene in Baltimore in June, and it was possible that the party would resolve the deadlock at that time, but also possible that it would split, with both northern and southern Democratic candidates nominated. Some observers thought that the Charleston impasse increased Seward's chances of securing the Republican nomination.[7]

One of Seward's key advantages at the convention would be Thurlow Weed, veteran of countless campaigns and conventions. Weed's approach in 1860 was quite unlike his approach in 1856; this year he was completely committed to Seward's nomination. Weed would bring with him to the convention not only hundreds of Seward supporters but also what one newspaper called "oceans of money." Money would be available for entertaining delegates in Chicago, and money would be available to help local candidates around the country, if they helped Seward secure the nomination.[8] But there was a cloud that went along with this silver lining, the cloud of corruption. Republicans generally saw themselves as the party of clean government, the answer to the infamous corruption of the Buchanan administration, but Weed was a glaring exception to this rule. The New York legislature had just passed bills to divide New York City into a "gridiron" of private rail lines; rail companies had generously bribed Republican legislators to secure passage of these bills; and Weed was viewed as the master hand behind both the bribery and the gridiron law. Weed's reputation naturally rubbed off on his best friend. James Dixon, a Republican senator from Connecticut, who was otherwise favorable to Seward, would not support him because "his administration would be the most corrupt the country has ever witnessed." Even Seward's friend Charles Francis Adams, son of the sixth president and now a member of Congress from Massachusetts, confided in his diary that "if I saw any better choice, the objections that I have to Mr. Seward on account of the lax influences around him in many matters would certainly avail."[9]

For many Republicans, Seward was entitled to the nomination by virtue of his clear, consistent, forceful argument against the extension of slavery. Almost every American knew that Seward believed that a "higher law" dedicated the territories to freedom. But others opposed him for precisely this reason; they believed he was a radical who could not win moderate or conservative votes. In Rhode Island in early April, a Republican candidate for governor closely identified with Seward was defeated by a moderate candidate backed by both Democrats and conservative Republicans. The *Providence Post* viewed the state election as a defeat for "higher lawism," and predicted that if Seward were nominated for president, he would carry neither Rhode Island nor Connecticut. Seward would also have difficulty in states such as Illinois and Indiana, whose southern regions were almost part of the South. Seward was aware of his reputation, and he resented those who (in his view) were prepared to discard the key principles of the party to find an acceptable, moderate nominee. In a letter congratulating his friend George Patterson on being elected local supervisor, he wrote that he had "half a mind to go back to Westfield, where it seems they don't think it an objection to a man that he is identified with their own party." And in a letter to Frances, he complained that he feared the party would seek "to disavow the cardinal article of uncompromising antagonism between freedom and slavery in the country."[10]

A few Republicans thought a Seward nomination would help the party gain strength among immigrants. One Wisconsin man, in a letter to the *New York Times,* argued that Seward would "receive the German and Irish vote throughout the entire West." A far larger group of Republicans feared that Seward would lose votes among nativists, especially in the critical states of Pennsylvania and New Jersey. Millard Fillmore, running as the Know Nothing candidate in 1856, had secured 18 percent of the vote in Pennsylvania and 24 percent in New Jersey; to prevail in those states in 1860, the Republicans would have to convince the former Know Nothings to vote Republican. A leading New Jersey Republican wrote to a friend that it was "conceded I think by all judicious and well advised men, that Mr. Seward's nomination will revive the divisions of 1856 in Pennsylvania and New Jersey, and will be fatal to us in those states." Thaddeus Stevens, Republican member of Congress from Pennsylvania, said bluntly that "Pennsylvania will never vote for a man who favored the destruction of the common school system in New York to gain the favor of Catholics and foreigners."[11]

Seward could have remained in Washington during the Republican Convention in Chicago—the Senate was still in session—but he found the political atmosphere too intense, and so he went instead to Auburn. At this stage of his life, Seward did not spend much time at his Auburn home, but he liked the town, and according to a visiting reporter was "beloved" by the people of Auburn "irrespective of partisan predelictions." The reasons for this affection included the way Seward treated his tenants—"as a landlord he is kind and lenient"—and his role in local affairs—"no philanthropic or benevolent movement is suggested without receiving his liberal and thoughtful assistance." Seward was thinking about the possibility that, if he was nominated, he would resign from the Senate and remain in Auburn through the campaign. Indeed, he reportedly drafted his farewell address to the Senate before leaving Washington. Adams noted in his diary that Seward had "left the city, expecting that his nomination will be followed by a resignation of his place in the Senate." [12]

Seward's neighbor John Austin recorded in his diary their frequent meetings during the critical week of the convention. Austin visited Seward on Monday evening and walked with him in the garden. "He appears entirely cool and calm, and not in the slightest degree excited." The next day, Seward "received a telegraphic dispatch from Chicago assuring him that everything looks promising for his nomination." On Wednesday, May 16, the first day of the convention, although Seward would "not express a positive opinion," Austin inferred that he considered "the probabilities to be strongly in his favor." Indeed, that same day, Webb telegraphed Seward from Chicago that there was "no cause for doubting" that he would be nominated. On the second day of the convention, Thursday, Seward received a similar telegram from Chicago, this time from his friend Elbridge Spaulding, Republican member of Congress from Buffalo: "Your friends are firm and confident that you will be nominated after a few ballots." Neutral observers reached similar conclusions. Murat Halstead, the convention reporter for the *Cincinnati Daily Commercial*, wrote that "every one of the forty thousand men in attendance upon the Chicago Convention will testify that at midnight of Thursday-Friday night, the universal impression was that Seward's success was certain." [13]

The Republican Convention was scheduled to select its candidates on Friday, May 18. On that morning, a pleasant spring day in Auburn, Seward received yet another telegram from Chicago, this one signed by his friends William Evarts, Preston King, and Richard Blatchford: "All right. Everything indicates your nomination today sure." Reverend Austin, knowing that the balloting was underway in Chicago, watched the telegraph office in downtown Auburn. "About 3 o'clock the account of the first ballot was received. I took it and went immediately to Gov. Seward's. [I] found him in his arbor in the garden. He received the statement without the movement of a muscle of his countenance."

The telegram reported that, on the first ballot, Seward had received 172 votes, about 60 short of the number he needed. Lincoln had received 102 votes, and the remaining votes were scattered among various candidates, including Cameron. Seward told Austin that this was "as favorable as could be expected for the first ballot."[14]

"We had been conversing some ten or fifteen minutes on the subject," Austin continued, "when Dr. Theodore Dimon came rushing into the garden with a statement of the second and third ballots. As he drew near us, he threw up his arms and exclaimed aloud: *'Oh God, it is all gone, gone, gone! Abraham Lincoln has received the nomination!'* " Austin looked from Dimon to Seward. "A deadly paleness overspread his countenance for an instant, succeeded instantly by a flush, and then all was calm as a summer morning." Seward "immediately commenced conversing in regard to the particulars of the ballot, and was the most composed of the three or four who were present." The telegram, which still survives among Seward's papers, was a short one, from Edwin Morgan, his friend and the chairman of the Chicago convention. It read simply: "Lincoln nominated third ballot." Dimon later recalled that, after reading the telegram, without any change in expression, Seward looked up at his friends and said: "Well, Mr. Lincoln will be elected and has some of the qualities to make a good president." There followed a little more "quiet conversation," and then Seward went inside to break the news to his wife and children. Fanny wrote in her diary that "father told Mother and I in three words, 'Abraham Lincoln nominated.' His friends feel much distress—he alone has a smile—he takes it with philosophical and unselfish coolness."[15]

———

Why did Seward lose the nomination? One reason is that the convention was held in Chicago, and Lincoln's men arranged details in ways that hurt Seward. The local committee printed extra tickets for the day of nomination, and distributed these to some of the midwesterners arriving on special trains, so that the convention hall was packed with Lincoln men, and many Seward men were left outside. At critical moments the roar for Lincoln was deafening. "Imagine all the hogs ever slaughtered in Cincinnati giving their death squeals together," Halstead reported, with "a score of big steam whistles going . . . and you conceive something of the same nature." Even more important, Lincoln's friend Norman Judd arranged the convention floor so that the New York delegation was separated, by several other states, from the New Jersey and Pennsylvania delegations. As Judd later recalled, "when the active excitement and canvassing in the convention came on, the Seward men couldn't get over among the doubtful delegations at all to log-roll with them, being absolutely hemmed in by their own followers."[16]

Another key reason why Seward lost was that Lincoln's manager Judge David Davis assured Cameron's manager Joseph Casey that, if Pennsylvania would give its votes on the second and later ballots to Lincoln, Cameron would have a key place in the Lincoln cabinet. On nomination day, the Pennsylvania delegation voted as expected for Cameron on the first ballot, but then surprised many by voting for Lincoln on the second and third ballots. Pennsylvania's sudden shift provided Lincoln with fifty-two delegates, more than one fifth of the total he needed. Davis later claimed that he had honored Lincoln's instructions—"make no contracts that will bind me"—but there is strong evidence that Davis made an agreement with the Cameron men. Late on the night before nomination day, when Joseph Medill of the *Chicago Tribune* asked Davis about Pennsylvania, the judge exclaimed, "Damned if we haven't got them." "How?" Medill asked. "By paying them their price," Davis replied. A few days later, Casey wrote Cameron that the Pennsylvania shift "was only done after everything was arranged carefully and unconditionally in reference to yourself." Casey contrasted the willingness of the Lincoln men to negotiate with the obstinacy of the Seward men, who "refused to talk of anything but his unconditional nomination." Ironically, it was Lincoln's men, representing "honest Abe," not Seward's men, with their reputation for corruption, who made the critical, questionable deal at Chicago.[17]

Seward had many opponents at Chicago, of whom the most visible was Horace Greeley. Greeley was at the convention in several capacities: as a reporter for his paper the *New York Tribune*; as a member of the Oregon delegation; and as a leader of those opposing Seward and supporting Judge Edward Bates of Missouri. Greeley's role was no secret;

even young Fanny, writing in her diary in Auburn, noted that Greeley, "having got himself appointed as delegate from Oregon, is acting against Father and for Bates." Greeley's argument was that Seward "cannot carry New Jersey, Pennsylvania, Indiana, or Iowa." More persuasive than Greeley, who was easy to dismiss as an eccentric, were the Republican leaders of these states. Henry Lane, the Republican nominee for Indiana governor, told all who would listen that Seward could not win in Indiana, and that a Seward nomination "would be the death" of Lane's own chances. Andrew Curtin, nominee for governor in Pennsylvania, made a similar argument about his state. Delegates from other states might not agree with the nativist views behind these arguments, but if they wanted to win the general election—and they desperately did—they had to listen. As Seward's friend Spaulding wrote him from Chicago, the key reason Seward lost was because of "the persistent cry that you could not carry New Jersey, Pennsylvania, Indiana and Illinois."[18]

Another way of explaining why Seward lost was that his views were better known in 1860 than those of Lincoln. For example, we know today that Lincoln opposed nativism. In 1855, in a personal letter to an old friend, Lincoln had written: "I am not a Know Nothing. That is certain. How could I be? How can anyone who abhors the oppression of negroes, be in favor of degrading classes of white people?" But this statement was not public in 1860. What *was* public was that Seward had spoken out against nativism and worked to help immigrants and Catholics on countless occasions. An opponent of Seward needed only to consult his published works, in which he declared that he would rather cut off his hand than act against fellow citizens "on the ground of the difference of their nativity or of their religion." Thousands of Republicans would not vote for a man with such views, and their leaders therefore favored Lincoln over Seward.[19]

As Herndon had noted in his letter to Seward in late 1858, Lincoln and Seward had very similar views on slavery. Both men viewed it as wrong; both were committed to preventing the spread of slavery into the national territories; and both were committed to allowing the southern states to maintain their slave systems, hoping southerners would gradually end slavery on their own terms. Lincoln's views on slavery were not secret, for his Cooper Union speech was only one of many on the subject. But Seward had a much longer and more quotable antislavery record than Lincoln. Republicans worried that Democrats would quote against them Seward's letters refusing to deliver up the Virginia fugitives, and his "higher law" speech, and his "irrepressible conflict" speech, and his Cleveland speech, in which he promised that slavery would be abolished. Republicans remembered the recent Rhode Island election, in which a candidate identified with Seward was defeated because of the defections of conservatives. Republicans read the Democratic papers, such as the *Albany Atlas & Argus*, which prayed for Seward's nomination because it "would unite and consolidate the whole . . . conservative vote of the Union" against Seward. The Chicago delegates opted for the man they perceived as moderate on the slavery issue, Lincoln, over the man they perceived as radical, Seward.[20]

A brief look ahead at the November election returns offers another way of analyzing the Chicago nomination. Lincoln prevailed in all the northern states but one, New Jersey, and even there he managed to secure four out of seven electoral votes. In several states, however, the margin of victory was slight. In both Indiana and Illinois, for example, Lincoln only received a few thousand votes more than his closest competitor, Stephen Douglas. In these states and others, Lincoln received many votes from moderates and nativists who would not have voted for Seward because of his reputation as a radical and an antinativist. If Seward as the candidate had won all the other states Lincoln won, but lost in a few key states such as New Jersey and Pennsylvania, he would not have secured the necessary majority in the electoral college. The presidential election would then have been decided in the House of Representatives, with each state's House delegation casting one vote. Lincoln carried eighteen states in the general election, but neither Lincoln nor Seward would have carried eighteen states in the House, for several of the states which voted for Lincoln were represented in the House by delegations with a majority of Democrats. In short, even if he had been nominated, Seward would probably not have been elected president.[21]

Seward himself once offered a similar explanation of why he lost in Chicago. Dr. Tullio Verdi, the Washington physician who frequently attended the Seward family, recalled that he asked Seward during the war how he had failed to secure the nomination that had seemed so certain. Seward replied that "the leader of a political party in a country like ours is so exposed that his enemies become as numerous and formidable as his friends, and in an election you must put forward the man who will carry the highest number of votes. Pennsylvania would not have voted for me, and without her vote we could not carry the election; hence I was not an available man. Mr. Lincoln possessed all the necessary qualifications to represent our party, and being comparatively unknown, had not to contend with the animosities generally marshaled against a leader. We made him the candidate; he was elected, and we have never had reason to regret it."[22]

——

Seward's remarks to Verdi were colored by later events, but even his immediate reactions in 1860 show that he accepted the convention's decision. Within hours of the nomination he wrote to his friend Weed: "You have my unbounded gratitude for this last, as for the whole life of efforts in my behalf. I wish that I was sure that your sense of disappointment is as light as my own." It should be, Seward said, because "I know not what has been left undone that could have been done or done that ought to be regretted." The editor of the *Auburn Daily Advertiser* could not find anyone to write the customary endorsement for Lincoln and Hannibal Hamlin of Maine, the vice-presidential nominee, until Seward agreed to perform the task. "No truer or firmer defenders of the Republican faith could have been found in the Union," he wrote, "than the distinguished and esteemed citizens on whom the honors of the nomination has fallen." A few days later, in a letter to the state's party committee, Seward declared that "I find in the resolutions of the convention a platform as satisfactory to me as if it had been framed with my own hands; and in the candidates adopted by it, eminent and able Republicans with whom I have cordially cooperated in maintaining the principles embodied in that excellent creed." He added that he hoped "no sense of disappointment" would cause his friends "to hinder or delay, or in any way embarrass" the Republican cause. The *New York Times* carried this letter on its front page.[23]

Seward's public endorsement of Lincoln did not prevent some of his supporters—generally not his close friends or major financiers—from writing to tell him that they were disappointed and embittered. A Michigan man wrote that "one thing and only one thing consoles me, our chance of being defeated this time and your sure chance of a nomination in '64." An Ohioan wrote to Frances Seward that he could not believe the delegates viewed Lincoln as "the suitable man for the presidency. The rail candidate forsooth! I confess to a disposition to rail at him, and much more at the convention for its self-stultification." Seward commented that, when he ventured out into Auburn, "I had the rare experience of a man walking about town, after he is dead, and hearing what people would say of him. I confess I was unprepared for so much real grief, as I heard expressed at every corner."[24]

A few days after the convention, Henry Raymond, the editor of the *New York Times*, arrived in Auburn to visit his friend. As Raymond reported the conversation in the *Times*, Seward said he would serve out the remainder of his term in the Senate, which would end in early 1861, but "he will not, in any event or under any circumstances, be a candidate for re-election." Moreover, although Seward favored Lincoln, "it is not likely that [Seward] will feel called upon, or that his friends will expect him, to take any active personal part in the pending canvass." Speculation about the place Seward would hold in a Lincoln cabinet was "idle and useless," for from this time forward "the only sphere of his labors will be his home and the society which surrounds it." Seward was done with politics. Frances was delighted to hear that her husband would soon spend full time at their home in Auburn. In a letter to him a few days later, she wrote that his determination to retire was "right and wise," since "thirty-five years of the best part of a man's life is all that his country can reasonably expect of him."[25]

Seward learned from Raymond and others about how Greeley had worked at Chicago against his nomination. In an effort to explain Greeley's animosity, Seward imprudently summarized for Raymond the letter he had received from Greeley in late 1854, the one which purported to dissolve "the political firm of Seward, Weed & Greeley." Seward may have asked Raymond not to mention the letter, but Raymond disregarded the request, for the *Times* reported that Greeley had "menaced

[Seward] with hostility wherever it could be made most effective, for the avowed reason that Gov. Seward had never aided or advised his elevation to office." Greeley immediately and angrily demanded that Seward provide him the original letter so that he could "print it verbatim in the *Tribune*, and let every reader judge how far it sustains the charges." After some back-and-forth, Seward provided the letter and it appeared in various papers. Weed, writing in the *Albany Evening Journal*, probably reflected Seward's own regrets about the letter and its publication: "It destroys ideals of disinterestedness and generosity which relieved political life from so much that is selfish, sordid and rapacious."[26]

On his way back to Washington at the end of May, Seward stopped in Albany, where Weed reported on a conversation he had had a few days earlier with Lincoln at his home in Springfield, Illinois. Weed later recalled that he and Lincoln had analyzed the election state by state, identifying which states "were safe without effort" and those that "required attention." Lincoln displayed "so much good sense, such intuitive knowledge of human nature, and such familiarity with the virtues and infirmities of politicians, that I became impressed very favorably." By the time Weed departed from Springfield, he was prepared to "go to work with a will." Weed probably advised Seward at their Albany meeting that he too would have to "work with a will" in order to elect Lincoln. Knowing that this would not be welcome news to his wife, Seward wrote to her only that Weed was "subdued, gentle, sad."[27]

Seward told Frances that when he arrived in the Senate chamber in Washington, a few Republicans "greeted me kindly," but others "showed a consciousness of embarrassment, which made the courtesy a conventional one." Several friends among the Democrats, however, including Jefferson Davis, "came to me with frank, open, sympathizing words." Seward dined that evening with Charles Francis Adams and his wife, whom he found "generous, kind, and faithful as ever." At this dinner and over the next days, Adams pressed on Seward the points he had made in a letter immediately after the nomination. "Your services are more necessary to the cause than they ever were," Adams wrote, and "your own reputation will gain more of permanency from the becoming manner with which you meet this disappointment than it would from all the brilliancy of the highest success."[28]

Charles Francis Adams knew about disappointment. Both his grand-father, John Adams, and his father, John Quincy Adams, had been one-term presidents, defeated in bitter reelection contests. John Adams had retired to his farm; but John Quincy Adams, whose portrait Seward still kept over his desk in Washington, had overcome his anger and served for seventeen useful years in the House of Representatives. Seward's duty, Charles Francis Adams insisted, was to return to the Senate and to cam-paign for Lincoln. These steps were important not just to secure Lincoln's election but also to secure Seward the proper place in a Lincoln adminis-tration. As Adams put it in his diary, "the cabinet of Mr. Lincoln cannot be left to itself, or to feeble men, without shipwreck."[29]

Seward was reluctant to accept the role that Adams and others were pressing upon him. He had meant what he had told Raymond, that he did not plan to "take any active personal part in the pending can-vass." Seward amplified this in a letter to his friend Benjamin Silliman, in which he (somewhat irreverently) compared his position to that of Moses, who died on the banks of the Jordan in sight of the Promised Land. "It is best that I be content to rest and wait, even if I am not ap-pointed to die on the bank. Who would be content to see me lead? Who would be satisfied with my lead? How could it be that I should not be-come the head of a faction or reduce the Administration to that condi-tion if I should remain in office?"[30]

In early June, Seward learned that his friend John Schoolcraft was near death at St. Catharine's, Ontario. He left Washington immediately, hoping to see Schoolcraft alive, but by the time he reached Albany, word had arrived there of his friend's death. Seward was devasted: he had known Schoolcraft for more than twenty years, had shared his Washington home with him in the early 1850s, and then watched with pleasure as Schoolcraft married his beloved niece, Carolyn. Seward stayed in Albany for the funeral service, then returned to Washington, writing somberly to Frances that this was the third funeral he had at-tended in four months, two of them for family members. He would resume "the Senate treadmill" the next day, taking some comfort in the thought that "responsibility has passed away from me."[31]

After ten days in Washington, Seward departed again, this time for Auburn, where his son William was about to marry Janet (Jenny)

Watson. Seward wrote Weed that he regretted he had been too busy to counsel his son "as a child has a right to expect, in so important a transaction." As for himself, "if I can rightly, and to the satisfaction of my friends, remain at rest, I want to do so. I am content to quit with the political world, when it proposes to quit with me. But I am not insensible to the claims of a million of friends, nor indifferent to the opinion of mankind." So Seward was prepared to take part in the campaign, although he hoped first to have a talk with Weed. Two days later, even before he spoke with Weed, Seward accepted an invitation to speak in Michigan. He explained to Weed that "some part, perhaps a considerable one, of the responsibility of electing [Lincoln] rests upon us." Moreover, like his friend Adams, Seward did not want to see a Lincoln administration under the influence of anti-Seward forces. So he told Weed he would "go to Chicago or any of the 'pivotal' states which may demand it," although he would wait a few weeks, because he did not want people to "suspect me of wanting something instead of willingness to do something."[32]

Seward remained in Auburn in July, leaving in early August to spend a few days with his friend William Evarts at his summer home in Windsor, Vermont. Several other political leaders were present, including Weed and Webb, and these men no doubt discussed the campaign in detail.[33] Perhaps because his friends were worried, Seward did not return home directly from Windsor but instead headed east, passing through New Hampshire to Maine. Although he arrived in Bangor without warning, in the midst of a heavy shower, he was welcomed by several thousand people. Seward explained to the crowd that he had yielded to the invitation of his friend Israel Washburn, Jr., Republican candidate for Maine governor, "to see something of the great eastern state." The interests of Maine were "all on the side of freedom and free labor," and its residents should therefore vote "for the able and upright statesman of the West, Abraham Lincoln of Illinois, and for your own talented and able citizen," the vice-presidential nominee Hannibal Hamlin. As Seward hoped, his remarks were picked up not only in local papers but by many national papers.[34]

After a brief visit with Washburn, Seward left on the morning train for Boston. As one paper reported, he was "called out by respectable

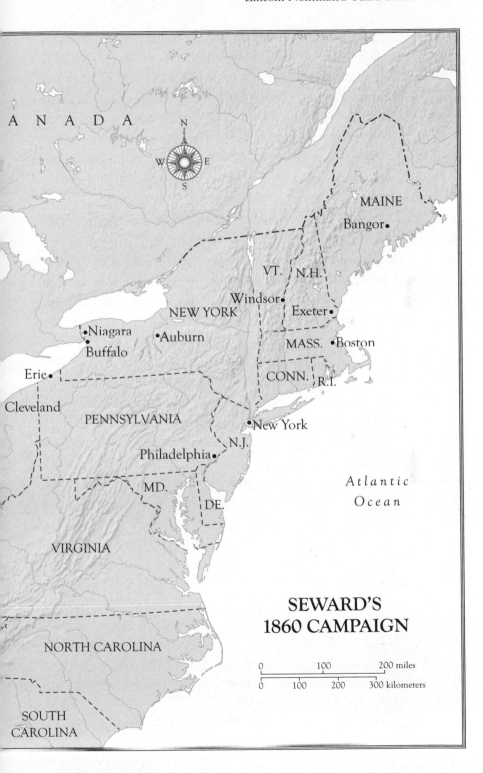

CANADA

N.W.E.S.

MAINE

Bangor•

VT. N.H.

Windsor•

Exeter•

NEW YORK

•Niagara

•Auburn

•Buffalo

MASS. •Boston

Erie•

CONN. R.I.

Cleveland

PENNSYLVANIA

•New York

N.J.

Philadelphia•

MD.

DE.

Atlantic
Ocean

VIRGINIA

SEWARD'S
1860 CAMPAIGN

NORTH CAROLINA

0		100		200 miles
0	100	200		300 kilometers

SOUTH
CAROLINA

congregations of people at the chief stations on the railroad, including Waterville, Portland, Dover, Exeter, Haverhill and Lawrence. At each of these places he made a brief speech." Seward was making what we would call a "whistle-stop tour," taking advantage of the railroad both to cover ground and to see people face-to-face. He arrived in Boston at about ten in the evening, was greeted by thousands and escorted to his hotel, the Revere House. In a brief but eloquent speech, he "confesse[ed] that if I have ever studied the interests of my country, and of humanity, I have studied in the school of Massachusetts." He recalled his early pilgrimage to visit John Quincy Adams, and linked the late Adams with Lincoln, saying both men were soldiers for freedom.[35]

Among those who met Seward at the station were Charles Francis Adams and his son Charles Francis Adams, Jr. Seward more or less invited himself to spend the next day with them, so the elder Adams picked Seward up early at his hotel and drove him by carriage to the family home in Quincy. Seward's purpose soon became clear: he wanted Adams to join his planned western political tour. It was, the senior Adams noted in his diary, "a duty for which I have not the smallest fancy" because "of all things I am the least fitted for electioneering." But Seward now turned upon Adams the same arguments that Adams had used on him a few weeks earlier: Adams had a *duty* to do his part to ensure that Lincoln was elected. Moreover, Seward also enlisted the younger Adams, at the time a bored lawyer in Boston and eager for the adventure. The junior Adams later recalled that when they returned Seward to the train station that afternoon, a "more unpromising looking subject for a great man than Seward didn't stand on the depot platform at that time." Seward was "small, rusty in aspect, dressed in a coat and trousers apparently made twenty years ago, and by a bad tailor at that, lolling against the partition as he talked with my father or those about him, with a face and head in no way striking." No one present, Adams suggested, "would have put his hand on that man—small and insignificant—as the first statesman in the country." Ten days after Seward's visit, the elder Adams, pressed by his son, wrote Seward to tell him they would both join the campaign.[36]

Seward left Auburn on September 1 for the most important campaign tour of his life. Republicans knew that they would not be able even to distribute their ballots in the Deep South, and that Lincoln would receive at most a handful of votes in the border states. In order to win a majority in the electoral college, therefore, and to prevent the election from going to the House of Representatives, Lincoln would have to carry almost every state in the North. As Seward left home, there were worrisome indications that the northern Democratic nominee, Stephen Douglas, would carry several northern states; the *New York Times* reported with dismay the "appalling strength of Douglas" in Illinois, Indiana, and Michigan. So Seward's mission was simple: to counter Douglas, and to build Republican enthusiasm, throughout the North.[37]

Seward was accompanied initially by his daughter Fanny, her friend Ellen Perry, and George Baker. At Syracuse, they were joined by James Nye and his daughter Mary. Nye was a minor but colorful New York politician, recalled by Charles Francis Adams, Jr., as "excellent company, full of stories," and Mary was "a pretty, bright girl of only seventeen, with whom I became very intimate during the trip." At almost every stop in upstate New York there was a crowd asking to hear from the governor. Seward excelled at long and serious speeches but could also give short and humorous ones. At Lockport, New York, he asked the crowd why they had gathered. "Is it an auction? I have no party to sell. What do I hear! The Whig party! Going, going, gone. The American party! Going, going, gone." Then, as the train started to move, he shouted: "This train, too. Going, going, gone!"[38]

Seward was greeted at Niagara, as he was at almost every stop of this tour, by hundreds of "Wide Awakes." The Wide Awakes were a quasi-military organization of young Republican men; they marched in military style, wearing dark caps and capes and bearing flaming torches. Although the Wide Awakes claimed that they were a peaceful political organization, they were viewed with understandable concern by southerners and southern sympathizers. One Indiana paper argued that the organization was "designed to support by force, if necessary to their plans, the measures of an Abolition Administration." The *Richmond Enquirer* claimed that the Wide Awakes "carry rails to break open our doors, torches to fire our dwellings, and beneath their long black capes the knife to cut our throats."[39]

From Niagara, Seward and his party traveled through Canada to Detroit, where he was greeted by cannons, rockets, and thousands of people. The next day, in spite of rain, tens of thousands assembled to hear him speak. As in his February speech, Seward adopted a moderate tone because "we love, and we ought to love, the fellowship of our slaveholding brethren." But the time had come, he said, for a Republican government to prevent the extension of slavery beyond its present borders, and Lincoln was the man who would do this. Thanks to the telegraph, the text of Seward's speech and descriptions of his enthusiastic reception appeared within a day or two in newspapers across the North.[40]

The party left Detroit on Wednesday by train, but the tracks ended after about a hundred miles, so they traveled the remaining miles to Lansing in carriages, escorted by Wide Awakes. The next morning, there was a procession through the state capital that Fanny and a reporter each estimated was about two or three miles long. There were Wide Awakes and others marching on foot, mounted riders, and "innumerable wagons carrying rail fences," a symbol of the rail-splitter Lincoln. From Lansing, Seward went on to Kalamazoo, which he did not reach until well after midnight. Even though it was so late, there were thousands at the train station to greet him. Seward commented that he seemed to meet a lot of Douglas Democrats, but he argued that a vote for "my excellent friend Stephen A. Douglas" was a wasted vote. Douglas could not become president, so northerners who voted for him were effectively voting for the southern Democratic candidate, John Breckinridge.[41]

The Seward party, now including the two Adamses, traveled by train through Michigan, Indiana, Illinois, and Wisconsin, arriving in Milwaukee at about two in the morning of Sunday, September 9. Here there was no public reception and no parade, for the city was in shock and in mourning. Less than twenty-four hours earlier the *Lady Elgin,* a passenger ship out of Milwaukee, had sunk in Lake Michigan with the loss of more than four hundred lives. "The angel of death passed just before me on the way," Seward remarked a few days later, "and instead of the greeting of thousands of my fellow citizens, I found only a thick

darkness [and] the weeping and wailing of mothers for the loss of children." Seward canceled his planned events and rested quietly for two
days.[42]

They traveled on to Madison, the state capital, where he responded
to the welcome in his own somewhat elaborate way, comparing the
young town with "the city of the ancient Aztecs, surrounded by beautiful lakes, and embowered in the richest vegetation." That evening, when
the Wide Awakes marched to his hotel, Seward said that it was appropriate that "young men should wake and watch on the eve of battle," and
"enjoined upon everyone present that this was a warfare ending only
with life." The next day, he noted that in his own travels he seemed to
be following the westward course of empire: from Athens to Rome to
London to Washington and now to the Midwest. The only threat to the
American empire was an internal threat, the "great and desperate effort"
of the southern slaveholders to establish slavery in the territories and ultimately to restore slavery throughout the nation. The responsibility for
resisting the expansion of slavery, and for making the United States "a
tower of freedom and a refuge for the oppressed from all lands," would
fall mainly "on the people of the northwest," and Seward said he did not
doubt that they would fulfill their historic role.[43]

The party left Madison the next morning, traveled a hundred miles
west by stage, and that evening boarded a Mississippi steamboat bound
upriver. The younger Adams found it incredibly exciting: the broad
river, the "high bluffs rising dim in the shadows," and the glare of the
steamer's fires, all "wonderfully picturesque." The elder Adams noted
only that he "slept very indifferently and was up soon after five." At the
insistence of Cadwallader Washburn, the local member of Congress, the
group tarried for a day at LaCrosse, Wisconsin. Seward and his friends
toured the local brewery where (Adams recorded) the German owner
"would not permit us to go without drinking three glasses apiece of his
beer." Perhaps because of the beer, perhaps because of the small setting, Seward's speech that afternoon was (again according to Adams)
"the most easy and agreeable address I have ever heard from him."[44]

A few days later, in St. Paul, Minnesota, a reporter thought the whole
state was in town for Seward's speech, "in spite of the mud and rain."
Seward did not disappoint. From these central northern highlands, he

said, he could see north into Canada, where enterprising people were building settlements which might one day become states of the United States. Looking even farther north, to Russian America, he could say to the settlers there that they could "build up your outposts all along the coast even up to the Arctic Ocean—they will yet become the outposts of my own country." Similarly, looking south, to the revolutionary unrest in Latin America, he could discern "the preparatory stage for their reorganization in free, equal and self-governing members of the United States of America." It was a grand, even grandiose, vision. Seward mocked the reports that the South would secede if Lincoln was elected; "nobody's afraid" of such threats, he said.[45]

The following day, Seward and his party left on the steamboat *Alhambra*, a vessel the younger Adams described as "in every respect a wretched one—old, dirty, and full of vermin." But as they floated and steamed down the Mississippi River, "the day was so fine and the scenery so pleasing" that even the elder Adams enjoyed himself. Seward had promised to speak in Dubuque, Iowa, on the afternoon of the 20th, but they did not arrive there until late at night, so he stayed on an extra day, speaking the next afternoon to an eager audience of several thousand. He stressed the economic aspects of slavery—"out of the million inventions which the American people enjoy, there is not one that was made by a slave"—and again denied any Republican intent to interfere with slavery in the slave states.[46]

At this point in the tour, the elder Adams, "having done all that my sense of duty required of me," left the group and returned east. Seward, the younger Adams, and the others continued south and west, heading for Kansas through Illinois and Missouri. The younger Adams later recalled how, as they approached Quincy, Illinois, the early morning sun "shone on Seward, wrapped in a strange and indescribable Syrian cashmere cloak, and my humble self, puffing our morning cigars in a baggage-car, having rendered ourselves, as he expressed it, 'independent on this tobacco question.' " Seward also indulged in alcohol, Adams remembered, and "at times his brandy-and-water would excite him, and set his tongue going with dangerous volubility, but I never saw him more affected than that—never anything approaching drunkenness." Adams was amazed at how much work Seward squeezed into the spare hours of the day. "I never could understand where, when or how he then prepared the really remarkable speeches he delivered in rapid succession."[47]

Kansas was still a territory, without a formal voice in the presidential process, but Seward was determined to speak there. In Lawrence, to an audience mainly of farmers and their wives, he presented his version of the territory's history and role: how it occupied the pivotal position in the nation's geography; how the free state settlers, though "reviled and despised" by the slaveholders, had "lifted the banner of liberty on high"; how their actions ensured that Kansas would "be forever free"; and how this meant that Nebraska and all other western territories would come into the Union as free states. At this point Seward bowed before his audience, "as I have never done before to any other people, in profound reverence. I salute you with gratitude and affection." The Kansas crowd responded with equal gratitude for the way in which Seward had defended them in the Senate and honored them now with his presence.[48]

Seward and his party started east the next day in order to reach Chicago in time for his promised speech there. Missouri was a slave state, dominated by Democrats, so Seward was surprised to be greeted at his St. Louis hotel by a large crowd. He responded with a short speech in which he argued against the Missouri statute making it a crime to speak against slavery. "The first duty you owe to your city and to yourselves is to repeal and abrogate every law in your statute book that prohibits a man from saying what his honest judgment and sentiment and heart tell him is the truth." A reporter noted that this was greeted with "mingled surprise and approbation." Seward continued in this vein, contrasting the progress he noted in the free territory of Kansas with the stagnation in the slave state of Missouri. This was met with "faint manifestations of approval." Seward urged his listeners to vote for Lincoln, and some of them would; St. Louis was one part of the state in which Lincoln received votes.[49]

On his way from St. Louis to Chicago, Seward stopped in Springfield, Illinois, where Lincoln was among those waiting at the train station. Adams noted that introductions were made "standing in the aisle of the car," with Lincoln seeming "embarrassed" and Seward "constrained." The two men then went out onto the platform, and Seward gave a ten-minute speech, in which he promised that the Republicans would have a majority of 60,000 votes in New York. When Seward and his friends arrived that evening in Chicago, the crowd was so dense that they needed the help of the local police to get into their hotel.[50]

For weeks, the *Chicago Tribune* and other Republican papers had been advertising Seward's speech to be given on October 2. Rail lines offered special discounted fares; Wide Awakes competed to bring the largest contingents; and the weather cooperated, providing what one paper called a "very fine" fall day. Seward cooperated as well, speaking from an open-air stage to tens of thousands, "holding the closest attention of the furthest men within reach of his voice." He traced the history of the conflict between freedom and slavery in American history and argued that only the Republican Party offered a solution to this conflict. The Constitutional Union Party and its candidate John Bell proposed simply to ignore the issue, but "it will not stay ignored; it will not rest." The southern Democrats proposed merely a continuation of the policies of James Buchanan, policies rejected not only by Republicans but also by Democrats. As for the northern Democrats and their candidate Douglas, Seward argued that their "territorial sovereignty" approach would not work because the North would not consent to the creation of new slave states and the South would not agree to new free states. Only the Republican Party would resolve the question of slavery in the territories, so that the American people could move on to build "a new and great empire."[51]

Several newspapers noticed that two senators, Douglas and Seward, were engaged in similar national railroad campaigns. The *New York Evening Post* praised Seward for the way in which, even though he had been "superseded" by Lincoln, he "throws himself into the canvass with all the ability and earnestness he can command." The *Post* criticized Douglas for violating the unwritten rule that candidates should not campaign for themselves, noting that "Seward speaks for a cause, Douglas speaks for Douglas." The two senators met by chance in LaPorte, Indiana, where Seward's train from Chicago stopped in the middle of the night and he was awakened by Douglas. Whiskey bottle in hand, Douglas asked Seward to come out onto the platform and "speak to the boys." When Seward said that he was too tired, Douglas relented, sipping from his bottle as he left. The next day, when Adams asked about the incident, Seward explained that it was his colleague's idea of "political courtesy," but that he "didn't mean to let Douglas exhibit him to his followers, just to make a little political capital for himself."[52]

Seward, exhausted by this point, somehow kept going for a few more days, speaking to large audiences in Cleveland and Buffalo, and smaller crowds in smaller towns along the way. As he approached Auburn, Adams noted in his diary, Seward "seemed to enlarge, and to dwell with real affection on every object along the road. He told me of the country, and gave me the names of lakes and bridges, and when we stopped at way stations, he would get out of the train . . . exchanging greetings with almost every man he met." They reached Auburn late on Saturday, October 6, where "a noisy throng was waiting for him." He was home.[53]

———

Seward did not rest for long. Although he had confidently predicted, while in Illinois, that Lincoln would carry New York, when he returned to Auburn he found the situation much more doubtful. The New York Democrats had managed to put together a Fusion ticket, so that voters would not have to choose among Lincoln's three opponents; they could simply vote *against* Lincoln. Democrats referred to this Fusion ticket as the "Union ticket" and insisted that the only way to save the Union from secession and civil war was for New Yorkers to "vote Union." Once the ticket was formed, Democratic merchants provided substantial financial assistance; it was reported that William Astor alone had given a million dollars to the Fusion cause. One Douglas paper was so confident that the Fusion ticket would prevail that it believed that it could "from this date proclaim the defeat of Lincoln." Another complication for Republicans in New York was that the ballot would include a proposed constitutional amendment to allow men to vote without regard to race, a sharp change from the current state constitution, which imposed a stiff property requirement upon free black voters. Democrats naturally linked this proposal to the Republicans; as one paper put it, "if you vote for the Republican ticket, you vote for universal negro suffrage in the state of New York!" It thus seemed quite possible that the Democrats would prevail in New York. If they did, Republicans could not win in the electoral college even if they carried every other northern state. From a Republican perspective, New York was essential.[54]

So Seward returned to the campaign trail, speaking first in Seneca Falls and other small towns in upstate New York. He did not mention the question of black suffrage, knowing that even among Republicans, this was a divisive issue. Instead, he stuck to what he called the "simple, only issue, the extension or non-extension of slavery throughout this great nation." Weed, writing from New York City, asked whether Seward could give a "soothing speech" there, one that would show "that it is the business of Republicans and the mission of the Republican party to preserve the Union." Seward agreed and, in early November, he told his audience at Castle Garden that Republican policy was "to leave things to go on just exactly as they have gone on hitherto." Republicans would leave slavery in the slave states "to be gradually, peacefully circumscribed and limited hereafter, as it has been hitherto," and Republicans would protect freedom in the western territories, "just exactly as it is now." He again dismissed the threat of southern secession after Lincoln's election. Even after returning to Auburn, Seward did not rest: he gave one final speech the night before the election, a conversational speech to hundreds of friends and neighbors.[55]

Election day, November 6, opened in Auburn with a snowstorm, but this did not deter Seward and others from going to the polls. Throughout the nation, turnout was high, exceeding 82 percent of eligible voters; more than 4 million men voted. Thanks to the telegraph, the main result was clear to Seward by early that evening: Lincoln would be president. Lincoln carried almost all the northern states; Breckinridge almost all the southern states; Bell carried three border states; and Douglas, although he received more than a million votes, carried only Missouri. Lincoln prevailed in New York, as Seward had promised, although at the same time New Yorkers roundly rejected the amendment to give blacks the vote. Lincoln also prevailed in every state in the Northwest, the region where Seward had spent so much of his time and effort, although some of the results were very close. In both Illinois and Indiana, for example, Lincoln received only 51 percent of the vote. A shift of a few thousand votes in a few key states, such as Illinois, Ohio, and Oregon, would have forced the presidential election into the House of Representatives. Since the House would have voted by state, and since most states had more Democrats than Republicans in their delegations, it is extremely unlikely that the House would have elected Lincoln as president in early 1861. Indeed, this was the stated goal of the New York Fusion ticket: to force the election into the House and thereby prevent the election of Lincoln.[56]

In September, while they were campaigning together along the the Mississippi River, Judge Aaron Goodrich had remarked to Seward that "you are doing more for Lincoln's election than any hundred men in the United States." Goodrich was right: in the final weeks of the campaign, Seward did more than any other man to achieve the election of Lincoln. Some Republican leaders, such as Edward Bates of Missouri, refused to give speeches at all; others such as Salmon Chase of Ohio gave one or two speeches; but Seward traveled thousands of miles and gave dozens of speeches. He campaigned for Lincoln in fifteen different states and territories, and Lincoln carried all of them except Missouri. Both through his speeches and through his presence, Seward helped generate enthusiasm, that essential but elusive ingredient, and thus secured for Lincoln the votes he needed to carry the close states.[57]

Now that the great campaign was over, however, the nation waited to see whether Seward was right in predicting there would be no secession.

CHAPTER 9

"Save the Union in My Own Way":

November 1860–March 1861

Many southerners were elated by Lincoln's election, for they believed, in the words of the *Charleston Mercury*, that "the South would soon govern the South." Within a few days after election day, the South Carolina legislature set an early date for a secession convention, and four other Deep South states soon set dates for their own conventions. Yet there were also many southerners who pleaded for delay and moderation, and these pleas too were reported in northern papers. As the *New York Times* noted, the contradictory southern news made it difficult to make any predictions, other than that South Carolina would probably secede. Seward, in Auburn, followed all these developments closely in the northern newspapers.[1]

Republicans soon divided over how to respond to the threat of secession. On the one hand there were those who opposed any conciliation, any compromise, with the southern traitors. Horace Greeley argued in the *New York Tribune* that before making concessions, the government should simply "let the erring sisters depart in peace." On the other hand there were those, led by Henry Raymond and Thurlow Weed, who advocated an attempt at compromise. Raymond wrote in the *New York Times* that Republicans should be moderate and conciliatory; they should revise the Fugitive Slave Law and repeal state laws designed to frustrate enforcement of the federal law. Weed went even further;

he suggested in the *Albany Evening Journal* that Congress reinstate the Missouri Compromise line so that new states formed north of the line would be free and states formed south would be slave. In a second article a few days later, Weed explained that even the territory south of the line would be effectively free because its climate and soil were unsuited to slavery, so the Republican Party could afford to be "tolerant" in this respect. Most Republicans condemned Weed's proposals.[2]

Although Seward and Weed later denied collaboration, it is almost certain they discussed at least the outlines of Weed's articles. Seward visited Weed in Albany on November 16, a few days before the first editorial appeared, and visited him again in New York City on November 29, the day before the second editorial appeared. Although less specific than Weed's editorials, Seward's first speech after the election was also a plea for moderation. Seward must have startled his immediate audience, a group of ardent young Wide Awakes, when he advised them to go home and forget politics for a while. The duty of Republicans in the current crisis, he told them, was "simply that of magnanimity. We have learned, heretofore, the practice of patience under political defeat. It now remains to show the greater virtue of moderation in triumph." Americans of different parties, he said, "are not, never can be, never must be, enemies, or even adversaries. We are all fellow-citizens, Americans, brethren."[3]

Seward had hoped to remain in Auburn through the end of the year, but in light of the alarming reports from the South, he decided he had to be in the nation's capital as Congress convened. So he was in Washington in early December when President Buchanan, in his last annual message, blamed the crisis on the "incessant and violent agitation of the slavery question throughout the North for the past quarter of a century." Buchanan condemned secession but claimed that the federal government could not prevent it. Seward quipped that the president's message "shows conclusively that it is the duty of the president to execute the laws—unless somebody opposes him—and that no state has the right to go out of the Union—unless it wants to." The New York lawyer George Templeton Strong, upon hearing this remark attributed to Seward, commented that he did not believe "Billy Seward ever said anything so clever."[4]

As soon as Seward arrived in Washington, his Republican colleagues demanded to know whether Weed's articles reflected his views. Seward reported to Weed that he told them he had not yet formed his views, that "they would know what I think and what I propose when I do myself." To counter reports that he would soon make a speech, Seward planted an article in the *New York Tribune*: "Mr. Seward will make no speech immediately, and will submit no proposition. All rumors to the contrary are entirely unfounded. He is in no manner or form responsible for the various suggestions recently put forward in various newspapers, which have been supposed to reflect his views, and was not consulted concerning, or in any way privy to, their publication." He wrote to his wife that he hoped the *Tribune* article would "throw all the dogs off my track."[5]

Even while Seward was publicly disclaiming Weed's articles, he was privately pressing Republicans toward moderation. James Harvey, a Washington reporter close to Seward, wrote to Lincoln that the senator's plan was "to watch and wait, and allow the storm, if possible, to spend its fury." Seward was especially concerned about the border states. He wrote to a friend that "whatever may be done or said now will not hold back either South Carolina or any Gulf State," but that the radical secession rhetoric would show "the Border States that they are to be ruined by the licentiousness of the Gulf States if they go with them." Similarly, he wrote to Frances that the "mad caps of the South want to be inflamed, so as to make their secession irretrievable," while the "good men there" wanted moderation, so they could "produce a counter-movement." By and large Seward succeeded in his effort to secure Republican silence; an Alabama congressman reported home that the Republicans "say nothing, promise nothing, threaten nothing."[6]

———

Seward spent much of the winter in the company of Massachusetts representative Charles Francis Adams, his wife Abigail Brooks Adams, and their children, including Henry Adams, a recent Harvard graduate. In a letter to his brother Charles, Henry described how Seward invited the four Adams children in Washington to a dinner without their parents. As they were leaving their house, Seward "patted mamma on the head like a little girl, and told her she might come down after dinner and pass the evening with us, if she felt lonely without her children." From any other man, Henry noted, "this would make our dear mother furious, but he is so hopelessly lawless that she submits and feels rather flattered." Seward served the children, including the two young teens, a fine Moselle wine, so that they were "pretty jolly." After dinner, he "made Loo [Louisa] and Mary play whist in spite of all resistance on their part." Seward "will have his way and treats us all as his children."[7]

Young Henry Adams was entranced by Seward. In early December, he wrote of a dinner party during which he carefully watched "the old fellow with his big nose and his wire hair and grizzled eyebrows and miserable dress, and listened to him rolling out his grand, broad ideas that would inspire a cow with statesmanship if she understood our language." A few days later, at a smaller dinner at Seward's, "the governor caused a superior champagne to be brought out"; he was "chipper as a lark," swearing "that everything was going on admirably." Seward and Adams shared a love of cigars, and after a dinner out "the Governor always finishes two and pockets a third for the way home." In his memoir, an older Adams was more critical, writing that Seward had "a head like a wise macaw; a beaked nose; shaggy eyebrows; unorderly hair and clothes; hoarse voice; off-hand manner; free talk; and perpetual cigar." He added that Seward "chose to appear as a free talker, who loathed pomposity and enjoyed a joke; but how much was nature and how much was mask, he was himself too simple a nature to know."[8]

In parallel with their debate about compromise, Republicans in late 1860 were also debating the composition of Lincoln's cabinet. Cabinet positions were the choicest of political plums, since each cabinet officer would make or influence hundreds of other appointments. The cabinet as a whole was expected to make many policy decisions, so that by appointing cabinet members with particular views or credentials, such as former Whigs or former Democrats, Lincoln would be signaling his policies. Geographic balance was another expectation, which raised the difficult question of whether and how to include border state men in the cabinet. Finally, by established tradition, the president generally offered the first position in the cabinet—secretary of state—to the leader of his political party. Since the days of Jefferson and Madison, the secretary of state had been the presumptive next president. Buchanan was merely the most recent example of a secretary of state who soon thereafter became president.[9]

Because of this tradition, and because of Seward's preeminent position in the Republican party, most people assumed Lincoln would offer Seward the post. After Lincoln's election, however, there was some doubt about whether the senator would accept the expected offer. The *New York Herald* reported that "by courtesy the State Department will be offered to Mr. Seward, who will decline it." Another paper carried a letter from an "independent" who claimed that "Mr. Seward will accept of no office whatever." Alarmed by such reports, friends insisted that Seward accept the position if it was offered. Charles Francis Adams wrote him immediately after the election: "Of course Mr. Lincoln will offer you the chief place in his Cabinet. I trust no considerations will deter you from accepting it. I know of no such faith existing in the competency of any other person." Senator Simon Cameron of Pennsylvania, who hoped that Seward would support his own candidacy for a cabinet post, wrote that "you will be offered the State Dept. within a few days and you must not refuse it. The whole victory achieved by the labor of so many years, will be lost if you run away now. My whole ambition is to see you in the Presidency." Seward did not commit himself in his responses to these and other letters.[10]

On or about December 12, Seward left the Capitol in the company of Hannibal Hamlin, senator from Maine and vice president–elect. As they walked toward Hamlin's hotel, Seward said that he was "tired of public life" and that "there was no place in the gift of the president which he would be willing to take." When they reached the hotel steps, Hamlin handed Seward two letters from Lincoln, still at home in Springfield. The first letter, as expected, was a brief formal offer of the position of secretary of state. The second letter, unexpected, was an informal note: "Rumors have got into the newspapers to the effect that the department named above would be tendered you as a compliment, and with the expectation that you would decline it." Lincoln assured Seward that "I have said nothing to justify these rumors." On the contrary, "it has been my purpose, from the day of the nomination at Chicago, to assign you, by your leave, this place in the administration." He pressed Seward to accept because "your position in the public eye, your integrity, ability, learning and great experience, all combine to render it an appointment preeminently fit to be made." And he added, in regard to patronage, that "I have prescribed for myself the maxim, 'Justice to all'; and I earnestly beseech your co-operation in keeping the maxim good." After reading the letters, Seward told Hamlin that he would have to "consult his friends before giving a final answer."[11]

Seward wrote to Lincoln within a day or two, thanking him for the offer, and for the kind way in which it was made, and asking for time to consider. He said that he wished he could meet with Lincoln, but he did not "see how it could prudently be [done] under existing circumstances." He assured Lincoln of his "hearty concurrence in your views in regard to the distribution of the public offices as you have communicated them." On the same day, Seward wrote Weed that they should meet the next evening in New York City. Seward learned from Weed that Lincoln had just invited Weed to his home in Springfield. This was perfect: it would allow Seward, through Weed, to learn how Lincoln viewed the secession crisis and how he intended to handle the cabinet. Even though Seward had told Lincoln that he shared his views on patronage, the truth was that Seward, and even more so Weed, had definite ideas about how Lincoln should form his cabinet. Seward wrote to Lincoln a second time, from Albany, saying that he would await news in Auburn while Weed went on to Springfield.[12]

There was, indeed, much news during the week Seward was at home. On December 17, only hours after he left Albany for Auburn, another editorial appeared in the *Albany Evening Journal*, in which Weed argued that the Republicans could afford to compromise and supported the Missouri Compromise line. Once again, many assumed that Weed's editorial reflected Seward's views. Israel Washburn, Jr., Seward's friend from Maine, wrote Seward from Washington that the politicians there were "*convinced*" that Seward had dictated Weed's column. The next day, Seward's friend and colleague John Crittenden, senator from Kentucky, outlined what was soon known as the "Crittenden compromise." Crittenden proposed several constitutional amendments, one of which would provide that in all territory "now held or hereafter acquired" north of the Missouri Compromise line, slavery would be prohibited, while in all such territory south of the line, slavery would be recognized and protected. Republicans found the words "hereafter acquired" worrisome, for they suggested that southerners planned to extend slavery by acquiring southern territory. On December 20, the Senate appointed a committee of thirteen members, including Crittenden, Seward, and Douglas, to consider compromise. Later in the day the telegraph reported that the secession convention in South Carolina, by a unanimous vote, had declared the state an independent nation. Georgia and other states would soon hold their own secession conventions; would they follow South Carolina or heed the advice of those who counseled delay and restraint?[13]

———

When Seward and Weed met again on December 22, on the train from Syracuse to Albany, they discussed these developments, but above all they talked about Weed's meeting with Lincoln in Springfield. Lincoln had roundly rejected the notion of extending the Missouri Compromise line, or indeed of offering any concession extending slavery. On that issue, Lincoln told Weed, as he had recently told Representative Elihu Washburne of Illinois, Republicans must "hold firm, as with a chain of steel." Lincoln did provide Weed with a single page on which he set out three points: that the fugitive slave clause of the Constitution should be enforced by federal law; that state laws in conflict with the federal law should be repealed; and that "the Federal Union must be preserved." Seward claimed, in a letter to Lincoln a few days later, that during their hurried railcar conference Weed did not provide him with a copy of Lincoln's three points. This is possible, but it seems more likely that Seward decided Lincoln did not appreciate how important it was for Republicans to at least seem conciliatory, and so he decided to explore slightly different ideas when he returned to Washington.[14]

Weed had hoped to persuade Lincoln to appoint a cabinet supportive of Seward, but he learned that this was not at all Lincoln's plan. When Weed suggested that New England be represented by Charles Francis Adams, Lincoln informed him that he was inclined toward

Gideon Welles, the Connecticut editor. Lincoln insisted that he would appoint former Democrats (such as Welles) as well as former Whigs (such as Seward). Lincoln also told Weed that he intended to appoint Salmon Chase, the former senator and governor from Ohio, and Montgomery Blair, a Washington lawyer and member of the powerful Blair family. Chase and Blair were former Democrats and already known as opponents of Seward. Weed tried to argue that the cabinet should have a consistent point of view—he meant a consistent Whig point of view—but Lincoln disagreed. The one point on which Lincoln and Weed *did* agree was the importance of naming at least one man from the border states. When Lincoln asked Weed for suggestions, Weed provided four names, including Representative John Gilmer of North Carolina. Lincoln was sufficiently intrigued that he authorized Weed to contact Gilmer; he also sent Gilmer a telegram directly, asking him to come to Springfield. Overall, however, Weed was quite discouraged about the composition of the cabinet—so discouraged that he told Seward he was not sure he should be part of it.[15]

After leaving Weed, Seward continued to New York City and checked in at his customary hotel, the Astor House. He had scarcely arrived when he was summoned to the ballroom, where the annual dinner of the New England Society was in progress, and his friends demanded an after-dinner speech. In impromptu and informal remarks, often interrupted by comments and applause, Seward tried to minimize the secession crisis. The Union was like a family, he said, and it was not odd that "in a family of thirty-four members there should be, once in the course of a few years, one, or two, or three, or four, of the members who would become discontented and wish to withdraw for a while." But he did not think that secession would last long because there was still such strong fraternal feeling among the states. If a foreign power were to "make a descent upon the City of New York tomorrow," he believed "the hills of South Carolina would pour forth their population to the rescue of New York." Equally, if a foreign power were to attack South Carolina, "I know who would go to their rescue." (This remark was greeted with "loud and prolonged cheers.") If people would simply wait patiently for another sixty days, Seward said, they would see "a brighter light" and "a more cheerful atmosphere."[16]

—

When Seward reached Washington early on December 24, and met with the four other Republican members of the Senate compromise committee, he learned that the committee had already rejected the key element of the Crittenden plan, the proposed Missouri Compromise line. Seward suggested, and the four agreed, that they should put forward three new points: that the Constitution should be amended to state that Congress could not abolish or interfere with slavery in the slave states; that the Fugitive Slave Law should be amended to grant the fugitive the right to a jury trial; and that all states should review their laws and repeal any that contravened the Constitution or federal laws. Seward's points were different from those Lincoln had shared with Weed, but in one essential respect they followed Lincoln: they did not suggest any territorial extension of slavery. When the whole committee met later that day, Seward recorded his vote against Crittenden's territorial compromise, again following Lincoln's lead on the central issue. Seward then put forward his own points, only the first of which was accepted by the committee. The compromise committee met a few more times, but with little progress, and on the last day of the year, the committee reported to the Senate that it had no recommendations and that it had disbanded.[17]

Although the compromise committee was not able to reach consensus, Seward tried to hold out hope to moderates. One paper reported that when asked in late December about the crisis, Seward said "in his oracular way that he is not a prophet; still he knows that . . . God meant this country to remain united and successful, and it can't happen otherwise." In a letter to Lincoln on December 26, he wrote that it now seemed likely that Georgia, Alabama, Mississippi, and Louisiana would secede. As to the border states, their course was more uncertain and in Seward's view more important. "While prudence and patriotism dictate adhesion to the Union, nothing could certainly restrain them but the adoption of Mr. Crittenden's compromise, and I do not see the slightest indication of its adoption on the Republican side of Congress." Seward admitted that, by inauguration day in March, Lincoln would face "several, perhaps all of, the slave states standing in a contumacious attitude," but he believed a southern reaction against secession would already be in progress. "Sedition will be growing weaker and loyalty stronger every day from the acts of secession as they occur."[18]

The next morning, Seward had a long talk with his friend Charles Francis Adams, in which he revealed what very few knew: that Lincoln had offered to make him secretary of state. As Adams recorded the conversation, Seward said that he had expected that, after offering him the position of cabinet leader, Lincoln "would have consulted him upon the selection of the colleagues with whom he was to act." But Seward had learned through Weed that Lincoln had already chosen most of the other members of the cabinet, and that many would be from other factions of the party. Seward especially regretted that there would be no cabinet position for Adams. The composition of the cabinet, Adams wrote, placed Seward "in great embarrassment what to do. If he declined, could he assign the true reasons for it, which was the want of support in it? If he accepted, what a task he had before him!" Always conscious of duty, Adams advised Seward to accept "in this moment of great difficulty and danger."[19]

Adams inferred from Seward's tone that he would accept, and any doubts Seward had were removed by alarming news reports. First there was news from Pittsburgh that Secretary of War John Floyd, one of several southerners in the Buchanan cabinet, had ordered a substantial transfer of arms to two southern forts. The attempted transfer led many to question whether Buchanan intended to help the secessionists rather than defend the Union. Then from South Carolina came the news that Major Robert Anderson, in charge of the federal forts and troops in and around Charleston Harbor, had moved his troops from the insecure Fort Moultrie to the more secure Fort Sumter. Northerners assumed that Anderson moved his troops because he feared an attack by the state militia, and the northern press praised the major for his courage and initiative. Southerners viewed the move as belligerent, and South Carolina retaliated by seizing Fort Moultrie and the federal arsenal in Charleston. President Buchanan and the cabinet were in intense meetings, and there were rumors that they would reprimand Anderson or even order him to abandon Fort Sumter.[20]

Seward wrote to Lincoln on December 28 that, in light of all the recent news, "there is a feverish excitement here which awakens all kind of apprehensions of popular disturbance and disorders, connected with your assumption of the government." Seward himself was not too worried, but he suggested that Lincoln consider arriving in Washington a week earlier, to calm the nerves of the capital. In a second letter, Seward continued the dialogue with Lincoln about the possibility of southern cabinet members, suggesting three names other than Gilmer. And in a third letter, he wrote that he had at last decided that, if named and confirmed as secretary of state, "it would be my duty to accept the appointment." He explained to his wife that "I have advised Mr. L. that I will not decline. It is inevitable. I will try to save freedom and my country."[21]

———

According to an anonymous but informed memoir, on the same day that Seward accepted Lincoln's offer, December 28, he met with James Orr, one of three commissioners in Washington seeking formal recognition of South Carolina as a separate nation. Orr told Seward that Major Anderson's recent movement had "immensely strengthened the war secessionists, not only in South Carolina but in other states, who were loudly proclaiming it as unanswerable evidence of an intention on the part of the United States to coerce South Carolina." Seward agreed with Orr that "Anderson's movement was a most unfortunate one," and he "suggested that the matter might be arranged if South Carolina would evacuate Fort Moultrie and allow Anderson to reoccupy that post, both parties agreeing that Fort Sumter should not be occupied at all by either." Henry Adams, in a letter to his brother, described how at dinner that day, when Adams expressed the conventional northern view that Buchanan should not dismiss Anderson, Seward expressed the opposite view, saying that it might be good if Anderson were dismissed and Sumter abandoned. "I *want* the North to be mad," Seward said, because "so long as the Democrats up there, and the great cities, stick to the South, they [the South] will bully us." If the North could only be "kicked hard enough" to reach a "war pitch," then the "South will learn manners." Seward's remarks about the fort showed that he had already begun thinking about Sumter in political rather than military terms.[22]

The secession winter was filled with sudden shifts, and one occurred in late December in Seward's views of the southern threat to Washington. He had minimized the threat in earlier letters, but now, on December 29, he informed Lincoln that "a plot is forming to seize the Capitol on or before" inauguration day and the plot "has its accomplices in the public councils." Seward explained that "at length I have gotten a position in which I can see what is going on in the councils of the President," and "it pains me to learn that things there are even worse than is understood." Buchanan "is debating day and night on the question whether he shall not recall Major Anderson and surrender Fort Sumter, and go on arming the South." Seward asked Lincoln to let him know, as soon as possible, whom he would name as secretaries of war and navy, so that Seward could coordinate with them. Seward did not even sign his name to this letter, saying that he trusted Lincoln would by now recognize his handwriting.[23]

Seward did not provide Lincoln with many details of the threat to Washington, but he amplified these in conversations with Lincoln's friend Leonard Swett, who in turn relayed them by letter to Lincoln. Seward, Swett noted, "thinks the southern plan now is to draw Maryland and Virginia into the revolution before the fourth of March, so as to get possession of the railroad from Baltimore to this place, and the telegraph wires. With these advantages, and these two states swept by the same mania that is now sweeping the South, they hope to prevent your inauguration." The southern men seem to "have taken exclusive possession, or nearly so, of the president," leading to fears that Buchanan would not oppose, might perhaps even support, southern designs on Washington. Swett conceded that the plan seemed "visionary," but he assured Lincoln that "all men here have serious fears of it." Seward continued, through Swett, to advise Lincoln about the cabinet, advising him to pick "men of strength, will, prudence and ability." He pressed Lincoln to reconsider Charles Francis Adams, and he also "approved" of Simon Cameron of Pennsylvania and Edward Bates of Missouri, whose names were in the papers as likely cabinet members.[24]

Seward's source of information from inside the Buchanan cabinet was Edwin Stanton, whom Buchanan had just appointed as U.S. attorney general. Stanton was a midwestern lawyer who had lived in

Washington for the past several years, practicing mainly patent law. Seward and Stanton knew one another through their patent work and had met from time to time in social settings, but they did not meet directly during the secession winter. They relied instead on an intermediary, Peter Watson, another patent lawyer. Seward's son Frederick recalled that, during these winter weeks, when his father returned home and asked if there had been any callers, the answer would generally be that "Mr. Watson was here to talk about the patent case." On one occasion, when Seward and Stanton met by chance on the street, they turned from one another and walked in opposite directions.[25]

On December 31, Seward received a letter from Frances, pressing him to avoid compromise and to come home to Auburn for a brief rest. Seward was continuing to explore the possibility of compromise; he had written to Weed a few days earlier that perhaps a constitutional convention, called for two years hence, would be well received by the border states and would settle them down. But he knew that his wife hated the very idea of compromise, so he wrote to her that "there is no fear of any compromise of principle or advantage to freedom." As to coming home, he wrote that he could not think about himself during "this emergency of probable civil war and dissolution of the Union. I could not be well or happy at home, refusing to do what I can, when called to the councils of my country."[26]

———

Early in January 1861, in another letter to Frances, Seward claimed that he had "assumed a sort of dictatorship for defense, and am laboring night and day, with the cities and states." Seward exaggerated, as he sometimes did, but he had recently asked at least two northern governors, John Andrew of Massachusetts and Edwin Morgan of New York, to have militia ready to move to Washington on short notice. He also worked with his old friend Winfield Scott, general-in-chief of the army, in trying to determine which of the local Washington militia units were reliable. Swett reported to Lincoln that it seemed the immediate danger to Washington had passed.[27]

On January 9, after weeks of rumors, Thurlow Weed announced in the *Albany Evening Journal* that Lincoln would name Seward as secretary of state. Weed predicted that Lincoln as president and Seward as "premier" would "discharge their duties, amid all the difficulties that surround them, so as to preserve the blessing of Union, and to deserve and receive the homage of their countrymen." January 9 was also the day on which Mississippi seceded from the Union; Florida followed on the 10th and Alabama on the 11th. Seward was more focused on the border states, especially Virginia and North Carolina, where legislatures were in session, debating whether they should call their own conventions. On January 10, the shocking news arrived that South Carolina had fired upon the American flag. The civilian ship *Star of the West,* chartered by the federal government to reinforce Major Anderson in Charleston Harbor, had encountered intense cannon fire as she approached Fort Sumter and turned back. The *Star of the West* incident enraged the North; James Watson Webb reported to Lincoln that everyone was demanding "the enforcement of the laws, the vindication of the Constitution, and punishment of the traitors."[28]

It was against this background that Seward let it be known that he would speak in the Senate on Saturday, January 12. The *New York Tribune* noted that "as the next premier his words will be scrutinized with much precision." The *Washington Evening Star* predicted that Seward's Senate speech would be "the most momentous one in its results ever delivered before that body." The *Star* believed that "he is about to extend the olive branch" and that "if he does the Union may yet escape destruction." One paper reported that two hours before Seward's speech, the lobbies and passages were already "densely thronged." Another estimated that when Seward started speaking at around one o'clock, there were 1,800 men and women packed into the small Senate chamber.[29]

Seward began by saying that, given the threats to the Union, "it is time for every Senator to declare himself." He himself would adhere "to the Union in its integrity and with all its parts . . . in any event, whether of peace or war, with every consequence of honor or dishonor, of life or death." In a passage closely based on John Jay's second *Federalist* letter, Seward analyzed the external and internal threats that would follow upon disunion. The separation of the United States into two or more confederacies, he predicted, would not be easy or peaceful. "Jealousies would bring on frequent and retaliatory wars." One reporter noted that "it was difficult to restrain oneself from tears, when at the allusion of Seward to the great men of the country now dead and gone, and at his vivid portrait of the horrors and evils of dissolution and civil war, we saw the venerable Senator Crittenden, who sat directly in front of Seward, shedding tears, and finally overcome by his feelings, cover his face with his handkerchief."[30]

In the second half of his speech, Seward outlined five concessions he was prepared to make to avoid dissolution and civil war. First, all state laws contrary to the U.S. Constitution (including the personal liberty laws designed to frustrate the federal Fugitive Slave Law) should be repealed. Second, the Constitution should be amended to confirm that Congress could not "abolish or interfere with slavery in any state." Third, Congress should admit Kansas under its free state constitution, and then organize the remaining western territory into two further states. He did not say, but his listeners assumed, that he was prepared for the southern state, New Mexico, to have a slave system. Alternatively, he proposed that in a few years, when passions had cooled, a constitutional convention be held to resolve the question of slavery in the western territories and all related questions. Fourth, to deter those like John Brown, Congress should pass a stiff law to "prevent mutual invasions of states by citizens of other states." Fifth, since physical bonds were even more important than written agreements, Seward would support the construction of two separate railroads to the Pacific, one northern and one southern.[31]

Seward noted that these were not the points he would have proposed if he had consulted only his own "cherished convictions." But he had "learned early from Jefferson" that in politics one must consider not only one's own views but also "those with whom we must necessarily act." He continued: "We must be content to lead when we can, and to follow when we cannot lead; and if we cannot at any time do for our country all the good that we would wish, we must be satisfied with doing for her all the good that we can." Seward would try to do what he could, but there were limits on his ability to do so, and he was all too aware of these limits.[32]

———

As he concluded his speech, the Senate chamber, in violation of the rules, resounded with applause. Seward's friend James Harvey wrote in the *Philadelphia North American* that "no recent event, among the many startling ones which have exercised the public mind, has excited more comment, or produced a profounder sensation, than Mr. Seward's speech." Even "radical secessionists, who professed an unwillingness to hear any terms," had listened to Seward carefully. The Washington correspondent for the *Dedham Gazette* conceded that Seward did not look or dress like a statesman; he wore for this great speech "the same morning coat that he always wears, not made by any fashionable tailor, certainly." But Seward was, for the *Gazette* reporter, "the most important man, by far, in the country," for he was "the man who holds now in his hand all the threads of our fate. Other men act; he stands behind them and above them; pushes them forward or draws them back, as circumstances demand."[33]

Other papers were more reserved. The *New York Times* commented that the speech proved that the new administration would "consult, with scrupulous care, the interests, the principles, and the sentiments, of every section of the Union." The *Times* also noted that many would be disappointed that Seward had not outlined a compromise that could end the crisis. The *New York Evening Post* believed that people were unreasonable in their expectation that Seward would have a magic solution for the crisis; he had gone as far as he could go consistent with Republican policy, and perhaps too far, given the "recent insult to the flag at Charleston." Radical Republicans denounced the speech. Senator Charles Sumner wrote to a friend that when Seward had read out the speech to him in draft form, and reached his five concessions, Sumner protested against them "with my whole soul—for the sake of our cause, our country and his own good name, and I supplicated with him to say no such thing."[34]

Frances Seward agreed with her friend Sumner. "Eloquent as your speech was," she wrote to her husband, "it fails to meet with the entire approval of those who love you best." She feared that her husband was "in danger of taking the path which led Daniel Webster to an unhonored grave" ten years earlier. "Compromise based on the idea that the preservation of the Union is more important than the liberty of nearly 4,000,000 human beings cannot be right," she wrote. "The alteration of the Constitution to perpetuate slavery—the enforcement of a law to recapture a poor, suffering fugitive—giving half of the territories of a free country to the curse of slavery—these compromises cannot be approved by God or supported by good men."[35]

The next day, in a postscript to a letter from their daughter, Frances softened her tone. Her earlier letter was written under the influence of a "violent headache," it was "exaggerated," and she wished her husband "would destroy it." Seward responded that he was "not surprised that you do not like the 'concessions' in my speech. You will soon enough come to see that they are not compromises, but explanations, to disarm the enemies of Truth, Freedom, and Union, of their most effective weapons." He was, he claimed, "the only *hopeful, calm, conciliatory* person" in all of Washington. "Mad men North, and mad men South, are working together to produce dissolution of the Union, by civil war." He was striving to avert such a disaster and he was "looking, or rather leaving, to posterity to decide upon my action and conduct. I must gain time for the new administration to organize and for the frenzy of passion to subside. . . I am doing this without making any compromise whatever, by forbearance, conciliation, and magnanimity."[36]

Eleven years earlier, when Daniel Webster had proposed compromise in March 1850, the poet John Greenleaf Whittier had denounced him in verse. "So fallen! So lost! The light withdrawn which once he wore!" Now in January 1861, with war imminent, Whittier praised Seward in a similar poem, saying that if he could manage, without yielding freedom, to save the Union from "a baptism of blood," Seward would be entitled to wear "a wreath whose flowers no earthly soil have known." Henry Adams wrote that the only moment during the whole winter when he saw Seward show strong emotion was when "he opened the envelope and read the sonnet which the poet Whitter sent to him from Amesbury."[37]

Seward was pleased by the praise of Whittier and others, and troubled by the criticism of his wife, but the audience about which he was most concerned was in the border states, the states that he was so desperate to hold in the Union. Reaction here was mixed. In Virginia, the *Alexandria Gazette* regretted that Seward did not recommend an immediate constitutional convention; a convention in a few years time, the paper argued, would be too late. The *Richmond Whig* lamented that Seward had provided "empty rhetoric and stale platitudes" rather than a "feasible and satisfactory plan for settling the pending difficulty." One member of the Virginia legislature, writing home from Richmond, commented that "Seward's last speech is, to be sure, somewhat conciliatory, but it falls far below the demands of the occasion." Others were more positive. The *Fayetteville Observer* printed the speech on its front page and praised Seward's moderation. The *Baltimore American* argued that the speech "surrenders much, concedes much, and if generously and justly received, may be made the basis for the adjustment of our sectional differences"; as to the specifics, the *American* commented that "except upon the third point, that relative to the territories, Mr. Seward's propositions are practical and sufficient." The *New York Times* reported from Washington that the leading border state men were "highly pleased" and "the people of [Washington], who represent the conservative spirit of the South, are in fine spirits."[38]

———

Within a few days after this speech there were some positive signs from the border states. The Virginia legislature rejected the suggestion that it should give a convention the authority to secede immediately; instead, the legislature set an early February date to elect delegates for a convention, but provided that any decision to secede would be subject to a second statewide vote. In another victory for moderates, the Virginia legislature invited the legislatures of all the other states to appoint delegates for a peace convention, to meet in Washington starting on February 4. Some have credited Seward with the idea for the peace convention; Henry Adams later wrote that Seward "caused" the convention to be summoned. Although the evidence for this seems rather thin, there is no question that Seward supported the convention, because it allowed him to insist, in his many letters to and conversations with border state men, that there was still a process in place for conciliation and compromise, that it was too early for Virginia and other border states to secede.[39]

Knowing that Lincoln's cabinet choices would signal the new administration's policies, Seward persisted in his efforts to influence these choices. In early January, for example, when many papers criticized Lincoln's intended choice of Simon Cameron for the cabinet, Seward was among those who defended Cameron in letters to the president-elect. One of the charges against Cameron was that he was too close to Seward. Lyman Trumbull, a Republican senator from Illinois, wrote Lincoln that "another very serious objection to Cameron is his connection to Governor Seward. The governor is a man who acts through others, and many believe Cameron would be his instrument in the cabinet." James Shepherd Pike, Washington correspondent for the *New York Tribune*, wrote to Salmon Chase that if both Cameron and Seward were part of the cabinet, Chase would have to join it as well, to counteract their corruption by "the superior blaze" of his honesty. Seward was not completely committed to Cameron, however, telling the Adams family at this same time that he "would have preferred any other man" for Treasury, the position the press believed Cameron would receive.[40]

The question of Cameron in the cabinet was linked with the question of Chase. Salmon Chase was viewed as the leader of the hard-line Republicans, those who would not compromise with the South, while Seward, especially after his Senate speech, was seen as the leader of the more conciliatory faction. Chase and Seward themselves were still somewhat friendly; on January 10, just after it was confirmed that Seward would be secretary of state, Chase had written him that "the post is yours by right and you will honor the post. My best wishes go with you." But the supporters of Chase and Seward were already bitter enemies, with Chase's more ardent supporters hoping not only to see Chase included in the cabinet but Seward excluded. Lincoln wanted both men in the cabinet, and Seward knew this, not only through the papers but also from Weed's meeting with Lincoln. In late January, when word leaked that Weed was about to go to Springfield again, people instantly assumed that he was going there to oppose Chase. There was a furious reaction; Weed canceled his trip; and Seward approved of his decision not to go. "Mr. Lincoln," Seward wrote to Weed, "has undertaken his cabinet without consulting me. For the present I shall be content to leave the responsibility on his own broad shoulders." Weed and Seward knew that this was not quite true—Lincoln had consulted with Seward both by letter and through Weed—but perhaps what Seward meant was that Lincoln had not listened to his advice to the extent he had expected.[41]

As the southern states seceded from the Union, their representatives resigned their seats in Congress. Five senators resigned on January 21, including Seward's friend Jefferson Davis. "I am sure there is not one of you," Davis said solemnly, "whatever sharp discussion there may have been between us, to whom I cannot now say, in the presence of my God, I wish you well; and such, I am sure, is the feeling of the people whom I represent towards those whom you represent." The departure of the southerners shifted power, allowing passage of some bills they had long opposed. On the very day of Davis's speech, for example, the Senate passed the bill for the admission of Kansas as a free state. The vote was 36 to 16; all the senators who voted against were Democrats from southern and border states. Seward lamented the departure of Davis and other friends, but rejoiced that, five years after he had proposed its immediate admission, Kansas was at last a state.[42]

Seward continued his efforts to explore compromise with key senators. He apparently met several times in late January with Senators Douglas, Crittenden, and James Dixon, a Republican from Connecticut. On January 25, a Washington lawyer wrote to Buchanan that "Gilmer of North Carolina informed me that Messrs. Seward, Douglas, Crittenden and Dixon of the Senate had a private meeting last night for the purpose of coming to some definite arrangement on our present national difficulties." A similar report, dated January 26, appeared in the *Chicago Tribune*: "Messrs. Douglas, Seward, Crittenden and Dixon held an important meeting last night on compromise. Crittenden says he has great hopes of its results. It is believed a modification of the Crittenden resolutions will be agreed on." In a public letter to John Barbour, a leading moderate in Virginia, and evidently based on their discussions with Seward, Senators Douglas and Crittenden wrote that they could "say with confidence that there is hope of adjustment, and the prospect has never been better than now since we first assembled." And on January 29, the diarist George Templeton Strong recorded that a friend claimed to have "authentic, private, confidential information that Seward, Crittenden, [Representative Robert] Hunter of Virginia, and Douglas agreed last night on certain 'conciliatory' measures, and the whole slavery question is settled."[43]

These reports make it clear that Seward was in close touch with key senators and border state representatives. What is less clear is whether he intended to compromise, or merely to *discuss* compromise in a way that would influence the imminent elections in the key border states. Elections were set for February 4 in Virginia and February 9 in Tennessee to select delegates for state conventions to debate secession. Henry Adams wrote home in late January that he was "inclined to believe that all Weed's motions, compromises and all, have been feelers on Seward's part. He will not compromise, himself, but he'll let others believe he will, and anyway, this disunion matter must be stopped, is his theory." James Ogden, a New York merchant visiting Washington at the same time, wrote to Crittenden that "a gentleman this morning told me that a perfectly reliable party assured him that Seward said, two days since, that his speech in the Senate contained nothing of conciliation and that he was inclined not to yield an inch. Whereas, three days since, another reliable party assured him that he had just had a long conversation with the same *statesman* and that he speaks in decided terms of the necessity of compromise." Ogden's report is hearsay, but it sounds very much like Seward, who was certainly quite able to talk down compromise with a Radical Republican and then talk up compromise a few hours later with a border state man.[44]

If Seward was going to go beyond talking about compromise and actually negotiate some kind of compromise, he would need support from Lincoln, and he sought such support through a letter of January 27. Seward described for Lincoln the "very painful" appeals of the border state Unionists, who warned that without "something of concession or compromise," their states would "go with the tide" of secession. The problem, Seward continued, was that "much the largest portion of the Republican party are reckless now of the crisis before us—and compromise or concession though as a means of averting dissolution is intolerable to them." These Republicans believed that civil war "will not come at all, or be less disastrous than I think it will be." Seward was not prepared to yield everything to the South: he wrote that he believed that "we must collect the revenues, regain the forts in the Gulf, and if need be maintain ourselves here [in Washington]." In general, however, "every thought we think ought to be conciliatory forbearing and patient, and so open the way for the rising of a Union Party in the seceding states which will bring them back into the Union."[45]

———

During the last week of January 1861, Washington was filled with delegations from the northern states pressing for compromise. One member of the Boston group recorded that when they asked Seward what could be done, he responded that he could not "advance farther or faster than he could carry his party," and suggested testily that they should ask Sumner "and others like him what they are willing to do." The New York committee included two dozen prominent business leaders, bringing with them a petition signed by nearly 40,000 New Yorkers. Seward, according to a letter home from Frederick, shocked these financiers "by telling them that the best thing they can do to save the Union is to lend it money at seven percent, instead of increasing the panic and difficulties by extorting twelve [percent]." Although the New Yorkers understood the background of Seward's request—the federal debt had doubled during the Buchanan years and the government was having difficulty selling even short-term high-interest notes—they nevertheless did not appreciate his effort to push them to lend at less than market rates. The New Yorkers pressed Seward to endorse their petition, which itself endorsed a variation of the Crittenden compromise. Seward declined. As Henry Adams wrote, Seward told the group that if he went along with their request, he would sacrifice himself politically and "would have to go back to Auburn and amuse myself with writing history the rest of my life." When the visitors protested that they had no such course in mind, Seward smiled and said that, if that was so, they would just have to "let me save the Union in my own way."[46]

In the Senate the next day, Seward presented the New York petition, calling it a fair summary of the views of the commercial men of New York City and indeed of the entire North. He carefully avoided supporting the petition or the compromise plan it embodied, but he praised the committee's spirit of "conciliation and affection." He had asked the leaders, Seward said, to continue in this same spirit by "voting for the Union," by "lending and even giving their money for the Union," and in the very last resort by "fighting in it." Seward also underlined that he still hoped and expected there would be a peaceful resolution of the crisis. The moment he sat down, Senator James Mason of Virginia was on his feet, denouncing Seward for raising money to subjugate the South and for wanting to solve the crisis "with blood." Both Mason and Seward were trying, through their remarks, to influence the Virginia voters: Seward to persuade them that compromise was possible, and to vote for Unionist delegates; Mason to persuade them that compromise was impossible, and to vote for secessionists.[47]

Because he soon would be secretary of state, foreign diplomats began seeking Seward out to ascertain and report home on his views. The most important of these was Lord Lyons, a middle-aged bachelor recently appointed as the minister to the United States for the United Kingdom. Lyons had entered the British diplomatic service immediately after graduating from Oxford, starting as an unpaid aide to his diplomat father, and advanced slowly, serving in various smaller European courts. Lyons was diligent, careful, and calm, but something of a prig; he neither smoked nor drank, and never really relaxed in Washington. He was also prejudiced against Americans, and especially against Seward, whom he viewed as an excitable, unpredictable, political American.[48]

In his reports to the British foreign minister in early February, Lyons echoed Adams over why Seward would not endorse a specific compromise plan. "He is sure that at this moment no plan would be accepted by both parties—and he does not choose to weaken his position by making himself responsible for a rejected plan." Seward believed, Lyons wrote, that "in a few months the evils and hardships produced by secession will become intolerably grievous to the southern states; that they will be completely reassured as to the intentions of the administration; and that the conservative element which is now kept under the surface by the violent pressure of the secessionists, will emerge with irresistible force." Seward predicted that Unionists would win the southern fall elections and bring the seceding states back into the Union. "He then hopes to place himself at the head of a strong Union party, having extensive ramifications both in the North and the South, and to make Union or Disunion not Freedom or Slavery the watchword of political parties." Lyons added that "in all of this" Seward apparently believed that "Lincoln will leave the whole management of affairs to him."[49]

Lyons was concerned that Seward "would not be very reluctant to provide excitement for the public mind by raising questions with foreign powers." Seward recounted to Lyons a conversation with Rudolf Schleiden, the minister for Bremen, in which Seward had said that "nothing would give [him] so much pleasure as to see a European power interfere in favor of South Carolina—for then he should 'pitch into' the European power, and South Carolina and the seceding states would soon join him in doing so." Schleiden's reports from this period to the Bremen foreign minister, although not as negative about Seward as those of Lyons, confirm that Seward made such remarks. Schleiden quoted Seward as saying that "if the Lord would only give the United States an excuse for a war with England, France, or Spain, that would be the best means of re-establishing internal peace." Lyons, summing up, regretted that Seward "takes no other view of foreign relations than as safe levers to work with upon public opinion here."[50]

———

February 4, 1861, was a busy and important day in American history. In Montgomery, Alabama, representatives of the seven states that had already seceded met to start forming a Confederate government. In Virginia, voters went to the polls in what one paper called the most important election in the state's history, to select delegates for a secession convention. In Washington, the national peace conference started, although few states were as yet represented. And on that evening, James

Shepherd Pike, a leader of the Chase forces, organized a Washington meeting of about twenty Republican members of Congress, all opposed to Seward's inclusion in Lincoln's cabinet. George Fogg, a New Hampshire editor who was visiting Washington, summarized the views of this group in a long letter to Lincoln. Fogg was blunt: "Mr. Seward's selection as secretary of state was a mistake"; Seward "would insist on being master of the administration, and would utterly scorn the idea of playing a subordinate part"; the senator was so eager to compromise that he would give up "every principle to which yourself and the Republican party stand pledged." Moreover, Seward allegedly spoke about the Republican Party as having "fulfilled its mission, and not being worth preserving," and he and Cameron had talked about "the early formation of new combinations, under the name of a 'Union party' or something of the kind." Seward did not know the precise allegations against him, but he did know about the Pike meeting; he wrote to Weed that he half-wished Pike's plot to "denounce me and exclude me from the cabinet" would succeed. "I am sure it would save the country, and as for me, what could be better?" [51]

Seward was elated on February 5 by the election news from Virginia: fewer than one third of the delegates elected to the convention were in favor of immediate secession. Moreover, the Virginia voters insisted that any decision to secede should take effect only if it was ratified by a second popular vote. The *New York Evening Post* reported that "Mr. Seward, with his characteristic hope and confidence, is particularly pleased with the result. He pronounces the Union safe, and that all the border states will follow the example of the Old Dominion." One of Seward's Virginia correspondents wrote him that "the Gulf Confederacy can count Virginia out of their little family arrangement—*she will never* join them." Another Virginian was more cautious, telling Seward that the secessionists "would have carried the recent election if we had not been able to hold out tolerable evidences that there was a hope of obtaining . . . constitutional guaranties of our slave property rights." He mentioned as being especially important the Douglas-Crittenden letter, based on their compromise talks with Seward. A few days later, news arrived in Washington that voters in Tennessee had also decided against holding any kind of convention, at least not yet. Henry Adams reported to his brother that "the ancient Seward is in high spirits and chuckles himself hoarse with his stories. He says it's all right. We shall keep the border states, and in three months or thereabouts, if we hold off, the Unionists and Disunionists will have their hands on each other's throats in the cotton states. We have weathered the storm."[52]

It was at about this time, early February, that Seward received Lincoln's response to the late January letter in which he had tried to persuade Lincoln of the necessity of compromise. Lincoln started by insisting that "on the territorial question, that is, the question of extending slavery under the national auspices—I am inflexible." Lincoln was especially opposed to any suggestion that slavery should extend to territory "hereafter acquired," for this would "put us again on the high-road to a slave empire." He added that "as to fugitive slaves, [the] District of Columbia, slave trade among the slave states, and whatever springs of necessity from the fact that the institution is amongst us, I care but little, so that what is done be comely, and not altogether outrageous." This was helpful, but the key for Seward was in the next sentence: "Nor do I care much about New Mexico, if further extension were hedged against." This suggested that Lincoln was open to the possibility that New Mexico would be admitted as a slave state, the possibility that Seward had floated in his speech. After receiving the letter, Seward told Charles Francis Adams that Lincoln "approved his course, but was so badgered at Springfield that he felt compelled to keep uncommitted on it at present." Since the peace convention was just getting started, however, there was no need for Seward to do anything about New Mexico, no need for him to change the approach he had outlined to Lord Lyons of not yet settling upon any specific compromise plan. Indeed, according to a letter from Sumner, who viewed the New Mexico plan as a "fatal dismal mistake," Seward would not vote for the plan if it ever came to a vote; he was merely using it "as a lure."[53]

February 13 was the date fixed by statute for the electoral votes to be counted and the next president officially designated. For weeks, Lincoln and Seward had worried that there would be a southern attempt to disrupt the process outlined in the Constitution, of counting the votes in the presence of both houses of Congress, in order to deny Lincoln the legitimacy of being declared president. "If the two Houses refuse to meet at all," Lincoln wrote Seward in early January, "or meet without a quorum of each, where shall we be? I do not think that this counting is constitutionally essential to the election; but how are we to proceed in the absence of it?" On the appointed day, Seward and the other senators joined the representatives in the House chamber; the *New York Times* reported that they watched "with almost breathless interest and silence." Vice President John Breckinridge presided over the counting, in which Breckinridge received more electoral votes than any candidate other than Lincoln. After all the votes were counted Breckinridge solemnly pronounced that Lincoln was elected president and Hamlin vice president. Frederick Seward, who was in Washington to help his father as private secretary, wrote home that although the day was uneventful, there had been careful preparations. "General Scott had his troops all under arms, out of sight, but ready, with guns loaded and horses harnessed; so that they could take the field at a few minutes' notice. But there was no enemy."[54]

Seward was also relieved, writing to tell his wife that "we have passed the 13th safely." He claimed that "I am, at last, out of direct responsibility. I have brought the ship off the sands, and am ready to resign the helm into the hands of the captain whom the people have chosen." At the same time, Seward was telling others that he would keep control. Schleiden reported to his ministry that Seward "consoled himself with the clever remark that there is no great difference between an elected president of the United States and a hereditary monarch"; in both cases, "the actual direction of affairs belongs to the leader of the ruling party." In a meeting with several southerners, Seward reportedly boasted that "if this whole matter is not satisfactorily settled within sixty days after I am seated in the saddle, and hold the reins firmly in my hand, I will give you my head for a football."[55]

Seward's desire to keep at least some control was heightened by Lincoln's remarks as he traveled by rail from Springfield toward Washington. In Indianapolis, Lincoln argued that it would not be "coercion" if the federal government "simply insists upon holding its own forts, or retaking those forts which belong to it." A few days later in Pittsburgh, he claimed that "*there is no crisis,* excepting such a one as may be gotten up at any time by designing politicians." And in a speech at Trenton,

New Jersey, he said he would try to "promote a peaceful settlement of all our difficulties," but added that "it may be necessary to put the foot down firmly." The papers reported that as he said this, Lincoln stamped his huge foot for emphasis, and the crowd erupted with "cheers so loud and long that for some moments it was impossible to hear."[56]

Lincoln's remarks distressed Seward, for the president-elect seemed to be mocking the concerns of moderate southerners and threatening the coercion they so feared and deplored. Charles Francis Adams, in his diary entry for February 20, reflected Seward's views as well as his own: "Nothing has so much depressed my spirits as the account of [Lincoln's speeches]. They betray a person unconscious of his own position as well as of the nature of the contest around him. Good natured, kindly, honest, but frivolous and uncertain." The next day, Adams wrote that Lincoln's remarks left people unsure what policy he would pursue: "If coercive, it is obvious Mr. Seward cannot go with him, and we may have war in thirty days." Charles Francis Adams, Jr., wrote home that "Seward's power has been impaired by the events of the last few days and especially by Mr. Lincoln's more early speeches. Ten days ago, I am assured, the game was in Seward's hands, the secessionists defeated and the agitation and excitement in the border states rapidly subsiding." Now, Adams continued, Lincoln's remarks "have spread the impression that Seward's policy is not to be followed out," and this impression had "seriously discouraged the Union men."[57]

———

On the morning of February 21, Seward received alarming news from General Scott: there was a plot to intercept and assassinate Lincoln as he passed through Baltimore the next day. Baltimore was a logical place for such an attack, both because many residents were ardent southerners, and because railroad passengers generally had to leave their trains and travel on foot or by carriage between the city's two train stations. Seward quickly assembled a few documents for Lincoln: a junior officer's report to Scott, a cover letter from Scott, and his own cover letter to Lincoln, pressing him to change his plans. For messenger, Seward selected his son Frederick. "Go by the first train," Seward instructed, as

Frederick later recalled. "Find Mr. Lincoln wherever he is. Let no one know your errand." Seward must have had several anxious hours after he sent his son on his way, not knowing whether Frederick would reach Lincoln or whether Lincoln would heed his advice. But on the afternoon of February 22, he received a telegram from his son with a code word they had previously agreed upon to inform him that Lincoln would alter his plans. Late that day, Seward summoned Lincoln's friend Representative Elihu Washburne to the Senate side of the Capitol, and the two men went to the train depot, hoping to meet Lincoln on the afternoon train. He was not on it. Not knowing when he would arrive, Seward and Washburne agreed they would meet again the following morning to meet the next Baltimore train.[58]

Lincoln arrived safely in Washington at six o'clock on the morning of February 23, and Washburne was at the station to meet him. Whether Seward was also there, or whether he met Lincoln and Washburne a few minutes later at the hotel, is a minor mystery. The sources are in conflict but it seems that Seward was not at the station, that he waited for Lincoln at Willard's Hotel, probably to avoid attracting attention at the station. The *Washington Evening Star* reported that Seward was in the Willard lobby at six in the morning, "solitary and alone, to the wonder of the few persons about at that hour, evidently looking for someone to arrive by the train momentarily expected." Lincoln arrived a few minutes later, the *Star* added, was greeted by Seward, and then went up to his room. Many of the press reports on Lincoln's arrival criticized his decision—heavily but silently influenced by Seward—to change his plans and slip through Baltimore by dark.[59]

After allowing Lincoln to rest a few hours, Seward picked him up in his carriage at eleven and escorted him to the White House. President Buchanan, who was meeting his cabinet, was surprised to be handed Lincoln's calling card, but he came out to meet with Lincoln and Seward for a few minutes, then took them into the cabinet room for another few minutes. From the White House, Seward and Lincoln drove to see General Scott; that evening, Lincoln dined at Seward's house. The next day was Sunday, and the two men went together to St. John's Episcopal Church, where, according to one paper, "not a dozen persons" recognized Lincoln, not even the pastor. On Monday afternoon, Seward escorted the president-elect to Capitol Hill, where they visited first the Senate, then the House of Representatives, and then the Supreme Court. A reporter commented that "faces in Washington are worthwhile studying, and Mr. Seward's, as he escorted Mr. Lincoln through the Capitol to-day, was fairly radiant. The 'irrepressible' senator thinks he has Mr. Lincoln sure, and delights in introducing him to everybody, on the same principle which leads children to display their new toys."[60]

At some point on Saturday or early Sunday, Lincoln provided Seward with a printed draft of the inaugural address and asked for his comments. Seward had been thinking about the address for weeks, writing Lincoln that "it is very important that your inaugural address be wise and winning," by which he meant "winning" to southern moderates. He must have been discouraged by the draft, for in many places it seemed partisan or bellicose. In one passage, Lincoln reminded his audience that he was elected on the Republican platform and "one so elected is not at liberty to shift his position." In the section on Fort Sumter, still in federal possession, and the other southern forts and arsenals, now generally in rebel hands, Lincoln's draft read: "All the power at my disposal will be used to reclaim the public property and places which have fallen; to hold, occupy and possess these, and all other property and places belonging to the government, and to collect the duties on imports; but beyond what may be necessary for these objects, there will be no invasion of any state." In reference to the Supreme Court and the *Dred Scott* decision, Lincoln denounced the "despotism of the few life officers composing the Court." And the last lines of his draft were a direct challenge to the South: "In *your* hands, my dissatisfied fellow countrymen, and not in *mine*, is the momentous issue of civil war. . . . *You* can forbear the *assault* upon [the federal government], I can *not* shrink from the *defense* of it. With *you*, and not with *me*, is the solemn question of 'Shall it be peace, or a sword?' "[61]

Seward immediately started revising Lincoln's draft to make it less partisan and more conciliatory. He numbered each of the more than two hundred lines of the draft, then marked up almost every line, providing Lincoln with more than fifty suggested changes and explaining them in a long cover letter. Seward started the letter by saying that his revisions were "of little importance severally," but were intended "to soothe the public mind." He advised Lincoln to think less about the Republican Party, for "they will be loyal, whatever is said," and focus instead on the "defeated, irritated, angered, frenzied party." In its current form, Lincoln's address would "give such advantages to the Disunionists that Virginia and Maryland will secede, and we shall within ninety, perhaps within sixty, days be obliged to fight the South for this capital, with a divided North for our reliance, and we shall not have one loyal magistrate or ministerial officer south of the Potomac." Lincoln should follow the example of Jefferson after the bitter election of 1800: "Partisan as he was, he sank the partisan in the patriot in his inaugural address, and propitiated his adversaries."[62]

Seward's list of specific changes, numbered to follow the lines of the draft, ran to six pages. He counseled Lincoln to delete the second and third paragraphs, in which Lincoln pledged himself to the Republican platform. Where Lincoln had called southern attacks on federal property "treasonable," Seward proposed the word "revolutionary." He recommended that Lincoln replace the strong sentence about the southern forts with something much softer, suggesting that enforcement of federal laws in the southern states would be tempered by consideration of "the circumstances actually existing, and with a view and a hope of peaceful solution of the national troubles and the restoration of fraternal sympathies and affection." Even though Lincoln's comments about the Supreme Court were similar to those Seward had made a few years back, Seward now deleted them entirely from the draft inaugural.[63]

Seward's most important suggested change came at the end of the draft. As he explained in his cover letter, the speech needed to end with "some words of affection," some words of "calm and cheerful confidence." Seward deleted Lincoln's final sentences, with their threat of war, and provided two alternative drafts. One draft, in Frederick's handwriting, suggested that Lincoln should reaffirm his affection for and commitment to all sections of the nation. The second draft, in Seward's handwriting, with his editing still visible, echoed his speech of a year earlier, about the bonds that tied the Union together:

I close. We are not we must not be aliens or enemies but ~~countrym~~ fellow countrymen and brethren. Although passion has

strained our bonds of affection too hardly they must not ~~be bro-~~
~~ken they will not~~, I am sure they will not be broken. The mystic
chords which proceeding from ~~every ba~~ so many battle fields and
~~patriot~~ so many patriot graves ~~bind~~ pass through all the hearts
and ~~hearths~~ all the hearths in this broad continent of ours will
yet ~~harmon~~ again harmonize in their ancient music when ~~touched~~
~~as they surely~~ breathed upon by the ~~better~~ guardian angel of the
nation.[64]

Seward's cover letter was dated "Sunday evening, February 24," and
he apparently gave it to Lincoln that evening or the next day. Then he
waited, with increasing impatience, for some indication that Lincoln accepted the suggested changes, or at least that he had excised the more
offensive passages. Yet it would appear that Lincoln and Seward did not
discuss the inaugural address during the next week and perhaps not
until *after* the inauguration on March 4. Instead, the week was devoted
to social events and to wrangles about who would be chosen for the
cabinet, including an intense effort to exclude Seward.[65]

———

Lord Lyons reported to the British foreign minister on February 18 that
"a not inconsiderable portion of the Republican party are disposed to
urge Mr. Lincoln to discard Mr. Seward altogether, on account of the
disposition he has already manifested to abandon the extreme anti-
slavery principles of the party." A few days later, an anonymous letter
from Seward's friend John Bigelow appeared in the *New York Evening
Post*: "The attempt to expel Mr. Seward from the Cabinet, futile as it is
likely to prove, is none the less a pregnant fact in the present condition
of the Republican party; and shows either a deliberate purpose to disor-
ganize and break up the party, or simply the selfishness of men who do
not know the consequences of succeeding in what they attempt." The
Albany Evening Journal joined the defense: Seward's opponents "were
ready to dissolve the Union, destroy the government, and bankrupt and
ruin the people to keep Seward out of the cabinet and secure for themselves and their adherents the 'spoils of office.' " The *New York Tribune*

alleged that Seward himself had dictated the letter in the *Evening Post*, and that he "regards himself as the center and soul of the incoming administration, and Mr. Lincoln but as an ornamental appendage thereto." Horace Greeley traveled to Washington to press Lincoln to drop Seward from the cabinet entirely; Weed was in Washington as well, defending Seward and attacking Chase.[66]

The peace convention concluded its work on February 27, recommending a constitutional amendment similar to the Crittenden compromise. Moderate papers rejoiced: the *Washington Evening Star* praised the "glorious result" and the *Albany Evening Journal's* headline read: "Brightly Breaks the Morning." Some expected that Congress would endorse the peace conference proposal and send it to the states for ratification. The Senate referred the proposal to a special committee of five, including Crittenden and Seward, with a request that the committee report the next day. Crittenden and two other senators endorsed the peace convention proposal, but Seward and one colleague were opposed, suggesting instead an immediate constitutional convention. Seward's proposal was similar to that which Chase had pursued in the peace convention, and one reporter noticed that "Mr. Chase was in friendly conversation with Mr. Seward just before that senator presented his proposition." Seward's failure to support the peace convention proposal disappointed and angered some: the *New York Herald* alleged that Seward's course over the past few months had "been a fraud and a cheat, from beginning to end," that he had merely "trifled with" the representatives of the border states. Other papers disagreed; the *New York Evening Post* said that Seward "has never meant to separate from his friends," meaning the Republican Party.[67]

This was a busy week in Washington. The thirty-sixth Congress was trying to wrap up its work, handling issues ranging from the trivial to the momentous. There were many social events as well, notably a grand dinner on February 28, hosted by Seward's friend Representative Elbridge Spaulding, with a guest list including all the men who would soon have cabinet positions: Seward, Chase, Cameron, Welles, Blair, Caleb Smith of Indiana, and Edwin Bates of Missouri, who arrived in town just minutes before the dinner started. Charles Francis Adams, Sr., was also there, but dismissed the dinner in his diary as "quite formal and a little dull." As they were leaving, Adams asked Seward "if things were right at headquarters." Seward answered that "they were not wrong, but they were not quite right." Charles Francis Adams, Jr., who had also recently arrived in Washington, wrote home that he found Seward "thin and worn and much aged since last summer." Seward told young Adams that "the majority of those around him are determined to pull the house down, and he was determined not to let them."[68]

Seward's house was filled with guests in town for the inauguration, including his Auburn friend John Austin. On March 2, Seward entered Austin's room early, cheerily telling him to "rouse up and go to market with me!" Austin complied, and watched in awe as Seward purchased "turtle, birds, ducks, turkeys, fish, pork, beef, tongue, etc. etc." Later that day a group from New York visited the house and Seward spoke to them from the steps. Austin noted that Seward's remarks were "bold and patriotic, yet kind and conciliatory," and that he had "rarely seen a body of men so affected by a speech, as were the New York delegation. Many of them wept like children." He reported a few days later in the *Auburn Daily Advertiser* that Seward's "heart revolts at civil war—at the thought that the land may be drenched with human gore, that brother may stain his hands with the blood of brother." Seward's "great aim and hope" was "to aid in preventing a catastrophe so awful." But his "principles, his devotion to the claims of liberty, he cannot abandon, even to avert evils so great as these." No northern man should believe, Austin insisted, that the Seward of early 1861 was any different from the Seward of 1860: he "is the same true son of freedom now as then."[69]

The struggle over cabinet positions continued up through the eve of the inauguration, with partisans of Seward trying to exclude Chase and partisans of Chase trying to exclude Seward. Some sources suggest that Seward met with Lincoln on March 1 or 2, and told him that "there were differences between himself and Chase which rendered it impossible for them to act in harmony." None of these sources, however, date from 1861, and it seems unlikely there was such a conversation.[70]

Instead, on March 2, Seward delivered to Lincoln a short resignation letter: "Circumstances which have occurred since I expressed to you in December last my willingness to accept the office of secretary of state seem to me to render it my duty to ask you leave to withdraw that consent." Many have viewed this resignation letter as a bluff and praised Lincoln for calling the bluff. The origins of this view date to an 1888 article about Lincoln by his two White House secretaries, John Nicolay and John Hay, in which they quote Lincoln as saying of Seward's letter: "I can't afford to let Seward take the first trick." More recent historians have stressed that Lincoln had not, in the ten days after his arrival, shown Seward any subsequent draft of the inaugural address. Seward thus did not know whether Lincoln had accepted his suggested changes, and more generally did not know what direction Lincoln intended to take in the secession crisis. In this view, Seward's letter was simply a strong way of saying that he was not willing to be part of a bellicose, radical administration; the letter was not a bluff, but an earnest effort to change the tone of Lincoln's inaugural address and the direction of the administration.[71]

Lincoln spent Sunday, March 3, "in comparative retirement, receiving only the visits of Mr. Seward and other intimate friends," according to one news report. If Seward visited Lincoln's hotel on this day, it seems likely they discussed the inaugural address, and this likelihood is supported by a few other bits of evidence. The first is the diary of Charles Francis Adams, Jr., one of Seward's dinner guests that afternoon. Adams noted that Seward was relatively subdued, but remarked to his guests that "he had been reading [the inaugural address] and that while it would [not] satisfy the whole country, it more than covered all his [Seward's] heresies." There is also a later memoir, stating that Seward wanted on March 3 to send an unsigned telegram to Jefferson Davis, to assure him that Lincoln's inaugural address would be conciliatory. Another version of this story, in the memoir of California senator William Gwin, claimed that Seward's friend and neighbor, the lobbyist Sam Ward, kept a draft of this Davis telegram in Seward's own hand.[72]

If the purpose of Seward's resignation letter of March 2 was to pressure Lincoln to moderate the inaugural address, and if Lincoln and Seward conferred about the address on March 3, so that Seward knew the address would be conciliatory, why did he not withdraw his resignation letter? We cannot be sure, but one plausible explanation is that Seward wanted to be certain that Lincoln would indeed deliver a moderate address. Seward knew that other people, especially Chase, wanted Lincoln to take a hard line in the inaugural, and that Lincoln could change his mind in response to their pressure. The back-and-forth on the address is indicated by a letter from an Illinois journalist helping Lincoln with the drafts. The draft address, the journalist wrote to his wife on March 3, "has been modified every day to suit the views of the different members of the cabinet. The amendments are principally verbal and consist of softening some of the words and elaborating more at length some of the ideas contained in the original draft."[73]

At seven o'clock that evening, the Senate gathered for the last session of the thirty-sixth Congress. Seward was present for at least the first part of the evening—he is recorded as voting on a motion to clear the galleries—and thus he probably heard the final Senate speech of John Crittenden—an impassioned plea to enact some form of compromise. After Crittenden spoke, it appears that Seward went home and to bed, for he did not vote at any later time during the all-night session. At about five in the morning of March 4, the Senate adopted the constitutional amendment to prohibit the federal government from interfering with slavery, and thereby opened the amendment for ratification by the states. Seward was not present for the vote, but he supported the amendment, for the wording tracked closely the amendment he had offered in December during the committee deliberations, and that he had urged again in January in his compromise speech. Indeed, one reporter referred to the amendment as the "Seward-Corwin amendment," suggesting that it was the joint product of Senator Seward and Representative Thomas Corwin of Ohio.[74]

———

Seward was up early on inauguration day, March 4. Two newspapers reported that he visited Lincoln at his hotel that morning to discuss the inaugural; other papers missed this meeting, if indeed it occurred. Seward's houseguest Reverend Austin did not mention Seward meeting Lincoln in his detailed account of inauguration day, and it seems likely that he would have noted such a meeting if there was one. Instead, he wrote in his journal that the day "opened cloudy and cheerless," but that at about nine "the sun broke forth bright and glorious," an omen, Austin prayed, of a successful administration. At about this time, a group of two hundred New Yorkers arrived at Seward's house, and Seward spoke to them from his steps. He started by observing that he had reached the end of his twelve years in Congress, "a period which seems in retrospect so short, and yet it has filled up the one-sixth part of the constitutional duration of this great empire." He had tried to represent not merely New York but "every state in every section," and every man and woman, free or slave, in every state. He feared that he had "done little good, indeed, far less than I have wished." But the senator trusted and expected that, under the president's guidance, "and with the blessing of God," the new administration would "close upon a reunited, restored, prosperous, free and happy Republic." A reporter noted that Seward was "greatly affected during the speech," even though he was "frequently applauded."[75]

At about eleven, Seward, accompanied only by his daughter-in-law Anna, left by carriage for the Capitol. He was at his desk on the Senate floor for one last time at about noon, as Vice President Breckinridge and Vice President–elect Hamlin entered, arm-in-arm. Breckinridge administered the oath of office to Hamlin, and after a brief delay Buchanan and Lincoln entered, also arm-in-arm. The whole party then went out in procession to the east side of the Capitol, to the sound of music and the cheers of the crowd. Senator Edward Baker, an old friend of Lincoln's from Illinois, introduced him with a few words, and Lincoln delivered his inaugural address. (The custom at the time was to deliver the address before taking the oath.) Lincoln spoke, according to Austin, in "a clear, ringing voice, and with much dignity and emphasis." He was interrupted a few times by applause, and at the conclusion "such shouts, such huzzahs, arose like mighty thunders, from the immense multitude, as [Austin] never heard before."[76]

As he listened to Lincoln deliver the address, Seward must have been pleased that most of his minor changes to the wording had been accepted, so that the address was less threatening and more conciliatory. Lincoln did not adopt all Seward's changes; he did not delete the sentence about Fort Sumter, for example, although he did delete the threat to reclaim forts in rebel hands. In its final form, this critical sentence read: "The power confided to me will be used to hold, occupy, and possess the property and places belonging to the government, and to collect the duties and imposts; but beyond what may be necessary for these objects, there will be no invasion, no using of force against or among the people anywhere." Lincoln also added several sentences regarding constitutional amendments, one supporting Seward's suggestion of a constitutional convention, and another saying he did not oppose the constitutional amendment just approved by Congress. This change must have been made at the last minute, since only a few hours elapsed between the Senate vote in the early morning and the inaugural at noon. This section may have been the result of a discussion between Lincoln and Seward, but it is also quite possible that there were no consultations that morning, that Seward learned the final form of the address only as he heard it delivered.[77]

Seward's most important suggestion had been to change the conclusion, and here Lincoln heeded his advice. He started with—and improved upon—Seward's handwritten paragraph about the mystic chords, passing through hearts and hearths, that bound the Union:

> I am loth to close. We are not enemies, but friends. We must not be enemies. Though passion may have strained, it must not break our bonds of affection. The mystic chords of memory, stretching from every battle-field, and patriot grave, to every living hearth and hearthstone, all over this broad land, will yet swell the chorus of the Union, when again touched, as surely they will be, by the better angels of our nature.

After Lincoln finished speaking, followed by another brief flourish of music, Chief Justice Roger Taney administered the oath of office and Lincoln was officially president.[78]

At some point in the early afternoon, Seward received a short note from the new president, asking him to reconsider his resignation. The public interest demanded Seward's services and "my personal feelings are deeply enlisted in the same direction." Lincoln asked him to respond by nine o'clock the next morning, the day on which Lincoln would have to submit his cabinet list to the Senate. Seward did not wait that long: he went to the White House in the early evening, met with Lincoln, and told him that he would serve. In a confirming letter to Lincoln the next day, Seward wrote that he had yielded to the "opinions and wishes as expressed in your letter of yesterday and in our conversation of last evening." In a letter to his wife, he explained that the president was "determined to have a compound cabinet," that is, one with disparate views, and that Lincoln hoped the cabinet would be "peaceful and even permanent." Seward was "at one time on the point of refusing—nay I did refuse, for a time, to hazard myself in the experiment. But a distracted country appeared before me; and I withdrew from that position." He did not "dare to go home, or to England, and leave the country to chance." Weed, who was in Washington in early March, related a slightly different version of these events a few weeks later to the New York lawyer John Bigelow. As Bigelow wrote it in his diary, Lincoln told Seward that "he could not get on without his help and begged him to hold on." After considering the issue overnight, Seward accepted on inauguration day, at which time the president "gave him to understand that whatever others might say or do, they two would not disagree but were friends."[79]

At about ten o'clock on the evening of inauguration day, Seward, accompanied by Frederick and Anna, left home to attend the inaugural ball. At Seward's suggestion, this was termed a "Union ball," and he had persuaded some leading members of other parties, including Edward Everett, the former senator from Massachusetts who had been the Constitutional Union candidate for vice president, to attend. Democratic senator Stephen Douglas, who had courted Mary Todd before Lincoln married her, accompanied Mary onto the dance floor when she arrived. Newspapers saw the presence of so many non-Republicans in the crowd as a hopeful sign of cooperation. As for Seward, one reporter noted that, "pale as a ghost, [he] moved timidly and shrinkingly through the throng." The reporter could not recall another inaugural ball at which there was "so little of joy, confidence, hope or congratulation."[80]

In the early afternoon of the next day, March 5, the president transmitted to the Senate his nominations for cabinet, including William Henry Seward. Within a few hours, with almost no discussion, the Senate confirmed all the nominations. Early the next morning, Seward went to the State Department, accompanied by Frederick, whose own nomination as assistant secretary of state, the number two position in the department, was submitted and confirmed later that day. There was thus almost no break between the end of one long phase of Seward's life, his twelve years as senator, and the start of another lengthy phase, his eight years as secretary of state.[81]

———

Was Seward a successful senator? If one looks only at his legislative record, it was not especially impressive. Many of the key laws passed during the twelve years he served, such as the Compromise of 1850 and the Kansas-Nebraska Act of 1854, were measures Seward strongly opposed. In the last few months of his Senate career, when many people looked to Seward to organize the Compromise of 1861, he would not commit himself to any one compromise plan. Some of the measures he strongly favored, such as legislation to support a transcontinental railroad or to encourage homesteads, did not pass while he was a senator. And the few measures of which Seward *was* the legislative parent, such as the subsidy for Field's telegraph and the guano islands bill, were comparatively modest, albeit with important long-term effects.

From another perspective, however, Seward was a good senator, perhaps even a great one. Senator Seward had a vision for the American empire: an immense empire, to which other parts of North America would gradually and willingly adhere; an interconnected empire, linked by canals and rails and telegraphs; an international empire, with strong trade ties to both Europe and Asia; a prosperous empire, with modern farms and factories; an open empire, one in which immigrants were welcomed and over time assimilated; a democratic empire, with key decisions made by the people's elected representatives in Washington; and a free labor empire, in which slavery would not exist in the national territories and would slowly and peacefully disappear in the southern states. Seward was not the author of all of these ideas, but he was their most prominent and articulate proponent in his decade in the Senate. The main legacy of his years as senator was this vision of American empire, a vision he would try to implement during his years as secretary of state, and a vision which would persist for many years thereafter.

Any assessment of Seward as senator has to consider in particular his work during the four months of the secession winter. Henry Adams, who observed Seward at firsthand, and who coined the term "secession winter," praised him to the skies. The senator was "cheerful where everyone else was in despair; cool and steady where everyone else was panic struck; clear-sighted where other men were blind." He avoided "harsh contact with all men, and steer[ed] with a firm and steady grasp between his friends who were ready to denounce him, and his enemies who were eager to destroy him." In sum, Seward "fought, during these three months of chaos, a fight which might go down in history as one of the wonders of statesmanship."[82]

Adams did not note, but he should have, that Seward was also at times during that winter arrogant, boastful, evasive, inconsistent, even dishonest. He talked about compromise with moderates and deprecated compromise with hard-liners. Other historians have faulted Seward for "greatly underestimat[ing] the force and stamina of the secession movement" and for "incredible blindness" in believing that reconciliation was still possible. Allan Nevins, writing in the late 1950s, when "appeasement" was the ultimate insult, called Seward's secession winter policy one of "appeasement." Seward, according to Nevins, "thought that any storm, even this, could be controlled by cunning management, party bargains, and dextrous maneuvering; he did not realize that he was facing men in deadly earnest, whose determination was fixed, and was dealing with a movement far too powerful for mere shrewd manipulation." But Nevins failed to distinguish between the most ardent secessionists—whom Seward knew were beyond persuasion—and the more moderate border state men—whom he hoped to keep in the Union in some way, and whose states did remain in the Union on inauguration day and for a while thereafter. Moreover, even if there was no way to avoid a civil war, were not Seward's efforts to find such a way necessary and praiseworthy? Henry Adams observed that Seward's conciliatory policy during the secession winter, "like all such attempts at wisdom and moderation in times of heated passions and threatening war," was soon "swallowed up and crushed under the weight of brute force." Yet, as Adams commented, "it is right to make the effort even if overruled."[83]

Perhaps the best way to assess Seward's work in this period is to descend from grand generalizations and look at details. The Virginia vote on February 4 ensured that the state would remain in the Union at least for another month or two, because even if the convention voted to secede, its vote would not take effect until after another general election. Virginia's vote not only saved the largest border state for a few critical weeks; it influenced other border states as well. Seward, through his speeches, through his work with Douglas and Crittenden, and through his contacts with key Virginians, helped to secure the Unionist victory in this critical election. Lincoln's safe arrival in Washington on February 23 was another turning point, and it was Seward who (through his son) persuaded Lincoln to change his plans, avoiding a public passage through Baltimore. We know today that there was a serious threat in Baltimore, that Lincoln might well have been killed or wounded if he had adhered to his original plans. The inaugural address on March 4 was also a critical moment. If the president had given the address in its original form, with its threatening final sentences, he would have strengthened those in the border states pressing for immediate secession. Seward provided Lincoln with the essence of his final paragraph, a poetic and conciliatory conclusion. Seward may not have saved the Union during the secession winter, as some have suggested, but on these and other occasions he made essential contributions to keeping the peace and maintaining the Union through inauguration day.[84]

CHAPTER 10

"I Must Do It":

March–April 1861

T he State Department of the Civil War era was not a large organization. The staff in Washington consisted of only thirty
clerks and a few translators; the overseas staff included thirty-
five ministers and about three hundred consuls, most of them unpaid
and part time. The Washington staff worked in a modest brick building
on the corner of Fifteenth Street and Pennsylvania Avenue, just north
of the larger and more elegant Treasury building. Indeed, the old State
building was already slated for demolition, to make room for expansion of the Treasury. The State Department was only a few steps from
the White House, and only a few steps from the house that Seward had
rented, but not yet occupied, on the east side of Lafayette Park.[1]

According to Frederick Seward's memoir, Lincoln told his father just
before inauguration that "there is one part of my work that I shall have
to leave largely to you. I shall have to depend upon you for taking care
of these matters of foreign affairs, of which I know so little, and with
which I reckon you are familiar." Seward was indeed more familiar
with foreign affairs than almost any Republican leader: he had traveled
widely, at a time when few Americans ventured abroad, and he had
served for the past four years on the Senate Foreign Relations Committee. Frederick's recollection is consistent with other comments Lincoln
made in early 1861. Rudolf Schleiden, the minister in Washington for the

German state of Bremen, reported in early March that Lincoln confessed to him that "I don't know anything about diplomacy. I will be very apt to make blunders." The historian John Lothrop Motley described in a letter to his wife a conversation with Lincoln in which the president said, of a foreign affairs question, "it does not so much signify what I think, you must persuade Seward to think as you do."[2]

On his first morning in his new office, the first person with whom Seward spoke was the chief clerk, William Hunter, who had served the department since 1829, and who would go on to serve until 1886. Frederick Seward, as assistant secretary, was number two in the department, but Hunter as chief clerk was number three, and with his long service he was already, according to Frederick, "an indispensable component part of its existence." Seward explained to Hunter that although in theory he could fire every clerk in the department and replace them from some of the hundreds of office seekers in Washington, he would not do so. He would insist, however, on absolute loyalty to the Union, and he quickly dismissed a few southern sympathizers. Those who remained on the staff through the war, Frederick recalled, were capable, experienced, and completely committed to the Union.[3]

Lincoln and Seward faced a far more difficult and important task in staffing the overseas side of the department. The ministers in foreign capitals were the government's eyes, ears, and voices abroad. The difficulties and delays of communication between Washington and foreign capitals, and the small size of the foreign missions, meant that the secretary of state depended heavily upon the ministers themselves, both as sources of information and as spokesmen for the United States. The loyalty of many of the ministers in place in early 1861 was questionable. In Paris, the U.S. minister was Charles Faulkner of Virginia, later arrested for arranging arms sales to the Confederacy; in Madrid, the minister was William Preston of Kentucky, later a Confederate general. All of this would suggest that Lincoln and Seward needed to appoint promptly a new set of loyal, intelligent, and industrious diplomats.[4]

Politics, however, interfered. American ministers in major foreign capitals were well paid: $17,500 per year in the case of the ministers in London and Paris, and $12,000 per year in the case of seven other posts. (Seward's salary as secretary of state was only $8,000.) Ministerial positions were also prestigious, eagerly sought by senators, representatives, editors, and political leaders. Whether a man spoke the local language, whether he could conduct a delicate negotiation, did not matter much; what mattered was whether he had political connections. As the *New York Tribune* observed a few years earlier, perhaps with some exaggeration, "diplomacy is the sewer through which flows the scum and refuse of the political puddle. A man not fit to stay at home is just the man to send abroad." An Alabama congressman, opposing an appropriation for the diplomatic service, complained that "our whole mission system is one grand humbug," intended mainly "to provide places for placemen, and to extend the patronage of the executive department."[5]

Lincoln's first diplomatic nomination was of his friend Norman Judd—the man who had arranged the seating at the Chicago convention to hamper Seward—to be the minister in Berlin. This cannot have been pleasant for Seward, but he did not object; he knew that he would have to pick his battles with care. On March 11, Lincoln wrote to Seward regarding four important ministerial posts: London, Paris, Madrid, and Mexico City. He suggested William Dayton, senator from New Jersey, for London; John Frémont, former senator and presidential candidate, for Paris; Cassius M. Clay, Kentucky abolitionist, for Madrid; and Thomas Corwin, congressman from Ohio, for Mexico City. "We need to have these points guarded as strongly and quickly as possible," Lincoln noted. Seward agreed on Clay and Corwin but questioned Frémont and Dayton. He feared that Frémont would bring prestige but nothing else to the post, and suggested instead that Dayton be sent to Paris. As to London, the most important post of all, Seward was adamant on Charles Francis Adams. He told Lincoln that Adams was "infinitely more watchful, capable, efficient, [and] reliable" than any other candidate. Moreover, New England was an important base for the Republican Party, while Dayton's state of "New Jersey gives us little, and that grudgingly."[6]

A week later, Lincoln wrote Seward again: they were agreed on Adams for London, Dayton for Paris, and two other European posts. Still unresolved was the question of Carl Schurz and "our German friends." Schurz, formerly a German revolutionary and now a leader of the German-American Republicans, arrived in Washington in early March determined to obtain for himself a major European post. Seward quite sensibly opposed the idea of sending a former revolutionary to a central European court, but Schurz and his allies believed they deserved a reward for their role in Lincoln's election. Schurz also hoped to break what he called "Seward's power over Lincoln," a "fatal influence" on the whole administration. There was a stormy meeting among Lincoln, Seward, and Schurz, at which Schurz refused to abandon his claim. Soon, however, Lincoln devised a solution: they would ask Cassius Clay to be minister to Russia, rather than Spain, and then appoint Schurz to Spain. Schurz exulted that "Seward's influence has been defeated, and I am master of the battlefield. There is rejoicing wherever the report has gone." At least one other observer agreed; a Massachusetts Radical wrote that it was "a source of congratulation today *among Seward's opponents* that he has suffered the first serious defeat which he has yet experienced in respect to any appointment—in the instance of Schurz, against whom for a European mission he had made an especial point."[7]

Schurz was only one of several anti-Seward men whom Lincoln appointed to senior foreign positions. James Shepherd Pike, the correspondent who had organized the meeting of congressmen opposed to Seward's inclusion in the cabinet, was appointed as the new American minister to the Netherlands. George Fogg, the editor who had written to Lincoln that Seward's appointment was a "mistake," was made the minister to Switzerland. But there were also a number of Seward men appointed to key foreign posts. Seward's friend James Watson Webb, the New York editor with whom he had worked since his first campaign for governor, wanted a European position but settled for minister to Brazil. John Bigelow, a friend with political, language, and academic skills, was appointed consul to Paris, where he would prove an invaluable backstop to the older and weaker Dayton. Henry Sanford, originally from Connecticut but now almost European because of his long residence there, was at Seward's suggestion appointed minister to Belgium.[8]

The struggle for foreign appointments involved not only the applicants themselves but also their political patrons. Treasury Secretary Salmon Chase wrote Seward to attack the appointment of a man from Maine, rather than from Chase's native Ohio, to be the consul general in London. "I think Ohio fairly entitled both as a state and as a Republican state to a fair share of the diplomatic appointments." Chase calculated

Ohio's share as being thirty-three of the appointments, and noted point-
edly that to date it had received only thirteen. Chase may well have
been behind an article that appeared a few days later in the *Cincinnati
Daily Gazette*, stating that Lincoln would allocate consular posts among
the states in accordance with their populations. Fortunately, Lincoln
never imposed such a procrustean framework.[9]

Seward and Chase clashed even more dramatically over the appointment of Chase's brother Edward as federal marshal for the northern
district of New York. Before raising the subject with Seward, Chase secured the support of Attorney General Edward Bates and several New
York members of Congress. He claimed in a letter to Seward that even
Seward had told him you should "insist on your brother." Seward responded that he had said no such thing; he had simply asked whether
Chase intended to insist upon his brother. Chase, Seward wrote him,
was just seeking a personal favor, but if Seward assented to the appointment, it would be "infidelity to party and friends." Chase replied
that he would not abandon his brother "or consent that the decision of
the Attorney General in his favor shall be rescinded." Seward, equally
outraged, wrote to Lincoln that "when Mr. Chase out of his department
demands as a personal favor an appointment in my state humiliating
to me, or the Attorney General assumes that he can better determine
who should be marshal in the very district in which I live, the thing becomes a scandal." Seward said he would "sooner attack either of those
gentlemen in the open street" than "oppose any local appointment they
might desire to make in their respective states." But perhaps because
he remembered his own troubles as governor, Seward added that he
would "cheerfully bear whatever you [Lincoln] require." The issue was
solved by naming Seward's candidate as minister to Nicaragua and
Chase's brother as marshal in New York, with the nominations carefully paired so the Senate could not approve one without approving the
other.[10]

Seward had his own family appointment to push through, that of
his son Augustus as an Army paymaster. Several months earlier, even
before he knew the election results, Augustus had written from his
remote New Mexico fort asking his father to secure him such an appointment. Augustus noted that he had watched as some of his West

Point classmates with Democratic connections had secured political promotions; if the Republicans gained power, Augustus wanted his own promotion. He followed this up with several letters—mail was erratic so he could not be sure his father had received his request—and one of the first letters Seward wrote to Lincoln after the inauguration asked for a conference to discuss a paymaster post. Frances feared that her husband was too polite, so she wrote herself from Auburn to Secretary of War Simon Cameron, pressing him to make the appointment. Cameron wrote back to assure her that Augustus would receive the post, adding: "In doing this I have had an opportunity of returning one of the many acts of personal civility received from your husband." [11]

Another early clash among Seward, Chase, and others involved a vacant seat on the Supreme Court. On the morning after the inauguration, apparently without speaking with Lincoln, Seward asked Edwin Stanton, still serving as attorney general, to draw up papers to nominate John Crittenden to the Supreme Court. By nominating the most visible congressional advocate of compromise to the Court, Seward hoped to send a signal to the border states that the administration would favor compromise. Stanton prepared the papers and submitted them to Lincoln. Almost immediately, Lincoln learned that Chase and several Republican senators objected. Chase was concerned that Crittenden was a Whig rather than a Republican, and Chase did not want to send a conciliatory signal. Lincoln did not sign or submit the nomination papers, explaining to one reporter that "he will not make any appointment which will be calculated to divide the Republicans in the Senate, as he desires to so act as to consolidate and strengthen the party." Seward did not give up on the idea of appointing moderate border state men. After the Crittenden proposal failed, he suggested to Lincoln that he consider George Summers, a prominent Virginia Unionist, for the vacant Supreme Court seat. At the end of the month, Seward forwarded to Lincoln a letter from the Maryland governor saying that "everything depends upon proper appointments to leading positions in border states." [12]

Even more coveted than a seat on the Court was the position of collector of customs for the port of New York. Not only did the collector receive thousands of dollars in salary and fees himself, but he appointed more than a thousand other men, who would return a small percentage of their income for political purposes. The struggle over this prized position started early, with Thurlow Weed leading the Seward forces, and William Cullen Bryant, editor of the *New York Evening Post*, and Horace Greeley, editor of the *New York Tribune*, leading the anti-Seward forces. Weed tried to persuade people, the *New York Herald* reported, that he was "the person that will deal out the soup for New York, and every person who is expecting to share in the good things of Lincoln's administration from the Empire State must apply through him." This led Lincoln to remind Weed that his approach would be "justice to all." As the struggle intensified in March, the *Cincinnati Daily Commercial* commented that "whether Fort Sumter shall be reinforced or surrendered, is less bruited than whether the strongholds of the New York custom house, post offices, etc. shall be surrendered to the 'irrepressibles' or held on to by the 'conservatives.'" Weed was disappointed when Lincoln nominated Hiram Barney, a leader of the anti-Seward faction, as collector of customs. In general, however, Seward and Weed controlled most of the New York appointments, to the dismay of Chase and their other opponents.[13]

Seward complained several times in March 1861 that Lincoln was devoting too much time to patronage. The president "takes that business up first which is pressed upon him most," Seward wrote his wife. "Solicitants for office besiege him, and he of course finds his hands full for the present." He told the senior Adams, when the minister visited Washington for a few days in late March, that Lincoln had "no conception of his situation—much absorption in the details of office dispensation, but little application to great ideas." These criticisms were somewhat unfair because Seward himself spent much of that month, during which the Senate was in special session, on patronage questions, especially foreign posts. As Frederick wrote home to his mother, "the rush for office is overwhelming. It begins at seven in the morning and lasts till late at night, grudging us even the time necessary for eating and sleeping, and to venture out in the street, even so far as from the house to the department, is to run the gauntlet of half a dozen aspirants for consulates in the Mediterranean or the Sandwich Islands."[14]

Lincoln met for the first time with his cabinet on the evening of March 6, in his second-floor office in the White House. Seward knew each of the men in the room. Salmon Chase, now Treasury secretary, had worked with him on the Van Zandt case fifteen years earlier and had corresponded with him in the intervening years. When Edward Bates, the attorney general, a Missouri Whig, had arrived in Washington a few days earlier, his first meeting was with Seward, who invited him to be his guest until his own house was arranged. Simon Cameron, the secretary of war, was the man whom Seward had visited twice in the hope of securing the delegates of Pennsylvania. Outsiders viewed Cameron as a Seward ally in the cabinet, but Seward's view of Cameron was more cautious; certainly they were not close personal friends. Gideon Welles, the secretary of the Navy, was a former Democrat from Connecticut, a leading editor there, and another person who had opposed the nomination of Seward for president and his inclusion in the Lincoln cabinet. Montgomery Blair, the postmaster general, was the son of Francis Preston Blair, with whom Seward had traveled to Canada during the summer of 1857. Seward knew the father better than the son, but he knew both Blairs. Finally, there was Caleb Smith, the secretary of the interior, another former Whig, a lawyer from Indianapolis, whom Seward may have met as early as 1849, when they overlapped at the end of Smith's and the start of Seward's congressional careers.[15]

This first cabinet meeting was, Bates noted in his diary, "formal and introductory only—in fact, uninteresting." Lincoln and Seward did not reveal to the whole cabinet the dramatic news they had received in the past two days: that Major Robert Anderson had reported that his limited supplies at Fort Sumter would run out within a few weeks, and that new southern defenses in Charleston Harbor would make it difficult or impossible to resupply the fort. The head of the Army, General Winfield Scott, advised Lincoln bluntly that "I see no alternative now but surrender" of the fort. Lincoln was understandably surprised and distressed by this news, for although Fort Sumter had been mentioned in the northern papers almost daily during January and February, nothing in the public reports had suggested that the situation was so precarious. Lincoln had just promised in his inaugural address that he would use all available power to "hold, occupy and possess" the few remaining federal forts in southern territory. Would he have to start his term by breaking his word?[16]

From Seward's perspective, the news from Anderson was less distressing because he had been thinking for weeks about the possibility of yielding Sumter as a way of placating the border states. There was a new reason to think about this possibility: Martin Crawford and John Forsyth, two of three commissioners appointed by the Confederate government to negotiate the separation of the Confederacy and the Union, had just arrived in Washington. Seward learned through his friend and neighbor Sam Ward that the commissioners intended to apply to the State Department to be formally received as representatives of a foreign nation. The commissioners told Ward that if their application was rejected, their government would probably not be able to prevent the angry residents of Charleston from attacking Fort Sumter.[17]

In one of their frequent letters to Robert Toombs, the secretary of state of the new Confederate government, the commissioners reported that Seward was boasting to friends that he had "built up the Republican party" and "brought it to triumph." Now, to save the party and the government, "war must be averted, the negro question must be dropped, the irrepressible conflict ignored, and a Union party, to embrace the border slave states, inaugurated." The commissioners also informed Toombs that, in a speech on March 7, Senator Stephen Douglas said that it was "admitted by all military men that [Fort Sumter] cannot be reinforced now, even by the use of the whole American Navy, without at least an army of ten thousand men on land to cooperate." Douglas added that "I believe it is admitted that there is not bread and salt enough in the fort to last more than thirty-one days." The details Douglas revealed were not known by many people; they were probably provided by his friend Seward, eager to reassure the border states.[18]

The full cabinet met again on March 9, when Scott and other military officers briefed the cabinet members on Fort Sumter. Bates recorded that he was "astounded" to hear that Sumter "must be evacuated." Within a few days, the news that Sumter would be surrendered was on the front pages of the nation's papers. The Boston Atlas & Bee declared that "there is little doubt that the government will order the evacuation of Fort Sumter." Radical Republicans greeted these reports with rage. Charles

Francis Adams noted in his diary that Seward had told him that "the violent remonstrances from the North and East against the abandonment of Fort Sumter had alarmed the President and delayed a decision. But circumstances must force it, and the only difference in the delay would be to destroy the effect it might otherwise produce as a voluntary act."[19]

At a meeting on March 15, the cabinet heard both from Gustavus Fox, a former naval officer now serving as adviser to Lincoln, who believed that it would be possible to use speed and darkness to get supplies in to Fort Sumter, and from General Scott, who had grave doubts about Fox's plan. At the end of the meeting, Lincoln asked the cabinet members for their written views: "assuming it to be possible to now provision Fort Sumter, under all the circumstances, is it wise to attempt it?" Seward's answer was an absolute no. He reminded the president that the ties binding the border states to the Union were tenuous; that a federal attack on Fort Sumter would quickly drive the border states into the Confederacy; that an armed attempt to provide arms and troops to the fort would be perceived as an attack; and that this would likely lead to civil war. The proper policy was delay. That would provide time for the "blind unreasoning popular excitement" in the South to subside, and for "devotion to the Union" to reassert itself, even in South Carolina. Near the end of his long letter Seward asked himself (as Lincoln probably asked him) whether there were any circumstances in which he would advise the use of force. Yes: Seward would use the Navy "to protect the collection of the revenue, because this is a necessary as well as a legitimate Union object." Ideally, any use of force should be defensive, so that the first blows were struck by "those who seek to dismember and subvert this Union." In this way, "we should have the spirit of the country and the approval of mankind on our side."[20]

Almost all the other cabinet members agreed with Seward in advising Lincoln against an attempt to reinforce Fort Sumter; only Blair disagreed. Seward believed, not unreasonably, that the Sumter issue had been decided, that Lincoln would now issue orders to evacuate the fort, since in Seward's words "without supplies the garrison must yield in a few days to starvation." He relayed some form of this news to the Virginian leader George Summers. A few days later, Summers reported indirectly to Seward from Richmond that the news of the imminent evacuation of Fort Sumter had "worked like a charm," allowing the Unionists to keep control over the ongoing state convention, which they hoped to end without a vote one way or the other on secession.[21]

On the same day as the cabinet meeting, March 15, Supreme Court justices Samuel Nelson and John Campbell visited Seward and advised him to receive and negotiate with the Confederate commissioners. Seward told them that he could not do this—it would essentially recognize the Confederacy as a legitimate foreign nation, and besides, "the surrender of Sumter is enough to deal with." The justices were instantly intrigued by Seward's remark, and Campbell offered not only to speak with the commissioners but also to write to their mutual friend Jefferson Davis, the new Confederate president. What, Campbell asked Seward, should he say to Davis? As Campbell later recalled, Seward started to answer, then asked how far it was to the Confederate capital in Montgomery, Alabama. Told it would take three days for a letter to reach there, Seward continued: "You may say to him that before that letter reaches him, the telegraph will have informed him that Sumter shall have been evacuated." The commissioners, hearing this from Campbell, were somewhat doubtful, but they were content to wait. They believed that delay would allow time for the Confederate government to strengthen itself and its army, just as Seward believed that delay would build up Union sentiment in the southern and border states.[22]

Seward may have viewed the cabinet meeting on March 15 and the responses to Lincoln's question as deciding the fate of Fort Sumter, but Lincoln did not. Lincoln knew that the fort had no military value but that it had immense symbolic value, for both North and South, as a Union fort in the very city where secession had started. Would surrendering the fort, as Seward predicted, strengthen Union sentiment in the border states, and ultimately lead to a peaceful restoration of the Union? Or would giving up the fort, as Blair predicted, merely encourage the Confederates, and thereby harden and perpetuate the division of the Union? To gather more information, Lincoln sent three men to Charleston: Gustavus Fox to assess the military situation of Fort Sumter; and Stephen Hurlbut and Ward Hill Lamon, friends from Illinois, to assess the political situation.[23]

Seward's comment about collecting federal revenues points to another problem, in many ways more serious than Fort Sumter, that the president and his administration now faced. The antebellum federal government was funded almost entirely by import duties. The southern states, as they seceded, continued to collect duties, but they kept the money for their own purposes rather than remitting it to Washington. Since the southern ports were not especially important in the nation's trade pattern, the federal government could perhaps forgo this revenue. But the trade pattern itself seemed likely to change, perhaps dramatically, perhaps immediately. A new and lower Confederate tariff would take effect on April 1. After that, the *New York Herald* predicted, "it will be cheaper for St. Louis and Cincinnati to import their goods via Savannah or New Orleans than via New York." It would be impossible, the *New York Evening Post* noted, for the United States to collect its tariff at the border with the Confederacy; the border was simply too long and too porous. Lincoln could perhaps face the political consequences of losing or surrendering Fort Sumter, but if the trade pattern changed so that goods entered through southern ports, without paying federal duties, the North would lose a large fraction of the federal revenue. The Treasury was nearly empty; congressional representatives had not been paid their salaries for months. So the potential loss of tariff revenue was an immediate, dramatic threat to the federal government.[24]

On March 18, Lincoln asked several cabinet members whether it would be legal and practical to use naval ships to collect the tariff outside southern ports. For some reason he did not pose this question to Seward, even though the secretary of state was learning that this approach would raise serious foreign policy questions. The British minister Lord Lyons warned Seward that if the United States tried "to stop by force so important a commerce as that of Great Britain with the cotton-growing states," it would lead to considerable domestic pressure within the United Kingdom to recognize the Confederacy. Lyons also reminded Seward of the position that the United States had recently taken with respect to a similar situation in Peru: that a foreign ship trading with a port controlled by a *de facto* government owed no tariff to the *de jure* government. This approach had served American interests in Peru, allowing Americans to trade with contested ports, but the precedent now threatened much more vital interests at home, for it would prevent the northern government from collecting duties outside the ports of the *de facto* southern government. Lyons inferred from Seward's comments that the government was considering "forcible collection of the duties in the southern ports" and also "a blockade of these ports." Lyons guessed (incorrectly) that Seward himself was opposed to both proposals.[25]

A few days later, on March 25, Lyons hosted a dinner party at which Seward, the French minister Henri Mercier, and the Russian minister Edouard de Stoeckl were present. Seward, according to the report by Lyons, alluded to the Peruvian precedent and announced that "I differ with my predecessor as to *de facto* authorities. If one of your ships comes out of a southern port without the papers required by the laws of the United States, and is seized by one of our cruisers and carried into New York and confiscated, we shall not make any compensation." Stoeckl reminded Seward of the well-known principle of international law: that a blockade had to be effective in order to be legitimate. Seward replied that what the United States had in mind was not a blockade—not an attempt to close the southern ports to all trade—but rather the use of naval vessels to collect duties from the ongoing trade in these ports. Lyons said that Seward's approach "seemed to me to amount to a paper [ineffective] blockade of the enormous extent of coast comprised in the seceding states" and would place the foreign powers "in the dilemma of recognizing the southern confederation or of submitting to the interruption of their commerce." At this, Seward lost his temper, or at least seemed to do so; Mercier and Lyons both reported that Seward nearly shouted. His anger, though, was understandable, for Seward knew his history. He knew that the critical moment in the American Revolution was when France recognized the United States as an independent nation; and he knew that if the Confederacy could secure recognition from a few major European powers, it would be essentially impossible to knit the American Union back together. His most important task as secretary of state was to prevent European recognition of the Confederacy, and if an occasional secretarial outburst was necessary to warn the Europeans against recognition, so be it.[26]

———

William Russell, a war correspondent for *The Times* of London already famous for his Crimean War reports, arrived in Washington on March 26. That evening, both Russell and Seward were dinner guests of Henry Sanford, the cosmopolitan Connecticut merchant just confirmed as the American minister to Belgium. In the book he published two years later, Russell described his initial impressions of Seward: a "slight, middle-sized man of feeble build, with the stoop contracted from sedentary habits and application to the desk." Seward was also "a subtle, quick man, rejoicing in power, given to perorate and to oracular utterances, fond of badinage [and] bursting with the importance of state mysteries." On this evening, Seward contradicted the recent newspaper reports that orders had already been given to evacuate Fort Sumter, insisting that "we will give up nothing that we have—abandon nothing that has been entrusted to us."[27]

Seward was telling a very different story to the Confederate commissioners, who were asking why the evacuation of Fort Sumter, which he had essentially promised them ten days earlier, had still not occurred. Through yet another intermediary, the Russian minister Stoeckl, Seward explained that he believed the southern states "would be permitted to depart in peace," but that he needed more time. As the commissioners put it in one of their reports, Seward said that "the Senate had not yet adjourned, he had to fight the ultra Republicans of his own party, he was daily gaining ground and would ultimately succeed, [but] the difficulties with which he was surrounded should be taken into consideration." Seward asked Stoeckl to arrange an informal meeting for him with one of the commissioners at the Russian's house; but then the next day Seward backed out, explaining to Stoeckl that he could not risk the possible press coverage.[28]

When Russell visited Seward at the State Department on March 27, he found the secretary in his office, a room of moderate size, "surrounded with book shelves and ornamented with a few engravings," comfortably "seated at his table and enjoying a cigar." Seward took the reporter across to the White House to introduce him to Lincoln, and that evening Russell dined with Seward at his home. Russell found, much as Lyons and Mercier were finding, that Seward's attitude toward the European nations "almost amounts to arrogance and menace." He insisted, for example, that "the southern commissioners who had been sent abroad could not be received by the government of any foreign power without incurring the risk of breaking off relations with the government of the United States." Seward was again taking a hard line against European recognition of the Confederacy, but it would have been more effective if he had delivered this message through American ministers abroad, rather than through a reporter. At almost this same time, however, he agreed that Charles Francis Adams could delay his departure for England until May 1, to allow Adams time to attend a family wedding. As the younger Charles Francis Adams would observe fifty years later, given the difficult domestic and international situation, it was inexcusable for Seward to allow Adams to "dawdle away weeks of precious time because of such a trifle." [29]

The next evening, March 28, Lincoln hosted his first state dinner. The guests included the cabinet members and several family members. While waiting for the arrival of the last few members of the party, Seward took Russell around "and introduced me to the ministers, and to their wives and daughters, among the latter Miss [Kate] Chase, who is very attractive, agreeable, and sprightly." The seating chart for the dinner party, in the neat handwriting of Lincoln's secretary John Nicolay, shows that there were about thirty people around the large table, with Secretary Seward seated between Lincoln's wife Mary and Chase's daughter Kate. One can readily imagine Seward amusing young Kate with his stories; one can also easily imagine the coldness between Seward and Mary, raised in a southern slaveowning family, who viewed Seward as an "abolition sneak." [30]

After dinner was over, as the guests were leaving, Lincoln asked his cabinet members to join him in another room. There he summarized for them a memorandum he had just received from General Scott, advising that it now seemed unlikely that "the voluntary evacuation of Fort Sumter alone would have a decisive effect upon the states now wavering between adherence to the Union and secession." Scott urged that Fort Pickens in Florida as well as Fort Sumter be surrendered in order to "give confidence to the eight remaining slave-holding states." Most of the cabinet members were stunned, although not Seward; the memorandum likely reflected conversations between Seward and Scott. Montgomery Blair later wrote that, after a silence, he told Lincoln and the others that Scott was "playing the part of the politician, not of a general," since no one believed there was any military reason to surrender the well-defended Fort Pickens. Blair did not need to remind his colleagues of Scott's reputation as the pawn of Seward.[31]

The cabinet met at noon on March 29, to consider not only Scott's memo but also the reports of the men whom Lincoln had sent to Charleston. Gustavus Fox said that the troops at Fort Sumter could survive on half-rations until April 15; he also believed that his plan to supply the fort with tugboats was workable. According to Stephen Hurlbut, "there is no attachment to the Union" among the residents of South Carolina; for them, the separate nationality of the Confederacy was a "fixed fact." Hurlbut advised that South Carolina would fight any attempt to send provisions, much less men or arms, to Fort Sumter. Lincoln and the cabinet were aware that northern public opinion was also growing harder. The day before, which was the last day of the special Senate session, Senator Lyman Trumbull of Illinois had introduced a resolution stating that "the true way to preserve the Union is to enforce the laws of the Union" and that "it is the duty of the President to use all the means in his power to hold and protect the public property of the United States and enforce the laws thereof." Trumbull's resolution did not pass—it was not even voted upon—but it underlined that there were now many Republicans who would insist on holding the forts and collecting the tariffs even if this course led to civil war.[32]

At this March 29 cabinet meeting, Lincoln again asked for views on whether to attempt to provision Fort Sumter. In light of the changing circumstances, it is not surprising that a number of the secretaries changed their minds, and favored sending the provisions. Welles suggested that Lincoln should notify South Carolina of his intent: "Armed resistance to a peaceable attempt to send provisions to one of our own forts will justify the government in using all the power at its command, to reinforce the garrison and furnish the necessary supplies." Chase viewed civil war as inevitable and thought it would be well to have it begin "in consequence of military resistance to the efforts of the administration to sustain troops of the Union stationed, under the authority of the

government in a fort of the Union, in the ordinary course of service."
Seward was one of only two cabinet members to argue in his letter
to Lincoln against attempting to provision Fort Sumter. He predicted
(rightly) that any attempt to provision the fort would trigger an attack
and start a civil war, perhaps even before the relief expedition reached
the fort. Seeking to keep at least a token federal force in the South,
Seward advised that Lincoln should "at once and at every cost prepare
for a war at Pensacola and Texas," where, according to reports, former
Governor Sam Houston was rallying the Unionists. Again, Lincoln made
no decision regarding Fort Sumter, although he did soon order that a
naval expedition be made ready to sail from New York to Charleston.[33]

———

One of the points in Seward's letter to Lincoln was that they should
seek the advice of Army captain Montgomery Meigs on Fort Pickens.
Meigs was a graduate of West Point, a veteran of the Mexican War, and
now in charge of the renovation and extension of the Capitol building.
More important, he had visited Fort Pickens during the past winter and
was a personal friend of Seward's. Seward summoned Captain Meigs
and together they went to see the president. Meigs recorded in his diary
that he told Lincoln that the fort was easily defensible; it could be held
indefinitely "if the Navy has done its duty and not lost it already." When
Lincoln asked Meigs to command an expedition to reinforce the fort,
Meigs responded that, as a mere captain, he could not give orders to the
senior officers already there. Seward suggested that Meigs be promoted,
and Lincoln said he would think on the matter. As they were leaving
the White House, Seward told Meigs that he "wished to hold Pickens
making the fight there and in Texas, thus making the burden of war,
which all men of sense saw must come, fall upon those who by revolting provoked it." Seward was thinking along the same defensive lines as
Welles and Chase, although Seward viewed the proper point of defense
as Pickens rather than Sumter.[34]

    Seward went the next day to Scott's headquarters on Seventeenth
Street and found the aged general at his desk amid his papers. As Frederick Seward later recalled, his father said to the general that although

they had advised the president to surrender both forts, the president "directs that Fort Pickens shall be relieved." Scott, with effort, stood up. "Mr. Secretary, the great Frederick used to say that 'when the King commands, nothing is impossible.' Sir, the President's orders shall be obeyed!" The two men then turned to a discussion of the situation, which was confused because of the lack of communications with the two forts.[35]

On March 31, Easter Sunday morning, Scott's military aide Erasmus Keyes showed up at Seward's house on F Street. As Keyes later recalled it, the discussion went as follows:

"Mr. Seward, I am here by direction of General Scott to explain to you the difficulties of reinforcing Fort Pickens."

"I don't care about the difficulties; where is Captain Meigs?"

"I suppose he's at his house, sir."

"Find him and bring him here."

"I'll call and bring him on my return from church."

"Never mind church to-day; I wish to see him and you here together without delay."

Major Keyes resented Seward's tone—he was after all merely a civilian—but he left, found Meigs, and returned to Seward's house in ten minutes. Seward continued to give orders: the two men were to prepare a plan to reinforce Fort Pickens, to discuss it with General Scott, and to present the plan that afternoon to Lincoln. Seward spent almost the entire afternoon with the president, from just after noon until five o'clock. Meigs and Keyes arrived at about three and, although they had not yet had time to talk with Scott, Lincoln insisted that they present their ideas anyway. Meigs proposed that Lieutenant David Dixon Porter should have command of the Pickens expedition. Lincoln approved their plans and instructed them: "I depend upon you gentlemen to push the thing through."[36]

At some point on this busy Easter Sunday—between meetings with Lincoln, Scott, Lyons, Meigs, and others—Seward found time to write the famous and mysterious document he titled "Some Thoughts for the President's Consideration."[37] He started boldly: "We are at the end of a month's administration, and yet without a policy either domestic or foreign." He admitted that a focus on appointments was understandable during the month that the Senate was in special session, but now that the session was over, the administration had to turn to "other and more grave matters." On the domestic front, Seward argued that Lincoln should try to *change the question before the public from one upon slavery, or about slavery,*" to the question of *"Union or Disunion."* Fort Sumter was perceived as a partisan issue and therefore the fort should be surrendered. At the same time, the administration should "defend and reinforce all the forts in the Gulf, and have the Navy recalled from foreign stations to be prepared for a blockade." On the foreign front, Seward recommended that the United States demand explanations from Spain, France, Great Britain, and Russia, for reasons he did not specify. If the explanations from France and Spain were not satisfactory, Seward suggested that the president should convene Congress and ask it to declare war against them. The memorandum concluded: "Whatever policy we adopt, there must be an energetic prosecution of it. For this purpose, it must be somebody's business to pursue and direct it incessantly. Either the President must do it himself and be all the while active in it, or devolve it on some member of his cabinet. Once adopted, debates on it must end, and all agree and abide. It is not in my especial province. But I neither seek to evade nor assume responsibility."[38]

Knowing that his handwriting was almost illegible, Seward asked his son to make a fair copy of the memorandum and deliver it to Lincoln. "It was not to be filed," Frederick recalled, "or to pass into the hands of any clerk." But Seward and his son were not the only people involved in this extraordinary effort. Seward discussed his ideas with Thurlow Weed, who was in Washington in late March for a few days, and with Henry Raymond, editor of the *New York Times,* who arrived in Washington at about midnight on April 1. Raymond went from the train station straight to Seward's house, where he conferred with Seward for four hours, and then met with James Swain, the local correspondent for the *Times.*[39]

Swain later recalled how Raymond revealed to him the outlines of Seward's memorandum and told him that he and Seward expected the president's reply would be "in accord" with Seward's suggestions. The plan was for Swain to send both documents by telegraph to New York, for publication in the *Times,* along with a "vigorous editorial endorsement of the program." Although the president's reply was not at all "in accord" with Seward's suggestions, both Raymond and Weed published editorials based on Seward's memorandum. The *Times* of April 3 ran an article entitled "Wanted—A Policy," which argued that Lincoln had to "decide whether he will *enforce the law* at the hazard of civil war—or whether he will waive the execution of the law, and *appeal to the people* of the seceded states on behalf of the Union." The *Evening Journal* of April 4 insisted that Lincoln had to take immediate steps to maintain peace, and that he should shun the advice of Republican "extremists" who wanted him to force the issue at Sumter.[40]

Seward's memorandum has puzzled and troubled historians ever since it was first published in 1888 as part of the biography of Lincoln by his secretaries, John Nicolay and John Hay. Did Seward really believe that abandoning Fort Sumter but retaining Fort Pickens would transform the debate from one about "slavery" to one about "Union"? Probably not: but he believed that surrendering Sumter was essential to keeping the border states, and he hoped that the Union argument would persuade Lincoln. Why did Seward want to "demand explanations" from Spain? Spain was at this moment violating the Monroe Doctrine by attempting to turn San Domingo (as the Dominican Republic was known at the time) back into a Spanish colony; the *New York Times* reported on March 30 that Spain was sending 5,000 troops for this purpose. What was Seward's disagreement with France? This is harder to answer: perhaps the issue was the reported French interest in Mexico; perhaps a rumored French plan to treat Haiti as Spain was treating San Domingo; perhaps a newspaper report that England and France were preparing fleets to send to the United States to "pick up any little advantages that may offer themselves" in the anticipated civil war. What was Seward's concern with England? Most likely he was horrified by the possibility Lord Lyons had raised, that Great Britain would recognize the Confederacy in order to secure an uninterrupted supply of cotton.[41]

What was Seward's dispute with Russia? Among the four foreign nations mentioned, this is the most difficult to explain. Frederic Bancroft, the late nineteenth-century biographer of Seward, was so puzzled that he sent a letter on this issue to Frederick Seward in 1894. Frederick replied that Stoeckl, the Russian minister, had "an intimate personal acquaintance" with leading southerners, that he worked closely with them during the secession winter, and that these southerners claimed "in their published correspondence" that Russia was about to "open diplomatic relations with the Confederacy." This is a creative argument, but one without support in the documents. The only recorded contact between Stoeckl and the southerners was his offer to invite one of the commissioners to his house for a meeting with Seward, an offer that Seward considered and rejected.[42]

The usual interpretation of Seward's memorandum is that Seward was insane to seek a foreign war and insane to think Lincoln would yield control of the administration. Although Seward used the word "war" in his memorandum, he did not really want to fight any of the major foreign powers; what he wanted was a foreign crisis that would rally Americans to the Union. He had been thinking about the domestic benefits of a foreign crisis since at least late December, when he mentioned this possibility in his speech at the Astor House. This interpretation raises another question, however: whether Seward was insane in thinking in April 1861 that a foreign quarrel would reunite the United States. He may well have been right, in December 1860, when he said that many in South Carolina would answer a call to defend New York City against foreign attack, just as New York would rally to defend Charleston if necessary. But the past four months had strained and broken many of the ties binding the Union together, and Seward did not adequately adjust his approach to reflect the new realities. It is also hard to understand how he could think that Lincoln would devolve onto him the main responsibility for administration policy. It is true that there were examples in recent history of strong secretaries of state who exercised considerable influence over weak presidents; Webster had dominated Franklin Pierce. It is also true that Lincoln did not demonstrate much executive ability in his first weeks in office; Lyons reported to London that the new president had not shown "any natural talents to compensate for his ignorance of everything but Illinois village politics." But Seward, so often referred to as subtle, in this case lost all his subtlety by putting in writing, rather than discussing in person, the ways in which he could help the overworked president.[43]

Lincoln wrote out a careful response to Seward's memorandum, but did not deliver it to Seward, wisely choosing to discuss the issues face to face. As to domestic policy, Lincoln reminded his secretary of state of the key sentence in his inaugural, the one in which he promised to hold, occupy, and possess the forts and to collect the tariffs. "This had your distinct approval at the time," Lincoln wrote, and it "comprises the exact domestic policy you now urge, with the single exception, that it does not propose to abandon Fort Sumter." As to foreign policy, Lincoln admitted that Spain's actions in San Domingo were a "new item," but he noted that in the past weeks he and Seward had cooperated in "preparing circulars, and instructions to ministers, and the like, all in perfect harmony, without ever a suggestion that we had no foreign policy." On the main point, overall control, Lincoln remarked simply that "I must do it."[44]

Seward's reaction to Lincoln's response is not recorded, other than through his actions: he continued to work with and for the president. Nicolay and Hay, who observed the two men closely, noted that both Seward's memorandum and Lincoln's response were soon forgotten, and that Seward served Lincoln for more than four years "without reserve" and indeed "with a sincere and devoted personal attachment." Lincoln, they added, "readily recognized the strength and acknowledged the services" of Seward, "to whom he unselfishly gave, to his own last days, his generous and unwavering trust." Although Seward's memorandum for Lincoln is interesting and revealing, it is far less important in the end than the warm friendship and close cooperation between the two men over four difficult years.[45]

———

On that same Monday, April 1, Seward summoned Navy lieutenant David Dixon Porter to the State Department to discuss the expedition to Fort Pickens. Porter later wrote that he advised Seward that it would be "necessary to adopt a very unusual course and that was to take a large vessel of the Navy without the knowledge of the Navy Department." It was necessary to go around the Navy, Porter explained, because "some of the clerks were known to be secessionists," and they would alert the South as soon as they learned of the expedition, with the result that "the fort would certainly fall into rebel hands." Porter proposed "that the *Powhatan*, then lying at New York navy yard, should be fitted out for this service without delay by a secret order of the president." Seward, Porter, and Meigs then went to the White House, where Lincoln "seemed well pleased with all the plans proposed." The president assured them that he would handle any issue with Welles; "I think I can smooth the old fellow," is how Porter recalled Lincoln's comment. The officers presented and Lincoln signed several orders: one directed Captain Samuel Mercer to yield command of the *Powhatan* to Lieutenant Porter; another directed Porter to take the *Powhatan* to Pensacola and defend Fort Pickens. "This order, its object, and your destination will be communicated to no person whatever until you reach the harbor of Pensacola." Porter left for New York that night or early the next day, and Meigs followed soon thereafter, with $10,000 in hand from Seward's secret service fund to cover expenses.[46]

Justice John Campbell, in his capacity as the Washington friend of the Confederate commissioners, visited Seward later on April 1 and asked about the evacuation of Sumter. Seward responded that Lincoln might provide supplies to the fort, but would not do so without notice to South Carolina's governor. "What does this mean," Campbell recalled asking Seward, "does the President design to attempt to supply Sumter?" Seward responded, "I think not. It is a very irksome thing to him to evacuate it. His ears are open to everyone, and they fill his head with schemes for its supply. I do not think that he will adopt any of them." Campbell stressed to Seward that southerners believed that the administration had already promised that the fort would be surrendered; if they now learned that the fort was to be reinforced, they might attack and capture it preemptively. Seward asked Campbell for a few minutes in which to confer with Lincoln. Whether he did confer with the president is doubtful, but he returned and gave Campbell a note in his own hand: "I am satisfied the government will not undertake to supply Fort Sumter without giving notice to [South Carolina] Governor Pickens."[47]

Seward soon followed up on one key point in his memorandum to Lincoln: Spain and San Domingo. On April 2, he sent a letter to Gabriel Tassara, the Spanish minister in Washington, warning him that the United States would view the reported Spanish actions in San Domingo as "unfriendly" and would work to counteract them with "prompt, persistent, and if possible effective resistance." Seward also informed both Mercier, the French minister, and Lyons, the British minister, of his message to Spain, partly in the hope that they would join in protesting the Spanish aggression in San Domingo, and partly to warn them against any plans their nations might have for similar actions in Latin America. Seward was thus "demanding explanations" from Spain, as he suggested to Lincoln, although events would soon prevent him from doing anything more by way of pressure against Spain's war on San Domingo.[48]

Seward also followed up on the Sumter issue by sending a telegram to the Virginia Unionist leader George Summers—the man whom he had suggested for the Supreme Court: "The president desires your attendance at Washington as soon as convenient." Summers responded that he was not sure the telegram was authentic, and in any case he could not leave Richmond at this moment, on the eve of a crucial vote in the state convention. Seward was nothing if not persistent. On April 3, he summoned Allan Magruder, a Virginian living and working as a lawyer in Washington, and they went together to see Lincoln, who explained that he wanted to see Summers as soon as possible. Although neither Lincoln nor Seward explained to Magruder why they wanted to see Summers, their different purposes are reasonably clear. Seward wanted to persuade Lincoln to surrender Fort Sumter by having him hear directly from the leading Virginia Unionist. Lincoln wanted to hear from Summers to judge whether there was any way to satisfy both the Virginia Unionists (who demanded at least the surrender of Fort Sumter) and the Radical Republicans (who demanded at least the retention of Fort Pickens and collection of the tariffs).[49]

Magruder returned to Washington early on April 4 with John Baldwin, another Virginia Unionist whom Summers had sent in his stead. The two men called first on Seward at the State Department, and Seward walked Baldwin to the White House, introduced him to Lincoln, then left the two alone. There is considerable controversy about Lincoln's conversation with Baldwin: some historians believe that Lincoln told Baldwin he would withdraw the federal troops from Fort Sumter if the Virginians would terminate their secession convention; others insist that Lincoln made no such offer. Whatever Lincoln said,

Baldwin told him that the surrender of Sumter would not be enough: the federal government would also have to abandon Fort Pickens and avoid any attempt to collect its tariff outside southern ports. Seward spoke with Baldwin at length later in the day, and presumably heard the same points; he must have been discouraged to learn how weak and conditional was the commitment of the Virginia "Unionists" to the Union. Baldwin later recalled Seward saying, sadly, that "the days of philosophic statesmanship [were] about to give way to the mailed glove of the warrior."[50]

Seward was well aware, in early April, of the work of Porter and Meigs in New York City to prepare a naval expedition to Fort Pickens. He was also probably aware, at least in general terms, that another naval expedition was being prepared in parallel, an expedition to relieve Fort Sumter in South Carolina.[51] At the latest, Seward learned of the Sumter expedition on the evening of April 5, when he received a confused and distressed telegram from Meigs. The *Powhatan* was nearly ready to sail from New York for Florida, but had been detained because of a telegram from Navy Secretary Welles. "What is to be done?" Meigs asked Seward in despair. Seward and Frederick went to see Welles at his room at the Willard Hotel, and read him Meigs's message. The *Powhatan*, Seward explained to Welles, was under Porter and bound for Pickens; no, no, Welles insisted, the *Powhatan* was under Mercer and bound for Sumter. Seward suggested that perhaps Silas Stringham, a senior Washington officer mentioned in the message from Meigs, could explain, but when Stringham was roused from his rest by Welles, he could not add anything. It was past eleven at night, but Welles insisted they resolve the issue with Lincoln immediately. As the four men were walking toward the White House, Welles later recalled, Seward remarked that "old as he was, he had learned a lesson from this affair, and that was, he had better attend to his own business and confine his labors to his own department. To this I cordially assented."[52]

The four men found the president awake and presented their arguments to him. Seward protested that the mission to Pickens was quite as important as the mission to Sumter, but Lincoln overruled him and directed him to telegraph to New York that the *Powhatan* should be part of the Sumter mission. Lincoln graciously accepted blame for the confusion, saying that he should have read the various orders more carefully. Seward returned to the State Department and sent a telegram to Porter: "Give the *Powhatan* up to Captain Mercer." When Porter received this message the next morning, he sent telegrams back to both Lincoln and Seward, asking them how to resolve the conflicting orders. Porter apparently received no response to his telegrams, and resolved "to obey the highest authority (the President) and not defeat the object of this expedition." He sailed in the *Powhatan* for Fort Pickens that afternoon.[53]

Many historians, starting with Gideon Welles in 1870, have argued that Seward selected the *Powhatan* for the Pickens expedition because he wanted to preclude or weaken any expedition to relieve Sumter. These historians contend that Seward signed his own name to the midnight telegram, rather than that of Lincoln, because Seward *wanted* Porter to disregard his message, and thus to obstruct the Sumter expedition. Seward could be devious, but these charges seem excessive. Admiral Porter, in his detailed account of these events, stresses that it was he who first suggested use of the *Powhatan* for the Pickens expedition, and that Seward was not aware of the intended use of the *Powhatan* for the Sumter mission. Moreover, it is hard to believe that the imperious secretary of state thought Porter would disregard his midnight order; he most likely simply forgot, at the late hour, that the prior order had been signed by Lincoln. The telegrams from Porter to Lincoln and Seward on April 6 show that Porter hesitated over what to do, and suggest that he did not receive any further orders from Washington.[54]

We have the Welles version of these events, but not the Seward version, because Welles kept a diary and wrote a memoir, and Seward did neither, except for the memoir of his early years in New York. Frederick recalled that his father asked him, not long after taking office as secretary of state, to obtain for him a large blank book, remarking that "as the epoch would probably be one of historic importance, he should begin to keep a diary." Frederick secured a suitable leather-bound book, but on the next day Seward handed it back to him. "There is the first page of my diary," Frederick recalled his father as saying, "and the last. One day's record satisfies me that if I should every day set down my hasty impressions, based on half information, I should do injustice to everybody around me, and to none more than my most intimate friends." Frederick wrote this years later, so the quote may not be correct, but the sentiment surely is; Seward did not want to record every petty issue in the Lincoln cabinet. Moreover, even after the war, he did not want to quarrel with Welles. Seward was alive in 1870 and 1871 when Welles published long articles attacking Seward's conduct with respect to Forts Sumter and Pickens, but he did not respond. The imbalance of the historical record—with Welles and other hostile observers providing so many of the details about Seward—makes it hard to provide a balanced picture of Seward in this instance, as in many others.[55]

On the day after the midnight meeting, the president asked Seward for a trusted messenger to send to South Carolina. Seward selected Robert Chew, a State Department clerk, and was probably present as Lincoln handed Chew his instructions. Chew was to proceed as fast as possible to South Carolina; if Fort Sumter was still in Union hands and not under attack, he was to inform the governor "to expect an attempt will be made to supply Fort Sumter with provisions only." On that same day, James Harvey, originally from South Carolina, recently appointed by Lincoln as minister to Portugal, sent a telegram to a friend in South Carolina: "Positively determined not to withdraw Anderson. Supplies go immediately, supported by a naval force under Stringham, if their landing be resisted." Seward's critics have charged that it was Seward who leaked news of the expedition to his friend Harvey and thereby betrayed the mission he had so long opposed. This seems unlikely. Seward knew that Stringham was not in charge of the naval force bound for Sumter; he was in Washington, where Seward had seen him the evening before. So unless Seward misled Harvey on this point, Harvey had some other source; he was after all a reporter in a capital rife with rumors.[56]

The Confederate commissioners, concerned about these rumors, asked Justice Campbell to ask Seward again about the promised withdrawal from Sumter. Campbell received from Seward an undated, unsigned response: "Faith as to Sumter fully kept. Wait and see." Campbell and the commissioners were not clear what Seward meant: did he refer to the earlier promise that Sumter would be evacuated? Or did he refer only to his more recent assurance that there would be some kind of *notice* before any attempt to provision the fort? That evening a messenger from the commissioners arrived at Seward's home, saying they now wanted Seward's written answer to a letter they had sent him a month earlier, in which they had requested a formal standstill agreement. The next day they had Seward's response: he politely but firmly declined to recognize the Confederacy or to negotiate with its commissioners. The commissioners and Campbell were outraged; Campbell wrote Seward a long letter accusing him of "systematic duplicity." But at this stage their outrage no longer mattered: what mattered was the southern reaction to Lincoln's message to the governor of South Carolina and to the naval expedition steaming toward Fort Sumter.[57]

On the rainy evening of April 8, the British reporter William Russell stopped by Seward's house, where he found himself pressed into service as a fourth player in a game of whist. Seward, as was his custom, talked as he played cards, telling Russell that the military preparations of which he heard meant only that the federal government, because the southern forts were "neglected and left without protection," intended to "relieve them from that neglect and protect them." It was all in accordance with Lincoln's inaugural address, Seward said: "we will not go beyond it—we have no intention of doing so—nor will we withdraw from it." Seward asked Frederick to find a document, and then read out to Russell "a very long, strong, and able dispatch," which he intended to send to London. After listening for a while, Russell told the secretary that the message would probably be well received in the United States, when it was eventually made public, but he doubted it would be appreciated in Britain, where it would sound bellicose. Both in his letter to Adams and his remarks to Russell, Seward claimed that he still viewed secession as temporary; the southern states would soon "see their mistake and one after another they will come back into the Union."[58]

———

As Seward had predicted, when the messenger bearing Lincoln's letter reached South Carolina, and the message was relayed to the

Confederate capital, President Davis and his cabinet decided not to wait for the arrival of the Union naval expedition. Davis instructed the local authorities in Charleston to demand the immediate surrender of the fort and, if this was refused, to attack the fort. The Confederate artillery attack on Fort Sumter began in the early morning hours of April 12, and the first confused and contradictory reports from Charleston started to arrive in Washington later that day. People gathered at telegraph offices; southern sympathizers rejoiced; northern conservatives like Seward lamented. Many feared that the capital itself was in danger. Lord Lyons reported to London that "the immediate apprehensions of the government are for this city. The chiefs of the Southern Confederacy loudly declare their intentions of attacking it immediately if the border states join them."[59]

By Sunday, April 14, it was known in Washington that, after enduring the artillery attack for more than a day, Major Anderson had surrendered. Lincoln, Seward, and the other members of the cabinet spent most of that anxious day in consultation. It was clear that the president should call for troops, but there was some debate within the cabinet as to just how many troops should be called. Some suggested that Lincoln should request that the states provide 50,000 men; Seward argued that the call should be for 100,000; Lincoln compromised on 75,000 men to serve for ninety days. Even more difficult was the question of calling a special session of Congress: should the president summon the members of Congress immediately to consider wartime legislation, or for some later date? Seward argued that it was pointless to "wait for 'many men with many minds' to shape a war policy." Alluding to Charles I of Britain, Seward commented that "history tells us that kings who call extra parliaments lose their heads." Lincoln agreed and delayed the start of the congressional session until the Fourth of July.[60]

Lincoln's proclamation did not explain at length the reasons for calling for troops; he did not have to, for he knew that the same newspapers that carried his proclamation would carry the detailed reports of the Confederate attack on the Union flag and fort at Sumter. The president appealed to "all loyal citizens to favor, facilitate and aid this effort to maintain the honor, the integrity and the existence of our national Union and the perpetuity of popular government." A fair copy of the proclamation was prepared. Lincoln signed it as president; Seward counter-signed as secretary of state and arranged for it to receive the great seal of the United States, making it official. Copies of the proclamation were then sent by telegraph to all the major newspapers, so that it could be published on Monday, April 15. The Civil War had started.[61]

CHAPTER 11

"Through the Fires of Tophet":

1861

E vents moved swiftly after Lincoln's April 15 proclamation. The
call for troops was met in most northern states with a wave of
patriotic enthusiasm; even previously hostile newspapers now
gave the president their full support. The border states, however, refused to provide any troops; the governor of Kentucky replied that his
state would "furnish no troops for the wicked purpose of subduing her
sister southern states." The most important of the border states, Virginia,
seceded. Virginia troops soon captured the federal arsenal at Harpers
Ferry and the federal shipyard at Norfolk. The Confederate government
announced that it would commission private vessels, known as privateers, to attack, capture, and if necessary destroy Union merchant vessels. On the afternoon of Friday, April 19, a friend rushed into Seward's
office to tell him that an angry mob had just attacked federal troops
passing through Baltimore. The troops had responded with their guns,
leaving four soldiers and perhaps a dozen locals dead. Within hours,
news arrived that mobs in Maryland, encouraged by their state government, had burned the bridges and cut the telegraph wires to the North.
Washington was now an isolated island, without news from or access to
the rest of the United States, defended by only a few thousand men of
doubtful loyalty.[1]

Lincoln, Seward, and the other members of the administration struggled to keep pace with these events. Over the objection of Navy Secretary Gideon Welles, Seward persuaded Lincoln that a naval blockade was the proper way to limit trade with the southern ports and prevent privateers from leaving those ports. Welles argued for closing the southern ports by a decree that did not use the word "blockade," but Seward knew, based on his recent conversations with the British minister Lyons and the Russian minister Stoeckl, that the major foreign powers would all regard such a decree as invalid. A blockade, Seward argued, was an internationally accepted form of warfare; it would avoid disputes between the North and foreign nations that could lead to their support of the South. Lincoln issued the blockade proclamation—almost certainly drafted by Seward—on April 19. The proclamation was deliberately vague as to when the blockade would take effect, both to give time to foreign merchants with ships at sea bound for southern ports, and to avoid questions about whether the blockade was effective enough to be recognized under international law. In response to the Confederate threat to commission privateers, the proclamation said that anyone who attacked a United States vessel under such "pretended authority" would be treated, tried, and perhaps executed as a pirate.[2]

Seward was also central in the response to the Maryland authorities, who insisted that no further federal troops pass through their state, and who suggested that Lyons be asked to mediate between North and South. Seward's informal reaction, as recorded by Lincoln's secretary John Hay, was that "Baltimore *delenda est*," that is, that the Union must destroy Baltimore just as Rome had destroyed Carthage. Lincoln asked Seward to draft a response to Maryland, soon published in the papers, in which Seward insisted that the troops passing through Maryland were only intended for the defense of the national capital, reminded Marylanders that they were still part of the Union, and rejected mediation. In conversations with Lincoln, Seward urged him to arrest members of the Maryland legislature, in order to prevent them from assembling and resolving upon secession. Lincoln did not accept this recommendation, but he did accept Seward's advice that he should suspend the writ of habeas corpus "on or in the vicinity" of the line between Philadelphia and Washington. To persuade a reluctant president to issue this decree,

Seward later recalled, he had to argue that "perdition was the sure penalty for further hesitation."[3]

Even as Seward, in his public letter to the Maryland governor, dismissed the suggestion of European mediation, he was privately exploring that very possibility with Rudolf Schleiden, the minister from Bremen. Schleiden approached Seward with the idea of an armistice that would last for a few weeks, until Congress convened in early July. The secretary did not reject the idea out of hand, but instead took Schleiden to see Lincoln, who was willing to allow Schleiden to go to Richmond to float the suggestion there. When Schleiden returned from Richmond in late April, he reported first to Seward. Nothing came of the mission, but it shows that Seward, even in late April, was still interested in peace and not afraid to be inconsistent.[4]

The week that started with the Baltimore riot, the week in which Washington was isolated and surrounded, was a stressful one for Seward and his family. Frederick tried to reassure his mother, writing to her one day that the city was "loyal, patriotic and enthusiastic," and on the next that "father is confident the whole storm will blow over without disaster here." It was only a few days later, after the arrival of troops via Annapolis and restoration of the telegraph, that Frederick's wife Anna could confess to her mother-in-law that "last week was a very anxious one for this city. All kinds of dangers threatening, no troops, no news from the North, no telegraph, no railroad." Seward later told the artist Francis Carpenter that, if he wanted to depict the most dramatic cabinet meeting of the war, he should forget the one at which emancipation was debated. Carpenter should instead "go back to the firing on Sumter, or to a much more exciting one than even that, the Sunday following the Baltimore massacre, when the Cabinet assembled or gathered in the Navy Department and, with the vast responsibility that was thrown upon them, met the emergency and its awful consequences, put in force the war power of the government, and issued papers and did acts that might have brought them all to the scaffold." Seward's reference to the scaffold may seem melodramatic, but he was right. If the Civil War had turned out otherwise, Seward and other senior leaders could have paid with their lives for their decisions to raise massive armies, to mount a naval blockade, to attack southern forces, and to imprison without charges hundreds of northern civilians.[5]

———

From April 1861 through February 1862, it was Seward who was in charge of the arrest and detention of suspected spies and southern supporters. He reportedly boasted to Lord Lyons in late 1861 that "I can touch a bell on my right hand, and order the arrest of a citizen of Ohio; I can touch a bell again, and order the imprisonment of a citizen of New York; and no power on earth, except that of the President, can release them. Can the Queen of England do so much?" In all likelihood Seward never said this to Lyons: there is no trace of the remark in the detailed reports of Lyons to the British foreign minister, and at a dinner party in early 1864 Lyons told an interlocutor that he remembered no such conversation. The quote first appeared in anti-administration newspapers in 1863, and it has been repeated regularly since then. Some historians have agreed with the sentiment if not the wording; one wrote that, during the first few months of the war, "Seward had more arbitrary power over the freedom of individual American citizens all over the country than any other man has ever had, before or since."[6]

More than eight hundred men, and a handful of women, were arrested and detained during the period in which Seward was responsible for domestic security. In almost all cases, Seward did not initiate the arrests; Army and Navy officers, federal marshals or local police officers decided on their own to make an arrest. In about a third of these cases, especially those involving remote prisons, Seward never even learned the names of those arrested. But in other cases, especially those in the eastern states, he learned of arrests soon after they were made. Seward would then generally issue orders directing that the prisoners be transferred to Fort Lafayette, in New York Harbor, or Fort Warren, in Boston Harbor, or the Old Capitol prison, in Washington itself. He received hundreds of letters—from prisoners, family members, friends, and foreign diplomats in the case of foreign prisoners—urging that particular prisoners be released or complaining about prison conditions. In some cases he would release prisoners quickly; in other cases he refused; and in many cases he simply did nothing, so the prisoners were still in custody when Seward transferred responsibility for the system to the war secretary in February 1862.[7]

Why were men arrested and imprisoned? In many cases it is hard to say, because the surviving records are so brief: "treasonable language" or "recruiting for rebel army." In other cases the reasons are clear. William Williams, a young British sailor, found himself in Charleston, South Carolina, when the Civil War started. He sailed for home on a British merchant ship that tried but failed to evade the federal blockade. Williams and all the other crew members were arrested and imprisoned at Fort Lafayette. Lyons learned about Williams and his British shipmates and raised the matter with Seward, who promptly ordered the British prisoners released. The Reverend K. J. Stewart, Episcopal priest of St. Paul's Church in Alexandria, was arrested by a federal officer in the congregation one Sunday morning for omitting the standard prayer for the president. Reverend Stewart was, according to a northern official, "an open and avowed secessionist." He too was soon released. But many were arrested on more serious charges: killing federal pickets, recruiting for the southern army, selling arms to the Confederates. Perhaps the most famous person Seward arrested was Rose Greenhow, a Washington hostess whom he knew well from prewar days. Greenhow was arrested at her home in August 1861, accused of spying for the Confederates, and she remained in prison until she was exchanged in June 1862. Greenhow's memoir and Confederate documents make it clear that she was indeed a spy, a determined and effective one.[8]

In late August and early September 1861, reports reached Seward that members of the Maryland legislature intended to gather to pass an ordinance of secession and to seek immediate Confederate military support. The sources differ somewhat on the military threat. In a letter to his mother in late September, Frederick wrote that the legislators planned "to pass the secession ordinance for Maryland and invite [Confederate general P. G. T.] Beauregard to take possession of Washington." In an 1864 letter, Union general George McClellan remembered that "intelligence reached us, I *think* through Seward, that the Secesh members of the Maryland legislature intended to meet at Frederick . . . secretly pass a secession ordinance, secretly send it to [Confederate general Joseph] Johnston, who was at once to move into Maryland and raise a general disturbance." The sources are clear, however, that Seward was deeply involved in deciding to make arrests and in implementing the decision. On September 4, the secretary traveled to Baltimore, where he spent the day with General John Dix, who made arrests in and around that city starting on September 13. And on September 8, he traveled to Rockville, where he spent several hours with General Nathaniel Banks, who made arrests in western Maryland starting a week later.[9]

As the arrests were made, Banks reported them to Seward by telegraph; Frederick summarized the messages as "four taken," "twelve more arrested," "clerks arrested," and finally, "Union men all gone home and secessionists all gone to Fortress Monroe." Seward probably drafted for Lincoln the letter justifying the arrests that appeared in the *Baltimore American*: "Of one thing the people of Maryland may rest assured: that no arrest has been made, or will be made, not based on substantial and unmistakable complicity with those in armed rebellion against the Government of the United States." Although the letter denied any political purpose, Seward told Lyons in November that the Maryland arrests had "almost all been made in view of the Maryland elections," and that he hoped immediately after the election "to be able to set at liberty all the British subjects now under military arrest." This may have been a convenient explanation for Lyons, but if Seward's purposes were political, he succeeded; Maryland voted for Union candidates in November 1861, and remained in the Union.[10]

A somwhat similar case involved seven political leaders of Maysville, Kentucky, including Colonel Richard Stanton, a former member of Congress. The seven were arrested on October 2, 1861, on orders of Union general William Nelson, who described Stanton as "the head of secession in Northeast Kentucky," and recommended that he be "removed farther from the scene of his villainies." Seward agreed and ordered that all seven men be held in Fort Lafayette. Both directly and indirectly, the Kentucky men pleaded with Seward for their release, claiming they never "engaged in the rebellion or intended to do so." In November, several men, including Frederick Stanton, brother of Richard and also a former member of Congress, came to Washington to meet with Seward.

According to one of those present, when Frederick Stanton asked Seward to list the charges against his brother, Seward responded that "there are no charges against him on file." One of the others then asked whether Seward intended to keep men imprisoned against whom no charges were made. Seward responded: "I don't give a damn whether they are guilty or innocent. I saved Maryland by similar arrests, and so I mean to hold Kentucky." When one of the group suggested that the secretary's arbitrary arrests would anger the residents of Kentucky, Seward continued: "I don't give a damn for the opinions of Kentucky." He intended simply to "hold her in the Union and make her fight for it." The men remained in prison for another few weeks, until Seward arranged for their release, again without explanation.[11]

Seward not only decided whether men should be freed; he decided on surveillance and prison conditions. In late October 1861, he ordered the provost in Washington to "establish a strict military guard over the residence of William M. Merrick," a federal judge who had angered the administration by a judicial decision in favor of a prisoner. The provost asked Seward whether the judge should be confined to his home. No, Seward replied, Merrick could move about the city, although it would be well that he should know that "his correspondence and his proceedings [are being] observed." Seward also instructed the Treasury Department to suspend payment of Merrick's salary, a clear violation of the constitutional requirement that judicial salaries be paid without interruption or reduction. The *New York Times*, in the same article that reported these actions against Merrick, declared that "the government will not in any way recognize the employment of counsel to procure the release of persons arrested and imprisoned for political offenses. The Secretary of State will consider it his duty to promptly investigate the case of any person arrested, and to act upon the facts obtained without argument by counsel." Seward was almost certainly the source for the *Times*. Fifteen years earlier, he had made himself famous by his ardent defense of prisoners; now he was making himself infamous by denying legal counsel to men imprisoned under his own authority. Seward did not care; he was determined to save the Union.[12]

———

Although prisoners occupied much of Seward's time in 1861, foreign affairs were even more important and time-consuming. The secretary of state devoted hours each day to reading reports from American ministers and consuls abroad, to sending them instructions, to meeting with foreign diplomats in Washington, and to responding to their various requests and complaints. Some of Seward's instructions and responses were brief, but many were long and detailed. In early April, for example, just before the attack on Fort Sumter, he sent Charles Francis Adams his initial instructions, more than 5,000 words, about the background of secession and the necessity of keeping Britain out of what Seward insisted was a temporary domestic disturbance. This was only one of dozens of papers of similar length and complexity (some might say verbosity) that Seward prepared and dispatched during the first few months of the war. He described the work in a letter to his daughter as an "oppressive labor."[13]

On April 24, one week after the Confederacy declared that it would authorize privateers, Seward sent dispatches to the relevant American ministers abroad, offering that the United States would become a party to the Declaration of Paris of 1856. The Declaration was an agreement among Britain, France, and several other nations, providing maritime rules for war, including a prohibition against privateers. Seward claimed that his purpose in now accepting the Declaration (which the United States had previously rejected) was to assure the European nations that their commerce would be safe from "depradations" by either side in the ongoing American conflict. Britain, however, viewed Seward's proposal as almost a trick; if the United States now entered the Declaration, and if the foreign powers accepted that the southern states were still part of the United States, then these nations would be obliged to treat southern privateers as pirates. Lyons, writing to the British foreign minister, Lord Russell, described Seward's proposal as "rather amusing." After some back-and-forth, Britain informed the United States that it would insist on a side letter, in which Britain would state that the Declaration would not apply to the "internal differences now prevailing in the United States." This was not acceptable to Seward, and he dropped the matter, annoyed but not too troubled.[14]

Far more worrisome to Seward were reports that started to arrive in

May 1861 suggesting that Britain and France might soon recognize the Confederacy as an independent nation. First came news that a member of the British Parliament had introduced a formal motion to recognize the Confederacy. The British government deferred consideration of the motion, but the deferral was only for two weeks. Then came a report that the French foreign minister M. Thouvenel had told the outgoing American minister that although France would not "act hastily" in the matter, the French practice was to recognize de facto governments once they were "clearly established," hinting that the Confederacy might soon meet this standard. Henry Sanford, the new American minister to Belgium, visited Paris at Seward's request and learned from Thouvenel that he would probably meet informally with the Confederate commissioners who were expected to arrive there soon. From London, Seward learned that the British government would also likely meet informally with the Confederate commissioners there. On May 16, a report reached the United States suggesting that Lord Russell had informed Parliament that the British government would recognize the Confederates as belligerents. The next day, the *New York Times* reported from London that "in the highest official circles" a war with the United States to obtain southern cotton was "already regarded as all but unavoidable, and such being the case, it may not be difficult to provoke." [15]

Seward was depressed and angered by these developments. He wrote to his wife that "they have misunderstood things fearfully, in Europe. Great Britain is in great danger of sympathizing so much with the South, for the sake of peace and cotton, as to drive us to make war against her, as the ally of the traitors." A few days later, in a private note to Henry Sanford, Seward commented that Britain and France "seem to have been in danger of getting committed. I trust, however, they have waited" for Charles Francis Adams to arrive as American minister in London. Seward told Sanford that Adams would be prepared because "I shall send him instructions bold and decisive tomorrow." [16]

As drafted by Seward, these instructions were indeed "bold and decisive," protesting strongly against the rumored unofficial discussions between Britain and the Confederates, and instructing Adams to "desist from all intercourse whatever, unofficial as well as official with the British government, so long as it shall continue intercourse of either kind with the domestic enemies of this country." This and other marks of favor by Britain toward the Confederacy would not "be borne by the United States." Seward conceded that the tension over British recognition of the southern rebels might lead to war between Britain and the United States, but insisted that such a war would be Britain's fault, and warned that the United States would do everything necessary to defend itself.[17]

Seward submitted his draft to Lincoln—as he generally did in the case of important letters—and Lincoln moderated it. For example, where Seward wrote that the British actions "would not be borne" by the United States, the president wrote that these actions "would not pass unquestioned." Lincoln suggested, and Seward agreed, that Adams should not deliver a copy of the letter itself to Lord Russell, but rather simply use it to guide him in his discussions. Seward sent the revised dispatch to Adams on May 21. Many historians have seen Lincoln's revision of Seward's draft as a critical moment in wartime diplomacy; one wrote that Lincoln "saved this nation from a war with England." But although Lincoln's changes were useful, they were not that substantial. The incident is better viewed as one example among many of the close working relationship that was developing between Seward and Lincoln. Seward wrote to Frances in May that "it is due to the President to say that his magnanimity is almost superhuman. His confidence and sympathy increase every day." In June, Seward told her that "you have no idea how incessant my labors are to keep the conduct of [the war] up to the line of necessity and public expectation. Executive skill and vigor are rare qualities. The President is the best of us; but he needs constant and assiduous cooperation. But I have said too much already. Burn this, and believe that I am doing what man can do."[18]

On May 22, the *New York Herald* ran an article which declared that "any act of intervention which affords direct advantage to the insurgent states, and which tends to hamper or obstruct the action of our government, will lead to the most decisive measures on the part of this administration." If England aided the Confederacy, the Union would "launch against her the thunderbolts of a war that would not cease till every power in Europe was involved. On this vital matter the President, the Secretary of State and all the cabinet entertain one view." The cabinet was confident, according to the *Herald*, that the people of the United States would "sustain them at every sacrifice against England and all the world." Many people, then and since, believed that Seward planted this article in the *Herald*. Lyons reported home that the article was "well known to have been written under Mr. Seward's own eye," and the French minister Mercier believed that Seward "proofread" it before it was published. But the *New York Herald* was not a paper with which Seward was at all friendly; indeed, the *Herald*'s editor, James Gordon Bennett, was one of his harshest critics. It seems more likely that the *Herald* obtained a copy of Seward's draft message to Adams and used it as the occasion for some anti-British rhetoric.[19]

Seward's friend Weed wrote him in late May to express concern that Seward's aggressive approach would lead to war with Britain and France. The secretary responded harshly to his friend: "Will you consent, or advise us to consent, that Adams and [American minister in Paris William] Dayton have audiences in the Minister's Audience Chamber, and [Confederate secretary of state Robert] Toombs' emissaries have access to his bedroom? Shall there be no compromise at home, and shall we have compromise on everything in Europe?" Seward's anger only intensified when he learned at the end of May that the British government had issued a royal proclamation regarding the hostilities between the United States and "certain states styling themselves the Confederate States of America." The proclamation declared that Britain would "maintain a strict and impartial neutrality in the contest," and reminded British citizens of the provisions of the Foreign Enlistment Act, including those which prohibited British citizens from enlisting in the Union or Confederate armies or from fitting out or arming ships to be used in the war by either side.[20]

The key point of the proclamation, from Seward's perspective, was that Britain had now recognized that the Confederacy was a belligerent. As a belligerent, the Confederacy could raise loans in Britain and Confederate ships could use British ports; moreover, recognition as a belligerent was a step toward recognition as a nation. Edward Everett, the former secretary of state, in a diary entry later in the year, noted that Seward's reaction to the British proclamation was: "God damn them, I'll give them hell. I'm no more afraid of them than I am of Robert

Toombs." Charles Sumner, after the war, recalled that he "never saw Mr. Seward more like a caged tiger, or more profuse of oaths in every form that the English language supplies, than when prancing about the room denouncing the Proclamation of Belligerency, which he swore he would send to hell." [21]

Seward's view, both at the time and for years thereafter, was that Britain acted hastily and unnecessarily in issuing its neutrality proclamation. In conversations with Lyons in Washington and letters to Adams in London, Seward insisted that the southern rebellion had been, in May 1861, a mere local insurrection, and thus that the rebels were not entitled to the elevated status of belligerents under international law. If there was a similar insurrection in Scotland or Ireland, Seward suggested, the British government would be outraged if the United States immediately declared that the Scottish or Irish rebels were "belligerents." Seward believed that the British proclamation encouraged the southern rebels; indeed, he sometimes claimed that the *only* thing sustaining the rebels was that they were recognized as belligerents by Britain and France. Over and over, throughout the war, Seward requested that Britain and France withdraw their recognition of belligerent status. Foreign Minister Russell wrote Lyons that Seward's request was "silly" because the American Civil War was not just some "local riot." [22]

Russell was right on this point and Seward was wrong. Looking across the Atlantic in May 1861, the British saw two substantial belligerent forces, the northern one instituting a blockade, and the southern one sending out privateers, both of which threatened British merchant ships. The British government, eager to avoid quarrels with either side, especially quarrels at sea, issued a proclamation of neutrality, as it had done in similar situations in the past. Indeed, the American government had issued similar neutrality proclamations in similar situations; Martin Van Buren had issued a proclamation in early 1838 reminding Americans that they had to remain neutral in the "civil war" in Canada. The British neutrality proclamation of May 1861 simply made explicit what was implicit in the American blockade proclamation of April, that the Confederates were belligerents. The United States would again implicitly admit that the Confederates were belligerents, not mere rebels, by exchanging prisoners with the Confederacy and by refraining from executing captured Confederate privateers as if they were pirates. The Supreme Court would later recognize that "the Confederate States were belligerents in the sense attached to the word by the law of nations."[23]

Seward acted more sensibly in his efforts to deal separately, rather than jointly, with the British and the French on the belligerency issue. On the morning of June 15, Frederick informed him that Lord Lyons and Henri Mercier had arrived to see him together. Frederick recalled that as his father approached the visitors, he smiled and shook his head. "No, no, no," Seward said, "this will never do." One of the diplomats admitted that it was unusual, but added, "we are just obeying our instructions." The other asked whether Seward would "at least allow us to state the object of our visit." "No," Seward said, "we must start right about it, whatever it is." He invited Mercier to dine with him that evening, then invited Lyons to join him in his office. Mercier persisted: "then you refuse to see us together?" Seward insisted: "certainly I do refuse to see you together, although I will see either of you with pleasure, here or elsewhere." In his separate meetings with Lyons and Mercier, Seward declined to receive the dispatches they wished to deliver to him regarding belligerency. As Lyons reported home, Seward explained that he "could not receive from us a communication founded on the assumption that the southern rebels were to be regarded as belligerents," and he "could not admit that recent events had in any respect altered the relations between foreign powers and the southern states."[24]

Seward overreacted to the British neutrality proclamation, but he also realized that what mattered most was what Britain and France did and not what they said. He was encouraged to learn from Adams that although Russell had met informally once or twice with the Confederate commissioners in London, he did not expect to meet with them again. Adams also reported that Britain did not intend to allow Confederate privateers to bring their captures into British ports and courts. This was a major advantage for the Union, because without ports into which to bring their prizes Confederate privateers could not operate profitably, and indeed Confederate privateers would have little effect during the war. Seward was also pleased to learn that the British and French governments would not claim that the Union blockade was ineffective and that their ships could disregard it. The line between an "effective" and an "ineffective" blockade was not especially clear in international law; certainly it would have been possible for the Europeans to argue in 1861 that the Union blockade was ineffective and thus invalid—but they did not do this, and indeed Britain ultimately defined "effectiveness" in a way quite favorable to the Union. By July 1861, Seward could write to Adams that if Britain continued to forbear from interference in the war, the United States would not be "captious" about the wording Britain used to describe its policies.[25]

Seward's foreign policy had many critics, but the most persistent and influential was Charles Sumner, his former friend, now chairman of the Senate Foreign Relations Committee. In late May, Sumner wrote to John Andrew, governor of Massachusetts, that Seward was guilty of the "grossest mismanagement" of foreign relations. Sumner made similar comments to Lyons and Mercier, and to his British correspondents, writing to one of them about the "evil influence" near Lincoln. Even Adams learned of Sumner's views, and he wrote privately to Seward that "the very hostile manner in which one of the senators of my state is in the constant habit of speaking about you everywhere in private must have become known to you. . . . All this is important only as explaining what I cannot fail to observe here, a prevailing tone of distrust of your policy and motives." Seward told Adams not to worry about what Sumner "can do here or near you," and described Sumner as a *cidevant* friend" whose anger was due at least in part to how Seward had ignored his protests against the appointment of Adams. Seward often claimed that he did not care about his critics, including Sumner, but Sumner's criticism impeded Seward's ability to conduct foreign policy and would, before long, threaten his place as secretary of state.[26]

————

By the summer of 1861, Seward's personal life had settled into the pattern it would follow throughout the war. He lived with his son Frederick and daughter-in-law Anna in a large rented house on Lafayette Square. When Augustus, serving as paymaster, arrived in late 1861, he would became a fourth, but almost invisible, member of the household. Frances and Fanny generally remained in Auburn; they visited only

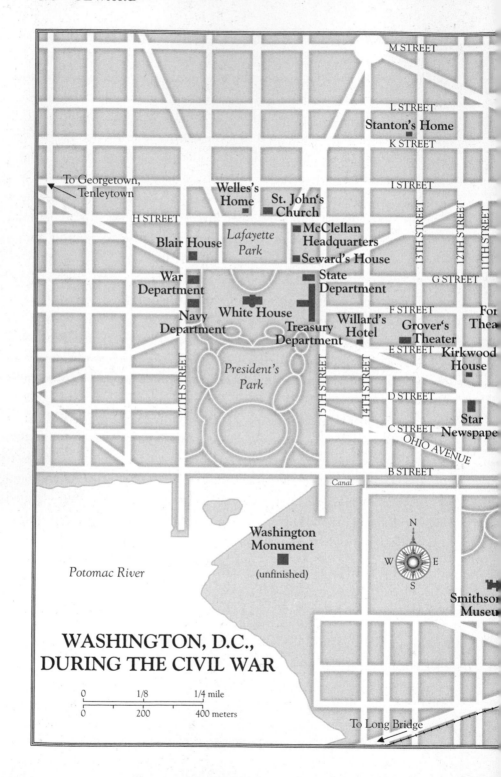

M STREET

L STREET

Stanton's Home

K STREET

I STREET

To Georgetown,
Tenleytown

Welles's
Home

St. John's
Church

H STREET

McClellan
Headquarters

Lafayette
Park

Blair House

Seward's House

War
Department

State
Department

G STREET

Navy
Department

White House

Treasury
Department

Willard's
Hotel

Grover's
Theater

For
Thea

F STREET

E STREET

Kirkwood
House

President's
Park

D STREET

Star
Newspaper

C STREET

OHIO AVENUE

Canal

B STREET

13TH STREET

12TH STREET

11TH STREET

17TH STREET

15TH STREET

14TH STREET

Washington
Monument

(unfinished)

N

W   E

S

Potomac River

Smithson
Museu

**WASHINGTON, D.C.,
DURING THE CIVIL WAR**

0   1/8   1/4 mile

0   200   400 meters

To Long Bridge

from time to time. Anthony Trollope, the British novelist, noted that the houses around Lafayette Square were "few in number—not exceeding three or four on each side, but they are among the best in Washington, and the whole place is neat and well kept." It was certainly, in the view of Trollope and others, the "most attractive part of the city." The Sewards' house was surrounded by leafy trees often filled with birds, so that Anna felt as if she was out in the country. Seward would rise early each morning and skim the papers as he ate breakfast, tossing each paper aside as he finished with it. He would then walk to the State Department, less than a block away, where he was generally in his chair before the first callers arrived. Before, between, and after visitors, he worked his way through his inbox, making notes on letters to indicate a response or drafting responses by hand.[27]

Much of his day was taken by meetings: with Lincoln, other cabinet members, military officers, foreign diplomats, reporters, and other visitors. "There was no time for lunch," Frederick recalled, "except four or five minutes snatched from other occupations." Anna would send over "some crackers and cheese," with cold tea in a flask, which led to rumors that Seward was drinking by day. (In response to a letter suggesting the arrest of an officer who claimed the secretary of state was "drunk from morning till night," Seward wrote loftily that "it has been a habit of my life to leave my conduct and character to the vindication of time and truth.") At about five in the afternoon, Seward would often suspend work and drive by carriage to one of the many military camps around Washington. There he would shake hands with the men and speak briefly with the officers; he was sometimes cheered as he arrived and departed.[28]

The secretary rarely dined with just his family during the war: either he was invited out or the Sewards would invite guests to their home. It was Anna who rented the house and decorated it with portraits of Washington, Jackson, Clay, and Webster from what she described as the "inexhaustible" collection of the State Department; it was Anna who supervised the servants; and it was Anna who presided as hostess at dinner and other parties. In late May 1861, for example, the *New York Times* reported on a "brilliant reception" at the Seward home, a party that included Lord Lyons and other diplomats and many military officers.

The house was "beautifully draped with flags," and the reporter found the sight "bright and beautiful and cheering." Seward moved among his guests with "a pleasant smile to one, a few words of kindly greeting to another, and a friendly shake of the hand to all." On other evenings, he would converse with friends over the dinner table, then enjoy a cigar on the back porch and a game of whist in the parlor. The card game was often interrupted by a visitor or a telegram from the War Office.[29]

———

By June 1861, more than 30,000 federal troops were encamped in and around Washington. The *New York Tribune* insisted in daily headlines that the Union Army should march "forward to Richmond." Frederick, in a letter home in late June, boasted that "we got Maryland in May, Missouri in June and probably shall get Virginia in July." Frederick's father was more cautious, like his friends Winfield Scott and Montgomery Meigs. At Seward's request, Meigs prepared a long letter advising against a premature advance into the South with untrained troops and inexperienced officers. Seward sent the letter to Lincoln and also persuaded the president, over the objection of Cameron, to make Meigs the quartermaster general. A few weeks later, secure in his new position, Meigs had a more aggressive view of the military situation: he argued in a cabinet meeting that the Union troops near Washington were better prepared and better equipped than the Confederates. Seward apparently agreed, as did Lincoln, who ordered Union general Irwin McDowell to attack the Confederates troops in and around Manassas, Virginia, about thirty miles west of Washington.[30]

After various delays, the Union troops attacked at Bull Run, near Manassas, on Sunday, July 21. Seward spent much of the afternoon in the War Department, smoking his cigar and reading the telegrams as they arrived. The early news was positive, but at around six a very different message arrived: "General McDowell's army in full retreat through Centreville. The day is lost. Save Washington and the remnants of this army." Seward grabbed the telegram and ran to the White House. Lincoln's secretary John Nicolay, in a letter to his fiancée, wrote that Seward demanded to know where the president was. "Gone to ride,"

Nicolay answered. "Have you any late news?" Seward asked. Nicolay started to read from a telegram. "Tell no one," Seward interrupted, "that is not so. The telegraph says that McDowell is in full retreat, and calls on General Scott to save the Capitol. Find the President and tell him to come immediately to General Scott's." Within a few minutes Lincoln, Seward, and the other cabinet members were gathered at Scott's office, where they remained until past midnight, reading the telegrams and debriefing men as they arrived back from the battlefield. Representative Elihu Washburne, after spending the day near the battlefield and then reporting to Lincoln and the cabinet, wrote home that he had never seen "a more sober set of men." [31]

Monday, July 22, was a dreary, rainy day in Washington. There was confusion about the details, but the main outlines of the disaster were clear enough: the Union troops had fled from the Confederates; hundreds of Union soldiers were dead and hundreds more captives. Seward was calm and philosophic. "One great battle has been disastrously lost," he wrote to his wife, "and nothing remains but to reorganize and begin again." He asked Governor Edwin Morgan of New York for help in raising more troops: "We will accept twenty-five or thirty thousand, but time is important. We want no three-months men, only three years or during war." (One factor in the defeat at Manassas was that men who had only enlisted for three months, knowing their terms were almost over, were reluctant to fight.) After consulting with Scott, Seward sent to Lincoln a list of "men fit to be generals," headed by George McClellan. Lincoln and Seward also spent several hours together, on the two days after the battle, visiting Union camps near Washington, first on the Virginia and then on the Maryland side of the Potomac. [32]

A week after the Bull Run disaster, Seward wrote to the American ministers abroad that the shock of the northern defeat had "passed away, producing no other results than a resolution stronger and deeper than ever to maintain the Union, and a prompt and effective augmentation of the forces for that end." Indeed, Lincoln had just signed into law bills calling for a million more men, and volunteers were pouring into northern recruiting offices. This letter from Seward was one of the first of many circular letters he would send to all the American ministers abroad, giving them an official perspective on developments, in order to correct the often erroneous or partial accounts that they would receive through newspapers or private letters.[33]

Many northerners were worried just after Bull Run about the security of Washington, but Seward was so confident that he asked his wife and daughter to visit, saying that although the weather was warm, their house was cool. Frances had not seen her husband in eight months, but she did not come immediately; she wrote to him that she would consider the question "when the weather is less oppressively hot." Perhaps realizing that she would not come to Washington on her own, Seward went to Auburn in late August. On the second evening of his short stay, a crowd gathered in his garden. The war, Seward told his neighbors, "may terminate next week, next month, next year. That depends on you. If you are brave, if you are loyal, if you are noble, the war will soon be brought to a successful issue." He urged the young men to enlist: "you could never fight for a cause more glorious; you could never fall for a country more worthy of sacrifice." As for himself, Seward said he would return to Washington, and "when I shall again see you, I know not." If he died, he hoped that his body would return to Auburn, but only if Auburn itself remained true to the Union. "May my bones never be laid in the midst of those who have proved false to their principles and unfaithful to their country."[34]

The next morning, Seward, Frances, Fanny, and his daughter-in-law Jenny departed from Auburn on an early train. (Jenny's husband William remained at home in Auburn, where he and a friend were now running a small bank.) They arrived in Washington in the late afternoon of the following day, ate dinner at their home, and then Seward took Fanny and Jenny (only sixteen and twenty at the time) across the street to the White House to meet the president. Fanny recorded in her diary that she was upset because they were still in "traveling attire," but Lincoln did not seem to mind; he "received us very cordially" and showed them his two kittens, a gift from Seward. "They were playing in one of the grand halls," Fanny noted, and "Mr. Lincoln seemed quite fond of them. Says they climb all over him."[35]

The next day was a Sunday, but the family did not attend church, for Seward was summoned to the White House, where he joined Lincoln and others in greeting General Benjamin Butler. In civilian life,

Butler was a lawyer, one with whom Seward had occasionally worked on legal cases; he was now one of the many political generals in the Union Army. Butler had already made his mark on the war by refusing to return slaves to their Virginia masters, arguing that they were a form of "contraband," a term that soon became shorthand for slaves who sought out the protection of the Union Army. Butler was just back from the Carolina coast, where he had led a highly successful expedition, capturing Forts Hatteras and Clark without a single Union casualty. In the afternoon, Lincoln joined the Seward family to visit two regiments camped south of the city. The colonel of one of these regiments, William Dwight of Massachusetts, reported in a letter home that Lincoln, Seward, and the whole family "came riding out to my camp today without the least notice." Although Dwight's men were just "lying about the camp" when Lincoln and the Sewards arrived in two carriages, Dwight had his men up and in line within ten minutes for inspection by the president. As Seward was leaving, he told the proud Dwight that this was "one of the best regiments we have seen," with men "more perfectly uniformed, cleaner and healthier looking than any I have seen."[36]

Fanny and her mother were in Washington for ten days, and according to Fanny's diary, her father saw Lincoln almost daily: at the White House, at the State Department, and especially in the afternoon, when they would drive out together to see the soldiers in their camps. Indeed, the diary gives the impression that Seward spent more time visiting with military men than dealing with diplomats. A whole day was devoted to a trip to Baltimore, where Jenny and Fanny toured Fort McHenry while Seward conferred with General Dix. On one evening, General Butler was the guest of honor for a dinner at the Sewards' house, and Fanny was delighted to meet this "man of note and renown." On another evening, General Scott, so stout he could barely walk, stopped by to pay his respects to Mrs. Seward.[37]

As she neared the end of this brief visit to Washington, Frances Seward felt that she had to call on Mary Lincoln, "especially as I went to see her husband." Having received word that Mrs. Lincoln would be available on a Monday evening after dinner, Seward, Frances, Fred, Anna, Fanny, Jenny, and William (in town for a few days) all presented themselves at the White House. The servant seated them in the Blue

Parlor, then went to inform Mrs. Lincoln of their arrival. "There we sat," Fanny wrote, until "after a lapse of some time the usher came and said Mrs. Lincoln begged to be excused, she was *very* much engaged." As Fanny observed, the truth was probably that Mary Lincoln did not want to see the Seward family; if she was really so busy, she would have given "general directions to the doorkeeper to let no one in." Mary Todd Lincoln never ceased to view Seward as her husband's rival, never accepted that the two men had become colleagues and close friends. She told her husband, at one point during the war, that she wished he had nothing to do with Seward, a "hypocrite" who simply "could not be trusted."[38]

Frances Seward hated making and receiving social calls of this sort; indeed, she hated Washington. This was the main reason why she visited the capital so rarely during the Civil War; but another was that she and her husband disagreed on the purpose of the war. For Frances, from the outset, the war was about slavery. After Fort Sumter she wrote to her husband that the "enthusiasm of the people—high and low rich and poor—[is] all enlisted at last in the cause of human rights. No concession from the South will avail to stem the torrent. No compromise will be made with slavery of black or white. God has heard the prayer of the oppressed and a fearful retribution awaits the oppressors." For Seward, the war was about the Union, and not about slavery. As he noted in a letter to Minister William Dayton in France, the condition of the slaves would not change, regardless of who won the war; Lincoln and the administration did not intend to interfere with slavery in the border or southern states.[39]

The slavery issue was raised while Frances was in Washington by a proclamation issued in Missouri by General John Frémont, declaring martial law in that state and purporting to free the slaves of all Confederate supporters there. Frances wrote to her sister Lazette praising the proclamation and hoping that the attorney general would not deem it improper or illegal. Lincoln and Seward had a very different view of Frémont's proclamation; they were worried (in Lincoln's words) that freeing slaves would "alarm our Southern Union friends and turn them against us." Lincoln first suggested and then ordered that Frémont rescind his decree. Although Seward must have discussed the issue with Frances while she was in Washington, she was not persuaded, for she wrote him immediately upon her return to Auburn that "I am sorry the President felt constrained to interfere with Frémont's proclamation—it was a measure so universally approved at the North that the President's action must give great dissatisfaction." Frances was wrong in thinking that the Frémont proclamation was universally approved in the North; most northerners still shared Seward's more limited view of the conflict. She was right, however, in thinking that the Union would ultimately have to deal with the issue of slavery.[40]

———

In late July, just after the Bull Run disaster, acting on the suggestion of Seward and others, Lincoln appointed George McClellan as commander of the Army of the Potomac. Although McClellan was only thirty-four years old, he had considerable military experience: second in his class at West Point, staff officer during the Mexican War, official observer of the Crimean War, and most recently leader of a small but successful campaign in western Virginia. Northerners had great hopes that McClellan would organize the eastern Union Army and lead it to victory. The *New York Tribune* ran an editorial entitled "Confidence Renewed," praising McClellan and his "admirable system of discipline." The *Chicago Tribune* happily reprinted an article from a southern paper calling McClellan an "officer of unquestioned capacity, an accomplished, enterprising, and successful soldier."[41]

Almost from the day he arrived in Washington, McClellan disliked Seward and denigrated him in private letters. The initial reason was Seward's old friend Scott, whom McClellan quickly decided was a "dotard" and perhaps even a "traitor." In early August, when Seward criticized McClellan for going around Scott to Lincoln, the young general wrote home to his wife: "how does he think I can save this country when stopped by General Scott?" A few weeks later, McClellan wrote his wife again that "I can't tell you how disgusted I am becoming with these wretched politicians—they are the most despicable set of men, and I think Seward is the meanest of them all—a meddling, officious, incompetent little puppy—he has done more than any other one man to bring all this misery upon the country and is one of the least competent to get us out of the scrape." And at the end of October, McClellan wrote that it was "terrible to stand by and see the cowardice of the President, the vileness of Seward, and the rascality of Cameron."[42]

McClellan disliked not only Seward but also Lincoln—whom he called "the original gorilla" in private—and the general did not especially hide his views. Lincoln's secretary Hay recorded an incident in November, when Lincoln, Seward, and Hay went to McClellan's house one evening. The servant said that the general was out but would be back shortly. After they had waited for an hour, McClellan returned, but instead of meeting them, went directly upstairs. The three men still waited, until the servant came to tell them that McClellan had gone to bed. Hay was horrified at what he viewed as an outrageous insult, a harbinger of military dictatorship, but Lincoln calmed him, "saying it was better at this time not to be making points of etiquette and personal dignity." Lincoln may or may not have said that he would "hold McClellan's horse if he would only bring us success"—the first source for this famous quote is a postwar letter from one who did not know the president well—but the president surely displayed incredible patience in dealing with the arrogant young general.[43]

One of McClellan's objections to Seward was his leading role in the "arbitrary arrests" of northern citizens; this was also a source of tension between Seward and the British. In an especially sharp letter in October, Lord Lyons complained about the arrest of two particular Britons, and more generally that Seward was arresting and imprisoning British citizens at "his own will and pleasure." The British government "cannot but regard this despotic and arbitrary power as inconsistent with the Constitution of the United States." Seward sent Lyons an equally sharp response, detailing the evidence against the two Britons and defending the constitutionality of the government's actions. The British could "hardly expect that the President will accept their explanations of the Constitution of the United States," especially when they would deprive the government of the power necessary to suppress the rebellion. When Seward published Lyons's letter and his response in the northern newspapers, most praised him for standing up to the British and many supported his policy of arrests. The New York Times commented that the war was "a life and death struggle, in which a resort to the extremest measures may become the highest of duties. It may seem hard to imprison an individual, but it is harder for a nation to be destroyed."[44]

Seward's publication of the Lyons correspondence was a minor public relations coup, but his publication at this same time of a letter to the northern governors, urging them to strengthen their harbors and coasts against possible foreign naval attacks, was a failure. Although he claimed that he was not acting because of any specific foreign threat, and indeed that foreign relations were in a better state than they had been for months, the letter naturally raised concerns. The stock market plunged and subscriptions to a pending federal loan dried up. Northern bankers complained to Chase that Seward's letter, and his decision to make it public, were "proof positive that Seward was unfit for his post."[45]

Seward was blamed not only for his own actions—and he deserves some for this letter to the governors—but also for the overall course of the war. George Fogg, the American minister in Switzerland, nominally reported to Seward, but this did not mean that his negative views of Seward had changed. In October, a friend wrote to Fogg that the Lincoln administration had been "an utter and palpable failure, and would be denounced by every body, but for the desire to sustain the government at this particular time." Seward was the cause of the failure, this friend continued, saying that his "whole course has been full of the most inexcusable blunders," and that the secretary "thought that all our difficulties could be settled on paper, when it was apparent to any one that they could only be settled at the point of the bayonet."[46]

After their victory at Bull Run, the Confederates believed that they had earned the right to full recognition from the European powers. To open diplomatic relations, the Confederacy appointed James Mason, former senator from Virginia, as its minister to Britain, and John Slidell, former senator from Louisiana, as its minister to France. Rumors and reports of these appointments reached the North in late September and early October, along with speculation about how the two ministers would escape the Union naval blockade, which was growing increasingly effective. Seward suggested to Welles that it would be useful to capture the two Confederate envoys from the Confederate warship on which they would presumably attempt to run the blockade, and Welles sent orders to this effect in mid-October. Seward was thus disappointed to learn, through the *New York Times* in late October, that Mason and Slidell had reached Cuba safely two weeks earlier. By the time this news reached Washington, it seemed likely the two Confederate ministers were on their way to Europe, perhaps almost there.[47]

On November 1, General Scott resigned and McClellan assumed his duties as commander of all the Union armies. A few days after his resignation, the aged and tired Scott wrote his friend Seward to inform him that he was going to Europe. The primary purpose of his trip was health, Scott wrote, but "it may be in my way, in private circles, to counter-act, in some degree, the machinations of those arch-traitors Slidell and Mason." Scott left for Europe at almost the same time as three other northern men whom Seward had recruited to serve as informal envoys: his friends Thurlow Weed and Archbishop John Hughes, and the Episcopal bishop of Ohio Charles McIlvaine. Some have suggested that Seward was reacting to the news of Mason and Slidell by sending his friends abroad, but this seems unlikely; he had been thinking for many months about the need to have informal as well as formal representatives overseas. As it turned out, the four northerners would be in Europe for the most dramatic and tense weeks in transatlantic relations of the entire Civil War.[48]

———

At about noon on November 16, Seward learned that the USS *San Jacinto*, under the command of Captain Charles Wilkes, had fired upon a British merchant ship, the *Trent*, and captured from her deck Mason, Slidell, and their two private secretaries. Seward had hoped, a few weeks earlier, that Mason and Slidell might be taken from a Confederate warship; he never imagined that the Navy would seize the men from an unarmed British vessel on its way between two neutral ports. His first action was to order the federal marshal in New York to intercept the *San Jacinto* before it could enter New York Harbor and to take the prisoners instead to Fort Warren, in a remote part of Boston Harbor. Seward feared that if the four Confederates were landed in New York City, they might be attacked by an angry mob.[49]

The *Trent* crisis was the Cuban missile crisis of the nineteenth century: a moment when the United States faced possible war with the world's other major power, a period of intense emotion and apprehension. The initial northern reaction to the news of the capture of Mason and Slidell was a combination of patriotic pleasure, deep concern, and legal research. "We do not believe the American heart ever thrilled with more genuine delight," the *New York Times* said, "than it did yesterday at the intelligence of the capture of Messrs. Slidell and Mason." The *Times* also noted that the streets were filled with lawyers and would-be lawyers, citing "Grotius, Puffendorf, Vattel and Wheaton" to support different views of the legality of the seizure. Frederick wrote home of this same sudden legal interest: "For twenty-four hours the town has teemed with international law disquisitions, Willard's Hotel and the streets being especial centers of learning, sage opinion and profound advice." Seward was engaged in his own quiet legal research, writing the scholar George Bancroft about prior cases. The *Boston Evening Transcript* expected there would be a "sharp exchange" with Britain, but insisted that Wilkes was within his legal rights to stop the *Trent* and to seize Mason and Slidell. Frederick's preliminary view was the same; he wrote the American consul in Havana that "the course adopted by Captain Wilkes in his late proceedings after consultation with you was entirely in accordance with the principles of international law laid down by the best and most authoritative writers on the subject."[50]

Gideon Welles later claimed that "no man was more elated or jubilant over the capture of [Mason and Slidell] than Mr. Seward, who for a time made no attempt to conceal his gratification and approval of the act of Wilkes." There is no contemporary evidence, however, that Seward was elated; on the contrary, he was almost instantly concerned. "After the first exultation was over," Frederick wrote his mother on November 17, "everybody began discussing the probable effect on English relations"; diplomats in Washington viewed the situation as "serious" and even "ominous." Lyons advised London that the federal government had "very serious apprehensions of the resentment which they suppose will be aroused in England." Mercier reported to Paris that Seward, unusually subdued, told him "how awful for the whole world would be an Anglo-American war." Seward informed Adams that Captain Wilkes had acted without instructions, and commented that "Lyons has judiciously refrained from all communication with me on the subject, and I thought it equally wise to reserve ourselves until we hear what the British government may have to say on the subject."[51]

On November 23, Frederick wrote Frances that, during the past week, "the whole community and the press have done little else but discuss diplomacy and the precedents of international law." The papers carried daily reports regarding the details of the seizure, speculations regarding the British reaction, and predictions regarding possible war with Britain. Frederick, likely reflecting his father's views, said that "there will be much scolding in England but I doubt if they really want to quarrel with us. We are more ready for war with them than they are for war with us." Given the delays in transatlantic communication, it would take several weeks for official British reaction to reach Washington, but even before then, the stock market in New York City declined and merchants in Boston fretted about their ships. One merchant wrote to Seward that he had sixteen ships at sea, which with their cargoes were worth more than a million dollars, and pleaded with him to avoid war, or at least postpone it for six months. Many papers, however, demanded that the United States resist any British demands, and proudly predicted that if there was a war, the United States would conquer Canada.[52]

When Captain Wilkes arrived in Boston in late November, he was hailed as a hero; he later received similar welcomes in New York and Philadelphia. One of the first actions of the House, after Congress assembled in early December, was to pass a resolution thanking Wilkes for his "brave, adroit, and patriotic conduct in the arrests and detention of the traitors James Mason and John Slidell." The *New York Tribune* reported from Washington in the middle of December that "the general feeling among Americans is that the United States can never give up Mason and Slidell." The *Chicago Tribune* agreed, saying that the rumor that the British government would demand the release of Mason and Slidell "causes a universal sentiment of defiance." The press in British Canada reacted with an equal and opposite fury. One Canadian paper assumed that Seward had personally ordered the seizure of Mason and Slidell, and denounced his "utter folly and desperate wickedness."[53]

Seward worked quietly to counter these belligerent reports with more moderate and conciliatory views. On December 9, the *Daily National Intelligencer*, often an administration mouthpiece, printed long excerpts from a letter from James Madison, when he was secretary of state, to James Monroe, when he was minister to England. The letter suggested, according to the newspaper, that the United States might be "estopped" by its own principles from holding Mason and Slidell. The *Intelligencer* did not find this ancient letter through its own research; Seward is the far more likely source. The *New York Times*, often a Seward newspaper, sounded a similar note. On December 17, the *Times* argued that Wilkes, instead of seizing Mason and Slidell from the deck of the *Trent*, should have brought the *Trent* into a port so that the legal issues could be properly determined by a prize court. The *Times* stressed that "the American people do not desire a war with England—that none but secessionists and those who sympathize with them, are disposed to a needless rupture of our friendly relations with any foreign power."[54]

———

The relative calm of late November and early December—while waiting for the official response from Britain to the *Trent* crisis—allowed Seward time to work on other issues. One task was to prepare the foreign policy section of Lincoln's annual message, which did not mention the *Trent*, a silence that Lyons thought showed "prudence and discretion."[55]

The message was accompanied by reports from several cabinet secretaries, including one from Secretary of War Simon Cameron, who argued that "it is as clearly a right of the government to arm slaves, when it may become necessary, as it is to use gun-powder taken from the enemy." When Lincoln saw this language, he was concerned about its effect in the border states and insisted that Cameron recall the report. Seward agreed with Lincoln, but it was too late, for Cameron's report was already in print in some newspapers. Soon a second version of the report was also in print, with Lincoln's more moderate wording. This airing of another policy dispute within the administration was, in the words of a Chicago editor, "a fiasco." As in the case of Frémont's proclamation purporting to confiscate slaves in Missouri, the Cameron incident highlighted the tensions between moderate Republicans, such as Lincoln and Seward, and more radical Republicans, who wanted to see a more aggressive war, and especially a war against slavery.[56]

In December 1861, Seward started an important custom that continues to the present day: the publication of American diplomatic correspondence. His predecessors had sometimes published a few selected letters, but Seward now printed a book of more than 400 pages containing mainly recent letters between himself and the American ministers abroad, but also including a few letters between himself and the ministers based in Washington. In succeeding years, he would publish more complete records; four volumes appeared at the end of 1864, including hundreds of recent letters with the principal foreign missions. Seward was publishing partly for history; although historians would have access to the full archives, he knew that they would turn first to the published volumes, so his selections would influence their histories. But he was mainly publishing for the present, seeking to influence domestic public opinion, knowing that American newspapers would print and comment on the letters. Those whose correspondence was published in this way were not always happy. Charles Francis Adams, writing from London to Edward Everett, a former secretary of state, was concerned that the "rather liberal publication of my more confidential dispatches may stand in the way of my future usefulness at this post." Everett agreed, writing Adams that Seward's practice of "emptying the pigeon holes of the Department of State into the street seems to me an entire novelty, and by no means an improvement on the former practice."[57]

Seward received at this time a letter that must have amused him: the members of the Seward Club of Philadelphia had resolved to elect him as U.S. president in 1864. Seward responded that he was not interested in the position, or indeed in any position other than his present one. When he became secretary of state, he "renounce[d] all ambition" so that "the counsels that I might give to the president in such a crisis should not only be, but be recognized as being, loyal and patriotic." Seward believed that the fate of the United States would be decided before the 1864 election. If the nation was saved, as he prayed and believed it would be, "I do not fear that my zeal in that great achievement will be overlooked by grateful generations to come after us." And if the nation should be lost, he did not want those who would "study the causes of the great ruin" to find among these causes "any want of self-sacrifice on my part." The *New York Times*, when it summarized Seward's letter, contrasted his approach with that of some of his cabinet colleagues, who "would not be indisposed to replace Mr. Lincoln." The *Times* did not give a name, but it was clearly referring to Salmon Chase, whose presidential ambitions were still strong.[58]

———

In mid-December, reports started to reach American newspapers of the British reaction to the arrests on the *Trent*. On December 13, the *New York Times* carried accounts of the "great excitement" in Britain over the "outrage on the British flag." The next day, the *Times* reprinted an article from the (London) *Morning Post*, a semi-official paper, insisting that the United States had no legal right to take the four men prisoner from a British merchant ship. "If we are right, the British Government will clearly be entitled to reparation and apology, and no reparation could be complete without the restitution of the passengers taken from under our flag." On the afternoon of December 15, Seward interrupted Lincoln while he was having tea with several midwestern politicians. According to the diary of Senator Orville Browning, one of those present, Seward said that he now had letters "stating that the British Cabinet had decided that the arrest of Mason and Slidell was a violation of international law, and that we must apologize and restore them to the protection of the British flag." Browning told Lincoln and the others that he did not believe the British government would do "so foolish a thing"; but he added that "if she is determined to force a war upon us why so be it."[59]

Northern newspapers were also filled, in mid-December, with detailed reports from British papers regarding preparations for war against America; the British government was sending thousands of troops to Canada, along with artillery, rifles, and ammunition. The British government had imposed an embargo on the export of gunpowder and the critical ingredients in making gunpowder—sulfur and saltpeter. This was a serious issue: Seward in fact had an agent in London, a member of the famous DuPont family, purchasing saltpeter in the name of the DuPont firm, but for the account of the U.S. government. DuPont had purchased more than 2,000 tons of saltpeter in November, and was in the process of having it loaded onto ships, when the government imposed the embargo. The northern newspapers merely mentioned the saltpeter embargo and gave considerable attention to the troop movements, but Seward was far more worried about the saltpeter shortage than the prospect of British troops arriving in icebound Canada.[60]

Seward was among the guests on December 16 at a reception hosted by the minister from Brazil. One of the other guests was George Bancroft, the Democratic politician and historian, who reported in a letter that Seward "looked dirty, rusty, vulgar, and low" and used words like "hell and damn." Another guest was William Russell, the British reporter, who later recalled that Seward predicted at this reception that, if there was war between the United States and Britain, the two nations would "wrap the whole world in flames! No power [is] so remote that [it] will not feel the fire of our battle and be burned by our conflagration!" Because these remarks do not appear in the diary Russell kept at the time, nor in Bancroft's account, it is open to question whether Seward made them, although perhaps he said something similar. Russell dined with Seward the next day and reported no such dramatic comments; he wrote to an American friend that Seward "said everything consistent with the honor of the United States would be done to make England feel U.S. did not mean to hurt her feelings or injure her prestige."[61]

On December 18, the newspapers reported that "the Queen's messenger" had just arrived in Boston and departed by train for Washington. Seward was thus not surprised when Lord Lyons showed up on December 19 to say that he finally had his official instructions from the British foreign minister Lord Russell regarding the *Trent* affair. Lyons summarized for Seward: the British government viewed the seizure of the Confederates from the *Trent* as a violation of international law; Britain expected the United States to apologize in appropriate terms and to deliver up the four prisoners. When Seward asked whether there was any time limit within which he had to respond, Lyons said that, although he did not want to appear to be giving an ultimatum, he was only allowed to wait seven days for an answer. Seward requested a copy of Russell's dispatch, since "so much depended upon the wording of it." Lyons hesitated, saying that once he gave him the dispatch, "the seven days would immediately begin to run." Seward persuaded Lyons to let him have an unofficial copy "on the understanding that no one but [Seward] and the president should know that [Lyons] had done so." Lyons reported to Russell that he was "glad to let him have it on these terms," for he hoped that it would give Seward, "who is now on the peace side of the Cabinet," time to work out an appropriate response.[62]

After Lyons left his office, Seward read and reread the British dispatch. The first paragraph detailed how the *San Jacinto* had stopped the *Trent* and seized the Confederates, "an affront to the British flag and a violation of international law." The second paragraph explained that, in light of the "friendly relations which have long subsisted between Great Britain and the United States," the British were prepared to believe that Captain Wilkes had acted without instructions or "greatly misunderstood his instructions." The British trusted that when the U.S. government considered the matter, it would provide Britain with the only acceptable redress: "the liberation of the four gentlemen" to Lyons or another British officer and "a suitable apology for the aggression which has been committed." Seward immediately went to the British legation where, according to Lyons, Seward told him how pleased he was that "the dispatch was courteous and friendly, and not dictatorial or menacing." Seward asked what would happen if, at the end of the seven days, he requested additional time or proposed negotiation. Lyons said that his instructions were clear: in that scenario, Lyons and the entire British delegation would have to leave immediately for Britain; they would break off diplomatic relations. The two men agreed to meet again in two days.[63]

When Lyons called upon Seward as agreed on Saturday, December 21, Seward admitted that he had not yet mastered the legal issues. As Lyons reported the conversation to Russell, Seward said that it would be "a great convenience to himself personally" if Lyons could postpone presentation of the dispatch, and thus postpone the date for Seward's response. The next day was Sunday; could Lyons wait till Monday? Lyons agreed, on condition that they meet early Monday morning. Later that same Saturday, Seward met with Henri Mercier and asked whether he thought the threatened departure of Lyons from Washington would "necessarily be followed by war." Mercier responded that he believed it would, based on the extensive British military preparations. Moreover, France would not blame Britain "for following a line of conduct which the French government would certainly follow in similar circumstances." If Mercier's views were indeed the views of the French government, they could be important in persuading Lincoln and the cabinet to adopt a moderate course, so Seward pressed Mercier: did he have any instructions from Thouvenel, the French foreign minister, on these points? No, Mercier confessed, he did not yet have Thouvenel's instructions, but he expected them any day. Seward thanked Mercier for his candor and suggested that they should wait to see the instructions, for "they may perhaps be different from what you suppose." [64]

From his comments to Mercier, Lyons, and others, it is clear that Seward by this date intended to surrender the prisoners. Lincoln, however, did not want to release the prisoners; he wanted to hold them captive while the legal issues were decided by international arbitration, perhaps with the French government serving as arbitrator, as proposed by the *New York Times*. Lincoln told Browning on Saturday, December 21, that "the question was easily susceptible of a pacific solution if England was at all disposed to act justly with us, and suggested that it was a proper case for arbitration." He then read Browning what the senator described as "a very able paper which he intends, at the proper time, shall go as a letter from the Secretary of State to Lord Lyons." In the draft, Lincoln proposed that Seward should tell Lyons that the United States did not believe Britain would demand a "categorical answer" based upon only a "partial record." Lincoln wanted Seward to request that both sides submit the facts and precedents to "such friendly arbitration as is usual among nations," and to assure Britain that the United States would "abide the result" of the arbitration. [65]

Early on Monday, December 23, as they had agreed, Lyons formally presented Seward with Russell's dispatch. In a separate private message, Russell had written Lyons that "what we want is a plain Yes, or a plain No to our very simple demands, and we want that plain Yes or No within seven days of the dispatch." Lyons almost certainly did not read this private message to Seward—he may not have received it yet—but he again told Seward that he needed a prompt answer, and that he would have to break off relations if the prisoners were not released. Lyons sensed, from Seward's tone, that he would recommend release. The regular day for a cabinet meeting was December 24, but Seward asked Lincoln to postpone it by one day, telling him (as Nicolay and Hay later recalled), "I shall then be ready." He needed more time to work on his draft response; he also wanted time to digest the many letters and reports that were arriving from Europe.[66]

Thurlow Weed, Seward's oldest friend and now his unofficial ambassador in Europe, was in Paris when news of the *Trent* seizure arrived there. Weed reported to Seward that the seizure caused a storm in both France and England, and warned that "if the taking of the rebels from under the protection of the British flag was intended, and is avowed, and maintained, *it means war.*" A few days later, writing from London, Weed reported that "everything here is on a war footing. Such prompt and gigantic preparations were never known." Charles Sumner also shared with Seward, on December 24, letters from two important British friends of America, the members of Parliament John Bright and Richard Cobden. Cobden argued that the United States should release Mason and Slidell and use the incident as an opportunity to develop a new and better system of belligerent rights. Bright wrote Sumner that "at all hazards you must not let this matter grow to a war with England. Even if you are right and we are wrong, war will be fatal to your idea of restoring the Union."[67]

Weed's letters informed Seward that not only was Britain angry at the United States; Seward himself was an object of especial anger. "There is general distrust of and hostility to yourself; how created or why, I know not," Weed wrote from London in early December. "I was told yesterday, repeatedly, that I ought to write the President demanding your dismissal." Weed mentioned that Seward had said something to the duke of Newcastle, when they dined together in Albany in October 1860 on the occasion of the visit of the Prince of Wales, that had just appeared in the British newspapers. Seward would have been mystified by Weed's remarks but for the *New York Times* of December 25, which reprinted an article from a British newspaper. According to this report, Seward had told the duke that "either Mr. Lincoln or myself will be the next president of the United States. If Mr. Lincoln be chosen, I shall be secretary, and we are determined to take the first opportunity that presents itself to insult your country." The duke said that he feared this would lead to war, to which Seward allegedly replied: "Oh no, there will be no war, but we will—we must insult you." Seward wrote back to Weed that "I saw the Duke of Newcastle only the one night at Albany, and then had only the few words possible on the way from the hotel to the cars. The whole of the story, as I see it here, is fabricated. I never said or thought a word like it." Other sources, however, including a letter from the duke to the Canadian governor, indicate that Seward had indeed spoken to the duke about the likelihood of American insults. Whatever was said in October 1860, Seward knew in December 1861 that the current crisis would be exacerbated by the British impression that he was a personal enemy of Britain.[68]

According to Orville Browning's diary, Christmas Day was a "bright, pretty and rather mild day," on which one could "walk without an overcoat." Seward walked that morning to the White House, where Lincoln and the cabinet gathered at ten o'clock and met for the next four or five hours. Seward started the discussion by reading first Russell's dispatch to Lyons and then his own lengthy draft response. Seward's draft began by restating the facts, noting that the British captain of the *Trent* was well aware that Mason and Slidell were enemies of the United States bound for Europe with enemy dispatches. He then argued that Mason and Slidell and their dispatches were "contraband of war," that Wilkes could lawfully stop and search the *Trent* for contraband, and that having found contraband, he could seize it. The most difficult question, Seward wrote, was whether Wilkes exercised the "right of capture in the manner allowed and recognized by the law of nations." He conceded that Wilkes, by allowing the *Trent* to proceed on her way to England rather than taking her into port for a legal trial of the issues, had violated the norms of international law. These were not merely international principles, Seward said, they were *American* principles, laid down by Jefferson, Madison, and Monroe. "If I decide this case in favor of my own government," Seward's draft response continued, "I must disavow its most cherished principles, and reverse and forever abandon its essential policy." This he would not do; instead, the four prisoners would be "cheerfully liberated" to Lyons, who had only to indicate "a time and place for receiving them."[69]

Seward's draft was not the only letter read to the cabinet; the members also heard letters from Adams and Weed, reporting on the mood in London and Paris, and the letters from Bright and Cobden, read by Sumner, who was present at Lincoln's invitation. Attorney General Edward Bates recorded in his diary that "there was great reluctance on the part of some members of the cabinet—and even the President himself" to accept Seward's arguments. Lincoln was concerned about "the displeasure of our own people—lest they should accuse us of timidly truckling to the power of England." This concern was justified; the next day, Republican senator John Parker Hale of New Hampshire would declare that "not a man can be found, who is in favor of this surrender [of the prisoners], for it would humiliate us in the eyes of the world, irritate our own people, and subject us to their indignant scorn." On the other hand, Lincoln and the cabinet were also worried about war with England and how it would affect the war with the South. "To go to war with England now," Bates wrote, "is to abandon all hope of suppressing the rebellion," for the British "would sweep us from all the southern waters" and "our trade would be utterly ruined and our treasury bankrupt." Chase's notes indicate that he had not made up his mind: he praised Wilkes, conceded that Seward was right on the law, but added that yielding to Britain would be "gall and wormwood," and that "rather than consent to the liberation of these men, I would sacrifice everything I possess."[70]

At some point during this discussion, Frederick Seward arrived, bearing a copy of the long-awaited letter from the French foreign minister Thouvenel. Although Thouvenel disagreed with Seward on some of the legal details—for example, he argued that Mason and Slidell could not themselves be viewed as contraband—he agreed that because Wilkes had not brought the *Trent* into port, he had violated international law. If belligerents could stop neutral ships and seize contrabrand in the way in which Wilkes had done in this instance, Thouvenel wrote, "we would be right back to the vexatious practices of earlier days against which no other power has protested more strongly than the United States." France expected that the United States would now yield up the four prisoners as Britain demanded. He added that "one would search in vain to find in what interest, for what objective, [the United States] would risk provoking a rupture with Great Britain by a contrary attitude." Thouvenel's letter allowed Seward to argue that there would be little point in the United States asking France to serve as arbitrator; France had already decided that Britain was right on the legal issues.[71]

Frederick recalled years later that at the end of the meeting, one cabinet member said, "we need not decide at once. Let us settle it that we won't surrender them today. We can meet again, and consider about it tomorrow." According to Frederick, after the other cabinet members left the room, Lincoln said to Seward: "You will go on, of course, preparing your answer, which, as I understand it, will state the reasons why they ought to be given up. Now I have a mind to try my hand at stating the reasons why they ought not to be given up. We will compare the points on each side." Frederick's recollection is probably not right on the details: if Bates is correct, Seward had already read out his entire draft, so Lincoln was not in any doubt about its terms; and if Browning is correct, Lincoln's own draft was prepared several days before the Christmas Day meeting. But it seems likely that Frederick is right that at some point there was a conversation in which Lincoln told Seward about his alternative draft, the one that would not yield up the prisoners, but would instead suggest arbitration.[72]

The cabinet met again on Thursday, December 26. Not long after these events, Seward told both Lyons and Weed that on this morning no one in authority, except himself, was prepared to surrender Mason and Slidell; if this is even close to correct, Seward still had considerable work to do to persuade Lincoln and the cabinet. He probably presented to the cabinet two more letters, one from Samuel DuPont and one from John Dahlgren, both discussing the saltpeter situation. In the end, as Bates recorded, "all yielded to the necessity, and unanimously concurred in Mr. Seward's letter to Lord Lyons, after some verbal and formal amendments." Seward later told Charles Francis Adams that, although all the other cabinet members opposed the release, none of them "could suggest any adequate form of policy," so "the discussion gradually subsided into modifications of the language" of Seward's draft. Seward happily agreed to change his draft in many minor respects, "until he had obtained the acquiescence of all."[73]

Frederick wrote that, after this second cabinet meeting, Seward reminded Lincoln about his promised draft. "You thought you might frame an argument for the other side?" Lincoln smiled and shook his head. "I found I could not make an argument that would satisfy my own mind, and that proved to me your ground was the right one." There are two other versions of the story about Lincoln's draft, perhaps more reliable if less quotable. Seward told Adams in 1870 that when he first read the president his own draft, Lincoln "declared that he could not agree with it at all, and he then undertook the task of preparing a substitute, to which Mr. S. immediately consented. But when the [Lincoln] substitute came and was compared with the [Seward] original, it was at once found so insufficient [that] the President voluntarily abandoned it, and acquiesced in [Seward's] draft with a few modifications." John Bigelow, in his memoir, recalled that Seward's friend Richard Blatchford, when he arrived in Paris in early 1862, related how Lincoln insisted that he would never give up the Confederate prisoners. Seward responded that, in that case, he would have to ask Lincoln to write the response to the British foreign minister, "for the strength of the argument from our own past policy, so far as I can see, is all in favor of a compliance with his demands." Lincoln agreed to prepare a draft, but he asked Seward to work on his own draft in parallel, and when Seward presented his draft to the president, the president discarded his own, saying Seward's argument was "unanswerable."[74]

Although they disagree in the details, these three versions agree on the main point: that Lincoln prepared a draft but decided, on reflection, to abandon it and adopt Seward's. It is fortunate that Lincoln did so, because the arbitration approach in his draft was anything but the "plain yes" or "plain no" within seven days that the British demanded. If the American response to the British had taken the form of Lincoln's draft, Lord Lyons would have been required, by his instructions, to leave Washington with all his staff and return to England; orders had already been sent to the British fleet to prepare to take Lyons on short notice. For all its politeness, Lincoln's draft would have been perceived in Britain as an attempt to avoid the issues, an improper effort to hold indefinitely four prisoners seized illegally from under the British flag. Lincoln's draft would probably have led Great Britain to declare war against the United States.[75]

The next morning, December 27, Seward invited Lyons to his office and told him, as Lyons reported to London, that "he had been able to effect a satisfactory settlement" of the crisis. Seward said that he had been "through the fires of Tophet" to get the men released, Tophet being the place where the ancient Canaanites sacrificed children by burning them alive. Not long afterward, Seward's messenger delivered the formal note to Lyons, who immediately dispatched a copy to London. Lyons explained in his covering note to the foreign minister that he viewed the key element of Seward's response as the surrender of the prisoners; that was enough to justify Lyons remaining in Washington, even if the British disagreed (as they later would) with some of Seward's legal analysis. Lyons wanted to discuss immediately with the secretary the arrangements for the release of the prisoners, but Seward put him off for a day or two, saying that he needed to address other issues first.[76]

Seward spent much of December 27 writing letters, including one to his friend Weed: "You will see what has been done. You will know who did it. You will hardly be more able to shield me from the reproaches for doing it, than you have been able to shield me in England for the reproaches of hostility to that country, and designs for war against it." He also gathered and delivered to the newspapers five key documents: his letter to Adams saying that Wilkes had acted without instructions; the letter from Russell demanding the prisoners; Seward's long response; Thouvenel's letter setting out the French views; and Seward's response to Mercier. Seward's decision to publish all these papers immediately, and to prevent any prior news report, shows that he was aware that he needed not merely to persuade the president and the British; he also needed to persuade the American public. Indeed, his long letter to Lyons, with its praise for Wilkes and its references to Jefferson and Madison, was written far more for the American public than for the British minister or legal scholars.[77]

That night, Seward hosted a dinner party at his home; the guests included Senators Preston King, Ira Harris, and Orville Browning, former Senator John Crittenden, and Anthony Trollope. Fanny Seward, who generally loved all things literary, did not like Trollope, whom she described in her diary as "a great homely, red, stupid-faced Englishman, with a disgusting beard of iron grey." She was also displeased by a negative remark by Crittenden about women; "so much for you," she wrote dismissively. After dinner, Seward took all the American guests into his library and read out to them the various letters, including his response to the British demands. Browning recorded that "we all agreed with him that in the present exigency [the prisoners] should be given up." Frederick recalled that "coupled with their compliments, however, were many regrets, that the act must inevitably doom [Seward] to unpopularity." Seward's response was that "if a sacrifice is required, it is for me to make it, for mine is the department to which the case belongs."[78]

In the event, no sacrifice was required. When the correspondence was published in the northern newspapers on December 28 and 29, the almost universal reaction was relief and praise. The *Daily National Intelligencer* lauded the "lucid dispatch" of Seward and the "firmness and sincerity with which the Administration, resisting a natural tendency impressed by the conceived drift of public opinion in our own country, has resolved to do what it believes to be right in the premises." The *Chicago Tribune* declared that the "settlement of the *Trent* affair affords much gratification among all classes, whatever their previous opinions, believing it has saved us from war with Great Britain, and possibly with France." The *New York Times* observed that there would be "profound satisfaction [in] the whole country" that the United States had "escaped the fearful perils of a war with England which, whatever might have been its ultimate issue, would have given a certain triumph to the southern rebellion." Lincoln's secretary and Seward's friend, John Hay, even wrote a poem for Seward, saying that a "grateful people" would some day "hail the power they did not comprehend."[79]

Meanwhile, Seward and Lyons worked out the details of the transfer of the prisoners to eliminate any chance of an angry scene. The four men were transferred first by tugboat from Fort Warren to Provincetown, on the remote tip of Cape Cod, where they boarded a British warship. A winter storm forced their ship to detour south, so it was not until January 29, 1862, that Mason and Slidell would reach Britain. Long before this, on January 9, news of Seward's response to Lyons had reached

Britain, where it was greeted with relief akin to that in the northern United States. British theaters interrupted their evening performances to announce the news, and men and women stood and cheered, for there would be no war.[80]

The *Trent* crisis, arising out of a seizure near Cuba, and the Cuban missile crisis, arising almost exactly a hundred years later out of missiles based on that island, were in many ways similar. Both involved a real risk of ruinous war. Bates noted in his description of the December 1861 cabinet meetings that "all of us were impressed by the magnitude of the subject and believed that upon our decision depended the dearest interest, probably the existence of the nation." A similar comment could have been made by a cabinet officer in October 1962. Lincoln is often credited with avoiding the possible war with Britain: "one war at a time," he is supposed to have said during the *Trent* crisis.[81] It was Seward not Lincoln, however, who insisted upon the immediate release of the prisoners. If Lincoln's draft dispatch, suggesting arbitration, had become the official American response to Lyons, it would have forced Lyons to break off diplomatic relations, and might well have led to war. Lincoln changed his mind, but it was Seward who convinced him to change his mind, and who persuaded the rest of the cabinet to go along. Seward also deserves considerable credit for the skillful way in which he managed the press, first preparing the public for the possible release of the prisoners, and then persuading the public to accept and even applaud that release. There were many points at which Seward changed the course of American history, but few as momentous as the *Trent* crisis.[82]

CHAPTER 12

"Remove Him!":

1862

F rances spent much of the first day of 1862 on a long letter from Washington to her sister Lazette. It was a "bright, beautiful morning" in the capital, she wrote, and "for the first time since we have been here the carriages are rolling along the streets as they used to do in old times." Four members of the family—her husband, Fred, Fanny, and their daughter-in-law Anna—had gone to the White House reception and then returned to host the family's own reception. For two hours the house was filled with diplomats, senior officials, military officers, and families. Frances did not mingle among the guests but remained in a back room, and their son Augustus, even more reclusive, "withdrew from the house after breakfast and has not returned." Later, after the reception was over, the Sewards drove north along Fourteenth Street, then explored what Fanny described in her diary as "all that beautiful neighborhood of Rock Creek." The weather was "really *warm*," Fanny noted, almost "too much so." They passed many Army camps, glimpsed a funeral procession, and on their return avoided a couple of drunken officers racing their carriages through Georgetown. In general, Fanny noted how orderly the camps were, especially for a holiday.[1]

Although the administration had been in office for less than a year, Simon Cameron had already proved himself incompetent as secretary of war; moreover, his department was awash in corruption. As Seward later told the story, one January evening Lincoln arrived at Seward's home, "sat down with me on this sofa upon which we are now sitting, and abruptly commenced talking about the condition of the War Department. He soon made it apparent that he had all along observed and known as much about" the problems in the department as any of the others in the administration. Lincoln and Seward agreed that Cameron should be removed and that Edwin Stanton—the diligent lawyer who had served as Seward's window into the late Buchanan administration—would be a good successor. Seward said that Stanton "was of great force—full of expedients, and thoroughly loyal."[2]

Lincoln wrote Cameron to say that he would "gratify" Cameron by appointing him as minister to Russia, a lucrative post in which Cameron had expressed some interest. The next day, while Salmon Chase and Seward were discussing Cameron at Seward's house, Cameron himself showed up, angered by Lincoln's letter, which he read as a rude dismissal. Seward and Chase calmed him down, and soon Lincoln mollified him with a warmer letter. Cameron resigned, Stanton was nominated and confirmed, and Seward chuckled to his wife that "not only was the press completely taken by surprise, but with all its fertility of conjecture, not one newspaper has conceived the real cause." Stanton immediately instituted changes that influenced not only his department; "the very atmosphere of the city breathes of change," the *New York Times* reported, "the streets, the hotels, the halls of Congress."[3]

At about this same time, late in January 1862, Ralph Waldo Emerson, the famous philosopher, arrived in Washington for a few days. Emerson recorded in his journal that when Charles Sumner took him on Saturday to Seward's "dingy" office, Seward told a convoluted story, then invited Emerson to join him for church. At St. John's on Sunday morning, Emerson was "a little awkward in finding my place in the common prayer book" and Seward "was obliging in guiding me." After church, Seward suggested they should go to see Lincoln, saying that "I almost always call on him at this hour." At the White House they visited first with the two Lincoln boys, Willie and Tad, who were having their hair dressed, and then with Lincoln himself. During dinner at Seward's house, Seward told many tales, including his version of the conversation with the duke of Newcastle. Seward's "manner and face were so intelligent and amicable" that Emerson, who had at first thought him ugly, "now thought him positively handsome."[4]

Emerson visited Seward at a good time: unlike the last weeks of 1861, with the *Trent* crisis, the first months of 1862 were a quiet period in foreign affairs. Britain and France were briefly excited by reports that the Union was sinking ships laden with stones in the channels of the Charleston Harbor. There was even some talk that the European nations might use this "barbarous" assault as an excuse to intervene in the war on the side of the South. Seward calmly explained to the European nations that the North was not trying to close the southern ports forever, merely to close certain side channels to simplify the blockade during the war. His explanations were accepted and the controversy subsided.[5]

More serious were reports which arrived in January that Britain, France, and Spain had sent dozens of ships and more than 50,000 soldiers to the coast of Mexico. The purported purpose of this expedition was to force the bankrupt Mexican government to pay its debts to the three European powers. Seward was naturally concerned that one or more of the European nations might use this as an excuse to conquer part of Mexico and turn it back into a European colony. In April, he was pleased to learn that Britain and Spain, satisfied with concessions made by the Mexican government, had withdrawn from the joint expedition. The French troops, however, continued to advance toward Mexico City, and there were reports that the French intended to install Maximilian, younger brother of Emperor Franz Joseph of Austria, as the emperor of Mexico. Some newspapers speculated that France's emperor Napoleon III intended to set up puppet states throughout Central America.[6]

Seward did what he could to caution France against its attempt to conquer Mexico. In early March, through William Dayton, the American minister in Paris, he warned that "no monarchical government established in Mexico, in the presence of foreign navies and armies in the waters and upon the soil of Mexico, would have any prospect of security or permanence." Baron Friedrich von Gerolt, the Prussian minister in Washington, reported that Seward told him that "the erection of a monarchy in the Mexican Republic must lead to serious consequences and without doubt, sooner or later, to serious conflict between the powers taking part in that act and the United States." Knowing that the

United States could not afford to fight France in Mexico, Seward stopped well short of threats. "France has a right to make war against Mexico," he wrote to Dayton, and the United States would avoid "intervention between the belligerents." This would remain Seward's Mexican policy until the end of the Civil War.[7]

Winter was the social season, and one evening in late January the Sewards hosted a party for several hundred people: diplomats, senators, representatives, officers, and their wives. Senator Orville Browning noted in his diary that it was "quite a brilliant affair." Winter was also the sickly season, and in early February Seward was alarmed to hear that Fanny, at school in Philadelphia, had a high fever. No doubt thinking of the tragic death of his first daughter, whose bedside he reached too late, Seward left Washington in haste for Philadelphia. He found there that Fanny, although suffering from typhoid, was not near death, and so after two days he returned to his work. Lincoln and his wife were not so fortunate: their son Willie died. In a letter to his wife explaining why he could not be with her and Fanny in Philadelphia, Seward said that he had to attend the funeral of "my friend" Willie, and also noted "the President's anxiety about his other sick child," Tad.[8]

In March, after Fanny was better, she and her mother traveled to Washington, where they remained for a month. Fanny recorded the constant stream of visitors to the Seward house, ranging from the president to minor military officers. Frances generally remained in her room, sometimes meeting one or two select friends there. Fanny was especially impressed by the nurse Dorothea Dix and General George McClellan. Nurse Dix had a "low voice, such as the watcher of sick beds should have" and her "whole mind seemed filled with the sufferings of others." McClellan was "taller, thinner in the face, and younger looking than I expected to see him." Fanny's warm words for McClellan are curious, given the general's views of her father and the almost daily messages from Lincoln to McClellan pressing him to move more quickly. McClellan's excuse was that he faced larger southern forces, but Seward laughed at his estimates of enemy numbers, telling a friend that the Union troops from the single state of New York probably outnumbered all the Confederate troops in front of McClellan's troops in Virginia.[9]

One visitor whom Fanny disliked was Edward Dicey, a young British reporter who spent several weeks in Washington in early 1862. Dicey was acceptable to her "as long as he kept still," but after dinner "his brilliant capability of making himself disagreeable show[ed] forth with undimmed lustre." Although Dicey did not record his impressions of the family, he did write perceptively about Seward: "I found him dressed in black, with his waistcoat half-unbuttoned, one leg over the side of his armchair, and a cigar stuck between his lips. Barring the cigar and the attitude, I should have taken him for a shrewd, well-to-do attorney, waiting to learn his new client's story: you are at your ease with him at once; there is a frankness and bonhomie about his manner which renders it, to my mind, a very pleasant one." Seward was good company: "A good cigar, a good glass of wine, and a good story, even if it is a little risqué, are pleasures which he obviously enjoys keenly. Still, a glance at that spare, hard-knit frame, and that clear, bright eye, shows you that no pleasure, however keenly appreciated, has been indulged in to excess throughout his long, laborious career." [10]

At the end of March, Union troops fought what Seward termed a "fearful battle" and gained a "brilliant victory" near Winchester, Virginia. Immediately afterward, Seward traveled by rail to tour the battlefield and inspect the hospitals. The distance was only a hundred miles, but the chaotic conditions prolonged the journey so that it took a whole day. The marks of the recent battle were "very visible," Fanny wrote, with the trees "broken down or pierced by balls." As for the wounded, they were "miserably provided for," with "no better beds than straw thrown on the floor" and "no ventilation." The only nurses were soldiers, for whom "the work was so distasteful that a guard was necessary to keep them from running away." Some of the soldiers' wounds were horrible, for instance, a rebel with "both eyes blown out." Such, wrote Fanny, "are the heart-rending details of war! Oh how long?" [11]

———

By early 1862, the lack of southern cotton was hurting the textile industries in England and France. When Henri Mercier, the French minister, raised this issue with Seward in late March, Seward showed him a letter he was about to send to Paris. Seward believed that the Union would

soon have possession of all the major southern ports, including New
Orleans, Mobile, and Savannah, and indeed predicted to Mercier that
"the insurrectionary government must very soon fall and disappear." A
few weeks later, Mercier told Seward that he was not so sure that the
Confederates were about to give up, that he would like to go to Richmond to see for himself. Seward quickly consented. The British minister Lord Lyons reported home that, as Mercier was about to leave for
Richmond, Seward told him he could "say to the southern leaders, not
of course from the United States government, but from him, Mr. Seward
personally, that they have no spirit of vengeance to apprehend, that they
would be cordially welcomed back to their seats in the Senate, and to
their due share of political influence." Seward added that "he was willing to risk his own political station and reputation in pursuing a conciliatory course towards the South, and that he was ready to make this
his policy and to stand or fall by it." Conciliation was Seward's approach
before the war; it was his approach during the war; and it would be his
approach after the war as well.[12]

Mercier reported immediately to Seward on his return, telling him
that all the leaders with whom he met in Richmond seemed determined
to continue the war. Judah Benjamin, the Confederate secretary of state,
essentially conceded to Mercier that the Union would soon control all
the southern ports, but Benjamin claimed that it would not matter. Even
if the Union forces took Richmond itself, he argued, the Confederates
would continue the war from the interior for as long as it took to achieve
their independence. Seward attempted to downplay the Confederate resolve, telling Mercier that it was like the excitement of an election campaign, that would pass once the votes were counted. Lyons reported to
London that Seward told him the Confederates were "about to make a
last effort; that their last resources were brought into play; that their last
armies were in the field." If the Union could defeat the Confederates
now, "they would accept the terms that would be offered to them."[13]

Although various Union advances were underway in May 1862, the
one that captured the most attention was that under McClellan, making its way toward Richmond up the peninsula formed by the York
and James rivers. Seward boasted to Charles Francis Adams on May 12
that "Richmond is practically held in close siege by General McClellan."

Seward was not alone in his overconfidence; the *New York Times* predicted that any day the news would arrive that "Richmond is ours." Perhaps hoping to be near the scene, Seward accepted an invitation from Welles to travel south by boat to inspect the naval forces and armies. The party included Secretary and Mrs. Welles, Attorney General Edward Bates, Secretary Seward, and Frederick and Anna Seward. They left Washington on the evening of May 13, and by the next morning were on the York River near Yorktown, Virginia, recently abandoned by the Confederates. They continued up the York River to McClellan's headquarters, described by Frederick as "a clearing in the woods containing two houses, suddenly transformed into a great city of a hundred thousand people." The three cabinet secretaries reviewed the troops in the rain, and Seward also conferred with General McClellan alone. At McClellan's request, Seward sent a telegram to Lincoln, urging him to transfer additional forces to McClellan as soon as possible. The general did not appreciate the visit, or the help from Seward, complaining in a letter to his wife that he "was very glad when I got through with them—such visits are always a nuisance."[14]

Seward and the others spent almost a week in Virginia, visiting Norfolk and Portsmouth, approaching within ten miles of Richmond, and watching a small naval battle from a distance. The towns were largely deserted, but the party was greeted by a few loyal Union men and many former slaves. Seward noted to Adams that "everywhere the American general receives his most useful and reliable information from the negro, who hails his coming as a harbinger of freedom." Dozens of former slaves showed up each day at Union Army camps or naval facilities, seeking food, shelter, work, and freedom. Seward had mixed feelings about these contrabands; he told his wife that "Virginia is sad to look upon; not merely the rebellion, but society itself, is falling into ruin. Slaves are deserting the homes entrusted to them by their masters, who have gone into the southern armies or are fleeing before ours." To Fanny he wrote that "we saw war, not in its holiday garb, but in its stern and fearful aspect. We saw the desolation that follows, and the terror that precedes its march."[15]

Seward hoped that the Union capture of New Orleans and its environs, a major cotton port and region, would simplify his life by providing European nations with some access to southern cotton. In the event, because of the chaos in the South, and the policies of both North and South, Union control of New Orleans did not lead to cotton exports on any significant scale. Instead, the Union military administration of New Orleans, under Seward's former dinner guest General Benjamin Butler, caused countless foreign complications for Seward. Within two weeks of his arrival in New Orleans, Butler had his troops forcibly search the Dutch consul to obtain the key to his vault, from which they seized thousands of Mexican silver coins. Butler believed the cash had been improperly transferred from a southern bank to the consul; the consul claimed it was the lawful property of a European trading firm. The consul complained to the Dutch minister in Washington, who complained to Seward, who ordered an investigation, then apologized to the Dutch minister, writing him that Butler's actions were "a violation of the law of nations and of the comity due from this country to a friendly sovereign state." [16]

The controversy over the Dutch consul was nothing compared to the commotion caused by Butler's infamous order regarding the women of New Orleans. After a number of incidents in which local women insulted federal troops, including one in which a woman emptied a chamberpot onto an officer's head, Butler ordered that "when any female shall by word, gesture, or movement insult or show contempt for any officer or soldier of the United States she shall be regarded and held liable to be treated as a woman of the town plying her avocation." Europeans were outraged by what they viewed as Butler's invitation to rape. Lord Palmerston, the British prime minister, took the unusual step of writing directly to Adams, without going through the foreign minister. "It is difficult if not impossible," he wrote, "to express adequately the disgust which must be excited in the mind of every honourable man by the general order of General Butler." It again fell to Seward to attempt to calm the British. Quoting the ancient motto of the Order of the Garter, Seward reminded Palmerston through Adams that *honi soit qui mal y pense*, in other words, the British should not assume an evil intent, but rather a charitable one. [17]

———

By late June, McClellan's Union Army of 100,000 men had reached the eastern outskirts of Richmond. There, starting on June 25 and continuing for seven days, Confederate forces under General Robert E. Lee attacked, in what is now called the Seven Days' Battle. Although the Union troops won several of the daily struggles, and although more than 20,000 Confederates were killed or wounded, severely depleting Lee's forces, McClellan could not bring himself to counterattack. Instead, he abandoned the attempt to capture Richmond and retreated to a safer position, all while writing bitter complaints to Washington. In one message, he wrote Stanton that "I have lost this battle because my force was too small." With 10,000 or 20,000 fresh troops, McClellan claimed, he "could take Richmond tomorrow," but he "had not a man in reserve." If he managed to save his men, McClellan wrote, he would "owe no thanks to you or to any other persons in Washington. You have done your best to sacrifice this army." [18]

The next day, June 28, Lincoln met with Seward to discuss the disastrous situation. There were no fresh troops to send to McClellan because Stanton, two months earlier, when the war was going well, had closed the recruiting offices. Lincoln feared that if he transferred troops to McClellan from other fronts, the Confederates would attack and capture those areas. If Lincoln himself called for additional troops just as the news of the reverses near Richmond reached the newspapers, it could cause a panic in the North. Seward told Lincoln that he would work with the northern governors and devise a way to raise at least another 100,000 men. Lincoln provided him a letter to share with the governors, explaining that he hoped with new troops "to take Richmond" and thus to "substantially end the war." But Lincoln's letter was clear that even if this did not occur, he would never give up. "I expect to maintain this contest until successful, or till I die, or am conquered, or my term expires, or Congress or the country forsakes me." Seward telegraphed to Thurlow Weed (recently returned to the United States) and New York governor Edwin Morgan to meet him at the Astor House in New York City. [19]

Seward arrived at the Astor House late on June 29 and worked around the clock for the next few days to line up support among the northern governors. Only three of them—Edwin Morgan, Andrew

Curtin of Pennsylvania, and Charles Olden of New Jersey for a few hours—were present in New York. He had to communicate with twenty other governors by telegraph, which was not always easy. He drafted a letter from the governors to Lincoln, asking the president to call out additional troops to follow up the "recent successes of the federal arms," and a response from Lincoln, calling for 150,000 volunteers. When Seward telegraphed the governors to ask them to subscribe their names to the draft letter, most readily agreed, but a few balked. Frederick Holbrook of Vermont responded that without the full text of the letter, and without more information about why it was necessary, "I must decline giving my name." John Andrew of Massachusetts informed Seward that he did not believe his state would provide any additional men unless the federal government offered immediate payment to new recruits.[20]

Late on the night of June 30, Seward telegraphed Stanton in Washington, asking for authority to promise an immediate advance of $25 to each volunteer, out of the $100 normally due at the time of discharge. Stanton responded the next morning that existing law did not allow for immediate payment to recruits; he also asked Seward whether it would be possible to raise twice as many troops. Seward wired back that the $25 bounty was "of vital importance," that "we fail without it," but that *with* the payment, the higher number of troops was possible. Stanton responded that he himself would take the responsibility for authorizing the $25 payment. Even this was not sufficient to persuade the reluctant Governor Andrew, so Seward left for Boston that evening.[21]

The result of Seward's labors appeared in the northern newspapers on the morning of July 2: a letter to Lincoln from almost all the northern governors (other than Andrew and a few who had not yet answered), asking him to call upon them for additional troops, and a response from Lincoln requesting 300,000 volunteers. The letter to Lincoln was backdated to June 28 so that it did not look like a response to recent events. Seward telegraphed Stanton from Boston that he could now add Andrew's name to the list of signatories. That evening Seward departed from Boston for Cleveland, where he intended to meet some of the western governors. He stopped for a few hours in Auburn, and the news reports he read while he was there—the papers were just starting to report the disasters near Richmond—convinced him that he had to return to the capital. He left Auburn at noon with Fanny; traveling for twenty-four hours almost without stop, they reached Washington late on July 4. It was not a happy Fourth: "the gloomiest since the birth of this republic," in the words of a Washington diarist. "Never was the country so low."[22]

Seward's efforts to strengthen the Union Army continued through the summer. He persuaded several New York congressmen to return to the state in order to raise regiments there. "All is well if we instantly show our strength," he wrote to one of the representatives, in a letter that soon made its way into the newspapers. At his own department, Seward encouraged the clerks to enlist or to find volunteers for military service, and on one occasion he ostentatiously gave $50 to each of several random recruits. This, too, was soon reported. Seward lobbied Congress for some form of draft, and the Militia Act of July 1862 established what one historian has termed a "quasi-draft" in the northern states. Reluctant men of military age now knew that if they did not volunteer, they could be drafted into the Union Army. As the *Albany Evening Journal* put it: "will you volunteer and receive all the bounties, or wait to be drafted and receive nothing?" The combination of bounty payments, patriotic appeals, and the draft threat slowly produced results: by year's end more than 400,000 men had volunteered. One of them was Seward's third son, William, appointed in August as the lieutenant colonel of the 138th New York Infantry Regiment.[23]

Seward returned home to New York for a few days at the end of August to check on recruiting and on his family; William and Jenny were expecting a child any day. The cabinet in Washington was debating whether to remove McClellan from command, and Welles—always ready to suspect Seward—assumed that he left in order to avoid having to participate in this debate. While Seward was in Auburn, word arrived of the disastrous defeat of the Union forces in the Second Battle of Bull Run. Seward again left Auburn in haste for Washington, arriving at about nine on the evening of September 3, driving immediately to see Lincoln at his suburban retreat, the Soldiers' Home, and remaining with him until midnight. Lincoln and Seward discussed not only the defeat at Bull Run but also the rumors (which soon proved true) that Lee's Confederate Army was crossing the Potomac into Maryland. Seward wrote home to Frances that this "news, added to what passed before, has produced much panic here, as it will through the country." He assured her that he did not fear for Washington, but admitted that he was "singular" in his attitude.[24]

Seward was correct in predicting that the Confederate invasion of the North would cause panic, especially in Maryland and Pennsylvania. After Lee captured Frederick, Maryland, on September 6, Seward wrote to the ministers abroad that the Confederates seemed "to be threatening alike Washington, Baltimore and Harrisburg." That same day, Seward and Frederick went out to watch some of the Union troops marching north to meet the enemy. Seward remarked to his son on the differences between the men at the head of the column—"the young, the strong, the energetic, pushing steadily forward"—and those at the rear— "shambling along and casting furtive glances over the fences and down the road behind them." Four hundred miles north, William and his regiment were preparing to hasten south to join the forces defending the capital. From this point onward, Seward would not only have a son in the Army, Augustus, and another in federal service, Frederick; he would also have a son on the front lines, his namesake William.[25]

———

Starting in late 1861, and continuing through 1862, Seward was involved in a series of decisions against slavery and in favor of former slaves. The first was to reverse the prior policy of the State Department denying passports to free blacks because they were not citizens under the *Dred Scott* decision. Charles Sumner requested that the State Department issue a passport for Robert Morris, a young black man in Boston who wanted to go to Europe for his college education. Seward did not want to highlight Morris's race in the passport, so he issued it without any racial description. After this the department quietly started issuing passports without regard to race.[26]

A second decision was to extend diplomatic recognition to Haiti and Liberia, two nations largely populated by former slaves and their descendants. At Seward's suggestion, Lincoln stated in his December 1861 congressional message that there seemed no good reason for "withholding our recognition of the independence and sovereignty of Haiti and Liberia." The *New York Times,* a paper often aligned with Seward, noted that the major European nations had recognized Haiti and Liberia, and commented that the only reason the United States had failed to do so was that "the slave-lords ruled in our legislative halls." There were still slaveholders in the halls of Congress, including Senator Garrett Davis of Kentucky, who claimed the recognition bill would mean that "full-blooded negroes" would soon be admitted as foreign ministers to the White House, and that their wives and daughters would be there as well for social occasions. With Seward's support, however, the bill passed both houses, and Lincoln signed it into law in June 1862.[27]

A third step, attempted but not accomplished, was compensated emancipation in the border states. In a special message to Congress in March 1862, Lincoln recommended that "the United States ought to co-operate with any state which may adopt gradual abolishment of slavery, giving to such state pecuniary aid, to be used by such state in its discretion, to compensate for the inconveniences, public and private, produced by such change of system." Lincoln's proposal was similar to the one Seward had made in his 1855 Senate speech, when he said that as a southerner he would favor compensated emancipation. The *New York Times*, again probably reflecting Seward's views, praised Lincoln's message to the skies. "The President has placed the Government on the side of Freedom. He has pronounced it to be better than Slavery. . . . In dealing with this vexed subject we think he has hit the happy mean, upon which all parties in the North and all loyalists in the South can unite." Unfortunately, the parties could not agree, and the proposal soon died in Congress.[28]

A fourth step was to free the slaves in the District of Columbia. This was another measure Seward had long advocated, at least since 1850, when he raised the issue in the debate on the compromise of that year. Legislation freeing the District's slaves and promising federal compensation to their owners passed in early 1862.[29]

A fifth measure, and the one of which Seward was most proud, was the slave trade treaty with Britain. Although it had long been illegal for Americans to participate in the slave trade, the trade still continued to some extent, often under an American flag, because slave traders knew that American ships, or those that were apparently American, would not be stopped by the British fleet. The British government had often suggested that the United States should allow Britain to stop and inspect ships its navy reasonably suspected of slave trading, but the Americans had consistently rejected the idea. Not long after he became secretary of state, Seward informed Lyons that he would not have the "squeamishness" of his predecessors about British searches of American ships suspected of bearing slaves. He even signed with Lyons a secret memorandum to this effect. The British were concerned, however, that the memorandum would not outlive Seward's tenure as secretary, and that even he might disregard it in a controversial case.[30]

In March, Lyons provided Seward with a draft treaty between Britain and the United States that would allow each nation to inspect ships of the other in certain defined cases. Seward reflected on the issue, conferred with a few friends on Capitol Hill, and then told Lyons that the United States would enter such a treaty, but only if it looked like the United States prepared the first draft. Seward was concerned, Lyons reported to London, that the "old jealousy of Great Britain on the subject of the right of search" would cause some senators to vote against the treaty if it was the result of "pressure from the British government." Lyons readily agreed to Seward's ruse. As he explained to the foreign minister, "Seward's long experience of the Senate, and his well-known tact in dealing with that body, gives his opinion on such a point much weight." Seward thus provided a draft treaty to Lyons, based on the British draft, but imposing a ten-year time limit on the arrangement. To create an appearance of negotiation, Lyons objected to the time limit. Seward insisted upon it, Lyons yielded, and they signed the treaty in early April.[31]

Seward promptly submitted the treaty to the Senate, where Sumner managed to secure unanimous ratification. When Sumner roused Seward from an afternoon nap with the news, Seward exclaimed, "Good God! The Democrats have disappeared. This is the greatest act of the Administration." A few days later, he wrote Frances that he was about to "sign, seal, and dispatch to Europe, our great treaty with Great Britain for the extirpation of the African slave trade. If I have done nothing else worthy of self-congratulation, I deem this treaty sufficient to have lived for." The slave trade was ending for other reasons, but this treaty, allowing Britain to inspect American ships, hastened its death. The number of slaves imported into Cuba, the last major importer, declined from more than 30,000 in 1860 to less than 200 in 1865.[32]

Seward wrote Weed in late April that "while there is much waste of talk upon abstactions, and flaming speeches in Congress, we have really succeeded in carrying practical measures of lasting importance" for slaves and former slaves. The "flaming speeches" were by Radical Republicans who insisted that the president issue a general emancipation proclamation. Lincoln resisted and Seward agreed, explaining in letters to Adams and others why he believed such a proclamation would be a grave error. The war was gradually ending slavery anyway, because slaves were fleeing to meet the Union armies, preferring life as a contraband to life as a slave. Five thousand contrabands were now attached to the Union armies in Virginia, Seward noted to Adams, and 9,000 more in coastal Carolina. An emancipation proclamation would also "deprive us of the needful and legitimate support of the friends of the Union who are not opposed to slavery" and "reinvigorate the declining insurrection in every part of the South."[33]

Most important, Seward believed that an emancipation proclamation would likely lead to "social revolution here, with all its horrors, like the slave revolution in San Domingo." (The Haitian Revolution, in both Haiti and San Domingo, was remembered as being especially violent.) "Servile war" was a recurring theme in Seward's letters that spring and summer. In May, he wrote Adams that if the insurgents attempted to prevent slaves from escaping to the North, "how could they hope to prevent the civil war they have inaugurated from degenerating into a servile war?" In early July, he wrote again to Adams: "It seems as if the extreme advocates of African slavery and its most vehement opponents were acting in concert to precipitate a servile war, the former by making the most desperate attempts to overthrow the federal Union, the latter by demanding an edict of universal emancipation as a lawful and necessary, if not, as they say, the only legitimate way, of saving the Union."[34]

The slavery issue divided not just the northern public; it divided the Seward family. In March, Frances wrote her husband that if "emancipating the slaves of the secessionists will hasten the close of this terrible war, it seems to me that the President will not much longer hesitate to do so." She believed that "the cry of the oppressed has reached the ear of God, and that He has 'come down to deliver them.' " In July, she wrote again: "I hope the time has come when you can conscientiously urge the President to issue a proclamation of immediate emancipation." In a draft letter that she may not have sent, Frances was even more adamant: "Whatever may be the principles in the determination of the President in this matter, you owe it to yourself and your children and your country and to God to make your record clear." If the president was not going to act soon to end slavery, "it would be far better for you to resign your place tomorrow than by continuing there seem to give countenance to a great moral evil."[35]

Seward disagreed with his wife. He wrote her in April that it was "too early, or too late, for a proclamation. Proclamations in each state recovered, issued by governors chosen from their own citizens, and sustained by the Army, are listened to." Frustrated with Congress, and with the way in which what he considered mere details interfered with more pressing issues, he wrote her in July: "I ask Congress to authorize a draft. They fall into altercation about letting slaves fight and work. Every day is a day lost, and every day lost is a hazard to the whole country. What if I should say that I concede all they want about ne-groes? One party has gained another partisan; the country has lost one advocate." (Seward saw himself not as a partisan but as a moderator like Lincoln. "Somebody must be in a position to mollify and moderate," he told Weed. "That is the task of the P. and the S. of S.") In another letter, Seward declared that "proclamations are *paper* without the support of armies." The slow pace of enlistment made him "mournful," for it sug-gested that the Union "shrinks from the war it has accepted, and insists on adopting proclamations, when it is asked for force."[36]

On Sunday, July 13, Lincoln, Welles, Seward, and his daughter-in-law Anna shared a carriage while riding out beyond Georgetown to attend the funeral of an infant child of Stanton's. Welles later recalled that it was during this carriage ride that Lincoln first suggested he was about to issue an emancipation proclamation. The president, according to Welles, said that he had "about come to the conclusion that it was a military necessity, absolutely essential for the preservation of the Union. We must free the slaves or be ourselves subdued. The slaves were undeniably an element of strength to those who had their service, and we must decide whether that element should be with us or against us." Welles remembered that Seward responded that the "subject involved consequences so vast and momentous, legal and political, that he should wish to bestow on it mature reflection." The president reverted to the topic of emancipation "two or three times" during the course of the carriage ride, saying that he was now convinced that "a change in the policy of the conduct of the war was necessary." [37]

This account by Welles, widely accepted and quoted by historians, should be questioned more closely. Although one version appears in the book now known as the *Welles Diary*, it is clear from the tone and tense that Welles wrote this account long after the war, as he worked on a series of articles. Moreover, although Lincoln often visited the Sewards' house, and thus knew Anna Seward well, it seems unlikely that he would bring up such a sensitive subject in her presence, especially if he had any hint of the views of Frances Seward on the issue. Welles mentioned the carriage ride in letters to his wife and his son, written on the same day, but did not mention emancipation, or indeed that Lincoln had brought up any important topic. In short, it seems that the famous carriage ride conversation is a later invention by Welles, perhaps to emphasize his own role in Lincoln's historic decision. [38]

On this same Sunday, Senator Orville Browning called at Seward's house in the late afternoon to talk about a bill just passed by Congress to confiscate the property of rebels, including their real estate and slaves. Browning was concerned that the bill violated the Constitution, and even more concerned about its political aspects. He noted in his diary that he told Seward that, if Lincoln vetoed the bill, "he would raise a storm of enthusiasm in support of the Administration in the border states which would be worth 100,000 muskets, whereas if he approved it I feared our friends could no longer sustain themselves [in the border states]." Seward agreed with Browning and promised to speak with the president. Even as Seward and Browning pressed Lincoln to veto the bill, however, others urged him to sign, insisting that a veto would destroy the Republican Party. The usually moderate *New York Times*

1

William Henry Seward, by Mathew Brady, circa 1863. Noah Brooks noted that Seward was "big as to nose, light as to hair and eyes, averse to all attempts upon his portrait." Henry Adams recalled that Seward had "a head like a wise macaw; a beaked nose; shaggy eyebrows; [and] unorderly hair and clothes."

2

ABOVE: The Miller-Seward family in about 1833, from left to right: Paulina Titus Miller (Miller's mother, 1751–1835); Judge Elijah Miller (1772–1851); Clarinda Miller (Miller's sister, 1794–1862); William Henry Seward (1801–1872); Augustus Seward (1826–1876); Frederick Seward (1830–1915); and Frances Miller Seward (1805–1865).

BELOW: They lived in the Miller-Seward house, on South Street, in Auburn, New York.

3

4

Frances Adeline Seward, by Nathaniel Jocelyn. Chester Harding, another artist, commented that she was "very beautiful; black eyes; dark hair; and a fine figure. She is very modest, and very intelligent; has read a great deal, and talks politics almost as well as her husband."

Henry Clay in the Senate, 1850, by Robert Whitechurch. Seward is at the far right, seated, facing Clay. Their desks were in fact side by side, so that Seward would have been closer to Clay than depicted.

Seward's colleagues in the United States Senate included, from the upper left to lower right: Daniel Webster, who called Seward "contemptible" during an 1840s dispute but then sought Seward's help in finding a federal position for his son; Charles Sumner, who aspired to Seward's position as secretary of state yet remained a close friend of Frances Seward; Stephen Douglas, with whom Seward collaborated on Kansas and then opposed as the Democratic presidential candidate in 1860; and John Crittenden, author of the "Crittenden compromise" debated during the secession winter of 1860–61.

Seward's New York friends included: Horace Greeley, editor of the *New York Tribune*; Thurlow Weed, editor of the *Albany Evening Journal*.

12

THE GREAT EXHIBITION OF 1860.

An 1860 Democratic cartoon shows Greeley calling the tune for Lincoln; Seward comments that it is "no use trying to keep me and the 'irreppressible' infant in the background, for we are really the head and front of this party."

ABOVE: The Capitol building was still under construction when Lincoln was inaugurated in March 1861.

RIGHT: Seward provided Lincoln many comments on his draft address, including this handwritten closing paragraph.

14

15 16

Seward's principal contacts with Britain during the Civil War were: Charles Francis Adams, the American minister in London, and Lord Richard Lyons, the British minister in Washington.

Seward lived during the war in a rented house on the east side of Lafayette Square.

17

Seward's cabinet colleagues included Gideon Welles, secretary of the Navy, and Salmon Chase, secretary of the Treasury.

Francis Carpenter gave Seward the central position in his painting of the cabinet discussion of emancipation.

In the summer of 1863, Seward took a party of diplomats on an extended tour of New York. Seward is at the far right of the group at Trenton Falls.

In February 1865, Lincoln and Seward met with Confederate commissioners on the *River Queen*.

Lincoln worked closely with his private secretaries, John Nicolay (seated) and John Hay (standing).

23

Seward's own principal aide was his son Frederick, shown here in Seward's State Department office.

24

25

26

President Andrew
Johnson and two of his
Radical Republican critics:
Benjamin Butler and
Thaddeus Stevens.

27

28

Seward with family and friends on the back porch and in the garden of their Washington home. In the upper photo, Seward leans against a pillar, facing his son Frederick; in the lower photo, Augustus, Anna, Frederick, and an unknown young woman are in the garden with Seward.

29

The women in Seward's life included, from upper left to lower right: Frances Seward, seen in the garden in about 1860; Charlotte Cushman, the actor whom both Seward and Lincoln admired; Fanny Seward, shown here with the family dog; and Olive Risley Seward, in whom Seward became interested after the death of his wife and daughter and whom he later adopted as his daughter.

ABOVE: Thomas Nast depicted Seward as the evil adviser to the Roman emperor Johnson. As Seward whispers into Johnson's ear, the two watch whites slaughter blacks in the amphitheater below.

BELOW: Emanuel Leutze painted Stoeckl (standing at globe) and Seward (seated with map) in their Alaska negotiation. The painting is somewhat fanciful; there is no evidence that Sumner (second from right) participated in the discussion.

36

Seward's face and neck were scarred by the assassin's knife. He also suffered, in later years, progressive paralysis of his hands and arms. Yet he managed to travel around the world.

called the bill "just and timely." Lincoln met with some key members of Congress to work out a compromise; he would sign the bill, but only if Congress would amend it to address his constitutional concerns. The compromise passed, over some Radical opposition, and Lincoln signed the bill into law.[39]

The Second Confiscation Act, as it is known, included a section authorizing the president to provide for "the transportation, colonization, and settlement, in some tropical country beyond the limits of the United States, of such persons of the African race, made free by the provisions of this Act, as may be willing to emigrate." Lincoln was strongly interested in colonizing the former slaves, for he believed that it would be impossible for black and white to live together peacefully in the postwar South. Seward was much more doubtful; he said not long after Lincoln's death that he and the president had "never disagreed but in one subject—that was the colonization of the negroes." One reason Seward opposed colonization was that he, more than Lincoln, knew of the foreign problems such a policy would create. Seward also believed that few former slaves would want to emigrate; as he put it to a British official, they generally had "great objections to leaving the country of their birth," and some would even prefer to "remain in slavery than start for a foreign land." Sending free blacks away from the United States was inconsistent with Seward's lifelong desire to encourage immigration in order to build up the American population and economy. As Frederick recalled, his father said, "I am always for bringing men and states *into* this Union" and "never for taking any *out*." For all these reasons, Seward never pursued colonization with the vigor that Lincoln would have wished.[40]

———

At a cabinet meeting on July 22, after brief discussions of other issues, Lincoln read out a rough draft of a proclamation. The first part was routine: it sounded as if it was merely the implementing order contemplated by one section of the recent Confiscation Act. The final sentence of Lincoln's draft, however, was anything but routine: "And, as a fit and necessary military measure for effecting this object [restoration of the Union,] I, as Commander-in-Chief of the Army and Navy of the United States,

do order and declare that on the first day of January in the year of Our
Lord one thousand, eight hundred and sixty-three, all persons held as
slaves within any state or states, wherein the constitutional authority of
the United States shall not then be practically recognized, submitted to,
and maintained, shall then, thenceforward, and forever, be free." Lincoln
was proposing to free not only the slaves of slaveowners engaged in the
rebellion; he was proposing to free all the slaves in the rebellious states.
Although the draft referred to the Confiscation Act, Lincoln did not follow the limits of that act; he was relying instead upon his war powers
as president. Because of this, and because of political concerns, he did
not propose to alter the status of slaves in the loyal states, such as Delaware or Kentucky; the proclamation would only affect the slaves in the
states still in rebellion. Indeed, if the rebellion ceased by the first day of
the new year, the proclamation would not have any effect at all.[41]

To reconstruct Seward's comments on Lincoln's draft, we need to
look at three sources. Edwin Stanton, in notes dated July 22, wrote:
"The President proposes an order declaring that all slaves in states in
rebellion on the —— day of ——. The Attorney General and Stanton
are for its immediate promulgation. Seward against it; argues strongly
in favor of cotton and foreign governments. Chase silent. Welles—.
Seward argues—that foreign nations will intervene to prevent the abolition of slavery for sake of cotton—argues in a long speech against its
immediate promulgation—wants to wait for troops—wants [General
Henry] Halleck here—wants drum and fife and public spirit—we break
up our relations with foreign nations and the production of cotton for
sixty years. Chase thinks it a measure of great danger—and would lead
to universal emancipation. The measure goes beyond anything I have
recommended."[42]

Whitelaw Reid, a journalist with good access to Lincoln and the
cabinet, reported in the *Cincinnati Daily Gazette* in early 1864 that after
Lincoln had read the draft to the cabinet in July 1862, Seward said: "I approve it, Mr. President, just as it stands. I approve of it in principle, and
approve of the policy of issuing it. I only object to the time. Send it out
now, on the heels of our late disasters, and it will be construed as the
convulsive struggle of a drowning man. To give it proper weight, you
should reserve it until some victory." The *Gazette*'s article was reprinted

in the *New York Times*, a paper edited by Seward's friend Henry Raymond, and the *Times* added that "we have reason to believe" the report "gives a substantially accurate account of the circumstances."[43]

The artist Francis Carpenter, who spent weeks in the White House in 1864 working on his painting of the Emancipation Proclamation cabinet meeting, wrote something similar in his book published in 1866. According to Carpenter, Seward's comment at the cabinet meeting was: "Mr. President, I approve of the proclamation, but I question the expediency of its issue at this juncture. The depression of the public mind, consequent upon our repeated reverses, is so great that I fear the effect of so important a step. It may be viewed as the last measure of an exhausted government, a cry for help; the government stretching forth its hands to Ethiopia, instead of Ethiopia stretching forth her hands to the government. While I approve the measure, I suggest, sir, that you postpone its issue, until you can give it to the country supported by military success, instead of issuing it, as would be the case now, upon the greatest disasters of the war!" Carpenter added that Lincoln told the artist that the "wisdom of the view of the Secretary of State struck me with very great force. It was an aspect of the case that, in all my thought upon the subject, I had entirely overlooked."[44]

These three sources conflict on one critical issue: Reid and Carpenter claim that Seward supported the preliminary emancipation proclamation but merely questioned its timing, whereas Stanton states that Seward opposed the proclamation in principle and *also* argued that it should be delayed. Stanton's notes should prevail on this issue, for several reasons. First, Stanton's notes were apparently written on the same day as the cabinet session; indeed, they may well have been written at the meeting, for they are on Executive Mansion notepaper. Reid and Carpenter were writing months and years later. Second, by the time Reid and Carpenter wrote, Seward's alleged opposition to the proclamation had itself become a political issue; Seward himself may have provided Reid and Carpenter with material to rebut criticism of his opposition to the proclamation. Third, Stanton's notes are consistent with Seward's comments both before and after the first cabinet discussion of emancipation.[45]

Just before the proclamation was discussed in the cabinet, Seward wrote Adams that it seemed as if the abolitionists wanted to start a servile war by "demanding an edict of universal emancipation." After Lincoln had issued the second and final Emancipation Proclamation, Browning noted in his diary that Seward "thought the proclamations unfortunate, and that we would have been nearer the end of the war and the end of slavery both without them, but that they were now past." A few weeks later Noah Brooks, a journalist close to both Lincoln and Seward, reported in the *Sacramento Daily Union* that "it is very well known that Seward yields a tardy and reluctant concurrence in the emancipation measures proposed by the president." In April 1863, Henry Bellows, a Unitarian minister, after a long evening with the secretary, wrote that Seward said he "had not been in favor of emancipation by proclamation, but of emancipation by force—freeing all slaves whether of the loyal or disloyal as our armies advanced, saying nothing to notify the enemy, but doing the thing." If Seward was prepared to concede to Bellows—who viewed emancipation as the greatest act of the Lincoln administration—that he had opposed the preliminary proclamation, there seems little reason to doubt that he indeed did so.[46]

Later still, but also relevant, is an 1867 letter from Francis Cutting of New York to Edwin Stanton, describing a visit to Washington in July 1862, at the time of the first cabinet discussion. On the morning after the cabinet meeting, Cutting met at his hotel with Weed, also in Washington at the time. Weed told Cutting that, the evening before, he had persuaded Lincoln to delay any emancipation proclamation. Cutting recalled that Weed said that such a proclamation "could not be enforced in the rebel states—that it would add to the intensity of their hatred, and might occasion serious disaffection to the Union cause in the border states; that it would work no good and probably would do much harm, and that it was more prudent to wait upon events." Cutting's letter does not mention Seward, but in light of the close relationship between Seward and Weed, and the close parallel between Seward's comments and those of Weed, it seems likely that Seward used Weed in July 1862 to reinforce his arguments with Lincoln against a proclamation.[47]

Whatever Seward and Weed said at and just after the July 22 cabinet meeting—and we will never know for sure—Lincoln did not issue his proposed proclamation but instead waited for military success. The

Union armies, however, did not achieve much success in the late summer and early fall of 1862. In the Battle of Cedar Mountain, Virginia, Confederate forces under General Thomas "Stonewall" Jackson defeated Union forces under Seward's friend General Nathaniel Banks. In the Second Battle of Manassas, the Confederates achieved another dramatic victory, leaving more than 10,000 Union men dead and wounded on the battlefield. In early September, General Robert E. Lee and his Confederate Army crossed the Potomac River into Maryland, captured Harpers Ferry, Virginia, along with 12,000 Union troops, and threatened Baltimore and Washington. But then, on September 17, along the Antietam creek near Sharpsburg, Maryland, Union troops under McClellan fought an all-day battle against the Confederates under Lee. The losses in this, the bloodiest day in American military history, were about equal, with more than 2,000 dead on each side. McClellan failed to achieve decisive victory, both because of his tentative tactics on the day of the battle and because of his failure to attack again on the days after the battle, a failure that allowed Lee and his troops to escape back across the Potomac. Lee's retreat, however, was enough to turn Antietam into a Union victory, or at least into what Lincoln could claim as a victory.[48]

Seward did not forget about emancipation during this two-month period; on the contrary, he sought to ascertain how the European powers would react to an emancipation proclamation. In a long letter to his friend John Stuart Motley, the historian who was America's minister in Vienna, Seward suggested that a proclamation at this stage of the war might well "leave us a nation divided into two nations, one of which would be a dangerous and aggressive slave nation under foreign protection and with foreign alliances." In a somewhat convoluted question, Seward asked whether Motley was sure that "under the reductions and pressures which could be applied to some European populations, they would not rise up and resist our attempt to bestow freedom upon the laborers whose capacity to supply cotton and open a market for European fabrics depends, or is thought to depend, on their continuance in bondage?" Motley simplified and restated the issue—would an emancipation proclamation encourage European intervention in the Civil War?—and answered, "a thousand times no!" Motley, who had good sources in England, told Seward that a "proclamation of emancipation to the blacks, with compensation to owners thenceforth loyal, even although it could not be everywhere immediately enforced, would strike the sword from England's hands." Many of England's leaders, including Prime Minister Palmerston, were strongly antislavery; an emancipation proclamation would make them realize that the North was fighting to free the slaves as well as preserve the Union; this would preclude British intervention in support of the South. Seward received similar advice from others he trusted, including Charles Francis Adams in London.[49]

In late August, Horace Greeley, in an open letter to Lincoln in the *New York Tribune*, castigated the president for failing to free the slaves. Greeley argued that Lincoln was listening too much to "certain fossil politicians hailing from the border states," and was ignoring the prayers of millions of other Americans. Lincoln decided to publish a reply to Greeley's letter so there could be no doubt about his policy. "My paramount objective in this struggle *is* to save the Union," Lincoln wrote, "and is *not* either to save or to destroy slavery. If I could save the Union without freeing *any* slave I would do it, and if I could save it by freeing *all* the slaves I would do it; and if I could save it by freeing some and leaving others alone I would also do that. What I do about slavery, and the colored race, I do because it helps to save the Union; and what I forbear, I forbear because I do *not* believe it would help to save the Union." Seward agreed with Lincoln; "the salvation of the nation," he later told Francis Carpenter, was "of vastly more consequence than the destruction of slavery." Frances Seward disagreed; in a letter to her husband she criticized Lincoln's letter to Greeley, saying it suggested "that the mere keeping together [of] a number of states is more important than human freedom."[50]

On Monday, September 22, Lincoln opened the cabinet session by reminding the members that they had not finished their discussion of emancipation. "When the rebel army was at Frederick," Lincoln said, according to Chase's diary, "I determined, as soon as it should be driven out of Maryland, to issue a proclamation of emancipation such as I thought most likely to be useful. I said nothing to any one; but I made a promise to myself, and (hesitating a little) to my Maker. The rebel army is now driven out, and I am going to fulfill that promise." Lincoln then read out to them his draft proclamation, which stated that, if any states or parts of states were still in rebellion on January 1, 1863, slaves in such regions "shall be then, thenceforward, and forever free." The proclamation promised that the federal government would "recognize the freedom of such persons, and will do no act or acts to repress such persons, or any of them, in any efforts they may make for their actual freedom." When Lincoln was done reading, Chase noted, there was a short silence, after which Seward remarked that because Lincoln had determined to issue the proclamation, "nothing can be said further about that." But Seward suggested that the sentence promising to "recognize" the freedom of the slaves would be stronger if the government also promised to "maintain" their freedom. (One might have thought that Seward, with his fear of servile insurrection, would have pressed Lincoln to weaken rather than strengthen this sentence.) He also advised Lincoln to delete a phrase that could be read as limiting the proclamation to the period in which Lincoln himself was in office. The other cabinet members agreed with Seward on these points and the changes were made. The next day, September 23, Lincoln's proclamation, countersigned by Seward as secretary of state, appeared in the nation's newspapers.[51]

It is not clear whether, at this point, Seward personally approved or disapproved of the proclamation. In his official letter to Adams and the other ministers abroad, in which he forwarded a copy of the proclamation, he asserted that the "good and wise men of all nations will confess that this is just and proper as a military proceeding for the relief of the country from a desolating and exhausting civil war." In a letter to Fanny, however, Seward was far more cautious: "The President's proclamation, so long and importunately clamored for by a portion of the people, has been issued at last. It is now evident [from the adverse press commentary] that the proceeding has not been delayed too long. In a short time we shall know whether it has come too soon. I hope that this may not prove to be the case. I was fearful of prematurely giving to a people prone to divide, occasion for organizing parties, in a crisis which demands union and harmony, in order to save the country from destruction." And the Russian minister Stoeckl, when he tried to get Seward's personal views on the proclamation, could only get a cryptic comment: "It is a *coup d'état*; let us see what results it will produce."[52]

———

Britain and France came closer to intervention in the American Civil War in 1862 than in any other year of the war. Although different terms were used—including "mediation," "recognition," and "intervention"— Seward knew well that any form of European involvement would harm the Union. If one or more of the major European powers offered to mediate between the North and the South, the offer itself would imply that both the United States and the Confederate States were separate, sovereign nations. Moreover, the mediating nation would almost certainly suggest that the dispute be resolved by allowing the Confederate States to remain in some form a separate nation. If the United States rejected this resolution, the mediator would likely recognize the Confederacy as a nation and perhaps enter the Civil War on the side of the Confederacy in order to punish the United States for its failure to abide by the results of the mediation. This type of armed mediation was quite common in the nineteenth century; the mediation by Britain and France in the late 1840s between Argentina and Uruguay was enforced by European fleets. Seward thus feared and discouraged any form of European intervention in the American war because he knew that even what started as a purportedly friendly mediation could lead to recognition and military support for the rebels.

Seward's most effective weapon against intervention by Britain or France was the close relationship between the United States and Russia. It is not easy to explain why the United States and Russia were so friendly in the mid-nineteenth century: one nation was a vibrant new democracy, the other an ancient monarchy, and their interests sometimes clashed, for example, in the northern Pacific, where American whaling vessels infringed on Russian waters. Yet there is no question that the two nations were firm friends. An English traveler in the United States in the early 1850s commented that she was "very much struck by the apparent *entente cordiale* that exists between Russia and the United States. There seems an inexplicable instinct of sympathy, some mysterious magnetism at work, which is drawing by degrees these two mighty nations into closer contact." During the Crimean War, from 1853 through 1856, the American press was generally sympathetic to the Russians in their war against Britain and France, and the United States stretched the limits of neutrality to provide arms and supplies to Russia. An American visitor, writing from St. Petersburg in 1858 for the *New York Times*, remarked that "the Russian people entertain for us sentiments of genuine admiration and regard," and that the emperor and his family were especially pro-American.[53]

While he was a senator, Seward was an exception to this pattern of Russian-American friendship. He had denounced the way in which Russia crushed the Hungarian Revolution in 1849, and he continued to criticize Russia thereafter. In the course of a speech in New York City in 1853, Seward called Russia an "unmitigated despotism" in which "four-fifths" of the people were mere slaves. In a Senate speech about Kansas, he argued that President Pierce's mistreatment of Kansas was as bad as the "despotism of the czar of Russia over the oppressed Poles." In one of his public letters, he commented that Russia "fills all southern Europe with terror." And in his famous Rochester speech, he said that "Russia yet maintains slavery, and is a despotism." Seward was not the only American with anti-Russian attitudes; during the Crimean War, as one scholar has noted, "a vocal group of liberals, merchants, and abolitionists, centered in New England, opposed Russia and sided with Britain for commercial and ideological reasons." Senator Seward's anti-Russian attitude was consistent with his attitudes toward slavery and commerce.[54]

As secretary of state, however, Seward realized the value of Russia, especially as a check upon Britain and France, and he completely changed course. In May 1861, in his initial instructions to the American minister to Russia, he noted that Russia had "always been a constant friend" of the United States, and that it would "be your pleasing duty to confirm and strengthen these traditional relations of amity and friendship." The Russian minister in Washington, Baron Stoeckl, did not especially like Seward; he wrote to the foreign minister in early 1861 that the secretary was "completely ignorant of international affairs," and yet "his vanity is so great that he will not listen to anyone's advice." Seward nevertheless tried to be Stoeckl's friend, inviting him and his American-born wife to his house and reminding him often of America's friendship for Russia.[55]

A welcome gift from Russia arrived in September 1861: a letter from the Russian foreign minister assuring Lincoln that the Russian emperor retained "the most friendly sentiments toward the American Union." The Union, in the emperor's words, was "an element essential to the universal political equilibrium." When Stoeckl told Seward about this letter, the secretary instantly recognized its value, writing to Stoeckl on the president's behalf to thank him for the "liberal, friendly, and magnanimous sentiments of His Majesty" and for this "new guaranty of friendship between the two countries." He also persuaded Stoeckl to allow both the Russian letter and Seward's response to be published immediately. The *New York Times* reported that the Russian letter caused "intense excitement" among diplomats in Washington. "It is the conceded opinion that [the letter] must cause England to think twice or three times before she attempts a recognition of the Southern rebels, even though she go without cotton for the next five years." The *Chicago Tribune* speculated that the letter meant that, if Britain or France intervened to support the South, Russia would intervene to support the North. Lord Lyons did not read the letter in this way—he wrote to the British foreign minister that the Russian letter was "little more than vague assurances"—but he was sufficiently concerned to send a copy home posthaste.[56]

Seward tried to reinforce, with Britain and France, the impression that intervention in the American war would cause Russian complications. In June 1862, for example, he wrote to John Bigelow, the American consul in Paris, that any European nation that intervened to support the Confederacy would "sooner or later fetch up in the arms of a native of an oriental country not especially distinguished for amiability of manners or temper." Seward did not name Russia, but his allusion would have been clear to Bigelow, and to the Frenchmen with whom he shared this comment. Seward also used every opportunity to remind Britain and France that intervention on the side of the South would lead to war with the North. In July 1862, he wrote to the American minister Dayton that France had no excuse for interfering in America's affairs: the United States had not interfered in France's war against Mexico, and had tried in making war against the Confederacy to avoid any collateral injury to France. French intervention on the side of the South would "bring out reserved and yet latent forces" in the North—forces that would not rest until the French were thrown out of North America. In August 1862, Seward wrote to Adams that, should Britain approach him with a proposal to "dictate, or to mediate, or to advise, or even to solicit or persuade, you will answer that you are forbidden to debate, to hear, or in any way receive, entertain or transmit, any communication of the kind." Any intervention by Britain in the American war would lead to war between the United States and Britain, and in such a war, Seward predicted, Britain would suffer severely.[57]

In October and early November 1862, the British cabinet seriously considered proposing either mediation or an armistice in the American Civil War. Given the delays in communication and the secrecy of the cabinet's discussions, Seward was only dimly aware of this debate, but he did have one worrisome indication: in late October, American papers reported a speech by William Gladstone, a senior member of the British cabinet, in which he said that the Confederate leaders "have made an army—they are making it appears, a navy—and they have made what is more than either, they have made a nation." Seward had no direct input into the British debate, but his prior statements and actions had their effect. One of the key arguments of those British leaders who opposed mediation was that there was no prospect that the North would accept mediation, and that any substantial aid to the South would lead to war with the North. The British cabinet could not help but be aware, after Seward's repeated warnings to Lyons in Washington and through Adams in London, that Lincoln and Seward would never accept foreign mediation, and that they were prepared to go to war against Britain if necessary. Seward often hinted to Lyons about the weaknesses Britain would have in such a war, especially its lightly defended Canadian provinces. Concerns about Canada were another factor in the British decision. Seward did not have any direct influence over Russia, but by publishing the Russian correspondence, he was able to highlight for the British leaders the likelihood that Russia would side with the United States.[58]

This mediation crisis ended, from Seward's perspective, in late November, with the publication in American newspapers of both the French mediation proposal and letters from Britain and Russia declining the French suggestion. The Russian foreign minister rejected the proposal strongly; the British foreign minister was more cautious, writing that "there is no ground at the present moment to hope that the federal government would accept the proposal suggested." The *Washington Daily Morning Chronicle* declared that "Russia has obtained the deep gratitude of this country, and should the occasion ever arise for practically showing how much we feel the obligation, we shall not wait to be reminded of it." Seward knew, from the wording of the British letter, and from his French reports, that this was not the last he would hear about mediation, but he also knew that this round of the debate was over.[59]

———

While the Europeans were debating whether to intervene, Americans were debating and voting in their fall elections. The Democratic newspapers argued that Lincoln, through the Emancipation Proclamation, was attempting to turn a war for Union into one against slavery. Democrats also criticized Seward for his disregard of civil liberties, and Lincoln for his alleged mismanagement of the war. The Democratic candidate for governor in New York, Horatio Seymour, campaigned largely against the administration's war policy, not on state issues.[60]

The 1862 election results were a disaster for the Republicans. Five major northern states that Lincoln had carried in 1860—New York, Pennsylvania, Ohio, Indiana, and Illinois—now elected House delegations in which Democrats would outnumber Republicans. Seymour was elected governor of New York by a margin of more than 10,000 votes. George Templeton Strong, the New York diarist, believed that people meant "to say by their votes, 'Messrs. Lincoln, Seward, Stanton & Co., you have done your work badly, so far. You are humbugs . . . and the war is no nearer an end than it was a year ago. I am disgusted with you and your party and shall vote for the governor or the congressman you disapprove, just to spite you.' " Seward was more optimistic, writing Adams that the differences between the Republican and Democratic parties were relatively modest, that neither the Democratic Party nor any substantial faction within that party favored disunion.[61]

On December 1, less than a month after the elections, Lincoln presented his second annual message to Congress. Seward certainly drafted the long section regarding foreign affairs, in which Lincoln dealt with details such as compensation for the owners of a Norwegian ship caught up in the blockade. He also likely reviewed and commented on the rest of the message, including Lincoln's renewed plea for compensated emancipation and his eloquent conclusion: "Fellow-citizens, *we* cannot escape history. We of this Congress and this administration, will be remembered in spite of ourselves. . . . In *giving* freedom to the *slave*, we *assure* freedom to the *free*—honorable alike in what we give, and what we preserve. We shall nobly save, or meanly lose, the last, best hope of the earth." In forwarding Lincoln's message to Adams and the other American ministers abroad, Seward remarked that Lincoln "grasps the subject of slavery earnestly and confidently." Whether Congress would accept the "bold suggestion of gradual and compensated emancipation," he could not say.[62]

———

"Remove him!" shouted a headline in the *Boston Commonwealth* on December 6. "William H. Seward stands before the American people today as the enemy of the public and it is the duty of every patriot to leave no stone within his or her reach unturned to secure his instant removal." The *Commonwealth*, which closely reflected the views of Sumner, listed Seward's various faults and crimes: "He has failed to comprehend the immensity and the character of the struggle now going on in this country. He has a right to be idiotic, undoubtedly, but he has no right to carry his idiocy into the conduct of affairs, and mislead men and nations by his twaddle about 'ending the war in sixty days.' " The editorial concluded that "we have had enough of his paralizing [sic] influence on the army and the president; let the watchword of the hour be, *remove Seward from the cabinet!*"[63]

This was far from the first attempt to oust Seward from his post. More than a year earlier, in September 1861, a group of New Yorkers had complained to Lincoln about the secretary's drinking and smoking. Lincoln responded, according to one of those present, that although Seward had faults, "I have been at work with him during a whole day and evening and never knew a man more ready to take up different subjects and to master them." In July 1862, the *New York Herald* published a report that Seward was about to resign because he disagreed with "the new and more vigorous war policy intended to be inaugurated by the late confiscation emancipation act." The *Herald* perhaps hoped that other newspapers would take up the call and press the secretary to resign. To head off any such movement, Seward gave an interview to the *Daily National Intelligencer* in which he claimed that there was no discord in the cabinet and that he had never suggested that he would resign. The *New York Tribune* concluded from this exchange that Seward "does not intend to retire from the cabinet so long as his remaining in it shall be desired by the president."[64]

Seward's strongest enemies were the Radical Republicans, those who favored immediate emancipation and a war of extermination against the southern rebels. The Radicals denounced Seward as having an improper and evil influence on the administration and the military. Zachariah Chandler, senator from Michigan, wrote to Lyman Trumbull, senator from Illinois, that nothing would save the nation other than "a change of policy and men [that] shall *instantly* be made." "For God and the country's sake," Chandler implored Trumbull, "send someone to *stay* with the President who will control and hold him." Joseph Medill, editor of the *Chicago Tribune*, wrote in similar terms to a Radical member of Congress: "McClellan in the field and Seward in the cabinet have been the evil spirits that have brought our grand cause to the very brink of death. Seward must be got out of the cabinet. He is Lincoln's evil genius. He has been president *de facto*, and has kept a sponge saturated with chloroform to Uncle Abe's nose all the while, except one or two brief spells."[65]

Salmon Chase, nominally Seward's colleague in the cabinet, was a key ally of his external enemies. In September 1862, a delegation of New Yorkers came to Washington to meet with Lincoln and to complain about Seward. One of the leaders of the group, James Hamilton, recalled later that he quoted to Lincoln from some of Seward's published letters, saying they proved that the secretary was "indulging in some idle theory that the traitors will, after sixty or ninety days, return to their allegiance." Lincoln reacted angrily, accusing Hamilton of quoting Seward out of context. "It is plain enough what you want," Lincoln continued, "you want to get Seward out of the cabinet. There is not one of you who would not see the country ruined, if you could turn out Seward!" That evening, over dinner, Hamilton reported this conversation to Chase, who apparently approved of all Hamilton had said. A few days later, Chase recorded in his diary another conversation, this time with Weed, in which Chase argued that Seward "adhered too tenaciously to men who proved themselves unworthy and dangerous, such as McClellan; that he resisted too persistently decided measures; that his influence encouraged the irresolution and inaction of the President with respect to men and measures." Chase complained even more strongly to his Radical friends on Capitol Hill about how Lincoln did not consult with the cabinet and how Seward manipulated the president.[66]

Chase was not Seward's only enemy within the cabinet. Gideon Welles noted in his diary in September 1862 that Seward "runs to the President two or three times a day, gets his ear, gives him his tongue, makes himself interesting, and artfully contrives to dispose of many measures or give them direction independent of his associates." Welles found the secretary's interference in the affairs of other departments especially annoying. "The qualities of Seward are almost the precise opposite of the President. [Seward] is obtrusive, never reserved, or diffident of his own powers, is assuming and presuming, meddlesome, unreliable, and uncertain, ready to exercise authority always, never doubting his right until challenged, then he becomes timid, doubtful, distrustful, inventive of schemes to extricate himself." Unlike Chase, however, Welles generally did not tell others about his views of Seward, at least until after the end of the Civil War.[67]

Montgomery Blair, the postmaster general, and his influential family were also enemies of Seward. In October 1861, Blair's father, Francis Preston Blair, wrote to Bigelow that "your friend, Seward, has been a nightmare for the administration." Blair claimed that, among his other errors, Seward had prevented the removal of Frémont from his command in Missouri, with the result that "we are now likely to have the abolition frenzy on an enlarged scale." Later that year, at the height of the *Trent* crisis, Blair's daughter Elizabeth Blair Lee wrote that Seward was "an arrant coward and will back down when bullied if he is allowed to do so by the country." Frank Blair (brother of Montgomery and Elizabeth) recommended to Lincoln that Seward should be removed from office before he could involve the United States in a war with Britain. Montgomery Blair, in a conversation with Welles, commented that Seward "is the least of a statesman and knows less of public law and administrative duties than any man who ever held a seat in the Cabinet," a comment Welles happily recorded in his diary.[68]

Mary Todd Lincoln was another enemy of Seward, viewing him as her husband's archrival. According to a postwar letter, when Mary learned that Lincoln intended to include Seward in his cabinet, her reaction was "Never!" She insisted that "if all things should go right—the credit would go to Seward—if they went wrong—the blame would fall upon my husband. Seward in the cabinet—*Never!*" Elizabeth Keckley, the White House seamstress, recalled a conversation in which Lincoln told his wife that she was mistaken about Seward. "Seward is an able man, and the country as well as myself can trust him." Mary responded that Seward was merely a "disappointed, ambitious politician." It outraged Mary to see Lincoln "let that hypocrite, Seward, twine you around his finger as if you were a skein of thread." Mary's hatred of Seward may have intensified in 1861 when he frustrated her efforts to abuse public funds, exposing an instance in which she overcharged the government for a dinner.[69]

The late 1862 attack on Seward would probably have faded if it had not been for a military disaster, the futile and fatal Union assault on December 13 against entrenched Confederates at Fredericksburg, Virginia. "In every attitude of death," one British observer wrote, "lying so close to each other that you might step from body to body, lay acres of the Federal dead." Within a few days after the battle, the dreadful evidence was everywhere in Washington, as the wounded filled every hospital and makeshift hospital in the capital. Lincoln was in despair. "If there is a worse place than hell," he told one visitor, "I am in it."[70]

On the afternoon of December 16, thirty Republican senators met in their caucus room to discuss the situation, and especially Seward. One of the senators, William Fessenden of Maine, wrote in his summary that a colleague had said that Seward "never believed in the war" and that "so long as he remained in the cabinet nothing but defeat and disaster could be expected." Another said that an unnamed member of the cabinet (almost certainly Chase) had told him "that there was a back-stairs influence which controlled the president." Only a handful of senators defended Seward, among them Preston King, who said that the charges were "mere rumors." The senators could not resolve the issue, so they agreed to meet again the next day.[71]

On December 17, the Senate Republicans resolved that "the public confidence in the present administration would be increased by a change in and partial reconstruction of the cabinet." They appointed a committee to meet with the president and press for him to remove Seward. Preston King went straight from this meeting to Seward's house. According to Frederick's memoir, after listening quietly to King's account of the meeting, Seward said: "They may do as they please about me, but they shall not put the President in a false position on my account." Seward and his son prepared and signed letters of resignation, which were promptly delivered to the president. Later that evening, Lincoln came to Seward's house to ask him to reconsider, but Seward said that it would "be a relief to be freed from official cares." Seward's friend Henry Raymond reported in the *New York Times* that Seward told Lincoln calmly that "he must be excused from holding any conversation with him upon the subject of the resignation—that it was based on what seemed to be a unanimous expression of opinion on the part of the Republican Senators that he ought no longer to hold the place." Seward added that "so far as his personal feelings were concerned, the happiest day of his life would be that which should release him honorably and without unmanly shrinking from labor or responsibility, from public office." Seward and Frederick spent much of the next two days boxing their papers at the State Department, preparing to leave Washington.[72]

On the evening of December 18, nine Republican senators met for three hours with Lincoln. Fessenden noted that the senators made the by now standard charges against Seward: that he was not in earnest about the war; that he interfered in military matters; and that he had an improper influence on the president. Sumner focused specifically on Seward's diplomatic dispatches, saying that he had disgraced himself and the United States, quoting the dispatch in which Seward charged that the abolitionists (with their zeal for emancipation) were hindering the war effort. Lincoln responded that "it was Seward's practice to read his dispatches to him before they were sent" but that he "did not recol-lect that [one] to which Mr. Sumner alluded." More generally, according to a report by Raymond in the *New York Times*, Lincoln told the sena-tors that "what the country wanted was military success. Without that nothing could go right:—with that nothing could go wrong. He did not yet see how the measure proposed by the Committee would furnish the remedy required; if he had a Cabinet of angels they could not give the country military successes, and that was what was wanted and what must be had."[73]

Lincoln met again with the senators on the evening of December 19, and this time the president had with him all his cabinet members other than Seward. Lincoln started with a long speech about the unity of the cabinet, saying that the cabinet had considered and agreed upon the most important issues. The president insisted, according to Fessenden's account, that Seward "had been earnest in the prosecution of the war, and had not improperly interfered—had generally read him his official correspondence, and had sometimes consulted with Mr. Chase." Lincoln then asked the cabinet members to comment on whether there was any lack of unity. As people turned toward him, Chase said that "he should not have come here had he known that he was to be arraigned before a committee of the Senate." And he conceded that "there had been no want of unity in the cabinet, but a general *acquiescence* on public measures." The Republican senators, accustomed to Chase's complaints about Seward, were shocked. When Lincoln asked them whether he should accept Seward's resignation, the senators divided; Sumner and the Radicals continued to argue against Seward, but others were now not sure. Although Fessenden was one of those who pressed Lincoln to remove Seward, he noted in a letter to his father that "Lincoln thinks he cannot get along without Seward" and that "our foreign affairs are too complicated for a fresh hand."[74]

Early on December 20, Gideon Welles called upon Lincoln and ad-vised him that it would be a mistake to accept Seward's resignation. Welles noted that he told Lincoln that he should "maintain the rights and independence of the Executive"; he should not allow the Senate to dictate to a president regarding his cabinet. Seward "had his infirmities and errors," Welles said, but he now realized that these "did not call for senatorial interference." Lincoln agreed, and asked Welles to talk with Seward. When Welles arrived at Seward's house, he found him talking with Stanton, who had come to similar conclusions. "This cabinet," Stanton said, "is like yonder window. Suppose you allowed it to be understood that passers-by might knock out one pane of glass—just one at a time—how long do you think any panes would be left in it?" When Welles told Seward what he had told Lincoln, Seward was "greatly pleased." Welles noted that Seward, under his mask of indifference, was "painfully wounded, mortified, and chagrined" by the senatorial attempt to oust him from office. Welles left, and not long thereafter, Montgomery Blair stopped by the house to tell Seward that he too objected to the proposed ouster of the secretary from the cabinet. Seward must have been gratified by the support of his three colleagues; but he still did not know whether Lincoln would accept his resignation or would yield to pressure from the Senate Radicals.[75]

Back at the White House, Welles found Chase and Stanton with Lincoln. Chase said that he had his resignation letter. "Where is it?," Lincoln demanded. "I brought it with me," Chase mumbled. "Let me have it," Lincoln said, as he grabbed the letter. The president scanned it and then looked up with a smile. "This," he said, "cuts the Gordian knot." Stanton said that he was also prepared to resign. "You may go to your department," Lincoln responded, "I don't want yours. This"—Chase's letter was still in his hand—"this is all I want; this relieves me; my way is clear; the trouble is ended." Lincoln then wrote letters to both Seward and Chase, asking them to withdraw their resignations and return to their duties. Seward responded immediately: "I have cheerfully resumed the functions of this Department in obedience to your command." Chase considered for a day before he reluctantly agreed as well. On December 22, unaware of this resolution, Lord Lyons wrote to London that "I shall be sorry if [the crisis] ends in the removal of Mr. Seward. We are much more likely to have a man less disposed to keep the peace than a man more disposed to do so." Lyons added, acknowledging how completely his own views of Seward had changed, that "I should hardly have said so two years ago."[76]

After a few days had passed, Seward could write to his friend Blatchford that the cabinet crisis, like the *Trent* crisis, "ought to be regarded as a proof of the stability of the country." In a letter to Sanford, Seward said that they were all merely players in a revolutionary drama. "The scenes are unwritten, the parts unstudied, the actors come on without notice, and often pass off in ways unexpected." Seward was also magnanimous, inviting Chase to join the family for dinner on Christmas Eve, an invitation Chase declined. Frances was with her husband in Washington for Christmas—she had arrived a week earlier to tend to William, who was recovering from a fever—but Fanny, daughter-in-law Jenny, and new granddaughter were not there, for they had received a telegram from Frederick instructing them to remain in Auburn. Fanny had followed the cabinet crisis from a distance, through the papers, "very anxious about father," for it seemed to her that "if he were to leave [Washington] the distracted state of affairs would prey upon his spirit all the more." She rejoiced to learn that the president had not accepted her father's resignation, and rejoiced again when Frederick wired that they should "come as soon as possible." It was not until New Year's Eve, however, that Seward was able to welcome Fanny, Jenny, and the baby to Washington.[77]

CHAPTER 13

"Ask Not Whether the Enemy Is Near":

1863

---

anuary 1, 1863, was a beautiful day in Washington, bright and clear
and warm. There had been some speculation that Lincoln would
not follow through on emancipation; some had read his December
message as indicating that he would wait for Congress to pass legislation rather than rely upon his military powers. Seward knew that Lincoln was determined, and in the last cabinet meetings of the year, he
suggested several small changes, which Lincoln accepted, to the final
proclamation. On the morning of the 1st, Seward went to his department to pick up the final document for Lincoln's signature. Lincoln, ever
the careful lawyer, noticed an error: the signature block was in the form
used for treaties rather than the proper form for a proclamation. Seward,
perhaps chastened, took the proclamation back for his staff to prepare
a corrected copy. Then he walked home to gather up Fred, Anna, and
Fanny, and take them to the White House reception.[1]

Fanny, who had just turned eighteen, was especially excited, for this
was her "coming out" day. She noted in her diary that she wore a light
blue dress and a "white hat trimmed with dark blue flowers." The first
hour of the presidential reception, starting at about eleven, was reserved
for the cabinet, diplomats, and their families. The diplomats in their full
court dress and the "gay and rich dresses of the ladies" made the "scene
a very brilliant one." Leaving the White House at noon, the Sewards

rushed home for their own reception. Their house was soon jammed with diplomats, officers, friends and total strangers, for the custom was that any decent person could call upon cabinet officers on this day. The young reporter Noah Brooks observed that although the "upstairs parlors were quite tastefully furnished," with "marble busts, engravings, flowers, and paintings," the most noticeable object was "the prodigious nose of Seward," as he greeted guests with his "matchless *suaviter in modo*," or graceful manner. "At two o'clock we were obliged to close the doors," wrote Fanny, "as the reception at the White House ceased then, and the whole crowd would have poured in here."[2]

After the family reception ended, Seward and Frederick walked to the State Department, picked up the revised proclamation, and returned with it to the White House. Lincoln paused before he signed. As Frederick recalled, Lincoln told the Sewards that he had never "felt more certain that I was doing right, than I do in signing this paper. But I have been receiving calls, and shaking hands since nine o'clock this morning, till my arm is stiff and numb." He feared that if his signature looked weak, people would say that he had hesitated. But, he said, "it is going to be done!" He signed with a firm, bold hand. Seward then countersigned and arranged for distribution.[3]

Seward had his whole family with or near him in early 1863. Frances, Augustus, Fred, Anna, and Fanny were in the house on Lafayette Square. William, Jenny, and their first child, Eleanor or Nellie, were nearby, in winter quarters at Fort Mansfield, about six miles north and west. When the weather and roads permitted, Seward would visit them in camp or they would visit the family in Washington. Frances remained largely in her room, leaving social duties to her daughter-in-law Anna. One evening when Anna was away, it was Fanny who had to preside over a diplomatic dinner, seated between the ministers from Peru and the Netherlands. She noted that this was "quite a stretch for my tongue, which is a little unpliable by nature."[4]

Henry Bellows, the Unitarian minister, after a family dinner with the Sewards, wrote home that Frances was "a dignified, simple, quiet person." She was "much more thorough in her religious and political radicalism than her husband," who jested to Bellows that "my wife doesn't think much of me." Augustus was "a quiet, country-looking fellow, who did not open his mouth," while Frederick was "a mild, intelligent young man who evidently hung on his father's every wish." Fanny struck Bellows as "rather pretty and very plainly dressed" but she "also said nothing." The abstemious minister observed that Seward drank "sherry, claret, perhaps half a dozen glasses," and did almost all the talking. On another evening, Bellows noted that two famous visitors, the historian George Bancroft and the judge Edward Loring, were just "shingles under [the] Niagara" of Seward's constant conversation.[5]

The Emancipation Proclamation did not end the debate over emancipation, for many denounced the proclamation, including the new governor of New York, Horatio Seymour, who called it "impolitic, unjust and unconstitutional." Clement Vallandigham, leader of the Copperheads, the northern opponents of the war, claimed on the House floor that the war was now pointless, that the North had no more chance of subduing the rebellious South than England once had of subduing the rebellious Americans. Others had more moderate views but were nevertheless tired of the war. "Exhaustion steals over the country," wrote Seward's friend Montgomery Meigs, and "confidence and hope are dying."[6]

This domestic dismay was the background for an unofficial mediation effort sponsored by a curious trio: Henri Mercier, the French minister to the United States; Horace Greeley, the editor of the New York Tribune; and William "Colorado" Jewett, an American adventurer recently returned from France. The three met in Washington in early January and soon thereafter the New York Tribune wrote favorably about Napoleon III and the possibility of French mediation. Seward responded through his friend Henry Raymond. Over dinner in Washington, Seward told Raymond that Greeley's conversations with Mercier were not only unwise, they were illegal under the Logan Act, which prohibited any American from attempting to influence a foreign government in its relations with the United States. The New York Times soon intimated that Greeley had violated the law by telling Mercier that "the people are tired of the war, that they desire peace above all things, and that they are ready to welcome the intervention of the French Emperor." Greeley responded with a public letter from Mercier denying that Greeley had been "a party to any scheme or proposal to bring about intervention or mediation." Seward also chastised Mercier, telling him that Greeley had "meddled in that which does not concern him" and that Mercier should speak directly with Seward in the future.[7]

Even before the dust settled on this dispute, there was another one, also involving Mercier. Seward had insisted, at the time of Mercier's April 1862 visit to Richmond, that Mercier went on his own and not as Seward's emissary. In early 1863, however, the American newspapers found, among the French diplomatic correspondence recently published in Paris, a letter from Mercier saying that it was Seward's suggestion that he go to Richmond, and that Seward told him the North would welcome back southern members of Congress. Radicals sensed this might provide a basis for a new attempt to remove the secretary. A reporter for the *New York Tribune* wrote his editor that "thank God—a new endeavor is to be made in the Senate to drive Seward out of the cabinet." One of the senators involved in this effort said that "if we go at Mr. Seward again we don't intend to flummox as we did before." Hoping to find additional ammunition, the Senate passed a resolution demanding that Seward provide all the correspondence related to the French mediation effort. Seward cleverly complied by providing not only the correspondence regarding April 1862, but also a masterful letter he had just posted to Paris, rejecting another mediation suggestion.[8]

In this letter, Seward disagreed with the French view that the United States was failing in its effort to subdue the southern rebellion. Given the immense territories and populations involved, the federal forces were making good progress in quelling the insurrection. There was, Seward asserted, no desire for compromise in the loyal states, nor any evidence of such a desire in the rebellious regions. The fundamental French error was their belief that there were already two American nations: "We have here, in a political sense, no North, no South, no Northern, no Southern States. We have an insurrectionary party, which is located upon, and is chiefly adjacent to the shores of the Gulf of Mexico; and we have, on the other hand, a loyal people, who constitute not only Northern States, but Eastern, Middle, Western and Southern States." Seward's firm response, and the favorable press reaction, quelled this second Senate effort to oust him; "good for Seward" was the reaction of George Templeton Strong.[9]

An opportunity arrived in 1863 for Seward to return the favor that

Russia had done the United States by refusing to join the French mediation effort in 1862. A rebellion was underway in Poland against its Russian rulers, and Seward personally sympathized with Poland, which he described privately as "the gallant nation whose wrongs, whose misfortunes, and whose valor have so deeply excited universal sympathy." Officially, though, he had to side with Russia, and so he refused a French proposal that the United States participate in a joint statement to the Russian emperor. Instead, he expressed confidence that the "enlightened and humane" emperor would treat his Polish subjects fairly. To be sure his message was not lost, Seward sent copies to various American ministers abroad, and it was soon published in the northern newspapers. The *Sacramento Daily Union* commented that the French proposal was just a "trick to commit our government against Russia" and that Seward deserved much "credit for avoiding the snare."[10]

———

Noah Brooks described Seward in early 1863 as being "small in stature, big as to nose, light as to hair and eyes, averse to all attempts upon his portrait, and very republican in dress and manner of living. He is affable and pleasant, accessible—from a newspaperman's point of view— smoking cigars always, ruffled or excited never, astute, keen to perceive a joke, appreciative of a good thing, and fond of 'good victuals,' if not of luxurious furniture." Seward was also "unpopular with Mrs. Lincoln, who would like to see Sumner in his place."[11]

Mary Lincoln was indeed still trying to get rid of Seward; a reporter quoted her as saying that "unless Seward was dismissed, the country would be ruined within three months." But Lincoln was not ready to part with his friend and valuable secretary of state. Brooks, who was close to both men, reported that Lincoln would not give up Seward's "wise and conservative counsels, and retains him against the wishes of a respectably large fraction of his own party friends, merely because he believes that to his far-seeing and astute judgment the administration has owed more than one deliverance from a very tight place." Brooks continued: "Seward's policy has always been of a character to avoid all things which might result in a divided North, and though it may have

been too emollient at times, it has resulted in retaining to the administration its cohesive strength, when it would have driven off its friends by
following . . . more arbitrary and rash measures." [12]

As Brooks noted, the relationship between Lincoln and Seward was
close, closer than that between the president and any other cabinet
member. The two men spoke often and on all issues, but they almost
never wrote about their conversations. To reconstruct their relationship
one must rely on other witnesses, such as Seward's son Frederick, who
recalled that as the two "sat together by the fireside, or in the carriage,
the conversation between them, however it began, always drifted back
into the same channel—the progress of the great national struggle. Both
loved humor, and however trite the theme, Lincoln always found some
quaint illustration from his western life, and Seward some case in point,
from his long public career, to give it new light." [13]

Lincoln's secretary John Hay described in his diary a carriage ride
the three men shared, during which Lincoln quoted a captured Confederate as saying that southern slavery had "gone to the Devil." Seward
agreed that slavery was dead, but said that the Democrats would not
recognize this, so their party "insists on devoting itself to guarding the
corpse." The situation was like the struggle between the Masons and
Antimasons in the 1820s, in which some die-hard Masons refused to
admit defeat even after most "had given up the fight and forgotten all
about it." Democrats like New York governor Seymour, Seward continued, were making a grave error in opposing the war, for it was a "fundamental principle of politics" that one should be "always on the side
of your country in a war." Lincoln agreed with Seward about Seymour,
and said this reminded him of a story. A Whig leader was once asked
whether he opposed the Mexican War. "No," said the Whig, he had opposed one war, and "that was enough for me. I am now perpetually in
favor of war, pestilence and famine." The three men laughed. [14]

Lincoln and Seward were so close that they could laugh at one another as well as with one another. Seward once remarked to a British
journalist, in Lincoln's presence, that he had "always wondered how
any man could ever get to be President of the United States with so
few vices. The President, you know, I regret to say, neither drinks nor
smokes." On another occasion, Lincoln told a visitor that "Mr. Seward is

limited to a couple of stories which from repeating he believes are true."
On yet another day, while riding with Noah Brooks in a mule cart to review some troops, Lincoln asked the driver, who was swearing loudly at
the mules, whether he was Episcopalian. The puzzled driver responded
that he was not, that he was raised as a Methodist. "I thought," Lincoln
said with a smile, that "you must be an Episcopalian, because you swear
just like Governor Seward, who is a churchwarden." [15]

Lincoln and Seward were close, but there were limits to their friendship. They did not know one another for that long—only from the time
of Lincoln's arrival in Washington in early 1861—so they did not have
the long history that leads to the warmest friendships. There is no suggestion that Lincoln ever spoke with Seward about the difficulties of his
marriage with Mary Lincoln, or that Seward ever spoke with Lincoln
about the difficulties of his own curious marriage with Frances Seward.[16]

Hay was aware of these limits, and of Seward's misguided early effort to control Lincoln, but for Hay there were "few instances of an official connection hallowed by a friendship so absolute and sincere as
that which existed between these two magnanimous spirits." Hay noted
that Lincoln and Seward were rivals for the presidential nomination, yet
Seward campaigned for Lincoln, and Lincoln named Seward to the first
place in his cabinet, and kept him there against all his critics. "Seward
had acumen and generosity enough to see that [Lincoln's] goodness of
heart, which everyone talked about, was the least of [his] claims to respect." Indeed, "from the beginning of the Administration to that dark
and terrible hour when they were both struck down by the hand of
murderous treason, there was no shadow of jealousy or doubt ever disturbed their mutual confidence and regard." [17]

———

In late April 1863, as better weather for marching and fighting approached, Seward traveled south to see the Union Army. He brought
with him a few members of his family and a few foreign diplomats, hoping they would report home on the strength of the Union forces. The
group departed from the Navy Yard, steamed down the Potomac River to
Aquia Creek, and went on from there by Army train to the headquarters

of General Joseph Hooker. Charles Francis Adams, Jr., a cavalry officer under Hooker, would later describe this headquarters as "a combination of bar-room and brothel," but Frederick and Fanny were both favorably impressed. Fanny noted that Hooker was an excellent host and that "the real affection with which he spoke of his men would do anyone good to hear." The Seward party slept in Army tents on the night they arrived, and on the next day there was a grand review of 15,000 soldiers. Many of the men whom the observers saw on that beautiful spring day would soon be dead. In the Battle of Chancellorsville, in the first week of May, Hooker's armies were badly mauled by Lee's Confederates, with hundreds of lives lost and thousands wounded. Many northerners despaired, but Seward maintained his calm, writing to John Bigelow, the consul in Paris, that "the army is capable and progress will be resumed." [18]

In late May, Seward accompanied Frances and Fanny on their rail trip home to Auburn. He spent a few pleasant days there, tending his garden, visiting with friends, and giving one short speech, in which he encouraged the young men of Auburn to enlist. Not long after he returned to Washington, some papers started to report rumors of another Confederate invasion of the North. Fanny wrote her father of the family's anxiety: "Although I don't consider myself a protection, Washington seems safer to me when I am there." Seward responded that there was no cause for concern: "Certainly the last thing that any one here thinks of nowadays is an invasion of Washington." [19]

A few days later, however, the papers confirmed that an invasion was in fact underway, and that the rebels had already captured Hagerstown in Maryland and Chambersburg in Pennsylvania. Seward wired his son William, who had just arrived in Auburn for a three-week home leave, that he should return to his regiment immediately. He also tried to calm his wife and daughter, writing that "the danger is neither so great nor so imminent as the popular apprehension would indicate." On the last day of June he wrote his friend Sanford: "it would be absurd to say we have no anxiety, but we certainly have grounds for expectation of a good result." He advised his wife that she should not "borrow much trouble from the military movements of the hour, which, even here, are imperfectly understood." He anticipated a major battle and "we must wait for results." [20]

There was indeed an epic battle at Gettysburg, Pennsylvania, on the first three days of July 1863, involving tens of thousands on both sides. Seward spent hours each day in the War Department telegraph office, but there was little news. As the *New York Times* reported from Washington late on July 2, "no reliable advices have been received here from the Pennsylvania battlefield. . . . Intense anxiety prevails." Then, early on the Fourth of July, a telegram arrived reporting that the Confederate forces had been "handsomely repulsed" the day before, with "severe loss." Lincoln composed and distributed a "press release," not quite claiming victory, but stating that the reports from Gettysburg "promise a great success for the cause of the Union." Seward was more cautious, writing to Frances that day that it "would be idle for me here to speculate upon what must become certain, and definitely known within a few hours after the sending of my letter. . . . The chances are largely in favor of the Union forces, in any stage of the conflict, and God is over all."[21]

By July 6, the *New York Times* could report that Lee had been "totally routed" at Gettysburg and was retreating towards Virginia. Then, on July 7, at about one in the afternoon, while Lincoln, Seward, and the cabinet were meeting, news arrived that, after a long siege, Union forces under Ulysses Grant had finally captured Vicksburg, the last major Confederate stronghold on the Mississippi. This news, coming just after Gettysburg, caused what Brooks described as "the wildest excitement throughout the city." In the government office buildings, "the announcement of the news was received with cheer upon cheer from the crowds of officers and clerks, and I do not believe that there was much work done in private or public offices during the rest of the day." That evening, crowds went from door to door, demanding and receiving remarks from their leaders. Seward's speech from his front steps was his best of the wartime years.[22]

He started with a review of recent history, from the secession crisis down to the present. The victories at Gettysburg and Vicksburg, in his view, were "the beginning of the end" of the war. He stressed that this was still a war for the Union, not a war against slavery. "The country shall be saved by the republican party if it will, by the democratic party if it choose, without slavery if it is possible, with slavery if it must." He predicted that the rebel states would soon start to rejoin the Union, like stars finding their proper places in a "glorious constellation." He knew that "these stars could not be altogether extinguished," and that "the attraction which brought them originally together, however weakened, cannot be utterly broken." But his listeners should not assume that these events would take place without further sacrifice. They must be prepared to vote for the Union, to fight for the Union, perhaps to die for the Union.[23]

For himself, Seward went on, he was determined to remain in the nation's capital, whatever its fate. "If I fall here let no kinsman or friend remove my dust to a more hospitable grave. Let it be buried under the pavements of the avenue, and let the chariot wheels of those who have destroyed the liberties of my country rattle over my bones until a more heroic and worthy generation shall recall that country to life, liberty and independence." This, Seward said, was his own resolution; "now, fellow-citizens, for yours." They must resolve that "you will not wait for draft or conscription. Ask not whether the enemy is near or whether he is far off. Ask only is there still an enemy in arms against the United States—a domestic one or a foreign one—array yourselves to meet that enemy." The American flag, he concluded, looking at all the flags above and around him, "must wave not only in the capital and in the free states, so-called," but throughout the Union, "until not one disloyal citizen remains in arms to oppose it."[24]

Seward's speech was in part a recruiting speech, for he was still concerned about the slow pace of enlistment. He expressed similar concerns in a letter to a northern black who had complained that although blacks could now enlist in the Union Army, they received lower salaries than white soldiers. The duty to defend one's country, Seward wrote, "does not depend on, nor is it affected by, what the country pays us, or what position she assigns us, but it depends on her needs alone."[25]

Frederick Douglass was making similar arguments: blacks should enlist regardless of the conditions, because by fighting in the Army they could win freedom for their enslaved brothers in the South and civil rights for themselves in the North. When Douglass met Lincoln for the first time, in August 1863, and started to introduce himself, Lincoln said that there was no need, for "Mr. Seward has told me all about you." Although Seward was still a common friend for Lincoln and Douglass, some Radicals worried that Seward's desire to reunite with the southern states would override his concern for blacks. Sumner wrote to Lincoln that Seward's comments about reunion with or without slavery caused concern, "which has been increased by reports that some of the cabinet wished the government to turn from the [emancipation] proclamation." In a letter to a British friend, Sumner explained more fully: "We are too victorious. If the Rebellion should suddenly collapse, Democrats, copperheads, and Seward would insist upon amnesty and the Union and 'no questions asked about Slavery.' God save us from any such calamity."[26]

——

The most serious foreign policy issue Seward faced in 1863 was how to prevent the construction in Britain and France of additional naval vessels for the Confederacy. Confederate agents in Britain had organized the construction of two such vessels in 1862: the *Florida* and the *Alabama*. To evade British neutrality laws, these ships were nominally built for foreign purchasers, and they did not receive their final arms until they were offshore. Charles Francis Adams protested, but the British government claimed that it could not arrest ships without solid proof that they were being built and armed for the Confederacy. By early 1863, northern newspapers were reporting almost daily on how the *Alabama* was capturing and burning northern commercial vessels. The *New York Times* complained that the Confederates "have inflicted with their one ship, in the short period of a few weeks, more damage upon our commerce and disgrace upon our Government, than our whole navy has done to them since the capture of New Orleans."[27]

Many believed that, if the Navy could not capture the *Alabama*, the government should commission privateers for the purpose. Working with Senator James Grimes of Iowa, chairman of the Naval Affairs Committee, and working against Charles Sumner, chairman of the Foreign Relations Committee, Seward pressed forward a bill to authorize the president to commission privateers. After the Senate passed the bill in February, Lord Lyons complained to Seward that "the Confederates had no merchant vessels," so the most likely targets of northern privateers would be British and French ships trading, or suspected of trading, with the Confederacy. Seward responded that since it did not appear that British law allowed the British government to prevent the construction there of Confederate cruisers, the United States might have to rely upon private enterprise—that is, privateers—to defend its commerce. Lyons reported regretfully to London that it seemed likely the legislation would pass Congress with Seward's strong support.[28]

The bill passed and Lincoln signed it into law in early March. A few days later, when Lyons again raised the privateer issue, Seward reminded him of newspaper reports that "six more armed vessels were building at Liverpool for the rebels." Allowing these vessels to go to sea would be a disaster for both nations: "If the [American] shipping interest was to be ruined by the depredations of pirates sailing from England, the indignation of the people would be beyond restraint." Seward again suggested that the best way for the United States to capture and destroy the *Alabama* would be to commission privateers for the purpose. Lyons said that Britain would not object to privateers directed solely at the *Alabama* and other Confederate raiders; Britain's concern was that the United States intended to allow privateers to stop and inspect neutral (British) vessels suspected of breaking the blockade. Seward acknowledged the dangers involved in this scenario, but he insisted that "unless some intelligence came from England to allay the public exasperation, the measure would be unavoidable." To be sure his message was heard, Seward made similar points in letters to Adams.[29]

Seward used not only sticks, such as the privateer threat, but also carrots in his effort to influence British policy. The dispute over the *Peterhoff* mails is a good example of his willingness to conciliate Britain. The *Peterhoff* was a British merchant ship that the American Navy stopped, seized, and forced into New York Harbor, on suspicion that the military goods on board were bound for the Confederacy. Lyons asked Seward to ensure that the *Peterhoff* mailbag was delivered to the British consul; this was the international custom, Lyons said, and what Seward had promised the prior year would be the American practice. When Seward asked Welles to telegraph orders to this effect to New York, he refused; Seward then telegraphed the district attorney himself, instructing him that the mailbag should "remain inviolate until further directions from me."[30]

Welles and Seward disputed this issue intensely over the next few days, writing letters and pleading with the president. Brooks, in his news report, described the protagonists as the "silky Secretary of State" and the "more resolute Secretary of the Navy," who insisted that "by all the principles of international law and common sense the mail must share the fate of all of the other papers found on board." According to Brooks, Lincoln was "inclined to the belief that a moderate degree of bluff will face down the piratical ship chandler across the water"; in other words, Lincoln supported Seward's threats to use privateers as a way to place pressure on Britain. Lincoln also agreed with Seward that "everything ought to be subordinated to the one leading purpose of crushing the rebellion," even if this meant that the United States had to swallow its pride in some cases. On April 22, at the request of Lincoln and Seward, and over the objection of Welles, the *Peterhoff* mails were delivered to the British consul in New York City.[31]

Seward realized how important it was, in his efforts to change British policy, to have the right Americans on the ground in Britain. He was fortunate in having Charles Francis Adams as the minister in London and Thomas Haines Dudley, a determined and diligent lawyer, as the consul in Liverpool. But he was concerned that Adams, although trained as a lawyer, did not have the skills necessary to work in the British legal system. So Seward summoned his old friend William Evarts, one of the leading members of the New York bar, and asked him to go as soon as possible to London. Seward told Lyons that Evarts "not only possessed his entire confidence, but might be considered as representing him personally." Seward was gratified to learn, not long after Evarts arrived in London, that leading British friends of America considered him "the right man in the right place."[32]

Some welcome news arrived in Washington in late April: the British authorities had arrested the *Alexandra*, a small cruiser under construction for the Confederates in Liverpool. The London reporter for the *New York Times* attributed the changed British attitude to the threat of American privateers. "There can be no doubt," the *Times* reported, "that

[Prime Minister] Palmerston and [Foreign Minister] Russell were helped to this wise conclusion by the [privateer] law lately enacted in Congress." At least two other factors may have influenced the British. First, Seward and Adams had been demanding that the British government compensate American owners whose vessels were destroyed by the *Alabama*. The Seward-Adams argument was that the British government, by allowing the Confederacy to build and equip the *Alabama* in Britain, had violated British and international law, and was thus liable for all the damage caused by the *Alabama*. Lord Russell politely disagreed, but he knew that the Americans would continue to press their claims after the Civil War, and that the American arguments might ultimately prevail. Russell did not want to increase the damages Britain might owe by allowing additional Confederate cruisers to be built in Britain. Second, Russell knew that although, in the current war, Britain was the neutral nation in which warships were being constructed for the Confederates, in the next war the roles could well be reversed, with warships being constructed in American shipyards for use against the British merchant fleet. Britain was generally a belligerent in nineteenth-century wars, not a neutral, and it did not want to lose sight of its long-term interests.[33]

Seward was pleased but not overjoyed at the news of the detention of the *Alexandra*, for he soon learned that the ship's owners had filed a lawsuit against the British government, claiming there was insufficient evidence upon which to seize the ship. At the trial in London, the judge charged the jury that it was perfectly lawful for a British shipbuilder to build a ship for the Confederates. Seward wrote to Adams that if the decision was not overturned on appeal, the United States would be forced to conclude that British law provided no protection "against the indiscriminate and unlimited employment of capital, industry, and skill, by British subjects, in building, arming, equipping and sending forth ships-of-war from British ports to make war against the United States."[34]

———

A few weeks later, news reached the United States of a new threat: the Laird shipyard at Liverpool was building two warships, each equipped with an underwater ram designed to pierce and sink enemy vessels.

Adams, ably assisted by Dudley and Evarts, gathered and presented evidence to the British authorities to show that these "Laird rams" were being constructed for the Confederates, not for foreign purchasers as claimed, and that the rams could have no possible peaceful purpose. As reports reached London that the first of the Laird rams was about to sail, Adams wrote to Russell almost daily, with increasing concern. If the British government allowed such dangerous warships to go to sea against the United States, he noted on September 5, Britain could no longer claim that it was neutral; it would be a *de facto* ally of the Confederacy. "It would be superfluous in me to point out to your lordship that this is war."[35]

Because of the communication delay, Seward was not aware of this letter for several weeks, but he and Adams were on the same page. Seward wrote to Adams on September 5 that he feared the Laird rams, once in Confederate hands, would be able to "enter Portland, Boston, New York, or, if they prefer, must attempt to break the blockade at Charleston, or to ascend the Mississippi to New Orleans." The British government must understand that such an assault by ships built in Britain for the Confederates would have the effect of "arousing the whole nation, and making a retaliatory war inevitable."[36]

A few days later, on September 10, Charles Sumner gave a four-hour speech on American foreign relations in New York City. The speech was an extended and strident attack on Britain: for its premature recognition of Confederate belligerency, for its hypocrisy in opposing slavery elsewhere but tolerating it in the Confederacy, for its role in the construction and support of the *Alabama*, and for the imminent release of additional Confederate cruisers. Although Sumner did not mention Seward by name, most people read the speech as an indirect attack on Seward, in which Sumner hoped to show that he was better qualified than Seward to lead American foreign policy, especially in the likely event of war against Britain.[37]

Seward, Adams, and Sumner were not aware, as they made these various statements in early September, that Palmerston and Russell had already decided to detain the Laird rams. Adams, when he heard the news on September 8, thanked God for "turn[ing] the hearts of the rulers at the critical moment." Seward somehow learned the fate of the rams ten days later, before the report from Adams arrived or any report had reached American newspapers. When Welles visited Seward on September 18 to discuss his concerns about the rams, Seward asked him a curious question: Was he a Mason? Welles responded that he was, but it did not matter, for they were discussing public business. Seward wanted Welles to assure him that he would not tell a living person what he was about to tell him: that the British cabinet had decided to detain the Laird rams. It would appear, from Seward's manner and from the timing, that he had some source within the British government.[38]

Sumner's bid to replace Seward backfired. Many American papers praised Sumner's early September speech; the *Chicago Tribune*, for example, called it a "statesmanlike document." But in Britain the speech was seen as mere bombast and belligerence. In a speech of his own in late September, Lord Russell deplored how Sumner had made "accusation after accusation, and misrepresentation after misrepresentation," which could lead to war between Britain and the United States. Russell contrasted Sumner's hostile approach with Seward's more diplomatic method: "the government of America discusses these matters very fairly with the English government. Sometimes we think them quite in the wrong; sometimes they say we are quite in the wrong; but we discuss them fairly, and with regard to the Secretary of State, I see no complaint to make." It was not only Russell whose attitude toward Seward was changed by Sumner's speech; Adams wrote a friend a few weeks later that Seward was now "considered as the best disposed to Britain of all our leading public men."[39]

Seward's own relationship with Sumner was complex. On the one hand, Seward knew that Sumner wanted to be secretary of state and that he was Seward's leading critic. On the other hand, Sumner was the chairman of the Senate Foreign Relations Committee, with whom Seward had to work on countless issues, including appointments, treaties, and legislation. Seward also knew that his wife continued to view Sumner as a personal friend. Seward therefore kept up at least the pretense that he and Sumner were friends, and Sumner was from time to time a guest at Seward's house. Seward even wrote Sumner to praise the New York speech: "You have performed a very important public service in a most able manner and in a conjunction when I hope it will be useful abroad and at home." He added, perhaps a bit patronizingly, that "you are on the right track, [to] rouse the nationality of the American People."[40]

Almost at the same time that Seward learned that the British would detain the Laird rams, he learned from the American minister in Paris, William Dayton, and the consul there, John Bigelow, that the Confederates were building armed cruisers in France. Bigelow provided Seward not only with rumors but with documents, which he received from a mysterious French informer, proving that the real purchasers of the vessels were the Confederates, not other foreign nations as claimed. The documents also showed that the Confederates (perhaps through misrepresentation) had obtained approval from the French government for building the ships. In later letters, Bigelow described the steps he took to stop the construction of these Confederate ships: hiring a top French lawyer, presenting the evidence to the French government, working to develop additional evidence, keeping up the pressure through the French press. In a sense, Seward did nothing to prevent the completion in France of the Confederate warships other than to approve of Bigelow's work. But in another sense, Seward was responsible, for it was Seward who arranged Bigelow's appointment in 1861, and Seward who persuaded Bigelow to remain in place rather than to resign as Bigelow requested early in 1863. Seward could thus take personal as well as official pleasure as it became clearer and clearer, in late 1863 and early 1864, that these French warships would never form part of the Confederate Navy.[41]

The Russians had given Seward a gift in 1862 when they refused French mediation, and they gave him another gift in late 1863, when Russian fleets sailed into both New York and San Francisco for friendly visits. The Russian fleets remained in American waters for the next few months, and when the eastern fleet visited Washington, Seward ensured that the Russian officers were entertained both at his own home and at the White House. There is some dispute today over the reasons why the Russian Navy visited the United States, with some arguing that Russians did not want their fleet to be "bottled up" in the Baltic if there was a war over Poland, and others arguing that the Russian admiralty merely wanted its navy to take long training voyages and visit foreign ports. In

1863, however, most people believed that the reason for the presence of the fleet was to underscore Russian support for the United States. Some even speculated that the vessels were intended to join the Americans in the event of naval war with Britain or France. Seward encouraged such speculations; a New York financier later recalled his saying that the Russian fleet would guarantee that no foreign power would recognize the Confederacy.[42]

———

Seward did not have much time to enjoy the news of the victories at Gettysburg and Vicksburg, for on July 13 there were deadly draft riots in New York City. A mob of five hundred people stormed the building in which names were being selected for the draft, beat the federal draft officers, destroyed the records, and burned the building for good measure. The rioters then took to the streets, beating and killing those they met, especially blacks. Many of the rioters were Irish Democrats, and they targeted Republicans and Republican newspapers. The rioting continued for several days, only gradually ending as federal troops arrived in the city. On July 17, Seward predicted to Lyons that the riots would strengthen the Lincoln administration by showing "the dangerous and abominable sentiments of the mob of Democratic voters." Seward wrote to his wife in similar terms, saying that "the thunder shower will clear the political skies."[43]

Seward was confident in Washington, but Frances was worried in Auburn. Noting signs of unrest among the Irish, she wrote that "we have been in daily apprehension of a riot here for some time, and even now fear an uprising when the commencement of the draft shall afford an excuse." Seward's daughter-in-law Jenny later recalled that, one morning during this period, Frances found that someone had thrown a rock through a window of their house. Frances told Jenny that there might be an attack, that she should remove anything valuable. "So that afternoon," Jenny wrote, "I took my husband's photograph down to my mother's house, it being, to my mind, the most valuable thing that I possessed." Seward, with an airy indifference that must have angered his wife, wrote her that "there will hardly be any body desperate enough to do you personal harm, and if the country, in its unwonted state of excitement, will destroy our home, the sacrifice will be a small one for our country, and not without benefit." A few days later, he wrote again, saying he hoped that "your alarm has passed by. If it recurs, you will do well to join us here, and leave what we have [in Auburn] to be a propitiation to faction." In the event, the draft passed off quietly in Auburn; the *New York Times* reported that "the best of order was observed and the best spirit was manifested."[44]

Even as the reports of draft riots were arriving, Seward was working to organize a grand tour of New York State for the foreign diplomats in Washington. The diplomats were in some cases reluctant; Lyons explained to Russell that he only agreed after Seward pressed him so hard that he could not refuse without personal insult. In the end, the group included all the major diplomats in Washington: Lyons of Britain, Mercier of France, Stoeckl of Russia, and Tassara of Spain. They visited Albany, Schenectady, and Auburn, which they reached at about six on the evening of August 19. Half of the foreign visitors stayed on that night in Seward's house, the other half at the nearby house of a friend. The next morning, Seward showed his foreign guests the sights of his hometown, then gave them a tour by boat of Lake Owasco. "Auburn is a quiet, modest town," the local paper declared, "but no one can blame her if she puts on airs on the present occasion." From Auburn, Seward and his guests proceeded to Rochester, Buffalo, and Niagara, returning to Washington via Pennsylvania.[45]

Seward had two purposes in this trip. First, he wanted to show the diplomats that, outside of the regions around Washington, the North was largely unaffected by the Civil War. Frederick later recalled that his father's foreign guests saw "hundreds of factories with whirring wheels, thousands of acres of golden harvest fields, miles of railway trains, laden with freight, busy fleets on the rivers, lakes and canals." Seward's second purpose was to improve his personal relations with the foreign diplomats. Even Lord Lyons, who had so distrusted and disliked Seward at the outset of their relationship, wrote to Russell after this trip that "when one comes really to know [Seward] one is surprised to find much to esteem and even to like in him."[46]

Seward returned to Washington in early September and devoted the month to diplomatic and military issues. An example of his military role was the midnight conference at the War Department during which Stanton recommended that 20,000 Union troops be transferred immediately by railroad from the eastern to the western front. Lincoln was initially doubtful; Salmon Chase wrote in his diary that the president remarked that the Army could not "get one corps into Washington in the time you fix for reaching Nashville." This "greatly annoyed" Stanton, who said that "the danger was too imminent and the occasion [too] serious for jokes." Chase suggested that they take a brief break to enjoy the meal Stanton had organized for them. When they returned to Stanton's office, "Mr. Seward took up the subject and supported Mr. Stanton's proposition with excellent arguments." Seward's comments turned the tide; Lincoln agreed and the orders were issued. Over the next few days, Stanton supervised the transfer of more than 20,000 men and their supplies, "the most successful and dramatic use of railroads in the war," in the words of one historian.[47]

In late September or early October, Seward interrupted Lincoln one morning in his office. According to Frederick, the conversation went something like this: "They say, Mr. President, that we are stealing away the rights of the states. So I have come today to advise you that there is another state right that I think we ought to steal." What state right, Lincoln asked, did Seward now want to take? "The right to name Thanksgiving Day!" Because the holiday was designated by several governors, it was observed on different days in different states. Would it not make more sense to have a single, national day? Seward presented Lincoln with a draft proclamation reciting the blessings the United States had enjoyed in the past year: bountiful harvests, domestic prosperity, and increasing population. Using Seward's draft, Lincoln designated the last Thursday of November as a day of thanksgiving, the first such national Thanksgiving.[48]

———

In the middle of October, Charlotte Cushman and her niece arrived at the Sewards' house in Washington and stayed for ten days. Cushman, forty-seven years old at the time, was one of the nation's most famous

Shakespearean actors, playing male as well as female roles. Seward had known and admired her for years; she had been his guest in Washington on at least two prior occasions. Cushman lived mainly in Rome during the Civil War years, but she returned to the United States in the summer of 1863 in order to raise funds, through benefit performances, for the relief of wounded soldiers. Lincoln was among those who was pleased to see the actor return to Washington; two years earlier, when Seward had first introduced Cushman to the president, Lincoln told her that *Macbeth* was his favorite play, and that he hoped some day to see her in the role of Lady Macbeth. Fanny was even more pleased at Cushman's return, for she viewed her as the model of the life she wanted to lead, that of a "useful unmarried woman."[49]

Although the term did not have its modern meaning, and indeed there was no accepted term, Cushman was a lesbian. She had a number of female lovers during her lifetime, including Emma Stebbins, the sculptor with whom she lived in Rome, and Emma Crow, now her niece by virtue of a marriage Cushman had arranged with her nephew. Cushman's trip to America was not only a way to raise funds for charity; it was a way to spend intimate time with Emma Crow. And Cushman's week in Washington had another purpose: to press Seward to appoint her feckless nephew to a diplomatic position in Rome so that Cushman's whole family—including both her lovers—could be together. It seems likely that Seward had at least some suspicion about Cushman's sexuality; there were after all no men in her life, only women, and she was known for the passion she brought to the role of Romeo. If Seward suspected anything, however, he did not care; he liked and respected Cushman and was happy to have her spend time with his daughter. Indeed, even though the theater was not a respectable profession, Fanny noted in her diary that her father said that "had he a son or a daughter with a talent for acting he would bid them go upon the stage."[50]

Fanny wrote pages in her diary about Cushman and her days in Washington: how her face was at times "girlish, from color and animation" but also "so full of grandeur that it cannot fail to be impressive." Fanny marveled at how the actor discussed finances and politics with her father "with the ease and air of habit which is usually confined to men." Lincoln was a frequent visitor at Seward's house during

Cushman's visit, and Crow later recalled that Seward would allow Cushman to remain in the room while the two men talked about politics and other issues. When Cushman asked Fanny when she might hope to see her in Rome, Fanny explained that she expected to visit Europe at the end of the war, for her father had promised that he would resign at that time and travel abroad with her. Cushman was doubtful; she believed that Seward "would feel that he must in duty see this thing through to the end—more than the end of the war—and that he never would retire, such a thing would never occur in his life." Cushman also commented that she viewed Seward as "the greatest man this country ever produced, because he is a *good* man." This affected young Fanny "to the heart," and she told the actor that "very few understood my father as she did and indeed, beyond our family, it is *very* few."[51]

The two leading theater managers in Washington, John Ford and Leonard Grover, both wanted Cushman to perform at their theaters. Ford gave Cushman and Fanny a personal tour of his new theater, which Fanny pronounced "tasteful and convenient." Cushman decided to perform at Grover's, however, in part because Grover had two excellent actors ready to play Macbeth and Macduff, and in part because of Ford's reported rebel sympathies. Cushman's benefit performance as Lady Macbeth at Grover's Theater was a great success. The theater was jammed: Lincoln, his wife, and his son Tad were in the presidential box; Seward, Fred, Anna, Fanny, and Emma Crow had the box opposite. Crow recalled that Cushman performed that night with special force, that her voice was so powerful it could be heard in the back of the theater, even when she spoke in a whisper.[52]

———

From the secession crisis onwards, Seward favored giving the Republican Party a new name, the Union Party, to emphasize that its main purpose was to save the Union, and to draw in some Democrats. This suggestion was implemented during the war, and by 1863, the National Union Party included not only almost all Republicans but also many prominent former Democrats. Although there were few federal offices at stake in that year, the fall elections were viewed as a referendum on the Lincoln administration. Moreover, to some extent, the 1863 elections were an early test of the candidates for president in 1864. More than twenty years had passed since an American president had received the nomination of his own party for a second term, so the newspapers naturally speculated about nominees other than Lincoln, especially Chase and Seward. It was perhaps to strengthen Seward's chances that his old friend Edwin Morgan, the former New York governor and now a Union Party leader, pressed him to speak during that state's campaign. Seward declined, writing Morgan that he worried about the tendency of the "friends of the Union to divide into contentious factions," and that he feared his campaign speeches would exacerbate this tendency. Chase, in contrast, accepted many invitations to speak in Ohio and exulted in the praise his speeches received in the press.[53]

In early November, Seward returned home to Auburn to vote and to check on his son William, who was convalescing from typhoid fever. Disregarding his own advice to Morgan, Seward gave an emotional political speech on the eve of the election, arguing that the Democratic candidates were really the candidates of the Confederates and other enemies of the Union. "If the ballot-boxes could be opened at Laird's shipyard in Liverpool, or in John Slidell's house in Paris, there would be a unanimous vote for [antiwar Democrats like] Seymour and Vallandigham." The Civil War would only come to an end when all the states recognized that Lincoln was the rightful president of the United States. As to slavery, Seward predicted that the "insurrection will perish under military power, and slavery will perish with it. Nevertheless, I am willing that the prodigal son shall return. The door, so far as I am concerned, shall always be open to him." The next day, Seward wired Lincoln to predict, correctly, that the Union Party would have a majority of about 25,000 votes in New York.[54]

Some papers praised but others criticized Seward's election eve speech, especially the comment that he was willing to welcome back the prodigal southern states. For the *Norfolk County Journal* in Massachusetts, Seward's ideas were "directly in conflict with those that the President has laid down as his own," and his speech provided "a new example of his waning judgment." William Lloyd Garrison, the abolitionist editor of the *Liberator*, contrasted Chase with Seward: to

Chase, "more than any other man in the cabinet, are we indebted for the president's proclamation, and the other executive acts which have struck the diabolical system of slavery." Seward, on the other hand, was an opponent of emancipation. Garrison cautioned that voters should consider "whether a vote for old Abe [in 1864] will not choose Seward to be again acting president." [55]

A few days after Seward arrived back in Washington, he received an urgent message from Lord Lyons: there were reliable reports from Canada of a Confederate plot to seize ships on Lake Erie, attack the large prison camp on Johnson's Island, free the hundreds of Confederate officers imprisoned there, and then use this force to attack Buffalo or other points. Although the hour was near midnight, Seward rushed from his home to that of Stanton, where he found the secretary of war reading Dickens. Seward relayed the British warning and Stanton went to the War Office to send out a series of telegrams: to the governors of the lake states, to the mayors of major cities, and to the military commanders. The next day, Seward sent his friend Preston King, senator from New York, to see the British governor in Canada and coordinate the American and Canadian responses to the Confederate threat. The Confederates did not launch this attack, but they also did not give up on the idea of using British Canada as a base from which to attack the North. [56]

————

On November 18, Lincoln, Seward, and a few others left Washington by special train, bound for Gettysburg, where Lincoln had agreed to speak at a ceremony to dedicate a national cemetery. The presidential party arrived in Gettysburg at around six that evening, with Seward wearing what one reporter called "an essentially bad hat," and ate dinner with the local organizers. After dinner, Lincoln and Seward retired to the adjoining private houses in which they were spending the night, but a crowd soon demanded that the president make a speech. He spoke for only a minute, saying that he had to be careful not to say foolish things, and that the best way to do that was often to say nothing at all, which is what he would do this evening. The crowd laughed and cheered, then moved next door to ask Seward if he would speak.[57]

Seward started by reminding his audience of how he had warned years ago that slavery should be ended gradually and peacefully, to avoid a sectional crisis and civil war. Now they were in the midst of that war. The war, however, would end, and with it would end its cause, slavery. After the war, "we shall know that we are not enemies, but that we are friends and brothers, that this Union is a reality, and we shall mourn together for the evil wrought by this rebellion." The key was to establish through Union victory the principle that "whatever party, whatever portion of the Union prevails by constitutional suffrage in an election, that party is to be respected and maintained in power until it shall give place, on another trial and another verdict, to a different portion of the people." With this central principle firmly in place, he concluded, "this Government of ours—the freest, the best, the wisest and the happiest in the world—must be, and, so far as we are concerned practically will be, immortal."[58]

John Hay complained in his diary that Seward "spoke so indistinctly that I did not hear a word of what he was saying." John Russell Young, however, a reporter for the *Philadelphia Press* who was present, later recalled that Seward "threw his sentences like clanging oracles into the night." Young also remembered that he was distressed, after the speech was over, that his notes of what Seward had said were so inadequate. Fortunately for Young, Seward had already given a copy of his text to the Associated Press, so that it would be printed in many northern newspapers over the next few days.[59]

The Harper house, where Seward was staying in the center of town, was crowded that evening; other guests included a few foreign ministers, the president's secretaries Nicolay and Hay, and Benjamin Brown French, the federal commissioner of public buildings. Seward, as was his custom, entertained the group with comments and stories. French recorded in his diary that the secretary's "conversation, no matter on what subject, is worthy of being written down and preserved, and if he had a Boswell to write, as Boswell did of Johnson, one of the most interesting and useful books of the age might be produced from the

conversation and sayings of William H. Seward. He is one of the greatest men of this generation." (Unfortunately, French did not go on to record Seward's comments that evening.) At about eleven o'clock, Lincoln
arrived at the house with a copy of his speech in hand and stayed in
Seward's room for about an hour. We assume, but do not know, that the
two men discussed and revised the speech, as they had discussed and
revised so many other documents.[60]

The next morning, Lincoln and Seward rose early and toured the
battlefield in a carriage. The sad debris of the battle was all around
them: the skeletons of dead horses, and the knapsacks, canteens, cups,
shoes, pants, and coats of soldiers. The corpses of many of the Union
dead had been removed, taken by their families back home for burial,
or taken by the Army to the new National Cemetery, where the cof-
fins were stacked high. Most of the dead Confederates, however, still
lingered in shallow graves on the battlefield. After this somber tour, Lincoln and Seward returned to their respective houses, put on their formal
clothes, then joined the procession to the cemetery, in which Seward
and the other cabinet members present rode on horseback just behind
Lincoln. At the cemetery, there was a raised platform for the speakers
and other visitors, from which Lincoln and Seward, seated side by side,
looked out over the crowd of perhaps 20,000 or 30,000 people.[61]

The main event of the day was an oration by Edward Everett, the
former secretary of state, an eloquent two-hour review of the battle and
the war. At one point during Everett's remarks, Lincoln leaned over and
whispered a comment in Seward's ear. After Everett's speech, Lincoln
rose to give his own immortal address. "Four score and seven years
ago," he began, and a few minutes later concluded: "that government
of the people, by the people, for the people, shall not perish from the
earth." The crowd responded with warm applause.[62]

According to a memoir by Lincoln's friend Ward Lamon that is not
generally considered reliable, Lincoln was dissatisfied with his speech,
and Seward agreed, telling Everett that Lincoln's speech was "a failure,
and I am sorry for it." According to a later letter, perhaps also unreliable,
Seward praised the speech, telling someone in the crowd that no man
other than Abraham Lincoln could have made such an oration. A better
way to measure Seward's approval of Lincoln's address may be to note

the similarity between Lincoln's speech and the speech Seward gave the previous evening: both spoke of the war as a test of whether democratic government could survive; and both spoke of the war as a way to secure freedom. The *Chicago Tribune* rightly observed that the two speeches complemented one another.[63]

———

For many months, Lincoln and Seward had been thinking and talking about Reconstruction: the process of bringing the rebel states and individual rebels back into the Union. In July 1863, Seward received a letter from a Tennessee lawyer urging the administration to proclaim amnesty to all southerners who would put down their arms, and predicting that such an amnesty would end the war. Seward passed the letter on to Lincoln, for it is now among the Lincoln Papers. In late November and early December 1863, Seward worked with Lincoln on his annual message, which included a proclamation of amnesty and reconstruction. Citing his broad authority to grant pardons, Lincoln promised a full pardon to most of the rebels if they would take an oath to abide by the laws of the United States *and* the Emancipation Proclamation. Certain men were not eligible for this general pardon; for example, those who had served in the Confederate government or above the rank of colonel in the Confederate Army. Once 10 percent of the prewar electorate of any southern state took the required oath, they could form a state government, and the president would recognize such government as legitimate. Lincoln also declared that he would not object to any southern state law "in relation to the freed people of such state, which shall recognize and declare their permanent freedom, provide for their education, and which may yet be consistent as a temporary arrangement with their present condition as a laboring, landless, and homeless class." He did not elaborate on this point, but it seems he had in mind laws like those of Illinois, which limited black mobility and rights.[64]

Most people in the North approved of Lincoln's message and 10 percent plan. The *New York Times*, often the best indicator of Seward's views, praised the plan as "simple and yet perfectly effective." Even Sumner, who had feared that Seward would persuade Lincoln to abandon or weaken emancipation, was pleased that Lincoln underscored in his message that he would never go back on his promise of freedom to the southern slaves. But there were dissenting voices. Wendell Phillips, the Boston minister, wrote to Benjamin Butler, the Radical general, that Lincoln's 10 percent plan "leaves the large landed proprietors of the South still to domineer over its politics, and make the negro's freedom a mere sham." There was also a tension between Lincoln and Congress over who should control the process of bringing the southern states and southerners back into the Union. Lincoln's proclamation implicitly claimed that the president would control the Reconstruction process through his pardon power and military authority. Congress naturally viewed itself as having the right to control the process through legislation and through its right to admit (or deny admission to) elected representatives. Lincoln's 10 percent plan also left many questions unanswered, such as how much discretion the southern states would have in their "temporary arrangements" for former slaves, and whether he would press the states to allow blacks to vote.[65]

Seward did not have much time for domestic issues in the last weeks of 1863, however, because he was caught up in another foreign policy crisis. On December 10, he learned of what the newspapers called a "daring act of piracy": sixteen passengers on the *Chesapeake*, bound from New York for Maine, had seized control of the vessel in the name of the Confederacy, killed the second engineer, and imprisoned the other officers. It soon emerged that these purported Confederates planned their attack in Canada, and that the *Chesapeake* was not far off the coast of Nova Scotia. The Union Navy sent ships to chase the vessel, and two of the Union ships found her in a remote Canadian harbor, taking on coal from a local ship, the *Investigator*. The Union ships captured the *Chesapeake*, but not before most of her crew had escaped ashore; the Union Navy also boarded the *Investigator* and seized from her one of the *Chesapeake* crew. The Union ships then towed the *Chesapeake* in to Halifax, Nova Scotia, to hand over ship and prisoners to the authorities there, but a pro-southern crowd helped one of the prisoners escape. The American consul in Halifax reported to Seward that one of the leaders of the *Chesapeake* pirates, a man who had spent time in Seward's prisons early in the war for sedition, was now walking around

Halifax boasting that he was perfectly safe. American newspapers complained that these events showed that the British in Canada were not neutrals; they were illicit supporters of the South.[66]

Seward's response to the crisis was calm and constructive. Even before Lord Lyons could protest about the American infringement of Canadian waters, Seward apologized, writing him that the government "has not authorized, nor does it propose to justify, any exercise whatever of authority, by its agents, within the waters or on the soil of Nova Scotia." On the other hand, Seward warned Lyons that the United States would not allow British Canada to become a base for Confederate attacks. Seward pressed the British authorities, both through Lyons and through Adams, to take the strongest possible steps to locate and bring to justice the *Chesapeake* pirates. The outrage on both sides soon died down.[67]

As 1863 ended, Seward could look back on a year in which his diplomatic work was less dramatic but more successful than in prior years. The *New York Times*, reviewing the diplomatic correspondence for the year, commended especially Seward's work in preventing the sailing of the Confederate warships from Britain, and thus avoiding the war the *Times* believed would have "inevitably followed." The *New York Herald* was less positive, noting that Seward's main focus seemed to be on writing "a mass of diplomatic correspondence which no living man will read through in ten years." But even his enemies had to admire the way in which the secretary not only prevented disasters—such as foreign recognition of the Confederacy—but managed even smaller incidents, such as the *Chesapeake*, in ways that helped the Union and harmed the Confederacy. The *Richmond Enquirer* noted that Seward, "by well timed, bold mendacity, and a well sustained system of deception and chicanery, has succeeded in outwitting every Cabinet in Europe." The new year, however, would bring new challenges.[68]

CHAPTER 14

"Firm and Hopeful":

1864

F rederick Seward wrote home in January 1864 that "we seem to have entered a new era of the war. Gaiety has become as epidemic in Washington this winter, as gloom was last winter. There is a lull in political discussions; and people are inclined to eat, drink, and be merry." The Seward family contributed to the gaiety by hosting three major receptions. One evening in early January, Seward welcomed the members of the National Academy of Sciences, including Professors Louis Agassiz of Harvard and Benjamin Silliman of Yale. A week later, he hosted a successful party for foreign ministers, members of the cabinet and Congress, and Army and Navy officers. "Who wonders," asked the *Daily National Republican*, "that the house of Governor Seward is a favorite resort, and who that enjoys his hospitality does not wish that he might be Secretary of State forever, and be 'at home' once a week?" At month's end Seward held what the *New York Times* called "the largest and most brilliant" event of the winter season. The guests included foreign ministers and secretaries, seven generals, and many other officers. "Mr. Seward was truly at home," the *Republican* reported. "He never seemed in better spirits nor appeared to be in more perfect health."[1]

According to Frederick, the family's "daily dinner was more hospitable and pleasant than these ceremonious ones." There were almost always a few guests: a cabinet colleague, an Army officer, a friend from New York. Seward would drink no more than a glass or two of wine, although "with cigars he was less abstemious, and after the ladies left the table, the conversation would often be continued for two or three hours in a cloud of smoke." Then the gentlemen would join the ladies for tea in the parlor, with the guests often staying "till near midnight."[2]

For Seward's daughter Fanny, the high points of the winter were two such evenings: one with the author George William Curtis and another with the actor Edwin Booth. Curtis, both a travel and a political writer, arrived in Washington in February to give a lecture on "The Way of Peace." Fanny was in the audience to hear him argue that the way to peace was not through compromise but by winning the war and reuniting the nation. A few days later, around the Seward dinner table, Curtis impressed Fanny with the "animation, intelligence and depth" of his conversation. Fanny wanted to be an author herself, and after meeting Curtis she wrote home to her mother that she was "full of the old literary fervor and anxious to be at work." She hoped that "I may yet make my life worth the living and be of some use in the world."[3]

Edwin Booth, the great Shakespearean actor, spent three weeks in Washington in early 1864, appearing night after night in different roles at Grover's Theater. Booth was the son of a famous actor and the older brother of another, John Wilkes Booth, who had played at Grover's in April 1863 and then at Ford's in November 1863. It seems likely that Seward, who loved theater and especially Shakespeare, saw John Wilkes Booth during one of these two runs, although there is no confirmation of this in the family letters or the newspapers. We do know that Seward was at Grover's at least five times in early 1864 to see Edwin Booth in various roles, and that he hosted Booth for dinner on Friday, March 11. According to Fanny's excited and detailed diary entry, when her father offered a few criticisms of his work, Booth accepted them "very gracefully," saying that "he had felt those defects himself." Dinner ended early, for Booth had to depart for the nearby theater. An hour later, the Sewards saw him again, "fully realizing, explaining [and] adorning the character of Hamlet," and yet somehow also "the same sad, sensitive, dignified gentleman who had just been our guest."[4]

During that same week, an even more famous visitor arrived in Washington: Ulysses S. Grant, fresh from military success in the west. With Grant in mind, Congress had recently revived the rank of lieutenant general, previously held only by George Washington and Winfield Scott. Lincoln nominated Grant for the post and asked him to come to Washington to take command of all the Union armies. Accompanied only by his teenage son, Grant arrived on the evening of March 8, checked in to Willard's Hotel, and presented himself at the president's weekly reception at about nine thirty that night. Lincoln welcomed Grant warmly, then passed him over to Seward, whom he asked to introduce Grant to others. Lincoln's secretary Nicolay recorded that "the general was taken by Seward to the East room, where he was greeted with cheer after cheer by the assembled crowd." Seward apparently stayed at Grant's side for the next hour, during which Grant met hundreds of people, and at the end of which he was "flushed, heated and perspiring." Seward was also present the next afternoon when Lincoln presented Grant with his commission as lieutenant general. "With this high honor devolves upon you a corresponding responsibility," said Lincoln to Grant, who responded modestly that with the help of God and the Army, he hoped "not to disappoint your expectations."[5]

During this same busy week, Salmon Chase announced that he would not be a candidate in the 1864 election. A pro-Chase anti-Lincoln circular, prepared by one of the committees working for Chase, had prompted Republican members of the legislature of Ohio to declare that they would support Lincoln. Without the support of his home state, Chase could not run. As the cabinet gathered just after the circular appeared, Welles observed Seward and Stanton having "a corner chat and laugh about Chase," who was not present, and "whom they appeared to think in a dilemma." Indeed, the next day, Chase wrote a public letter saying he would not run. Weed's view was that the Chase campaign for the nomination was not yet over; he told Lincoln that the letter was just a "shrewd dodge," and that Chase intended to reappear "with more strength than ever."[6]

———

Much of Seward's work in early 1864 involved Congress and legislation. In March, he presented to the cabinet a draft bill to encourage immigration to the United States. Welles was not impressed; he remarked that "we should be careful about meddling with the subject on many accounts." The other cabinet members agreed with Seward, however, and a Seward immigration bill was soon making its way through Congress. The *New York Times* supported it, writing that "we never needed [immigration] so much as we do now, when a million of producers have been withdrawn from the labor market." The bill passed in July, establishing a commissioner of immigration under the secretary of state, and allowing for labor contracts of up to one year to pay for passage to the United States. This legislation, inspired by Seward, was one reason that immigration to the United States increased substantially in 1864 and 1865, reaching a quarter of a million immigrants in the latter year.[7]

Seward also favored telegraphs, and he worked to secure congressional support for a telegraph that would connect the United States with Europe via Canada, Russian America, the Bering Strait, and Siberia. The Collins telegraph, as it was known, was the brainchild of Perry McDonough Collins, an adventuruous American who had already traveled much of the Russian part of the route. Collins had met Seward in Washington in the summer of 1862 and converted him into an enthusiast for the project. By 1864, with some help from Seward through introductions, Collins had secured agreements from the Russian and British governments allowing him to build his proposed telegraph line over their territories. Collins now asked Seward for help in obtaining from Congress not only permission but also a subsidy. Seward contacted his old friend Samuel Ruggles—who years earlier had helped with reports on canals and railroads in New York—and together Seward and Ruggles wrote a strong letter supporting the Collins line. Seward argued that the Collins telegraph would help to spread "American ideas and principles of public and private economy, politics, morals, philosophy and religion." The project would also cement America's friendly relations with Russia and Britain, "those two great and enlightened powers." Seward,

Collins, and Ruggles were able to achieve some but not all of what they wanted: Congress granted the right of way and agreed to a naval survey of the Bering Strait, but denied the subsidy. Collins nevertheless started construction, keeping Seward posted on progress with periodic letters.[8]

Seward's relations with Congress often took the form of defending his work as secretary of state, as in the Arguelles incident. The case started when the Spanish minister in Washington asked Seward to arrest and extradite a former Spanish official, Don José Arguelles, who was accused of violating Spanish law by selling blacks into slavery. Seward immediately arrested Arguelles in New York City and shipped him under guard to Spanish Cuba. When the arrest—or abduction, as some termed it—was reported in the papers, there was considerable criticism, and the Senate demanded the relevant correspondence. Seward complied, stating in a cover letter that "a nation is never bound to furnish asylum to dangerous criminals who are offenders against the human race." This was not enough for his critics: one member proposed that the House denounce the secretary's actions as illegal. Seward responded with a long letter, more than twenty printed pages, reviewing the domestic and foreign precedents, and arguing that Arguelles's extradition was lawful and appropriate. His critics were still not satisfied, but the session of Congress ended before they could take further action. Seward himself was proud of the arrest, telling one Spanish official that "so far as depends on me, as Secretary of State, Spanish slave-dealers who have no immunity in Havana, will find none in New York."[9]

The Arguelles case was soon forgotten, but Americans could not forget the ongoing French invasion of Mexico. By early 1864, the French Army was in control of most of Mexico, and Napoleon III was about to install Maximilian of Austria as emperor in Mexico City. The Juárez government, which the United States still recognized as the sole legitimate Mexican government, was a government-in-exile, based in northern Chihuahua. Seward's policy toward Mexico had not changed in the past two years: the United States was neutral in the war between France and Mexico, although it hoped and expected that Mexico would some day regain its independence. This approach was far too weak for many Americans: they wanted to support Mexico and oppose France. Resolutions to this effect were introduced in Congress and pressed by Mexico's tireless minister to Washington, Matías Romero, and by the chairman of the House Foreign Affairs Committee, Henry Winter Davis. Although Seward opposed these resolutions and lobbied some House members personally, the House unanimously adopted a Davis resolution in April 1864, declaring that the United States would not recognize a "monarchical government erected on the ruins of any republican government in America under the auspices of any European power." [10]

Seward tried to downplay the matter in a letter reporting the resolution to the American minister in Paris, noting that it was only the opinion of a single house, not binding legislation; and he asked the minister to assure the French government that the Lincoln administration did not plan to change American policy as a result of the Davis resolution. Seward was usually quite conscious of how his letters would read in the newspapers—indeed, he composed many letters with this in mind—but in this instance his inner ear failed him. Word of the letter leaked; the House demanded a copy; and as soon as Seward provided one, his critics were again upon him, arguing that the secretary of state was too eager to please France, too disrespectful of the unanimous resolution of the people's representatives. [11]

Seward was involved in a third controversy that spring: the suppression of two Democratic newspapers in New York City. On May 18, he received a telegram from John Dix, the general in charge in New York, asking whether a presidential proclamation that had appeared in a few morning newspapers was authentic. Another telegram provided the text of the purported proclamation, in which Lincoln, in light of "the situation in Virginia, the disaster at Red River, the delay at Charleston, and the general state of the country," demanded 400,000 more troops, and threatened to draft them if necessary. After sending a message to the press to declare the proclamation an "absolute forgery," Seward conferred hastily with Lincoln and Stanton. Soon orders were on their way: Dix should arrest and imprison the editors and owners of the two newspapers involved and seize their offices and printing presses. A few days later, after the perpetrator of the fraud was identified and imprisoned, the editors were released, and their newspapers resumed publication. Although the orders were signed by Stanton, Welles was sure that Seward was to blame. "The act of suspending these journals," Welles wrote in his diary, "and the whole arbitrary and oppressive proceeding, had its origin with the Secretary of State." [12]

For Seward's critics, these three incidents—the abduction of Arguelles, the disregard of the Davis resolution, and the arrest of the editors—were part of an ugly pattern. The *New York Evening Post* declared that Seward "appears to forget that in this country the people rule and that if they are unanimous upon any subject their desires or determinations deserve to be treated with respect and with very great attention." The people "are doubtless troublesome to a statesman who has the ambition to manage affairs himself, and without their interference," but they would not ignore actions such as "the abduction of Arguelles, the stoppage of newspapers, and the truckling to France." Democrats would soon make the alleged violation of constitutional rights by Seward one of their main arguments against the reelection of Lincoln. [13]

The false proclamation of May 18 was plausible only because the military news at the time was so discouraging for the North. The Red River campaign in Louisiana, led by Seward's friend Nathaniel Banks, was indeed a disaster, "one damn blunder from beginning to end," in the words of General William Tecumseh Sherman. (It is sometimes suggested that Seward insisted on the Red River campaign in order to plant the Union flag in Texas, but the documents do not bear this out.) The Union had been trying and failing to capture Charleston, South Carolina, for more than two years. And in Virginia, Grant and his army were advancing south, fighting almost daily battles against Lee and his Confederate Army, but the Union forces were paying a terrible price for each mile they advanced, losing roughly 2,000 soldiers killed or wounded each day. [14]

By late May, Seward's son William was on the front lines in Virginia. William had spent the first few months of 1864 near Washington, as one of the officers of the Ninth New York Heavy Artillery, at Fort Foote on the Maryland side of the Potomac River. William's wife Jenny and their infant daughter Nellie were with him in camp, and there were frequent visits back and forth to Washington; other officers also had their families with them and enjoyed their proximity to Washington. Perhaps not surprisingly, the Ninth New York was not in good fighting form; an

Army general reported in mid-May that he found the regiment "in point of discipline and drill" to be "much less efficient than any regiment in the line of [Washington] defenses." Then, just as hundreds of wounded Union soldiers were arriving in Washington from the Virginia campaign, orders arrived to prepare the Ninth New York to join the Union Army near Richmond. The regiment's colonel resigned because, as Jenny later recalled, "he would not go to the front." Her husband William, as the lieutenant colonel, suddenly found himself in charge of a regiment of 2,000 men. Many of the men probably wished that they could, like the colonel, resign and go home, but this would be desertion, punishable by death. As an officer at headquarters put it to a friend, "these heavy artillery men have been awfully deceived. They were enlisted as they supposed to garrison forts only, to have no field service, but General Grant has got them out here acting as infantry, and a sicker set of fellows you never saw." [15]

Frances Seward was also sick with worry. On May 15, before she heard that William would join Grant, she wrote to Augustus that she regretted the "immense sacrifice of life" in Virginia, and was pleased that "Will is not with the Army." Five days later, after she learned of William's orders, she wrote William that she could not "yet bring myself to the contemplation of your death or of your suffering as others have done." Frances would take such consolation as she could "in the reflection that you will be fighting for a holy cause," by which she meant freedom for the slaves, not preservation of the Union. William left Washington the next day, and then, for more than two weeks, his family waited without news of any kind. Seward wrote him in early June, trying to hide his anxiety, but closing warmly: "May God bless and preserve you my dear son." [16]

A few days before this letter, in the early morning of June 1, William and the Ninth New York had marched south for ten hours, reaching their position in Grant's line of battle that afternoon. At about six o'clock that evening the regiment, as ordered, charged forward into the battle. William and his men ran down into a ravine and up the other side, penetrating between two Confederate units, and thus finding themselves under fire from all sides. One of the men later recalled that "it seemed as though all the artillery of the enemy were massed at that particular spot, for had hell been turned up sideways, to our inexperienced eyes, the sight could not have been more fiery." In only a few minutes of intense fighting, thirteen men from the regiment were killed and more than a hundred wounded. William himself, according to a letter from a friend, "had a hard fight, in which most of his clothes were torn from him." Two days later, in the dawn assault at Cold Harbor, William and his men charged again, but they stopped after only two hundred yards, took cover, and suffered few casualties. Grant lost thousands of men at Cold Harbor, most of them in the first few murderous minutes.[17]

Seward and his family knew nothing of these events at the time. On June 6, Seward wrote Frances that he was sending her, in the form of a clipping from a Philadelphia newspaper, "the first clue I have found to the whereabouts of our son." The paper reported that two of the officers in William's regiment were injured on June 1. "From the absence of any mention of William among the casualties," Seward added, "it is justly inferred that he was left unharmed." Further word arrived a few days later in the form of a telegram from Charles Dana, an assistant secretary of war assigned to Grant's headquarters, to Stanton in Washington. In the course of his daily report, Dana mentioned that "Colonel Seward is well and with his regiment." Dana probably intended this news for Seward, whom he knew from New York before the war, and Stanton almost certainly shared it with Seward when it arrived early on June 10. But knowing that William was safe one day did not mean he would remain safe the next, for Grant was about to move south again, fighting his way toward Petersburg.[18]

Meanwhile, in Baltimore, the National Union Convention met on June 7 and 8 to make nominations and adopt a platform. There was no question that the Union Party would nominate Lincoln for president, but there was considerable question about the vice-presidential nomination, and this choice vitally affected Seward. The candidates included Hannibal Hamlin of Maine, the current vice president; Andrew Johnson, former senator from and now military governor of Tennessee; and Daniel Dickinson, a former senator from New York. As Noah Brooks reported from Baltimore, many believed it was "desirable that a War Democrat should be nominated," and this argued against Hamlin and for Dickinson or Johnson. Seward's enemies were among those who advocated Dickinson, knowing that if Dickinson became vice president, Seward would have to resign, because of the unwritten rule that no one state could have two senior federal positions. Noah Brooks reported that Weed and others at Baltimore opposed Dickinson, "reserving themselves for the contingency of Seward's again being the Premier, which he could not well be if a New York man were Vice President." Whitelaw Reid, another correspondent in Baltimore, also reported that Seward's friends gave their support to Johnson to prevent the nomination of Dickinson. Seward must have been pleased to learn, late on June 8, that Johnson had received the nomination.[19]

The platform also had implications for Seward. Lincoln and Seward had been silent in the spring on the subject of a constitutional amendment under consideration in Congress to end slavery. On the eve of the party convention, however, both men decided that the platform should support such an amendment, and they spoke with their friends to this end. It was Seward's friend Edwin Morgan, chairman of the convention, who declared on the first day of the gathering that the platform would support "an amendment to the Constitution as will positively prohibit African slavery in the United States." The platform also included two planks about which Seward was less enthusiastic: one calling for unanimity in the cabinet, and a second declaring that the "people of the United States can never regard with indifference the attempt of any European power to overthrow by force or to supplant by fraud the institutions of any republican government on the western continent." The *New York Evening Post* claimed that these two planks were "a blow between the eyes of the Secretary of State." Seward sidestepped the blow, however, by warmly endorsing the platform.[20]

The fighting in Virginia and the politicking in Washington and Baltimore might seem unrelated, but Seward was well aware of their close connection. He wrote to his wife that "the country is entering on a new and perilous time—a canvass for the presidency in a time of civil war. Faction is inventive, active, unscrupulous. It will avail itself of misfortunes in the field, if that shall happen." By "faction," Seward had in mind not only the Democrats but also other groups, such as the "Radical Democracy Convention," which had just met in Cleveland and nominated John Frémont for president as an alternative to Lincoln. Salmon

Chase was no longer the leader of a faction within the cabinet—he had resigned in May over a patronage question—but being outside the cabinet might make Chase an even more dangerous opponent for Lincoln and Seward.[21]

———

In late January 1864, Seward had received from Charles Francis Adams a letter reporting the comments and questions of a senior southerner in London. This southern leader claimed the Confederate government was interested to know the federal government's precise peace terms: would Lincoln insist that the southern states repudiate their war debts? And what would Lincoln allow the southern states to do with freed slaves? Seward conferred with the president and together they drafted the response. As to the debt, "no part of the insurgent debt, funded or unfunded, can be assumed by the government." As to the former slaves, however, "laws not inconsistent with their freedom may be passed to alleviate the inconveniences of sudden and universal emancipation." Seward did not elaborate, but it seems clear that he and Lincoln intended to signal that they would not object if, after the war, the southern states adopted "black laws" akin to those still in force in many northern states. In general, Seward discouraged Adams from discussing substance in London; it would be better to deal with such matters in the United States, after military victory.[22]

In early July, after months of debate, Congress passed the Wade-Davis bill, named after Senator Benjamin Wade of Ohio and Representative Henry Winter Davis of Maryland. Wade and Davis were Radical Republicans: less concerned than Lincoln and Seward about southern sensibilities, more determined to see a thorough reform and reconstruction of the South. Under Lincoln's 10 percent plan, new governments were forming in areas under federal control, such as Louisiana, after 10 percent of the prewar electorate took an oath of loyalty. The Wade-Davis bill, however, would prohibit a new state government until at least 50 percent of adult white males took such an oath. Lincoln's oath required only that former rebels promise to support the Constitution and the Emancipation Proclamation; Wade-Davis would require those who wanted to serve in a state constitutional convention or vote on a proposed constitution to take an "Ironclad Oath" that they had never fought against the Union. Lincoln's plan did not specify much about the new southern state constitutions, other than that they should not enslave those made free by the proclamation; Wade-Davis would demand that the new constitutions repudiate Confederate debts, prohibit high-ranking Confederates from voting or serving in state offices, and abolish slavery. Indeed, the Wade-Davis bill purported to abolish slavery immediately in all southern states, even in regions which, because they were under federal control on January 1, 1863, were not covered by the terms of the Emancipation Proclamation.[23]

On the morning of the Fourth of July, as Congress was about to depart for several months, Lincoln, Seward, and Hay were in the president's room in the Capitol building, reviewing the final flurry of bills. Several senators and representatives came to press Lincoln to sign the Wade-Davis bill, including Senator Zachariah Chandler of Michigan. As Hay recorded the conversation, Lincoln told Chandler that "this bill was placed before me a few minutes before Congress adjourns" and "it is a matter of too much importance to be swallowed in that way." Lincoln questioned whether Congress had the power to prohibit slavery; Chandler responded that it was no more than Lincoln himself had done; to which Lincoln replied: "I conceive I may in an emergency do things on military grounds which cannot be done constitutionally by Congress." After Chandler stormed out, Lincoln turned to his colleagues and said: "I do not see how any of us can now deny and contradict all we have always said, that Congress has no constitutional power over slavery in the states." Seward surely agreed: in his view, Congress had no general authority to abolish slavery; this could only be done by the states, by the president under his military authority in regions in rebellion, or by a constitutional amendment.[24]

Because the session was ending and Congress would not return to Washington until early December, Lincoln did not have to explain his veto; he could simply "pocket veto" the Wade-Davis bill by not signing it. Perhaps hoping to persuade some Republicans to his more moderate approach to Reconstruction, Lincoln issued a message on July 8 stating that he was not willing to be "inflexibly committed to any single plan of restoration." He was especially unwilling to declare that "the free-state constitutions and governments, already adopted and installed in Arkansas and Louisiana, shall be set aside and held for nought." Lincoln was willing to support the Wade-Davis approach as "one very proper for the loyal people of any state choosing to adopt it," although it seemed unlikely that any southern state would choose such an arduous path.[25]

The president's message did not attract much immediate press attention, perhaps because the papers were focused on Confederate general Jubal Early, who, with a force of thousands of Confederates, had crossed the Potomac, seized Frederick, Maryland, and now threatened Washington. William Seward and his regiment were among those rushed by steamboat from City Point, Virginia, to Baltimore, Maryland, and then by rail and foot to confront Early. On Saturday, July 9, William and the Ninth New York Heavy Artillery were part of the Union force of less than 6,000 men, under the command of General Lew Wallace, that fought an all-day defensive battle against more than twice as many Confederates along the Monocacy River in Maryland. William and his men were in the thick of the battle; more than fifty members of the regiment were killed that day or died soon thereafter, and another hundred and fifty were wounded less seriously.[26]

On that evening, according to a letter from Frederick to Frances, the family received "successive reports of the battle, the disaster and the retreat of General Wallace from Monocacy." Seward stayed at the War Department, reading the telegrams as they arrived. He had just returned home after midnight, when Stanton himself arrived to tell him that there was a report that "William was wounded and a prisoner. None of us slept much the rest of the night," Frederick wrote, "and it was arranged that Augustus should go over in the first train to Baltimore and make inquiries. He left at seven." After several anxious hours, during which Washington was filled with "panic rumors," Seward received a telegram from Augustus saying that William was injured but not captured. Hearing that part of the Ninth New York Regiment had arrived in Washington and was setting up camp, Seward and Frederick got into a carriage to ride out to see them. When Seward got home at about eight that evening, he found waiting a telegram from General Wallace. "I have the pleasure of contradicting my statement of last night. Colonel Seward is not a prisoner, and I am now told he is unhurt. He behaved with rare gallantry." Seward relayed this by telegraph to Frances in Auburn, who wrote back: "God be praised for the safety of our boy." [27]

William was safe, but Washington was not. By July 11, Early and his Confederates were just north of the city, approaching Fort Stevens. Lincoln and Seward went out to visit the fort where, according to Hay's diary, "a soldier roughly ordered [Lincoln] to get down or he would have his head knocked off." Lincoln and Seward also visited some of the other forts along the northern edge of the city. That evening, Lincoln told Hay he was "not in the least concerned about the safety of Washington," and Seward shared Lincoln's confidence, telling Frederick that there was a good chance of "overpowering the rebel force and capturing it." On July 12, Lincoln and Seward were again at Fort Stevens and Lincoln was again under fire. Lincoln and Seward were among the few calm men in the capital; the Russian minister Stoeckl reported that day that "it is impossible to describe the consternation which has prevailed and which still prevails in Washington. . . . The department offices are closed and the clerks, organized into companies, are drilling on the public square." But the next day, the threat was gone; Early had retreated overnight and soon crossed back into Virginia. [28]

———

In late July, Seward, Frederick and Anna boarded a small naval vessel and steamed south to visit Grant near Petersburg. The family arrived at City Point, and like other visitors were amazed to see that the Union had built a small city, complete with a mile of wharves, a railroad yard, and acres of tents. Frederick wrote home that General Grant "took us over his stronghold, up to the top of his signal tower, one hundred and seventy-five feet high, to look upon the spires of Petersburg and Richmond, then out to his front to look over the earthworks, [and] at the rebel picket lines in the woods." Petersburg was indeed close to Grant's front lines, only about ten miles away, and if Grant could capture Petersburg, he would capture Richmond, for Richmond depended upon rail lines through Petersburg. But capturing Petersburg was proving more difficult than Grant had expected; he might have captured it with a rapid attack in June, but by July and August it was well-defended with troops and trenches.[29]

Seward also took time, while on this trip, to visit with General Benjamin Butler, his former dinner guest, who was now in charge of the Army of the James River and based near Chester, Virginia. Butler had not achieved much military success, but he was nevertheless the favored presidential candidate of many Radicals, including Horace Greeley of the *New York Tribune* and Representative Thaddeus Stevens of Pennsylvania. It seems likely that Seward visited Butler in order to take his presidential temperature, but Butler was puzzled about his visit. "I could in no way learn what [Seward] came for," he wrote his wife; "I do not believe he came for nothing."[30]

The military news for the Union in the summer of 1864 was generally grim. There were to be sure a few successes: news arrived in early July that the USS *Kearsarge* had sunk the infamous *Alabama* off the French coast. But Grant's great army was stalled in front of Petersburg and in late July suffered a disastrous defeat when an attempt to blow up a section of the Confederate defenses failed miserably. General William Sherman and his army were similarly stalled in front of Atlanta. After his raid on Washington, Confederate general Early attacked and burned Chambersburg, Pennsylvania, reinforcing the sense that the North was not safe from southern attacks. The *New York Times* reported on August 19 that the Confederate raider *Tallahassee* was in Halifax, Nova Scotia, "after having destroyed between sixty and seventy merchant ships and fishing smacks, in four or five days' time." The report was exaggerated—the *Tallahassee* had only captured about thirty vessels—but the *Times* feared that "we shall have a fleet of pirates on our coast in six months, sufficient to sweep our commerce from the seas."[31]

The political news was also dismaying for Lincoln, Seward, and the Union Party. One evening in early August, Seward visited Lincoln at the White House and read to him from the *New York Tribune* of that morning, in which Senator Wade and Representative Davis launched an all-out attack on the president. Lincoln's veto of their bill was a "rash and fatal act," a "blow at the friends of his Administration, at the rights of humanity, and at the principles of Republican government." The real reason Lincoln vetoed their bill, they alleged, was to secure the electoral votes of the southern states in his favor, and his veto would start a "civil war for the Presidency." The *New York Herald* noted that even the most ardent Democrats had not charged Lincoln in such harsh terms as those now used by his fellow Republicans Wade and Davis. The *Herald* predicted that this rebellion among Republicans would lead to a call for a new convention to revoke the nominations of both Lincoln and Frémont, and to nominate a new Republican candidate for president. Even Lincoln must see, the *Herald* argued, that "under no circumstances can he hope to be the next President of the United States."[32]

It was not only Lincoln's critics who believed in August 1864 that he could not be reelected; many of his friends agreed. Thurlow Weed was in Washington in early August and chanced to meet one of Butler's supporters. "Lincoln is gone," Weed told him, "I suppose you know as well as I. And unless a hundred thousand men are raised sooner than the draft, the country's gone too." Weed told Lincoln and Seward the same thing: Lincoln's election was impossible. John Martindale, a Rochester friend of Seward's, wrote Butler that there was "very great discouragement over the North, great reluctance to recruiting, strong disposition for peace, and even among republicans of long standing inclination *for a change of rulers.*" Seward was one of the very few who continued to believe in Lincoln's chances. He wrote his wife that "the signs of discontent and faction are very numerous and very painful. But it is not necessary to regard them as alarming. We know that any considerable success would cause them all to disappear, and we have a right to hope for success." Whatever happened, he declared to Frances, "we have a simple line of action to pursue, and that is to be faithful; faithful to the country and to its cause, and those to whom that country has committed the precious charge of its defense." Seward echoed here, probably without realizing it, his closing argument in the Freeman trial, when he said that he wanted his epitaph to read simply: "he was faithful."[33]

On August 23, two discouraging letters arrived in Washington, one from Weed and one from Raymond. Weed wrote Seward that "when, ten or eleven days since, I told Mr. Lincoln that his re-election was an impossibility, I also told him that the information would soon come to him through other channels. It has doubtless, ere this, reached him. At any rate, nobody here doubts it; nor do I see any body from other states who authorises the slightest hope of success. The People are wild for Peace." Raymond wrote Lincoln that "I am in active correspondence with your staunchest friends in every state and from them all I have but one report. The tide is setting strongly against us." This was the view of Representative Elihu Washburne in Illinois, of former Senator Simon Cameron in Pennsylvania, and of Governor Oliver Morton in Indiana. There were two causes for their pessimism about Lincoln's chances: "the want of military success," and the belief that the administration would insist, as the price of peace, on the abandonment of slavery. Raymond urged Lincoln to offer peace to the Confederates *on the sole condition of acknowledging the supremacy of the constitution,*" with "all other questions to be settled in a convention of the people of all the states." He predicted that the Confederates would reject this offer, and that this rejection would "dispel all the delusions about peace" in the North and "take the wind completely out of the sails" of the Democrats. At a cabinet meeting that afternoon, Lincoln made a curious request. He had a short paper, he said, which he would like all the cabinet members to sign, without having read it. One by one the secretaries, including Seward, signed as Lincoln requested, not knowing what they were signing or why.[34]

Two days later, Raymond was in Washington for the meeting of the National Union Executive Committee—the body charged with coordinating the state efforts to reelect Lincoln—and he met with Lincoln, Seward, and others. Seward, who had known Raymond longer than any of the others, probably took the lead in the conversation. According to Nicolay's notes, Lincoln and Seward explained to Raymond that they had thoroughly considered his idea of proposing peace, and that Lincoln had even started to draft a letter to Raymond authorizing him to go to Richmond for this purpose. On further consideration, however, they had decided against the idea, and now explained to Raymond why they believed that "to follow his plan of sending commissioners to Richmond, would be worse than losing the presidential contest—it would be ignominiously surrendering it in advance." After some discussion, Raymond agreed with Lincoln and Seward, and he and his colleagues "went home much encouraged and cheered up."[35]

In a letter to Frances explaining why he had not yet come home to

Auburn, Seward wrote that "one difficulty no sooner passes away than another arises, and I find my responsibilities increasing on every side." But he assured her that in spite of all the military and political troubles, he was "firm and hopeful."[36]

———

One reason that Seward was hopeful was that the Democrats were about to gather in Chicago for their national convention, and their debates might show that the Democrats were as divided as the Union Party. So it proved. War Democrats, who favored continuation of the war to restore the Union, secured the nomination of General George B. McClellan for president, but Peace Democrats largely controlled the platform, which declared that "after four years of failure to restore the Union by the experiment of war," the time had come "for a cessation of hostilities." The platform was internally inconsistent, however, for it also professed strong commitment to the Union and the Constitution. Republican papers immediately noticed the tensions within the Democratic Party, underscored by the long delay between the end of the convention and McClellan's letter accepting the nomination but rejecting the "peace plank" in the platform.[37]

The Democrats were still meeting when Seward left Washington in late August for Auburn. Stanton kept him posted with daily telegrams, one of which said "nothing new from any quarter." Then, on the morning of Saturday, September 3, Seward received a message that Stanton had sent late the day before: "Sherman's advance entered Atlanta about noon today. Particulars not received yet." Soon another telegram, sent by the War Department to all points, arrived in Auburn, announcing that Sherman had captured Atlanta. People celebrated across the North, and in Auburn a large group moved in procession to Seward's house for a speech. Seward started by praising Admiral David Farragut, who had recently captured Mobile, Alabama, and Sherman, who had "performed the most successful and splendid march through a mountainous and hostile country recorded in modern history." He went on to praise Welles and Stanton: "Farragut's fleet did not make itself, nor did he make it. It was prepared by the Secretary of the Navy. And he that shall record the history of this war impartially will write that, since the days of Carnot," who raised and organized the great revolutionary armies of France, "no man has organized war with ability equal to that of Stanton." [38]

Seward did not limit himself to pleasant praise, however; he launched into an ardent attack on the Democrats. This civil war, he said, was a war between Abraham Lincoln, the rightful president of the entire United States, and Jefferson Davis, the "usurper" set up by some southerners after they lost the election of 1860. The Democrats, with their peace platform, would allow the South to secede, so to vote for the Democrats "would be nothing less than to give up the very object of the war at the ballot box." Moreover, a Democratic victory would lead not just to one division of the nation but to a series of rebellions and secessions, as in the fragile states of South America. How, Seward asked his audience, can we "save our country from this fearful danger?" A voice called out: "vote Lincoln in again!" Seward responded: "you have hit it exactly my friend. We must vote Lincoln in again, and fight him in at the same time." [39]

The main Democratic argument, Seward said, was that Lincoln would not accept peace on the basis of integrity of the Union, that he also insisted on the abolition of slavery. Seward pointed out that the rebels had never offered peace on the basis of a single Union; they insisted that there had to be two separate nations. He added: "When the insurgents shall have disbanded their armies, and laid down their arms, the war will instantly cease, and all the war measures then existing, including those which affect Slavery, will cease also, and all the moral, economical and political questions, as well questions affecting Slavery as others which shall then be existing between individuals and States and the Federal Government, whether they arose before the civil war began, or whether they grew out of it, will, by force of the Constitution, pass over to the arbitrament of courts of law, and to the councils of legislation." Like many of Seward's sentences, this one was vague and complex, but he seemed to suggest that the courts or Congress or perhaps even Lincoln would allow slavery to persist in some form after the end of the war. [40]

Sherman's victory at Atlanta ended the effort to find a Union Party nominee other than Abraham Lincoln. Weed reported on September 10, in a letter Seward passed on to Lincoln, that "the conspiracy against Mr. Lincoln collapsed on Monday last. It was equally formidable and vicious, embracing a larger number of leading men than I supposed possible." On September 13, after Union candidates prevailed in local elections in Maine and Vermont, Seward made another short campaign speech, this time from his doorstep in Washington: "Sherman and Farragut have knocked the bottom out of the Chicago [Democratic] nominations; and the elections in Vermont and Maine prove that the Baltimore [Union] nominations are staunch and sound. The issue is thus squarely made up: McClellan and dissolution, Lincoln and Union."[41]

———

Seward's work for Lincoln's election was not limited to speeches; he was also active behind the scenes. He was deeply involved, for example, in efforts to get Union votes at the Brooklyn Navy Yard. Many of the thousands who worked there were hostile to the administration, and Seward and Raymond believed they should be presented with a simple choice: vote Union or lose their jobs. Welles, as secretary of the Navy and a former Democrat, resisted these efforts, denouncing the "vicious New York school of politics" that would "compel men to vote." Raymond spent much of his time in Washington, meeting with Seward and others and pressing Lincoln on the Navy Yard. Exactly what was agreed about the Yard is unclear. John Hay recorded in his diary that Assistant Navy Secretary Gustavus Fox assured Lincoln that the department "stands ready to turn out any man hostile to the Administration," but Welles insisted in his diary that Lincoln "expressed his intention of not further interfering but will turn the whole matter over to me." The Democratic *Brooklyn Daily Eagle* had no doubts, complaining bitterly that "no man who will not vote for Lincoln can get work in the Navy Yard."[42]

Lincoln, knowing that the election in New York would be close and that he needed Weed to exert every effort, appointed a few Seward-Weed men to key posts in New York City. Welles groused about the "miserable intrigues of Weed and Seward," but Welles was not doing much to secure votes; Weed and Seward were. Welles was also unhappy when Lincoln and Seward descended upon him one day in October to

ask that a naval vessel be put at the service of a Union committee soliciting votes among the sailors of the Mississippi squadron. This was only
one instance of Seward's work in getting out the vote among the soldiers and sailors; in another, he wrote to General Butler, asking him to
help a friend who "comes to the Army to aid in collecting the soldiers'
vote of the state of New York."[43]

Military developments continued to influence the political campaign.
On September 20, the *National Republican* trumpeted the victory of
Union general Philip Sheridan over Confederate general Jubal Early in
the Shenandoah Valley. But on this same day, at the cabinet meeting,
Stanton read telegrams reporting that Confederate agents had seized
two commercial ships on Lake Erie, apparently intending to use them to
attack the Union prison on Johnson's Island. The Confederate attempt
had failed, the ships involved had been scuttled, and the attackers had
scattered, but Stanton wanted immediate action to strengthen northern
defenses. Welles reminded Stanton that there was a treaty with Britain
limiting naval forces on the Great Lakes; Stanton admitted that he "knew
nothing" of the treaty, so Seward summarized its contents for all present. At least initially, Seward was not too concerned by the Lake Erie
attack, assuming that the British would do what they could to punish
those involved and prevent similar attacks.[44]

A few days after this, Seward traveled south again to visit with Grant
at his City Point headquarters and with Butler at his own headquarters
nearby. A reporter for the *New York Times* observed the secretary on
the deck of his naval steamboat on September 26, "pacing backward
and forward alone, hands plunged deep in his pockets and cigar in
mouth; doubtless enjoying with its fragrance the good things that General Grant has been pouring into his ear." Seward dined that day with
Butler, who was again mystified by the mysterious secretary of state.
"I spent two hours with him in very friendly chat," Butler wrote his
wife, "and he said nothing to the purpose, only that Stanton would not
be removed." Speculation about cabinet changes after the election had
already started.[45]

State elections were held in Indiana, Ohio, and Pennsylvania on
October 11. Many people, Seward included, believed that these elections would predict the national result in November, that if the Union

Party could carry these three states, it would win across the North. Seward was at home in Washington that evening, hosting a varied group: General Nathaniel Banks and his wife, the minister from Chile and his wife, and John Hay. After his guests left, Seward joined Lincoln in the War Department telegraph office, where welcome election news was arriving: the Union candidates would win in Indiana and Ohio and were very close in Pennsylvania. Welles noted that "Seward was quite exultant over the elections—feels strong and self-gratified. Says this Administration is wise, energetic, faithful, and able beyond any of its predecessors."[46]

On October 20, the northern newspapers reported another Confederate raid from Canada: two dozen armed men had attacked the town of St. Albans, Vermont, killing one resident, wounding others, robbing the local banks of thousands of dollars, then retreating across the border. Union general John Dix immediately issued an order from New York City to the local officers in Vermont: they should "pursue [the raiders] into Canada if necessary and destroy them." Seward sent a long message to Adams, complaining both of this attack and the Lake Erie attack, arguing that the British authorities in Canada were not taking neutrality seriously, and asking Adams to give formal notice to Britain that the United States would start to fortify the Great Lakes. When Dix's order made its way into the newspapers, Lyons complained to Seward, who refused to apologize; it was up to Britain, he insisted, to ensure that Canada ceased to be a safe base for rebel raiders.[47]

A few days later, on November 1, Seward received an alarming telegraph from the American consul in Halifax, Nova Scotia: there was a plot to set fire to the principal northern cities on election day. In light of the raids on Lake Erie and at St. Albans, Seward had no choice but to take this threat seriously; he sent a telegram to warn the mayors of New York and other large cities. At the same time, Stanton received word that there was a plot to organize in New York City an election riot even more destructive than the draft riots of July 1863. Stanton summoned Butler to Washington and directed him to go to New York City with several thousand federal troops and ensure that law and order were maintained there. Some Democrats denounced Seward's telegram, and Butler's presence, as an attempt to influence the election. In an order of November 5, published in the papers, Butler denied the charge. "If it were not within the information of the government that raids, like in quality and object to that made at St. Albans, were in contemplation, there would have been no necessity for precautionary preparations."[48]

Seward was concerned about election violence, but he also believed that he should vote, so he returned to Auburn, while Lincoln in Washington kept him posted with daily telegrams. In an Auburn speech on the eve of the election, Seward attempted to place recent events in historical context: "Every country that has existed, especially every free country, has passed through the fiery furnace of civil war." In every civil war, there were factions and traitors, such as the Americans who had helped to organize the rebel attacks on Lake Erie and St. Albans. Seward's friends should not despair, however, for he was sure that Lincoln would be reelected, and that soon thereafter there would be messengers from the rebel states, seeking peace. Seward predicted that these messengers would say something like: "Father Abraham, we have sinned before God and against our brethren. We repent our error; we disavow and offer up the traitors who have led us into crime. Extend your protection over us, and give us once more peace and communion with you at our altars and our firesides." The audience responded with "prolonged and vehement cheers." Seward provided Raymond with an early copy of the speech so that it could appear in the *New York Times* on the morning of the election.[49]

Election day, November 8, was quiet in Auburn, quiet in New York City, quiet throughout the North. More than 4 million Americans voted and more than 55 percent of them voted for Abraham Lincoln. The election in New York state was very close—the result there would not be known for several days—but the results in other states were sufficiently clear that by late on the night of the election, Seward knew that Lincoln had prevailed. An elated Seward left Auburn by rail early on the 9th and was back in Washington by the 10th.[50]

After hearing a speech from Lincoln at the White House that evening, a large crowd walked to Seward's house, where the secretary appeared at an upper window and was "greeted by three tremendous cheers." Now that the election was over, Seward told the crowd, it was time to be friends with the Democrats, and friends soon with the South.

He predicted that the "stars and stripes shall again wave over Richmond, the rebellion will go down, and within three years you will have to look mighty hard to find a secessionist." He closed with an eloquent tribute to Lincoln, reported in the papers as: "The re-election of the president had placed him beyond the pale of human envy or detraction, as he was above human ambition; all would soon learn to see him, as the speaker and the audience had seen him—a true patriot, benevolent and loyal, honest and faithful. Hereafter all motive of detraction of him would cease to exist, and Abraham Lincoln would take his place with Washington, Jefferson and Adams, among the benefactors of his country and the human race." Then, after the "loud and prolonged cheers" died down, Seward urged his listeners to visit other cabinet members, including Stanton and "my excellent compatriot Gideon Welles," and cheer them as well.[51]

———

On November 11, at the first cabinet meeting after the election, Lincoln reminded its members that in late August he had asked them to sign a paper without letting them read it. Lincoln now asked Hay to open the paper, which he did with some difficulty, and the president read it aloud: "This morning, as for some days past, it seems exceedingly probable that this Administration will not be re-elected. Then it will be my duty to so cooperate with the President elect, as to save the Union between the election and the inauguration; as he will have secured his election on such ground that he cannot possibly save it afterwards." Lincoln explained that he had fully expected, in late August, that McClellan would be the president-elect in early November. He had planned to tell McClellan that they should work together, "you with your influence and I with all the executive power of the Government, try to save the country. You raise as many troops as you possibly can for this final trial, and I will devote all my energies to assisting and fighting the war." Seward, in a light tone, said that if Lincoln had approached McClellan in this way, the general would have told the president "yes, yes," and "on the next day when you saw him again and pressed these views upon him he would say 'yes, yes,' and so on forever and would have done nothing at all." Lincoln, still serious, said that in this case, "I should have done my duty and have stood clear before my own conscience."[52]

Seward devoted much of November and early December to working with Lincoln on the annual message and preparing the annual volumes of diplomatic correspondence. Although the message alluded to the recent attacks from Canada, it downplayed them, saying there was "every reason to expect" that the British authorities would "take the necessary measures to prevent new incursions." The message noted the increase in immigration and declared that immigrants were "one of the principal replenishing streams which are appointed by Providence to repair the ravages of internal war and its wastes of national strength and health." A long section discouraged those who hoped that Lincoln was about to negotiate peace with Confederate leader Jefferson Davis. "No attempt at negotiation with the insurgent leader could result in any good. He would accept nothing short of severance of the Union—precisely what we will not and cannot give." The difference "between him and us is distinct, simple, and inflexible. It is an issue that can only be tried by war, and decided by victory." As to individual rebels, Lincoln stressed that the amnesty under his 10 percent plan remained available, and that he would extend pardons to some individual southerners who did not come within the plan's precise terms. "The door," Lincoln declared, is "open to all," although he warned that the time would probably come for "more rigorous measures."[53]

By the time this message was presented, in early December 1864, Seward and Welles were the only members of the president's original cabinet still in place. There was considerable speculation about further cabinet changes, with some Radical papers arguing that Lincoln had to remove Seward and Welles in order to comply with the party platform calling for unanimity in the cabinet. Seward was not troubled by such comments, telling Welles that "he did not care a damn about himself— if the President wanted him he would remain, and would go if he did not." Seward could afford to be relaxed, for he knew how much Lincoln relied upon him, not only for foreign affairs but also for domestic advice.[54]

The most interesting and intense patronage battle of late 1864 was started by the death of Chief Justice Roger Taney. The candidates to succeed Taney on the Court included Salmon Chase, Montgomery Blair, Edward Bates, Edwin Stanton, and Seward's friend William Evarts. We know that Lincoln discussed the issue with Seward, for Welles complained that in the "matters of the greatest importance," Seward was the president's only "confidant and adviser," but we do not know exactly what Seward advised the president. Some historians believe that Seward supported Blair, but the sole evidence for this is a letter from Sumner, months later, reporting that Blair complained that Seward had not, as he said he would, pushed Blair's candidacy. Given the antipathy between Seward and Blair by late 1864—Blair believed that Seward was one of those who had urged Lincoln to remove him from the cabinet— Sumner's letter seems a rather slight basis for concluding that Seward was a "Blair supporter." Lincoln ended the debates in early December by naming Salmon Chase. "Probably no other man than Lincoln," Nicolay wrote to his fiancée, "would have had, in this age of the world, the degree of magnanimity to thus forgive and exalt a rival who had so deeply and so unjustifiably intrigued against him."[55]

A week later, Seward was outraged to learn that the men who had attacked St. Albans had been freed by a Canadian court on a technicality. Even worse, the Canadian people seemed to approve of their release. The *Chicago Tribune* demanded that the government send troops to Montreal "or any other place where the St. Albans pillagers may have taken refuge, to take them out and hand them over to a Vermont jury, to be dealt with according to the law." General Dix seemed to contemplate just such a march in an order he issued from New York, and released to the newspapers, authorizing federal troops to proceed into Canada. A month earlier, at the time of the St. Albans raid, Seward had supported Dix's orders, but now he believed there was no need to threaten invasion, and much reason for calm. After Seward conferred with Lincoln and Stanton, an order was sent to Dix: he was not to send troops into Canada. Lincoln reinforced the point with a general order two days later: no federal forces were to enter any foreign nation without specific instructions from the secretary of war. Seward quietly reassured the British that the United States would not invade Canada, but he also pressed them to better enforce their own neutrality laws.[56]

On the morning of December 25, the Sewards and others in

Washington were roused early by the booming of celebratory cannon fire. Sherman and his Union Army, after marching more than two
hundred miles from Atlanta, out of touch with Washington and the rest
of the world, had reached and captured the port of Savannah. While
Washington celebrated, Seward worked on his foreign correspondence,
writing to John Bigelow in Paris that "I am keeping my secular Christmas as I did the religious one—by working at my desk. There is no end
to work in these revolutionary times." Indeed, when one reviews the
four thick volumes of diplomatic correspondence Seward published in
late 1864, and contemplates that these volumes contain only a fraction
of the letters and papers he drafted and received during the year, one
wonders how he ever found time to leave his desk.[57]

CHAPTER 15

"I Am Not Dead":

1865

The key issues facing the Congress in early 1865 related to Reconstruction. The Democrats favored "the Union as it was, the Constitution as it was." Unanimously opposed to the Emancipation Proclamation, Democrats were also generally against the proposed constitutional amendment to abolish slavery nationwide. At the other extreme were the Radical Republicans, who favored not only a constitutional amendment against slavery but also an aggressive federal program to reform southern society and protect the former slaves. Radicals were in no rush to welcome the southern states back into the Congress: when Louisiana, under federal control, formed a state government and sent representatives to Washington, the Radicals prevented them from taking their seats. Some Radicals argued that unless southern blacks were given the vote, the southern states would not have "republican governments" as required by the Constitution, even though many northern states still prohibited or limited black suffrage. Radicals wanted not just a temporary Freedmen's Bureau, but a permanent independent federal agency charged with helping and protecting southern blacks. Democrats were horrified by the Radical approach, both because it would represent a dramatic increase in federal power at the expense of the states, and because it would turn the southern states from Democratic into Republican states, with Republican blacks outvoting Democratic whites.[1]

Lincoln and Seward advocated a middle course between the Radicals and the Democrats. They favored a constitutional amendment to end slavery, and Seward led the lobbying effort for the amendment. They also favored admitting the senators and representatives from the reformed southern states; Seward's friend Nathaniel Banks was in Washington all through the winter of 1864–65, working as Lincoln's lobbyist to persuade Congress to seat the Louisiana legislators. Lincoln and Seward opposed a perpetual, independent Freedmen's Bureau. Above all, they believed that as soon as possible after war ended, the federal government should cease to interfere in the southern states, allowing them to resume their proper roles, both within their borders and within the national government. Lincoln and Seward had a traditional view of the relative roles of the federal and state governments; the Radicals wanted a much more extensive role for the federal government, taking control of issues that had been reserved to the states, such as civil and voting rights.[2]

To secure the votes necessary in the House of Representatives to pass the constitutional amendment to end slavery, Seward had to look beyond just the Republican Party, because there were not enough Republicans in the House to provide the two-thirds majority required. The only way to obtain approval would be to persuade some northern Democrats and some border state Unionists to vote in favor, or at least to absent themselves and thereby reduce the number of votes necessary to reach a two-thirds majority. In the event, the House vote on the afternoon of January 31 was very close; the amendment only passed because it received the votes of fifteen Democrats, six of them from New York, and of eighteen Unionists.[3]

Seward was the leader of the effort to persuade reluctant representatives, and for this purpose he assembled a team of lobbyists, many with tarnished reputations. One of these lobbyists, William Bilbo, a colorful Tennessee lawyer, while working for Seward among the New York City Democrats, was arrested by General John Dix on suspicion of being a rebel agent, and only released after Seward obtained an order from Lincoln. There is considerable evidence that Seward and his lobbyists talked about using bribes to secure the votes of Democratic members of Congress; one even wrote Seward that he "had no doubt" about passing the amendment, because "money will certainly do it, if patriotism fails." Yet there is little evidence that bribes were paid. The *Cincinnati Daily Gazette* reported after the vote that the New York lobbyists had offered up to $50,000 to Unionist members of Congress to cover their "expenses." One of these members, not named by the *Gazette*, when pressed by the lobbyists, said that his expenses amounted to twenty-seven dollars. "Good lord," the lobbyist exclaimed, "that isn't the way they do things in Albany!"[4]

There is better evidence that Lincoln and Seward offered to reward editors and members of Congress with appointments if they would write or vote in favor of the amendment. For example, Anson Herrick, an upstate New Yorker who was both an editor and a representative, was promised that if he voted in favor, his brother would be appointed a federal revenue assessor. George Yeaman, a Kentucky Unionist who voted in favor of the amendment, was soon appointed minister to Denmark. Not long after the *New York Herald* published an editorial supporting the amendment, Lincoln offered its editor James Gordon Bennett the prestigious post of minister to France. Fortunately for Seward, Bennett declined the offer, allowing Seward to promote John Bigelow, already in Paris and serving ably as the acting minister.[5]

Seward's surviving letters do not explain why he worked so hard to secure House approval of the constitutional amendment. For his wife Frances, the answer was simple: to abolish slavery. After the House vote she wrote to congratulate her husband on the passage of the measure, "which I know you had so much at heart." The *New York Herald*, however, believed Seward's reasons were more complex; it reported on the eve of the vote that the secretary was "exceedingly anxious for the passage of this constitutional amendment as the initial point of a great peace compromise with Jeff. Davis embracing the reconstruction of the Union." Samuel "Sunset" Cox, a leading Democrat from Ohio, had a similar view, writing later that Seward "regarded the acceptance of such an amendment as absolutely needed in all negotiations for peace, as the emancipation proclamation was of doubtful validity, whereas an amendment would be organic, indisputable law." Seward and Cox had worked closely in the weeks before the critical House vote, but Seward did not explain to Cox, or at least Cox did not record, why he believed that an amendment would hasten the peace process. Perhaps Seward's reasons were similar to those of Lincoln, as later recalled by James Rollins, a Missouri representative. "If the members from the Border States would unite," Lincoln told Rollins, "at least enough of them to pass the 13th amendment to the Constitution, [the Deep South] would soon see they could not expect much help from that quarter, and be willing to give up their opposition."[6]

––––

The newspapers covered the debates on the constitutional amendment, but they covered far more eagerly the rumors of peace, especially two visits to Richmond by the elder statesman Francis Preston Blair. Lincoln provided Blair a letter that he could show the southern leaders, saying that he would always be ready to discuss peace between the two sections of our "one common country." In his discussions in Richmond, Blair floated the idea that the North and South should suspend their war and make common cause against the French in Mexico. Some newspapers discounted the prospect of peace; others believed an armistice was imminent; and by late January there were rumors that southern peace commissioners were on their way to Washington. Representative James Ashley of Ohio, floor manager in the House for the constitutional amendment, feared these rumors would cost him votes among Democrats who believed that a constitutional amendment would complicate peace talks. Ashley wrote to Lincoln, pleading for him to deny the rumors. Lincoln responded on January 31 that "so far as I know, there are no peace commissioners in the city, or likely to be in it."[7]

Lincoln's letter to Ashley was disingenuous. It was true that southern commissioners were not on their way to Washington, but three senior Confederates were on their way to Fort Monroe, in Hampton Roads, to negotiate there with Seward. The three southerners were Alexander Stephens, formerly a Whig member of Congress from Georgia, now the Confederate vice president; Robert Hunter of Virginia, formerly a federal senator and now a Confederate senator; and former Supreme Court Justice John Campbell, now a Confederate assistant secretary of war. Indeed, on the same day that Lincoln wrote Ashley, the same day as the historic House vote, Lincoln was working on his instructions for Seward's imminent meeting with the southern commissioners.[8]

Some historians have suggested that Seward was in the House chamber on January 31, as members voted on the constitutional amendment.[9] But the contemporary newspapers do not mention his presence in the House, and it seems more likely that he spent the afternoon at the State Department finishing up his correspondence, and at the White House discussing his instructions with the president. Lincoln's written instructions to Seward specified three "indispensable" points: that the national authority be restored throughout the United States; that the Emancipation Proclamation not be varied or abandoned; and that there be "no cessation of hostilities short of an end of the war, and the disbanding of all forces hostile to the government." Any other suggestion not inconsistent with these three key points would be "considered and passed upon, in a spirit of sincere liberality," Lincoln wrote. But he cautioned Seward that "you will not assume to definitely consummate any thing." Late that evening Seward sent Lincoln a note telling him that he would leave the next morning at eight and hoped to reach Fortress Monroe by the end of the day.[10]

Ice made it too dangerous to travel by boat on the Potomac, so Seward arose early on February 1 and went by train from Washington to Annapolis. During his brief stop there, he visited the governor, handed him a copy of the constitutional amendment, and pressed to have it approved by the state legislature as soon as possible. He then boarded the Union steamer *River Queen* and headed south, through the ice floes, reaching Fort Monroe at about ten that night. When he arrived, he telegraphed Lincoln that he hoped to meet with the three Confederate commissioners the next day.[11]

Early on February 2, Seward met with Major Thomas Eckert, who had been discussing with the Confederates the terms on which they could pass through Union lines. Lincoln had instructed Eckert that he should allow the Confederates to proceed only if they agreed to negotiate on the basis of Lincoln's letter, that is, toward peace for "one common country." The Confederates would not agree to this, so Seward began preparing to return to Washington. But before he could leave, a telegram came from Lincoln saying that he should remain. Lincoln, on the basis of a message from Grant, had decided that he would also come down to Fort Monroe and join Seward in meeting the Confederates. The three southern commissioners reached Fort Monroe in a boat provided by the Union Navy at about five o'clock that afternoon, and one paper reported that Seward hosted them to a fine dinner that evening. In his official report to Congress, however, Lincoln stated that when he arrived at Fort Monroe after ten that same night, he learned that "the Secretary of State had not yet seen or communicated" with the three Confederates, strongly suggesting there was no such dinner.[12]

———

On the next day, February 3, the five men—Lincoln, Seward, Stephens, Hunter, and Campbell—talked for four hours in the comfortable rear cabin of the *River Queen*. As Seward noted in a letter a few days later to Adams, there were no "secretaries, clerks, or other witnesses. Nothing was written or read." The only other person present, Stephens later recalled, was the black steward, "who came in occasionally to see if anything was wanted, and to bring in water, cigars, and other refreshments."[13]

The discussion opened with inquiries after mutual friends and pleasant recollections of the times the five men had shared in Washington before the Civil War. Stephens, according to his memoir, then asked Lincoln whether there was not some "way of putting an end to the present trouble, and bringing about a restoration of the general good feeling and harmony *then* existing between the different states and sections of the country?" Lincoln responded that there "was but one way he knew of, and that was for those who were resisting the laws of the Union to cease that resistance." Stephens persisted: would it not be possible to postpone that divisive question, and pursue an issue upon which the parties had a common interest, namely, Mexico? Lincoln said that whatever Francis Blair had said about Mexico during his recent visits to Richmond was merely Blair's personal view and not official policy. The administration would not consider an armistice until the war ended by "the re-establishment of the national authority over the United States."[14]

After a brief pause, Campbell asked how Reconstruction would occur, assuming that the southern states surrendered. Seward suggested that before discussing this, Stephens should explain his ideas more fully, since they seemed to have "a philosophical basis." Lincoln may have been annoyed at Seward for continuing a pointless discussion of Mexico, but he and Seward listened while Stephens explained at length his proposal for a joint military mission to expel the French from Mexico. Seward asked Stephens about arrangements between the Union and Confederacy in the interim. How would they deal, for example, with states in which there were two state governments, one Union and one Confederate? Stephens, knowing the North would not accept the idea of a treaty between two sovereign governments, responded that these points could be resolved by a military convention between two belligerents, arguably preserving the northern position that there was only one nation. Lincoln said he would "make no treaty with the Confederate States because that would be a recognition of those States." Hunter pressed the point, noting that Charles I, while insisting that he was the sole sovereign, had entered into temporary military arrangements with his adversaries during the English Civil War. "I do not profess to be posted in history," Lincoln said. "On all such matters I will turn you over to Seward. All I distinctly recollect about the case of Charles I, is, that he lost his head in the end." [15]

Campbell now returned to Reconstruction; how did Lincoln and Seward envisage that this process would work? Lincoln said that it was simple: the southern rebels had to lay down their arms and allow the national authorities to resume their rightful roles. Seward added that Lincoln had already answered these questions in his recent annual message. Campbell insisted, though, that there were important issues that the president had not addressed in the message, such as the status of property subject to conflicting claims under conflicting laws. Seward said property questions would be settled in the courts after the war; he expected that Congress would be "liberal in making restitution of confiscated property, or providing indemnity, after the excitement of the times had passed off." [16]

The discussion of property naturally led to the question of the status of the slaves. Seward informed the commissioners that the House had just approved the amendment to end slavery; because of delays in communication, this was the first they had heard of the House vote. Sources differ as to what Seward said next. In his letter to Adams a few days after the conference, he wrote that he told the southerners that "there is every reason to expect that [the amendment] will be soon accepted by three-fourths of the states, so as to become a part of the national organic law." Campbell recalled Seward's comments very differently; Seward said that the amendment was "passed as a war measure, and under the predominance of revolutionary passion, and if the war ended, it was probable that the measures of war would be abandoned," and that he lamented the way in which extreme measures were often adopted "in revolutionary times." Stephens similarly remembered that Seward suggested that "if the Confederate States would then abandon the war, they could of themselves defeat this amendment by voting it down as members of the Union." The Confederate version of Seward's remarks seems more reliable than Seward's letter to Adams, in part because it squares with Lincoln's remarks, as reported after the conference to a southern editor and printed in June 1865. According to this source, Lincoln' told Stephens that the Confederate states could, by ending the rebellion soon, gain the right to vote on the pending amendment; he added that "it would be desirable to have the institution of slavery abolished by the consent of the people as soon as possible—he hoped within six years."[17]

If these sources are right about Seward's remarks about the constitutional amendment—if he indeed suggested that the southern states could delay or even defeat the amendment—they raise difficult questions about his motives. Why would a man who had argued against slavery for twenty years, and who had just devoted a month to an all-out effort to pass a constitutional amendment to end slavery, suggest that the southern states should obstruct that very amendment? One possibility is that Seward was using the amendment as a lure, a way to entice the southern states to the peace table. More plausible, in light of Seward's general views on slavery and reconciliation, is that by this time Seward believed slavery was dying a rapid death, and that it did not matter much whether the process ended in one year or ten years. What mattered most to Seward was to end the war and to bring the southern states back into the Union, and he was prepared to delay ratification of the antislavery amendment in order to hasten the reunification of the nation. Before the war, Seward had insisted that only the southern states could abolish slavery within their borders, and he still wanted, as the war ended, to see that the southern states were part of the constitutional process of abolishing slavery.[18]

Stephens later recalled that he had argued, after Seward mentioned the constitutional amendment, that immediate emancipation would be cruel to the blacks, leaving them "helpless and suffering." Lincoln admitted that their condition might be hard; he was reminded of a story about an Illinois farmer who bragged to his neighbor about a new and better way to feed the hogs. The trick, the farmer said, was "to plant plenty of potatoes, and when they are mature, without either digging or housing them, turn the hogs in the field and let them get their own food as they want it." When asked by his neighbor what the hogs would do "when the winter comes and the ground is hard frozen," the farmer replied: "let 'em root." Again, it is tempting to disbelieve the southern sources, but it is likely that Lincoln did tell this rather crude story, and that it reflected his view of how southern blacks would have to fend for themselves after the war.[19]

Hunter expressed regret that the North had offered the South no peace terms other than "unconditional submission to the mercy of conquerors." Seward instantly disagreed; neither he nor Lincoln had used the words "unconditional submission." The southern states, in returning to the United States, would do so "under the Constitution of the United States, with all its guarantees and securities for personal and political rights"; this could not "properly be considered as unconditional submission to conquerors, or as having anything humiliating in it." Lincoln said that if the southern states would abolish slavery on their own, he believed the federal government would compensate them (and through them the slaveowners) for the lost value of the slaves. He mentioned the figure of $400 million as an amount Congress might appropriate for this purpose. The sources conflict as to Seward's reaction to Lincoln's comment. According to Stephens, Seward said that the northern people were "weary of the war," and he believed they "would be willing to pay as an indemnity for the slaves, what would be required to continue the war, but stated no amount." According to Hunter, however, Seward did not approve of the suggestion of compensated emancipation, insisting that the North had already spent and suffered enough to end slavery. Lincoln sighed and disagreed with Seward, saying, "you may talk so about slavery, if you will; but if it was wrong in the South to hold slaves, it was wrong in the North to carry on the slave trade and sell them to the South."[20]

As the five men stood up to part ways, Stephens asked whether they could not at least do something about an exchange of prisoners, who were suffering in camps both North and South. Lincoln agreed and said that he would instruct Grant to renew efforts on a general prisoner exchange and, in particular, promised to release the nephew of Stephens. Hunter asked Seward about the Capitol building; was it finished? It was indeed, Seward said, and was now "one of the most magnificent edifices in the world." After the three Confederates returned to the federal steamboat that was to take them back to Confederate territory, Seward sent a black sailor after them by rowboat to present them with a case of champagne. The man reached the steamboat, delivered the gift, and the commissioners waved their handkerchiefs in grateful acknowledgment. Seward then borrowed the boatswain's trumpet and shouted across the open water: "Keep the champagne, but return the negro."[21]

Lincoln and Seward traveled overnight by the *River Queen* back to Annapolis, arriving at daybreak. A special train was waiting to take them to Washington, which they reached at ten o'clock that morning. The cabinet, the city, and the nation were all eager to hear about their conversations with the Confederates. The two men met the cabinet at noon, reported in detail, and persuaded even Welles (who had opposed the trip) that no harm had been done. "No results were obtained," Welles noted in his diary, but Lincoln's "honest sincerity" in going almost to Richmond "may have a good effect." The papers soon started to print their various versions of the events. The *New York Times*, apparently after an interview with Seward, reported that there was a "radical and irreconcilable difference" between the two sides, so that the nation must "rouse itself to renewed efforts, and prepare to make fresh sacrifices in defense of the integrity of the Union."[22]

In most winters of the war there was little fighting, but in the first months of 1865 the Union forces continued their progress against the Confederacy. In mid-January, the Union captured Fort Fisher in North Carolina, cutting off access to Wilmington, the last major port of the southern Confederacy. In late February, Sherman and his army captured Columbia, South Carolina; northern newspapers predicted that from there, Sherman would march for Raleigh, North Carolina. Grant and his army continued their siege of Petersburg, unable to attack because of the cold and wet weather, but it seemed almost certain that in the spring Grant would break through the long, weak line of Confederate defenses there.[23]

As the war seemed to near its end, Seward looked forward to retirement, telling friends that "he had accomplished his object as secretary of state in keeping foreign powers out of our conflict." Frances was also thinking about her husband's possible retirement, and dreading his plans to add substantially to their Auburn home. Frances had lived in the house all her life and she loved it just as it was. She wrote to Fanny in Washington that "after mature consideration of the matter and supposing all parties to consent, I advise that your father, instead of building an addition to this house, should unite with Fred and build somewhere on the Hudson, or any other place they should prefer, a house which will be a home for you all like that in Washington, where you all seem happy." Frances would "reserve in this house so much as Aunty and I need to be comfortable, letting William take the remainder." Frances believed William intended to live in Auburn, but she questioned "whether my other children would find it so agreeable here as we who have never *lived* elsewhere." Fanny surely shared this remarkable letter with her father, but whether Seward responded in any way is not recorded.[24]

Inauguration day, Tuesday, March 4, started with a dreary rain in Washington. Seward was with Lincoln that morning in the Capitol building as the president signed into law the last few bills of the thirty-eighth Congress. The most important of these measures was the Freedmen's

Bureau Bill, creating a temporary one-year agency within the War Department to provide help to the former slaves. Lincoln and Seward may not have been enthusiastic about this bill, but Lincoln signed the measure because he believed that it was constitutional, and because he—like Seward—believed that presidential vetoes should be rare.[25]

At noon, Seward was in the Senate chamber for a familiar ceremony: the swearing-in of the new vice president and the new senators. The Senate chamber was crowded with what Brooks described as "the good, the brave, the beautiful, the noble of our land, and the representatives of many foreign lands." Unfortunately, the leading character in the ceremony, the new vice president, Andrew Johnson, "was in a state of manifest intoxication." After Hannibal Hamlin, the outgoing vice president, made a few gracious remarks, Johnson rose and rambled on for twenty minutes, talking about his humble background in rural Tennessee, how he was a man of the people who had fought all his life against the aristocrats. As this sorry speech continued, Brooks noted that almost all the cabinet officers had pained expressions—all except Seward, who was "bland and serene as summer."[26]

After Johnson finished and the new senators had taken their oath of office, the whole group moved outside, to the east front of the Capitol, for the inauguration of the president. A crowd of 40,000 people, including many soldiers and many blacks, cheered as Lincoln and the others appeared and took their seats. A few minutes later, as Lincoln rose to speak, "the sun, which had been obscured all day, burst forth in its unclouded meridian splendor," Brooks reported. Seward was in the front row of the dignitaries, looking out over the immense crowd, listening to Lincoln's speech, in which it appears that neither Seward nor any other adviser played any role. Lincoln closed his short speech, more like a sermon, with compassion: "With malice toward none; with charity for all; with firmness in the right, as God gives us to see the right, let us strive on to finish the work we are in; to bind up the nation's wounds; to care for him who shall have borne the battle, and for his widow, and his orphan—to do all which may achieve and cherish a just, and a lasting peace, among ourselves, and with all nations."[27]

Almost everyone who heard it praised Lincoln's address. Charles Francis Adams, Jr., wrote to his father that "this inaugural strikes me in its grand simplicity and directness as being for all time the historical keynote of this war." Isaac Arnold, a member of Congress from Illinois, later recalled a conversation between a minister and "a distinguished statesman from New York," quite possibly Seward. The minister called Lincoln's speech "the finest state paper in all history." The statesman agreed and added that "as Washington's name grows brighter with time, so it will be with Lincoln's. A century from to-day that inaugural will be read as one of the most sublime utterances ever spoken by man. Washington is the great man of the era of the Revolution. So Lincoln will be of this, but Lincoln will reach a higher position in history." [28]

——

As his second term began, Lincoln made very few changes in his cabinet and his staff. His two private secretaries wanted to move on, however, and Seward found excellent positions for both of them. John Nicolay was appointed consul at Paris—the position Bigelow had filled before he was promoted to minister—and John Hay was appointed principal secretary in Paris. Seward was especially close to young Hay, who had spent many evenings during the war at Seward's house, and who would go on to become secretary of state himself under presidents William McKinley and Theodore Roosevelt. [29]

Not long after the inauguration, Lincoln left for City Point, Virginia, to confer with Grant. A few days later, Seward also headed south by steamboat, accompanied by Fanny, her friend Mary Titus, the Spanish minister, and the interim British minister. (Lord Lyons had by this time returned to Britain.) Seward claimed that this was only a pleasure excursion, but the papers speculated that he was going to join Lincoln in peace talks. "We sat on the deck till long after twilight," Fanny wrote, thinking about all the young men who had passed down this same river on their way to war "full of high desire, strong in courage and hope and daring." Fanny's reverie was ended by a call to join her father and the two diplomats in a game of whist. Seward met with Lincoln and Grant at City Point before starting back for Washington on April 1 and arriving late the next day. [30]

On Monday, April 3, a little before noon, news reached Washington that Union troops had entered and captured Petersburg and Richmond. "The great news spread like wildfire through the city," Brooks reported, and "almost by magic the streets were crowded with hosts of people, talking, laughing, hurrahing, and shouting in the fullness of their joy." Seward was at the War Department when the welcome news arrived; he joined Stanton on the balcony as the war secretary honored all those who had bled and died for the Union. After Stanton finished, the crowd called for Seward, whose speech was shorter and lighter. "I started to go to the front, the other day," he said, "and when I got to City Point they told me it was out to Hatcher's Run, and when I got out there, I am told it wasn't there, but somewhere else; and when I got back [to Washington] I am told by the Secretary that it is at Petersburg; but before I can realize that, I am told again that it is at Richmond, and west of that. Now I leave you to judge," Seward concluded, "what I ought to think of such a Secretary of War as that." The crowd roared its approval, and Stanton led them in singing "The Star-Spangled Banner."[31]

One speech was not enough for this great day. An hour or two later, a crowd called for Seward at the State Department, and he obliged with a few remarks. He said that he could not speak long, for he was busy with his foreign correspondence. "What shall I say," he asked the crowd, "to the Emperor of China?" He answered his own question: "I shall thank him, for he never allowed the rebel flag to be raised in any of his ports." (This was a not so subtle criticism of the port privileges that the Europeans had provided to the Confederates.) "What shall I say," Seward asked, "to the Emperor of France?" A voice called out: "to get out of Mexico!" Seward pretended not to hear; he said that he would tell Napoleon that "he can go tomorrow to Richmond and get his tobacco so long held under blockade there." And what, Seward asked, should he say to John Bull? A voice: "Give him hell!" Again, Seward opted for a more pacific remark, saying that he would tell the British that they could get cotton more easily by trading with the United States than by running the blockade. Seward concluded by saying the United States wanted only "peace and good will to all mankind, and no interference in our affairs by any one." The cheers were "loud, long, and lusty."[32]

———

On the morning of April 5, Seward sent a telegram to Lincoln, who was still in Virginia, near Richmond. "We need your personal sanction to several matters here," he wrote, "which are important and urgent . . . but not at all critical or serious. Are you coming up or shall I go down to you with the papers?" Although Lincoln responded that he expected to be back in Washington in two or three days, Seward asked Welles to arrange a ship that could take him south; he wanted to be with Lincoln if there were to be any serious peace talks. "He is filled with anxiety to see the President," Welles complained to his diary, "and these schemes are his apology."[33]

Seward would not get to see Lincoln for several days. At about four that afternoon, Seward, Frederick, Fanny, and Mary Titus set out from home in their carriage, heading north along Vermont Avenue. As Fanny recalled, "the carriage door not being tightly shut kept flying open," and Seward asked the coachman to dismount and shut the door. While the man was on the ground closing the door, the horses startled and started to run. Frederick jumped out, thinking to slow the horses, but he fell to the ground. According to a newspaper account, the horses gained speed and turned a corner, "swinging the driver by the reins as one would swing a cat by the tail." Fanny wrote that her father "had some idea of being able to stop them and sprang from the carriage in spite of my entreaties." Fanny could not see what happened to him, but a paper reported that he "fell violently to the ground upon his right side, break-ing his arm close to the shoulder joint [and] bruising his nose, cheek, and jaw in a terribly painful manner." Several strangers picked up the unconscious Seward and carried him back to his house. The family doc-tor, Tullio Verdi, who arrived a few minutes later, recalled that he found Seward in his bed with "his lower jaw completely fractured on both sides, his right arm also fractured, near the shoulder." Verdi's opinion was that Seward's condition, "considering his age, was perilous in the extreme." Frederick sent a telegram to his mother in Auburn: she should come to Washington at once.[34]

For the next several days, Seward was confined to his bed, in dread-ful pain, often delirious at night. Dr. Verdi recalled that his jaw "was in such a condition that it was a difficult problem for the surgeons" how best to keep its parts together and promote proper healing. Frances wrote to her sister that she found her husband worse than she had expected. "His face is so marred and swollen and discolored" that she could hardly recognize him; he could barely speak or eat because of his painful broken jaw. But Frances was encouraged by her conversations with the doctors, and with her husband, whom she described as "patient and uncomplaining."[35]

One of the most frequent visitors to Seward's bedside in these days was his cabinet colleague Edwin Stanton. Fanny wrote that Stanton "wiped his lips—spoke gently to him—and was like a woman in the sickroom." On the day of the accident, Stanton had sent a telegram to Lincoln in Virginia, describing Seward's injuries, and telling the president that "I think your presence here is needed." The next day, however, Stanton sent another telegram: Seward's condition was better and Lincoln need not return immediately. "I have seen him and read him all the news. . . . His mind is clear and his spirits good." The news was indeed encouraging: Grant was fighting Lee west of Richmond and it seemed that any day might bring news of Lee's surrender. Fanny recorded how, a few days later, Seward tried to thank his friend. "God bless you Stanton—I can never tell you half—," Seward started to say. Stanton, "much affected," told him that he should not try to speak. But after a moment Seward continued, "You have made me cry for the first time in my life I believe."[36]

Lincoln arrived back from Virginia late on Sunday, April 9, and he immediately went to Seward's house. "It was in the evening," Frederick recalled, "the gas-lights were turned down low, and the house was still, every one moving softly, and speaking in whispers." Lincoln entered Seward's room "with kindly expressions of sympathy," and sat down on the edge of his friend's bed. "You are back from Richmond?" Seward asked, his voice a mere whisper. "Yes," said Lincoln, "and I think we are near the end, at last." To converse more comfortably, Lincoln stretched himself out on Seward's bed and rested his head on his elbow, near Seward's head on the pillow. When Fanny entered the room and slipped around the bed, Lincoln somehow managed to reach out his long arm and shake her by the hand, "in his cordial way." Fanny recalled that Lincoln described for her father how, earlier that day, he had visited a Union hospital near Richmond and shaken the hands of hundreds of invalids. "He spoke of having worked as hard at it as sawing wood, and seemed, in his goodness of heart, much satisfied at the labor." Seward could not say much, but he listened to Lincoln talk for about an hour, after which the president left. It was the last time the two men would see one another.[37]

At around ten that evening, Stanton woke Seward with the news that Lee had surrendered to Grant at Appomattox a few hours earlier. "God be praised!" was Seward's reaction; he then listened eagerly as Stanton read to him the details, fresh off the Army telegraph.[38]

All of Washington heard the news the next morning when there was celebratory cannon fire. The cannonade was followed by a hard rain, but the people did not care; they rushed out, laughing, crying, celebrating. The federal departments did not even attempt to open for work. Fanny noted that her father "felt better" and "sat up twice during the day." During the afternoon, Frances and Fanny sat at the open window in Seward's room, looking out at the happy crowds "marching about with flags and bands of music." On the next day, Tuesday, April 11, her father "did not seem so well." Fanny read a bit to him from Tennyson's long poem *Enoch Arden*, but then Fred arrived with the newspapers, and Seward listened to those instead.[39]

When Lincoln spoke that evening to an exuberant throng in front of the White House, Seward could surely hear the crowd from his room, although not Lincoln's words. The president did not give the rousing speech the audience expected, but instead talked seriously about the problems of Reconstruction. He noted that some people were disappointed that Louisiana had not extended the right to vote to all its black residents, and for the first time he stated that he personally favored giving the vote to "very intelligent" blacks and to "those who serve our cause as soldiers." But these issues were, in his view, for the states to decide, not the national government. Lincoln cautioned against approaching Reconstruction with any one "exclusive and inflexible plan"; each state was different and would approach these issues differently.[40]

One of those listening to Lincoln was John Wilkes Booth, the brother of Edwin Booth, whom Seward had hosted a year earlier. The younger Booth, an ardent southerner, had been thinking for months about kidnapping Lincoln and had been recruiting colleagues for some such desperate effort. Two of Booth's men were with him in the audience that evening: David Herold, a young pharmacist's assistant; and Lewis Powell, also known as Lewis Payne, a solid six-foot Confederate veteran. When Lincoln reached the part of his speech in which he spoke about extending the vote to certain blacks, Booth turned to Powell and muttered: "that means nigger citizenship. Now, by God, I'll put him through."[41]

Over the next few days, Booth would perfect his plan: to kill, at one time, the president, the vice president, and the secretary of state. Some have suggested that Booth targeted Seward because, in the statute regarding presidential succession, the secretary of state was tasked with organizing an election in the event of the death of both the president and the vice president. This seems implausible: Booth was an actor, not a lawyer. Moreover, if he had been a lawyer, he would have known that in the absence of the secretary of state, the assistant secretary or the department's chief clerk would serve as acting secretary. It seems far more likely that Booth targeted Seward because he believed that if both Lincoln and Johnson were killed, Seward would take over as de facto president. Killing Seward would contribute to the chaos that was Booth's main goal. Booth may also have wanted retribution for all the southerners whom Seward, by ringing his infamous if fictional bell, had arrested and imprisoned.[42]

Lincoln and Seward were aware that there were men who wanted to kill them, but both were careless about personal security. Lincoln told Noah Brooks midway through the war that "I long ago made up my mind that if anybody wants to kill me, he will do it." Seward wrote to Bigelow in 1862 that "assassination is not an American practice or habit, and one so vicious and so desperate cannot be engrafted into our political system." He noted that Lincoln, during the summer, "occupies a country house near the Soldiers' Home, two or three miles from the city. He goes to and fro from that place on horseback, night and morning, unguarded"; Seward himself traveled the same road "unattended at all hours, by daylight and moonlight, by starlight and without any light." But years later, James Speed, who was the attorney general in early 1865, recalled Seward telling him after the fall of Richmond that "if there were to be assassinations, now was the time." Seward urged

Speed, who was on his way south to see Lincoln, to "warn the president of the danger."[43]

———

Fanny noted in her diary that on April 12 each of Seward's three doctors visited him several times. To hold the jaw in place more firmly, one of the doctors removed the bandages and "secured the fractured jaw by wire from one tooth to the other." Seward's right foot started to hurt him on this day; he was suffering from gout in addition to his injuries. To help him sleep better, the doctors that evening gave him a sleeping potion of valerian. The medicine did not agree with Seward; he suffered a delirious night and was "still confused when morning came." Frances, Fred, Anna, and Fanny took turns sitting with the patient and reading to him; the doctors visited and examined him; and Stanton came by with the news that the Union had captured Lynchburg, Virginia. On the evening of the 13th, Seward was better, and Frances and Fanny enjoyed watching, from the window of his sickroom, the celebratory fireworks in Lafayette Square. George Robinson, one of two male nurses assigned to Seward by the Army, told Fanny that the fireworks resembled skirmish fire.[44]

Seward slept well, and on the morning of Friday, April 14, he ate a solid breakfast for the first time since his carriage accident: a "soft egg, milk toast, shad and coffee." Fanny read to her father again from Tennyson, of whom her father "spoke very highly." A bit later, Frederick returned from the White House, where he had attended a cabinet meeting in his father's stead, and reported to Seward on the discussion. "We can't undertake to run state governments in all these southern states," Frederick later recalled Lincoln as saying. Lincoln had expressed "kindly feeling toward the vanquished, and [a] hearty desire to restore peace and safety at the South, with as little harm as possible to the feelings or the property of the inhabitants." Seward agreed with the president's approach; it was Seward who had declared, two years earlier, that he would always welcome back the prodigal sons.[45]

From Seward's perspective, the assassination attempt against him later that day probably started and ended in less than a minute. He was dozing in his bed at about ten o'clock in the evening; sitting nearby were his daughter Fanny and the male nurse Robinson. Seward perhaps heard something of the fight between his son Frederick and the assassin Powell in the corridor—the sounds that made Fanny think that the servants "were chasing a rat in the hall." More likely, Seward had no notice that anything was amiss until Robinson opened the door and a six-foot stranger, with a pistol in one hand and a Bowie knife in the other, rushed into his room. Powell slashed at Robinson with the knife and knocked him down, and also brushed aside Fanny, who was screaming at him not to kill her father. Then he pinned Seward to the bed with his left arm, and with his powerful right arm slashed several times at his face and neck.[46]

Fortunately for Seward, Powell's technique was wrong; instead of a theatrical downward stab, he should have plunged his knife into Seward's gut (where an infection would likely have led to death) or stabbed him through the eye into the brain. Seward was also fortunate to be wearing the brace on his jaw: although accounts differ on this point, it seems likely that the brace deflected one or more of Powell's blows. Finally, Seward was fortunate that his doctors (in order to allow his broken arm to hang freely) had placed him on the edge of his bed farthest from the door. This may well have caused Powell's first blow to miss; it also allowed Seward to fall or to roll himself off the bed, out of Powell's reach, at least for a moment. But Powell had already severely slashed Seward's face and neck. Seward later recalled that the blade was cold, and then there was what seemed like a rainfall—a rainfall of his own blood.[47]

Although Robinson had no weapon, he grabbed Powell from behind, pulled him away from Seward, and the two men grappled in the dark. Fanny's screams brought her brother Augustus, in his nightshirt, into the room. Powell stabbed at both men with his knife, cutting each of them. They wrestled him out into the hallway, where Powell finally gave up the fight and fled down the stairs. But before leaving he also stabbed Emerick Hansell, a young State Department messenger who was cowering on the stairs as he listened to the screams upstairs. Fanny ran back into Seward's room and, seeing her father's bloody body on the floor, screamed: "Oh my God! Father's dead!" She rushed to his side;

Robinson followed a few seconds later. "Father seemed to me almost dead," Fanny wrote a few weeks later, "but he spoke to me, telling me to have the doors closed, and send for surgeons, and to ask to have a guard placed around the house." George Robinson, in an interview published four days after the attack, recalled almost these same words: "I am not dead. Send for the police and a surgeon, and close the house." Robinson picked Seward up and placed him gently on the bed.[48]

Dr. Verdi arrived a few minutes later to find blood throughout the house and especially in Seward's room. Verdi wrote a few days later to a medical friend that Seward was "lying in his bed, covered with blood, a fearful gaping gash marking his chin and extending below the maxillary bone." But his patient was the only one in the room whose face "did not express fear." Verdi hastily examined Seward and "had the joy to bring the first consolation to that anxious family, in announcing to them that his wounds were not mortal." Fanny recalled that her father, who could not speak, reached "out his hand towards me in a soothing way, as if to bid me to be calm and reassure me." Frances asked Verdi to attend next to Frederick, whom Powell had beaten about the head with his pistol butt; Verdi's initial view was that Frederick's wounds were fatal. Then the doctor examined Augustus and was relieved to see that his wounds were "comparatively light," and Robinson, whose wounds were also slight, and finally the young messenger Hansell, who had "a deep gash just above the small of the back, near the spine." Because the knife had not penetrated the intestine, Hansell would make a "miraculous escape." All of this violence, Verdi later marveled, was "the work of one man—yes, of one man!"[49]

Seward spent the remainder of the night and the next few days in his bed. His room was quiet but the house was busy, with military guards at the doors, and doctors, nurses, and family members tending Seward and especially Frederick, who was for several days unconscious and for several weeks in grave danger. Weed, who was in Washington at the time of the attacks, told Sanford that he feared that, even if Frederick somehow survived, he would never recover his mental abilities.[50]

Exactly when and how Seward learned of Lincoln's death is unclear. Fanny recalled that on the morning after the attack, her mother said "very gently" to her father. "Henry, the President is gone." Seward "received the news calmly, but seemed to know the meaning of the words." The *New York Tribune* reported on April 17 that "the terrible news of Mr. Lincoln's death was broken to [Seward] last night, but he bore up under the depressing announcement with remarkable fortitude." Brooks reported on April 20 that, a few days before, Seward had asked to have his bed moved near the window. "His eye caught the stars and stripes at half-mast on the War Department," and Seward told his attendant: "the President is dead." The attendant, according to Brooks, "stammered and changed color as he tried to say nay," but Seward continued: "If he had been alive he would have been the first to call on me; but he has not been here, nor has he sent to know how I am, and there's the flag at half-mast." Then Seward "lay in silence, the great tears coursing down his gashed cheeks, and the dreadful truth sinking into his mind."[51]

By April 27, William Hunter, the acting secretary of state, could report to Bigelow that Seward "has been able to ride out yesterday and today, and it is quite probable that in the course of a fortnight he will be able to a certain extent to attend to business." As for Frederick, Hunter wrote that he was "in a condition to inspire good hopes of his ultimate recovery, though the process must of course from the nature of his injuries be slow." Two weeks later, Hunter told Bigelow that Seward's main concern was the condition of his son, who had suffered several serious hemorrhages and was "by no means out of danger." The *New York Herald* reported on May 13 that Frances "has been made quite ill by mental anxiety and unremitting attention to her husband and son." In late May, Frances admitted in a letter to a friend in Auburn that she had been confined to her bed for more than a week. "The wearing anxiety I feel about Mr. Seward and Frederick consumes my strength."[52]

As Seward and Frederick improved, Frances worsened, and on the morning of June 21, at the age of fifty-nine, she died. Fanny wrote that "the day before she died all pain seemed to leave her," and on the morning of her death, she "lay still and beautiful, only breathing more and more lightly till she ceased to breathe at all." The press reports, almost without exception, attributed her death to the assassination attempt. Weed wrote in the *New York Times* that "infirm and feeble as she had been for years, while those she loved so devotedly were in danger, disease had no power over the wife and mother. But when the strain was off, her over-taxed powers, mental and physical, gave way."[53]

The relationship between Seward and his wife was in many respects curious: from the time he went to Washington in early 1849 until her death in 1865, the two were apart far more often than they were together. Frances was not able to play the role of the senator's wife, or the secretary's wife, because of her frequent illnesses and her dislike of Washington society. Yet in spite of their differences and frequent separations, Seward relied upon Frances, especially on moral issues. Thurlow Weed, who knew the Sewards almost from the time of their marriage in 1824, wrote in his obituary that Frances was "the companion, counselor, and friend to whom her husband turned, and upon whom he relied, on all occasions. Between them there was a perfect trust." Charles Sumner, in a letter to Seward, wrote that Frances was "a noble woman—all that you once told me she was, when you first spoke to me of her, before I even saw her. I shall never forget her goodness to me, her kind counsels when I was an invalid, and her sympathy in my trials." Seward did not write much about his wife after her death, but he endorsed the comments of his friend George William Curtis, who described Frances in an obituary as "the tenderest of mothers, the truest and wisest of counselors, the most retiring, faithful, and patient of women." Curtis added that "her religious faith, her intelligent political confidence, her gentle and pervasive sympathy cheered her long hours of seclusion and illness, and strengthened the heart and hope of those even who seldom saw her." Seward forwarded a copy of this obituary to Fanny with a note: "he says just what I feel."[54]

Not long before Frances died, Weed wrote, she told her husband that she would "like to see the flowers and hear the birds in the garden once more." Seward therefore arranged that, on the day of the funeral in Auburn, his wife's body would rest a few hours in the family garden. "Amid those pleasing shades," the *Albany Evening Journal* reported, Seward received hundreds of visitors. "Among them were the poor and the rich, the black and the white. The hearts of all were alike in sympathy with him; and he received them with equal composure and courtesy. While few dared, in their grief for him, venture upon more than a pressure of the hand, he had a word of kindness and comfort for all."

The funeral was conducted in St. Peter's Episcopal Church, the church in which Frances had worshipped all her life. A local paper believed the crowd was "the largest assemblage that ever attended the funeral of a woman in America, outside of the great seaboard cities," and suggested that they were brought there by their love for Frances even more than by respect for her husband. From the church the mourners processed to Fort Hill Cemetery, to a hillside site purchased by Frances's late father. "At the cemetery a bird perched in a tree directly over the grave," the *New York Times* reported, "and mingled its clear, cheerful, ringing melody with the solemn tones of the clergyman, as he committed the body to the earth, with the words 'Dust to dust, ashes to ashes.' " [55]

Seward was tested in 1865 as few men are ever tested: by the carriage accident, by the attack of the assassin, by the near death of his son Frederick, by the death of his good friend and leader Lincoln, and then by the death of his wife Frances. Although he attended church regularly, he was not an especially religious man, and it does not seem that he found much solace in religion in this hour of trial. He seems instead to have found comfort in his work, to which he returned as soon as possible after his own injuries and his wife's funeral. The *New York Times*, often a good guide to his thinking, stated in July that during Seward's months of suffering his "mind has been engaged in the transaction of public business—a fact which will enable him, with comparative ease, to resume the active and laborious duties of his department." [56]

The most difficult foreign policy problems facing the secretary of state in 1865 came from Mexico. There were four foreign governments involved: Emperor Maximilian's government in Mexico City (supported by France but not recognized by the United States); Benito Juárez's government in Chihuahua City (recognized by the United States and at war with Maximilian and the French); France (with about 30,000 troops in Mexico); and Austria (with several thousand "volunteers" in Mexico). Even more difficult for Seward was dealing with the various Americans involved: the new president Andrew Johnson; his Radical critics in Congress; and especially General Ulysses Grant. In one sense, Seward's

Mexican policy did not change during 1865: he wanted the United States to remain neutral in the war between Juárez and Maximilian; he cautioned the French that their intervention in Mexico would ultimately fail; and he hoped to see France leave Mexico. In order to maintain American neutrality, however, Seward now had to fend off Grant, who seemed determined to provide American military support for the Juárez government, even if such support meant war with France.[57]

In March 1865, Seward wrote to Bigelow in Paris that "France, while she cannot have the sympathies of this country in regard to Mexico, has no ground for that reason to apprehend hostility in any form from this government." American interference in the Mexican civil war, he added, would be inconsistent with its refusal to allow European interference in its own civil war. In early June, in one of the first letters he was able to dictate after the assassination attempt, and after the accession of Andrew Johnson, Seward wrote to Bigelow that he could assure France that American policy with respect to Mexico "has undergone no change by the change of administration, but will continue as heretofore."[58]

Even Seward, perpetually confident, would perhaps have been less confident of his control over Mexican policy if he had known of the actions of Johnson, Grant, and the tireless and audacious Mexican minister in Washington, Matías Romero. As early as January, Grant had sent General Lew Wallace to the Mexican border with informal instructions to speak with both the Confederates and the Juárez forces. Wallace reported to Grant from the border that he had spoken at length with Confederate general James Slaughter, who "entered heartily into the Mexican project. It is understood between us that the pacification of Texas is the preliminary step to a crossing of the Rio Grande." According to the Confederate report of this conversation, which made its way into northern newspapers, Wallace declared that Grant was determined to drive the French out of Mexico, and that "whatever Grant recommends, Lincoln will do." In April, only days after Lincoln's death and Seward's near death, Romero had a long private meeting with the new president, in which Romero pressed Johnson to take a more active, more pro-Juárez policy toward Mexico. Romero reminded Johnson of anti-French and pro-Mexican remarks he had made in the summer of 1864, before he was vice president, and Johnson was flattered to learn

that Romero had arranged for these remarks to be translated and published in Mexico.[59]

Nothing came of Wallace's conversations with the Confederates, but
he was right on one cardinal point—that Grant was keen to enforce the
Monroe Doctrine in Mexico. Sumner wrote a British friend that Grant
thought "many officers and men will insist upon driving Maximilian out
of Mexico." Romero informed the foreign minister in late April that he
had spoken with Grant, who declared that "although he is tired of war,
his major desire is to fight in Mexico against the French, that the Monroe Doctrine has to be defended at any price." A week later, Romero
wrote that Grant had said that "60,000 veterans from the United States
would march into Mexico as soon as they were mustered out, and this
government would not oppose that action." Romero and Grant even discussed the possibility that Grant would lead these troops into Mexico.[60]

Grant ordered General Philip Sheridan, in mid-May, to go to the Rio
Grande River with tens of thousands of Union troops. There were legitimate reasons at this time to fortify the border—to prevent Confederate
military units from moving into Mexico—but it is remarkable how open
Grant was about his foreign policy objectives. He directed one of the
generals under Sheridan to move as far as possible up the Rio Grande,
and to practice neutrality "in the *French and English sense* of that word."
Sheridan later recalled that Grant told him, before he left Washington,
that "he looked upon the invasion of Mexico by Maximilian as part of
the rebellion itself, because of the encouragement that invasion had
received from the Confederacy, and that our success in putting down
secession would never be complete till the French and Austrian invaders
were compelled to quit the territory of our sister republic." Grant encouraged Sheridan to keep arms at or near the Rio Grande, and to provide them quietly to the Juárez government; in one of his orders, Grant
wrote that a "war on the part of the United States is to be avoided, if
possible, but it will be better to go to war now when but little aid given
to the Mexicans will settle the question than to have in prospect a
greater war, sure to come, if delayed until the Empire is established."[61]

Seward was confined to bed by his injuries for most of April and
May: "my house continues to be both a garrison and a hospital," he
wrote to Bigelow; "my studies and official labors are tentative only,

rather than real; my limbs and muscles require to be further strengthened and habituated to their ancient exercise." Yet even in his illness, he learned something of what was afoot with respect to Mexico. It was likely at Seward's request that General Grant attended the cabinet meeting on June 16 to discuss Mexico. In a letter to Johnson summarizing his views, Grant argued that neither France nor Imperial Mexico had been neutral in the Civil War; they had both aided the Confederates at every opportunity. Grant was especially outraged by recent reports that "large organized and armed bodies of rebels have gone to Mexico to join the Imperialists." Grant recommended that the government allow both Mexican sides to purchase arms in the United States, which would in practice help the Juaristas more than the French. Grant also advised that the United States should "interpose no obstacle to the passage into Mexico of emigrants to that country," by which he really meant that Americans should be allowed to enlist in the Juarista Army.[62]

At this cabinet meeting, Romero reported—apparently on the basis of a leak from Grant—that Seward pretended to agree that the United States must require the French to get out of Mexico, but differed only as to the means to be used to achieve this goal. Grant's approach, Seward insisted, would "wound French pride and produce a war with France." Seward stressed that Maximilian's empire "was rapidly perishing, and, if let alone, Maximilian would leave in less than six months, perhaps in sixty days, whereas, if we interfered, it would prolong his stay and the Empire also." Welles did not usually agree with Seward, but in this case he commented that Seward "acts from intelligence, Grant from impulse." Romero reported home that he feared that, if Seward prevailed, Mexico would "remain in the same situation as during the darkest days of the Lincoln administration. We will be unable to acquire a dollar, a rifle or a man here."[63]

On July 14, President Johnson read to the cabinet a letter from Sheridan to Grant, supported by Grant, which Welles described as "strongly hostile to the French and Maximilian." Sheridan boasted that he had his troops "in their magnificent trim" and hoped soon to "have the pleasure of crossing the Rio Grande with them with our faces turned towards the city of Mexico." Welles noted that Seward "was astounded" by this letter, and argued at length that if the United States sent troops to Mexico and drove out the French, "we could not get out ourselves." As he put it a few days later to Romero, Seward did not see why invaders from the United States would be more welcome in Mexico than the French; the United States would find itself in a long and expensive war with Mexico. There was no resolution at this cabinet meeting, nor did Grant get the answer he wanted when he wrote Johnson a few days later asking for permission to send troops to Mexico.[64]

Seward at this point cleverly captured one of Grant's chess pieces: General John Schofield, whom Grant and Romero were grooming to lead the joint American-Mexican force. Seward and his family were on their way in late July to Cape May, New Jersey, for a week of vacation, and Seward invited Schofield to join him there. During this visit, as Schofield later recalled, Seward asked him to undertake a special mission to France. "I want you to get your legs under Napoleon's mahogany," Seward said, "and tell him he must get out of Mexico." Schofield was flattered by the offer and in early August he wrote Seward to accept. Rather than send Schofield to Paris immediately, however, Seward delayed, claiming he needed to wait for word from Bigelow on Napoleon's latest views on Mexico. When Schofield finally left New York for Paris in November, he did not have specific instructions from Seward, nor did Seward charge Bigelow with ensuring that Schofield would meet and negotiate with Napoleon. Schofield would have a pleasant time in Paris, but he would meet Napoleon only once, at a social function. Seward later admitted to Bigelow that his only purpose in sending Schofield to Europe had been to "squelch the wild scheme" of Grant in Mexico.[65]

Seward also moved to limit Matías Romero's access to Johnson. He sent a circular to all the senior diplomats in Washington, reminding them that they were required to conduct diplomacy through the State Department, and that they were only allowed to visit with the president on rare ceremonial occasions. Romero complained to the foreign minister that it seemed that he was the only person addressed by what was called the "Romero circular." In October, Romero told Grant that nothing useful could be done to help Mexico as long as Seward was secretary of state, and suggested that Grant should ask the president to remove Seward. Grant and Schofield explained to Romero why this would not be possible: Johnson relied heavily upon Seward, whose "influence increased very considerably after the attempt to assassinate him." In conversations with Grant, Seward softened him with assurances that he would get the French out of Mexico through diplomacy, without the need for military action.[66]

Seward not only countered Grant's Mexican policy; he also used the threat of Grant's policy in his negotiations with France. In November, Seward asked Bigelow to inform the French foreign minister that the American people viewed the French attempt to force Maximilian upon the Mexican people as "disallowable and impracticable," and that Americans would not wait forever to see the French depart from Mexico. Two weeks later, the administration announced that it would appoint General John Logan, a protégé of Grant and known as friendly to Mexico, to be the new American minister to the Juárez government. The *New York Times* probably spoke for Seward when it declared that the proposed appointment of Logan was "a new notification to Maximilian that his Imperial rule is not and will not be recognized." Welles noted that the marquis de Montholon, the new French minister in Washington, was "scared out of his wits" by Logan's appointment and by the press commentary. When Montholon asked Seward who was behind the appointment, and whether it should be viewed as adverse to France, all he could get out of Seward was a cryptic comment.[67]

In early December, Montholon presented to Seward a proposal from the French foreign minister: France would withdraw its troops from Mexico if the United States would recognize the government of Maximilian. Seward declined. As he explained in a long note to Montholon, the French seemed to misunderstand the reasons for America's concern about Mexico: the United States had no interest in Mexico other than in seeing Mexicans ruling themselves as they had before the French invasion. Seward hoped that France would soon realize that it was in its own interest to withdraw its troops. There were some signs that this might occur: Seward heard from Bigelow that the "universal unpopularity of the Mexican expedition" among the French public was forcing Napoleon to consider bringing home the troops. But there were also contrary signs, such as press reports that several hundred fresh Austrian troops had just arrived in Mexico. In short, as the year ended, Seward had not solved the Mexican crisis, but he had prevented Grant from leading the United States into a second Mexican war, and he had increased the pressure on France to get out of Mexico.[68]

————

The year 1865 was one of dramatic change for Seward: Lincoln was killed; Johnson became president; Frances died; the Civil War ended. But 1865 was also a year of continuity: he remained in the same home and the same position in the government. One area in which Seward's views did not change in 1865 was reconciliation; he believed it essential, as soon as possible, to bring both the southern states and individual southerners back into the political process. While Seward was convalescing, his friend John Forney spent several "interesting and memorable evenings" at the Seward home, on which he reported in his paper the *Philadelphia Press.* "The southern people will come back in peace, and in obedience," Seward told Forney. "They have been defeated by the ballot-box and on the battlefield. Having resisted the one and resorted to the other, they are now left completely prostrate; and in this condition they have neither interest nor real inclination to renew a conflict which has only brought beggary to their households, destruction to their favorite institution, and ruin to their colossal fortunes. On our part, having proved our strength, it is right that we should now prove our wisdom. Patience, forbearance, magnanimity—these are the instrumentalities which, backed by unlimited and unexampled strength, will reestablish the Republic on enduring foundations." Moreover, as Seward wrote to a French friend, southerners "acting politically in their respective states must reorganize their state governments. We cannot reorganize for them." The national role was a limited one—to maintain order until new southern state governments were formed and represented—but "when that is done we may close the work of amnesty and restoration."[69]

One key change in Seward's life was in his relationship with the president. Seward mourned Lincoln's death for many months. "His name is to grow greater," Seward wrote in July, "and that of all contemporaneous magistrates and sovereigns to grow smaller, as time advances.

Nothing that men or monarchs of this generation can do could affect, in any way, a fame that, through process of immolatory sacrifice for human rights, has become imperishable." Although Seward had played a major role in selecting Andrew Johnson as vice president, and thus in making him president, he did not know Johnson well at the time he became president, and the two men never became close. Seward was educated, polished, and cosmopolitan; Johnson was self-taught and provincial, often speaking as if he were still a minor rural southern politician. Seward was sociable, while Johnson was aptly described by one historian as "the loneliest individual ever to inhabit the White House." Lincoln had conferred with Seward at all hours and on all issues, whereas Johnson, as Welles observed, had "no confidants and [sought] none." And yet Seward would serve Johnson ably and faithfully through his controversial presidency, and Johnson would stand by his secretary of state. Even before Seward emerged from his bed, Johnson tried to quell rumors that he would replace Seward by telling a reporter that he "entertains for him the deepest sympathy in his sufferings" and "impatiently awaits the time when he will have the benefit of Mr. Seward's counsel."[70]

Some of Andrew Johnson's remarks before and just after he became president suggested that he would take a different approach than Seward toward the South. In October 1864, addressing an audience of free blacks in Nashville, Johnson had denounced the "damnable aristocrats" of the South, and said that "humble and unworthy" as he was, he would "indeed be your Moses, and lead you through the Red Sea of war and bondage to a fairer future." In April 1865, immediately after the assassination, Johnson declared that "the American people must be taught—if they do not already feel—that treason is a crime and must be punished." Such remarks led Radicals to believe that Johnson would support them in punishing the rebels and protecting the southern blacks. But other actions suggested that Johnson, who was after all a southerner and a Democrat, would take a far more moderate approach. He quickly appointed southerners as provisional governors for all the southern states, and suggested that the only conditions for the new state constitutions would be that they should repudiate secession, slavery, and the Confederate debt. Johnson was generous with pardons for individual rebels, granting thousands by the end of the year. Seward was deeply involved in the pardon process—both the formalities and the informal conversations. It was Seward, for example, who secured the release from prison and a pardon for Alexander Stephens, the former Confederate vice president and Hampton Roads commissioner. Writing to Fanny in November, Seward told her that she would find their house in Washington to be "the chief resort of the recently rebels."[71]

————

The elections of 1865, the first after the end of the war, were an important test for both Johnson and Seward. In New York, Democrats and Republicans alike claimed to be the true party of Andrew Johnson. As the *New York Herald* noted, the state offices at issue were insignificant; the question was which party would gain the "inside track" with Johnson and thus establish itself as "the ruling party for the next fifty years." Democrats argued that Johnson was not really a Republican; he was a former Democrat who had joined the Union Party only for the 1864 election, but would now govern on the basis of his traditional, Democratic views. Republicans responded that the Democrats could not now claim Johnson as one of their own; Lincoln and Johnson were elected mainly by Republican votes in 1864, and Johnson was carrying out the moderate, conservative policies of Lincoln.[72]

In the South, in the fall of 1865, voters went to the polls to select new state legislatures and new federal representatives. The campaigns were marred by white violence against blacks and in some cases against northern visitors to the southern states. Another complication was the "Ironclad Oath" that Congress now required of its members and federal employees: they had to swear that they had never voluntarily borne arms against the United States. Southern papers reported that Seward told friends that, although he would not have voted to impose the oath requirement, the oath was now the law, and southern states would do better to "send an idiot or a child to Congress who can take it [the oath] than to send a wise man who cannot." Johnson remarked that "there seems, in many of the [southern] elections something like defiance, which is all out of place at this time." But neither Seward nor Johnson devoted much effort to the southern elections, and even if they had, they probably would not have had much effect. Southerners generally elected men who were their leaders before and during the Civil War: those elected to Congress included Alexander Stephens, many others who had served in the Confederate government, and four generals and five colonels from the Confederate Army.[73]

Seward's main contribution to the campaign was a speech in Auburn in late October. Although nominally non-partisan, the speech was a subtle attack on both the Democrats and the Radicals, and printed and praised in moderate Republican newspapers. Seward argued that the administration's plan of restoration (he avoided the word "reconstruction") was not really Johnson's plan but Lincoln's, and indeed "the only feasible plan." To make the process work, southerners had to trust that the North would treat them fairly; northerners had to trust the South to manage its own affairs; in short, "we must trust each other." Seward noted that he had recently entertained, at his home in Washington, a hundred prominent southern men. "They were frank, unreserved and earnest in their desire of acquiescence and reconciliation, as I was also of mine." Some voters might be confused by the way in which the Democrats now claimed Johnson as one of their own, even though they had opposed his administration and that of Lincoln. There was no reason to doubt, however, that Johnson would remain true to the Lincoln administration's policies of war and reconciliation. Seward praised Johnson lavishly, saying that among all those with whom he had worked over many years, none "has seemed to me to be more nobly free from personal caprice and selfish ambition than Andrew Johnson; none to be more purely and exclusively moved in public action by love of country and good will to mankind."[74]

Seward had kind words for Johnson in private as well. In early October, Seward was the guest of honor at a small dinner in New York; the Reverend Henry Bellows was one of the other guests. Bellows noted that Seward said that the president was "as dignified and decorous as any man in the White House in his day." He added that he "had trusted Mr. Johnson ever since he found him the only southern man in the Senate right on the slavery question—and he saw no change in him now." As to Seward himself, Bellows observed sadly the effects of the assassination attack: he looked "five years older than when I last saw him six months ago. His right cheek was swollen with the bulging scar of a wound that looked two or three inches long, and must continue permanently to disfigure that side of his face." His friend was still "erect, self-possessed, easy and talkative," but Bellows found that he was also "the least bit *senile*."[75]

When the votes were counted in November, Republicans had prevailed in New York, and former Confederates had prevailed in many southern states. Seward was concerned that Congress, when it assembled, would quarrel within itself and with the president. "The approach of Congress prognosticates trials of many sorts," he wrote Fanny, "from the ill-assortment of tempers, and the absence of a spirit of conciliation, when conciliation is the interest and duty of all."[76]

Observers on all sides looked forward to Johnson's first annual message; the *New York World* anticipated that the message would end "the present unnatural state of things, in which men holding the most conflicting views on the most fundamental questions, are alike courting and claiming the President." At Johnson's request, Seward prepared not only the foreign policy section of the message but also a draft discussion of reconciliation. He suggested that Johnson should state that the power to admit representatives from the southern states rested with Congress, and that the president would "leave it there in entire confidence in the wisdom, prudence, and patriotism of the national legislature." Seward also proposed that Johnson should say that, in order for the southern representatives to resume their places in Congress, the southern states had to meet only three conditions: to repeal their secession statutes; to repudiate the Confederate debt; and to adopt the constitutional amendment abolishing slavery. "With the fulfillment of these conditions," Seward's draft continued, "I shall be content, so far as depends upon the executive department of the government, to accept and recognize the lately insurgent states, as loyal members of the national Union, and their citizens as brethren in full standing in the national family."[77]

Johnson did not accept much of the draft, not because he disagreed with it, but because he wanted to be more ambiguous. The president hoped to prolong his popularity with both parties, and so he tried in his message to please Democrats (by pressing Congress to admit the

southern members) and Republicans (by apparently endorsing protection for the freed southern blacks). Newspapers from all perspectives
praised Johnson's first annual message: the Democratic *New York World*
claimed the message endorsed Democratic principles and the Radical
New York Tribune said that few prior messages "contained so much that
will be generally and justly approved, with so little that will or should
provoke dissent."[78]

Rather than seat the southern delegates immediately, or debate their
qualifications one by one, Congress appointed a Joint Committee on Reconstruction, and asked it to determine the basis on which southern representatives should be seated. Although Johnson disliked the committee
from the outset, Seward was prepared to give it a chance. The *New York
Times* declared that the proposed committee made good sense: it would
allow "the main question involved [to] be discussed and decided upon
its intrinsic merits, without being complicated or embarrassed by questions of regularity or returns in the case of individual members."[79]

A few days before Johnson's message, the legislature of Mississippi
passed a law that, along with parallel laws soon passed in other southern states, would become a major issue in Reconstruction. The Mississippi Black Code, as it became known, provided that any black under
the age of eighteen who was an orphan or whose parents could not
support him or her was to be apprenticed to a white person. Any black
over eighteen who committed any of a long list of offenses, and who
could not pay the required fine, would be hired out to a white person.
Blacks could not practice a skilled trade without a license; they could
not possess guns or other weapons; they could not rent land outside of
an incorporated town. The Mississippi law was to some extent modeled
on northern laws that discriminated against blacks, but the northern
newspapers did not notice this. "The men of the North will convert the
State of Mississippi into a frog pond," the *Chicago Tribune* declared,
"before they will allow such a law to disgrace one foot of soil in which
the bones of our soldiers sleep and over which the flag of freedom
waves." Other states soon passed similar laws. Seward did not, as far as
the record shows, comment on the Black Codes, but for the Radicals the
codes proved that the southern states were far from ready for admission
to Congress or for reconciliation.[80]

A conversation between President Johnson and Senator Sumner in early December illustrated well the emerging divide between the president and the Radicals. When Sumner complained that "the poor *freedmen* in Georgia and Alabama were frequently insulted by rebels," Johnson asked whether murders ever occurred in Massachusetts. Yes, Sumner conceded, they did. And did people ever knock one another down in the streets of Boston? Yes, Sumner conceded, they sometimes did. "Would you consent," Johnson asked, "that Massachusetts should be excluded from the Union on this account?" No, Sumner replied, "surely not." Seward was not present for this conversation, but he would have agreed with Johnson: the occasional violence against blacks, and the election of some rebel leaders, were no excuse for northern Radicals to attempt to impose their social theories upon the South, or to deny the southern states their places in Congress and the southern people their political rights. Seward would also have advised Johnson, however, that to achieve his goals he would have to work with the moderate Republicans; he would have to ensure that the moderates sided with him rather than with the Radicals.[81]

On December 18, Seward certified that a sufficient number of states had ratified the Thirteenth Amendment, the amendment abolishing slavery, so that it was now part of the Constitution. Twenty-seven out of thirty-six states had approved, Seward noted, counting all the southern states in his calculation, including those whose representatives were not yet admitted to Congress. One could question whether these were legitimate states for this purpose, but Seward did not; he believed the executive branch could form its own views on whether to recognize a state government, as it had during the Civil War in the cases of West Virginia, Louisiana, and other states. "It was with especial gratification," Frederick later recalled, that his father "affixed his name to this crowning and closing act of the long struggle." Frederick's language here reflected his father's views: Seward believed that, with the adoption of the Thirteenth Amendment and the formation of new southern state governments, the process of Reconstruction was almost complete. The Radicals believed the struggle had only begun.[82]

CHAPTER 16

"Political Apostasy":

1866

A common and erroneous view about Seward is that he was always an expansionist, always interested in adding new territory to the United States. In fact, before the Civil War, Seward generally opposed efforts to expand, saying that the United States had sufficient territory and that he wanted "no enlargement of territory sooner than it would come if we were contented with a masterly inactivity." It is true that he would sometimes predict eventual expansion, such as when he declared in 1846 that "our population is destined to roll its resistless waves to the icy barriers of the north, and to encounter oriental civilization on the shores of the Pacific." But when faced with concrete proposals, Seward would vote against them, as he did in the case of the Gadsden Treaty to purchase additional territory from Mexico, and in the case of President Buchanan's attempt to acquire Cuba from Spain. Seward's prewar attitudes were shaped by the knowledge that any acquired southern territory would become slave territory. After the Civil War, and after the Thirteenth Amendment, this was no longer a concern.[1]

There were a number of other reasons why Seward became, after the end of the war, eager to acquire territory. One was his wartime experience of how the American Navy had been weakened, especially vis-à-vis Britain, by its lack of offshore naval bases. There was a commercial as well as a military aspect to Seward's interest: he believed

the United States would some day be the world's leading trading nation, and that this day would be hastened by acquiring foreign ports
and territories. The end of the war brought an increased popular interest in expansion. The *Chicago Tribune* claimed that "California alone
would drive Maximilian from Mexico if our government would give her
permission." Many papers agreed with the *Charleston Daily Courier* in
predicting that Canada would soon "form one of the commonwealths
of this great Republic." Welles wrote in his diary in the summer of 1866
that "Seward is a monomaniac almost on the subject of acquisition, that
being the hobby on which he expects to be a candidate for President."
Welles was wrong to think that Seward still aspired to the presidency—
Seward knew that he had far too many enemies—but right to think that
he was interested in making history by adding to the American empire.[2]

An area of special interest for Seward was the Caribbean, where he
believed the United States needed a naval base. During the war, Lincoln and Seward had asked Admiral David Dixon Porter to consider
the various alternatives; Porter recommended that the United States
acquire St. Thomas, in the Danish West Indies, because it was centrally
located with an excellent harbor. In January 1865, Seward raised the
possibility of purchase with Waldemar Raasloff, the Danish minister
in Washington. According to the State Department summary of the
conversation, Seward assured Raasloff that the negotiations would be
conducted "in the most generous, chivalrous, and delicate manner." The
initial response was that the Danes could not enter into a negotiation
"at present" but would "regard with favor, at some future date, the re-
newal of this proposal." In December 1865, Raasloff told Seward that his
government was prepared to consider the transaction if the price was
sufficient to compensate Denmark not only for the island but also for
the anticipated displeasure of Britain and France. Seward told Raasloff
that he was about to leave for a few weeks in the Caribbean and would
perhaps go to St. Thomas, but that his visit would have "no connection
whatever with the proposed purchase."[3]

Seward departed from Washington on the last day of December, accompanied by Frederick, Anna, and her younger sister Molly Wharton.
The first few days of the trip were cold and rough, but within a few
days Seward was sitting in the winter sunshine on deck, wearing an

immense straw hat, and chatting with the naval officers. He told the press that this was a family vacation, but he was using a Navy steamship, something he could properly do only if this was an official trip. It was, indeed, the first time that an American secretary of state had traveled outside the United States on official business, a minor distinction of which Seward was perhaps not aware.[4]

When the Sewards arrived at St. Thomas in early January 1866, they were favorably impressed. Frederick noted that the main harbor was a "great basin, capacious enough for a small navy," but with a narrow entrance, "which even the diminutive forts and antiquated ordnance of the Danes are able to defend." The people were energetic and enterprising. After several pleasant days on St. Thomas, the party went over to the neighboring Danish island of Santa Cruz, where they visited the quaint capital of Christiansted and met with the Danish governor. The governor and his aides joined the Sewards for the twenty-mile carriage ride back to their ship, and the secretary learned much from "the conversation of these intelligent and well-informed Danes."[5]

Seward was interested in purchasing one or more islands, but he was not interested in negotiating with only the Danes. Rather, he wanted to have parallel negotiations with several sellers in order to keep his options open and to keep the sellers honest. His next stop, therefore, was the Dominican Republic, which had recently prevailed in its war against Spain and formed a new government. Seward knew that there had been serious talks in the past about the possibility of the United States acquiring Samaná Bay from the Dominicans and that the government there was now willing to consider a sale. Seward met with the president and his ministers at the presidential palace, and the president pressed him on the question of when the United States would recognize the Dominican government. Seward responded in his somewhat florid way, saying that the American empire would require "outward buttresses" in the form of republican governments in nearby countries and islands. The United States would therefore recognize the Dominican Republic "as soon as it shall afford us the necessary guarantee of its own stability." Perhaps to pave the way for territorial negotiation, perhaps simply to carry out this promise, Seward arranged for American recognition of the Dominican Republic as soon as he returned to Washington.[6]

From San Domingo, Seward sailed west to Port-au-Prince, the capital of Haiti. It does not appear that the secretary had territorial designs on Haiti, but rather wanted to see for himself this self-governing black nation. Here again the Sewards met with the president and toured the capital. They were struck by the poverty of Haiti, the modest buildings and unpaved streets. But as Anna noted in her journal, Seward believed that the proper comparison was not between Haiti and "white nations older and more advantageously situated"; the proper comparison was between the condition of Haiti and "what it was when they were slaves." Haiti had made "a vast stride in advance," and he believed that it would continue to do so if it could establish a "permanent and tranquil government."[7]

The Sewards' next stop was Havana, capital of the Spanish colony of Cuba. They lingered here for several days, meeting local residents and expatriate Americans, attending a grand state dinner hosted by the governor general and touring two cigar factories. As senator, Seward had spoken against an appropriation toward the purchase of Cuba, but this did not mean that as secretary, he opposed the American acquisition of Cuba. On the contrary, Seward expected that Cuba would some day be part of the United States. As he explained to the Spanish minister in Washington, Cuba would "by means of constant gravitation, fall into the United States." Seward was prepared to see Cuba remain a Spanish colony—he said while in Havana that "Spain is the only European power that has any right to a footing in America, since Spain has always been eminently American"—but he adamantly opposed the transfer of Cuba to any other European power. Seward's visit was thus not about the acquisition of Cuba but about building better relations with Spain, relations that could be used to smooth the eventual purchase of Cuba or perhaps other Spanish territory in the Caribbean.[8]

After returning to Washington at the end of January, Seward continued his efforts to acquire either islands or ports. In late March, at a cabinet meeting, he proposed paying $10 million to acquire St. Thomas, "three times as much as the amount" that Welles thought would be an appropriate offer. To support his position, Seward arranged for both a senior admiral and a senior general to confirm the military value of the Danish islands. In July, Seward made a written offer to Raasloff: the

United States would pay Denmark $5 million in gold for the three is-
lands in the Danish West Indies. Raasloff was about to depart for home
leave in Denmark, where he remained for the rest of the year, during
which the negotiations stalled.[9]

Meanwhile, Seward received indications that the Dominican Republic was willing to sell Samaná Bay to the United States. "We are very
poor indeed," the Dominican foreign minister confessed to the American representative. In early December 1866, Seward caused some excitement by appearing in the House of Representatives, walking to the
desk of the Radical Republican Thaddeus Stevens, and sitting down to
talk with him. Seward persuaded Stevens to include in the pending ap-
propriations bill an additional $250,000 "for the contingent expenses of
foreign intercourse." Seward bragged to Welles about how he had met
not only with Stevens but also with Senators William Fessenden and
James Grimes, "and had got each of them evidently enlisted" behind the
proposed purchase of Samaná Bay. When Welles told Seward that he
did not favor the purchase, that Seward was offering too much, Seward
responded that "he did not doubt it, but then we ought to be liberal and
not take advantage of a poor, weak neighbor who was in need." [10]

Later in the same month, Seward appointed Frederick to go to San
Domingo and offer up to $2 million for either the purchase of, or a long
lease on, Samaná Bay. Over the objection of Welles, Seward also arranged that Admiral Porter would accompany Frederick, in order that
the purchase would appear to be "a naval affair." When Porter and Frederick returned to Washington early in the new year of 1867, however,
they had to report that they could not reach terms with the Dominicans.
As Porter later recalled, the problem was the weak Dominican government, which feared that any agreement with the Americans would lead
to yet another new government.[11]

———

On the day after he returned to Washington in late January 1866, Seward
had a long conversation with President Johnson, who told a reporter
that the secretary found "all his foreign matters in first rate condition on
his return." Domestic affairs were another story. Congress had still not

seated any of the representatives sent to Washington by the southern states. Instead, Congress was considering a civil rights constitutional amendment, with the suggestion that the southern states would not be admitted back until after the states ratified this new amendment.[12]

Congress was also working on a bill to strengthen and extend the Freedmen's Bureau, a bill that passed with almost unanimous Republican support in February. If Seward had been president, he might well have signed the Freedmen's Bureau bill into law. His closest friend in Congress, Henry Raymond of New York, commented on the House floor that "we owe, as a duty to those who have been set free, the protection which this bill affords." But Seward was not president, and Johnson had no intention of signing the bill. Southern whites hated the Freedmen's Bureau, which they saw as northern meddling in their domestic affairs. Democrats also opposed the Bureau, which they viewed as an expensive, unnecessary, and improper expansion of federal authority. Johnson shared these concerns and wanted the support of these groups in his 1868 election campaign, so he asked several advisers, including Seward, to prepare draft veto messages, from which Johnson would cut and paste to form the final message.[13]

Seward's draft strongly endorsed the bill's objective: "Freedmen who were emancipated by the nation as a means of suppressing the civil war are entitled to national protection until the country shall have resumed its normal and habitual condition of repose." His main argument for the veto was that the bill was premature. Under current law, the Bureau would continue to exist for one year after the end of the Civil War, and since neither the president nor the Congress had declared a formal end of the war, the Bureau had at least a year to function. Would it not be better to revisit these issues in a few months' time, Seward asked, as the Bureau approached the end of its term? Johnson adopted many of Seward's technical arguments but rejected his moderate tone. The central argument in Johnson's veto message was that Congress should not legislate *at all* on Reconstruction until it admitted the southern representatives. The authority of each house of Congress to judge its members' qualifications could not be stretched to allow Congress to "shut out in time of peace any state from the representation to which it is entitled by the Constitution."[14]

Moderate Republican leaders, several of whom had discussed the issues with the president, were surprised and distressed by Johnson's message. On the day after the message was issued, the Senate considered whether to pass the bill over the president's veto. Thirty Republican senators voted in favor of the motion to override, but ten Republicans sided with eight Democrats to support Johnson, so the motion failed by two votes.[15]

Johnson, ignoring the narrow margin, and ignoring the press criticism, exulted in his victory. When a celebratory crowd arrived at the White House, the president compared the current Radical leaders in Congress with the southern rebels. The secessionists had tried to tear the Union apart; the Radicals were trying to concentrate power in the central government and in their own hands, "equally objectionable," in his view. A voice called out for names and Johnson readily obliged: the men whom he viewed as "being opposed to the fundamental principles of the government and as now laboring to destroy them" included Representative Thaddeus Stevens and Senator Charles Sumner. The crowd cheered. Johnson suggested that these men were trying to remove him from power, perhaps even to have him killed. "Are they not satisfied with the blood which has been shed? Does not the murder of Lincoln appease the vengeance and wrath of the opponents of this government?" The crowd cheered again.[16]

A few hours later, not yet aware of Johnson's remarks, Seward spoke in New York City to an educated and enthusiastic audience at Cooper Union. Seward argued that the differences between the president and Congress were slight, mere questions of detail. Some Radicals wanted to keep the southern states out of Congress, but this would not work for long, because "you can never keep states out of this Union, no never." As to the Freedmen's Bureau veto, Seward tried to characterize it as merely Johnson's way of declining additional authority. "It will be a sad hour for the Republic when the refusal of unnecessary powers, treasure and patronage by the President shall be held to be a crime."[17]

Seward's speech was an elegant argument for the administration position, far more persuasive than Johnson's crude comments. The *Albany Evening Journal,* though no longer edited by Weed, remained quite friendly to Seward, and it applauded his speech as "able, statesmanlike, comprehensive." Seward offered "soothing and amiable prophecies," the *Chicago Tribune* noted, while Johnson used "threats and violence." Whatever good was done by Seward's speech, however, was largely undone by a telegram he sent to Johnson, calling the president's speech "triumphant" and claiming "the country will be happy." Seward's telegram was printed in the papers, and *The Nation* observed that it would "always remain among the curiosities of telegraphic literature." It is indeed hard to understand. A clue is provided by a telegram from Weed to Johnson, also sent from New York, within a few minutes of Seward's message. "I want to thank you with my whole grateful heart," Weed wrote, "for that glorious speech of yesterday." Weed and Seward were trying to persuade Johnson to appoint a Seward Republican to the key position of collector of customs for the port of New York; Democrats were trying to secure this powerful post for one of their own. Perhaps Seward and Weed sent their obsequious messages as part of their effort to secure this patronage post.[18]

In March, both houses of Congress passed, with substantial Republican majorities, a civil rights bill designed to protect former southern slaves. The bill declared that all persons born in the United States (other than foreign citizens and American Indians) were citizens of the United States. All citizens (without regard to their race) would have the right to make and enforce contracts, to sue and be witnesses in court, and to enjoy the equal protection of the laws. To ensure that these provisions were not disregarded in southern state courts, the bill allowed and indeed required federal criminal authorities to prosecute violations of these federal rights. Johnson was determined to veto the bill, and perhaps he was right to do so: it is an interesting question whether the Constitution, at the time, authorized such a bill. Seward advised Johnson to use measured language in his message: "If you could find a way to intimate that you are not opposed to the policy of the bill but only to its detailed provisions it will be a great improvement and make the support of the veto easier to our friends in Congress." Seward also forwarded to Johnson a letter from Weed, who counseled that the president should, if he vetoed the bill, "evince his paternal regard" for the southern blacks. And Seward provided Johnson with a detailed draft veto message along these lines.[19]

The draft suggested that Johnson should agree with the general purpose of the bill, "to secure all persons in their civil rights without regard to race or color." Seward's objections to the bill were technical concerns about its enforcement provisions; in effect, he would have invited Congress to amend the bill and promised that the president would sign the amended bill. Again, Johnson adopted some of Seward's arguments but rejected his tone, issuing a message that disagreed with almost every aspect of the civil rights bill. Johnson insisted that the federal government had no role in civil rights; these were questions for the state governments alone. If Congress could pass this bill, Johnson argued, it could pass a bill giving blacks the vote not only in the southern states but in *all* the states. Far from showing "paternal regard" for the southern blacks, Johnson vilified them, suggesting they were far less ready to become American citizens than recent European immigrants.[20]

Johnson's harsh veto message angered not only the Radicals but also many moderate Republicans who had expected that he would work with them toward some kind of civil rights compromise. On April 6, thirty-three senators voted to override the veto and only fifteen voted to sustain it. Seward's friend Edwin Morgan was among the senators who voted against Johnson. Morgan explained in a letter to Weed that Johnson had refused to even talk with him about compromise. "It was then *this* bill or *nothing*," Morgan wrote, and he believed that it was imperative that Congress pass some form of civil rights legislation. On April 9, the House also voted to override the veto, and the bill became law, the first major piece of legislation in American history to take effect over a presidential veto.[21]

———

Johnson's civil rights veto was a turning point in 1866, and in the Reconstruction era, for it separated Johnson not only from the Radicals but from essentially all Republicans. Historians have agreed that Johnson should have heeded Seward's advice, that he should have worked with rather than alienated the moderate Republicans. "Johnson lacked the finesse and flexibility to follow the course marked out by Seward," one historian wrote, because the president "preferred all-out enemies to lukewarm friends." The two veto messages of early 1866, both rejecting Seward's moderate approach, raise questions not only about Johnson but also about Seward: Why did Seward remain in Johnson's cabinet? Why didn't he speak out in defense of the rights of southern blacks? Had Seward lost his compassion?[22]

There is some evidence that by 1866 Seward was not especially concerned about southern blacks, or at least was less worried about them than about other issues. In March 1888, the *New York Evening Post* published what it claimed were notes of an April 1866 conversation between Seward and Charles Eliot Norton, at the time an editor of the *North American Review*, and Edwin Godkin, at the time the editor of *The Nation*. According to the *Post*, Seward told the two men that "the North has nothing to do with the negroes. I have no more concern for them than I have for the Hottentots. They are God's poor; they always have been and always will be so everywhere. . . . The South must take care of its own negroes as the North did and does." It is possible that Seward said this in 1866, but it is also possible that these "quotes" were created in 1888. After all, if Seward had made these comments in 1866, why would two journalists not have published them at the time? Godkin and *The Nation* were harsh critics of Johnson and Seward; it seems especially unlikely that he would have withheld these comments if Seward in fact made them. In short, although memorable, the 1888 article is not very reliable.[23]

More reliable is a letter to the French philosopher the comte de Gasparin, in which Seward wrote that what was needed "immediately, urgently, and indispensably" was to get the southern states back into the national government. "This work cannot wait without danger of disorganization, anarchy, imbecility and ultimate disunion." To condition admission of the southern states on black voting, as many Radicals wanted, would require Congress to coerce the southern states to ratify a constitutional amendment, perhaps through military force. This would involve "centralization, consolidation, and imperialism" utterly foreign to the American system. Seward was worried that the Radical approach could lead to a second civil war. He was willing to leave the treatment of southern blacks to the southern state governments, in the same way that the treatment of northern blacks was handled by the northern state governments. Seward no longer had a Radical in his own household, in the form of his wife Frances, who would surely have shared the Radical concern for the fate of southern blacks. Unlike Frances, Seward was never an abolitionist who insisted on the immediate end of slavery; he was prepared before the Civil War to wait for decades to see the gradual but inevitable end of the slave system. It is thus not surprising that after the war and his wife's death, he was prepared to wait for gradual social and political processes to improve the lives of former slaves and their descendants.[24]

The plight of southern blacks was highlighted in early May by racial riots in Memphis, Tennessee. Different newspapers had different versions of how the riots started, but almost all agreed that white Memphis residents had raged through black sections of the city, killing and wounding dozens. Seward did not even mention Memphis, however, or southern blacks, in a speech he gave in Auburn later in the month. Instead, he compared the state of the Union to a ship after a life-threatening storm, now entering a safe harbor. There were minor disputes about how best to enter the harbor, but they would be resolved. The key task for Congress was to admit the southern states back into Congress, or at least provide a clear and short path to their readmission. Echoing the Bible, Seward said that "neither hope nor fear, nor anger, nor ambition, nor height, nor depth, nor any other creature, can separate [the states] from this inherent, life-saving love of Union." Because there was, in his view, no prospect of obtaining approval of a constitutional amendment providing blacks the vote, Congress should not even consider that issue.[25]

Seward claimed in his Auburn speech that he was speaking for the Union Party, but the press reaction showed that the Union Party had more or less dissolved into its Republican and Democratic elements, and that Seward no longer represented the Republicans. The *Albany Evening Journal* read the speech as warning Johnson that he should not form a personal political party, but rather must adhere to the Union Party, and on this basis called Seward's speech "able, moderate, and politic." More typical of Republican reactions was the *New York Tribune,* which charged Seward with effectively telling 4 million blacks that they would have only such rights as their former masters would grant them. The central issue, according to the *Tribune*, was whether southern blacks would "be left entirely at those Rebels' mercy," and on this issue "Seward clearly places himself in line with the Copperheads and Rebels," using the derogatory term for northern allies of the southerners. The *Chicago Tribune* contended that Seward's eagerness for reconciliation with the rebels was just like his eagerness to avoid war in the days before Sumter; in both cases, Seward showed "mere cowardice." The *New York Independent* declared that Seward "once earned honor by remembering the negro at a time when others forgot him; he now earns dishonor by forgetting the negro when the nation demands that the negro should be remembered." [26]

———

Seward devoted much of 1866 to domestic politics, but there were serious foreign policy issues as well during this critical year. [27] On February 6, the *New York Times* reported what it viewed as the most important news since the downfall of the Confederacy: Napoleon III had announced that "preparations are being made to withdraw the French troops from Mexico." The *Times* considered this a vindication of Seward's Mexican policy, but Seward himself was more cautious, noting that the emperor's statement included no specifics about when and how the French would withdraw. Details arrived in late April, when the secretary received official word that the French troops would leave Mexico in three tranches: one in November 1866; a second in March 1867; and a third and final group in November 1867. To ensure that the French would not change their mind, Seward immediately published this correspondence, and for good measure his correspondence with the American minister in Austria in which he insisted that Austria withdraw at the same time. [28]

The French declaration did not silence the American critics of the secretary of state's Mexican policy. Thaddeus Stevens declared in a House speech that it was a "blunder" and a "crime" for the United States to rely upon "a promise to withdraw the invading forces in eighteen months' time." Stevens suggested that the United States should loan $2 million to the Juárez government to enable it to defeat Maximilian.

If the loan provoked a war between the United States and Maximilian's army, Stevens would welcome it, for it would give the United States "an opportunity to vindicate her honor, which has become dim under the Micawber policy of our Foreign Secretary." Stevens apparently meant that Seward, like the character in Dickens, lived on hope rather than reality.[29]

As the date approached for the first French troops to depart, there were worrisome indications that Napoleon was having second thoughts, and so Seward carefully increased the pressure on the French to abide by what he now termed the "agreement" for their three-stage withdrawal. He arranged that Thomas Campbell, the new American minister to the Juárez government, would be accompanied there by General William Sherman as military adviser. Seward's instructions to Campbell, which he shared through Bigelow with the French, asked him to explore whether American military forces could "be useful in favoring the restoration of law, order, and republican government" in Mexico. The French interpreted Sherman's presence and Campbell's instructions as a threat that, if the French troops did not withdraw soon, the United States would begin to provide military advice to the Mexicans. When Seward learned that the French would not withdraw any troops in late 1866, but instead start in early 1867, he sent a long protest to Bigelow, using the recently opened transatlantic telegraph. Seward's message may have been meant more for domestic than foreign purposes, however, for when Bigelow reported back that the reason for the French decision was military, not political, and that the entire force would withdraw in early 1867, Seward did not object.[30]

In March 1867, more than five years after the first French troops landed in Mexico, the last of these troops departed. The republican government of Mexico was restored without a war between the United States and France or between the United States and the Maximilian government. There were many reasons for the French defeat in Mexico, but historians have credited Seward's cautious but persistent Mexican diplomacy. Two recent historians observed that "the drumming of Seward's fingers in Washington had increasingly reverberated through the salons of the Tuileries and had inexorably indicated to Napoleon III that time, which has no allies, had run out for his Grand Design for the Americas."

Another author remarked that Seward assisted Juárez "parsimoniously but successfully, refusing to recognize any other government or pretender, forcing the evacuation of the French by a diplomatic pressure that increased steadily as Napoleon weakened." Seward indeed managed the Mexican issue well, not only by pressuring the French to leave Mexico but also by countering General Grant and others who courted a second Mexican war.[31]

———

As the Civil War ended, many Irish-American soldiers joined the Fenian Brotherhood, an association dedicated to Irish independence. Some of the Fenians started talking about and planning for attacks on Canada and Ireland, and these plans were far from secret; indeed, they were reported and derided in the major American newspapers—"brag and bluster," in the words of the *New York Times*. The British were concerned, however, and in the summer of 1865, the new British minister in Washington, Sir Frederick Bruce, asked Seward what steps the government was taking to ensure that the Fenians did not violate American neutrality laws. Bruce was not at all pleased to learn from Seward that the Johnson administration did not intend to suppress what it viewed as a political rather than a military organization. After his conversation with Seward, Bruce reported to London that "the Irish party, owing to their compact organization, exercise, unfortunately for us, a powerful influence in American politics."[32]

The Irish-Americans were well aware of their political power, and when Bernard Killian, a Fenian leader, met with Johnson and Seward in late 1865, he asked their views on plans to set up a Fenian republic within Canadian territory. The president and secretary responded vaguely but positively, saying they would "acknowledge accomplished facts." Killian then tried and failed to get Seward to commit himself on paper, but even after his cold official response, the Irish-Americans viewed the secretary as a friend. The British also viewed Seward as their friend, however. In one of his private letters to the foreign minister, Bruce reported that Seward advised against any formal correspondence on the Fenian issue, "on the grounds that it would reanimate their cause and tend to secure for them the sympathy of those who hate England but have no friendly sentiments towards the Irish." Bruce agreed: "our policy in this harassing business is to act in concert with Mr. Seward." Johnson told Bruce, in a private conversation in early 1866, that the Fenian movement "met with no sympathy on the part of the Government, which on the contrary was anxious to discourage it."[33]

In February 1866, the British authorities in Ireland arrested a large number of Fenians, many of them naturalized American citizens. At the same time, Parliament suspended the writ of habeas corpus in Ireland, so the Fenians faced indefinite arrest without trial. When the American consul in Dublin attempted to visit the Fenians in prison, the authorities refused permission because British law viewed British citizenship as "inalienable," so that these men were British citizens and not Americans. Seward immediately raised his concerns with both Bruce in Washington and Adams in London. He argued that British severity toward the prisoners, especially those who had fought on the northern side in the Civil War, would only strengthen the Fenian movement in the United States. It would be far better, Seward said, for the United States and Britain to resolve the legal question of dual citizenship through a treaty or through arbitration. The British did not accept the American views, but they did release the arrested men, on condition that they return immediately to the United States.[34]

In the early hours of June 1, 1866, about one thousand armed Fenians crossed the Niagara River, near Buffalo, into Canada. Perhaps as a result of orders from Washington, perhaps as a result of local naval initiative, the USS *Michigan* soon appeared on the Niagara River, where it blocked any Fenian reinforcements. On June 2, British-Canadian forces defeated the Fenians in the Battle of Ridgeway; some of the Fenians were captured in Canada, others returned to the United States and dispersed. Seward followed these events closely from Washington but argued against any kind of presidential proclamation. On June 6, however, worried about further Fenian invasions of Canada, and pressed by Bruce through Seward, Johnson at last issued a proclamation reminding Americans that they could not lawfully attack Canada.[35]

If Seward hoped, by delaying and toning down this proclamation, to avoid Fenian anger against himself and Johnson, he failed. The *New York Times* reported that "Irishmen universally denounce the government for its action in the matter, and the invectives they hurl at the offending heads of President Johnson and Secretary Seward are scarcely excelled by those they launch against the British authorities." The *Chicago Tribune* observed that Irish-Americans were "ravenous for revenge on the President, and if an election were held tomorrow they would go *en masse* against the Administration party." Over the summer and fall, Seward tried to recover some goodwill among Irish voters by pressing the British to show mercy to the captured Fenians. Seward ensured that his letters to the British minister were printed in American newspapers; his second long letter appeared only days before the November elections. A few Irish-Americans praised his efforts on behalf of the Fenian prisoners, but many others were still outraged at the way in which they believed he had betrayed their cause.[36]

———

In June 1866, after months of proposals, debates, and compromises, Congress approved a civil rights amendment to the constitution. The amendment granted citizenship to all those born in the United States and prohibited states from depriving "any person of life, liberty, or property, without due process of law" or from denying any person "the equal protection of the laws." Radicals were disappointed that the amendment did not also address black voting rights, but almost all the Radicals in Congress voted for the amendment. Moderates also supported the amendment; those who voted yes included Seward associates Edwin Morgan in the Senate and Henry Raymond in the House. Seward played no role in the debate, but after the amendment passed, he transmitted it officially to the states for their consideration, as the secretary of state was required to do by federal law. Johnson was annoyed with Seward for taking even this modest step, so the president issued his own message, describing Seward's action as ministerial, and arguing that Congress should not have amended the Constitution without first seating the southern delegates. Johnson did not mention it, but observers understood that if the southern delegates had been seated, Republicans could not have obtained the required two-thirds majorities to approve a constitutional amendment.[37]

The passage by Congress of the amendment intensified discussions among Johnson, Seward, and others about a National Union convention, an attempt to bring together all those who approved the administration's reconciliation policy. Even as they were drafting the call for the convention, however, Johnson's supporters disagreed about the new movement. Democrats and former Democrats like Gideon Welles wanted the call letter to attack the civil rights amendment; Republicans and Union Party men like Seward strongly opposed this suggestion, saying that the only way to entice Republicans into the movement was to avoid this issue. Welles fretted that the movement would be "perverted to an intrigue in behalf of the old Whig party, on which Weed and Seward rely." Henry Raymond, on the other hand, worried to Seward that the convention would be controlled by "former Rebels and their Copperhead associates, and used for purposes hostile to the Union party." Seward had to use all his persuasive powers, and those of Johnson, to convince Raymond that the movement was not a new party, and that he could and should participate.[38]

As Seward insisted, the call letter said nothing about the civil rights amendment; it simply asked delegates from all states to assemble "as friends and brothers under the national flag" in Philadelphia. Johnson asked his cabinet members to support the call. Three Republicans refused and resigned: Postmaster William Dennison, Interior Secretary James Harlan, and Attorney General James Speed. War Secretary Edwin Stanton, although he increasingly sided with the Republicans and refused to support the convention, did not resign, and for some reason Johnson did not remove him.[39]

Seward supported the convention in a strong public letter in which he criticized Congress for failing to admit representatives of the southern states. His letter was attacked by many papers. The *New York Tribune* argued that the question was not whether the South should be represented in Congress, but rather whether it should be represented by unrepentant rebels or by representatives elected by all southerners, black and white together. The *Albany Evening Journal*, which had supported Seward for more than three decades, now declared that "the great mass of those who have always acted with Gov. Seward will find themselves dissenting from him," because they were not willing "to go into council with those whose hands are stained by loyal blood." The *Journal* was referring to the likelihood (which apparently did not trouble Seward) that many of the southern delegates would be former Confederate military officers.[40]

Seward wrote to Fanny, who was living at home in Auburn with her brother William, that he regretted the departure of his Republican cabinet colleagues. "It does not surprise me, although it pains me, that all of my associates have not been able to see it their duty, as I see it mine, to sustain" the president. In another letter to Fanny, Seward said he would not bother her more with politics. "I am quite willing that you should be spared anxieties, in a field in which you can do no effectual labor." Fanny, who knew well that her mother and father had often discussed politics, responded that she liked to learn about political issues. Her father obliged with a letter in which he characterized his southern policy as an application of the "Christian precepts." He was trying to preach "forgiveness to enemies—magnanimity to the conquered—equality to all," and although many resisted this message, their "resistance will not continue." When Congress at last admitted representatives from Tennessee, on the basis of the state's approval of the constitutional amendment, Seward celebrated and hosted the Tennessee representatives at his home. "I had a calf served up in many ways," Seward wrote Fanny, "and they accepted it as 'returned prodigals.' " President Johnson did not share in Seward's pleasure: he was so opposed to the constitutional amendment that he had tried to prevent Tennessee from ratifying it, even though he knew ratification was the price his home state had to pay to have a voice again in Congress.[41]

Seward commented to his daughter that, during the eight months Congress had been in session, "slavery has been extirpated throughout the United States" and "peace has been completely restored." The very next day, however, an attempted convention in New Orleans led to a vicious racial riot that left more than a hundred blacks dead, many at the hands of the white police force. Johnson, on the day of the riot, sent a telegram to Louisiana directing the federal military to support the local authorities "in suppressing all illegal and unlawful assemblies." The national newspapers immediately assigned blame according to their politics. The *New York Tribune* declared that the massacre was "President Johnson's responsibility"; the editors contrasted Johnson's lenient treatment of Fenian conventions with his vindictive treatment of New Orleans blacks. The *New York Times*, on the other hand, absolved Johnson and blamed the Radicals, "who would not be unwilling to precipitate a state into civil war to accomplish negro suffrage." In a letter to his daughter, Seward called the riot in New Orleans "a sad affair" but did not comment further.[42]

Seward did not attend the National Union Convention in Philadelphia in August, but he was there in spirit, represented by friends like Raymond and Weed. The convention was also known as the "arm-in-arm" convention because, at its outset, the northern and southern delegates entered the hall arm-in-arm, as thousands of spectators cheered. Raymond wrote in the *New York Times* that the message of the convention was simple: "every Congressional District in the country is called upon to return only members who are favorable to the policy of representation and reconciliation." Although Seward was pleased with the work of the convention, he was also troubled that there were so few Republicans present, and that there were no Republican candidates for Congress who favored Johnson's policies. In supporting candidates who would support the president, therefore, Seward was supporting the Democratic Party, the party against which he had fought for almost his entire political life.[43]

One reason that Seward did not attend the convention was that he was busy in Washington planning a post-convention political tour for Johnson, himself, and others. The nominal purpose of this tour was to attend the dedication in Chicago of a memorial to Stephen Douglas, but the presidential party would take a slow and circuitous route, giving the tour its name, the "swing around the circle." Seward organized the group that traveled with the president (including Secretary Welles, General Grant, and Admiral Farragut) and corresponded with those who would welcome them in various cities and towns. The trip started well enough: the president was warmly greeted in Philadelphia, New York City, and Albany. At each stop Johnson gave more or less the same speech: he thanked the audience for its welcome, declared that he was a man of the people, and insisted that the Union had to be saved by reconciliation with the South. Seward sometimes made brief remarks. In New York City, for example, he said he was sure that New York would "give a certificate at the polls that the Union of the United States consists not of twenty-five but of thirty-six states."[44]

The high point of the trip for Seward was on August 31, when the presidential party arrived in his hometown of Auburn at about three in the afternoon. The *New York Times* noted that "the entire population seemed to be in the streets and equally excited." Johnson, Seward, and the others drove in carriages from the train station to the park just south of Seward's house, where the mayor welcomed the president and the president responded by thanking Auburn and praising its "distinguished statesman." The party then drove another two miles south to the shore of Lake Owasco for an open-air dinner, with many toasts and short speeches. After dinner they returned to Auburn, where there were fireworks and Johnson was the house guest of Seward. The party left Auburn early the next morning and, after short stops at various stations along the railroad's route, reached Niagara Falls that evening. Seward, in his remarks there, compared Lincoln and Johnson, noting that before his death Lincoln had many critics, just as Johnson had now.[45]

The first low point of the "swing around the circle" was at Cleveland on September 3, where Johnson responded to hecklers as he used to do on the campaign trail in Tennessee. The president claimed that a "subsidized gang of hirelings have traduced me and maligned me ever since I have entered upon the discharge of my official duties, yet I will say had my predecessor lived the vials of wrath would have been poured out on him." The crowd called out: "never, never, never." Johnson challenged any member of the crowd to "place their finger upon one single hair breadth of deviation from one single pledge I have made." A voice called out: "Hang Jeff Davis." Johnson responded in kind: "Why don't you? Have you not got the Court? Have you not got the Attorney General?" After this unfortunate dialogue, reported in the newspapers,

Welles pleaded with Seward to control Johnson. Seward answered that "the President was doing good and was the best stump speaker in the country." Perhaps no one could have restrained Johnson, but Seward should have tried.[46]

The tour reached an even lower point at St. Louis, where Johnson accused the Radicals in Congress of causing the New Orleans riot: "Every drop of blood that was shed is upon their skirts, and they are responsible for it." The president claimed that he had been "traduced" and "slandered" and "maligned" and "called Judas—Judas Iscariot, and all that." He continued: "If I have played the Judas, who has been my Christ that I have played the Judas with? Was it Thad Stevens? Was it Wendell Phillips? Was it Charles Sumner? (Hisses and cheers.) Are these the men that set up and compare themselves with the Savior of men, and everybody that differs with them in opinion, and try and stay and arrest their diabolical and nefarious policy, is to be denounced as a Judas?"[47]

Johnson's speeches may have amused his audiences but they outraged the northern press. Even previously supportive newspapers, such as the *New York Herald* and the *New York Times*, now criticized the president. When Johnson remarked that he "did not care about his dignity," the *Times* reminded him that the American people could never see the dignity of the presidency disregarded "without profound sorrow and solicitude." The *New York Herald*, seeking to protect Johnson, asked whether the "Mephistopheles Secretary" planned the grand tour "for the purpose of damaging the President," and whether Seward "still has ambition to take the Presidential chair." Seward's speeches during the tour were far more temperate than those of Johnson, but they too were attacked. The *Chicago Tribune* commented that Seward's remarks about the loyalty and humility of the southern states "surpass[ed] the ravings of Johnson in their wicked and deliberate perversion of the truth." *The Nation* was especially angered by Seward's suggestion that the Republican Party would soon find itself without leaders. The editors predicted that it would be Seward, not the party, who would soon found himself alone. "Distrusted by his old friends, he will never be taken to the bosom of his old enemies. His trouble is not that the party to which he once belonged is without a leader, but that he wanders about, like a restless ghost—a leader without a party."[48]

Seward probably did not read these articles because, not long after the presidential party left Louisville, he became seriously ill, perhaps with food poisoning. By the time they reached Harrisburg, Pennsylvania, on September 14, he was near death. As Welles described the scene in his diary, he and Johnson visited Seward in his railcar sickbed and found he could hardly speak. Seward took Johnson's hand and whispered: "My mind is clear, and I wish to say at this time that your course is right, that I have felt it my duty to sustain you in it, and if my life is spared I shall continue to do so. Pursue it for the sake of the country; it is correct." It is interesting that Welles does not indicate that he or Johnson said any words to comfort Seward; perhaps this was because Welles disliked Seward so intensely, or perhaps because Johnson never really liked Seward in the way that Lincoln had liked him.[49]

Augustus, who was traveling with Seward, sent telegraphs to summon his siblings, and Fred, William, and Fanny arrived in Harrisburg early on September 15. They found their father "very cold and purple" but "all tenderness and consideration," urging Fanny not to fatigue herself. Seward was determined to return to Washington and, although the children "had but little hope" he would survive the journey, they agreed to make the attempt. Seward seemed to travel well, so they continued to Washington, where Stanton met them at the station, with kind words for all of them. The doctors attended Seward closely over the next few days, during which his condition varied. One day a paper reported that he was "mending rapidly" and that his doctor "pronounces him now out of danger"; the next day another paper reported that his friends were "much alarmed." By Monday September 24, however, Seward could resume his work at the State Department.[50]

The press attacks on Seward were not suspended by his illness: indeed, one paper suggested that his problem was just drunkenness, which would wear off with rest and plain soda. As the *Chicago Tribune* observed, the reason for the harsh comments was simple: Seward had committed the sin of "political apostasy," renouncing his Republican faith. In an era in which party identification was even more important for the average American than it is today, political apostasy was a rare and unpardonable sin. Seward was aware of the anger against him but reacted with his customary calm. When a friend forwarded reports that

Republicans were claiming that the nation was now run by two drunk-ards, Johnson and Seward, Seward wrote back: "I have no remembrance of a time, during my public life, in which less charitable views of my public and private character were taken, by those who differed from me, than those which are now presented, by the opponents of the policy which it is my duty to maintain. My first complaint of unkindness at the hands of my fellow citizens remains yet to be made, and I think it may with safety be still longer deferred."[51]

———

Fanny Seward suffered from a chronic cough, almost certainly from tu-berculosis. She was at home in Auburn for much of 1866, but after the hurried trip to Harrisburg, she stayed with her father in Washington. In early October, in a cheerful letter to her brother William, Fanny wrote that she was "very much stronger" and could "see marked improve-ment in everything but my cough—and that is not any worse." Not long afterward, however, she sickened; and early on the morning of October 29, she died. She was only twenty-one. The *New York Times* noted that she was "eminently quiet and unobtrusive" but also had a "strength of character far beyond what a casual observer would detect," a strength shown when she "threw herself between her father's breast and the uplifted knife of the assassin." The assassin Lewis Powell later said, according to the *Times*, that "if he could have made up his mind to strike her out of his way he could have accomplished his purpose upon the Secretary, but that her face, between his weapon and her father, disarmed him." None of the obituaries mentioned Fanny's literary ambi-tion and skill, but it is for the journal she kept from the age of fourteen onwards that she is rightly remembered today.[52]

The funeral service for Fanny Seward was held in Washington on the afternoon of October 31. The mourners gathered at the house, then pro-cessed behind the casket the short way to St. John's Episcopal Church. The rector met them at the church door and, as prescribed by the prayer book, pronounced: "I am the resurrection and the life, saith the Lord." The church was crowded with mourners, including President Johnson, the entire cabinet, most of the foreign diplomats, and some of Fanny's own youthful friends. After the service, Seward accompanied his daughter's body by special train from Washington to Auburn. At the reception in the family home there, when the coffin was opened, Seward looked down at her face and said, "there she is, come and see her." A reporter noted that "there was not, there could not have been, a dry eye in the room." Fanny was buried quietly on a Saturday afternoon in the same beautiful graveyard where the family had buried her mother just a year earlier.[53]

Seward told Sanford that he was not "altogether unprepared" for Fanny's death, but it was still hard upon him. He wrote to his friend Bigelow that "no one can ever know or conceive how precious in my sight was the treasure that you so truly say was removed that I might look elsewhere for its restoration." He explained to Charlotte Cushman, the actor whom Fanny had so admired, that "I had during the last ten years dreams which formed themselves into schemes of retirement, of travel, of study at the approaching end of a life which has been active from motives of duty, but as the world will probably insist motives of ambition. Those dreams and schemes were entirely free from all impurity and all selfishness, perhaps so entirely free, because she was associated with them all." Seward knew that he should "rejoice that she was withdrawn from me to be reunited with the pure and blessed spirit that formed her own." But "I am not spiritual enough to find support in these reflections."[54]

Fanny's death coincided with the fall elections, which were a political disaster for Johnson and Seward. They had pleaded with voters to elect moderate Democrats, men who would support Johnson's reconciliation policy; instead, the voters generally elected Radical Republicans, men utterly opposed to Johnson and his policies. In Seward's own New York, after a campaign focused far more on national than state issues, the Republican candidate for governor prevailed, and Republicans gained control of both houses of the state legislature. Similar results obtained in other states. It was, according to the *New York Times*, the "final repudiation of the Democratic party." Seward wrote to a friend that "responsibilities are removed to the shoulders which ached for them. Before long we shall know whether you and I have been right hitherto or otherwise."[55]

There were some indications, after the election, that Johnson was considering compromise with Congress on Reconstruction. The *New York Times* reported hopefully on November 16 that Chief Justice Salmon Chase, still viewed as a strong Republican, had visited the White House and met with Johnson, Seward, and others. A few days later, the *Times* noted that Johnson had stopped at Seward's home in the evening and stayed for about an hour. Johnson again asked Seward to help him draft his annual message, and Seward prepared a moderate draft, starting with an optimistic description of the national condition. Seward acknowledged that each house of Congress had the exclusive right to determine when and on what terms to admit members. The draft noted that six states had already ratified the pending constitutional amendment, and pledged that the president would give his "cheerful concurrence and co-operation" in all "judicious and constitutional measures" designed to restore national peace and prosperity. Seward's draft intimated a grand compromise: Johnson would accept the civil rights amendment if Congress would admit the southern representatives.[56]

Johnson, however, once again rejected Seward's conciliatory tone and did not pursue compromise. In part this was a matter of personality—Andrew Johnson was not a statesman of the compromising kind—and in part it was a matter of calculation. Three border states had already rejected the pending civil rights amendment, and it seemed unlikely that any southern states (other than Tennessee) would ratify it. Without these votes, the constitutional amendment would not secure approval from three fourths of the states, unless Congress used harsher measures to coerce the southern states, such as imposing military rule or granting blacks the right to vote. Johnson thought that it was unlikely that Congress would take such radical steps and thus likely that the amendment would fail. Alternatively, if Congress imposed military rule on the southern states, Johnson believed northern moderates would react against Congress, and support him in his 1868 presidential campaign. Seward may not have fully agreed with Johnson on his approach, but he did not disagree either, and so he remained at Johnson's right hand.[57]

CHAPTER 17

"Let Us Make the Treaty Tonight":

1867

The conflict between the Johnson administration and the Republican Congress intensified in early 1867. At their first meeting of the year, Johnson and his cabinet considered whether to veto a bill to extend voting rights to blacks in the District of Columbia. According to Welles, Seward said that "he had always advocated negro suffrage and voted for it in New York," but he distinguished between New York, where blacks were a small minority, and the District, where they would form a near majority. Although Seward told his colleagues that he believed that universal suffrage would eventually prevail, he supported Johnson's veto. Congress immediately overrode the veto.[1]

By early 1867, most Republicans were convinced that only military rule would stop southern violence against blacks and loyalists. In late February, Congress passed and presented to Johnson a military reconstruction bill that would place ten southern states under military governors with the power to arrest and try civilians in military courts. These southern states could only have civilian governments again, and only be represented in Congress again, if they adopted new constitutions with black voting, and ratified the pending civil rights constitutional amendment. All men disqualified from holding office by the pending amendment—roughly all southerners who had held state or federal office before the war—would be disqualified from participating in the process of forming new state constitutions. By any standard, this bill was an extreme measure, placing millions of American citizens under military governors and denying them their political rights unless and until they adopted certain laws.[2]

Congressional Republicans were also concerned that Johnson would abuse his power to remove federal officials. Their concerns were not without basis: Johnson had already forced three Republicans out of his cabinet and replaced them with Democrats; he had also removed hundreds of Republicans from lower federal positions. As governor, Seward once remarked that it was impossible to please people with patronage; for every friend one made through an appointment, one also made five new enemies. Johnson could have made a similar remark, for his patronage policy was unpopular not only with Republicans but also with Democrats, who wanted him to remove more Republicans and especially Seward. *The Nation* remarked that Seward was the "particular aversion" of the Democrats: "Their leaders hate him cordially, but the rank and file abhor him with an intensity which the leaders could not control if they would."[3]

The Republican remedy for Johnson's removals was a tenure of office bill, also passed and presented to Johnson in February 1867. The bill would prohibit the president from removing, without the prior consent of the Senate, any official whose initial appointment had required Senate consent. Many Republicans were especially concerned to protect Stanton: the secretary of war was a critical figure in military reconstruction and Stanton was working well with the Radicals. Other Republicans, however, believed that even Johnson deserved the right to remove his senior advisers. The result of this dispute was an awkward compromise in the section of the tenure of office bill on cabinet officers, saying they could hold office during the term of the president who appointed them. Did this language mean that Johnson could remove Stanton because he had been appointed by Lincoln? Or did it mean that Johnson could not remove Stanton until March 1869, because that would be the end of Lincoln's second term? Even as the bill passed, the answer was not clear.[4]

Johnson and Seward believed that both the military reconstruction bill and the tenure bill were unwise and unconstitutional. Although Stanton often disagreed with his colleagues and the president, he agreed with them that the tenure bill was unconstitutional, and Johnson asked him to draft the veto message. Perhaps sensing a trick—an attempt to divide him from his Radical friends in Congress—Stanton pleaded that he had too much other work. Johnson then asked Seward to draft the message, which he did, with some help from Stanton. As drafted by Seward and presented by Johnson, the veto message was moderate and learned, quoting legal authorities to prove that Congress could not limit the president's removal power as the bill attempted to do. Scholars now generally agree that Johnson and Seward were right—that the tenure bill was unconstitutional—but this Congress did not care about such details and soon passed both bills into law over Johnson's vetoes.[5]

———

Congress was also engaged in the spring of 1867 in its first serious effort to impeach a president. The House Judiciary Committee investigated rumors that Johnson had corresponded improperly during the war with Confederate officials, that he had used federal funds without congressional approval, and that he had appointed unqualified men as governors of the southern states. As Welles noted, the Republicans had "no facts, no charges, no malconduct," but they were determined to find something "which can be tortured or twisted against [the President]." Seward testified before the committee for a full day in May, responding to a range of hostile but inept questions. One representative was convinced that the secretary had misused his influence to prevent publication of a damaging book. Other representatives tried through their questions to prove that Johnson and Seward had aided and abetted southern men in perjuring themselves in taking federal oaths of office. In June, on a narrow vote, the committee decided against recommending impeachment, but this did not end the threat against Johnson; Radicals were determined to resume their impeachment effort in the fall and winter.[6]

Johnson and Seward did score one major political victory during this spring: in April, the voters of Connecticut elected a Democratic governor and three Democratic members of Congress. Johnson told Welles that he was "much gratified" by the result and saw it as "the turn of the current." Others agreed: the *Charleston Mercury* viewed the election as a rebuke of the Republicans, who had "abolished the governments of ten states," placed them "under military despotism," and "dictated to them the terms of their admission into the Union." Seward asked Welles, whose home state was Connecticut, whether there was not some good man from the state who wanted a diplomatic position. "He felt anxious," Welles wrote, "to give recognition to Connecticut for the good work she had done."[7]

It is not surprising, given Seward's strong support for Johnson, that Seward as well as Johnson were targets for severe attacks. Representative Glenni Scofield of Pennsylvania assailed Seward for including the southern states not admitted to Congress when he counted votes on the constitutional amendment. Seward was like an old English hunting dog, Scofield said, only kept on because he "never bit the hand that fed him, nor barked on a false trail." The canine comparison elicited "laughter and applause," which the Speaker of the House checked with his gavel. When Scofield asked the Speaker whether his time had expired, Thaddeus Stevens interjected that "the Chair called you to order for doing injustice to the dog," which prompted "renewed laughter."[8]

Seward was also criticized for his role in the removal of John Lothrop Motley, the American minister in Vienna. Johnson received a letter in late 1866 from George McCracken, an American traveling in Europe, complaining about various American diplomats. According to McCracken, Motley would tell "every traveler" that Johnson had "deserted [his] pledges and principles" and that Seward was "hopelessly degraded." At Johnson's request, Seward asked Motley for his side of the story. Motley responded with a resignation, insisting that as an American he had a right to discuss public issues "within my own walls." Seward asked Motley to reconsider: he did not see any reason for Motley to resign. Seward told a friend that, when he showed a copy of this letter to the president, "to my surprise and regret" Johnson "insisted upon Motley's resignation being accepted." Seward was thus forced to intercept his letter by telegram to London. Charles Sumner, Motley's friend and patron, obtained the correspondence and denounced Seward on the Senate floor. The *Chicago Tribune* said that Motley was right: Seward was "hopelessly degraded."[9]

Some critics suggested that it was Seward and not Johnson who was to blame for the administration's policies. Stevens told the House that Seward had possessed Johnson like the devils in the Bible. "While [Johnson] was 'clothed and in his right mind,' he uttered the thoughts and sentiments of a statesman; but Seward entered into him, and ever since they have both been running down steep places into the sea." Thomas Nast made a similar point in a political cartoon, depicting Johnson as a Roman emperor, with Seward as the evil adviser hovering over him and whispering into his ear, as both watched whites slaughtering blacks in the amphitheater below.[10]

John Hay, recently returned from Paris and visiting Washington, wrote to John Nicolay that their friend Seward was "splendid in his present temper—arrogant, insolent, implacable—thoroughly in earnest— honest as the day." John Bigelow, also recently returned from Paris, noted that in spite of his scars, Seward's overall health was good, and he asked their mutual friend Weed whether Seward still had a chance for a presidential nomination. "None whatever," replied Weed, for "he is one of the most unpopular men in the country."[11]

———

Seward's initial interest in Russian America—the region we now know as Alaska—stemmed from his interest in whaling, which he viewed as both an important industry and an element of national naval power. In 1852, in the course of a Senate speech on whaling, Seward had recommended that the Navy survey the waters around the Bering Strait, already a favorite ground for American whalers. Seward was probably aware of the discussions in the late 1850s between his friend Senator William Gwin and the Russian minister Stoeckl about the possible American purchase of the Russian colony. Such awareness could help explain Seward's bold statement in his 1860 campaign speech that the towns and forts of Russian America would "yet become the outposts of my own country." In late 1864, when Seward learned that Russia might be prepared to sell the territory, he invited the czar's brother, Grand Duke Konstantin, the leading proponent of the sale, to come to the United States. Face-to-face talks, Seward wrote the American minister in Russia, "would be beneficial to us, and by no means unprofitable to

Russia. I forbear from specifying my reasons. They will readily occur to you." Konstantin did not come to America, but Seward did not forget the issue.[12]

In early 1866, Johnson received a petition from the legislature of the territory of Washington, asking the federal government to "obtain such rights and privileges of the government of Russia, as will enable our fishing vessels to visit the harbors of its possessions." As Seward later explained, he used this petition to raise with Stoeckl "the importance of some early and comprehensive arrangements between the two countries to prevent the growth of difficulties in the Russian possessions." Stoeckl's postwar reports to the Russian foreign minister show that he was worried that American settlers would soon take over Russian America, more or less as they had taken over the Mexican territories of California and Texas earlier in the century. Indeed, by the time Stoeckl departed Washington in late 1866 for a few months of home leave in St. Petersburg, he was convinced that Russia should sell Russian America to the United States. Seward almost certainly encouraged Stoeckl in these views.[13]

Stoeckl arrived back in the United States in the middle of February 1867, but remained in New York City for several weeks nursing an ankle he had sprained during the passage across the North Atlantic. As Stoeckl later reported to the Russian foreign minister, "I put myself in contact with the Secretary of State by the intermediary of one of his political friends who exercises great influence over him," and hinted that he was now ready to talk. This unnamed friend was probably Thurlow Weed, now living in New York City and editing the *Commercial Advertiser.* Weed's newspaper would soon emerge as one of the main advocates of the proposed Russian treaty.[14]

When Stoeckl at last returned to his post in Washington, he met with Seward, probably on March 11. After preliminary pleasantries, Stoeckl alluded to the Washington fishing petition and to other American efforts to obtain rights in the Russian territory, and said that Russia would never grant such rights. As Stoeckl hoped, Seward then raised the question of whether Russia would be prepared to sell the territory. As Seward hoped, Stoeckl responded that the Russian government had now authorized him to negotiate the terms of a sale. Seward said that before they started negotiations, he would need to speak with Johnson.[15]

At a second meeting a few days later, Seward told Stoeckl that al-though the president was "not inclined to the transaction," he would allow the secretary to negotiate terms. Seward would still need to confer with the cabinet, and Stoeckl offered to confer in parallel with key sena-tors and representatives. Seward instantly objected; as Stoeckl reported the conversation, he insisted that "this negotiation must be conducted in the greatest secrecy. Let us first see if we can agree. It will be time then to consult with Congress." Seward was surely right to prevent Stoeckl from talking with senators, for such discussions would have led to press reports, which would have led to criticism even before Seward and Stoeckl agreed on terms. As to price, Seward first mentioned $5 million, but before Stoeckl even reacted, he added that "we might even go to $5,500,000, but no more." Stoeckl may have countered with $7 million; he at least indicated that he was not prepared to accept Seward's price. Seward also made a curious request: he asked whether Russia would place pressure on Denmark to sell the Danish West Indies to the United States. Stoeckl was not at all enthused about this idea, but he agreed to raise the issue with St. Petersburg, which he dutifully did.[16]

On March 15, Seward presented to the cabinet "the draft of a treaty with Russia for the purchase of her American possessions on the Pacific for the sum of $7,000,000 in gold." Orville Browning, at the time the in-terior secretary, noted in his diary that "we all approved of the purchase but made some minor criticisms of the treaty, which is to be modified." A comparison of the draft treaty Seward presented at this meeting with the final text suggests that these criticisms were minor indeed, the ad-dition of a word here and there. Seward and Stoeckl had not yet agreed on price, but Seward presumably believed that he would not have to pay more than $7 million, so he sought cabinet authority for this sum. With cabinet approval in hand, he continued his negotiation with Stoeckl; it appears that it was only at this stage that Seward presented Stoeckl with a draft, which led to some questions about the wording. Stoeckl ob-jected, for example, to Seward's suggestion that the transfer take place upon the exchange of ratifications, even though payment would not occur for several months thereafter. Seward explained that payment could not occur in the next few months because the House of Represen-tatives, which would need to approve the expenditure, would not be in

Washington until December. He assured Stoeckl that once the treaty was signed, the faith of the United States would be pledged.[17]

Seward presented a revised draft to the cabinet on March 19. Again, the discussion was very brief: Browning noted that the treaty "was agreed by us all and is to be sent to Russia for approval," and Welles that "there was no division of opinion on the measure." Seward led his colleagues to believe that the treaty was already "concluded" between himself and Stoeckl, but in fact there were some open issues, including price. After the cabinet meeting, Seward told Stoeckl that he had faced significant opposition in the cabinet—a fiction—and that he could not go above $6,500,000. After some back-and-forth, Seward agreed to increase the price to $7 million and Stoeckl agreed to include the buildings of the Russian American Company, the state-sponsored privately owned company that had a monopoly on trade in Russian America. Stoeckl also accepted language drafted by Seward confirming that the transfer was "free and clear" of any claims of the Company or any other company associated with Russia. Stoeckl explained in his report to St. Petersburg that the Company's buildings "cannot be of great value," and certainly not the $500,000 Seward had effectively offered for them and for his legal language.[18]

On March 26, Stoeckl sent a long coded message to the Russian foreign minister to summarize the terms he and Seward had reached. These included the precise definition of the territory; the rights of the Russian citizens in the territory (either to stay and become American citizens or to return to Russia); the transfer process; and the price of $7 million. "I send this telegram," he wrote, "at the request of Seward who pays for it and who said to me that he has met with great opposition in the cabinet because of the sum agreed on and that for the affair to succeed it will be necessary to make haste and have the treaty confirmed by the Senate which is to sit for two weeks longer." Stoeckl may have thought Seward agreed to pay for the telegram, but Seward later denied it, with the result that an annoyed Stoeckl had to pay the telegraph company more than $9,000.[19]

At about ten o'clock on the evening of Friday, March 29, Seward was playing whist in his library with a few family members when Stoeckl was shown into the room. Stoeckl said that he had received telegraphic permission to sign the treaty, and suggested that they meet the next day to work out the details. As Frederick later recalled, his father pushed himself back from the card table with a smile:

"Why wait till tomorrow, Mr. Stoeckl? Let us make the treaty tonight."

"But your department is closed," Stoeckl responded. "You have no clerks, and my secretaries are scattered about the town."

"Never mind," said Seward, with a wave of his hand. "If you can muster your legation together before midnight, you will find me awaiting at the department, which shall be open and ready for business."[20]

Seward realized that the time had arrived to start conferring with Congress, and in particular with Sumner, who chaired the Senate Foreign Relations Committee. He sent Frederick to Sumner's house with a short note, asking Sumner to come to his house as soon as he could to discuss "a matter of public business." By the time Sumner arrived, Seward himself had left for the State Department, but Stoeckl was still at Seward's, and he and Frederick outlined the proposed treaty to Sumner. The senator listened and asked a few questions, but he expressed no opinion on the purchase.[21]

As promised, Seward and a few key colleagues were waiting for Stoeckl and his colleagues at midnight. Stoeckl said that his government had instructed him to seek several changes: Russia wanted an earlier payment date; it wanted to be paid in London instead of in Washington; and it wanted the United States to commit that it would not disturb for one year the existing arrangements to provide San Francisco with Russian American ice. Seward refused the ice contract request, standing by his position that the transfer must be "free and clear." As to payment, he explained again that it would be impossible to obtain payment before December, and that payment in London would be inconvenient for the U.S. government. Seward prevailed on all these points, but to persuade Stoeckl to sign, he agreed to increase the purchase price to $7,200,000, apparently without any authority from the president or the cabinet. The clerks prepared the final drafts in English and French, compared them carefully, and Seward and Stoeckl signed the treaty at about four o'clock on the morning of March 30, 1867.[22]

The Senate was set to end its session at noon on that same day, and Seward was at the Capitol early. Welles, who was also there, observed how Seward "made special confidants" of several senators, speaking with each of them separately, and Welles was both "amused" and "disgusted" by "the little acts and overpowering egotism he exhibited." The president arrived at the Capitol not long after Seward and Welles, and formally submitted the treaty for the Senate's consideration under a short cover note, no doubt prepared by Seward. For some reason, Seward thought it possible that the Senate would approve the treaty that morning, but there was no chance of this; Sumner insisted that the treaty be referred to his committee, and other senators needed time to review and consider the matter. Seward yielded, but he arranged for Johnson to summon the Senate into a special session, to start two days later, to consider both the Russian treaty and nominations.[23]

On the evening of this eventful day, Seward's dinner guests included John Bigelow, Gideon Welles, and Alexander Cattell, a Republican senator from New Jersey. Bigelow noted in his diary that Seward said the Russian treaty was just "part of a system of negotiations which he was conducting, he thought to a successful issue." Seward was alluding here to his discussions with the Danes and the Dominicans, through which he hoped soon to add tropical islands as well as northern lands to the United States. He boasted that his successes would force those "who used to say that our flirtations with Russia could never have any practical result" to reconsider their opinions. Welles was less charitable, complaining in his diary that Seward spent the whole evening "talking of himself and his doings and his plans."[24]

———

The one "fact" that most Americans know about Seward is that the press immediately mocked the proposed purchase of Alaska as "Seward's folly." This turns out to be incorrect. The phrase "Seward's folly" was not used in the spring of 1867—it was a much later invention—and the initial press reaction to the Russian treaty was almost entirely supportive. It was only in the latter part of 1867, as the nation learned of Seward's other proposed purchases, that the press started to criticize his territorial ambitions, and by the end of the year some newspapers were hostile to the Russian treaty as well. It appears that the only newspaper that said anything in early 1867 about the "folly" of the treaty was the *New York Tribune*, which asserted that "there is not, in the history of diplomacy, such insensate folly as this treaty." In 1874, *The Nation* claimed that at the time of the treaty debate, "Mr. Seward was much laughed at for his folly," and in 1880 a book by an Alaskan pioneer commented that Alaska was originally viewed "as Secretary Seward's folly." In 1891, in his biography of his father, Frederick wrote that the treaty was immediately denounced as "Seward's folly" and the territory mocked as "Johnson's polar bear garden." The myth that the press immediately denounced the treaty as "Seward's folly" is alive and well; it appears in standard textbooks and in the recent Oxford history of American foreign policy.[25]

Most newspapers in April 1867 supported the proposed purchase of Russian America. The *New York Herald* praised the agreement, especially because it increased the likelihood that the United States would acquire British Columbia. The *Daily Alta California* declared that "it is of the highest importance to the whole country, and to the interests of this Coast particularly, that the territory should be consolidated as soon as possible. The Stars and Stripes should fly without rival from Behring's Straits to Cape St. Lucas," that is, to the southern tip of Baja California. The *Chicago Tribune*, although it almost always opposed Johnson and Seward, nevertheless favored the treaty. Many papers emphasized that the treaty would strengthen the relationship between the United States and Russia. The *National Republican* declared that "if this country ever had a national friend it has been Russia," and commended the way in which the treaty would bring the two nations into friendly contact in the North Pacific, calling it "the greatest diplomatic achievement of the age."[26]

There were, to be sure, a few dissenting voices, notably the *New York Tribune,* still edited by Seward's former friend Horace Greeley. The *Tribune* opposed the treaty on every possible ground: that the territory was worthless; that it would be expensive to administer and defend; that the purchase would involve the United States in complications with Great Britain; that Seward and Johnson were merely trying to divert attention from their domestic difficulties. A few other papers could not resist the opportunity for humor. The *New York Herald* supported the

treaty but also printed a mock advertisement, stating that any impov-
erished foreign nation, wishing to sell excess territory, could apply to
Seward in Washington.[27]

Seward started his public relations campaign for the Russian treaty
within hours after he signed it. He immediately sent an outline by telegraph to Weed in New York, with the result that headlines in the late
Saturday edition of the *Commercial Advertiser* proclaimed a "grand acquisition of territory." The *Washington Evening Star* also reported and
commended the treaty on the day it was signed. The *New York Times*
extolled the treaty in several articles, saying it would provide ports
along the trading routes to Japan and China. The *Times* noted that the
United States would now possess territory on three sides of British Columbia, hinting that the treaty would lead to acquisition of that territory;
many papers made this same argument in favor. Indeed, the *Daily National Intelligencer* thought that the Russian territory alone "would be of
little value"; its acquisition only made sense if added to the intervening
British territory so that the United States could "possess the entire shore
of the Pacific."[28]

Seward realized that his own name did not have much weight any
longer, so he sought and obtained supportive letters from others, including Army generals Montgomery Meigs and Henry Halleck and naval
commodore John Rodgers. Spencer Baird, assistant secretary of the
Smithsonian, praised the possibilities of the Russian territory for fishing,
whaling, and trapping fur animals. Baird also noted that "surface wash-
ings of gold have been discovered on the headwaters of streams on the
east side of the coast range of mountains." Perry Collins, who knew the
territory from his work on the (now suspended) Russian telegraph, reported the presence of gold, copper, coal, and timber. "Taking it, then,
as a whole," Collins wrote, "the country of Russian-America cannot be
considered, as some would have it, a dreary waste of glaciers, icebergs,
white bears and walrus, and only fit for the Esquimaux." Seward ensured that these supportive letters were published in the newspapers.
He also gathered some of the key letters into a short pamphlet published by the State Department just before the Senate vote.[29]

Seward had some unlikely allies in this process. Representative
Thaddeus Stevens, who had recently denounced Seward as the devil,

now declared himself "unqualifiedly in favor" of the Russian treaty. Chief Justice Salmon Chase, with whom Seward had quarreled often under Lincoln, and who was now an opponent of Johnson, was also reported to support the treaty. Charles Sumner opposed Johnson and Seward almost reflexively, but at least at first he maintained a careful neutrality on the issue.[30]

During the ten days the treaty was pending in the Senate, Seward hosted four or five dinner parties for senators, in which he argued his case. Some of the newspapers mocked these parties; the *New York Herald* joked that "terrapin and Château Margaux will doubtless assist in the elucidation of this already knotty subject." The *New York Tribune* reported worriedly that "the influence of these Russian treaty dinner parties can be measured from day to day. Senators can be named who were positively against the treaty when it was sent to the Senate, and who now when interrogated half-apologetically confess their purpose to vote for it." Even senators who declined Seward's dinner invitations, like James Harlan of Iowa, asked him to come discuss the matter with them during the day.[31]

While Seward was hosting his dinners, Sumner was presiding over meetings of the Senate Foreign Relations Committee. According to notes by the committee secretary, Senator William Fessenden of Maine told the committee that he would support the treaty "with an extra condition," namely, "that the Secretary of State be compelled to live there, and the Russian government required to keep him there." Senator Reverdy Johnson of Maryland agreed, saying that the amendment would be "carried unanimously." These men were not strangers to Seward: he had been their colleague in the Senate and Fessenden's colleague in the cabinet. But Seward had become so unpopular that senators could tell such jokes, at least in the privacy of the committee room.[32]

In the first few days after the treaty was signed, many papers predicted the Senate would postpone consideration until December, when it would return to Washington for its regular session. Seward wanted an immediate vote, well aware of how events in the intervening eight months could change the political landscape. As the days passed in early April, the newspapers reported that it seemed more likely that the Senate would approve Seward's treaty. Even the correspondent for the hostile *New York Tribune* was forced to admit, in his report of April 7, that "the chances of ratification of the Esquimaux Acquisition Treaty, which were utterly desperate when it was presented to the Senate, improve daily."[33]

On the morning of April 8, Reverdy Johnson sent a brief note to tell Seward that the committee would probably approve the treaty that day. At one o'clock that afternoon, Sumner presented the treaty to the Senate and spoke for two hours in its favor. One paper reported that "Seward had his messengers in the lobby all afternoon, carrying letters to and fro, and distributing gorgeous invitations to his fourth Russian treaty dinner, given at 6 p.m." The next day, Fessenden moved to delay consideration; his motion failed by a vote of 29 to 10. Sumner then moved that the Senate approve the treaty, and his motion passed by a vote of 37 to 2. The vote on Fessenden's motion is probably a better measure of Senate support for Seward's treaty than the vote on Sumner's motion: substantial but not overwhelming.[34]

Two days later, Stevens wrote Seward to "congratulate you and rejoice at your safe deliverance." Alluding to the process of obtaining House approval for an appropriation to pay the purchase price, Stevens said he hoped the "afterbirth" would prove simple. He urged Seward to "go ahead and put through [the acquisition of] Samaná [Bay] and you may well sleep with your fathers. As I intend to out-live you I will deliver your eulogy of unmingled praise—the other little matters I will drop out." Stevens probably knew that he would not outlive Seward— he was already quite ill—but he was prescient in seeing that Seward's purchase of Alaska would prove to be his great accomplishment.[35]

———

Seward joined the president on two political tours during the summer of 1867, both of which proved far more successful than their disastrous "swing around the circle" in 1866. In the first week of June, they traveled to Raleigh, North Carolina, stopping as well in Chapel Hill, where they attended graduation at the University of North Carolina. In one of Seward's short speeches, he seemed to suggest that North Carolina should hasten along the path outlined by the Military Reconstruction

Act, even if this meant that its representatives in Congress would be black. "Come white, come black, come mixed, come altogether," Seward said, "only come, and all will be well again." The *Charleston Mercury* noted that Seward did not make a good first impression: one would never believe that the "careless looking old man, with a dingy beaver [hat] half covered with dingier crape, his clothes hanging so loosely around a hundred and forty pounds of flesh that they fit nowhere, a cigar between his teeth and a walking stick in his hand," was the great secretary of state. A closer acquaintance, however, revealed that Seward was "kind, genial, approachable and humorous—full of good points, diplomatic to a fault."[36]

Two weeks after their return to Washington, Johnson and Seward were off again, this time to New England, where Johnson was to dedicate a Masonic memorial in Boston. Seward, ever the Antimason, missed this ceremony, but he was otherwise generally at the president's side, often alluding to territorial expansion. In Baltimore, Seward said that "if we of the northern and eastern states have not room enough to live together without cutting each other's throats, why we will extend the area of freedom a little downward towards the tropics [and] up to the Arctic Ocean." In Hartford, he declared that "the people of the United States have now before them a prospect the most glorious that ever dawned upon any nation on the globe," the prospect of a free nation "extending from the Atlantic to the Pacific Ocean and approaching the shores of Japan and China." This line of Seward's speech was greeted with "great applause."[37]

Seward spent a quiet Sunday with the Adams family in Quincy, Massachusetts, attending church services in the morning and sitting on the house porch in the afternoon. Benjamin Brown French, the commissioner of public buildings in Washington, was among those present, and French noted in his diary that he could "hardly remember ever to have spent a more pleasant hour" than listening to Seward talk about statesmen now past such as Daniel Webster and Edward Everett. When French suggested that Johnson, unlike these men, seemed to speak without preparation, Seward said that he was mistaken, that "he had often been surprised at finding how much President Johnson relied on his previous reading and study for what appeared to be extemporaneous speaking." Charles Francis Adams, Jr., in a letter about this same visit, observed that Seward seemed to have aged considerably. He "speaks and thinks slowly, repeats himself, gets wound up and doesn't seem to have a clear idea what he is after." For Adams there were "few things sadder than the decay of a great mind."[38]

Seward found a cabinet crisis underway when he returned to Washington. Johnson and Stanton had been fighting a low-level war for months over Reconstruction policy, with Stanton often siding with the Radicals. Finally fed up, Johnson wrote to Stanton on August 5 that "considerations of public interest will persuade me to accept your resignation, if tendered." Equally fed up, Stanton wrote back that "considerations of public interest" dictated that he remain in office until Congress returned to Washington. Some newspapers and diaries suggest that Seward urged Johnson not to take any action against Stanton. If so, Johnson did not listen, for on August 11 he wrote Stanton again, suspending him from his office and naming General Grant as interim secretary of war. The reason for suspending rather than removing Stanton was to avoid any issue under the Tenure of Office Act. There was a very good argument that the act did not apply to Stanton, but even if it did, there was no question that the act allowed Johnson to suspend Stanton while Congress was not in session.[39]

Stanton's suspension led to speculation about Seward's fate. The *Chicago Tribune* claimed that "the report that Secretary Seward intends to resign his seat in the cabinet and retire to the shades of private life at Auburn, is received with the utmost indifference by the country." Seward was no longer an important political figure, the *Tribune* said, because he had with his steady support of Johnson "effectually committed political suicide." Johnson commented to his private secretary, William Moore, that he had "the kindest feelings" toward Seward, and would even "help him to the extent of his ability in reaching a nomination for the presidency." Johnson realized that Seward's prospects were slight, for he had "lost all strength in his own state," so that he was "rather a dead carcass." Still, Seward was a carcass that Johnson wanted to keep in his cabinet: when Seward offered his resignation on August 23 (perhaps to give the president flexibility to create an entirely new cabinet), Johnson refused it.[40]

Seward must have considered insisting upon that resignation, so that he could at last retire. Although he never criticized Johnson, at least not in surviving letters, he must have been frustrated with the way the president so often ignored his moderate tactical advice. He must also have been annoyed with how Congress impeded his ability to conduct foreign policy. Yet Seward remained in office for several reasons. He disagreed with Johnson on minor issues, but believed he was correct on the major issue: that the southern states should be allowed to govern themselves, not subjected to military rule. Seward also had much that he wanted to accomplish in foreign affairs, including the purchase of one or more islands in the Caribbean. On a personal level, after the deaths of Frances and Fanny, there was not much to draw him back to Auburn. He was happier in Washington, in the company of Frederick and Anna, and of politicians and diplomats, than he would be in the quiet of Auburn, in the company of William, his daughter-in-law Jenny, and their children, Nellie (five) and Willie (two). Charlotte Cushman, Seward's theater friend and Fanny's role model, had been right when she predicted that Seward would never willingly leave the stage.[41]

———

In the summer of 1867, a small item in the *New York Times* reported that the Pacific Steamship Company would establish a coaling station on what was then known as Brooks Island, now known as Midway Island. Seward must have been gratified: this was one of the many islands Americans had claimed under Seward's guano island law, and now some were being used for other purposes. The U.S. Navy soon took formal possession of Midway and advised Congress that the island would provide a key point, "especially in the event of a foreign war."[42]

In late October, Seward learned by telegraph that George Yeaman, the American minister in Denmark, had at last signed a treaty to purchase the Danish islands of St. Thomas and St. John for $7,500,000. Seward had been watching over Yeaman's shoulder for many months, sending him frequent instructions by letter and telegram. The signed treaty was, in the words of its leading historian, "a monument to

Seward's patience and spirit of conciliation." The *New York Times* praised the purchase, calling the harbor of St. Thomas "the finest and safest in all the Windward Antilles." The *Times* added (in words it would soon regret) that "the famous hurricanes of the Caribbean Sea, of which everybody has heard, and which prevail all the latter half of the year, are not known in this magnificent harbor."[43]

The news of the Danish treaty coincided with other good news for Seward: the fall elections. Although only state offices were at issue, the elections were viewed as a referendum on the dispute between Johnson and the Radical Congress, and Johnson prevailed throughout the North. More Democrats were elected than in previous elections, and three northern states rejected proposals to allow blacks to vote, a clear rebuke to the Radical program of imposing black voting nationwide. Johnson remarked to friendly crowds that "the people have spoken in a manner not to be misunderstood," and that he had faith the people would continue to support his approach to national reconciliation.[44]

Another piece of good news was that the United States had taken formal possession of the territory now known as Alaska. Seward had pressed the Russians to exchange the ratifications as soon as possible, and then pressed the Army and Navy to take possession of Alaska, which they did in Sitka on October 18. An American Navy ship in the harbor boomed salutes as the Russian flag was hauled down and the American flag raised. Because there was no telegraph, the news did not reach Washington until late November, along with reports of the first American settlers in the region. Seward knew that it would be difficult for the House to refuse to pay for territory over which American flags were waving and within which Americans were settling.[45]

At about the time he learned of the Alaskan ceremony, however, there was bad news for Seward, both from home and abroad. From St. Thomas there were reports first of a hurricane and then a devastating earthquake. In Washington on November 25, the Judiciary Committee voted five–four to recommend that the House impeach President Johnson. The committee did not give its reasons, but the critical member explained in the *New York Times* that he switched his vote because it now seemed Johnson intended to "prevent the reorganization of the southern states upon the plan of Congress." On this same day, November 25, Representative Cadwallader Washburn of Wisconsin—the former Wisconsin friend whom Seward had favored with a day's visit during the 1860 campaign—introduced a resolution to limit Seward's territorial plans. Washburn said that his resolution was not aimed at the purchase of Russian America, although he would oppose that purchase in time; what Washburn wanted was "to serve notice upon the Kingdom of Denmark that this House would not pay for that purchase; and to serve notice upon all the world that we will pay for no purchase that the Secretary of State, on his own motion, may see proper to make." There was no debate: Washburn demanded an immediate vote and secured the support of ninety-three members, all of them Republicans.[46]

Historians have attributed the substantial vote for Washburn's resolution to the news of the hurricane and earthquake, and no doubt some members voted for this reason. Others probably voted yes as an indirect attack on Johnson. Many representatives, however, voted with Washburn because they agreed with the newspapers that opposed any further territorial purchases. The *Hartford Courant* reported that Seward was attempting to buy Baja California and claimed he would "buy up the whole hemisphere from the glaciers of Greenland to the volcanoes of Terra del Fuego, if he only lives long enough and the credit of the nation holds out." The *Sacramento Daily Union* predicted that, if Seward was allowed to continue making purchases, there would be members of Congress from "Hawaii, Fiji, Madagascar . . . and perhaps Iceland and Greenland." Seward was aware of the shifting sentiment, writing to Yeaman that "the desire for the acquisition of foreign territory has sensibly abated" and that people seemed to "value dollars more, and dominion less."[47]

While Radicals worked to gather votes in favor of impeachment, Johnson and Seward worked on the president's annual message. Seward prepared a full draft that criticized Congress for excluding the southern states but expressed the hope that Congress would now admit them under their new constitutions, so they could participate in the 1868 presidential election. Johnson adopted a much harsher tone, especially on the way in which Congress had imposed black voting upon the southern states. He argued that blacks had "shown less capacity for government than any other race of people" and "wherever they have been left to their own devices they have shown a constant tendency to relapse into barbarism." However odious Johnson's remarks seem today, they reflected the views of many whites at the time, such as the thousands who had just voted against black voting in the northern states. In the foreign policy section of the message, which followed Seward's draft much more closely, Johnson emphasized the importance of obtaining a Caribbean port and reminded the House that it would soon have to appropriate funds for Alaska.[48]

The overall tone of Johnson's message was harsh and unrepentant; it was not a message to persuade moderates to vote against his impeachment. Four days later, however, they did just that; only fifty-seven Radicals voted for impeachment, while sixty-eight moderate Republicans voted against. Many Republicans agreed with James Wilson of Iowa, who argued that impeachment of a president required more than mere political disagreement, that it required some serious crime, of which there was as yet no evidence.[49]

———

The hostile newspapers were right to think that Seward was working on several fronts to acquire additional territory. Especially interesting, in part because of its relationship with Alaska, is Seward's effort to acquire British Columbia.

At the outset of 1867, British Columbia was a struggling colony stretching from Washington territory to Russian America, with a population of only about 10,000 people. Many of the residents were unhappy with the colonial administration and hoped to become part of the United States. The American consul at Victoria, the main town of the colony, wrote to Seward in late 1866 that the locals were "almost unanimous in their desire for annexation to the United States." A Victoria newspaper, reprinted in the *New York Times*, claimed in early 1867 that "nine out of every ten of our people—sick of the present misrule—look to annexation to the United States as the only hope for our Colony."[50]

Seward was engaged at this time in an apparently unrelated negotiation with Great Britain over the *Alabama* claims, claims against Great Britain for the damage done to the United States and its citizens by the *Alabama* and other Confederate cruisers during the Civil War. These ships, as Seward wrote to Adams, still the American minister in London, were "built, armed, equipped, and fitted out in British ports . . . and were harbored, sheltered, provided, and furnished, as occasion required, during their devastating career, in ports of the [British] realm." There were strong indications in early 1867 that Britain was prepared to pay the United States a reasonable amount for what might be called direct damages, such as the destruction of particular ships by the *Alabama*. This was not good enough for Seward, however. He instructed Adams that, if there was an arbitration or mediation, the arbitrators had to consider the whole controversy, as reflected in the wartime diplomatic correspondence, without "imposing restrictions, conditions, or limitations upon the umpire, and without waiving any principle or argument on either side." Since Seward had claimed, in this correspondence, that the premature British recognition of Confederate belligerency prolonged the Civil War, the British viewed Seward's suggestion as raising the possibility of immense indirect damages. Although Seward did not mention British Columbia in this connection to Adams, the astute minister suspected that the secretary was deliberately prolonging the *Alabama* claims negotiation in order to seek some British territory.[51]

Adams guessed correctly, for Seward had been thinking along these lines since at least early 1866, when his favorite newspaper, the *New York Times,* quoted and praised an obscure government report regarding Canada. "If Great Britain desires to propitiate this country," the report read, "would it not be her true policy to cede to us a portion of her remote territories, valuable to us, but of little value to her? Were she to cede us Vancouver's Island and British Columbia . . . might she not easily bring our claims to a peaceful solution?" Indeed, it seems that one key reason Seward was interested in Alaska is that he thought it would help the United States acquire British Columbia. In April 1867, John Bigelow, during a visit to Washington, suggested to Seward that "he should buy the British possessions on the Pacific and pay for them with the *Alabama* claims, of which bills for about $11 million have already been presented." Seward responded that he had already "sounded" the British government on this possibility, "but they dared not." A few weeks later, in a conversation with Charles Francis Adams, Jr., Seward said that there was now only one way in which the *Alabama* claims would be settled: by British territorial concessions that would enable the United States to "round off our North Western territory."[52]

The possible trade of the *Alabama* claims for British Columbia was soon in the newspapers on both sides of the Atlantic. *The Times* of London reported in May 1867 that "Secretary Seward has his eye on British Columbia and desires to obtain it." A complicating factor arose, however: the Canadian Confederation. The British North America Act, signed in March and effective in July 1867, created a national government for four eastern provinces, including Quebec and Ontario, and these eastern provinces started to "reach out" to British Columbia, inviting it to join them. A Montreal newspaper insisted in May that the new confederation must stretch from ocean to ocean, just like the United States. A Victoria paper predicted at about the same time that, in order to entice British Columbia, the new confederation would agree to assume the colony's substantial debts.[53]

There was a further complication: British honor. Adams wrote Seward in August 1867 to warn that "the maintenance of the connection with Canada is a matter of pride with the British nation," and that the British would only become "more stubborn" if there was "the smallest indication" that the United States intended to impair the connection. Perhaps because of this warning from Adams, perhaps because he expected that pro-American sentiment would increase in British Columbia over time, Seward did not press the British on the issue during the remainder of the year. It is clear, however, that he continued to believe that a trade was likely. Orville Browning recorded in his diary that at a cabinet meeting in January 1868, Seward expressed the view that "we would ere long get" the British territory "from the island coasts to the mountains." Seward suggested that all "grievances on both sides would be thrown into a heap and one would be taken out to balance another until all were disposed of. In this way we would pay for Columbia with the *Alabama* claims."[54]

Even as Seward was making these comments in Washington, a public meeting in Victoria was resolving in favor of "the immediate admission of this Colony into the Dominion, on fair and equitable terms." The one "essential condition" set out in this resolution was the "construction by the Dominion Government of a transcontinental wagon road." The *Daily Alta California* reported that the Victoria resolution was far from unanimous, that there were still many people in British Columbia who favored annexation to the United States rather than incorporation into Canada. But the trend in British Columbia, to the extent it could be discerned in the United States, seemed to be toward Canadian confederation and against American annexation.[55]

Seward was interested in Alaska and British Columbia in part for their own resources and in part because of their potential role in trade with East Asia. For similar reasons, he was keenly interested in the Hawaiian Islands (an independent kingdom at this time) and the Panama isthmus (part of Colombia at this time).[56]

In early 1867, American newspapers reported that the Sandwich Islands, as Hawaii was known, wanted to negotiate a treaty of reciprocity with the United States, to reduce or eliminate tariffs between the two nations. The trade treaty was signed in San Francisco in May. Seward approved, both because he desired to see more trade with the islands and because he hoped they would some day become part of the United States. The *Daily Alta California* commented that reciprocity with Hawaii "would be the first step toward an eventual peaceful acquisition of that territory, now regarded with covetous eyes by France and Great Britain." But there was opposition in the United States to the reciprocity treaty, not only from southern states whose sugar interests would be harmed but also from those who favored immediate annexation. Seward was aware of this, writing to the American minister in Honolulu that "if the policy of annexation should really conflict with the policy of reciprocity, annexation is in every case to be preferred." He pressed quietly for ratification, but in the end he was able to secure neither reciprocity nor annexation; the treaty was still languishing in the Senate when Seward retired in early 1869. As one historian has noted, however, "the groundwork for the acquisition of Hawaii had been laid; the Islands were just too important to remain independent."[57]

Like many Americans, Seward was fascinated by the possibility of a canal connecting the Atlantic and Pacific oceans. As early as 1856, he had argued in the Senate in favor of an appropriation for survey work toward "a ship canal near the Isthmus of Darien [Panama] to connect the waters of the Pacific with the Atlantic." After the Civil War, Seward conferred with senior military officials about the various possible routes. In March 1866, the Colombian minister in Washington asked Seward whether the United States would be interested in arranging and paying for a canal survey of the isthmus. Seward was definitely interested; he replied only three days later, committing the Johnson administration to work with Colombia toward a treaty along these lines. After this letter, however, there was a long silence, during which there was a change of government in Colombia. Impatiently, Seward instructed the American minister in Colombia to press the new government on the canal question, but there was no progress during 1867.[58]

Seward's interest in Latin America was not limited to possible acquisitions—either of islands or of the isthmus; he wanted to see the United States emerge as the leading nation of the American hemisphere. It was partly with this in mind that he proposed, in December 1866, that the United States host a peace conference among all the belligerents involved in the ongoing war between Spain, on the one hand, and Chile, Peru, Ecuador, and Bolivia, on the other. This was not an especially violent war—the fighting was limited to a few attacks by the Spanish Navy on South American ports—but there was the prospect of fighting as well as the certainty of trade disruption. By February 1867, Seward had reason to believe that the belligerents would accept his invitation, and the Spanish minister reported that Seward was gratified that Washington would be the center of these discussions. But in May, Seward learned that Chile, after previously indicating that it would accept the invitation, had now imposed conditions which were (in the words of the American minister) "equivalent to a rejection of the proposed conference altogether." There was not much press coverage of Seward's proposed mediation, but what there was fell into a predictable pattern: the New York Tribune opposed him and the New York Times supported him, calling his effort "noble and philanthropic." Undaunted by the adverse comments and the reluctance of the belligerents, Seward persisted in pushing them toward the conference table, but the issue was not resolved until after his retirement and indeed his death.[59]

———

As far back as 1852, Seward predicted that American trade with East Asia would some day be as important as its trade with Europe. He had a chance to show his interest in Japan in the summer of 1867 when an official Japanese delegation arrived in Washington, intent on learning about the American Navy and purchasing one or more naval vessels. He greeted the Japanese delegation warmly and drafted a speech in which the president noted that "we are advancing our frontiers near to Japan" and that the two countries were now connected by a "regular and frequent steamship line." Seward hosted the Japanese for a dinner at his house; he arranged for them to tour the Naval Academy; and he facilitated their discussions with the Navy, which resulted in an agreement to purchase the Confederate ram *Stonewall*.[60]

In early 1867, Seward learned that a few French missionaries and American merchants had been killed in Korea, a country at the time closed to all foreigners. Seward met with the French minister in Washington and suggested that their two nations should send a joint military expedition to "chastise" the Koreans and force them to accept trade treaties along the lines of those with China and Japan. Seward insisted that only the United States and France should participate in this expedition; this would counteract the impression, after the forced French exit from Mexico, of tension between the two nations. Nothing came of Seward's proposal, nor of another similar suggestion he made at the time: that the United States, in order to prevent attacks on Western shipping by pirates based on the island of Formosa, should "acquire and hold some strong naval port in the region these outrages so habitually occur." Both Seward's proposed Korean expedition and his suggested Taiwanese acquisition would have required force. Seward often talked of expanding the American empire only through peaceful means, but he was prepared in some circumstances to use force.[61]

Seward was always sensitive to the difficulties faced by immigrants.

In his initial instructions to George Bancroft, the new minister to Prussia, Seward explained that there was only one major issue between the two nations: naturalization. Prussia did not admit that its citizens could become naturalized American citizens, and so, when such citizens returned home for visits, they were often arrested for failure to fulfill their military obligations. Seward asked Bancroft to attempt to reach a fair resolution of this question with Prussia, expressing the hope that "other German states and possibly the governments of other countries would imitate her example," since similar issues affected naturalized American citizens from other European nations. Bancroft, a scholar who had studied in Germany in his youth, started work on the problem as soon as he arrived in Berlin, and signed the resulting treaty in early 1868. The treaty provided that Prussians who had lived in the United States for at least five years, and who had been naturalized as American citizens, would not be liable for Prussian military service upon their return to Prussia unless they stayed for more than two years, in which case they would be presumed to have renounced their U.S. citizenship. Similar provisions applied to Americans who moved to Prussia, although there were very few such persons. As Seward hoped, this was the first of more than thirty similar "Bancroft treaties," treaties that substantially simplified and improved travel for naturalized American citizens.[62]

At the end of 1867, the *New York Times* observed that Seward was almost as busy now as he had been during the war years. But whereas during the war he had worked to prevent European interference, he was now working "with extraordinary success to extend American influence round the globe, and to negotiate treaties of commerce, amity and relationship with all those powers and peoples with which we have heretofore had no intercourse, or with which it has been limited and imperfect." The *Times* noted that Seward had four treaties pending before the Senate—with Japan, the Sandwich Islands, Madagascar, and Venezuela—as well the treaty to acquire the Danish West Indies that would be submitted soon. Although some laughed that "Secretary Seward is traveling to the furthest ends of the earth to make treaties and establish relations with countries of which they never heard," the *Times* disagreed: "Nothing could be more important in regard to the growth of American influence and the extension of American power in the future." The United States would "raise up a vast commerce, extending over all the oceans and covering the Pacific with ships far more numerous than now sail on the Atlantic." America's extensive foreign trade would require treaty relationships. Thus, for the *Times*, Seward's diplomacy was not folly: it was "far-sighted and comprehensive."[63]

Historians have agreed that Seward deserves credit for laying, as the title of one book put it, "the foundations of the American empire." Another author has called Seward "the central figure in nineteenth century American imperialism." It is true that, in the end, Alaska was the only territory that Seward himself managed to add to the nascent American empire. But he placed markers on many other territories that the United States would later acquire: the Hawaiian Islands, the Panama Canal Zone, Puerto Rico, and the Virgin Islands.[64] Many of the men who followed through on his imperial vision were Seward men. One of his old New York friends, Hamilton Fish, was secretary of state from early 1869 through 1877: under Fish, the United States signed a reciprocity treaty with the Hawaiian Islands, signed a treaty (disapproved by the Senate) to acquire Samaná Bay, and attempted (both with diplomats and by force) to establish diplomatic relations with Korea. Another Seward friend, William Evarts, was secretary of state from 1877 through 1881; he signed a treaty of friendship with Samoa, establishing America's claims in that part of the world. Yet another protégé, John Hay, was secretary of state from 1898 to 1905, when the United States acquired control of Cuba, Puerto Rico, Guam, the Philippines, and the Canal Zone.[65]

Seward believed not only in territorial expansion but also in a commercial and diplomatic empire. He encouraged immigration to the United States, always seeing immigrants as a source of strength; he fostered international communication systems, such as the Field and Collins telegraphs; he wanted trade relationships with East Asia, and was prepared to back up words with arms; and he believed that Washington was the natural center for inter-American and international discussions. If he were alive today, he would not be surprised to learn that the United States has more trade with East Asia than with Europe, or that many of the most famous Americans are first- or second-generation immigrants, or that New York City is the world's financial center, or that the headquarters of the World Bank and the Organization of American States are both in Washington. Seward would not be surprised by these developments: he would be pleased.

"I'll See You Damned First":

1868–1869

As 1868 started, the Alaska appropriation bill was stalled in the House of Representatives. The opponents of the bill, led by Seward's former friend Cadwallader Washburn, argued that Alaska was worthless and that the House had the right to deny the appropriation even though the Senate had ratified the treaty and the United States had taken possession of the territory. The supporters, led by Seward's friend Nathaniel Banks, chairman of the Foreign Affairs Committee, responded that the territory was valuable and that the United States was morally and legally bound to pay Russia the promised purchase price. The *New York Tribune* had come around to reluctant support of the Alaska appropriation, noting that Russia was America's "most powerful friend" and that the Senate had "ratified the treaty by a nearly unanimous vote." The *Chicago Tribune*, however, insisted that Alaska was "a barren waste, which must be held forever at an annually increasing cost to the country." The *Boston Daily Advertiser* reported that Seward himself was more concerned about Senate approval for the Danish treaty than he was about House approval for the Russian bill. "With that wise shake of the head and knowing wave of the hand for which he is noted," Seward dismissed concerns about the Alaska appropriation, telling the reporter that "the matter's settled, the matter's settled."[1]

The Alaska appropriation not only faced substantive opposition; it was also threatened by efforts to link it with the Perkins claim. The widow of the late Benjamin Perkins claimed that the Russian government owed her hundreds of thousands of dollars, based on an oral agreement between her husband and Stoeckl for providing arms and powder during the Crimean War. The Perkins family had enlisted as lobbyists several prominent congressmen in its effort to press the claim, including Nathaniel Banks, Benjamin Butler, and Thaddeus Stevens. Stoeckl reported to his government that if anything was now paid on the Perkins claim, three fourths would go to the lawyers and lobby- ists; Butler alone would receive $30,000 if the claimants prevailed in their "swindle." Stoeckl had written to Seward in September 1867 to express his concern that those interested in this "pretended and stale claim against the Russian government" would try to force Congress "to withhold a portion of the consideration money of the Russian treaty." Although Seward assured Stoeckl that the United States would honor all its obligations under the treaty, it in fact required some work on Seward's part to persuade Banks and Stevens to abandon their prior support of the Perkins claim and to support a clean Alaska appropria- tion, without any Perkins deduction.[2]

Impeachment was also stalled in the House at the outset of 1868. Most Republicans hated Johnson, but moderate House Republicans did not believe that he had yet committed a "high crime or misdemeanor," the constitutional standard for impeachment. Moreover, because there was no vice president, the outcome of a successful impeachment would be to install as president the Radical Ohio senator Benjamin Wade, the president *pro tempore* of the Senate. Moderate Republicans, those who favored Grant for president, worried that if Wade became president, he would contrive to secure the Republican nomination, or that his radi- calism would enable the Democrats to prevail in the fall election. This was another reason why many Republicans were prepared to wait out Johnson's few remaining months in office; they were confident that he would soon be replaced by Grant.[3]

Grant started the year as interim secretary of war. In mid-January 1868, however, the Senate rejected Johnson's request that he be allowed to retain Grant in this role and insisted that Stanton be reinstated as secretary of war. Johnson believed that Grant had promised that, in this

scenario, he would hold on to the office for a few days in order to give
Johnson time to name another interim secretary. Instead, when Grant
learned of the Senate's decision, he quickly handed the keys to his office back to Stanton, who ensconced himself there with guards. Johnson
was apoplectic: he called Grant into the cabinet room and grilled him
in front of Seward and the other cabinet members. After Grant had departed, all the secretaries other than Seward agreed with Johnson that
he should remove both Stanton and Grant. Seward, Welles noted, was
"very reticent," saying that "on grave and important questions he always
preferred to take a night's sleep." Welles suspected that Seward, even
though he had supported Democrats in the most recent elections, was
at heart still a Republican, and in this case Welles was probably right:
Seward never abandoned the Republican Party, and he was thinking
ahead to Grant's likely tenure as the next Republican president.[4]

On a Friday in late February, the president issued two orders: one
notified Stanton that he was dismissed; and the other appointed General Lorenzo Thomas as interim secretary of war. If Johnson had discussed these orders with Seward, the latter almost certainly would have
advised against them; Stanton was not doing much harm at the War
Department, and he could not do much harm in the last few months of
Johnson's term. But Johnson did not confer with Seward, or with any
other member of his cabinet; he simply acted, confident as always that
he was right and his critics were wrong. When word of these orders
reached Capitol Hill, senators and representatives were shocked and
enraged. The Senate immediately went into executive session and, late
on the evening of the same day, resolved with only a few dissenting
votes that Johnson had no legal authority to remove Stanton and install
Thomas. In the House, Thaddeus Stevens limped from desk to desk
telling his colleagues that "if you don't kill the beast, it will kill you."
On Monday, February 24, after a brief but passionate debate, the House
voted to impeach Johnson. The vote was not even close: 126 in favor
and 47 against.[5]

In the days after this vote, the House drafted and adopted eleven
articles of impeachment, specifying the charges against the president.
Most of the articles were based on Johnson's attempt to remove Stanton,
but there was an eleventh, catch-all article that charged Johnson with

disrespecting Congress and violating the Military Reconstruction and Tenure of Office laws. The House selected seven managers, the lawyers who would argue the case before the Senate, including Benjamin Butler, an able trial lawyer before his Civil War service, and Thaddeus Stevens, the most ardent advocate of impeachment but now limited by failing health. In parallel, Johnson selected his defense lawyers, including Benjamin Curtis, a former Supreme Court justice, and Henry Stanberry, who resigned as U.S. attorney general to avoid any conflict between the two roles. At Seward's suggestion, almost insistence, Johnson added Seward's friend the New York lawyer William Evarts to the defense team.[6]

———

Seward strongly supported Johnson throughout the impeachment process. Frederick later recalled that his father, at some point during this spring, remarked that "if this impeachment should be successful, the presidency would become as uncertain a tenure in the United States, as in some of the South American republics." Johnson's secretary William Moore recorded in his diary that when one senator suggested to Seward that he could remain in office after the president's removal, "provided he did nothing to interfere with the progress of impeachment," Seward replied, "I'll see you damned first. The impeachment of the President is an impeachment of his Cabinet."[7]

Seward's main role in the impeachment was not selecting defense counsel or speaking with senators, but raising funds to pay for Johnson's lawyers and lobbyists. In a long article in late 1869, the *Cincinnati Daily Gazette* reported that Seward and two other cabinet members were approached in early 1868 by an "expert in all such matters," who claimed that men close to Radical senators were prepared to bet $50,000 that Johnson would be acquitted in the Senate. This unnamed expert asked if Seward and others were prepared to take the other side of the bet. Why would Seward and his colleagues enter such a bet? If Johnson prevailed, they would owe the expert $50,000, and the expert could use that money to pay the friends of the senators, who in turn could pay senators for voting for acquittal. The *Gazette* reported that Seward and Postmaster General Alexander Randall were in favor of the proposal, but that Treasury Secretary Hugh McCulloch was opposed, and the plan was not implemented.[8]

Not long after this incident, according to the *Gazette*, Seward and others summoned the lobbyist Cornelius Wendell to discuss ways to influence the Senate. Wendell's advice to Seward and the others was simple: "Buy your way out."

"How much will it cost?"

"Two hundred thousand dollars."

"We can't raise it."

"Then you can't acquit."

After considering the issue for a few days, however, Seward and his colleagues reportedly spoke with Wendell again and told him they had decided to attempt to raise the funds. Wendell claimed in an 1869 interview, also printed in the *Gazette*, that this group and its friends raised more than $150,000 for the president's defense, and that although much of the money "went into the pockets of those who raised it," tens of thousands of dollars were paid to agents who claimed they could influence senators. Johnson, according to Wendell, "knew nothing about" this sordid process, but Randall "was ready from the first," and Seward "also looked at matters in a business-like way."[9]

Seward's own papers contain glimpses of his role in raising and disbursing funds for the president's defense. One of his lobbyists, Richard Schell, wrote Seward from New York in March to report that he had raised $6,000; Schell said that, on the advice of Weed, he would not send it to Washington immediately, but give it to Seward when they met in a few days. In early April, Weed wrote that "the matter about which you feel so much solicitude is progressing, though not as rapidly as I hoped and expected. But I trust that you will not be disappointed." A few days later, Seward's Albany friend Robert Pruyn forwarded to Seward a check for $500 "for the object indicated." In mid-May, Johnson's lead defense lawyer Henry Stanberry presented Seward with a set of accounts for "the portion of the defense fund which came to my hands." The accounts show that Stanberry received more than $7,000 from Seward, and that in total Stanberry paid about $11,000 to himself and the other lawyers on the defense team. If only $11,000 was spent on defense lawyers, and if many times this amount was raised for the president's defense, it seems almost certain that much of the money went to lobbyists, and likely that some of it wound up with senators.[10]

The House managers hoped to start the Senate impeachment trial on March 13, but Johnson's defense lawyers obtained first one delay and then another. It was during this period of preparation and anticipation that the House Committee on Foreign Affairs had its first debate on the Alaska appropriation. When Chairman Banks presented a draft report to the committee in favor of the appropriation without deduction, Washburn presented his own draft report opposing any payment. After what one newspaper described as an "animated discussion" that showed the Banks report "could not be carried through the committee at present," Banks agreed to postpone consideration of the appropriation, until at least the first week of May. In a letter to Seward, Banks tried to put the best face on the setback, saying that he believed the House would not do any serious work during the imminent Senate trial of Johnson. Banks assured Seward, who in turn assured Stoeckl, that the House would ultimately approve the Alaska appropriation.[11]

Stoeckl was still worried that the House would insist upon deducting a sum for the Perkins claim. A deduction would not only reduce the amount paid to Russia, from which Stoeckl expected to receive a personal bonus; it might prevent passage of the bill entirely if the Senate, which also had to approve the appropriation bill, insisted upon payment in full. Apparently at Seward's suggestion, Stoeckl hired lawyers to help him in the Russian lobbying effort. The lead lawyer was Robert J. Walker, a former senator and Treasury secretary, and a personal friend of Seward's for many years. The second was Frederick P. Stanton, a former representative from Kentucky, the man whom Seward had rebuffed in his 1861 effort to secure the release of his imprisoned brother. A third member of the team was Robert W. Latham, one of the dubious lobbyists with whom Seward had worked to secure House approval for the Thirteenth Amendment. Although it was Stoeckl who retained the lawyers, his reports to the Russian foreign minister make clear that he and they worked closely with Seward. In one such letter, Stoeckl wrote that he had hired several "sure men," including Walker, "a very influential man in whom I can place full confidence." Seward, "in concert" with Walker, "employs all sorts of means in respect of members to range them on our side when the vote occurs." Seward and Walker, Stoeckl added, were working "with the greatest circumspection" to avoid compromising Stoeckl in any way.[12]

———

On March 30, before a packed Senate chamber presided over by Chief Justice Salmon Chase, Butler opened the formal impeachment trial by arguing for the conviction and removal of President Johnson. Butler stressed the charges relating to Johnson's attempt to remove Stanton, arguing that Johnson was seeking an unlimited and unrestrained ability to remove any executive officer. Over the next few days, Butler and the other House managers presented their case, and the defense lawyers harassed them by interposing objections, some of which led to lengthy legal debates among the senators. On April 9, in a far less crowded Senate chamber, Benjamin Curtis opened the case for the Johnson defense. In a quiet but persuasive tone, Curtis argued that the Tenure of Office Act did not apply to Stanton, and that even if it did, the act was contrary to the U.S. Constitution. Curtis insisted that Johnson did not have to be right on the legal questions: he just had to have a reasonable legal argument, for surely it was not a "high crime or misdemeanor" for the president to act upon a reasonable legal position.[13]

Curtis and the other defense lawyers then presented their witnesses, including Gideon Welles, who testified on the afternoon of April 17. Seward expected to be called as a witness for the defense immediately after Welles, so he spent the whole day on the Senate floor, chatting with friendly senators. The defense planned to have Seward testify that the entire cabinet, including Stanton, viewed the Tenure of Office Act as unconstitutional. Seward never got his chance, however, for the prosecution objected to similar testimony from Welles, and after losing the evidentiary argument, the defense lawyers decided against calling the other cabinet members. As the leading historian of the Johnson impeachment has noted, the House managers and Senate Radicals, by "muzzling some of the most prominent men in the nation," gave moderates the impression that the Radicals were "more interested in covering up than revealing the truth." Seward's willingness to testify, and then the evidentiary decision that precluded his testimony, may thus have helped Johnson more than Seward's testimony itself would have done.[14]

For some Republican senators, one of the main practical arguments for removing Johnson was that he effectively had no secretary of war. Lorenzo Thomas attended cabinet meetings, but he had no access to the War Department, where Edwin Stanton managed to retain the secretary's office and to continue issuing orders, although he had no contact with the president. Johnson discussed his options with Seward, and a compromise candidate emerged: John Schofield, the New York general whom Seward had sent to Paris in late 1865 as his informal emissary. Johnson was not especially keen about Schofield, but Seward vouched for him and Seward's friend Evarts acted as intermediary between the president and the general. On April 24, Johnson through Seward sent the Schofield nomination to the Senate, where it reassured moderate Republicans. Johnson's lawyer Curtis told his secretary Moore that "during the last twenty-four hours impeachment had gone rapidly astern."[15]

Closing arguments started in late April and continued into early May; as the future president James Garfield noted, Washington was "wading knee deep in words, words, words." The longest but perhaps best speech was given by Evarts, who skillfully used humor against Butler and his arguments. When Johnson praised the Evarts speech to Seward, the secretary responded with a smile that his friend "kept in pretty close touch with me." As they waited for a cabinet meeting to start, Seward mocked the worries of Interior Secretary Orville Browning and offered to bet him a case of champagne that Johnson would be acquitted. Treasury Secretary McCulloch shared Seward's cheerful optimism. Welles noted, suspiciously, that he could "get no facts to justify the confidence of the State and Treasury, farther than that they have talked pretty freely with Members." Perhaps one reason Seward was so confident was that, on that same day as the cabinet meeting, Weed and several other Seward associates met in New York City to discuss ways to raise and deploy further defense funds.[16]

At the request of the House managers, the Senate voted first on the catch-all impeachment article, the one thought most likely to succeed. On the morning of May 16, the day of the anticipated vote, Seward wrote to his friend Gertrude Sanford that if Johnson was convicted, "before the sun sets I shall retire from a public life now protracted too many years." The Senate was jammed with spectators; but Seward remained at the State Department, which is where he learned, in the early afternoon, that nineteen senators had voted against impeachment, just enough to acquit Johnson on this article. Seward immediately sent a short note to Johnson, congratulating him "upon the day's result." Not long thereafter, one of Seward's aides came into his office, where he found the statesman "lying on the sofa, with a copy of Rousseau in his hand, smoking and reading." The aide asked the secretary what had happened. Seward smiled and answered, then "went on reading, as if the country had not just passed through a crisis of tremendous importance." [17]

———

Two days later, on May 18, Nathaniel Banks secured the approval of the House Foreign Affairs Committee for the Alaska appropriation. Only two committee members voted against the bill: Cadwallader Washburn and George Morgan of Ohio. Their minority report argued that Alaska had no agricultural, mineral, or other resources to make its purchase worthwhile. Banks notified the House, when he reported the bill, that he would be away for several weeks, so that the final vote would not occur until at least the second week of June. [18]

The impeachment process was not yet over: the Senate had decided that it would vote on the remaining impeachment articles on May 26, and the House had appointed Butler and others as a special committee to investigate whether "improper or corrupt influences" had affected the initial Senate vote. The charitable view of Butler's goal is that he hoped to find evidence against Johnson that would persuade at least one additional senator that Johnson should be impeached and removed; the cynical view is that he hoped to find something with which to blackmail one or two senators. Butler summoned various witnesses to Washington, including Weed and Wendell, but none of them provided the damning details Butler needed. He issued a preliminary report on May 25, and pressed the Senate to delay its vote, so as to allow more time to investigate. [19]

There was thus great anxiety and uncertainty early on May 26 about what would happen: would the Senate vote as planned on the remaining impeachment articles, or would the Radicals secure a delay? It was a regular cabinet day, and Seward and the other cabinet members were with Johnson that afternoon at the White House, receiving reports by telegraph from Capitol Hill. At the outset of the Senate session, a Radical moved to postpone the impeachment issue for a month, but the votes on this motion were evenly split, and it was thus defeated. Several of the senators who had voted in favor of impeachment were now tired of the process, eager to have it come to an end, one way or the other. The senators then considered another impeachment article, voting in exactly the same way that they had ten days earlier, so this article also failed by one vote. Then the Senate voted on a third article, with the same result. After the third article failed, the House managers abandoned their effort and the Senate impeachment court adjourned indefinitely. Andrew Johnson had survived.[20]

After these final votes, there were rumors that the president would placate moderate senators by removing the unpopular Seward from the cabinet. Welles did not credit the rumors; he thought Johnson appreciated all the work Seward had done in his defense. "There has been money raised in New York," Welles wrote in his diary, "to assist the president in defraying his expenses in the impeachment trial, and Seward has been the channel of communicating, etc." Georges Clemenceau, the future French prime minister, was in Washington as a journalist, and he made a similar entry in his journal: "The influence, or at least the maneuvers, of the Secretary of State played a considerable part in the President's acquittal, and one does not shut the door of one's house on a man who has just saved one's life." Indeed, Seward's position in Johnson's cabinet was strengthened a few weeks later by the addition of his friend William Evarts as attorney general. Welles groused that the Evarts appointment reflected "the finger of Weed and Seward."[21]

———

Seward and Banks had hoped that the House would approve an Alaska appropriation by the middle of June, but perhaps because they did not yet have the votes in hand, Banks did not start the debate until the last day of June. On the eve of the debate, Banks wrote to Seward that he now counted a slight majority of the House in favor of the bill. Banks did not calculate, however, on developments during the debate. William Loughridge of Iowa offered as an amendment a lengthy preamble asserting that the treaty, because it required an appropriation, would not become effective and binding until it had the consent of both houses of Congress. Banks knew that this language would not be acceptable to the Senate, but it was hard for him to oppose, in the House of Representatives, an assertion of the House's own rights.[22]

Cadwallader Washburn spoke in favor of Loughridge's amendment, but added that if the House approved the Alaska appropriation, nothing could stop Seward's territorial ambitions. The secretary would secure Senate approval for his purchase of the Danish West Indies, Washburn said, and he was also negotiating a treaty to purchase Greenland and Iceland from Denmark. When this remark was greeted with skeptical laughter, Washburn waved a few sheets of paper which he said were an advance copy of a report being printed at the request of the State Department, showing that Seward was indeed working toward the purchase of the two islands. (Washburn obtained these pages from a reporter, who likely obtained them improperly from a clerk.) Seward was sufficiently concerned after this debate to ask Johnson to appeal *"personally"* to several specific Democrats to support the appropriation. He also forwarded to Johnson a letter from Robert Walker saying that "immortal as will be the vetoes of the president, sublime as his conduct during the impeachment, yet the great *act* of his presidency will be the acquisition of Alaska."[23]

In early July, Butler offered another amendment to the appropriation bill, this time to require that $500,000 be withheld from the purchase price in order to pay the Perkins claim. Butler is usually characterized as an opponent of the Alaska appropriation, and he did ridicule the purchase and the purchaser, saying that only Seward would be "insane enough to buy the earthquakes in St. Thomas and ice-fields in Greenland." But perhaps, if Stoeckl was right that Butler had an interest in the Perkins claim, Butler hoped that the Alaska appropriation would pass with the Perkins deduction. The chair ruled Butler's amendment out of order, and Banks mustered the votes necessary to sustain the ruling. Banks could not prevent the House from adopting Loughridge's amendment, however, and with that amendment the House passed the bill on July 14. Reporters noticed that both the lobbyist Robert Walker and the Russian secretary Waldemar Bodisco were busy on the House floor on this critical day.[24]

A few days later, the Senate also passed the appropriation, but without the House language about the House's constitutional role. The newspapers now predicted that the impasse over this issue would likely result in the Alaska bill being delayed until the next session of Congress, which would not start until December. Even Seward had to know that his Alaska appropriation was in trouble. What would happen if Alaska became an issue in the presidential campaign? What would happen if the president-elect, probably Grant, opposed the purchase? Fortunately for Seward and for Alaska, the small conference committee—including Sumner for the Senate and Banks for the House—was able to devise language acceptable to both sides. Over the vociferous opposition of Washburn, Butler, and a few others in the House, the conference version of the bill passed both houses and was signed into law by Johnson on July 27. Seward, greatly relieved, immediately left Washington for a few days of vacation in Auburn.[25]

On August 1, the Treasury Department presented Stoeckl with a check for the full purchase price, $7,200,000. Stoeckl wired $7 million to Russia, retaining $200,000 in the United States to cover expenses. Some of these expenses were quite legitimate; Stoeckl owed more than $20,000 as counsel fees to Walker. It appears, however, from two statements made by Seward, that other expenses were questionable. On September 6, during a Sunday outing, Seward described for Johnson various payments by Stoeckl. Johnson took the (for him) unusual step of recording the conversation in a memorandum. He wrote that Seward told him that John Forney, editor of the *Daily Morning Chronicle*, demanded that Stoeckl pay him $30,000 to support the Russian treaty. Since Stoeckl believed that "there was no chance of the appropriation passing the House of Representatives without certain influence [being] brought to bear in its favor," he paid Forney this amount. Moreover, "$20,000 was paid to R. J. Walker and R. P. Stanton for their services—N. P. Banks chairman of the committee on foreign relations $8,000, and that the incorruptible Thaddeus Stevens received as his 'sop' the moderate sum $10,000." All these sums, Johnson noted, "were paid by the Russian minister directly and indirectly to the respective parties to secure appropriation of the money the government had stipulated to pay the Russian government."[26]

Two weeks later, Seward's friend John Bigelow, the former minister to France, recorded in his diary a similar conversation with Seward. Bigelow was dining at Seward's house and admiring Leutze's painting of the Alaska negotiation when Seward asked if he would like to know how the treaty was consummated. When Bigelow said that he would, Seward said, "then I must put you under oath. Before that money could be voted $20,000 had to be given to R. J. Walker $10,000 to his partner F. K. Stanton $10,000 to ten members of Congress, and $20,000 to Forney who had lost $20,000 by the defalcation of his clerk." Seward continued: "$10,000 more were to be given to poor Thad Stevens but no one would undertake to give that to him so I undertook it [my] self. The poor fellow died [on August 11] and I have it now."[27]

Seward's reported statements to Johnson and Bigelow are troubling, and even more so when compared with his sworn response to questions from a House investigating committee in December 1868. "I know nothing whatever," Seward then declared, "about the use the Russian Minister made of the fund." If we believe Bigelow and Johnson, Seward's testimony was perjury.[28]

Seward did not explain to Bigelow or Johnson why he participated in Stoeckl's effort to purchase House votes for the Alaska appropriation; nor did he defend himself against the newspaper reports about his role in raising and distributing funds for the Johnson defense. It is not hard, however, to surmise his motives. Seward believed that it would be a national disaster for the Senate to remove Johnson from office; there would be unrest and instability, perhaps even a civil war between Johnson's supporters and opponents. Turning impeachment into a means of removing an unpopular president would weaken the United States for decades as future presidents would face similar political impeachments. Seward knew from history about the instability and fragility of republican governments: he feared that the removal of Johnson would lead the United States on a destructive path like that of the Roman Republic.

The defeat of the Alaska appropriation would not threaten the republic in this way, but Seward believed it would be an error: not only would it lead to the loss of a valuable territory, but it would limit the ability of future secretaries of state to make similar territorial agreements. Last but not least, Seward knew that Butler and his other opponents would use every weapon available in order to defeat Johnson and the Alaska purchase. In short, Seward was not a saint, he was a practical politician, and he was prepared if necessary to use dubious means to achieve great goals.[29]

———

Although Seward is rightly known today for the Russian treaty, he worked during his last year in office on more than a dozen other treaties, with nations as disparate as Britain, China, Colombia, and Denmark. In some cases these treaties were signed and approved by the Senate; in other cases they were signed but not approved; and in still other instances Seward was not able to reach any agreement. In early 1869, he boasted to the cabinet that he was about to send to the Senate the fifty-sixth treaty that the United States had signed during his tenure as secretary of state, "about as many [treaties] as had been made during the whole previous existence of the government." Welles could not resist remarking that President Washington had warned in his farewell address against "entangling alliances," a remark that "vexed" Seward.[30]

Seward hoped, through parallel negotiations with several sellers, to secure at least one port in the Caribbean. In early 1868, however, the separate strands of his policy came into conflict. A minister from the Dominican government arrived in Washington and was reported to be negotiating with Seward toward the sale of Samaná Bay. Since it seemed the United States would acquire a Dominican port for much less than the $7.5 million purchase price in the Danish treaty, the Senate had a perfect excuse to delay its debate on the latter treaty. Even Seward conceded, in a letter to Yeaman in Denmark, that it seemed the Senate would "prefer to wait for the result of my conferences with the Dominican minister before proceeding to a final consideration of the Danish treaty." The Dominican option was not the only problem for the Danish treaty, however. As Seward noted in a letter that summer, both parties in the presidential campaign were stressing economy rather than "the higher, but more remote, questions of national extension and aggrandizement." Because he did not have the votes to ratify the Danish treaty, Sumner was simply holding it in his committee, thinking it was "better to have it fail through oblivion rather than by an adverse vote."[31]

Late in 1868, Seward learned that it might be possible, instead of purchasing a single Dominican port, for the United States to annex the entire island, both Haiti and the Dominican Republic. Seward persuaded Johnson to include in his December message a statement that the United States should seek to acquire "the several adjacent continental and insular communities as speedily as it can be done peacefully, lawfully, and without any violation of national justice, faith, or honor." Seward and Johnson added that "even so direct a proceeding as a proposition for an annexation of the two republics of the island of St. Domingo would not only receive the consent of the people interested, but would also give satisfaction to all other foreign nations." In late January 1869, Seward informed Banks that he had just received "a reliable and confidential proposition" from the Dominican Republic, "which proposes immediate annexation, waives all preliminary stipulations, and addresses itself simply to the discretion and friendship of the United States." Banks offered a resolution to support annexation in the House, but it was defeated in early February. Seward, as always, was not easily discouraged, and he continued during his last days in office to work toward annexation, hoping it would occur early in the Grant administration.[32]

He had more success with China, where he drafted and signed what is now known as the Burlingame Treaty. The treaty is named after Seward's friend Anson Burlingame, who had served ably as America's minister to China from 1861 through 1867, and late in that year informed Seward that he had resigned his post and accepted an appointment to serve as China's minister to the Western powers. Seward, who had wanted for some time to improve upon the existing American treaty with China, welcomed Burlingame's new status. When Burlingame and his Chinese colleagues arrived in Washington in June 1868, Seward pulled out all the stops: he arranged for a formal state dinner at the White House, for informal visits to Capitol Hill and Mount Vernon, and for a reception at his own home, complete with "two instrumental bands."[33]

Amidst all this celebration, Seward and Burlingame discussed and negotiated their treaty, which they signed in Washington at the end of July. Scholars believe that Seward prepared the first draft of the Burlingame Treaty, and there are provisions which certainly *sound* like Seward, such as the section in which the two nations recognized "the inherent and inalienable right of man to change his home and allegiance, and also the mutual advantage of the free migration and emigration of their citizens and subjects respectively from one country to the other." The treaty committed the United States to respecting the sovereign rights of China within its territory and committed both nations to allowing migration and residence on a "most favored nation" basis for the other's nationals. Given the anti-Chinese sentiment in California, and given the ancient Chinese laws against emigration, the Burlingame Treaty was an important step for both sides, and it facilitated substantial Chinese immigration over the next few years.[34]

In early August 1868, on their way to Niagara, Burlingame and the Chinese delegation stopped for a day at Auburn, where they were entertained by Seward. His guest list included not only various local leaders but also such national leaders of the women's movement as Elizabeth Cady Stanton, Susan B. Anthony, and Martha Coffin Wright. When one of the senior Chinese praised the intelligence of the American women, Seward's sister-in-law Lazette Worden responded that "Chinese women would be intelligent also, if they were allowed to come into the parlor, instead of being kept in the back part of the house." Stanton recalled that the only answer of the Chinese delegates to the women's questions about Chinese society was "immoderate laughter." The interpreters explained that the Chinese had never before heard "women in all earnestness ask such profound questions."[35]

Seward was ambitious but not unrealistic in his treaty negotiations. He realized early in 1868 that he was not going to persuade the British government to part with British Columbia, and that he probably could not persuade Congress to ratify a treaty that abandoned the *Alabama* claims for what some would deride as mere territory. He therefore turned his attention to naturalization, pressing the British to sign a treaty along the lines of the Bancroft agreements. Many Americans, and not only Irish-Americans, were angered that the British were holding in their prisons men whom the United States viewed as naturalized American citizens, but whom the British insisted were still British citizens. In July 1868, in his initial instructions to Reverdy Johnson, the former senator from Maryland who was the new American minister to Britain, Seward stressed that his first priority should be to reach an agreement on naturalization. Johnson's second priority, Seward instructed, was to resolve the disputed boundary in the San Juan Islands, between British Columbia and Washington, by referring the issue to international arbitration. Only if he could resolve these two questions should Johnson turn his attention to the *Alabama* claims, perhaps referring them to arbitration as well.[36]

In early October, Reverdy Johnson and the British foreign minister signed a protocol in which Great Britain agreed that British citizens who were properly naturalized in the United States would be treated as American citizens. Seward commended Johnson for what he called a "brief, simple, and effective" document. Johnson then turned to the San Juan issue, and within a week he signed an agreement providing that it would be resolved through arbitration. Seward was pleased and excited: he wired Johnson in late October to ask him to hasten work on the claims convention. Johnson made haste and on November 10 signed a convention providing for an international arbitration to resolve the various claims pending between Britain and the United States.[37]

When he received the text of the claims convention, however, Seward was displeased. He told his cabinet colleagues that Reverdy Johnson had "exceeded his instructions and assented to terms which were inadmissible." This was rather unfair because Seward's initial instructions on the claims convention were vague indeed. Seward now instructed Johnson that the convention had to be amended to remove what he viewed as invidious distinctions between the *Alabama* claims and other claims. After a few weeks of back-and-forth, Seward realized that he would have to reverse himself if he wanted to have any agreement signed by the end of his term. He yielded on all but a few trivial points, and Johnson signed the convention in London on January 14, 1869. The American press reaction was almost entirely adverse. The

New York Tribune called it "an utter failure, a fraud on American claimants, and a treaty which the Senate will overwhelmingly refuse to sanction." Even the *New York Times*, after initially positive reports, was soon expressing doubts about whether the Senate should approve the convention. To some extent these comments reflected concerns about the details of the convention, and to some extent hostility toward Seward, who was viewed as subservient to British interests. The Senate rejected the claims convention in April 1869, but two years later it approved a similar treaty, providing Seward some measure of vindication.[38]

As the end of Andrew Johnson's presidency approached, Seward was especially interested in securing from Colombia rights to build a canal across the isthmus at Panama. When the negotiation faltered, he decided to send a more senior minister—Caleb Cushing, the eminent Massachusetts politician—to the remote Colombian capital. Armed with broad authority from Seward, Cushing arrived in Bogatá in the first days of 1869 and managed to draft, negotiate, and sign the treaty within two weeks. He then rushed back to Washington and delivered the document to Seward, who presented it immediately to the Senate. The *New York Times* exulted that "every political obstacle to the construction of the great inter-oceanic ship-canal across the Isthmus of Darien is now removed; it remains only to attack the physical obstacles forthwith." The *Times* predicted that there would be an operational canal within a decade.[39]

In late February, while the canal treaty was pending in the Senate, Seward explained his vision of the canal to a group of New York financiers. "We are Americans," he declared, "charged with responsibilities of establishing on the American continent a higher condition of civilization and freedom than has ever before been attained in any part of the world." (Was he aware of the echo of his first message as governor, in which he said that "our race is ordained to reach, on this continent, a higher standard of social perfection than it has ever yet attained"?) The canal was necessary to achieving America's mission, Seward argued, because "commerce can no longer afford to use the circuitous and perilous navigation around the Capes. It must and will have shorter channels of transport, and of these there can be but two—the one across the Isthmus of Suez, the other across the Isthmus of Darien."

The French were about to open the Suez Canal, which would allow ships easier access to Asia. "It would be a reproach to American enterprise and statesmanship to suppose that we are thus to become tributaries to ancient and effete Egypt, when by piercing the Isthmus of Darien we can bring the trade of even the Mediterranean . . . through a channel of our own." For Seward, "the Darien ship canal is the only enterprise connected with the great work of civilization which remains to be undertaken." Americans would complete the canal, he predicted, and it would be "transcendently profitable and transcendently useful."[40]

Both Seward and the *New York Times* underestimated the difficulties. Sumner's Foreign Affairs Committee approved the Cushing treaty and reported it to the Senate in early March, but the full Senate did not take up the issue immediately. Then, in mid-April, news arrived that the Colombian congress had rejected the treaty on various grounds. The real reason for the Colombian vote, the *Daily Alta California* said, was a "belief that they can get a higher price." The Senate deferred action on the Cushing treaty and never ratified it. Even after his retirement, Seward remained passionate about the canal, mentioning it often in speeches and letters, encouraging younger men to see the work through. He would have been proud that, after the unsuccessful French attempt to build a Panama Canal, Americans resumed the effort, and that his protégé John Hay handled the final treaty negotiations.[41]

———

Although Seward had less of a role in the 1868 presidential election than in previous ones, he could not keep himself entirely out of the fray. Early in the year, Andrew Johnson and Seward hoped that the Democratic Party, when it met in July in New York City, would nominate Johnson for president. Johnson had some supporters, especially among southern delegates, but he had many more enemies, including men who opposed him, in the words of Welles, because "he had retained Seward, whom they abominated, and to whom they could not be reconciled." After several days of balloting, the Democratic Convention nominated former New York governor Horatio Seymour. Johnson was not pleased by the nomination, but he much preferred Seymour to Grant, whom he thought had supported impeachment.[42]

Seward's position was more difficult: he was personally friendly with Grant and utterly unfriendly with Seymour, because of their long history in opposite parties in New York and Seymour's more recent attacks on Lincoln and Seward. Republican newspapers were soon saying that Seward would support Grant and that Johnson was annoyed with Seward. The *New York Tribune* reported that Johnson was putting his cabinet officers "upon the rack" and requiring them to swear allegiance to Seymour, but that Seward had refused, for "he rather thinks that he prefers Grant." But the papers may have exaggerated the tension between Johnson and Seward. Isabel Barrows, who worked for Seward for two months in 1868 as his stenographer, later recalled that Seward took the president for a picnic one Sunday, "away from all the cares and pomp of state." Seward told Barrows that he thought the president was "lonely" and that the outing "did the poor man good."[43]

Seward himself was lonely at this time; Isabel Barrows found him "much more cheerful" at his office than at his home, for "the shadow left by the death of a beloved wife and daughter seemed to linger in the house." When Henry Sanford, on leave from his post in Belgium, visited Washington in early 1868 with his young wife Gertrude, Seward took an instant liking to Gertrude. "All the affection you have bestowed upon me," he wrote to her as the Sanfords returned to Europe, "is heartily reciprocated." A few weeks later, in the summer of 1868, Seward started paying attention to Olive Risley, the twenty-four-year-old daughter of Hanson Risley, a minor political and personal friend from Chautauqua County. Seward had first met Risley thirty years earlier, when Seward was the land agent at Westfield; they had stayed in touch thereafter; and during the Civil War Seward had helped Risley obtain a position as a Treasury agent in Washington.[44]

Although Hanson Risley was by no means a close friend of the secretary, Seward became very close with his daughter Olive, taking her for long carriage rides while she was in Washington and writing to her often when she was out of town. Olive signed her letters "affectionately yours," and she and her younger sister Hattie stayed with Seward in Auburn for two weeks that summer, a period Olive described to Seward as "one of the brightest and happiest of our lives." By October, papers were commenting upon the "contemplated marriage." "He is lonely in his great establishments here and at Auburn," one paper reported, "and being an amiable, sportive, frisky, foxy, and infatuating man of fame and place, who would not marry him that was ambitious and the daughter of a politician?" Seward indeed loved Olive, but in many ways—as a companion, a daughter, a secretary, and (as time passed) a nurse. Moreover, Seward did not want, by marrying Olive, to deprive his sons of their rightful place and inheritance. So he waited; he was in any case far too busy with work to think about marriage.[45]

One of Seward's tasks that fall was to prepare a long speech he intended to give on the eve of the national election. His aide at the time, Samuel Barrows, recalled the care with which Seward worked: dictating to Barrows, marking up the drafts, then dictating additions. Barrows traveled with Seward to Auburn, where Seward put the full text aside— it would be given to the press—and started work on a short summary, just a few pages, from which he would speak on the day. Another visitor recalled that Seward's daughter-in-law Janet barred the doors to his office, but somehow Seward's four-year-old grandson Willie found his way to his grandfather's knee. "The revision of the speech went on," the visitor wrote, with the pages in one hand and the grandson in the other, "and I did not discover that the great speech suffered one bit from Willie's childish interruptions."[46]

Seward argued in his election speech that Johnson had merely followed the policy of Lincoln, a policy of "opening the easiest and shortest way for a return into the national family of the people of the southern states, who now repented their attempted separation." Johnson was opposed by the Radicals, who "entertained wild propositions of retaliation, confiscation, proscription, disenfranchisement, and other penalties, as conditions of reconciliation," and hindered by some Democrats, who insisted that "all conditions whatever were unnecessary, unreasonable, and unconstitutional." In the current presidential contest, because the Democratic Party had not yet proven that it would adhere without conditions to the Union, nor that it fully accepted the abolition of slavery, Seward said he would support the Republicans.[47]

The newspapers interpreted Seward's speech for their own purposes.

The *San Francisco Evening Bulletin* reported that "the venerable Secretary of State had declared himself emphatically for Grant." The *Cleveland Herald* characterized Seward's speech as a "direct and earnest protest against the Democratic party and the principles avowed by its leaders." The *National Intelligencer*, a Johnson paper, emphasized the way in which Seward defended Johnson and suggested that Seward still favored the Democrats. The *New York Sun* reported that "the speech does not meet the approval of Mr. Seward's patron in the White House, who, while appreciating the compliments, differs from him widely as to his conclusions."[48]

———

Grant prevailed in the November election, winning almost all the northern states and even a few southern states. Soon after the election, Seward traveled from Washington to New York City to attend the funeral of the wife of his longtime friend Richard Blatchford. Grant chanced to be on the same train, riding in the presidential car, and he invited Seward to join him. The two men spent several hours together, sharing cigars and stories. When Seward returned to Washington and mentioned this meeting to his colleagues, the Democrats among them were horrified. Interior Secretary Browning noted in his diary that, after all the conflict between Johnson and Grant, he found Seward's willingness to talk with Grant quite remarkable.[49]

In January 1869, Seward hosted an elegant dinner for Grant and his wife. The papers viewed this as an attempt by Seward to obtain a place in Grant's cabinet; one commented that Seward was a "simpleton" if he thought he could stay on as secretary into a third administration. Welles feared that Seward did have some chance, noting that he had "crawled abjectly to the man who for two months had not spoken to him." If Seward did hope to remain in office, his son Frederick did not recall such hopes; what he recalled was how his father commented sadly that he would soon leave Washington and probably never again see the city in which he had lived so much of his life.[50]

As inauguration day approached, there was an intense discussion within the Johnson administration about whether the president and cabinet should participate in Grant's inauguration. Welles, who hated Grant, argued that there was no need to join the ceremony; he reminded the president that his hero Andrew Jackson had refused to call upon John Quincy Adams, and that Adams then "very properly declined to attend the inauguration" of Jackson. Although Seward faulted Grant for his hostility toward Johnson—he noted that Grant disregarded the custom of appointing an intermediary to make arrangements with the outgoing administration—he urged Johnson to participate in the inauguration, as almost every president other than Adams had done. Even after Grant indicated that he would not follow the tradition of sharing a carriage with Johnson from the White House to the Capitol, so that the two men would have to proceed in parallel carriages, Seward pressed Johnson to accept the compromise, pointing out that the inaugural committee had assigned Johnson the place of honor, on the right side of the road.[51]

On the day before inauguration, Seward received a letter signed by all the senior officers of the State Department. Many of these men had worked for and with Seward for the full eight years of his tenure, and they now expressed their appreciation for his kindness toward them. Seward responded with equal warmth, thanking his staff for their long and faithful service. As to assessing what he and they had accomplished, "that will be the task of history, which delights in contemplating studiously the vicissitudes of nations; and that task can only be performed when we shall have ceased to be." To an Auburn friend who asked when the town should greet him at the train station, Seward wrote that he must "decline any public meeting, speech, drive, procession, ceremony, or demonstration." He wanted to return quietly and live quietly among his friends and neighbors.[52]

On the gloomy rainy morning of March 4, 1869, Johnson and most of his cabinet gathered at the White House at about nine. The fortieth Congress was coming to a close, and a number of bills awaited the president's review and signature. "The members of the cabinet were busy in reading and examining the bills," Browning noted, "and the president in approving, and in performing other duties." Seward arrived at ten, apologized for being late, and asked if they were now ready to leave for the Capitol. Johnson kept working without a word. At last Seward said that they would be late; "ought we not to start immediately?" Johnson responded, Welles wrote, that "he was inclined to think we would finish up our work here by ourselves." Johnson, Seward, and the others remained in the cabinet room until about half past twelve, when, knowing that Grant had been inaugurated, Johnson rose and shook hands with his former cabinet members. Then they all walked out under the north portico, where their carriages were waiting. Seward left Washington later the same day, pausing only briefly in New York before reaching Auburn, where he found a foot of snow.[53]

The end of Seward's long government career prompted a few reviews, one of which noted that the "great mystery of his life is involved in the question, how he could stand the wear-and-tear of association, politically, with Andrew Johnson, generally endorsing his policy, or what was called his policy." Although Seward's relations with Johnson will always involve some mystery, the main reasons he supported the president are clear enough. Seward disapproved of some of his tactics, but he agreed with Johnson that the southern states should be allowed to govern themselves, and to rejoin the national government, without undue delay or onerous conditions. Seward was especially reluctant to desert a president under attack, and he saw impeachment as an improper and dangerous attack, not just on the man but on the institution of the presidency. Seward hoped to strengthen the United States through additional territory and new treaties, and he believed, perhaps immodestly, that he was the best secretary of state available to Johnson. (In a conversation with Bigelow not long after his retirement, Seward said that only three men were qualified to serve as secretary of state: himself, Charles Francis Adams, and Charles Sumner.) After the deaths of his wife and daughter, Seward's work became even more important to him; he had little reason to return to Auburn. For all these reasons, he supported Johnson and stayed in his administration. Seward thus has the curious distinction of having worked with and admired both Abraham Lincoln, considered one of the greatest if not the greatest of all American presidents, and Andrew Johnson, generally considered one of the worst.[54]

CHAPTER 19

"Nothing Remained . . . But to Keep in Motion":

1869–1872

W hen Seward arrived home in March 1869, the family in Auburn consisted of the elder statesman himself; his third son William, now a banker; his daughter-in-law Janet; his granddaughter Eleanor, or Nellie, age seven; and his grandson Willie, age four. Seward's sister-in-law Lazette Worden lived a few blocks away in her own small house, but she was with the Sewards almost every day. Frederick and Anna lived in Montrose, a day's train trip away on the Hudson River, and they visited Auburn often. Seward's Army son Augustus was on leave in Europe for most of 1869, and after that on duty in distant posts, so his visits were rare. During Seward's first few weeks at home, he busied himself in arranging his books and papers and in remodeling the house to create a larger library. In the evenings he played whist; when he did not have enough family members to fill the table, he would summon a neighbor.[1]

Seward turned sixty-eight in the spring of 1869. His health was generally good, but he suffered from a progressive paralysis of his hands and arms, which made it first difficult and later impossible to write. He relied increasingly on others to write for him and help him with other tasks, although he did not like the resulting loss of privacy and independence. Seward claimed to Frederick that he would avoid politics, but he could never leave political issues entirely. Even before he arrived home, Republican papers reported that the former secretary, while passing through New York City, had voiced his approval of Grant's cabinet. Soon Democratic papers printed a letter Seward wrote to decline an invitation to a banquet to honor Johnson, in which he called the former president "the great statesman of Tennessee."[2]

Seward had been thinking for months if not years about an extended western and southern trip. He told Welles that he expected, within a few weeks after he left office, to be in Mexico City. Just after the inauguration, a paper reported that he would depart soon for the West and South America in order to round out his "personal knowledge of the most interesting portions of the world." Seward may have delayed a few weeks so that he could travel by the transcontinental railroad, for which he had argued as a senator and which finally opened in May 1869. He persuaded Fred and Anna to join him, but the traveling companions he really hoped to have were his friend Hanson Risley and daughters Olive and Hattie Risley. Even though the girls were eager and Risley was not occupied, having lost his job with the change of administration, he declined. Olive could not hide her dismay, writing to Seward that she dreaded being separated from him by the Rocky Mountains.[3]

On the day that the Sewards were set to leave, Seward drove from his house to the local cemetery where his wife and daughter were buried. A paper reported that he "reverently removed the faded flowers with which the tombs were yet strewn," then scattered new flowers on the two graves, "while his friends stood around with heads uncovered, and hearts overflowing with sympathy." Turning from the graves, Seward declared he was now ready to go to the Pacific.[4]

———

The Sewards started west by rail on June 7, stopping for brief visits in Detroit, Chicago, Cheyenne, Denver, and Salt Lake City. They attended services at the Mormon Tabernacle in the afternoon and chatted with Brigham Young in the evening. Former California governor Leland Stanford sent Seward both an invitation to speak in Sacramento on the Fourth of July, which he declined, and a special railcar, which he gratefully accepted. Seward informed friends that he did not want a grand public reception in San Francisco, but "it was of no use," as one local paper reported, for "the popular enthusiasm was irrepressible." Californians viewed Seward as their friend, both for the way he had defended their interests in the past and for his acquisition of Alaska, a region they expected would be a great benefit in their future. So he was greeted in San Francisco with cannons, fireworks, bands, and huge crowds anxious, in the words of one newspaper, "to catch a glimpse of the man who had done so much to glorify and aggrandize his country."[5]

Such crowds and press reports naturally raised questions. The *New York Sun* wrote that "those who suppose that Mr. Seward has finally retired from the political arena are mightily mistaken. He is as much a candidate for the presidency as ever, and it is as such that he is now traveling." The *New York Times* defended Seward, saying that if there was "such a thing as earning an exemption from personal abuse, by faithful public service, one would suppose that Mr. Seward has earned it." But speculation about Seward's political future would not die. The *Daily Alta California* argued that he was the right man for president for 1872: "He has stamped his name indelibly upon the records of his time, and upon the geography of his country, while too many of our presidents have been mere tallies by which the nation may vaguely determine its age."[6]

When Seward mentioned to friends in San Francisco that he would like to see Alaska, he was offered a ship and crew by one of the wealthy merchants, and soon he and his party were traveling up the California coast in the steamboat *Active*. After a day in Victoria, British Columbia, where he made gracious remarks about the friendship between the United States and Britain, Seward spent two days exploring the American side of Puget Sound, stopping at the tiny settlements of Port Townsend, Port Ludlow, Steilacoom, and Seattle. In his speech at Olympia, the capital of Washington territory, which at the time had a total territorial population of only 20,000, he declared that Washington would have "a destiny as great and glorious as that of any portion of our national domain." His presence and remarks proved to one local reporter that "although our territory, in point of numbers, is futile and weak, we were not forgotten."[7]

Seward and his party steamed slowly north through the magnificent scenery of the Inland Passage. When they reached Sitka, the largest town in Alaska, they spent their first three hours walking about the muddy streets, meeting what Frederick recalled as "Russians in their national dress, United States soldiers in their blue uniforms, Indians in blankets and feathers, and traders and travelers clad in the latest style" of San Francisco. Over the next few days Seward explored Sitka thoroughly: he attended services at both the Lutheran and Russian Orthodox churches, reviewed a military dress parade, toured the sawmill and the brewery, and was the guest of honor at a grand reception. He joked with one reporter that there was "no person in town of whom he did not know everything that was to be known."[8]

The general in charge of the region suggested that he and Seward should go yet farther north, to see the camp of George Davidson, a government scientist with whom Seward had worked in 1867 and who was in Alaska to record an imminent solar eclipse. Seward readily agreed. As they steamed along, Seward commented that the scenery surpassed anything in Europe and predicted that Americans would soon be spending their summer vacations in Alaska. After the *Active* anchored in the mouth of the Chilcat River and received confirmation that Davidson was not far away, Seward and a few others started upriver in canoes paddled by local Indians. They were about halfway from the *Active* to the Davidson camp when one of the Indians noticed the first signs of the eclipse. A reporter in the party wrote that the Indians "refused to row any further, so the party went ashore, and were soon seated around a fire in a most picturesque little dell on the river bank, between high mountains." After observing the entire eclipse, Seward and his companions resumed their voyage and reached camp, where they were entertained first by Davidson and then by local Indians.[9]

When Seward returned to Sitka, the residents pleaded with him to give them a speech, and he agreed, probably because he had been working on such a speech for some time. He reviewed the resources of Alaska: the animals, timber, and minerals, including coal, iron, and gold. He was confident that settlers would come to Alaska, he said, just as they had come to other western regions. After all, he had seen in his own lifetime "twenty new states added to the eighteen which before that time constituted the American Union, and I now see, besides Alaska, ten territories in a forward condition of preparation for entering into the same great political family." He predicted that Congress would soon grant Alaska a territorial government and that one or more American states would be formed out of the immense territory.[10]

Seward and his friends and family returned by steamer to Victoria, where he was honored with a grand banquet hosted by the chief justice of the colony. In his remarks, Seward praised the richness of the region through which he was passing, and predicted that it would grow even greater after "the extinguishment of the colonial system of continental Europe in the West Indies, and the construction of a ship canal, adequate to modern navigation, across the Isthmus of Darien." He then spent ten days exploring Oregon: walking and driving around Portland, traveling by steamboat up the Columbia River, and touring the rich farmland of the Willamette Valley. In the state capital of Salem, he gave another speech, predicting that Oregon, with its fertile soil and "vast hydraulic power," would serve as the "granary and manufactory" of the Pacific Coast. Seward's friend Weed, commenting on these western speeches in his newspaper, said that Seward seemed to have "grown young in his Pacific tour, and his nature is as fresh now as in his most vigorous days."[11]

———

Before leaving New York, Seward had assured his sister-in-law that he would return by September; he had business to attend to in Philadelphia, he said. Not long after he arrived in California, however, he changed his mind and decided to winter in California and Mexico, to which he had been invited by the government. In the latter part of September, the three Sewards traveled south by boat to San Diego, and then north by coach back to San Francisco: through Los Angeles, Santa Barbara, and San Luis Obispo. The trip was not easy or especially safe; Frederick recalled that their stage was once stopped by three grim men with rifles who proved to be "not highwaymen, but honest citizens, in hot pursuit of horse thieves, with the laudable intent of hanging them on the nearest tree." On another occasion, a burglar entered the rooms where the family was sleeping; Anna awoke and ordered him out. "The rascal left," a paper reported, "and it was fortunate for him that he did so, as the fearless lady, who is said to be a good shot, would doubtless in a few seconds have given him proof of her skill." [12]

During the first part of his western tour, Seward did not send many letters to Olive Risley, and her letters to him grew somewhat shrill. "I shall be terribly disappointed if my first letter from you is not a very long one," she wrote, asking him to describe "all that has happened to you since you left Denver." As if to make up for his silence, in the latter months of his trip Seward kept a daily journal for Olive, and sent her pages upon pages. In September, he described Southern California as consisting of orange groves and cattle ranches and said he wanted her to join him in Mexico. In October, he wrote that travel was difficult because "we speak no Spanish, except Fred, who cannot talk for six persons. No one understands us or speaks to us in intelligible English." (The Mexican government soon solved this problem by giving the Sewards the services of a young diplomat who "spoke English fluently and perfectly.") In early November, Seward wrote to Olive that "the illegible and ragged manuscripts which I sent you yesterday will show you how tenaciously I adhere equally to a purpose of my will or an affection of my heart. When shall I cease to regret that I have not the use of your flexible hand, instead of this enfeebled one of my own, to recreate the facts and record the observations which have made this last five months one of the most instructive periods of my whole life?" A few weeks later he closed his letter by telling Olive that he was "as anxious as you can be that we may meet again and not be separated." [13]

The Sewards arrived in Mexico in early October and remained three months, traveling slowly west across the country and stopping for long stays in the principal cities. Mexicans believed that Seward had played a critical role in forcing French and Austrian troops to leave their country, and thus in securing their independence, so he was hailed in every village and town as a great national hero. "Cordially as he had been invited and welcomed by the government of Mexico," Frederick later wrote, "Seward was hardly prepared for the warmth and depth of popular feeling, which he everywhere encountered." In many ways, Seward's tour of Mexico in 1869 and 1870 was like Lafayette's grand tour of the

United States in 1824 and 1825, during which the young Seward had first met the French hero. In both cases, an elder foreign statesman was greeted with almost excessive enthusiasm, in part because of his role in the war of independence, but also because the statesman proved by his presence that the young nation mattered in the world at large.[14]

In early January 1870, the Sewards sailed from Veracruz to Havana. Cuba was in the early stages of what is now known as the Ten Years' War, an unsuccessful rebellion against the Spanish colonial rulers. Seward, who was the guest of the Spanish and their local supporters, carefully avoided any comments such as those he had made just a few months earlier in British Columbia, about the "extinguishment of the colonial system of continental Europe in the West Indies." Instead, in the words of the *New York Times*, his rare remarks were "strictly non-committal in the matter of the insurrection." Seward spent much of his time on the remote sugar plantation of an American acquaintance, where he enjoyed what Frederick later recalled as quiet nights and "sunny days on the broad shaded verandah."[15]

When Seward arrived in Baltimore in late February, his first impulse was to return to Auburn. But after learning that the rail line was blocked by snow and the temperature in Auburn near zero, he decided to "tarry a while" in Baltimore and New York. Hanson Risley sent word from Washington to Baltimore that Olive was in bed with typhoid fever, but for some reason Seward did not make the short trip to see her. Perhaps he was concerned that he would catch the fever; perhaps he was embarrassed by the warmth of his Mexican letters. Olive wrote him later, when she could finally sit up to write, that she was "dreadfully disappointed." Seward's days in New York City were filled with visitors and dinners: it was in Anna's words "a levée every day and all day long—a regular State Department without the clerks and doorkeepers." Seward reached Auburn in early March and was greeted by friends and a severe snowstorm. He was "in good health and spirits after his long journey," according to the local paper, and "entertained his friends with all his usual hospitality during the evening."[16]

———

Seward spent five months in Auburn in 1870 between his two long foreign trips. He received many invitations to speak but declined all but one: that of the New-York Historical Society. After working on the draft speech with the aid of a local girl as secretary, however, Seward realized that he was not up to the task, and he sent an apology to the society. Seward's health was still generally good, but his hands and arms had grown weaker. He wrote to a friend that the best remedy was exercise: "raising blisters upon the palm of the hand" by rowing a small boat on Lake Owasco and by working in his garden in Auburn. Another form of exercise was a daily drive behind the two fine sorrel horses he had purchased in California. They were as "fleet as deer," Lazette reported to Augustus, and his father drove them far too fast for her taste.[17]

There were many visitors to the house that spring and summer. A delegation from Syracuse arrived one evening and Seward, while pleading that he would not give a speech, in fact gave one, talking about all that he had recently seen: "the glaciers, mountains, forests and tablelands, of the mines and caves, of the cataracts, rivers, lakes, seas and oceans, their majesty, beauty and riches." Henry Sanford, the former minister to Belgium, and his wife Gertrude visited, bringing from Florida two young alligators that they intended to send to the zoo in Paris. Mrs. Sanford played with the creatures "as if they were kittens," prompting Lazette to remark in a letter that "they would soon be old enough to devour their children."[18]

Charles Francis Adams and his son of the same name, on their way back to Boston from Niagara Falls, also stopped off in Auburn to visit with Seward. The senior Adams noted in his diary that "the first thing I noticed was the absence of that vivacity sometimes approaching even to hilarity which distinguished him formerly. His tone was subdued even grave. But his mind appeared as vigorous as ever, and his processes of ratiocination just as peculiar as they had been." Seward told Adams long stories about wartime Washington, about how he had persuaded the cabinet to declare a naval blockade of the southern ports and later, in the *Trent* crisis, to yield up Mason and Slidell. Seward's remarks about Lincoln confirmed for Adams "all my ideas of his entire unfitness for an executive position," and those on Johnson suggested "a man of low views, limited ideas and strong personal prejudices and passions." Since Seward admired both Lincoln and Johnson, it seems likely that Adams was reflecting his own prejudices rather than Seward's views. By the end of the stay, Adams was convinced that Seward was "the only really great man left in the country," although the country did not appreciate him and would not until after his death. Adams urged his friend "not to lose any more time but commit to paper his reminiscences of the events of that critical period." But he "seemed to shrink from it as too laborious a task." [19]

Seward had been thinking about a trip to South America, but he now started planning a much more extensive journey: to Asia and perhaps around the world. Hanson Risley agreed that he would join the first portion and his daughters the whole of this tour. The plan was that Olive would take notes that she and Seward would work up together, after their return, into a book. For the portion from San Francisco onwards, the party would also include the former postmaster general, Alexander Randall, and his wife, and the consul at Shanghai—Seward's nephew George—and his wife. According to the *New York Times*, all these people would "accompany [Seward] on his entire trip to China and India." [20]

———

There was a cheering crowd at the Auburn train station in August 1870 to send Seward and the Risleys on their way. In Salt Lake City, Brigham Young introduced them to eleven of his sixteen wives and almost all of his forty-nine living children. When Seward and his friends attended services at the Tabernacle, in the midst of 10,000 worshippers, Seward decided to take the Mormon communion, writing home that he did so "regardless of the religious and political differences." From Salt Lake, they continued by rail to San Francisco, where they toured the environs for a few days. On the morning of September 1, 1870, they boarded the commercial steamship *China* and sailed through the Golden Gate. [21]

After an uneventful passage across the Pacific, Seward arrived in Japan, where he remained for five weeks. Japan was in the midst of the Meiji Revolution, a period of rapid modernization and Westernization under the leadership of the Meiji emperor. Seward met with the Japanese foreign minister and, in an unprecedented honor, with the emperor himself, with whom he exchanged short scripted speeches. A working session with the senior ministers followed, at which they asked Seward questions about such arcane topics as the federal census. Seward remarked later that the emperor and his ministers were "sincerely emulous and progressive," and that the only danger was popular reaction against an excessively rapid change. Olive was especially interested in and troubled by the place of women in Japan. In the book she and Seward wrote upon their return, they recorded that she and her sister joined Seward to visit the foreign minister, in spite of the sign declaring that "neither horses, cattle, nor women, [are] admitted here." The "debasement of women," they wrote, "has tainted and corrupted the whole state." [22]

From Japan, the party crossed the China Sea to Shanghai, where they found the foreign community greatly agitated by the recent massacre of Catholics in Tientsin. Even though many Westerners were leaving Tientsin and Peking, Seward insisted that he would proceed as planned through those cities and others. As the party entered Peking with an armed escort, they were somehow split into small groups. It later emerged that the Chinese guides thought this would be a safer way to travel, but Seward wrote that he could not forgive those who allowed their carefully planned and armed group to be "scattered through the lanes, alleys and ditches of a semi-barbarian city." It was not easy to see the sights. The Temple of Heaven was officially closed, so the Sewards had to wait until the guard was looking the other way, rush past him, then bribe him to let them out. To reach the Great Wall, they traveled by mule litter, at a pace of about two miles per hour, and stayed in a rude country inn. [23]

Although Seward wrote home that his health was good, he was more and more dependent upon others. Alexander Randall reported that Seward was "suffering from a complete paralysis of both arms, so that he is deprived of the use of them in performing the most ordinary offices of nature." Not long after reaching China, Seward learned that the Randalls intended to return home in December, and that his nephew George and his wife would remain in Shanghai. Seward now faced a serious problem: how to continue his trip around the world with the two young women without offending Victorian propriety? He solved the problem in an unusual way: by adopting Olive as his daughter. In a new will, signed at Peking in early November, Seward left his home and real estate in Auburn in three equal shares to his sons, and all his other property in four equal shares to his sons and Olive. He waited a month to write to his sons about what he had done, and even then he was vague: "I have thought it just and convenient that Olive Risley who stands with me now as she has for a long time past in the relation of a daughter shall assume the family name." Frederick wrote back to his father that "the arrangement with Olive about her name seems to me judicious and sensible," suggesting that Frederick did not yet understand that Olive was to have a share of the estate. William, the banker, sensed that money was involved, but he heartily approved: "We are certainly under many obligations, as you are, to Olive for her kind care and affection for you, and I see no better or delicate way than this of rewarding its continuation."[24]

With this change made, Seward, Olive, Hattie, and Seward's servant continued their tour of China, exploring far up the Yangtze River. From Hong Kong they headed south: to Saigon, Singapore, Java, and Penang, reaching Madras, in British India, in early February, 1871. Here they rested for two weeks at the home of Seward's good friend Lord Francis Napier, whom he had known as the British minister to Washington and who was now president of Madras. Over the next three months, the party made a thorough tour of India, seeing everything and meeting everyone. Each night, Seward would dictate to Olive, sometimes for hours, so that she could not write her own letters, even to her father. In late April they departed for the Middle East, where Seward studied with particular interest the Suez Canal. They spent the month of May in Egypt, traveling up the Nile on a boat provided by the Khedive. Hattie Risley wrote home that after surviving the Egyptian heat, she believed she "could live in a red hot oven. The flies are swarming in thousands, and as I write my left hand is occupied in trying to keep them away."[25]

Seward did not have a fixed itinerary and he thought about spending a second winter abroad, in southern Italy or France. Hanson Risley, whom Seward invited to join the group in Constantinople, wrote back demanding that Seward bring his two daughters home immediately, without seeing Europe. But Seward ignored Risley's plea and they went on to visit Athens, Budapest, Vienna, Venice, Florence, Rome, Naples, Geneva, Berne, Paris, Berlin, Hamburg, and London.[26] Nathan Appleton, a wealthy young American in Paris, marveled at how Seward, when meeting other Americans, could "recall the time, place, and circumstances of their former acquaintance, no matter how slight it had been." Even though Seward needed the help of a servant to cut his food or raise his glass, Appleton noted that he would "talk away with a zest, and after dinner smoke his cigar, which he hardly ever took from his mouth on account of the difficulty of getting at it with his hand."[27]

Benjamin Moran, the secretary at the U.S. Embassy in London who had found Seward annoying when he visited before the war, now wrote in his diary that he was "a really handsome and memorable old man, with graceful manners and pleasing address." Like Appleton, Moran remarked on the contrast between Seward's illness and his energy. "His hands are crippled past use, his face is scarred, and he eats with difficulty; but his mind and body are vigorous, his eyes are bright and blue, and he can walk with ease." Moran added that "Miss Risley Seward is not handsome, but very intelligent, observant, and agreeable," and that her sister Hattie was "pleasing but by no means refined."[28]

Seward wrote his sons that, if possible, he would prefer to avoid New York City upon his return, and they arranged for him to bypass customs formalities and proceed straight to Frederick's house at Montrose, where he rested for a few days. The hour was late and the rain was heavy when he arrived in October 1871 at the Auburn train station, but there was a large crowd to meet him, and another crowd in his house on South Street. In his remarks, Seward said that "we are met together, I trust not to part again." He acknowledged that many had viewed his intended journey as "eccentric," but he hoped they would now see that it was reasonable. Upon his retirement he had realized that "at my age, and in my condition of health, 'rest was rust,' and nothing remained, to prevent rust, but to keep in motion." Now he was home, in Auburn, where he looked forward to enjoying "the same affection and friendship which have been the great happiness of my life."[29]

———

According to an account in the *New York Sun* by Henry Stanton, friend of Seward and husband of Elizabeth Cady Stanton, on the morning after his return Seward walked around his house and garden. He was greeted by his dogs and his servants, but he kept asking people to "show me the bird." Stanton was puzzled until they reached a large cage, about ten feet square, in which lived an eagle Seward had brought home from Alaska. The eagle "winked at Mr. Seward with his weather eye and seemed to say 'Mr. Secretary, you and I understand each other.' " Inside the house, Seward showed Stanton many boxes containing years of letters, a collection that suggested to Stanton that Seward's biographer would "not be at a loss for materials," but would instead have difficulty "to reduce even the most important and interesting of them within a compass suited to the mass of readers." Seward estimated for Stanton that in the months since his retirement, he had traveled more than 72,000 miles, and claimed that he only missed one meal because of illness during his entire trip around the world.[30]

Seward soon started to work with Fred and Anna on the memoir of his early years. Lazette reported to Augustus in early December that "the book progresses rapidly and will be a very interesting history of the events of father's political life." Seward had only reached 1834 in his narrative when Olive arrived, after a long visit with her father and family, and he suspended work on the memoir in order to work with Olive on their joint travel book. The two of them, often with a few others, spent much of the winter and spring at the family's small second house on Lake Owasco, where there were fewer interruptions. Lazette wrote in February 1872 that the "book of travels is progressing but not as rapidly as he would like." A few months later, Frederick visited the publishers in New York and reported to his father that they were "much pleased with what they have seen of the book, and were confident of a large sale."[31]

One reason that Seward was delayed was that he had so many visitors. His oldest and best friend Thurlow Weed came to Auburn, as did his friends John Hay and Charlotte Cushman. In spite of ever weaker hands and arms, and the pain in his face and neck, he exercised every day, explaining in a letter to Cushman that "the more sickness and infirmity chain [me] down, the more determination [I] summon to resist the fetters." He also devoted some time each day to the pleasures of the table and conversation, and Frederick recorded some of his table talk for posterity. "Work does not seek the idle man," Seward commented, "but thrusts itself upon the industrious one." On another occasion he remarked that "women are equal to men and have equal rights. But the rights they have are not precisely the same ones. The right of fighting, for instance, is not one of them."[32]

The year 1872 was an election year, and Seward was again involved, although in a very limited way. The Republicans nominated Grant for a second term, and the Democrats nominated Horace Greeley. There was much that Seward disliked about the Grant administration, but he was sure that Grant was more presidential than Greeley. Partisans on both sides sought Seward's support; some even suggested that he should go on the campaign trail. Finally, Seward wrote a public letter, published in early October: "I have seen no sufficient reason to withdraw [my vote] from the support of the principles and policy which carried the country safely through the civil conflict, or from the party organization and candidates who represent them." This was hardly an enthusiastic endorsement of Grant, although some papers chose to read it that way.[33]

Seward was busy in the early fall weeks with the travel book; a reporter noted that he was working on it five or six hours each day. "He expects to do a great deal of work before he dies," the reporter added, "and I hope he may be spared to accomplish his desire." He caught a chill and cough one evening, but there is no sense of concern in the family letters until October 10, when William sent a telegram to Frederick: "I consider father's condition quite alarming; a fever has set in which can not be controlled." Frederick and Anna left Montrose as soon as they could, but they did not make it to Auburn in time to see Seward die—apparently as the result of an infection in his lungs—at three in the afternoon on that same day. Seward was in his small library, surrounded by family members, including his adopted daughter Olive. As his eyes closed and his breath failed, his daughter-in-law Jenny asked him whether he had anything to say to them. "Nothing," he said, "only love one another."[34]

Four days later, the family opened the doors of their Auburn home at nine in the morning, and for the next four hours mourners processed by the open coffin. Most were ordinary people from the town and nearby: among those who sent flowers were Harriet Tubman, the former slave whom Seward had helped to purchase her Auburn house. There were also famous men among the mourners, including Thurlow Weed. President Grant sent the family a telegram to express his regret that he could not be in Auburn for the funeral of the "distinguished patriot statesman." At 2 p.m. the casket was taken by hearse the few blocks north to St. Peter's for the service, which included one of Seward's favorite hymns, "I Would Not Live Always." Hundreds of people then followed the casket to the cemetery, where Seward was buried next to his wife Frances. Not long after the grave was filled, the *New York Times* reported, "the rain recommenced, and darkness quickly came, gloomily closing the mournful scene."[35]

———

Seward was controversial in death as in life.

He had delivered an official funeral oration for John Quincy Adams, and in the spring of 1873 Adams's son Charles Francis Adams delivered the official oration for Seward in Albany. Adams of course praised the life and work of Seward, but he also made a few critical remarks about Lincoln. Gideon Welles, as soon as he read this address, started work on a response, which he published in early 1874 as a pamphlet of more than 200 pages. After claiming that he would not denigrate the dead, Welles did just that, saying that if it was not quite true (as Henry Clay purportedly said) that Seward had no convictions, then his convictions were neither deep nor durable. Seward, according to Welles, was arrogant, ambitious, meddlesome, unpleasant. For Welles, the only mystery about the scheming Seward was how he had been able to deceive the far wiser and better Lincoln. Jeremiah Black, the former secretary of state and attorney general, in a long letter published in 1874, wrote that Seward "knew less of law and cared less about it than any other man who has held high office in this country. If he had not abandoned the law, he might have been a sharp attorney; but he could never have risen to the upper ranks of the profession."[36]

The controversy continued. Henry Adams, in his essay on the secession winter, published early in the twentieth century, praised Seward's management of the crisis, saying that he "fought, during these three months of chaos, a fight which might go down in history as one of the wonders of statesmanship." Henry's brother Charles, however, concluded in his published memoir that Seward was "an able man, a specious and adroit, and a very versatile man; but he escaped being really great." Seward pretended to be a philosopher, Charles Adams wrote, but his philosophy "was not the genuine article." He was instead, "as men instinctively felt, more of a politician than a statesman." Charles Dana, the former assistant secretary of war, writing at about the same time as Adams, disagreed strongly, finding that Seward had "the most cultivated and comprehensive intellect in the administration" and also "what is very rare in a lawyer, a politician, or a statesman—imagination." [37]

Some elements of the indictment of Seward are correct: he was indeed ambitious and he was sometimes untruthful. His ambition was in many cases reasonable, but in some cases far from it, as when he tried in early 1861 to wrest control of the administration from Lincoln. His dishonesty was perhaps most dramatically evident when he denied, to the congressional committee, that he had any knowledge of how Stoeckl had used his share of the Alaska purchase payment. But the suggestion that Seward was an unpleasant person is quite wrong. Almost everyone who met him over the course of his long life liked him, for he was friendly and sociable. Even those who were his political enemies were often his personal friends. Seward's ability to get along with people of all classes and backgrounds, and to inspire among his friends fierce loyalty, were key elements of his success, along with his intelligence, diligence, persistence, and perpetual if sometimes excessive optimism. Black's criticism of Seward as a lawyer is also wrong, for Seward handled many major cases during his legal career, ranging from the dramatic Freeman murder trial to patent appeals in the U.S. Supreme Court. He may not have especially enjoyed his legal work, but he was good at it, as proven by the many clients who sought out his services.

Was Seward a statesman? He was an important governor of New York, in part because of what he did in building canals and railroads, but especially because of his defense of the disadvantaged: immigrants and their children, free blacks and slaves. When he moved to

Washington in 1849 as senator, Seward immediately established himself as the national leader of those who opposed the extension of slavery into the western territories. Although he is often called an abolitionist, he was not one: he did not share the intense moral outrage of the abolitionists, nor did he advocate an immediate end of slavery. Rather, Seward believed that slavery should disappear gradually, through the actions of slaveowners and southern state legislatures, a more practical approach than those of either the northern abolitionists or the southern extremists. He also believed, right up to the eve of the Civil War, that there would be no war over slavery. He was wrong in this belief, and wrong in his prediction that slavery would end peacefully, but he nevertheless deserves substantial credit for building the national consensus in favor of limiting and ending slavery.

Both as governor and then as senator, Seward had a grand vision of what the United States would become: an extensive territory, peacefully acquired, connected with rails, roads, and telegraphs, prosperous because of its vigorous free market economy, with extensive international trade, and open to immigrants from all lands. There were several reasons why Seward did not obtain the 1860 presidential nomination, but the main ones were that many Republicans disliked how he welcomed Catholic and other immigrants and feared his "radical" views on slavery. Rather than nominate Seward, whose views on slavery and Catholics were well known, the Republicans opted for the comparatively unknown Lincoln. Seward showed rare qualities in the summer and fall of 1860 in mastering his disappointment and in campaigning tirelessly for his rival. More than any other man, Seward ensured that Lincoln was elected president.

Seward's service to the nation continued during the secession winter when, even if his hope of compromise was unrealistic, he managed to keep the prospect of compromise alive, and thereby to keep the border states in the Union through Lincoln's inauguration. Seward slipped in early 1861 when he suggested to Lincoln that he rather than Lincoln should guide the administration, but what is remarkable is how well and how closely the two men worked together thereafter. Seward was the indispensable man of the Lincoln administration: the man who managed to keep the European nations out of the American Civil War;

the man who avoided war with Britain during the *Trent* crisis; the man who advised Lincoln on every aspect of domestic and foreign policy; the man who somehow kept his sense of humor and hope through the darkest days. Many people helped to ensure that the Union emerged from the Civil War as one nation, rather than splitting into two or more rival nations, but it is hard to name a single northern civilian other than Lincoln who contributed more than Seward.

Seward continued to serve as secretary of state through the controversial administration of Andrew Johnson. Many believed that Seward, in supporting Johnson's Reconstruction policies, abandoned his defense of the disadvantaged, leaving the southern blacks to be mistreated by their former masters. Seward did not see it this way; he saw himself as continuing the moderate reconciliation policies of Lincoln, which would allow the southern states to resume their proper places in the Union, and allow southerners to govern themselves. It was during the Johnson administration that Seward managed to pressure the French out of Mexico, without a war, and to arrange the purchase of Alaska, his greatest single accomplishment. As Dana observed, Seward's purchase of Alaska showed great imagination, an ability to see how that distant territory would strengthen the United States. Seward also started the process for other American acquisitions, including Hawaii, the Virgin Islands, and the Panama Canal Zone, and men whom he trained or influenced, such as John Hay, would complete the process. In one of his Kansas speeches, Seward declared that "heaven cannot grant, nor man desire, a more favorable occasion to acquire fame, than he enjoys who is engaged in laying the foundations of a great empire." Although "empire" is today generally not considered a positive term, Seward used it often, and he would be proud to be known today, as he should be, for his central role in founding the American empire.[38]

In sum, although Seward was far from perfect, his talents and accomplishments more than entitle him to be called a statesman. Indeed, other than presidents, Seward was the foremost American statesman of the nineteenth century.

ACKNOWLEDGMENTS

It is customary to thank librarians, and I am indeed grateful to the many librarians who helped me and my research assistants. But I am also thankful to the financial supporters of the libraries in which we worked. In this age of austerity, the friends of the library are more important than ever. The libraries and archives whose resources enabled me to write this book include: the American Antiquarian Society, Auburn Public Library, Boston Public Library, Bowdoin College Library, British Library, Buffalo & Erie County Historical Society, Cayuga County Historian's Office, Cayuga County Historical Society, Columbia University Library, Cornell University Library, Dartmouth University Library, Dauphin County Historical Society, District of Columbia Public Library, Duke University Library, Goshen Historical Society, Harvard University Library, Historical Society of Pennsylvania, Huntington Library, Library of Congress, Massachusetts Historical Society, Missouri Historical Society, National Archives, New Hampshire Historical Society, New-York Historical Society, New York Public Library, New York State Library, Oakland University Library, Phillips Exeter Academy Library, Sanford Museum, Schenectady Historical Society, Seward House, Smith College Library, Union College Library, University of California at Irvine Library, University of Chicago Library, University of Maine Library, University of Michigan Library, University of New Hampshire Library, University of North Carolina Library, University of Rochester Library, University of Washington Library, Wells College Library, Wisconsin Historical Society, and Yale University Library.

My research assistants allowed me to work in more libraries than I could have reached on my own. Thank you to Ange Clayton, Jeremy

Dibbell, Maggie Flamingo, Emily Freilich, Tom Guthrie, Molly Hassell, Kristi Martin, Sophia Palenberg, and Rohan Pavuluri. Theresa Palenberg helped with antique German handwriting.

Several people graciously shared their research notes with me. Thank you to Larry Denton, Jennifer Haines, Maury Klein, and Mark Stegmaier. A special thank you to Ken and Audrey Mochel for their work on John Austin.

Other friends read chapters and commented. I am especially honored that Donald Cole, my history teacher at Exeter years ago, reviewed and commented on the entire manuscript. Others who critiqued chapters include Dan Crofts, Larry Denton, John Evans, Jack Herney, Russell McClintock, John McGinnis, and David Stewart. None are responsible for the errors that remain.

My agent, Scott Waxman, deserves credit for choosing Seward from among the ideas I presented when we met years ago. My first editor at Simon & Schuster, Roger Labrie, improved every page of this book with his careful reading and editing. Ann Adelman was an excellent copy editor. Alice Mayhew and others at Simon & Schuster, including Rachelle Andujar, Rachel Bergmann, Jonathan Cox, Michelle Jasmine, Karyn Marcus, and Julia Prosser have also been quite helpful.

This book is dedicated to my wife. Masami was born in Japan, and does not know much about American history, other than what she has been forced to learn through her husband. She has not read this book, but she has supported it in so many other ways. Thank you, Masami-san.

NOTES

The principal collection of Seward Papers is at the University of Rochester; most of this material is available on microfilm, and to simplify life for future researchers, I have cited the reel numbers. The Rochester Seward Collection generally contains letters received by Seward from third parties and letters among the Seward family; it generally does *not* contain Seward's letters to third parties, except for some drafts. To compensate for this, it is necessary to turn to other sources, such as the Weed Papers at Rochester; the National Archives (for letters sent while Seward was secretary of state); and Frederick Seward's three-volume biography of his father. In many cases, Frederick's biography contains the only extant copy of letters from Seward. In some cases, when the manuscript copy survives, it is possible to see how Frederick edited these letters, sometimes significantly. When no other source is available, however, we must depend on Frederick, although he is not completely reliable.

For the period during which Seward was secretary of state, his official correspondence is available in two main places: the National Archives, in manuscript form, and *Foreign Relations of the United States* (FRUS), the published correspondence, now available online. Again, there are sometimes differences between the manuscript and the published version, but in cases where the precise wording is not critical, I have often cited to FRUS, since it is more accessible.

As Seward himself admitted from time to time, his handwriting was poor, and as he got older it became almost illegible. Quotations from his letters should therefore be treated with caution; others may read the same lines differently than I have. I should also note that I have

sometimes modernized spelling, punctuation, italicization, and capital-
ization, to make it easier for us to understand Seward.

In the notes which follow, if papers are cited without a place, the citation is to the principal collection of papers, such as the Seward Papers
and the Weed Papers at Rochester, or the Lincoln Papers at the Library
of Congress. Other collections, such as the Seward Papers at the Library
of Congress, are cited more specifically.

The following abbreviations are used:

Baker: George E. Baker, ed. *The Works of William H. Seward.*
          5 vols. (New York: Redfield, 1853–84)

CWL: Roy Basler, ed. *The Collected Works of Abraham Lincoln.*
          8 vols. (Washington, DC: Lincoln Sesquicentennial Com-
          mission, 1959)

FRUS: *Foreign Relations of the United States*, with year, volume,
          and page numbers

LC: Library of Congress, Manuscript Room

MHS: Massachusetts Historical Society

NA: National Archives, with microfilm publication and reel
          numbers

NYPL: New York Public Library

NYSL: New York State Library

OR: *Official Records of the Rebellion: A Compilation of the Offi-
          cial Records of the Union and Confederate Armies*, 128 vols.
          (Washington, DC: Government Printing Office, 1880–1901),
          with series, volume, and page numbers

Seward: Frederick W. Seward. *William H. Seward*, 3 vols., with dif-
          ferent subtitles. The first includes Seward's autobiography
          through 1834; the second two volumes are titled *Seward at
          Washington* with dates (New York: Derby & Miller, 1891).

UR: University of Rochester

NOTES FOR INTRODUCTION

1 For newspaper accounts of Seward's accident and recovery, see *Daily National Republican*, Apr. 6, 8, & 12, 1865; *New York Times*, Apr. 5, 7, 8, 10, 12, & 14 ("unable to leave his bed as yet"). On Booth and his colleagues, see Michael Kauffman, *American Brutus: John Wilkes Booth and the Lincoln Conspiracies* (New York: Random House, 2004); Edward Steers, *Blood on the Moon: The Assassination of President Lincoln* (Lexington: University Press of Kentucky, 2001); and James Swanson, *Manhunt: The 12-Day Chase for Lincoln's Killer* (New York: William Morrow, 2006).

2 Primary sources for the Seward assassination attempt include: Fanny Seward's account, in Patricia Johnson, "I Have Supped Full of Horrors," *American Heritage* 10 (1959): 60–65, 96–101; Frances Seward's letter, in Seward 3:278–80; testimony from William Bell, George Robinson, Augustus Seward, Frederick Seward, and T. S. Verdi in Benn Pitman, *The Assassination of President Lincoln and the Trial of the Conspirators* (Cincinnati: Moore, Wilsatch & Baldwin, 1865), 154–59; Ben Perley Poore, *The Conspiracy Trial for the Murder of the President* (Boston: J. E. Tilton, 1865–66), 1:471–80, 2:3–9, & 156–57; and *Trial of John H. Surratt in the Criminal Court for the District of Columbia* (Washington, DC: Government Printing Office, 1867), 1:249–55, 260–65; newspaper accounts such as *New York Times*, Apr. 15, 1865; *Washington Evening Star*, Apr. 18, 1865; and *Cincinnati Commercial*, Dec. 8, 1865 (Seward's own account); Seward 3:276–80 (Frederick's account). Secondary accounts include: Kauffman, *American Brutus*, 22–24; John Lattimer, "The Stabbing of Lincoln's Secretary of State on the Night the President Was Shot," *Journal of the American Medical Association* 192 (1965): 99–106; Betty Ownsbey, *Alias "Paine": Lewis Thornton Powell: The Mystery Man of the Lincoln Conspiracy* (Jefferson, NC: McFarland, 1993), 76–85; Swanson, *Manhunt*, 49–61; T. S. Verdi, "The Assassination of the Sewards," *Republic* 1 (1873): 289–97.

3 Fanny Seward Diary, Apr. 14, 1865, in Johnson, "I Have Supped Full," 99.

4 *Alexandria Gazette*, June 4, 1863; *Harrisburg Weekly Patriot & Union*, May 7 & June 4, 1863 (little bell); *Liberator*, Nov. 13 & Dec. 4, 1863 ("acting president"); Asia Booth Clark, *John Wilkes Booth: A Sister's Memoir*, ed. Terry Alford (Jackson: University of Mississippi Press, 1996), 124 ("other brains").

5 On Lincoln as Caesar, see Kauffman, *American Brutus*, 104, 116, 212–13, 353, 444 n. 40. On Booth and his family, see Nora Titone, *My Thoughts Be Bloody: The Bitter Rivalry Between Edwin and John Wilkes Booth That Led to an American Tragedy* (New York: Free Press, 2010).

6 Charles Francis Adams, Jr., *Charles Francis Adams, 1835–1915: An Autobiography* (Boston: Houghton Mifflin, 1916), 59–61; Baker 1:417 ("image of our Maker"); *New York Evening Post*, Mar. 24, 1888 ("Hottentots"); Henry Adams, *The Education of Henry Adams* (Cambridge, MA: Riverside Press, 1918), 104.

NOTES FOR CHAPTER 1

1 Seward 1:19–21; Baker 1:xii–xv; Frederick W. Seward Jr., *Obadiah Seward of Long Island, New York, and His Descendants* (Goshen, NY, 1949), 90–92; William H. Seward Jr., "Early Days and College Life of the Late William H. Seward," *Collections of Cayuga County Historical Society* 7 (1889): 24–25; Isaac Jennings, Probate Record, Orange County, New York; E. M. Ruttenber and L. H. Clark, *History of Orange County, New York* (Philadelphia: Everts & Peck, 1881), 585; Oliver Popenoe, *The Jackson Family*, on Poppino/Popenoe/Popnoe family Web site.

2 Seward 1:27–28 (quote); Federal Census 1820, Orange County, NY; *New York Times*, Apr. 28, 1872 (obituary of Polydore); Seward, *Obadiah Seward*, 92; Shane White, *Somewhat More Independent: The End of Slavery in New York City, 1770–1810* (Athens: University of Georgia Press, 1995).

3 Seward 1:20–28; Herbert Mapes, "A Short History of the Birthplace of William Henry Seward," 1936 (MS at the Seward House).

4 E. M. Ruttenber, *History of Orange County . . . and City of Newburgh* (Newburgh, NY: Ruttenber & Son, 1875), 265–72; New York State Department of Economic Development, *Population of New York State by County, 1790–1990* (on NY State Web site); Gordon Wood, *Empire of Liberty: A History of the Early Republic, 1789–1815* (New York: Oxford University Press, 2008), 314–29.

5 Seward 1:20–21; Seward, "Early Days," 26; Seward Notebook, Seward House.

6 George Baker, *The Life of William H. Seward* (New York: J. S. Redfield, 1854), 19; Seward 1:20–21; Seward, "Early Days," 26; Seward Notebook, Seward House.

7 Seward to Samuel Seward, Sept. 11, 1816, Seward Papers, Union College; Seward to Samuel Seward, Sept. 14, 1816, Samuel Seward Papers, Goshen Historical Society; Seward 1:29–30.

8 Seward to Samuel Seward, Nov. 22, 1816, Seward Papers, Union College; Seward to Samuel Seward, Oct. 21, 1817, & May 1820, Samuel Seward Papers, NYSL; Seward to Daniel Jessup, Mar. 10, 1817, & July 3, 1818, Seward Papers reel 1; Seward 1:25; Thomas Harding, *College Literary Societies: Their Contribution to Higher Education in the United States, 1815–1876* (New York: Pageant Press, 1971); James McLachlan, "The *Choice of Hercules*: American Student Societies in the Early 19th Century," in Lawrence Stone, ed., *The University in Society*, 2 vols. (Princeton: Princeton University Press, 1974), 2:449–94; Wayne Somers, ed., *Encyclopedia of Union College History* (Schenectady, NY: Union College Press, 2003), 459–61.

9 Seward to Samuel Seward, Jan. 10 & Feb. 18, 1817, Samuel Seward Papers, NYSL; Seward to Daniel Tuthill, Feb. 29, 1818, Samuel Seward Papers, Goshen Historical Society; Baker 1:xx; Seward 1:31–35; *A Catalogue of the New-York Alpha of the Phi Beta Kappa; Union College, Schenectady* (Schenectady, NY: Riggs, 1852), 15.

10 Seward to Samuel Seward, Sept. 30 & Nov. 18, 1818, Samuel Seward Papers, NYSL; Somers, ed., *Encyclopedia*, 425–26. The textbook for Nott's course was *Elements of Criticism* by Lord Kames.

11 Seward to Samuel Seward, Nov. 22, 1816, May 28, July 1, & Sept. 24, 1817, Mar. 5, 1818, Samuel Seward Papers, NYSL; Seward 1:32, 36.

12 John Wheeler to Samuel Seward, Jan. 25, 1819, B. Richardson to Samuel Seward, Feb. 15, 1819, Benjamin Hopkins to Samuel Seward, Jan. 18, 1820, all in Samuel Seward Papers, NYSL; Seward to Samuel Seward, Feb. 2, 1819, George Grier Papers, UR; Seward 1:36–40; E. Merton Coulter, "Seward and the South: His Career as a Georgia Schoolmaster," *Georgia Historical Quarterly* 53 (1969): 147–64.

13 [*Milledgeville*] *Georgia Journal*, Mar. 2, 9, & 16, 1819.

14 Seward to Samuel Seward, Mar. 9, 1819, Samuel Seward Papers, NYSL; Seward to Mary Seward, Mar. 11, 1819, Seward Papers reel 121 folder 4934.

15 Seward to Samuel Seward, Apr. 24, 1819, Samuel Seward Papers, NYSL; Rosetta Alexander to Seward, Apr. 11, 1866, Seward Papers reel 94; Coulter, "Seward," 160–61; Seward 1:40–42.

16 Seward to Samuel Seward, June 12, 1819 (from Savannah), Samuel Seward Papers, NYSL; Jane Westcott to Seward, Feb. 15 & May 17, 1820, Samuel Seward Papers, Goshen Historical Society; Seward 1:43–44.

17 Seward to Samuel Seward, Jan. 11 & May 4, 1818, Samuel Seward Papers, NYSL; Seward 1:47; *New York Spectator*, Sept. 23, 1834; Peter Bernstein, *Wedding of the Waters: The Erie Canal and the Making of a Great Nation* (New York: W. W. Norton & Co., 2005).

18 Annals of Congress, 15th Cong., 2d sess. 1204–05; Robert Forbes, *The Missouri Compromise and Its Aftermath: Slavery and the Meaning of America* (Chapel Hill: University of North Carolina Press, 2007); Sean Wilentz, *The Rise of American Democracy: Jefferson to Lincoln* (New York: W. W. Norton & Co., 2005), 222–40.

19 Seward to Samuel Seward, May 1820, Samuel Seward Papers, NYSL; Seward 1:25, 45–47; Somers, ed., *Encyclopedia*, 459–61.

20 Seward to Samuel Seward, June 6, 1820, Samuel Seward Papers, NYSL; Seward, "Oration on the Probable Permanency of the Union," July 1820, Abraham Lincoln Collection, Yale; *Schenectady Cabinet*, Aug. 2, 1820; Somers, ed., *Encyclopedia*, 176, 180. Seward's oration has not been noticed by prior biographers.

21 Seward, "Oration," Yale.

22 Seward to Samuel Seward, Mar. 19, 1822, Seward Papers Addition, UR; David Berdan to Seward, Aug. 1822, quoted in Baker 3:121; Seward to Kennedy Furlong, June 15, 1855, Seward Papers, NYPL; Seward 1:47–51.

23 Seward to Samuel Seward, May 11, 1825, George Grier Papers, UR; Seward to H. V. Howland, Apr. 21, 1850, Seward Papers, NYSL; Seward 1:55; Scott Anderson, *Entrepreneurs and Place in Early America: Auburn, New York 1783–1880*, PhD thesis. (Syracuse University, 1997).

24 *Auburn Free Press*, July 5, 1826; Seward to Samuel Seward, Oct. 12, 1826, & Apr. 22 & June 5, 1829, Samuel Seward Papers, NYSL; Seward to James Berdan, Jan. 20, 1828, Seward Papers, NYSL; Seward Legal Letterbook, 1827–30, Seward Papers reel 192; Robert T. Swaine, *The Cravath Firm and Its Predecessors*, 3 vols. (New York: Ad Press, 1946–48), 1:59–60.

25 David Berdan to Seward, May 4, 1822, & Jan. 22, 1823, Seward Papers reel 121.

26 Seward to Samuel Seward, June 3, 1823, Samuel Seward Papers, NYSL; Seward 1:55; Mrs. A. W. Fairbanks, ed., *Emma Willard and Her Pupils, or Fifty Years of Troy Female Seminary* (New York: Margaret Sage, 1898); Anne Scott, "The Ever Widening Circle: The Diffusion of Feminist Values from the Troy Female Seminary," *History of Education Quarterly* 19 (1979): 3–25.

27 David Berdan to Seward, July 22, 1823, Seward Papers reel 121; Seward to Samuel Seward, Aug. 12 & 15, 1823, Seward Papers reel 121, folder 4934.

28 *Cayuga Republican*, Oct. 27, 1824 (marriage); Frances Seward to Seward, Feb. 13, 1829, Seward Papers reel 113; Seward to Samuel Seward, July 9 & 22, 1830, Samuel Seward Papers, NYSL (Frederick's birth). The best study of the Sewards' marriage is Patricia Johnson, " 'I Could Not be Well or Happy at Home' . . . Politics and the Seward Family," *University of Rochester Library Bulletin* 31 (1978) (available online).

29 David Berdan to James Marshall, Feb. 23, May 23 & June 19, 1825, Berdan Papers, Michigan; Seward to Adelphic Society, Sept. 3, 1827, Seward Papers reel 1; Seward memoir of Berdan, Berdan Papers; Seward to James Berdan, Jan. 20, 1828, Seward Papers, NYSL.

30 Seward 1:53; Alexis de Tocqueville, *Democracy in America*, ed. Phillips Bradley, 2 vols. (New York: Alfred A. Knopf, 1945), 1:250; William E. Gienapp, " 'Politics Seem to Enter into Everything': Political Culture in the North, 1840–1860," in Gienapp, et al., *Essays on American Antebellum Politics, 1840–1860* (College Station: University of Texas, 1982).

31 *Cayuga Patriot*, July 5, 1825, & Dec. 1, 1830; *Cayuga Republican*, July 5, 1825; Seward to Samuel Seward, June 28, 1828, Samuel Seward Papers, NYSL.

32 The quote is from the *Cayuga Republican*, Nov. 7, 1827. See also Donald Cole, *Martin Van Buren and the American Political System* (Princeton: Princeton University Press, 1984); Evan Cornog, *The Birth of Empire: De Witt Clinton and the American Experience, 1769–1828* (New York: Oxford University Press, 1998); Jabez Hammond, *The History of Political Parties in the State of New-York*, 2 vols. (Albany: Van Benthuysen, 1842); and Craig and Mary Hanyan, *DeWitt Clinton and the Rise of the People's Men* (Montreal: McGill-Queen's University Press, 1996).

33 *Auburn Free Press*, June 13 & 20, July 18, 1827, & Sept. 2, 1829; *Reformer*, Oct. 1828; Seward to Samuel Seward, Aug. 16, 1828, Samuel Seward Papers, NYSL; Seward 1:53, 193–94.

34 Seward to Samuel Seward, Dec. 20, 1823, June 21 & Aug. 5, 1824, George Grier
    Papers, UR; *Cayuga Patriot*, Oct. 27, 1830; Hanyan and Hanyan, *DeWitt Clin-
    ton*, 117–80; Hammond, *History of Political Parties*, 2:163–67; Wilentz, *Rise of
    American Democracy*, 248–51.

35 Baker 3:335–37 (reprints address); Seward 1:55; *Auburn Free Press*, Oct. 6, 1824;
    Cayuga Republican, July 14, Oct. 13, & Nov. 10, 1824.

36 *Auburn Free Press*, June 8 & 15, 1825; *Cayuga Republican*, June 8 & 15, 1825;
    Seward 1:64–65; Stanley Idzerda, Anne Loveland, and Marc Miller, *Lafayette,
    Hero of Two Worlds: The Art and Pageantry of His Farewell Tour of America,
    1824–1825* (Hanover, NH: University Press of New England, 1989).

37 Baker 3:193–96; *Auburn Free Press*, July 6, 1825; *Cayuga Republican*, July 6,
    1825; *Cayuga Patriot*, July 6, 1825.

38 *Auburn Free Press*, Oct. 25 & Nov. 15, 1826; Hammond, *History of Political Par-
    ties*, 2:235–36; Seward 3:482–83.

39 Seward to Samuel Seward, Apr. 13, 1828, Seward Papers; Seward 1:71; Michael
    Holt, "The Antimasonic and Know Nothing Parties," in Arthur Schlesinger Jr.,
    ed., *History of U.S. Political Parties*, 4 vols. (New York: Chelsea House, 1973),
    1:576–77; Daniel Howe, *What Hath God Wrought: The Transformation of Amer-
    ica, 1815–1848* (New York: Oxford University Press, 2007), 266–69; William
    Vaughn, *The Antimasonic Party in the United States, 1826–1843* (Lexington:
    University Press of Kentucky, 1983), 26–29.

40 Seward 1:66–67.

41 Hammond, *History of Political Parties*, 2:256; Seward to Samuel Seward, Dec. 8,
    1827, Samuel Seward Papers, NYSL; *Cayuga Patriot*, Oct. 15, 1828, & Oct. 27,
    1830; Glyndon Van Deusen, *William Henry Seward* (New York: Oxford Univer-
    sity Press, 1967), 12.

42 Seward 1:69; *State Convention: Proceedings and Address of the Republican Young
    Men of the State of New-York: Assembled at Utica on the Twelfth Day of August,
    1828* (Utica, NY: Northway & Porter, 1828); *New York Spectator*, Sept. 25, 1834.

43 *Auburn Free Press*, Oct. 15 & Nov. 12 & 19, 1828; *Cayuga Patriot*, Oct. 8, 15,
    22, & 29, 1828; *Cayuga Republican*, Oct. 1, 8, & 15, 1828; Donald B. Cole,
    *Vindicating Andrew Jackson: The 1828 Election and the Rise of the Two-Party
    System* (Lawrence: University of Kansas Press, 2009); Seward 1:72–73 (memoir);
    Vaughn, *Antimasonic Party*, 28–32.

44 *Proceedings of a Convention . . . February 1829* (Albany: Weed & Sprague,
    1829); *Auburn Free Press*, Apr. 1 & Nov. 11, 1829; *Cayuga Patriot*, Apr. 8 & Nov.
    11, 1829; *Onondaga Register*, Mar. 4, 1829; Seward to Samuel Seward, Aug. 21,
    1829, Samuel Seward Papers, NYSL.

45 *Proceedings of the Anti-Masonic Republican Convention . . . January 1, 1830*
    (Auburn: T. M. Skinner, 1830); *Albany Argus*, Feb. 27, Mar. 1 & 23, 1830; *Albany
    Evening Journal*, Mar. 22, 1830 (1st issue); Charles McCarthy, *The Antimasonic*

Party: A Study of Political Antimasonry in the United States, 1827–1840 (Washington, DC: Government Printing Office, 1903), 392–94; Seward 1:76–77; Glyndon Van Deusen, *Thurlow Weed: Wizard of the Lobby* (Boston: Little, Brown, 1947), 54–55.

46 *Albany Evening Journal Extra*, Nov. 1830; Harriet A. Barnes, ed., *Autobiography of Thurlow Weed* (Boston: Houghton Mifflin, 1883), 167; Seward 1:55–56, 76–77; Van Deusen, *Weed*, 55–57.

47 *Cayuga Patriot*, Feb. 10, 1830; *Cayuga Republican*, Feb. 17, 1830; *Onondaga Republican*, Mar. 24, 1830.

48 Ward to Seward, June 21, 1830, Seward Papers reel 1; *Auburn Free Press*, July 7, 1830; *Onandaga Republican*, June 23 & 30, July 7, 14, & 21, 1830; *Ontario Phoenix*, July 14, 1830.

49 Seward 1:78–79; *Cayuga Patriot*, Aug. 25, 1830; *Cayuga Republican*, Sept. 1, 1830; *Proceedings of the Anti-Masonic Convention . . . August 11, 1830* (Utica: W. Williams, 1830); McCarthy, *Antimasonic Party*, 395–97; Vaughn, *Antimasonic Party*, 30–39.

50 *Proceedings of the United States Anti-Masonic Convention Held at Philadelphia, September 11, 1830* (Philadelphia: Trimble, 1830); Vaughn, *Antimasonic Party*, 54–55; Seward to Samuel Seward, Oct. 1, 1830, Samuel Seward Papers, NYSL.

51 In his memoir Seward recalled that, before Philadelphia, Weed asked whether he could afford public service and intimated that he would be nominated— Seward 1:79–80. Many have assumed from this, and from their later relationship, that Weed played a major role in Seward's campaign. One author asserts that Weed was "managing every step of the campaign"—Doris Kearns Goodwin, *Team of Rivals: The Political Genius of Abraham Lincoln* (New York: Simon & Schuster, 2005), 71. But Weed was in Albany, a long way from Seward's senate district, and Weed's paper, the *Albany Evening Journal*, said almost nothing about his campaign.

52 Seward to Samuel Seward, Oct. 1, 1830, Samuel Seward Papers, NYSL; Franklin Hough, *The New York Civil List* (Albany: Weed Parsons, 1858); *Cayuga Patriot*, Nov. 11 & Dec. 9, 1829; *Onondaga Register & Syracuse Gazette*, Dec. 2, 1829.

53 *Onondaga Republican*, Sept. 22, 1830; *Ontario Phoenix*, Sept. 22, 1830.

54 *Cayuga Patriot*, Sept. 22 & 29, 1830; *Cayuga Republican*, Sept. 22 & 29, 1830; *Lyons Countryman*, Oct. 12, 1830; *Onondaga Republican*, Sept. 22, 1830; *Ontario Phoenix*, Sept. 29, 1830; *Wayne Sentinel*, Oct. 22, 1830; *Yates Republican*, Oct. 26, 1830; "To the Candid of All Parties," October 1830 (Seward pamphlet collection, UR).

55 *Albany Argus*, Oct. 14, 1830 (McNeil a "merchant, of good talents"); *Lyons Countryman*, Oct. 12, 1830; *Onondaga Register & Syracuse Gazette*, Oct. 6 & 20, 1830; *Wayne Sentinel*, Oct. 15, 1830.

56 Seward to Samuel Seward, Oct. 1, 1830, Samuel Seward Papers, NYSL.

57 Seward to Weed, Nov. 8 & 23, 1830, Weed Papers; Seward to Samuel Seward, Nov. 5 & 7, 1830, Samuel Seward Papers, NYSL; *Cayuga Patriot*, Dec. 1, 1830; Vaughn, *Antimasonic Party*, 38–39.

58 Barnes, ed., *Weed Autobiography*, 465; *Onondaga Republican*, Sept. 22, 1830.

NOTES FOR CHAPTER 2

1 Seward to Frances Seward, Jan. 2 & 9, 1831, Seward 1:162–63; see ibid. 191–92 (debt).

2 Seward to Frances Seward, Jan. 12, 1831, Seward 1:166; Tracy to Seward, Feb. 7, 1831, Seward Papers reel 1; Seward to Tracy, Feb. 11, 1831, Tracy Papers, NYSL; see Kenneth R. Bowling, *Peter Charles L'Enfant: Vision, Honor and Male Friendship in the Early American Republic* (Washington, DC: George Washington University Libraries, 2002).

3 Seward to Frances Seward, Jan. 12, 1831, Seward 1:166.

4 Seward to Frances Seward, Jan. 15 & 18 & Feb. 16, 1831, Seward 1:168–70 & 182.

5 Seward to Frances Seward, Aug. 24 & Sept. 14, 1831, Seward 1:196 & 206; Seward to Weed, July 19, Aug. 2, Sept. 10 & Oct. 19, 1831, Weed Papers.

6 Frances Seward to Lazette Worden, Feb. 7, Mar. [undated] & Mar. 18, 1832, Seward Papers reel 118; Seward to Tracy, June 17, 1832, Tracy Papers, NYSL; Tracy to Seward, Sept. 24, 1832, Seward Papers reel 1.

7 *Speech of William H. Seward, on the Resolution Against Renewing the Charter of the United States Bank* (Albany: Packard, Hoffman, 1832); *Albany Evening Journal*, Feb. 13 & Apr. 26, 1832; Seward to John Quincy Adams, Feb. 18, 1832, Adams Papers, MHS, reel 495; Howe, *What Hath God Wrought*, 373–86; Wilentz, *Rise of American Democracy*, 359–70.

8 Alden Chester, *Courts and Lawyers of New York: A History*, 4 vols. (New York: American Historical Society, 1925), 1:792–803.

9 *Davis v. Packard*, 10 Wendell 50 (1832); Court of Errors Minutes, Apr. 1, 1833, NYSL.

10 *Parks v. Jackson*, 11 Wendell 442 (1833); Court of Errors Minutes, Dec. 26, 1833, NYSL; Seward 1:142–44. For a list of Seward's other opinions in the Court of Errors, see Swaine, *Cravath Firm*, 1:64.

11 Seward to Frances Seward, June 21 & Nov. 10 & 19, 1832, Seward 1:216, 218, 221; Peter Porter to Henry Clay, Aug. 30, 1832, in James Hopkins, et al., eds., *The Papers of Henry Clay*, 11 vols. (Lexington: University Press of Kentucky, 1959–92), 8:568; Howe, *What Hath God Wrought*, 383.

12 *Albany Evening Journal*, Feb. 19, 1833; Cole, *Martin Van Buren*, 238–42; Richard Ellis, *The Union at Risk: Jacksonian Democracy, States' Rights, and the Nullification Crisis* (New York: Oxford University Press, 1987), 141 57, Howe,

What Hath God Wrought, 395–410; Jon Meacham, *American Lion: Andrew Jackson in the White House* (New York: Random House, 2008), 222–47; Seward 1:228–29.

13 John Jenkins, *History of Political Parties in the State of New York* (Auburn: Alden & Markham, 1846), 376–77, 381, 388–90; *Albany Evening Journal*, Feb. 21 & 22, 1833.

14 Seward to Samuel Seward, Apr. 8, 1833, Samuel Seward Papers, NYSL; Seward to John Quincy Adams, Apr. 8, 1833, Adams Papers, MHS reel 497; Seward to Albert Tracy, May 22, 1833, Tracy Papers, NYSL; *Albany Evening Journal*, June 4, 1833 (reports sailing).

15 Baker 3:514, 520, 523, 547, 590–91.

16 Seward 1:128–29.

17 Ibid., 1:141; *Albany Evening Journal*, Nov. 7, 1833; Frances Seward to Lazette Worden, Nov. 11, 1833, Seward Papers reel 118. Goodwin suggests that there was an improper correspondence between Frances and Tracy while Seward was in Europe—Goodwin, *Team of Rivals*, 74. In the letter she quotes, however, Frances merely expresses annoyance with Tracy about forwarding Seward's letters. Later letters, cited in note 19, show a continuing close relationship. The impropriety was thus in Albany in early 1834, not while Seward was away in 1833.

18 *Albany Evening Journal*, Mar. 6 & Sept. 8, 1834; Jabez Hammond to Seward, Aug. 28, 1834, Seward Papers reel 2.

19 Frances Seward to Lazette Worden, Nov. 17 & Dec. 20, 1833, Jan. 8 & Feb. 7, 1834, Seward Papers reel 118; Frederick Seward, *Reminiscences of a War-Time Statesman and Diplomat, 1830–1915* (New York: G. P. Putnam's Sons, 1916), 2–3; Seward to Tracy, June 1 & 15, 1834, Tracy Papers, NYSL; Seward to Frances Seward, Dec. 1, 1834, Seward Papers reel 112; Seward to Tracy, Dec. 29, 1834, ibid. reel 3.

20 Bayard Tuckerman, ed., *The Diary of Philip Hone, 1828–1851*, 2 vols. (New York: Dodd Mead, 1889), 1:86; *New York Commercial Advertiser*, Jan. 25, 1834; Donald Cole, *The Presidency of Andrew Jackson* (Lawrence: University Press of Kansas, 1993), 192–207; Howe, *What Hath God Wrought*, 386–93; Leo Hershkowitz, *New York City, 1834–1840: A Study in Local Politics*, PhD thesis (New York University, 1960), 1–19; John Morris, *The New York State Whigs, 1834–1842: A Study of Political Organization*, PhD thesis (University of Rochester, 1970), 56–72.

21 *Albany Evening Journal*, Jan. 16 & 17, 1834; Frances Seward to Lazette Worden, Jan. 18, 1834, Seward Papers reel 118; Seward to Samuel Seward, Jan. 29, 1834, Samuel Seward Papers, Goshen; *Speech of William H. Seward on the Resolutions Concerning the Removal of the Government Deposites* (Albany: Hoffman & White, 1834).

22 Baker 1:37–50 ($6 million loan), 3:349–55 (end of session); *Albany Evening Journal*, Mar. 24, Apr. 4, 5, & 12, 1834; Ivor D. Spencer, *The Victor and the Spoils: The Life of William Marcy* (Providence, RI: Brown University, 1959), 79–80.

23 James Mowatt to Seward, Sept. 20, 1834, Seward Papers reel 3; Michael Holt, *The Rise and Fall of the American Whig Party: Jacksonian Politics and the Onset of the Civil War* (New York: Oxford University Press, 1999), 25–30; Morris, *New York State Whigs*, 56–81.

24 Seward to Samuel Seward, May 5, 1834, Samuel Seward Papers, Goshen; Weed to Seward, May 20, 1834, Seward Papers reel 2; Seward to Weed, May 25, 1834, Weed Papers; Albert Tracy to Seward, May 26, 1834, Seward Papers reel 2; Seward to Albert Tracy, June 1, 1834, Tracy Papers, NYSL; Morris, *New York State Whigs*, 82–88.

25 Seward to Albert Tracy, July 19, 1834, Tracy Papers, NYSL; Frederick Whittlesey to Seward, July 24, 1834, Seward Papers reel 2; Seward to Samuel Seward, July 25, 1834, Samuel Seward Papers, Goshen; Weed to Seward, July 30, 1834, Seward Papers reel 2; Seward to Weed, Aug. 3, 1834, Weed Papers; Seward to Frances Seward, Aug. 22 & 26, 1834, Seward Papers reel 112; Frances Seward to Lazette Worden, Sept. 1, 1834, ibid. reel 118; *Cayuga Democrat*, Aug. 13, 1834.

26 Weed to Seward, Sept. 8–12, 1834 (multiple letters), Seward Papers reel 2; Trumbull Cary to Seward, Sept. 11, 1834, ibid.; Seward to Weed, Sept. 12, 1834, Weed Papers; Van Deusen, *Thurlow Weed*, 86–88.

27 *Albany Evening Journal*, Sept. 13 & 15, 1834; *New York Spectator*, Sept. 25, 1834; *New York Commercial Advertiser*, Sept. 30, 1834 (youth).

28 *Albany Evening Journal*, Sept. 22, 1834; *Albany Argus*, Sept. 13 & 22, 1834; Seward to the Citizens of Tioga County, Oct. 20, 1834, Baker 3:417–19; Major Wilson, "The 'Country' versus the 'Court': A Republican Consensus and Party Debate in the Bank War," *Journal of the Early Republic* 15 (1995): 619–47.

29 Seward to Samuel Seward, Sept. 28, 1834, Samuel Seward Papers, Goshen; Frances Seward to Lazette Worden, Oct. 2, 1834, Seward Papers reel 118; Seward to Simeon Bloodgood, Oct. 14, 1834, ibid. reel 3; Joseph Root to Seward, Oct. 23, 1834, ibid. (from Ohio).

30 Weed to Seward, Oct. 21, 1834, Seward Papers reel 3; Frederick Whittlesey to Seward, Oct. 27, 1834, ibid.; Weed to Seward, Nov. 1, 1834, ibid.; *Albany Evening Journal*, Nov. 10, 1834; *Albany Argus*, Nov. 25, 1834.

31 Seward to Weed, Nov. 6, 1834, Weed Papers; Dudley Selden to Seward, Nov. 12, 1834, Seward Papers reel 3; Henry Raynor to Seward, Nov. 13, 1834, ibid.; Jonathan Burnet to Seward, Nov. 16, 1834, ibid.; Abraham Thompson to Seward, Nov. 17, 1834, ibid.; Michel Chevalier, *Lettres sur l'Amérique du Nord* (Paris, 1837), 269–70 (author's trans.); Greeley, *Recollections of a Busy Life*, 112; Hershkowitz, *New York City*, 88–90.

32 Seward to Frances Seward, Nov. 28 & Dec. 1, 1834, Seward Papers reel 112.

33 Frances Seward to Seward, Dec. 5, 1834, Seward Papers reel 113; Seward to Frances Seward, Dec. 8, 1834, ibid. reel 118; Albert Tracy to Seward, Dec. 29, 1834, ibid. reel 3; Seward to Tracy, Dec. 29, 1834, ibid.; Seward to Frances Seward, Dec. 30, 1834, ibid. reel 118.

34 Seward to Weed, Feb. 8 & Apr. 12, 1835, Weed Papers; Seward to Samuel Seward, Feb. 1, Mar. 2 & 22, 1835, Samuel Seward Papers, Goshen; Meacham, *American Lion: Andrew Jackson in the White House*, 298–301.

35 Seward 1:260, 456–57; Seward to Samuel Seward, Mar. 22 & June 5, 1835, Samuel Seward Papers, Goshen; Frances Seward Journal, June 1835, Seward Papers reel 197; Seward to Weed, June 12, 1835, Weed Papers; *New York Spectator*, June 22, 1835 (quoting *Harrisburg Chronicle*).

36 Seward 1:267–68; Seward to Albert Tracy, June 24, 1835, Tracy Papers, NYSL; Frances Seward to Lazette Worden, June 1835, Seward 1:272.

37 Seward 1:269–70, 274, 276; Seward to Weed, June 21, 1835, Weed Papers.

38 Seward to Weed, July 5 & 19 & Sept. 5, 1835, Weed Papers; Seward 1:286.

39 Seward to Samuel Seward, Oct. 29 & Dec. 11, 1835, Samuel Seward Papers, Goshen; *Address Delivered by William H. Seward at the Commencement of the Auburn and Owasco Canal, October 14, 1835* (Auburn: Ivison & Co., 1835).

40 Seward to Trumbull Cary, June 13, 1836, Cary Papers, Buffalo & Erie County Historical Society; Seward to Weed, June 14, 1836, Weed Papers; *Fredonia Censor*, July 13 & 20, 1836; Charles Brooks, *Frontier Settlement and Market Revolution: The Holland Land Purchase* (Ithaca, NY: Cornell University Press, 1996), 185–219.

41 Seward to Samuel Seward, July 7, 1836, Samuel Seward Papers, Goshen; Trumbull Cary to John Van Der Kamp, Dec. 23, 1836, Cary Papers, Buffalo & Erie County Historical Society; Seward to Van Der Kamp, Feb. 17, 1837, Patterson Papers, UR.

42 Seward to Samuel Seward, Aug. 23, 1836, Samuel Seward Papers, Goshen; Seward to Frances Seward, July 24 & Oct. 30, 1836, Seward 1:306, 316–17; Seward to Weed, Nov. 17, 1836 & Jan. 3, 1837, Weed Papers; *New York Daily Express*, Nov. 1, 1836 (Seward spoke prior evening); *New York Evening Post*, Nov. 2, 1836 (quoting unnamed Whig paper quoting Seward on Van Buren).

43 Seward to Weed, Jan. 16 & Mar. 26, 1837, Weed Papers; Seward to Frances Seward, Feb. 12 & Mar. 26, 1837, Seward 1:325, 329; Frances Seward to Seward, Apr. 2, 1837; Robert C. Ayers, *From Tavern to Temple, St. Peter's Church, Auburn: The First Century* (Scottsdale, AZ: Cloudbank Creations, 2005).

44 Seward to Samuel Seward, May 13, 1837, Samuel Seward Papers, NYSL: Seward to Frances Seward, June 1837, Seward 1:331–32; Seward to Weed, June 20, 1837, Weed Papers; Howe, *What Hath God Wrought*, 502–05.

45 Baker 3:135–52 (education); *Auburn Journal & Advertiser*, Oct. 11, 1837; *Address of the New-York & Erie Railroad Convention to the People of the State*

of New-York (Auburn: Oliphant & Skinner, 1837); Seward to Samuel Seward, Nov. 28, 1837, Samuel Seward Papers, Goshen.

46 Seward to Weed, Nov. 12 & 17, 1837, Weed Papers; Seward to Frances Seward, Nov. 19 & 23, 1837, Seward 1:346–47; Seward to Samuel Seward, Nov. 28, 1837, Samuel Seward Papers, Goshen; Hammond, *History of Political Parties*, 2:479.

47 Seward to Samuel Seward, Dec. 31, 1837, Samuel Seward Papers, Goshen.

48 Jennings Seward to Jared Rathbone, Apr. 21, 1837, Patterson Papers, UR; Weed to Seward, Mar. 8, 1838, Weed Papers; Seward to Jennings Seward, 1837–38, Seward Papers reel 120.

49 Seward to Weed, Jan. 25, 1838, Weed Papers; *Jeffersonian*, Feb. 17, 1838; Seward to Samuel Seward, Feb. 25, 1838, Samuel Seward Papers, Goshen; *New York Herald*, Apr. 25, 1838; Seward to Frances Seward, Apr. 26, 1838, Seward 1:364; Seward to Weed, Mar. 19, 1838, Weed Papers; Seward to Weed, June 1838, Seward 1:367 (missing from Weed Papers); *New-Yorker*, May 19, 1838.

50 Seward to Weed, Dec. 24, 1837, Weed Papers; *Jeffersonian*, Feb. 17, 1838; Seward to Weed, Mar. 19, 1838, Seward 1:363; Robert C. Williams, *Horace Greeley: Champion of American Freedom* (New York: New York University Press, 2006).

51 Seward to Weed, Nov. 17, 1837, Weed Papers; *Buffalo Commercial Advertiser*, July 24, 1838; *Albany Argus*, Aug. 7 & 20, 1838; Weed to Seward, Aug. 16, 1838, Seward Papers reel 5; Edward Marvin to Weed, Aug. 31, 1838, Weed Papers; Ernest G. Muntz, *The First Whig Governor of New York, William Henry Seward, 1838–1842*, PhD thesis. (University of Rochester, 1960).

52 Weed to Seward, Sept. 15, 1838, Seward Papers reel 5; *Albany Evening Journal*, Sept. 13 & 14, 1838; *Auburn Journal*, Sept. 19, 1838; *Morning Courier & New-York Enquirer*, Sept. 14, 1838.

53 *Jeffersonian*, Sept. 22 & 29 & Oct. 6, 1838. For background, see Cole, *Martin Van Buren*, 285–316.

54 Baker 3:356–62 (address drafted by Seward); *Albany Evening Journal*, Oct. 3, 1838; *Baltimore Sun*, Oct. 27, 1838; *Jeffersonian*, Oct. 28, 1838.

55 Seward to Biddle, Sept. 20 & 22, 1837, Biddle to Seward, Sept. 21 & 24, 1837, all in Patterson Papers, UR; *Albany Argus*, Oct. 3, 5, & 8, 1838; Seward to Citizens of Chautauque County, Oct. 15, 1838, Baker 3:457–64; Weed to Seward, Oct. 23, 1838, Seward Papers reel 6.

56 *United States Democratic Review*, Oct. 1838, p. 111; *Jeffersonian*, Oct. 6 & 13, 1838; Poughkeepsie Handbill, Oct. 27, 1838, Seward Papers reel 6; Holt, *Whig Party*, 64–76 (quote p. 67); Rush Welter, *The Mind of America, 1820–1860* (New York: Columbia University Press, 1975), 165–89.

57 Allan Nevins and Milton Thomas, eds., *The Diary of George Templeton Strong, 1835–1875*, 4 vols. (New York: Macmillan Co., 1952), 1:94; Edwin Burrows and Mike Wallace, *Gotham: A History of New York City to 1898* (New York: Oxford

University Press, 1999), 622; Simeon Bloodgood to Christopher Morgan, Sept. 27, 1838, Seward Papers reel 5; Seward to Weed, Oct. 5, 1838, Weed Papers.

58 William Jay and Gerrit Smith to Seward, Oct. 1, 1838, Seward Papers reel 6; Seward to Weed, Oct. 5 & 8, 1838, Weed Papers; Luther Bradish to Gerrit Smith, Oct. 13, 1838, Bradish Papers, NYHS; Weed to Seward, Oct. 23, 1838, Seward Papers reel 6; Seward to Luther Bradish, Oct. 27, 1838, Bradish Papers, NYHS.

59 Seward to Jay and Smith, Oct. 22, 1838, Baker 3:426–32.

60 *Emancipator*, Nov. 1, 1838; *New York Herald*, Nov. 5, 1838; Seward to Weed, Nov. 4, 1838, Weed Papers; Weed to Seward, Nov. 4, 1838, Seward Papers reel 6; Ralph Harlow, *Gerrit Smith: Philanthropist and Reformer* (New York: Henry Holt & Co., 1939), 140.

61 Stephen Tompkins to Seward, Nov. 12, 1838, Seward Papers reel 6; *Albany Argus*, Nov. 28, 1838 (county by county); James C. Derby, *Fifty Years Among Authors, Books and Publishers* (New York: G. W. Carleton & Co., 1884), 58.

62 Seward to Weed, Nov. 11 & 19, 1838, Weed Papers; Seward to Jennings Seward, Nov. 12 & Dec. 17, 1838, Seward Papers reel 120.

63 Muntz, *First Whig Governor*, 73; Seward 1:381–83.

64 Seward to Weed, Nov. 20 & Dec. 14, 1838, Weed Papers; Derick Stockholm to Seward, Dec. 7, 1838, Seward Papers reel 7; Samuel Lyman to Seward, Dec. 14, 1838, ibid.; Samuel Ruggles to Seward, Dec. 17, 1838, ibid.; Seward to Frances Seward, Dec. 25 & 27, 1838, Seward 1:383–84.

NOTES FOR CHAPTER 3

1 Seward to Weed, Dec. 8, 1838, Weed Papers; Seward to Frances Seward, Jan. 1, 1839, Seward 1:385; *New York Herald*, Jan. 4, 1839.

2 Augustus Seward to Lazette Worden, Jan. 7, 1839, Seward Papers reel 116; *New York Herald*, Jan. 5, 1839 ("turkies, geese") ("broke his chandeliers"); *Albany Evening Journal*, Jan. 18, 1839.

3 Baker 2:197; John L. O'Sullivan, "The Great Nation of Futurity," *United States Democratic Review* 6 (November 1839): 426–30; Howe, *What Hath God Wrought*, 700–07; Warren Zimmerman, *First Great Triumph: How Five Americans Made Their Country a World Power* (New York: Farrar, Straus & Giroux, 2002), 33–34.

4 Baker 2:190, 197–99.

5 Ibid., 196–97; Ray Billington, *The Protestant Crusade, 1830–1860: A Study of the Origins of American Nativism* (New York: Macmillan Co., 1938); Howe, *What Hath God Wrought*, 319–23; Nancy Schultz, *Fire and Roses: The Burning of the Charlestown Convent, 1834* (New York: Free Press, 2000); Kenneth Silverman, *Lightning Man: The Accursed Life of Samuel F. B. Morse* (Cambridge, MA: Da Capo Press, 2004), 132–42.

6   Baker 2:200–05.

7   Ibid., 191–93; 268–70; Muntz, *First Whig Governor*, 97–99.

8   *Albany Evening Journal*, Jan. 1, 1839; *Albany Argus*, Jan. 4, 1839; *Daily National Intelligencer*, Jan. 5, 1839; *Baltimore Sun*, Jan. 5, 1839; Seward to Christopher Morgan, Jan. 15, 1839, Seward Papers reel 8.

9   Seward to Hiram Ketchum, Feb. 15, 1839, Seward Papers reel 8; Muntz, *First Whig Governor*, 75–87.

10 *New York Herald*, Feb. 7, 1839; *New-Yorker*, Feb. 16, 1839; *Albany Evening Journal*, Feb. 27 & 28, Mar. 4 & 6, 1839; Muntz, *First Whig Governor*, 85–89.

11 *Albany Argus*, Jan. 12 & 24 & Mar. 7, 1839; *Albany Evening Journal*, May 9 & 10, 1839; Charles McCurdy, *The Anti-Rent Era in New York Law and Politics, 1839–1865* (Chapel Hill: University of North Carolina Press, 2001), 8–9.

12 Baker 2:592–97 (prison) & 3:208–10 (Sunday School); *Christian Watchman*, July 19, 1839; *New York Evangelist*, May 25, July 20 & Aug. 10, 1839; *New York Herald*, July 6 & 8, 1839; *Niles' National Register*, Aug. 17, 1839; Richard Cawardine, *Evangelicals and Politics in Antebellum America* (New Haven: Yale University Press, 1993).

13 Seward to Frances Seward, July 30, 1839, Seward 1:429; Seward remarks, Seward 1:431, 435; Seward to Luther Bradish, Aug. 18, 1839, Bradish Papers, NYHS; Seward to Weed, Aug. 25, 1839, Weed Papers; Frances Seward to Lazette Worden, Oct. 29, 1839, Seward Papers reel 118.

14 Seward 1:395; Barnes, ed., *Memoir of Thurlow Weed*, 99–101.

15 Seward to Thomas Tallmadge, June 30, 1839, Martin Van Buren Papers, LC, reel 32; *Morning Courier & New-York Enquirer*, July 6, 1839; *New York Express*, July 6, 1839; *New-Yorker*, Aug. 3, 1839; Cole, *Martin Van Buren*, 346–51; Seward to Weed, Aug. 15, 1839, Weed Papers; Seward to Henry Clay, Aug. 17, 1839, in Hopkins, ed., *Papers of Henry Clay*, 9:335; Holt, *Whig Party*, 99–100. Although some have suggested that Seward favored Scott (Van Deusen, *Seward*, 61–62), it seems more accurate to characterize him as neutral in 1839.

16 Seward to Henry Hopkins, Sept. 16 & Oct. 24, 1839, in Baker 2:449–56; Leonard Curry, *The Free Black in Urban America: The Shadow of the Dream* (Chicago: University of Chicago Press, 1986); Paul Finkelman, "The Protection of Black Rights in Seward's New York," *Civil War History* 34 (1988): 211–34; Stephen Valone, "William Henry Seward, the Virginia Controversy, and the Anti-Slavery Movement, 1839–1841," *Afro-Americans in New York Life and History* 31 (2007): 65–80.

17 *Morning Courier & New-York Enquirer*, Sept. 10, 1839; Frances Seward to Lazette Worden, Nov. 11, 1839, Seward Papers reel 118; Richard Blatchford to Seward, Dec. 19, 1839, Seward Papers reel 12; Muntz, *First Whig Governor*, 107–10; Thurlow Weed, *Selections from the Newspaper Articles of Thurlow Weed* (Albany, 1877), 91–95.

18 Baker 2:352–53 (proclamation); ibid. 2:354–69 (summary); NY Senate Doc. No. 70 (Mar. 15, 1841) (correspondence); McCurdy, *Anti-Rent Era*.

19 Christopher Morgan to Seward, Dec. 26, 1839, Seward Papers reel 12; Joseph White to Crittenden, June 28, 1847, Crittenden Papers, LC; Greeley, *Recollections of a Busy Life*, 131; Holt, *Whig Party*, 100–05.

20 Frances Seward to Samuel Seward, Jan. 26, 1840, Samuel Seward Papers, NYSL; Holt, *Whig Party*, 100–13; McCurdy, *Anti-Rent Era*, 32–33.

21 Baker 2:227–28; Joel H. Silbey, *Martin Van Buren and the Emergence of American Popular Politics* (Lanham, MD: Rowman & Littlefield, 2002), 145–47.

22 Baker 2:237, 241–42; *New York Evening Post*, Jan. 14, 1840; *Albany Argus*, Jan. 14, 1840; McCurdy, *Anti-Rent Era*, 35–36, 54; Jay Sexton, *Debtor Diplomacy: Finance and American Foreign Relations in the Civil War Era* (New York: Oxford University Press, 2005), 26–28.

23 Baker 2:217; Muntz, *First Whig Governor*, 121–22.

24 Baker 2:215; Burrows and Wallace, *Gotham*, 500–01, 629–31; Diane Ravitch, *The Great School Wars, New York City, 1805–1873: A History of the Public Schools as Battlefield of Social Change* (New York: Basic Books, 1974), 33–45.

25 Draft Veto, Mar. 27, 1840, Baker 2:379–83; Weed to Francis Granger, Apr. 1, 1840, in Barnes, ed., *Memoir of Thurlow Weed*, 86–87; James Watson Webb to Seward, Apr. 1, 1840, Seward Papers reel 15; Seward to Christopher Morgan, Apr. 8, 1840, ibid.; *Albany Argus*, Mar. 28–Apr. 2, 1840; *Albany Evening Journal*, Mar. 28–31, 1840; *New York Herald*, Mar. 28–Apr. 2, 1840; Van Deusen, *Seward*, 72–73.

26 Baker 2:221–23; Seward 1:464 ("informal conferences"); *Christian Reflector*, Aug. 14, 1839 ("diabolical"); Finkleman, "Black Rights," 212, 221–22; Thomas Morris, *Free Men All: The Personal Liberty Laws of the North, 1780–1861* (Baltimore: Johns Hopkins University Press, 1974), 81–84.

27 Washington Irving to Seward, Oct. 27, 1839, Seward Papers reel 11; Winfield Scott to Seward, Nov. 27 & 28, 1839, ibid.; Seward to Christopher Morgan, Apr. 8, 1840, ibid. reel 15; Seward to John Scoles, May 26, 1840, ibid.; Seward to Thomas Chittenden, Nov. 19, 1840, ibid. reel 17; Muntz, *First Whig Governor*, 89–94.

28 John Hughes to Seward, Aug. 29, 1840, Seward Papers reel 16; Seward to Hughes, Sept. 1, 1840, ibid.; Henry Browne, "Public Support of Catholic Education in New York, 1825–1842: Some New Aspects," *Catholic Historical Review* 39 (1953):1–27.

29 *Albany Evening Journal*, Aug. 14 & 23, 1840; *New-Yorker*, Aug. 1 & Sept. 26, 1840; *Niles' National Register*, Oct. 31, 1840; *Log Cabin*, Sept. 26 & Oct. 10, 1840; Baker 3:224–28 (Otsego).

30 *Correspondence Between the Governors of Virginia and New York*, New York Senate Doc. No. 1 (1841); Baker 3:471–88; Seward to Daniel Webster, Aug. 25, 1840, in Harold Moser, ed., *The Papers of Daniel Webster: Correspondence,*

Vol. 5: 1840–1843 (Hanover, NH: University Press of New England, 1982), 55–56; Webster to Seward, Sept. 29, 1840, Seward Papers reel 17.

31 *Albany Argus*, July 7, Sept. 15 to Nov. 5, 1840; *Albany Evening Journal*, Sept. 10, 1840; Muntz, *First Whig Governor*, 191–97.

32 *New York Herald*, Nov. 9, 1840; *Log Cabin*, Nov. 9, 1840; Silliman to Seward, Nov. 9 & 14, 1840, Silliman Papers, UR; Seward to Silliman, Nov. 12 & 15, 1840, Seward Papers reel 17 (cc of Nov. 12 in Silliman Papers); John Hughes to Seward, Nov. 29, 1840, ibid. Seward's friend Benjamin D. Silliman was a New York City lawyer, nephew of the more famous Professor Benjamin Silliman of Yale.

33 Seward to Seth Hawley, Nov. 1840, Seward 1:508; Seward to Christopher Morgan, Jan. 3, 1841, Seward Papers reel 19; Seward to William Henry Harrison, Feb. 6, 1841, ibid. reel 19; Seward to Francis Granger, Apr. 2 & 5, 1841, ibid. reel 20; Holt, *Whig Party*, 125–26; Muntz, *First Whig Governor*, 205–07; Aida Donald, *Prelude to Civil War: The Decline of the Whig Party in New York 1848–1852*, PhD thesis. (University of Rochester, 1961), 126–28.

34 Seward to Francis Granger, Apr. 12, 1841, Granger Papers, LC.

35 Seward to Mordecai Noah, Aug. 29, 1840, Seward Papers reel 16; Baker 2: 279–80.

36 William Bourne, *History of the Public School Society of the City of New York* (New York: William Wood & Co, 1870), 350–73 (includes Spencer report); Ravitch, *Great School Wars*, 58–64.

37 Bourne, *History of the Public School Society*, 373–402; Muntz, *First Whig Governor*, 276–82; Ravitch, *Great School Wars*, 64–66.

38 Baker 2:390–93; Lewis Tappan to Seward, Apr. 27, 1841, Seward Papers reel 20; Seward to Austin Pray and Thomas Paul, July 13, 1841, Baker 3:435; Seward to John Rutherford, Oct. 8, 1841, Seward Papers reel 22; Finkelman, "Protection," 233–35.

39 *Journal of Commerce*, June 5, 1841; Seward to Christopher Morgan, June 10, 1841, Seward Papers reel 21.

40 Seward to Frances Seward, Sept. 10 & 15, 1841, Seward 1:563–64; Seward to John Spencer, Aug. 25, 1841, Gratz Collection, Historical Society of Pennsylvania; Holt, *Whig Party*, 122–39; McCurdy, *Anti-Rent Era*, 74–81; Robert V. Remini, *Daniel Webster: The Man and His Time* (New York: W. W. Norton & Co., 1997), 523–34.

41 Seward to John Collier, Aug. 1 & 4, 1841, Seward Papers, NYSL; Seward to John Spencer, Baker 2:608–09; James Richardson, ed., *Messages and Papers of the Presidents* (Washington, DC, 1901), 4:47, 82; McCurdy, *Anti-Rent Era*, 74–81; Reginald McGrane, *Foreign Bondholders and American State Debts* (New York: Macmillan Co., 1935).

42 Seward to Samuel Ruggles, Nov. 4, 1841, Huntington Library; Seward to Adams, Nov. 6, 1841, Adams Papers reel 519; Hughes to Seward, Nov. 0, 1041, Seward

Papers reel 23 ("chafed and jealous"); Seward to Hughes, Nov. 10, 1841, quoted in John Hassard, *Life of the Most Reverend John Hughes* (New York: Appleton & Co., 1866), 248; Seward to Spencer, Nov. 11, 1841, Seward Papers reel 23; Holt, *Whig Party*, 139–40; Ravitch, *Great School Wars*, 67–70.

43 Elmer Plischke, *U.S. Department of State: A Reference History* (Westport, CT: Greenwood Press, 1999), 195 (no "prior foreign relations experience"); Zimmerman, *First Great Triumph*, 83; Cong. Globe, 35th Cong., 1st Sess. 38 & 2d Sess. 45; Cong. Globe, 36th Cong., 1st Sess. 198 & 2d Sess. 23 (Foreign Affairs Committee assignments).

44 Seward to Weed, Mar. 10, 1838, Weed Papers; Howard Jones and Donald Rakestraw, *Prologue to Manifest Destiny: Anglo-American Relations in the 1840s* (Wilmington, DE: Scholarly Resources, 1997), 28–33, 43–51; Muntz, *First Whig Governor*, 99–100; Kenneth Stevens, *Border Diplomacy: The Caroline and McLeod Affairs in Anglo-American-Canadian Relations, 1837–1842* (Tuscaloosa: University of Alabama Press, 1989), 1–17, 71–72.

45 Henry Fox to John Forsyth, Dec. 13, 1840, and Forsyth to Fox, Dec. 26, 1840, both in *The Albion*, Jan. 9, 1841; Seward to Forsyth, Feb. 24, 1841, in *New York Tribune*, May 24, 1841; Stevens, *Border Diplomacy*, 13–21, 74–82.

46 *Philadelphia Public Ledger*, Dec. 21, 1840; *The Times* (London), Mar. 18, 1841; *Morning Courier & New-York Enquirer*, Mar. 11 & 16, 1841; *New York Evening Post*, Feb. 15 & 18 & Mar. 15, 1841; Palmerston to Fox, Feb. 9, 1841, in Henry Bulwer, *The Life of Henry John Temple, Viscount Palmerston*, 3 vols. (London: Richard Bentley & Son, 1874), 3:49; Jones and Rakestraw, *Prologue*, 48.

47 Webster speech, July 15, 1839, in Remini, *Daniel Webster*, 494; Webster to Crittenden, Mar. 15, 1841, in Kenneth Shewmaker, ed., *The Papers of Daniel Webster: Diplomatic Papers, Vol. 1: 1841–1843* (Hanover, NH: University Press of New England, 1983), 45–48; John Spencer to Crittenden, Mar. 1841, Webster Papers reel 14; Webster to Seward, Mar. 17, 1841, in *Webster: Diplomatic Papers*, 49; Seward to Webster, Mar. 22, 1841, ibid. 53; Seward to Webster, Mar. 22, 1841 (second letter), in *New York Tribune*, May 24, 1841; Seward to Crittenden, May 31, 1841, Crittenden Papers, LC; Albert Kirwan, *John J. Crittenden: The Struggle for Union* (Lexington: University of Kentucky Press, 1962), 145–47.

48 Seward to Legislature, Apr. 6, 1841, Baker 2:394; Seward to Francis Granger, Apr. 12, 1841, Granger Papers, LC; Winfield Scott to Seward, Mar. 27, 1841, Seward Papers reel 20; Seward to Tyler, May 4, 1841, *Webster Diplomatic Papers* 68–69; Scott Kaufman and John Soares, " 'Sagacious Beyond Praise'? Winfield Scott and Anglo-American-Canadian Border Diplomacy, 1837–1860," *Diplomatic History* 30 (2005): 57–82.

49 Tyler to Seward, May 7, 1841, *Webster: Diplomatic Papers*, 69–70; Seward to Tyler, May 10, 1841, ibid. 70–72; Webster to Fletcher Webster, May 10, 1841, ibid. 72 n.5; Tyler to Seward, May 25, 1841, ibid. 77–80; Seward to Tyler, June 1,

1841, ibid. 85–94; Seward to Samuel Lyman, June 7, 1841, Huntington Library (hopes correspondence closed).

50 *New York Tribune*, May 4, 18–20, & July 14, 1841; Seward to Frances Seward, July 13, 1841, Seward 1:552; Webster to Joseph Story, July 16, 1841, *Webster: Diplomatic Papers*, 99; Webster to Hiram Ketchum, July 1841, ibid., 99–100; Seward to Christopher Morgan, Aug. 9, 1841, Seward Papers reel 21; Stevens, *Border Diplomacy*, 111–15, 120–23.

51 Seward to Weed, Aug. 12, 1841, Weed Papers; Webster to Seward, Aug. 24, 1841, *Webster: Diplomatic Papers*, 101–02; Seward to Webster, Sept. 3, 1841, ibid., 108–14; Stevens, *Border Diplomacy*, 123–25.

52 Seward to Frances Seward, July 13, 1841, Seward 1:552; Samuel Blatchford to Seward, Sept. 20, 1841, Seward Papers reel 22; Winfield Scott to John Bell, Sept. 21, 1841, *Webster: Diplomatic Papers*, 146–48; Willis Hall to Seward, Oct. 12, 1841, Seward Papers reel 22; *New York Tribune*, Oct. 7–14, 1841; Stevens, *Border Diplomacy*, 136–55.

53 Baker 2:306–08.

54 Bourne, *History of the Public School Society*, 501–06 (report); Muntz, *First Whig Governor*, 289–94; Ravitch, *Great School Wars*, 70–74.

55 Hughes to Seward, Mar. 22, 1842, in "Archbishop Hughes to Governor Seward on the School Question, 1842," *Records of the American Catholic Historical Society of Philadelphia* 23 (1912): 36–40.

56 Seward to Samuel Lyman, June 7, 1841, Huntington Library; Seward to Hughes, Apr. 10, 1842, quoted in Hassard, *Life of Hughes*, 250–51; *New York Tribune*, Apr. 11, 1842; Ravitch, *Great School Wars*, 74–75.

57 Baker 2:409–12; Horace Greeley to Seward, Jan. 7, 1842, Seward Papers reel 24; Muntz, *First Whig Governor*, 235–37.

58 Baker 2:298–99, 413–14, 433–35; Finkelman, "Black Rights," 227–28, 232.

59 *Albany Weekly Argus*, Feb. 5, Mar. 7 & 26, 1842; *New York Tribune*, Mar. 7, 11, & 29, 1842; Baker 2:316, 320; McCurdy, *Anti-Rent Era*, 80–84.

60 Seward 1:609–14; Baker 2:23, 73; *North American Review* (December 1842): 664–65.

61 *Albany Evening Journal*, Nov. 10, 1842; Muntz, *First Whig Governor*, 301–02.

62 Seward to Eliza Allen, Mar. 12, 1842, Baker 2:646–47; Seward 1:628–35 (letters and narrative); *New York Tribune*, Nov. 14–19, 1842.

63 Seward 1:636–37; Baker 2:661–63; Nevins and Thomas, eds., *Diary of George Templeton Strong* 1:193–94; Seward to James Bowen, Dec. 3, 1842, Seward Papers, NYPL.

64 Seward to Weed, Dec. 31, 1842, Weed Papers.

65 Seward to Weed, Jan. 8, 1843, Weed Papers (added to Dec. 31 letter); *Albany Evening Journal*, Jan. 4 & 7, 1843; Seward 1:642–45.

NOTES FOR CHAPTER 4

1 Seward to Weed, May 13, 1843, Weed Papers; Frances Seward to Lazette Worden, May 14, 1843, Seward Papers reel 119; Seward 1:704.

2 Seward to Richard Blatchford, Feb. 1, 1843, Seward Papers reel 29; Receipts, Seward House; Seward 1:646, 651 ($400,000); Van Deusen, *Seward*, 88 ($200,000); *Schermerhorn v. American Life Insurance & Trust Co.*, in Oliver Barbour, ed., *Reports of Cases in Law and Equity in the Supreme Court of the State of New York*, 67 vols. (1848–1888) 14:131.

3 *Auburn Journal & Advertiser*, Jan. 18, 1843; Seward to James Bowen, Jan. 19 & May 31, 1843, Seward Papers reel 29; Seward to Weed, Jan. 28, 1843, Weed Papers; Swaine, *Cravath Firm*, 82.

4 Frances Seward to Lazette Worden, May 7, 1843, Seward Papers reel 119; Seward to George Grier, May 18, 1843, Grier Papers, UR.

5 Chester Harding to daughter, Mar. 10, 1843, quoted in William H. Gerdts, "Heads or Tails: The Seward Portrait in City Hall," *Art Quarterly* 21 (1958): 75; *Hudson River Chronicle*, Mar. 16, 1843; Francis Seward to Lazette Worden, Aug. 10, 1843, Seward Papers reel 119; Seward to Weed, Aug. 11, 1843, Weed Papers.

6 John Quincy Adams Diary, July 28 & 29, 1843, MHS; Seward to Weed, July 31, 1843, Weed Papers; Frances Seward to Lazette Worden, Aug. 1, 1843, Seward Papers reel 119; Seward 1:671–73.

7 Frances Seward to Lazette, Dec. 26, 1843, Apr. 8, 1844, June 23 & Aug. 13, 1845, June 14, 1846 (quoting Augustus), & Apr. 3, 1847, Seward Papers, reel 119; George W. Cullum, *Biographical Register of the Officers and Graduates of the U.S. Military Academy at West Point, New York*, 3 vols. (Boston: Houghton Mifflin, 1891), 2:204.

8 Seward to Weed, Mar. 25, 1843, Weed Papers; Eliphalet Nott to Seward, Feb. 4, 1847, Seward Papers reel 29; Frances Seward to Lazette Worden, Feb. 6, 1847, ibid. reel 119; Seward to William Seward Jr., c. 1844, Seward Papers (not on film); Seward to Frances Seward, May 11, 1848, Seward 2:67.

9 Seward to Frances Seward, Nov. 16, 1844, Seward 1:735; Seward to Samuel Seward, Dec. 10, 1844, Samuel Seward Papers, Goshen; Seward to Augustus Seward, Dec. 11 & 15, 1844, Seward Papers reel 112; Seward to Frances Seward, Dec. 20, 26, & 29, 1844, Seward 1:736–37; *New London Morning News*, Dec. 30, 1844; Frances Seward to Lazette Worden, Jan. 10, 18, & 28, 1845, Seward Papers reel 119; Seward to Samuel Seward, Jan. 13, 1845, Samuel Seward Papers, NYSL.

10 Martha Coffin Wright to Lucretia Mott, July 13, 1846, quoted in Sherry H. Penney and James D. Livingston, *A Very Dangerous Woman: Martha Wright and Women's Rights* (Amherst: University of Massachusetts Press, 2004), 56; Seward 1:461 ("inevitable cigar") & 577 (reception); *Liberator*, Jan. 21, 1842; *Christian Watchman*, Feb. 11, 1842. I cannot find, in the Garrison Papers at Smith College, the quoted language in the letter Penney and Livingston cite.

11 Seward to Frances Seward, Jan. 1, 1846, Seward 1:768; Frances Seward to Lazette Worden, June 11, 1847, reel 119.

12 Seward to Frances Seward, July 17, 1845, Jan. 21, 1846, May 9 & 13, 1846, Seward 1:752, 778, 804–06; Seward to Weed, Apr. 11, 1846, Weed Papers.

13 Seward to James Bowen, Mar. 30, 1843, Seward Papers reel 29; *United States Gazette*, Apr. 13, 1843; Seward to Weed, June 24, 1843, Weed Papers; Seward 1:740–42; *New York Tribune*, May 17, 1845.

14 Seward 1:670–71.

15 *Scientific American*, Dec. 16, 1848, Oct. 6, 1849, June 12 & Aug. 7, 1852; see Carolyn C. Cooper, "A Patent Transformation: Woodworking Mechanization in Philadelphia, 1830–1856," in Judith A. McGaw, ed., *Early American Technology: Making and Doing Things from the Colonial Era to 1850* (Chapel Hill: University of North Carolina Press, 1994). Wilson deserves a biography.

16 Seward to Frances Seward, Jan. 8 & 15, 1846, Seward 1:773–74 & 798; Seward to Wilson, Mar. 22, 1846 (bill), quoted in Swaine, *Cravath Firm*, 103; Seward to Weed, Nov. 21, 1848, Weed Papers; James Wilson to Seward, Apr. 19, 1849, Seward Papers reel 29; Seward to Frances Seward, Apr. 28 & May 6, 1849, ibid. reel 112; *Wilson v. Rousseau*, 45 US 646 (1846); cases reported in Samuel Blatchford, ed., *Reports of Cases Argued and Determined in the Circuit Court of the United States for the Second Circuit* (Auburn: Derby & Miller, 1852), 3–172; *Wilson v. Simpson*, 50 US 109 (1850); *Wilson v. Sandford*, 51 US 99 (1851); Samuel S. Fisher, ed., *Reports of Cases Arising Upon Letters Patent for Inventions Determined in the Circuit Courts of the United States* (Cincinnati: Robert Clarke & Co.), 2:635–60; *Charleston Courier*, May 7, 1849; *Charleston Mercury*, May 8 & Aug. 7, 1849; *Scientific American*, May 31, Oct. 6, & Nov. 17, 1849.

17 Seward 1:671; Frank Gilbert, *Jethro Wood: Inventor of the Modern Plow* (Chicago: Rhodes & McClure, 1882), title page; Irene McNeu, *Erastus Corning: Merchant and Financier, 1794–1872* (Ithaca, NY: Cornell University Press, 1960); William Seward, *The Steam Engine: Hon. William H. Seward's Argument in the Circuit Court of the United States* (Providence, RI: Knowles, Anthony & Co., 1853); Blatchford, *Reports*, 467–79.

18 Seward to Frances Seward, Apr. 26, 1847, and June 19, 1849, Seward 2:46 and Seward Papers reel 112; Swaine, *Cravath Firm*, 87–89.

19 Seward to James Bowen, Jan. 28, 1843, Seward Papers reel 29; Seward to Weed, Jan. 24, June 18, Sept. 17, & Oct. 8, 1843, Weed Papers; Seward to the *Courier*, Oct. 1843, Seward 1:683. I have not found this letter in the *Morning Courier & New-York Enquirer*.

20 Seward to Weed, Aug. 29, 1846, Weed Papers; Gideon Welles, *Lincoln and Seward: Remarks Upon the Memorial Address of Charles Francis Adams* (New York: Sheldon & Co., 1874), 23.

21 *Albany Evening Journal*, Nov. 10, 1843; *New York Tribune*, Sept. 29 & Nov. 9, 1843; Seward 1:684–85.

22 Seward to Christopher Morgan, Nov. 8 & 25, 1843, Seward Papers reel 29; Holt, *Whig Party*, 162–68, 190–91.

23 Baker 3:239–45; *New York Tribune*, Feb. 27, 1844.

24 William H. Seward, *The Elements of Empire in America* (New York: C. Shepard, 1841). On the timing of the two speeches, see *New York Tribune*, July 17 & 29, 1844.

25 Seward to Weed, Mar. 24, 1844, Weed Papers; Holt, *Whig Party*, 168–72; Frederick Merk, *Slavery and the Annexation of Texas* (New York: Alfred A. Knopf, 1972).

26 Seward to Weed, June 20, 1844, Weed Papers; Holt, *Whig Party*, 171–79; Charles G. Sellers, *James K. Polk: Continentalist* (Princeton: Princeton University Press, 1966), 56–107.

27 Baker 3:246–53; Seward, *Elements of Empire*, 10; see also Seward to Chautauqua convention ("I want no enlargement of territory sooner than it would come if we were contented with a masterly inactivity"), Seward 1:791. For arguments which (in my view) ignore Seward's early reluctance, see Ernest N. Paolino, *The Foundations of the American Empire: William Henry Seward and U.S. Foreign Policy* (Ithaca, NY: Cornell University Press, 1973); Walter G. Sharrow, "William Henry Seward and the Basis for American Empire, 1850–1860," *Pacific Historical Review* 36 (1967): 325–42. For Whig views on territory, see Michael Morrison, "Westward the Curse of Empire: Texas Annexation and the American Whig Party," *Journal of the Early Republic* 10 (1990): 221–49; Major L. Wilson, *Space Time and Freedom: The Quest for Nationality and the Irrepressible Conflict, 1815–1861* (Westport, CT: Greenwood Press, 1974), 115–19.

28 Martha Wright to Lucretia Mott, Dec. 1841, Garrison Family Papers, Smith College (teatime debate); Seward 1:729 (speech quote); Margaret H. Bacon, *Valiant Friend: The Life of Lucretia Mott* (New York: Walker & Co., 1980); Sally G. McMillen, *Seneca Falls and the Origins of the Women's Rights Movement* (New York: Oxford University Press, 2008); Penney and Livingston, *Very Dangerous Woman*; Melissa Wraalstaad, *Frances Seward and Lazette Worden: Two Sisters' Approaches to Activism*, MA thesis (SUNY Oneonta, 2002).

29 Clay to Stephen Miller, July 1, 1844, in Hopkins, ed., *Papers of Henry Clay*, 10:78–79; Clay to Thomas Peters and John Jackson, July 27, 1844, ibid. 89–91; Seward to Weed, Sept. 2 & 15, 1844, Weed Papers; Holt, *Whig Party*, 180–86; Howe, *What Hath God Wrought*, 686–87.

30 Baker 3:254–59; Seward to Frances Seward, July 6, 1844, Seward 1:720; *New York Tribune*, July 13, 1844; Michael Feldberg, *The Philadelphia Riots of 1844* (Westport, CT: Greenwood Press, 1975); Holt, *Whig Party*, 190–92; Ira M. Leonard, "The Rise and Fall of the American Republican Party in New York City, 1843–1845," *New-York Historical Society Quarterly* 50 (1966): 151–92.

31 Seward to Whigs of Orleans County, May 13, 1844, Baker 3:394–96; Seward to Benjamin Squire, June 7, 1844, Baker 1:396–98; Seward to Whigs of Michigan, June 12, 1844, Baker 1:399; Seward to Calvin Townsley, June 12, 1844, Baker 1:400–01; Seward to Weed, July 24, 1844, Weed Papers; [*Brattleboro*] *Vermont Phoenix*, Aug. 23, 1844; Seward to Weed, Sept. 30, 1844, Weed Papers.

32 Seward to Weed, Oct. 22, 1844, Weed Papers; Seward to Clay, Oct. 25, 1844, *Clay Papers* 10:135; Holt, *Whig Party*, 194; Howe, *What Hath God Wrought*, 689–90 (Clay victory "would probably have avoided the Civil War").

33 Seward to Weed, Nov. 7, 1844, Weed Papers; Seward to Clay, Nov. 7, 1844, *Clay Papers* 10:141–42.

34 *Report of the Trial of Henry Wyatt, a Convict in the State Prison at Auburn, Indicted for the Murder of James Gordon, Another Convict Within the Prison* (Auburn, NY: J. C. Derby, 1846); *Auburn Journal & Advertiser*, Feb. 18 & 25, 1846; Andrew W. Arpey, *The William Freeman Murder Trial: Insanity, Politics, and Race* (Syracuse, NY: Syracuse University Press, 2003), 2, 15; Seward 1:785.

35 Frances Seward to Seward, Mar. 1846, Seward 1:787.

36 *New York Tribune*, Mar. 20, 1846; *New York Morning Express*, Mar. 21, 1846; *Albany Weekly Argus*, Mar. 18, 1846.

37 Seward to Alvah Worden, March 22, 1846, Weed Papers; Seward to Weed, March 28, 1846, ibid.; Arpey, *Freeman*, 15–40.

38 Seward to Weed, May 29 & June 10, 1846, Weed Papers; John Austin Journal, May 29, 1846, Harvard Divinity School Library.

39 Benjamin F. Hall, ed., *The Trial of William Freeman for the Murder of John G. Van Nest . . . and Others* (Auburn, NY: Derby, Miller & Co., 1848), 26–27; Seward 1:811.

40 John Austin Journal, June 1846, Harvard (day-by-day account); *Auburn Journal & Advertiser*, June 3, 17, & 24, & July 1, 1846; Frances Seward to Lazette Worden, July 1, 1846, Seward Papers reel 119; Arpey, *Freeman*, 60–61. This letter provides a telling example of how Frederick Seward edited his family's letters: he not only omitted his mother's reference to "three hundred female barbarians" at the courthouse; he added a sentence in which "Wyatt is made to answer for the murder committed by Freeman." In this case we have the original, but in many cases, especially letters from Henry to Frances, the version in Frederick's books is the only one that survives—Seward 1:813.

41 Hall, *Freeman*, 36–37, 57–59, 94–96.

42 John Austin Journal, July 4, 1846, Harvard; *New York Tribune*, Nov. 27, 1846 (apparently based on article by Austin).

43 Hall, *Freeman*, 143–44; John Austin Journal, July 6, 1846, Harvard.

44 John Austin Journal, July 6, 1846, Harvard; *New York Tribune*, Nov. 27, 1846. Goodwin erroneously places this episode at the outset of the Freeman trial—Goodwin, *Team of Rivals*, 85.

45 Baker 1:411–18, 474–75; Hall, *Freeman*, 473–75. For some interesting incidents around the trial, see Martha Wright to Lucretia Mott, July 13 & 20, 1846, Garrison Family Papers, Smith College.

46 John Austin Journal, Aug. & Sept. 1846, Harvard; Martha Wright to Lucretia Mott, Aug. 15, 1846, & Feb. 7, 1847, Garrison Family Papers, Smith College; Seward to Silas Wright, Aug. 17, 1846, and Wright to Seward, Sept. 7, 1846, both in Baker 1:475; Frances Seward to Lazette Worden, Oct. 3, 1846, Seward Papers reel 119; Frances Seward to Seward, Aug. 21, 1847, ibid. reel 113 (death); *Albany Evening Journal*, Sept. 14, 1846 (stay); Arpey, *Freeman*, 117–40; Hall, *Freeman*, 479–94 (state supreme court opinion).

47 *In the Supreme Court of the United States: John Van Zandt, ad sectum Wharton Jones: Argument of William H. Seward* (Albany: Weed & Parsons, 1847); Seward to Salmon Chase, Dec. 9 & 26, 1846, Feb. 18 & Mar. 24, 1847, Chase Papers, LC.

48 Seward to Weed, Aug. 29, 1846, Weed Papers.

49 Seward to Frances Seward, Jan. 2, 4, & 6, 1846, Seward 1:769–72.

50 Seward to Frances Seward, May 13, 1846, Seward 1:806; *New Orleans Picayune* (May 1846); Seward to Weed, May 28, 1846, & Aug. 15, 1847, Weed Papers; Frances Seward to Seward, Apr. 7 & Aug. 18, 1847, Seward Papers reel 113.

51 Seward to Weed, Jan. 1847, Weed Papers (filed as Feb.) (Seward quotes Adams).

52 Seward to Frances Seward, Mar. 31, 1847, Seward 2:42; Seward to Weed, Aug. 27, 1847, Weed Papers; *Albany Weekly Argus*, June 20, 1846 (soup letter); Robert W. Johannsen, *To the Halls of the Montezumas: The Mexican War in the American Imagination* (New York: Oxford University Press, 1985), 114–21; Charles W. Elliott, *Winfield Scott: The Soldier and the Man* (New York: Macmillan Co., 1937), 429–31.

53 *New York Tribune*, Sept. 3, 1847; Seward to Frances Seward, Oct. 14, 1847, Seward 2:55; Seward to Frances Seward, Jan. 29, 1848, ibid., 62; Seward to Weed, Feb. 5, 1848, Weed Papers; Holt, *Whig Party*, 275–82.

54 Patterson to Weed, Jan. 23, 1848, Weed Papers; *Albany Evening Journal*, Feb. 17 & 24, 1848; Van Deusen, *Seward*, 108; Holt, *Whig Party*, 300.

55 Seward to Weed, Sept. 26, 1847, Weed Papers (apparently not interested in being governor again); *New London Morning News*, Oct. 2, 1847; Seward to Frances Seward, Oct. 14, 1847, Seward 2:55; *Baltimore Sun*, Nov. 17, 1847; Clay to Greeley, Nov. 22, 1847, *Clay Papers,* 10:378–79; Greeley to Clay, Nov. 30, 1847, ibid., 381–82; *Boston Post,* Feb. 2, 1848.

56 Seward to Weed, Nov. 6, 1847, Weed Papers; Greeley to Schuyler Colfax, Oct. 2, 1848, Greeley Papers reel 3.

57 *New York Tribune*, Feb. 23–29, 1848; *Albany Evening Journal*, Feb. 29, 1848; Samuel F. Bemis, *John Quincy Adams and the Union* (New York: Alfred A. Knopf, 1956), 534–37; Holt, *Whig Party,* 310–12; John H. Schroeder, *Mr. Polk's War: American Opposition and Dissent, 1846–1848* (Madison: University of Wisconsin Press, 1973), 156–59.

58 *New York Tribune*, Apr. 8, 1848; Seward 2:64; Baker 3:75–76, 281.

59 Seward to Weed, Mar. 29 & May 27, 1848, Weed Papers; Harry Bradley to Millard Fillmore, June 20, 1848, Millard Fillmore Papers, LC; Holt, *Whig Party*, 327–29. See *Albany Morning Express*, June 4, 1849 (Weed "moved heaven and earth to obtain the nomination of WH Seward for the Vice Presidency" but was "checked in the most masterly manner by John A. Collier").

60 Seward to Weed, June 10, 1848, Weed Papers.

61 Weed to Seward, July 29, 1848, Weed Papers ("things are going very wrong"); Patterson to Weed, Aug. 24, 1848, ibid. (Whigs would have to "work in order to save our troops from going to Van Buren"); Seward to Weed, Aug. 31, 1848, ibid.

62 Seward to Frances Seward, Sept. 24, 1848, Seward 2:79; *Boston Daily Atlas*, Sept. 23, 1848; *New York Tribune*, Sept. 25, 1848; *Albany Evening Journal*, Sept. 26, 1848.

63 Francis Carpenter, "A Day with Governor Seward at Auburn," July 1870, Seward Papers reel 198. For other accounts, see Michael Burlingame, *Abraham Lincoln: A Life*, 2 vols. (Baltimore: Johns Hopkins University Press, 2008), 1:283; Goodwin, *Team of Rivals*, 127; Seward 2:79–80; John M. Taylor, *William Henry Seward: Lincoln's Right Hand* (New York: HarperCollins, 1991), 174; Van Deusen, *Seward*, 110. Some authors treat Frederick Seward as an independent source on this, but his account is clearly based on Carpenter, although he obfuscates the date, probably because he realized his father was not in Worcester on the night in question.

64 *Boston Daily Atlas*, Sept. 25, 1848 (reporting Lincoln's departure); *Springfield [MA] Republican*, Sept. 22, 23, & 25, 1848 (reporting Seward's speech); [*Worcester*] *National Aegis*, Sept. 25, 1848 (no mention of Lincoln in MA).

65 Seward to Frances Seward, Oct. 1 & 5, 1848, Seward 2:80–81; *Miner's Journal & Pottsville General Advertiser*, Sept. 30 & Oct. 7, 1848; *North American & U.S. Gazette*, Sept. 28, 1848.

66 Seward to Frances Seward, Oct. 6 & 27, 1848, Seward 2:82–84; Seward to Weed, Oct. 9, 27, & 29, & Nov. 6, 1848, Weed Papers; Baker 3:303–05; *New York Tribune*, Oct. 6, 1848; *North American & U.S. Gazette*, Oct. 9, 1848.

67 Seward to Frances Seward, Oct. 27, 1848, Seward 2:85; Baker 3:291–302.

68 Seward to Frances Seward, Oct. 1848, Seward 2:83 ("very weary of this roving life"); Seward to Weed, Nov. 6, 1848, Weed Papers.

69 Seward to Weed, Oct. 29 & Nov. 8, 1848, Weed Papers; Aida Donald, *Prelude to Civil War: The Decline of the Whig Party in New York 1848–1852*, PhD thesis (University of Rochester, 1961), 108–16; Holt, *Whig Party*, 368–69, 379, 394–96, 416–17.

70 *New York Herald*, Dec. 2, 1848; *Albany Evening Journal*, Dec. 9 & 22, Jan. 8, 12, 13, & 31, 1849; *Rochester American*, Jan. 11, 13, 16, 20, & 25, 1849; *Whig or Abolition: That's the Question* (New York, January 1849),

71 *Albany Evening Journal*, Jan. 9, 22, & 27, 1849 (quote from *Saratoga Whig* on Jan. 22); *Buffalo Commercial Advertiser*, Jan. 30, 1849; William Cornwell to Samuel Blatchford, Jan. 20, 1849, Seward Papers reel 30; Seth Hawley to Seward, Jan. 23, 1849, ibid.; Frothingham Fish to Seward, Feb. 6, 1849, ibid.

72 *Albany Evening Journal*, Jan. 24, 1849; *Rochester American*, Jan. 26, 1849; Webb to Seward, Jan. 28, 1849, Seward Papers reel 30; Weed to Seward, Jan. 28, 1849, ibid.; Seward to Webb, Feb. 1, 1849, Baker 3:414–16.

73 *Albany Evening Journal*, Feb. 2, 1849; *Morning Courier & New-York Enquirer*, Feb. 2, 1849; Weed to Seward, Feb. 4, 1849, Seward Papers reel 30; Fish to Seward, Feb. 6, 1849, ibid.; Holt, *Whig Party*, 394–96.

74 *New York Tribune*, Feb. 7, 1849; John Hughes to Seward, Feb. 7, 1849, Seward Papers reel 30; Eliphalet Nott to Seward, Feb. 13, 1849, ibid.

75 *Albany Evening Journal*, Feb. 8, 1849 (reprinting *Evening Post*); *Mississippi Free Trader & Natchez Gazette*, Feb. 17, 1849.

NOTES FOR CHAPTER 5

1 Seward to Frances Seward, Feb. 25 & 27, Mar. 1 & 2, 1849, Seward 2:99–102; Seward to Weed, Feb. 27 & Mar. 3, 1849, Weed Papers; Harriet Weed, ed., *Autobiography of Thurlow Weed* (Boston: Houghton Mifflin, 1883), 586. Weed's memoir is probably right in saying the meeting was pleasant; the three men continued to exchange letters at this time; see, e.g., Fillmore to Weed, Oct. 22 & Nov. 21, 1847, Weed Papers.

2 *Cong. Globe*, 30th Cong., 2d Sess. App. 326–27 (special session of 31st reported with 30th); *Daily National Intelligencer*, Mar. 6 & 8, 1849; *New York Tribune*, Mar. 6 & 8, 1849; Seward, *Reminiscences*, 70; William Allen, *History of the United States Capitol* (Washington, DC: Government Printing Office, 2001), 132–33. Clay was a member of the Senate in early 1849 but did not attend the session. See Robert Remini, *Henry Clay: Statesman for Union* (New York: W. W. Norton & Co., 1991), 716–17.

3 Seward to Frances Seward, Mar. 6, 1849, Seward Papers reel 112; *Daily National Intelligencer*, Mar. 6 & 8, 1849; *New York Tribune*, Mar. 6 & 8, 1849; Holman Hamilton, *Zachary Taylor: Soldier in the White House* (Indianapolis: Bobbs-Merrill Co., 1951), 156–61; Robert Scarry, *Millard Fillmore* (Jefferson, NC: McFarland & Co., 2001), 143–45.

4 Seward to Weed, Mar. 8, 1849, Weed Papers; Seward to Frances Seward, Mar. 8 & 15, 1849, Seward Papers reel 112.

5 Donald Cole, *Vindicating Andrew Jackson: The 1828 Election and the Rise of the Two-Party System* (Lawrence: University Press of Kansas, 2010), 125; Holt, *Whig Party*, 416–18 (quote 417); Mark Summers, *The Plundering Generation:*

Corruption and the Crisis of the Union, 1849–1861 (New York: Oxford University Press, 1987), 23–40.

6 Seward to Frances Seward, Mar. 9 & 10, Seward Papers reel 112; Seward to Weed, Mar. 21 & 29, 1849, Weed Papers; *Albany Morning Express*, May 16, 1849; *New York Evening Post*, May 29, 1849; Holt, *Whig Party*, 432–33.

7 Webster to Fletcher Webster, Mar. 27 & 28, 1849, in Charles Wiltse, ed., *The Papers of Daniel Webster: Correspondence, Vol. 6: 1844–1849* (Hanover, NH: University Press of New England, 1974–82), 323–25; Seward to Frances Seward, Mar. 26, 1849, Seward Papers reel 112; Lincoln to Seward, June 4, 1849, CWL, 8:414; Holt, *Whig Party*, 425–26; Remini, *Daniel Webster: The Man and His Time*, 659–60; David Donald, *Lincoln* (New York: Simon & Schuster, 1995), 138–41. It is possible that Lincoln and Seward met in Washington in late 1848 or early 1849; they were both there for much of this period.

8 Seward to Frances Seward, Apr. 29 & 30, May 3 & 6, 1849, Seward Papers reel 112; Seward to George Grier, June 17, 1849, George Grier Papers, UR; *Charleston Courier*, May 7, 1849.

9 Seward to Fitz-Henry Warren, Sept. 4, 1849, Seward Papers Addition; Clarence Seward to Seward, May & June 1870, Seward Papers reel 124; *New York Times*, May 25, 1870 (court decision); Seward 2:109–10; Van Deusen, *Seward*, 116. Almost all the letters from Seward to Grier, in the Grier Papers, and from Grier to Seward, in the Seward Papers, relate to the estate.

10 Frances Seward to Lazette Worden, Jan. 15, Dec. 14 & 21, 1849, & Feb. 13, 1850, Seward Papers reel 119; Seward 2:111–12 (house).

11 *New York Tribune*, Nov. 12, 1849; David Potter, *The Impending Crisis, 1848–1861* (New York: Harper & Row, 1976), 90–96.

12 *New York Tribune*, Nov. 12, 1849; Don Fehrenbacher, *The Slaveholding Republic: An Account of the United States Government's Relations to Slavery* (New York: Oxford University Press, 2001), 269–71; Mark Stegmaier, *Texas, New Mexico, and the Compromise of 1850: Boundary Dispute and Sectional Crisis* (Kent, OH: Kent State University Press, 1996), 85–88, 92–93.

13 Seward to Weed, Nov. 30, 1849, Weed Papers; Cong. Globe, 31st Cong., 1st Sess. 28 (Toombs); James McPherson, *Battle Cry of Freedom: The Civil War Era* (New York: Oxford University Press, 1988), 67–68.

14 Robert Toombs to John Crittenden, Apr. 25, 1850, in Mrs. Chapman Coleman, ed., *The Life of John J. Crittenden: With Selections from his Correspondence and Speeches*, 2 vols. (New York: Da Capo Press, 1970), 1:364–66; *New York Herald*, Dec. 6, 1849; Myrta Avary, ed., *Recollections of Alexander Stephens* (New York: Doubleday, Page & Co., 1910), 25; Potter, *Impending Crisis*, 96 ("Seward had incurred the distrust of southerners, who saw him as a backstair manipulator of Old Rough and Ready"); Stegmaier, *Texas, New Mexico*, 87 ("positively alarming to Southerners was the extraordinary amount of

influence that New York's new antislavery Whig senator William H. Seward seemed to exercise over Taylor").

15 Seward to Weed, Nov. 30 & Dec. 3, 1849, Weed Papers; *New York Tribune*, Dec. 25, 1849; Richardson, ed., *Messages and Papers*, 6:2556–57, 2564–68; Remini, *Clay*, 736–42.

16 Seward to George Patterson, Feb. 9, 1850, Patterson Papers, UR; Frances Seward to Lazette Worden, Feb. 10, 1850, Seward Papers reel 119; *New York Evening Post*, Mar. 14, 1850; Remini, *Clay*, 730–38.

17 Cong. Globe, 31st Cong., 1st Sess. 451–55; Merrill Peterson, *The Great Triumvirate: Webster, Clay and Calhoun* (New York: Oxford University Press, 1987), 460–61.

18 Cong. Globe, 31st Cong., 1st Sess. 476–83; Remini, *Daniel Webster*, 669–72.

19 Frances Seward to Lazette Worden, Mar. 10, 1850, Seward Papers reel 119; *Boston Semi-Weekly Atlas*, Mar. 9 & 13, 1850; *New York Tribune*, Mar. 9, 1850; *New York Evening Post*, Mar. 14, 1850; Peterson, *Triumvirate*, 464–66; Remini, *David Webster*, 675–78.

20 Frances Seward to Lazette Worden, Mar. 10, 1850, Seward Papers reel 119; *New York Tribune*, Mar. 12 & 15, 1850.

21 Cong. Globe, 31st Cong., 1st Sess. App. 260–63.

22 Ibid., 264–65; *New York Tribune*, Mar. 12, 1850.

23 Cong. Globe, 31st Cong., 1st Sess. App. 265; Van Deusen, *Seward*, 127–28.

24 Cong. Globe, 31st Cong., 1st Sess. App. 268–69; McPherson, *Battle Cry of Freedom*, 73.

25 Frances Seward to Lazette Worden, Mar. 10, 1850, Seward Papers reel 119; *New York Tribune*, Mar. 12 & 15, 1850; *New York Evening Post*, Mar. 14, 1850.

26 *New York Evening Post*, Mar. 14, 1850; Seward to Weed, Mar. 22 & 31, 1850, Weed Papers.

27 Samuel Lyman to Seward, Mar. 11, 1850, Seward Papers reel 36; *Boston Semi-Weekly Atlas*, Mar. 16, 1850; *Brattleboro Semi-Weekly Eagle*, Mar. 18, 1850; *New York Tribune*, Mar. 19, 1850; Salmon Chase to Charles Sumner, Apr. 13, 1850, in John Niven, ed., *The Salmon P. Chase Papers*, 5 vols. (Kent, OH: Kent State University Press, 1993–98), 2:287.

28 *New York Herald*, Mar. 13, 1850; *New Hampshire Patriot*, Mar. 28, 1850; *New Orleans Daily Picayune*, Mar. 22, 1850; *Washington Daily Union*, Mar. 13, 1850.

29 The memoir was not published until 1873, by a reporter who was not present at the conversation between Taylor and Bullitt (Theodore Parmalee), "Recollections of an Old Stager," *Harper's New Monthly Magazine* 47 (1873): 589. Relations between Taylor and Bullitt were strained in this spring, and within a few weeks Taylor would arrange to have Bullitt fired—Hamilton, *Soldier in the White House*, 321–23; Holt, *Whig Party*, 491, 501–02. For the article and reaction, see *Washington Republic*, Mar. 15, 1850; *Brooklyn Eagle*, Mar. 18, 1850;

Pittsfield [MA] Sun, Mar. 21, 1850; Frances Seward to Lazette Worden, Mar. 21, 1850, Seward Papers reel 119; *Albany Morning Express*, Mar. 18 & 19, 1850 (suggesting Seward would lose patronage).

30 Weed to Seward, Feb. 8, Mar. 14, 15, & 17, 1850, Seward Papers reel 36; Seward to Weed, Mar. 31, 1850, Weed Papers. Holt's argument about the state political background of the Weed-Seward disagreement makes Seward (in my view) too much the creature of his supporters. See Holt, *Whig Party*, 491–93.

31 Cong. Globe, 31st Cong., 1st Sess. App. 859–63.

32 Cong. Globe, 31st Cong., 1st Sess. App. 1021–24; *Poughkeepsie Weekly Eagle*, July 11, 1850.

33 *Albany Evening Journal*, July 5, 1850; *Albany Morning Express*, July 6, 1850; *Boston Semi-Weekly Atlas*, July 6, 1850; *New York Tribune*, July 4, 1850; Weed to Frances Seward, July 4, 1850, Seward Papers reel 38.

34 *New York Tribune*, July 6, 1850; & Seward to Frances Seward, July 6, 9 & 10, 1850, Seward 2:143–44; Hamilton, *Zachary Taylor*, 388–93.

35 Seward to Frances Seward, July 12 & 15, 1850, Seward 2:145–46; Seward to Weed, July 20, 1850, Weed Papers; Paul Finkelman, *Millard Fillmore* (New York: Times Books, 2011), 72–84.

36 *New York Tribune*, July 27, 1850; *New York Evening Post*, July 29, 1850; *Albany Evening Journal*, July 31, 1850 (quotes *Atlas*); Cong. Globe, 31st Cong., 1st Sess. App. 1442–47; Seward to Weed, July 27, 1850, Weed Papers; Seward to Frances Seward, July 26, 1850, Seward 2:149 (misdated); Stegmaier, *Texas*, 184–86.

37 Seward to Weed, Aug. 2, 1850, Weed Papers; *Albany Evening Journal*, Aug. 2, 1850; *New York Tribune*, Aug. 2, 1850; *New York Express*, Aug. 2, 1850; Stegmaier, *Texas*, 193–200.

38 Thomas Rusk to James Brooks, Sept. 11, 1850, Rusk Papers, University of Texas; Stegmaier, *Texas*, 144, 157.

39 Seward to Frances Seward, Aug. 7, 1850, Seward 2:153; "H" to Millard Fillmore, Aug. 14, 1850, Fillmore Papers reel 20; *Baltimore Clipper*, Aug. 17 & Sept. 3, 1850; Seward to Patterson, Aug. 21, 1850, Patterson Papers, UR (Seward in Auburn); *New Orleans Picayune*, Aug. 28, 1850; Thomas Rusk to James Brooks, Sept. 11, 1850, Rusk Papers, University of Texas; *New Hampshire Patriot*, Oct. 17, 1850; George Poage, *Henry Clay and the Whig Party* (Chapel Hill: University of North Carolina Press, 1936), 258–61; Stegmaier, *Texas*, 272–73.

40 Allan Nevins, ed., *The Diary of Philip Hone*, 2 vols. (New York: Dodd, Mead, 1927), 2:902; Nevins and Thomas, eds., *Diary of George Templeton Strong*, 3:19; Stegmaier, *Texas*, 279–94.

41 Cong. Globe, 31st Cong., 1st Sess. App. 1642–49 (quote 1649); *Albany Evening Journal*, Sept. 12, 1850.

42 Seward to Weed, Sept. 21, 1850, Weed Papers; Fillmore to Daniel Ullman, Sept. 22, 1850, Ullman Papers, NYHS; *Albany Evening Journal*, Sept. 16, 1850;

New York Evening Post, Sept. 28, 1850; *New York Tribune*, Sept. 30, 1850; *Washington Republic*, Sept. 30 & Oct. 1, 1850; Holt, *Whig Party*, 583–91.

43 Hamilton Fish to Seward, Oct. 24, 1850, Seward Papers reel 39; Seth Hawley to Seward, Mar. 29, 1851, Seward Papers reel 40; *Boston Post*, Dec. 11, 1850 (Seward "very quiet"); *Detroit Free Press*, Jan. 8, 1851; Cong. Globe, 31st Cong., 2d Sess. App. 88–92, 257–58, 374–75; *New York Tribune*, Apr. 10, 1851 (fugitive slaves); Holt, *Whig Party*, 592–97, 644–50.

44 Seward to Frances Seward, May 11, 1851, Seward 2:164; *New York Tribune*, May 16 & 19, 1851.

45 Seward to Weed, June 3, 1851, Weed Papers; Seward to Frances Seward, Aug. 10 & Sept. 4, 1851, Seward 2:167; T. C. Leland, ed., *Argument of William H. Seward in Defence of Abel F. Fitch and Others* (Detroit: F. B. Way & Co., 1851); Charles Hirschfield, *The Great Railroad Conspiracy: The Social History of a Railroad War* (Kalamazoo: Michigan State College Press, 1953).

46 Scott to Seward, Nov. 9, 1839, Gratz Collection, Historical Society of Pennsylvania; Scott to Seward, July 8, 1851, Seward Papers reel 41; *Savannah Daily Republican*, July 1, 1851; Seward to Weed, Dec. 26, 1851, Weed Papers; Holt, *Whig Party*, 698–99.

47 *Philadelphia Public Ledger*, Jan. 8, 1852; Holt, *Whig Party*, 692–97; Donald Spencer, *Louis Kossuth and Young America: A Study of Sectionalism and Foreign Policy, 1848–1852* (Columbia: University of Missouri Press, 1977).

48 "Kossuth in America," *Mercersburg Review* 4 (1852): 81–90; *Brownson's Quarterly Review* (April 1852); *New York Times*, Jan. 5, 1852; Holt, *Whig Party*, 692–97; Spencer, *Louis Kossuth*, 136–44.

49 Cong. Globe, 32d Cong., 1st Sess. 89, 310; Frances Seward to Lazette Worden, Jan. 3 & Apr. 17, 1852, Seward Papers reel 119; *New York Times*, Jan. 9, 10 & 21, Apr. 13 & 17, 1852; Spencer, *Louis Kossuth*, 89–90, 151.

50 Frances Seward to Lazette Worden, Dec. 29, 1849, Jan. 3, Mar. 18, & Apr. 12, 1852, Seward Papers reel 119; Cong. Globe, 32d Cong., 1st Sess. 2371; Frances Seward to Charles Sumner, Aug. 26, 1852, Sumner Papers, reel 9; David Donald, *Charles Sumner and the Coming of the Civil War* (New York: Alfred A. Knopf, 1960), 208, 225–37.

51 *Propeller Genesee Chief v. Fitzhugh*, 53 US 443 (1852); Cong. Globe, 32d Cong., 1st Sess. 1198–202, 1873–76, 1974–76; David Currie, *The Constitution in the Supreme Court: The First Hundred Years* (Chicago: University of Chicago Press, 1985), 257–58; Howard Kushner, "Visions of the Northwest Coast: Gwin and Seward in the 1850s," *Western Historical Quarterly* 4 (1973): 295–306; Paolino, *Foundations of the American Empire*, 25–40.

52 Seward to Frances Seward, June 10, 17, & 25, 1852, Seward 2:185–88; Holt, *Whig Party*, 712–25.

53 *New York Tribune*, June 21, 1852; *New York Times*, June 29, 1852; *Daily National Intelligencer*, July 3, 1852; Peter Harvey, *Reminiscences and Anecdotes of Daniel Webster* (Boston: Little, Brown, 1909), 200; Holt, *Whig Party*, 725–33.

54 *New York Times*, Sept. 4, 1852; *Rutland Herald*, Sept. 4 & 16, 1852; Seward to Hamilton Fish, Sept. 17, 1852, Fish Papers, LC; Allan Nevins, *Ordeal of the Union*, 2 vols. (New York: Charles Scribner's Sons, 1947), 2:61–69.

55 Schuyler Colfax to Seward, Aug. 2, 1852, Seward Papers reel 44; Charles Sumner to Charles Adams, Aug. 25, 1852, Adams Papers, MHS; William Gienapp, *The Origins of the Republican Party, 1852–1856* (New York: Oxford University Press, 1987), 19.

56 P. C. H. Harris to Seward, Sept. 24, 1852, Seward Papers reel 44; *New York Times*, Oct. 16, 1852; Gienapp, *Origins*, 23–25; Holt, *Whig Party*, 741–46. For an amusing example of anti-Scott, anti-Seward rhetoric, see the "Life and Exploits of Gen. Scott, Respectfully Dedicated to his Commander, Gen. Bil. Seward," in the collection of the American Antiquarian Society.

57 *New York Times*, Jan. 5, 1853; Seward to Weed, Nov. 4, 1852, Weed Papers; Charles Sumner to Seward, Nov. 6, 1852, in Beverly Wilson Palmer, ed., *The Selected Letters of Charles Sumner*, 2 vols. (Boston: Northeastern University Press, 1990), 1:373; Seward to Sumner, Nov. 9, 1852, Sumner Papers reel 9; Henry Raymond to Seward, Nov. 6, 1852, Seward Papers reel 45; Seward to Raymond, Nov. 1852, quoted in Francis Brown, *Raymond of the Times* (New York: W. W. Norton & Co., 1951), 118.

58 Cong. Globe, 32d Cong., 2d Sess. 285, 765–67, 907–09 & App. 140–47; *New York Times*, Feb. 10, 1853.

59 *New York Times*, Dec. 16, 24, & 27, 1852, Feb. 25 & 28, 1853; *Wiswall v. Sampson*, 55 US 52 (1853); *Troy Iron & Nail Factory v. Corning*, 55 US 193 (1853); *Huff v. Hutchinson*, 55 US 586 (1853).

60 *New York Times*, Sept. 16, 1853; Baker 4:121–43.

61 Seward to Frances Seward, Mar. 17, 1853, Seward 2:202; George Baker to Seward, Nov. 1852 to Feb. 1853, Seward Papers reels 45–46 (more than twenty letters); Baker to Weed, July 20, 1853, Weed Papers; Baker 1:lxxix, 2:379–83 & 3:386–90. At Webb's request Seward omitted mention of the pardon. Seward to Webb, Jan. 15, 1853, Webb Papers Yale.

62 *New York Times*, Apr. 1, 1853; *Daily Chicago Journal*, May 17, 1853; *The Nebraska Question: Comprising Speeches in the United States Senate* (New York: Redfield, 1854) (backmatter quotes reviews of Baker); George Baker, "William Henry Seward: A Religious Man," *Unitarian Review* 23 (1885): 163–70.

63 Seward to Frances Seward, Jan. 4, 1854, Seward 2:216; Potter, *Impending Crisis*, 158, 166.

64 Seward to Weed, Jan. 7 & 8, 1854, Weed Papers; Seward to Frances Seward, Jan. 29, 1854, Seward 2:217–18; Cong. Globe, 33d Cong., 1st Sess. 175; Potter,

Impending Crisis, 158–63. As Holt notes, Seward's claim that it was he who urged Dixon to offer his amendment "has provoked considerable dispute among historians" because the sources, "mostly consisting of reminiscences written much later, conflict with each other"—*Whig Party*, 1138 n. 11. The sources are Charles Francis Adams Diary, Sept. 19, 1860, Adams Papers reel 75; Gideon Welles, *Lincoln and Seward* (New York: Sheldon & Co., 1874), 68–69; and Mrs. Archibald Dixon, *The True History of the Missouri Compromise and Its Repeal* (Cincinnati: Robert Clarke, 1899), 437–44.

65 George Baker to Frances Seward, Feb. 17, 1854, Seward Papers reel 48; Cong. Globe, 33d Cong., 1st Sess. App. 150–54.

66 John Forney, *Anecdotes of Public Men*, 2 vols. (New York: Harper & Bros., 1873–83), 2:164; Cong. Globe, 33d Cong., 1st Sess. App. 154–55.

67 *New York Times*, Feb. 18, 1854; *New York Herald*, Feb. 21, 1854; William Herndon to Seward, Mar. 21, 1854, Seward Papers reel 48; Seward to Frances Seward, Mar. 3 & 5, 1852, Seward 2:224; Holt, *Whig Party*, 818–19.

68 George Baker to Seward, May 10 & 14, 1854, Seward Papers reel 48; Seward (from Albany) to Hamilton Fish, May 19, 1854, Fish Papers, LC; Cong. Globe, 33d Cong., 1st Sess. 1321 (vote) & App. 768–70 (speech); Robert Johannsen, *Stephen A. Douglas* (New York: Oxford University Press, 1973), 434.

NOTES FOR CHAPTER 6

1 Key secondary works include: Tyler Anbinder, *Nativism and Slavery: The Northern Know Nothings and the Politics of the 1850s* (New York: Oxford University Press, 1990); Gienapp, *Origins of the Republican Party*; Holt, *Whig Party*; Potter, *Impending Crisis*.

2 Henry Wilson to Seward, May 28, 1854, Seward Papers reel 48; *New York Tribune*, May 29 & June 13, 1854; *New York Times*, June 10 & July 18, 1854; *Albany Evening Journal*, July 13, 1854.

3 Seward to Weed, May 29, 1854, Weed Papers; Gamaliel Bailey to James Pike, May 30, 1854, Pike Papers, University of Maine; Seward to Theodore Parker, June 23, 1854, Parker Papers, MHS; Seward to Weed, June 24, 1854, Weed Papers.

4 Seward to Edward Everett, June 19, 1854, Everett Papers, MHS; *National Era*, May 4 & Nov. 9, 1854; Gienapp, *Origins of the Republican Party*, 82–87; Holt, *Whig Party*, 830–34.

5 William Hodge to Millard Fillmore, Sept. 26, 1853, Fillmore Papers, LC; John Krout, "The Maine Law in New York Politics," *New York History* 17 (1936): 260–72; Gienapp, *Origins of the Republican Party*, 39–43, 147–49; Holt, *Whig Party*, 894–901.

6 Patterson to Weed, May 8, 1854, Weed Papers; Weed to Patterson, May 10 & 29, 1854, Patterson Papers, UR; *New York Times*, May 26, 1854; Charles Adams to

Weed, July 16, 1854, Weed Papers; Henry Wise to Edward Everett, Mar. 3, 1860, Everett Papers, MHS ("one of these days he will be found drunk in a gutter"); Gienapp, *Origins of the Republican Party*, 39–43, 147–49; Holt, *Whig Party*, 689–92, 894–901; Ian Tyrell, *Sobering Up: From Temperance to Prohibition in Antebellum America, 1800–1860* (Westport, CT: Greenwood Press, 1979), 252–82.

7   On the Know Nothings, see Anbinder, *Nativism and Slavery* (quotes on 23 & 31); Thomas Curran, "Seward and the Know-Nothings," *New-York Historical Society Quarterly* 51 (1967): 141–59; Gienapp, *Origins of the Republican Party*, 92–102; Michael Holt, "The Politics of Impatience: The Origins of Know Nothingism," *Journal of American History* 60 (1973): 309–31 (quote on 317); Holt, *Whig Party*, 845–50; and Bruce Levine, "Conservatism, Nativism, and Slavery: Thomas R. Whitney and the Origins of the Know-Nothing Party," *Journal of American History* 88 (2001): 455–88.

8   Cong. Globe, 33d Cong., 1st Sess. 1708; Lyman Spalding to Weed, Aug. 3, 1854, Weed Papers; Horace Greeley to Schuyler Colfax, Aug. 24, 1854, Greeley Papers, NYPL; Seward to ?, Sept. 1854, Seward 2:237. The newspaper from which Seward quoted was the July 15 issue of the *Know-Nothing and American Crusader.*

9   *New York Times*, July 14, Aug. 16 & 17, 1854; Weed to Patterson, July 11, 1854, Patterson Papers, UR; Greeley to Schuyler Colfax, July 26, 1854, Greeley Papers, NYPL; Seward to Frances Seward, Aug. 20, 1854, Seward 2:237; Greeley to Seward, Nov. 11, 1854, Seward Papers reel 48; Hendrik Booraem, *The Formation of the Republican Party in New York: Politics and Conscience in the Antebellum North* (New York: New York University Press, 1983), 52–55; Brown, *Raymond of the Times*, 134–35; Holt, *Whig Party*, 895–96.

10 Weed to George Patterson, Sept. 17, 1854, Patterson Papers, UR; *New York Times*, Sept. 20 & 21, 1854; *New York Herald*, Sept. 21, 1854; Seward to ?, Sept. 1854, Seward 2:236; Gienapp, *Origins of the Republican Party*, 153–54; Holt, *Whig Party*, 900–02.

11 *New York Times*, Sept. 27 & Oct. 13, 1854; *New York Herald*, Sept. 27 & 28, 1854; Charles Conrad to Millard Fillmore, Sept. 28, 1854, Fillmore Papers, LC; George Comstock to Daniel Ullman, Oct. 6, 1854, Ullmann Papers, NYHS; Gienapp, *Origins of the Republican Party*, 154; Holt, *Whig Party*, 902–03. Ullman's name is spelled "Ullmann" in some sources, including the NYHS Catalogue.

12 Seward to Ullman, Dec. 30, 1834, Nov. 19, 1838, & Feb. 21, 1852, Ullmann Papers, NYHS; Anbinder, *Nativism and Slavery*, 78–86; Holt, *Whig Party*, 899–907.

13 Alonzo Johnson to Weed, Oct. 14, 1854, Weed Papers; *New York Herald*, Oct. 23, 1854 ("every candidate for the state assembly is required to pledge himself in Mr. Seward's favor"); Andrew Hodges to Weed, Oct. 25, 1854, Weed

Papers (asking if a candidate could be trusted if he pledged); Booraem, *Republican Party*, 64–67; Curran, "Know-Nothings"; Holt, *Whig Party*, 905–06.

14 "Saratoga Springs," *Harper's Magazine* 53 (1876): 392 (quote); Irving Browne, "Reuben Hyde Walworth," *The Green Bag* 7 (1895): 266; Henry Stanton, *Random Recollections* (New York: Harper & Bros., 1887), 141–43; *The Reaper: Argument of William H. Seward in the Circuit Court of the United States* (Auburn, NY: William Finn, 1854).

15 *Albany Evening Journal*, Oct. 23, 27, & 28, 1854; *New York Herald*, Oct. 23, 25, & 27, 1854; *New York Times*, Oct. 10 & 30, 1854.

16 Baker to Seward, Nov. 10, 1854, Seward Papers reel 48; *Albany Evening Journal*, Oct. 12 & 16, 1854; *New York Times*, Dec. 21, 1854 (results); Anbinder, *Nativism and Slavery*, 78–86; Holt, *Whig Party*, 899–907.

17 *Boston Daily Atlas*, Nov. 13, 1854; *Buffalo Commercial Advertiser*, Nov. 17, 1854; *Rochester Daily American*, Nov. 20 & 21, Dec. 12, 1854.

18 Greeley to Seward, Oct. 25 & Nov. 11, 1854, Seward Papers reel 48; see Greeley, *Recollections of a Busy Life*, 315–20; Williams, *Horace Greeley*, 176–79.

19 Seward to Weed, Dec. 2, 1854, Weed Papers; Horace Greeley to George Baker, Feb. 8, 1855, in Derby, *Fifty Years Among Authors*, 135; Goodwin, *Team of Rivals*, 215–16.

20 Daniel Barnard to Hamilton Fish, Jan. 30, 1855, Fish Papers, LC; James DePeyster to James Beekman, Feb. 18, 1855, Beekman Papers, NYHS; W. S. Tisdale, ed., *Know Nothing Almanac and True Americans' Manual for 1855* (New York: DeWitt & Davenport, 1855), 53; Anbinder, *Nativism*, 148–49; Curran, "Know-Nothings," 155–57; Brown, *Raymond*, 142–43.

21 *United States Senatorial Question* (Albany: Weed, Parsons, 1855), 11, 13, & 26.

22 *Albany Evening Journal*, Feb. 5, 1855; Thomas Newman to Seward, Feb. 6, 1855, Seward Papers reel 49; Anbinder, *Nativism*, 149; Curran, "Know-Nothings," 160.

23 *Albany Evening Journal*, Feb. 8, 1855; Seward to Henry Raymond, Feb. 1855, quoted in Brown, *Raymond*, 143; Seward to Weed, Feb. 7, 1855, Weed Papers.

24 *Albany Evening Journal*, Feb. 5 & 8, 1855 (8th quotes other papers); *Boston Daily Atlas*, Feb. 7, 1855; *Cleveland Herald*, Feb. 6, 1855 (quotes *Richmond Whig*); *Springfield [MA] Republican*, Feb. 7, 1855; Frances Seward to Augustus Seward, Feb. 7, 1855, Seward Papers reel 115; Seward to Frances Seward, Feb. 18, 1855, Seward 2:246 (thanking for lost letter).

25 *New York Times*, Feb. 7, 1855; *Washington Daily Union*, Feb. 6, 1855; Theodore Parker to Seward, Feb. 11, 1855, Seward Papers reel 49.

26 Cong. Globe, 33d Cong., 2d Sess. 299 & App. 216, 240–42; Weed to Seward, Feb. 27, 1855, quoted in Wayne Miller, *The Emergence of William H. Seward as a National Political Leader, 1847–1859*, PhD diss. (University of Southern California, 1957), 166 (no longer in Seward Papers).

27 Frederick Douglass to Seward, July 31, 1850, Seward Papers reel 38; John Austin Journal, Sept. 13, 1855, Harvard; Seward to Frances Seward, Nov. 18, 1855, Seward 2:258; Kate Clifford Larson, *Bound for the Promised Land. Harriet Tubman: Portrait of an American Hero* (New York: Random House, 2004), 163–66, 184.

28 George Baker to Seward, May 14, 1855, Seward Papers reel 49; Seward to Baker, May 1855, Seward 2:252.

29 George Baker, ed., *The Life of William H. Seward* (New York: Redfield, 1855); pamphlet count based on the catalogues of the American Antiquarian Society and Cornell University.

30 *Albany Evening Journal*, July 20, 1855; Seward 2:254; Gienapp, *Origins of the Republican Party*, 224–228; Holt, *Whig Party*, 945–49; Miller, *Emergence*, 169–71.

31 Baker 4:225–40; *New York Tribune*, Oct. 15, 1855.

32 Frances Seward to Charles Sumner, June 9, 1853, Mar. 27, 1854, Sumner Papers reel 10; Seward to Sumner, Mar. 26, 1855, ibid. reel 12; Sumner to Hamilton Fish, Apr. 28, 1855, ibid. reel 71; Sumner to Seward, Oct. 15, 1855, Seward Papers reel 49; Henry Adams to Charles Francis Adams Jr., Feb. 8, 1861, in Worthington Ford, ed., *Letters of Henry Adams (1858–1891)* (Boston: Houghton Mifflin, 1930), 87.

33 Baker 4:241–52; *Boston Daily Atlas*, Oct. 18, 1855; *Raleigh Register*, Oct. 20, 1855.

34 Seward to Frances Seward, Nov. 8 & 10, 1855, Seward 2:258; Seward to William McKinstry, Nov. 8, 1855, Seward Papers reel 49; Anbinder, *Nativism and Slavery*, 183–87; Gienapp, *Origins of the Republican Party*, 189–237; Holt, *Whig Party*, 929–50.

35 Gamaliel Bailey to George Julian, Mar. 9, 1856, Giddings-Julian Papers, LC; *New York Times*, Apr. 18, 1856; Gienapp, *Origins of the Republican Party*, 305–29.

36 Seward to Weed, Dec. 31, 1855, & Jan. 6, 1856, Weed Papers; Weed to Seward, Jan. 3, 1856, Seward Papers; Gienapp, *Origins of the Republican Party*, 250–51; Michael Holt, "Another Look at the Election of 1856," in Michael Birkner, ed., *James Buchanan and the Political Crisis of the 1850s* (Selinsgrove, PA: Susquehanna University Press, 1996).

37 Cong. Globe, 34th Cong., 1st Sess. 921, 1698–99; Sen. Exec. Doc. 25, serial 879, 93–95; *New York Times*, Apr. 17, 1856; Jimmy Skaggs, *The Great Guano Rush: Entrepreneurs and American Overseas Expansion* (New York: St. Martin's Press, 1994).

38 Cong. Globe, 34th Cong., 1st Sess. 1698–99, 1740–41.

39 Cong. Globe, 34th Cong., 1st Sess. 1743, 2212, 2227; *New York Times*, July 25 & Aug. 18, 1856; U.S. Statutes at Large 11 (1856): 199–200; U.S. Code, vol. 48, secs.

1411–19; Walter Nugent, *Habits of Empire: A History of American Expansion* (New York: Alfred A. Knopf, 2008), 251–54; Skaggs, *Great Guano Rush*.

40 *New York Times*, July 27, 1855; Nevins, *Ordeal of the Union*, 2:380–93, 408–11; Potter, *Impending Crisis*, 199–209.

41 Richardson, ed., *Messages and Papers*, 5:352–60; Cong. Globe, 34th Cong., 1st Sess. 399–404; Nevins, *Ordeal of the Union*, 2:416–31; Potter, *Impending Crisis*, 215; Van Deusen, *Seward*, 168–69.

42 Weed to Seward, Mar. 5, 1856, Seward Papers reel 50; Greeley to Baker, Mar. 7, 1856, quoted in Baker, "Seward, Weed, and Greeley," *The Republic* 1 (1873): 199; Seward to Weed, Mar. 13, 1856, Weed Papers; Weed to Seward, Mar. 15, 1856, Seward Papers reel 50; *Washington Daily Union*, Apr. 10, 1856; *New York Tribune*, Apr. 10, 1856.

43 Seward to Weed, Apr. 14, 1856, in Seward 2:270; Weed to Seward, Apr. 18 & May 11, 1856, Seward Papers reel 51; Seward to Weed, Apr. 30, 1856, quoted in Miller, *Emergence*, 213; Seward to Weed, May 4 & 15, 1856, Weed Papers; E. Peshine Smith to Henry Carey, June 7, 1856, Carey Papers, Historical Society of Pennsylvania.

44 Cong. Globe, 34th Cong., 1st Sess. App. 529–47; Donald, *Sumner*, 282–87.

45 Donald, *Sumner*, 290–307; William Hoffer, *The Caning of Charles Sumner: Honor, Idealism, and the Origins of the Civil War* (Baltimore: Johns Hopkins University Press, 2010).

46 The best proof of Seward's absence is the detailed account by his friend Representative Edwin B. Morgan, which does not list Seward among those present—Morgan Papers, box 15, Wells College.

47 Frances Seward to children, May 22, 1856, Seward Papers reel 115; Cong. Globe, 34th Cong., 1st Sess. App. 663–64; Seward 2:271–73; William Gienapp, "The Crime Against Sumner: The Caning of Charles Sumner and the Rise of the Republican Party," *Civil War History* 25 (1979): 218–45.

48 *New York Evening Post*, May 23, 1856; *New York Herald*, May 27, 1856 (quoting *Richmond Whig*); *Richmond Enquirer*, June 3, 1856; *Ohio State Journal*, June 4, 1856 (quoting *Petersburg Intelligencer*).

49 *New York Evening Post*, May 23, 1856; *New York Times*, May 26 & 27, 1856; *New York Tribune*, May 26, 1856; Potter, *Impending Crisis*, 208–14.

50 Frederick Seward to Frances Seward, June 14, 1856, Seward 2:277–78; Jeremiah Wilbur to Seward, June 20, 1856, Seward Papers reel 52; Gienapp, *Origins of the Republican Party*, 301–03; Nevins, *Ordeal of the Union*, 2:451–60.

51 Webb to Seward, June 16, 1856, Seward Papers reel 52; Schoolcraft to Seward, June 16, 1856, ibid.; Seward to Frances Seward, June 17, 1856, Seward 2:278; Seward to Webb, June 17, 1856, Webb Papers, Yale; Gienapp, *Origins of the Republican Party*, 339. Seward's letter to Schoolcraft is no longer available, and all he wrote to Webb was that he had written Schoolcraft what was necessary.

It seems likely that Seward's letter to Schoolcraft was not quite the "peremptory declension" Seward described to Frances, and thus that even if Weed had Seward's letter in hand, he did not want to read it out to the convention.

52 Thomas Miller to Frances Seward, July 19, 1856, Seward Papers reel 52; Frances Seward to Seward, July 27, 1856, Seward Papers reel 114; Gienapp, *Origins of the Republican Party*, 343.

53 Seward to N.Y. Committee, June 21, 1856, in *Cleveland Herald*, June 27, 1856; Frances Seward to Seward, July 20, 1856, Seward Papers reel 114; Frances Seward to Augustus Seward, Sept. 8 & 15, 1856, Seward Papers reel 115; Seward to Samuel Wilkeson, Sept. 10, 1856, Weed Papers; Sumner to Seward, Sept. 18, 1856, Seward Papers reel 52; Seward to Webb, Sept. 28, 1856, Webb Papers, Yale; Gienapp, *Origins of the Republican Party*, 341–43; Miller, *Emergence*, 223–25.

54 Charles Dana to James Pike, Aug. 9, 1856, Pike Papers, University of Maine; Seward to Frances Seward, Aug. 17, 1856, Seward 2:287; Weed to Seward, Oct. 3, 1856, Seward Papers reel 52; Gienapp, *Origins of the Republican Party*, 36–82. Seward's first speech was before Weed's letter, but it seems likely Weed raised this issue earlier.

55 Seward spoke in Auburn, Buffalo, Cooperstown, Detroit, Lyons, Oswego, and Rochester—*Albany Evening Journal*, Oct. 15, 18, & 27, 1856; Seward to Frances Seward, Oct. 27, 1856, Seward 2:293; Gienapp, *Origins of the Republican Party*, 401 ("October elections all but extinguished Frémont's chances").

56 Caleb Henry to Seward, Nov. 6, 1856, Seward Papers reel 53; Samuel Blatchford to Seward, Nov. 7, 1856, ibid.; Martha Coffin Wright to W. R. G. Mellen, Nov. 14, 1856, Garrison Family Papers, Smith College; Gienapp, *Origins of the Republican Party*, 413–43.

NOTES FOR CHAPTER 7

1 Frederick Seward to Seward, Dec. 2, 1856, Seward Papers reel 116; Frances Seward to Augustus Seward, Apr. 19, 1853, & Dec. 16, 1856, ibid. reel 115; Anna Seward to Frances Seward, Mar. 26, 1857, ibid. reel 116; Mary Grier to family, Jan. 10 & Feb. 26, 1857, Grier Papers, UR; Martha Coffin Wright to Lucretia Mott, Sept. 8, 1855, Garrison Family Papers, Smith College ("not to be married"); Deirdre Stam, "Growing up with Books: Fanny Seward's Book Collecting, Reading, and Writing in Mid-Nineteenth-Century New York State," *Libraries and Culture* 41 (2006): 189–218.

2 *New York Times*, Jan. 10 & Feb. 26, 1857, Aug. 16, 1858; Cong. Globe, 34th Cong., 3d Sess. 393–95, 758–59; John Steele Gordon, *A Thread Across the Ocean: The Heroic Story of the Transatlantic Cable* (New York: Walker & Co., 2002), 69–72.

3 *New York Times*, Mar. 4 & 5, 1857; Cong. Globe, 35th Cong., Spec. Sess. App. 371–72; Kenneth Stampp, *America in 1857: A Nation on the Brink* (New York: Oxford University Press, 1990), 63–67.

4 *New York Times*, Mar. 7, 1857; *New York Tribune*, Mar. 9, 1857; Stampp, *America in 1857*, 93–100; Don Fehrenbacher, *The Dred Scott Case: Its Significance in American Law and Politics* (New York: Oxford University Press, 1978), 314–15.

5 *New York Tribune*, Mar. 7, 1857; *Chicago Tribune*, Mar. 12, 1857; *New York Times*, Apr. 11, 1857; Potter, *Impending Crisis*, 280–81; Stampp, *America in 1857*, 104–09.

6 Seward Journal, Seward 2:301–22; Seward to Hamilton Fish, Sept. 21, 1857, Fish Papers, LC; *Albany Evening Journal*, Sept. 22, 1857. A version of the journal appeared in the *Albany Evening Journal* from Sept. 5 to Sept. 22.

7 *Albany Evening Journal*, Sept. 17, 1857; *New York Times*, Jan. 13, 1862 (reprint).

8 *Chicago Tribune*, Oct. 14 & 23, 1857; Seward to Patterson, Oct. 26, 1857, Patterson Papers, UR; Seward to Frederick Seward, Oct. 26, 1857, Seward 2:324; Seward to James Watson Webb, Nov. 12, 1857, Seward Papers reel 55; Frances Seward to William Seward, Nov. 19, 1857, ibid. reel 115; David Donald, *Lincoln's Herndon* (New York: Alfred A. Knopf, 1948), 107–11; James Huston, *The Panic of 1857 and the Coming of the Civil War* (Baton Rouge: Louisiana State University Press, 1987), 14–34; Johannsen, *Douglas*, 583–84.

9 Seward to Frances Seward, Dec. 10, 1857, Seward 2:330; Cong. Globe, 35th Cong., 1st Sess. 14–22 & App. 4–5; Johannsen, *Douglas*, 306–17, 588–92; Stampp, *America in 1857*, 281–303.

10 Cong. Globe, 35th Cong., 1st. Sess. 412–13 & App. 5–6; Michael Burlingame and John Ettinger, eds., *Inside Lincoln's White House: The Complete Civil War Diary of John Hay* (Carbondale: Southern Illinois University Press, 1999), 73; Stampp, *America in 1857*, 201–08; Mark Stegmaier, "Intensifying the Sectional Conflict: William Seward versus James Hammond in the Lecompton Debate of 1858," *Civil War History* 31 (1985): 200–01.

11 Cong. Globe, 35th Cong., 1st Sess. 518–21; *New York Evening Post*, Feb. 17, 1858; *New York Times*, Feb. 5, 1858.

12 George Baker to Seward, Feb. 4, 1858, Seward Papers reel 56; *Albany Evening Journal*, Feb. 6, 1858; *New York Tribune*, Feb. 6, 1858; Seward to Richard Blatchford, Feb. 13, 1858, Greeley Papers, NYPL.

13 Weed to Seward, Mar. 11, 15, & 31, 1858, Seward Papers reel 56; Seward to Weed, Mar. 13, 18, & 24, 1858, Weed Papers; Blatchford to Seward, Apr. 12, 1858, Seward Papers reel 56; Samuel Wilkeson to Seward, June 1, 1858, ibid. reel 57.

14 Cong. Globe, 35th Cong., 1st Sess. 941–43.

15 Fehrenbacher, *Dred Scott*, 307–15, 473–74; McPherson, *Battle Cry of Freedom*, 178–79; Potter, *Impending Crisis*, 288; Samuel Tyler, *Memoir of Roger Brooke Taney* (Baltimore: John Murphy & Co., 1872), 391; Van Deusen, *Seward*, 190.

The relationship with Nelson is evidenced by Seward to Frances Seward, July 6, 1844, Seward 1:720; Nelson to Seward, Feb. 10, 1857, Seward Papers reel 54.

16 Cong. Globe, 35th Cong., 1st Sess. 698; *New York Times*, Feb. 17, 22, & 25, 1858; Seward to Frances Seward, May 20, 1858, Seward 2:344.

17 Cong. Globe, 35th Cong., 1st Sess. 943–45.

18 Ibid., 1894–98; Allan Nevins, *The Emergence of Lincoln*, 2 vols. (New York: Charles Scribner's Sons, 1950), 1:291–301; Potter, *Impending Crisis*, 322–26.

19 *Pittsfield Sun*, Jan. 25, 1857; Seward to Hamilton Fish, Sept. 21, 1857; Seward to Frances Seward, Dec. 14, 1857, & June 10, 12, & 13, 1858, Seward 2:331, 346–47; Haskell Monroe and James McIntosh, eds., *The Papers of Jefferson Davis*, 11 vols. (Baton Rouge: Louisiana State University Press, 1971–99), 6:196 n. 6; Varina Davis, *Memoir of Jefferson Davis*, 2 vols. (New York: Belford & Co., 1890), 1:579–81.

20 Undated article by William Wilkinson, Frederic Bancroft Papers, Columbia University; for background on this election, see Robert Imholt, *Beyond Slavery: The Transformation of Issues in the Politics of New York, 1857–1860*, PhD thesis (University of Kentucky, 1974).

21 Baker 4:292–93.

22 Undated article by William Wilkinson, quoted in Frederic Bancroft, *The Life of William H. Seward*, 2 vols. (New York: Harper & Bros., 1900), 1:191.

23 *New York Tribune*, Oct. 28, 1858; *New York Times*, Oct. 28, 1858; *New York Herald*, Oct. 28, 1858; *New York Evening Post*, Nov. 15, 1858; Seward to Theodore Parker, Nov. 19, 1858, Seward Papers reel 57.

24 William Herndon to Theodore Parker, Nov. 8 & 23, 1858, Parker Papers, MHS; Herndon to Seward, Dec. 28, 1858, Seward Papers reel 57; Seward to Herndon, Dec. 31, 1858, Herndon Papers, LC; Herndon to Seward, Jan. 17, 1859, Herndon Papers, NYHS.

25 Timothy Jenkins to Seward, Nov. 12, 1858, Seward Papers reel 57.

26 Fanny Seward Diary, Dec. 25, 1858, Feb. 20 & 25, 1859, Seward Papers reel 198; Amanda Foreman, *A World on Fire: An Epic History of Two Nations Divided* (London: Allen Lane, 2010), 3–6; Patricia Johnson, *Sensitivity and Civil War: The Selected Diaries and Papers, 1858–1866, of Frances Adeline Seward*, PhD thesis (University of Rochester, 1964). Johnson's transcribed, annotated version of Fanny's diary is invaluable.

27 Cong. Globe, 35th Cong., 2d Sess. 538–40, 1352–54; Nevins, *Emergence*, 1:444–55.

28 Seward to Patterson, Apr. 6, 1859, Patterson Papers, UR; Patterson to Seward, Apr. 7, 1859, Seward Papers reel 58; Cong. Globe, 36th Cong., 1st Sess. 164 (quoting Seward); Hinton Helper, *The Impending Crisis of the South* (New York: Burdick Brothers, 1857); David Brown, *Southern Outcast: Hinton Rowan Helper and the Impending Crisis of the South* (Baton Rouge: Louisiana State University Press, 2006).

29 *Philadelphia Public Ledger,* Apr. 2, 1859; Seward to Weed, Apr. 11, 1859, Weed Papers; *New York Herald,* May 3, 1859.

30 Frederick Seward to Frances Seward, May 8, 1859, Seward Papers reel 116; *New York Times,* May 9, 1859.

31 Benjamin Moran Diary, May 21, June 2, 6, & 7, 1859, Moran Papers, LC; Seward to Fanny Seward, June 1859, Seward Papers reel 112; Seward 2:362–90 (excerpts from letters without dates); Palmerston Memorandum, May 23, 1861, quoted in Gordon Warren, *Fountain of Discontent: The Trent Affair and Freedom of the Seas* (Boston: Northeastern University Press, 1981), 86; Weed to John Hughes, Dec. 7, 1861, Weed Papers. Amanda Foreman has a good description of Seward's 1859 visit to London, but relies too much on 1861 documents— Foreman, *World on Fire,* 38–47 & 847 n. 47.

32 Seward to E. D. Morgan, Nov. 16, 1859, Morgan Papers, NYSL; Seward to Fanny Seward, July–Nov. 1859, Seward Papers reel 112; excerpts in Seward 2:391–435.

33 John Bigelow to William Cullen Bryant, Nov. 1859, quoted in Margaret Clapp, *Forgotten First Citizen: John Bigelow* (Boston: Little, Brown, 1947), 124; Seward to Bigelow, Nov. 13, 1859, Bigelow Papers, NYPL; *New York Herald,* Oct. 20, 1859; *Brooklyn Daily Eagle,* Nov. 2, 1859; *New York Times,* Nov. 5, 1859; Larson, *Harriet Tubman,* 153–78 (describing role of Seward's tenant Tubman in Brown's plot).

34 Seward to Fanny Seward, Dec. 1859, Seward 2:436; Seward to John Bigelow, Dec. 13, 1859, Bigelow Papers, NYPL; John Austin Journal, Dec. 30, 1859, Harvard; *New York Times,* Dec. 28, 1859, & Jan 4, 1860.

NOTES FOR CHAPTER 8

1 Cong. Globe, 36th Cong., 1st Sess. 37–39, 68–70, 164–65, 931; Potter, *Impending Crisis,* 378–91.

2 Fanny Seward Diary, Feb. 29, 1860, Seward Papers reel 198; Frances Seward to William Seward, Feb. 29, 1860, ibid. reel 113; Cong. Globe, 36th Cong., 1st Sess. 910–14; *New York Times,* Jan. 6 & Mar. 1, 1860; *Washington Evening Star,* Feb. 29, 1860.

3 Fanny Seward Diary, Feb. 29, 1860, Seward Papers reel 198; Cong. Globe, 36th Cong., 1st Sess. 914.

4 *New York Times,* Mar. 1, 1860; *New York Evening Post,* Mar. 2, 1860; *New York Journal of Commerce,* Mar. 2, 1860; Gary Ecelbarger, *The Great Comeback: How Abraham Lincoln Beat the Odds to Win the 1860 Republican Nomination* (New York: Thomas Dunne, 2008), 147–48; Harold Holzer, *Lincoln at Cooper Union: The Speech That Made Lincoln President* (New York: Simon & Schuster, 2004), 155–70.

5 Seward to Weed, Mar. 10 & 15, Apr. 5 & 25, 1860, Weed Papers; Elbridge Spaulding to Weed, Apr. 29, 1860, ibid.; Weed to Cameron, Apr. 27, 1860,

Cameron Papers, LC; Joseph Casey to Simon Cameron, May 24, 1860, Cameron Papers, Dauphin County Historical Society (suggests Weed unwilling to discuss cabinet); Van Deusen, *Thurlow Weed*, 248–49 (suggests Weed did not want to get in middle of Cameron-Curtin dispute).

6 *Daily National Intelligencer*, May 19, 1860; *Harper's Weekly Magazine* (May 1860); *New York Times*, Mar. 24 & Apr. 17, 1860; *Providence Post*, Apr. 13 & May 15, 1860; *Washington Evening Star*, May 10, 1860; Ecelbarger, *Great Comeback*, 160–63, 188–92; Potter, *Impending Crisis*, 424–25.

7 William Fessenden to Family, May 7, 1860, Fessenden Papers, Bowdoin ("the Charleston denouement has improved Mr. Seward's chance"); *Washington Evening Star*, Feb. 24, 1860; Potter, *Impending Crisis*, 405–13; Roy Nichols, *The Disruption of American Democracy* (New York: Macmillan Co., 1948), 288–319.

8 Ecelbarger, *Great Comeback*, 201–02; William Heseltine, ed., *Three Against Lincoln: Murat Halstead Reports the Caucuses of 1860* (Baton Rouge: Louisiana State University Press, 1960), 159–62 (quote on 162); Reinhard Luthin, *The First Lincoln Campaign* (Cambridge, MA: Harvard University Press, 1944), 138–48; Van Deusen, *Thurlow Weed*, 248–52.

9 *New York Evening Post*, May 23, 1860 (Seward would have been nominated but for the corrupt legislature); *New York Times*, Apr. 19, 1860; James Dixon to Gideon Welles, Apr. 26, 1860, Welles Papers, LC; Charles Francis Adams Diary, May 11, 1860, MHS; Mark Summers, "'A Band of Brigands': Albany Lawmakers and Republican National Politics, 1860," *Civil War History* 30 (1984): 10–13; Mark Summers, *The Plundering Generation: Corruption and the Crisis of the Union, 1849–1861* (New York: Oxford University Press, 1988).

10 Seward to Patterson, Feb. 27, 1860, Patterson Papers, UR; Seward to Frances Seward, May 4, 1860, Seward 2:448; *Providence Post*, Apr. 6 & 13, 1860; James L. Huston, "The Threat of Radicalism: Seward's Candidacy and the Rhode Island Gubernatorial Election of 1860," *Rhode Island History* 41 (1982): 87–99; Luthin, *First Lincoln Campaign*, 141; Potter, *Impending Crisis*, 425.

11 James Sherman to John Tweedy, Tweedy Papers, Wisconsin Historical Society; Elbridge Spaulding to Seward, May 18, 1860, Seward Papers reel 59; *New York Times*, Apr. 17, 1860; Anbinder, *Nativism and Slavery*, 264–70; Bancroft, *Life of Seward* (Stevens quote); William E. Gienapp, "Who Voted for Lincoln?" in John Thomas, ed., *Abraham Lincoln and the American Political Tradition* (Amherst: University of Massachusetts Press, 1986), 57; Charles Hamlin, *The Life and Times of Hannibal Hamlin* (Cambridge, MA: Riverside Press, 1899), 342.

12 Seward to Frances Seward, May 5, 1860, Seward 2:449; John Austin Journal, May 12, 1860, Harvard; C. F. Adams Diary, May 13, 1860, MHS; *New York Herald*, Aug. 27, 1860.

13 John Austin Journal, May 14–17, 1860, Harvard; James Watson Webb to Seward, May 16, 1860, Seward Papers reel 59; Elbridge Spaulding to Seward, May. 17, 1860, ibid.; Hesseltine, ed., *Three Against Lincoln*, 161.

14 Evarts, King, and Blatchford to Seward, May 18, 1860, Seward Papers reel 59; Elbridge Spaulding to Seward, May 18, 1860, ibid.; John Austin Journal, May 18, 1860, Harvard. The numbers in the text are taken from Spaulding's telegram; in fact Seward received 173.5 votes—see Ecelbarger, *Great Comeback*, 225.

15 John Austin Journal, May 18, 1860, Harvard; Edwin Morgan to Seward, May 18, 1860, Seward Papers reel 59; Fanny Seward Diary, May 18, 1860, ibid. reel 198; Theodore Dimon to *Auburn Advertiser*, n.d., quoted in Van Deusen, *Seward*, 225. Austin's account, especially the reference to "the three or four who were present," shows there was no large crowd at Seward's house, nor were there three telegrams. The key source for the large crowd/three telegrams is Stanton, written years after the fact—Henry Stanton, *Random Recollections* (New York: Harper & Bros., 1887), 215–16; Goodwin, *Team of Rivals*, 12, 250.

16 Ecelbarger, *Great Comeback*, 204–05, 218–19; Michael Burlingame, ed., *An Oral History of Abraham Lincoln: John G. Nicolay's Interviews and Essays* (Carbondale: Southern Illinois University Press), 46–47 (Judd interview); Hesseltine, ed., *Three Against Lincoln*, 165; Luthin, *First Lincoln Campaign*, 160–62.

17 Lincoln endorsement, May 17, 1860, CWL 4:50; Joseph Casey to Simon Cameron, May 24, 1860, Cameron Papers, Dauphin County Historical Society; *Chicago Tribune*, Feb. 7, 1909, page Hb (Medill's quotes); Erwin Bradley, *Simon Cameron: Lincoln's Secretary of War: A Political Biography* (Philadelphia: University of Pennsylvania Press, 1966), 148–51; Ecelbarger, *Great Comeback*, 211–14 & 263–64; William Harris, *Lincoln's Rise to the Presidency* (Lawrence: University Press of Kansas, 2007), 206–07; Luthin, *First Lincoln Campaign*, 157–58. The deal was questionable not because it was unethical but because Cameron proved unfit for a cabinet position.

18 Fanny Seward Diary, May 17, 1860, Seward Papers reel 198; Elbridge Spaulding to Seward, May 18, 1860, ibid. reel 59; Joseph Casey to Simon Cameron, May 24, 1860, Dauphin County Historical Society; Ecelbarger, *Great Comeback*, 200–01, 208–10; Hesseltine, ed., *Three Against Lincoln*, 163; Luthin, *First Lincoln Campaign*, 154–60; Addison Proctor, *Lincoln and the Convention of 1860* (Chicago: Chicago Historical Society, 1918), 8 (Greeley quote).

19 Lincoln to Joshua Speed, Aug. 24, 1855, CWL 2:323; Seward to Benjamin Silliman, Nov. 12, 1840, Baker 3:388; Anbinder, *Nativism and Slavery*, 264–70; Gienapp, "Who Voted for Lincoln?" 57.

20 William Herndon to Seward, Dec. 28, 1858, Seward Papers reel 57; *Albany Atlas & Argus*, May 5, 1860; Ecelbarger, *Great Comeback*; Holzer, *Lincoln at Cooper Union*; Huston, "Threat of Radicalism"; William Lee Miller, *Lincoln's Virtues: An Ethical Biography* (New York: Alfred A. Knopf, 2002), 395: ("Lincoln

had the advantage, as well as the disadvantage, of being less well-known than others: he had not acquired their enemies.").

21 Gienapp, "Who Voted for Lincoln?" 67–68; Potter, *Impending Crisis*, 429–30.

22 Dr. T. S. Verdi, "The Assassination of the Sewards," *The Republic* 1 (1873): 289–90.

23 Seward to Weed, May 18, 1860, Weed Papers; *Auburn Daily Advertiser*, May 19, 1860; *New York Times*, May 25, 1860.

24 George Pomeroy to Seward, May 21, 1860, Seward Papers reel 59; William Mellen to Frances Seward, May 21, 1860, ibid.; Richard Blatchford to Seward, Aug. 8, 1861, ibid. reel 65; *New York Herald*, May 21, 1860; Seward 2:453–54.

25 *New York Times*, May 24, 1860; Frances Seward to Seward, May 30, 1860, Seward Papers reel 114.

26 *Albany Evening Journal*, June 14, 1860; *New York Times*, May 24 & 26, June 1 & 15, 1860; *New York Tribune*, May 25 & June 14, 1860; Van Deusen, *Seward*, 229–30.

27 *Illinois State Register*, May 25, 1860; Seward to Frances Seward, May 30, 1860, Seward 2:455; Barnes, ed., *Autobiography of Thurlow Weed*, 602–03.

28 Seward to Frances Seward, May 30, 1860, Seward 2:454–56; Charles Francis Adams to Seward, May 22, 1860, Seward Papers reel 59.

29 C. F. Adams Diary, June 21, 1860, MHS; Richard Brookhiser, *America's First Dynasty: The Adamses, 1735–1918* (New York: Free Press, 2002); Martin Duberman, *Charles Francis Adams, 1807–1886* (Boston: Houghton Mifflin, 1961).

30 *New York Times*, May 24, 1860; Seward to Benjamin Silliman, July 3, 1860, Seward Papers reel 60.

31 *Albany Evening Journal*, June 9 & 11, 1860; *New York Times*, June 9 & 11, 1860; Seward to Frances Seward, June 13, 1860, Seward 2:458; Van Deusen, *Thurlow Weed*, 77. For Seward's relations with Schoolcraft and Caroline, see Caroline Canfield to Seward, Sept. 26, 1849, Seward Papers reel 122 (hopes to leave Florida); Seward to Mahlon Canfield, Oct. 14, 1849, ibid. (insists that Caroline attend school in Georgetown); Caroline Canfield to Seward, June 3 & Oct. 28, 1850, ibid. reel 123 (from school in Georgetown); Frances Seward to Lazette Worden, Mar. 18, 1852, Seward Papers reel 119 (Schoolcraft like a family member), Caroline Canfield to Seward, June 9 & 15, 1853, ibid. reel 123 (needs money to travel).

32 Seward to Weed, June 26, 1860, Seward 2:459; Seward to J. W. Tillman, June 28, 1860, in *New York Times*, July 4, 1860; Seward to Weed, July 6, 1860, Weed Papers; Seward to Aaron Goodrich, July 10, 1860, in *New York Times*, July 30, 1860.

33 Seward to Richard Blatchford, July 10, 1860, Seward Papers Addition; Seward to William Evarts, July 10, 1860, ibid.; *Bellows Falls Argus*, Aug. 16, 1860; *New Hampshire Statesman*, July 18, 1860; *New York Herald*, July 9, 1860.

34 *Albany Evening Journal*, Aug. 13, 1860; *Bangor Daily Whig & Courier*, Aug. 13, 1860; *New Hampshire Statesman*, Aug. 18, 1860; *New York Times*, Aug. 15, 1860; *New York Tribune*, Aug. 16, 1860.

35 *Boston Daily Atlas & Bee*, Aug. 14, 1860; *Chicago Tribune*, Aug. 17, 1860; *New York Herald*, Aug. 15, 1860; *New York Times*, Aug. 15, 1860.

36 C. F. Adams Diary, Aug. 14 & 15, 1860, MHS; *New York Times*, Aug. 15, 1860; Charles Francis Adams to Seward, Aug. 25, 1860, Seward Papers reel 60; Adams, *Autobiography*, 59–61.

37 *New York Tribune*, July 27, 1860; *New York Times*, Sept. 5 & 19, 1860; Harris, *Lincoln's Rise to the Presidency*, 224–25; Luthin, *First Lincoln Campaign*, 192.

38 Fanny Seward Diary, Sept. 1, 1860, Seward Papers reel 198; *New York Times*, Sept. 5, 1860; Adams, *Charles Francis Adams*, 61–62.

39 Fanny Seward Diary, Sept. 1, 1860, Seward Papers reel 198; *New York Times*, Sept. 5, 1860; *Indiana Old Line Guard*, Sept. 27, 1860; *Richmond Enquirer*, Sept. 28, 1860; Gienapp, "Who Voted for Lincoln?" 60–62; Jon Grinspan, "Young Men for War: The Wide Awakes and Lincoln's 1860 Presidential Campaign," *Journal of American History* 96 (2009): 357–78.

40 Fanny Seward Diary, Sept. 2–4, 1860, Seward Papers reel 198; *Boston Daily Advertiser*, Sept. 5, 1860; *Chicago Tribune*, Sept. 5, 1860; *Daily Cleveland Herald*, Sept. 5, 1860; *Milwaukee Daily Sentinel*, Sept. 6, 1860; *New York Times*, Sept. 5, 1860.

41 Fanny Seward Diary, Sept. 5–8, 1860, Seward Papers reel 198; *Chicago Press & Tribune*, Sept. 8 & 10, 1860; *Janesville [WI] Daily Gazette*, Sept. 9, 1860; *Hartford Courant*, Sept. 12, 1860; *New York Times*, Sept. 13 & 15, 1860.

42 Fanny Seward Diary, Sept. 8–11, 1860, Seward Papers reel 198; *Chicago Press & Tribune*, Sept. 10, 1860; *New York Times*, Sept. 12 & 13, 1860; Baker 4:92.

43 Fanny Seward Diary, Sept. 11–12, 1860, Seward Papers reel 198; *Janesville Weekly Democrat*, Sept. 21, 1860; *Madison Daily Argus & Democrat*, Sept. 12–13, 1860; *Milwaukee Daily Sentinel*, Sept. 14, 1860; *New York Herald*, Sept. 13, 1860; Baker 4:90–92, 319–29.

44 Fanny Seward Diary, Sept. 13–14, 1860, Seward Papers reel 198; C. F. Adams Diary, Sept. 8 & 14, 1860, MHS; Baker 4:409; Theodore Blegen, "Campaigning with Seward in 1860," *Minnesota History* 8 (1927): 157, 167. The diary of Charles Francis Adams Jr. appears only in the Blegen article and Adams autobiography.

45 *Chicago Press & Tribune*, Sept. 21 & 24, 1860; *St. Paul Times*, Sept. 22, 1860; *New York Times*, Sept. 29, 1860.

46 Baker 4:95–96; Blegen, "Campaigning," 162–64, 169–70.

47 C. F. Adams Diary, Sept. 21–23, 1860, MHS; Adams, *Charles Francis Adams*, 61–62; Fanny Seward Diary, Sept. 21–23, 1860, Seward Papers reel 198.

48 Fanny Seward Diary, Sept. 26, 1860, Seward Papers reel 198; *Oskaloosa [KS] Independent*, Oct. 3, 1860; *New York Times*, Oct. 3, 1860; Baker 4:101, 385–96.

49 Fanny Seward Diary, Sept. 27–Oct. 1, 1860, Seward Papers reel 198; *New York Times*, Sept. 29 & Oct. 1, 1860; *Hartford Daily Courant*, Oct. 6, 1860; Baker 4:102–07.

50 Fanny Seward Diary, Oct. 1, 1860, Seward Papers reel 198; *Chicago Tribune*, Oct. 2, 1860; *Illinois State Journal*, Oct. 2, 1860; *Illinois State Register*, Oct. 2, 1860; *New York Times*, Oct. 6, 1860; Adams, *Charles Francis Adams*, 64–65; Baker 4:107–08.

51 *Chicago Tribune*, Sept. 7 & 12, Oct. 1–3, 1860; *New York Times*, Oct. 3 & 6, 1860.

52 *Baltimore Sun*, Oct. 6, 1860; *Chicago Tribune*, Sept. 28, 1860; *New York Evening Post*, Sept. 17, 1860; *New York Times*, Oct. 6, 1860; Adams, *Charles Francis Adams*, 65–66; Johannsen, *Douglas*, 778–95.

53 *Chicago Tribune*, Oct. 5, 1860; *New York Times*, Oct. 5 & 6, 1860; Adams, *Charles Francis Adams*, 67; Baker 4:111, 384; Seward 2:470.

54 *Wayne Democratic Press*, Sept. 26 & Oct. 17, 1860; Phyllis Field, *The Politics of Race in New York: The Struggle for Black Suffrage in the Civil War Era* (Ithaca, NY: Cornell University Press, 1982), 114–27; Philip Foner, *Business and Slavery: The New York Merchants and the Irrepressible Conflict* (Chapel Hill: University of North Carolina Press, 1941), 169–207; Harris, *Lincoln's Rise to the Presidency*, 238–40; Luthin, *First Lincoln Campaign*, 210–11, 216–17.

55 Weed to Seward, Oct. 25, 1860, Seward Papers reel 60; *Auburn Daily Union*, Nov. 6, 1860; *New York Herald*, Oct 29, 1860; *New York Times*, Oct. 22, 25, & 31, & Nov. 2 & 3, 1860; *New York Tribune*, Oct. 30 & Nov. 3, 1860; Eli Goldschmidt, *Northeastern Businessmen and the Secession Crisis*, PhD thesis (New York University, 1972), 166–68.

56 *Auburn Daily Union*, Nov. 6, 1860; *New York Times*, Nov. 7, 1860; *New York Tribune*, Nov. 7, 1860; Harris, *Lincoln's Rise*, 242–43; *Presidential Elections, 1789–2000* (Washington, DC: Congressional Quarterly Press, 2002), 121.

57 *New York Times*, Sept. 29 & Oct. 22, 1860; Luthin, *First Lincoln Campaign*, 171.

NOTES FOR CHAPTER 9

1 *Albany Evening Journal*, Nov. 14, 1860; *Charleston Mercury*, Nov. 8, 1860; *New York Times*, Nov. 19, 1860; Daniel Crofts, *Reluctant Confederates: Upper South Unionists in the Secession Crisis* (Chapel Hill: University of North Carolina Press, 1989); William Freehling, *The Road to Disunion*, Vol. 2: *Secessionists Triumphant, 1854–1861* (New York: Oxford University Press, 2007).

2 *New York Tribune*, Nov. 9 & 27, 1860; *New York Times*, Nov. 14, 19 & 21, 1860; *Albany Evening Journal*, Nov. 17, 24, & 30, 1860; Russell McClintock, *Lincoln and the Decision for War: The Northern Response to Secession* (Chapel Hill,

University of North Carolina Press, 2008), 57–58; David Potter, *Lincoln and His Party in the Secession Crisis* (New Haven: Yale University Press, 1942), 70–74.

3 Seward to Weed, Nov. 15, 1860, Weed Papers; Seward to Frances Seward, Nov. 30, 1860, Seward 2:478; Hiram Barney to George Fogg, Dec. 10, 1860, Fogg Papers, New Hampshire Historical Society; *Albany Evening Journal*, Nov. 19 & 30, 1860; *Lowell Daily Citizen*, Nov. 26, 1860 (speech); *New York Times*, Nov. 24, 1860 (speech). On Seward's connection with the editorials, see McClintock, *Lincoln and the Decision*, 71 & 294; Patrick Sowle, *The Conciliatory Republicans During the Winter of Secession*, PhD diss. (Duke University, 1963), 34–35.

4 Seward to Weed, Nov. 18, 1860, Weed Papers; Seward to Frances Seward, Dec. 5, 1860, Seward 2:479; Cong. Globe, 36th Cong., 2d Sess. 3 & App. 1–7; Nevins and Thomas, eds., *Diary of George Templeton Strong*, 3:71.

5 Seward to Weed, Dec. 3, 1860, Weed Papers; Lyman Trumbull to Lincoln, Dec. 4, 1860, Lincoln Papers; Seward to Frances Seward, Dec. 5, 1860, Seward 2:480; *New York Commercial Advertiser*, Nov. 30, 1860 (Seward will make an early speech); *New York Tribune*, Dec. 3 & 5, 1860.

6 Preston King to John Bigelow, Dec. 3, 1860, in John Bigelow, *Retrospections of an Active Life*, 3 vols. (New York: Baker & Taylor, 1909), 1:317; James Harvey to Lincoln, Dec. 5, 1860, Lincoln Papers; Seward to Frances Seward, Dec. 7, 1860, Seward 2:480; Seward to Fish, Dec. 11, 1860, Fish Papers, LC; David Clopton to Clement Clay, Dec. 13, 1860, Clay Papers, Duke University.

7 Henry Adams to C. F. Adams Jr., Jan. 17, 1861, in J. C. Levenson, ed., *The Letters of Henry Adams*, 6 vols. (Cambridge, MA: Harvard University Press, 1982–88), 1:223.

8 Henry Adams to C. F. Adams Jr., Dec. 9 & 29, 1860, in ibid., 1:204–05, 215; Henry Adams, *The Education of Henry Adams: A Centennial Version* (Boston: Massachusetts Historical Society, 2007), 80–81.

9 William Baringer, *A House Dividing: Lincoln as President Elect* (Springfield, IL: Abraham Lincoln Assoc., 1945); Harry Carman and Reinhard Luthin, *Lincoln and the Patronage* (New York: Columbia University Press, 1943); Harold Holzer, *Lincoln President-Elect: Abraham Lincoln and the Great Secession Winter, 1860–1861* (New York: Simon & Schuster, 2008). Some assert that Weed urged Lincoln, immediately after the election, to travel to Auburn to confer with Seward—e.g., Goodwin, *Team of Rivals*, 283. The only source for this is an 1866 entry in the diary of Welles, an ardent enemy of Weed—Beale, ed., *Welles Diary*, 2:388–89. There is no trace of such an invitation in the papers of Lincoln or Weed or Seward, all of which are reasonably complete for this period— Weed to Lincoln, Nov. 3, 1860, Lincoln Papers; Weed to David Davis, Nov. 17, 1860, ibid.; Lincoln to Weed, Dec. 17, 1860, CWL 4:154. There were, however,

reports that Seward would travel to Springfield to confer with Lincoln—*Albany Evening Journal*, Nov. 12, 1860.

10 Adams to Seward, Nov. 11, 1860, Seward Papers reel 60; Seward to Adams, Nov. 12, 1860, Adams Papers, MHS; Simon Cameron to Seward, Nov. 13, 1860, Seward Papers reel 60; Seward to Cameron, Nov. 15, 1860, Cameron Papers, LC; Seward to Israel Washburn Jr., Nov. 17, 1860, Washburn Papers, LC; C. F. Adams Diary, Nov. 16–17, 1860, MHS (Adams quotes a letter to "the Journal" but the quoted language is not in the *Albany Evening Journal*); *New York Herald*, Nov. 23, 1860; *New York Times*, Nov. 10, 1860.

11 Abraham Lincoln to Seward, Dec. 8, 1860, CWL 4:148–49 (two letters). There are three versions of the conversation between Hamlin and Seward. The first is in the diary of Gideon Welles, based on a late 1865 conversation with George Fogg, based on a conversation between Fogg and Hamlin at the same time— Beale, ed., *Welles Diary*, 2:389. The second and third versions, published in 1883 and 1899, seem even less reliable—Howard Carroll, *Twelve Americans* (New York: Harper & Bros., 1883), 152–54; Charles Hamlin, *The Life and Times of Hannibal Hamlin* (Cambridge, MA: Riverside Press, 1899), 372–73 (cites and follows Carroll). December 12 seems a likely date because Seward would not have waited long before writing Weed.

12 Leonard Swett and David Davis to Weed, Dec. 10, 1860, in Barnes, *Memoir of Thurlow Weed*, 301–02; Seward to Lincoln, Dec. 13, 1860, Lincoln Papers; Seward to Weed, Dec. 13, 1860, Weed Papers; Seward to Lincoln, Dec. 16, 1860, Lincoln Papers.

13 Seward to Israel Washburn, Dec. 16, 1860, Washburn Papers, LC (from Albany); *Albany Evening Journal*, Dec. 17, 1860; Cong. Globe, 36th Cong., 2d Sess. 112–14, 158; Israel Washburn to Seward, Dec. 19, 1860, Seward Papers reel 60; George Fogg to William Butler, Dec. 19, 1860, Fogg Papers, New Hampshire Historical Society; *New York Times*, Dec. 21, 1860.

14 Lincoln to Elihu Washburne, Dec. 13, 1860, CWL 4:151; Lincoln Resolutions, Dec. 20, 1860, ibid. 156–57; Lincoln to Lyman Trumbull, Dec. 21, 1860, ibid., 158; Weed to Lincoln, Dec. 23, 1860, Lincoln Papers; Seward to Lincoln, Dec. 26, 1860, ibid.; *New York Times*, Dec. 24, 1860 (timing of Seward-Weed meeting); Goodwin, *Team of Rivals*, 287–89; Holzer, *Lincoln President-Elect*, 165–70; McClintock, *Lincoln and the Decision*, 93–94, 103; Barnes, ed., *Autobiography of Thurlow Weed*, 603–14.

15 Weed to Seward, Dec. 25, 1860; C. F. Adams Diary, Dec. 27, 1860, MHS; Crofts, *Reluctant Confederates*, 221–25; Daniel Crofts, "A Reluctant Unionist: John A. Gilmer and Lincoln's Cabinet," *Civil War History* 24 (September 1978): 225–49; Barnes, ed., *Autobiography of Thurlow Weed*, 603–14.

16 *New York Times*, Dec. 24, 1860 (Seward's speech).

17 Seward to Frances Seward, Dec. 24, 1860, Seward 2:483; Seward to Lincoln, Dec. 26, 1860, Lincoln Papers; *Journal of the Proceedings of the Special Committee Under the Resolution of the Senate of the 18th of December 1860*, 36th Cong., 2d Sess. (Washington, DC, 1861); Potter, *Secession Crisis*, 170–74, 186–87.

18 Seward to Lincoln, Dec. 26, 1860, Lincoln Papers; Seward to Frances Seward, Dec. 26, 1860, Seward 2:485–86; *Journal of the Proceedings; Dedham [MA] Gazette*, Jan. 5, 1861; Potter, *Secession Crisis*, 186–87.

19 C. F. Adams Diary, Dec. 27, 1860, MHS.

20 Ibid.; *New York Times*, Dec. 26–29, 1860; *Washington Evening Star*, Dec. 26–29, 1860; Maury Klein, *Days of Defiance: Sumter, Secession, and the Coming of the Civil War* (New York: Alfred A. Knopf, 1997), 162–66; McClintock, *Lincoln and the Decision*, 107–12; Benjamin Thomas and Harold Hyman, *Stanton: The Life and Times of Lincoln's Secretary of War* (New York: Alfred A. Knopf, 1962), 94–97.

21 Seward to Lincoln, Dec. 28, 1860, Lincoln Papers (three letters); Seward to Frances Seward, Dec. 28, 1860, Seward 2:487.

22 Daniel Crofts, *A Secession Crisis Enigma: William Henry Hurlbert and "The Diary of a Public Man"* (Baton Rouge: Louisiana State University Press, 2010), 80–82, 218–20; Henry Adams to C. F. Adams Jr., Dec. 29, 1860, in Levenson, ed., *Letters of Henry Adams*, 1:214–15.

23 Seward to Lincoln, Dec. 29, 1860, Lincoln Papers; Seward to Weed, Dec. 29, 1860, Seward 2:487–88; Seward to Frederick Seward, Dec. 30, 1860, ibid., 489.

24 Leonard Swett to Lincoln, Dec. 31, 1860, Lincoln Papers.

25 Seward to Henry Wilson, May 28, 1870, Seward Papers reel 108; Seward 2:492; Thomas and Hyman, *Stanton*, 98–100; William Hutchinson, *Cyrus Hall McCormick: Seed-Time, 1809–1856* (New York: Century Co., 1930), 427.

26 Seward to Weed, Dec. 29, 1860, Weed Papers; Seward to Frances Seward, Dec. 31, 1860, Seward 2:489. The letter from Frances to Seward is not among the Seward Papers.

27 Seward to Frances Seward, Jan. 3, 1861, Seward 2:491; C. F. Adams Diary, Jan. 3–5, 1861, MHS; C. F. Adams to John Andrew, Jan. 4, 1861, Andrew Papers, MHS; Edwin Morgan to Seward, Jan. 5, 1861, Seward Papers reel 61; Leonard Swett to Lincoln, Jan. 5, 1861, Lincoln Papers; Klein, *Days of Defiance*, 192–93.

28 *Albany Evening Journal*, Jan. 9–11, 1861; *New York Times*, Jan. 9–11, 1861; *New York Tribune*, Jan. 9–11; James Webb to Lincoln, Jan. 12, 1861, Lincoln Papers; Crofts, *Reluctant Confederates*, 136–47; Klein, *Days of Defiance*, 191–205.

29 *Boston Atlas & Bee*, Jan. 16, 1861; *New York Evening Post*, Jan. 14, 1861; *New York Tribune*, Jan. 11, 1861; *Washington Evening Star*, Jan. 11–12, 1861.

30 Cong. Globe, 36th Cong., 2d Sess. 341–42; *Boston Atlas & Bee*, Jan. 16, 1861 ("difficult to restrain"); *New York Evening Post*, Jan. 14, 1861; *New York Times*, Jan. 16, 1861.

31 Cong. Globe, 36th Cong., 2d Sess. 343–44.

32 Ibid. 344; cf. Thomas Jefferson to Thomas Cooper, Oct. 7, 1814, in Joyce Appleby, ed., *Jefferson: Political Writings* (Cambridge: Cambridge University Press, 1999), 289.

33 *Boston Daily Advertiser,* Jan. 14, 1861; *Philadelphia North American,* Jan. 14, 1861; *Dedham Gazette,* Jan. 19 & 26, 1861; *Norfolk County Journal,* Jan. 19, 1861 (Seward established his "reputation for enlightened, comprehensive, and liberal statesmanship by his speech of Saturday last"). Mark Stegmaier, ed., *Henry Adams in the Secession Crisis: Dispatches to the Boston Daily Advertiser* (Baton Rouge: LSU Press, forthcoming), has detailed and useful notes on Seward's speech.

34 *New York Times,* Jan. 14, 1861; *Chicago Press & Tribune,* Jan. 14, 1861; *New York Evening Post,* Jan. 14, 1861; Charles Sumner to Samuel Howe, Jan. 17, 1861, Sumner Papers reel 64; Fessenden to Elizabeth Warriner, Jan. 12, 1861, Fessenden Papers, Bowdoin (speech was "spiritless" and "pleased no one but the ladies").

35 Frances Seward to Seward, Jan. 19, 1861, Seward Papers reel 114; see also Martha Coffin Wright to Marianna Pelham Mott, Feb. 28, 1861, Garrison Family Papers, Smith College (Lazette Worden "wants no compromises").

36 Seward to Frances Seward, Jan. 13, 18, & 23, 1861, Seward 2:496–97; Fanny Seward to Seward, Jan. 20, 1861, Seward Papers reel 116. It seems that there is a letter missing, or misdated, because Henry's letter of Jan. 18 is a response to some letter from Frances.

37 Henry Adams, "The Great Secession Winter of 1860–61," in George Hochfield, ed., *The Great Secession Winter of 1860–61 and Other Essays* (New York: Sagamore Press, 1958), 29; Horace Scudder, ed., *The Complete Poetical Works of John Greenleaf Whittier* (Boston: Houghton Mifflin, 1894), 186, 332.

38 *Alexandria [VA] Gazette,* Jan. 15, 1861; *Baltimore American,* Jan. 14 & 15, 1861; *Fayetteville [NC] Observer,* Jan. 21, 1861; *New York Times,* Jan. 16, 1861; *Richmond Whig,* Jan. 15 & 17, 1861; Edward Burks to Rowland Buford, Jan. 15, 1861, in James Walmsley, "The Change of Secession Sentiment in Virginia," *American Historical Review* 31 (1925): 85; Donald Reynolds, *Editors Make War: Southern Newspapers in the Secession Crisis* (Carbondale: Southern Illinois University Press, 2006), 185–86.

39 For evidence of Seward's communications with Virginians, see Henry Adams to C. F. Adams Jr., Jan. 24, 1861, in Levenson, ed., *Letters of Henry Adams,* 1:225 (Seward "receives as many letters from Virginia as he ever did from New York"); Seward to Lincoln, Jan. 27, 1861, Lincoln Papers (recent events have "opened access to me for Union men in Virginia"). See Adams, "Great Secession Winter," 24; Crofts, *Reluctant Confederates,* 138–49; McPherson, *Battle Cry of Freedom,* 256 ("Seward's conciliation policy also bore fruit in the form of a 'peace convention' "); Potter, *Secession Crisis,* 306–09; Sowle, *Conciliatory Republicans,* 276.

40 Lincoln to Cameron, Dec. 31, 1860, CWL 4:168; James Pike to Salmon Chase, Jan. 4, 1861, Chase Papers reel 14; Henry Adams to C. F. Adams Jr., Jan. 11, 1861, in Levenson, ed., *Letters of Henry Adams* 1:220; Seward to Lincoln, Jan. 13 & 15, Lincoln Papers; George Fogg to William Butler, Jan. 17, 1861, Fogg Papers, New Hampshire Historical Society; Lyman Trumbull to Lincoln, Jan. 21, 1861, Lincoln Papers; Holzer, *Lincoln President-Elect*, 181–83, 201–05; McClintock, *Lincoln and the Decision*, 122–25.

41 James Pike to Salmon Chase, Jan. 4, 1861, Chase Papers reel 14; Salmon Chase to Seward, Jan. 10, 1861, Seward Papers reel 61; George Fogg to William Butler, Jan. 17, 1861, Fogg Papers, New Hampshire Historical Society; George Fogg to Gideon Welles, Jan. 18, 1861, ibid.; Weed to Seward, Jan. 19 & 20, 1861, Seward Papers reel 61; Seward to Weed, Jan. 21, 1861, Weed Papers; Crofts, *Reluctant Confederates*, 227–29; Holzer, *Lincoln President-Elect*, 201–10.

42 Cong. Globe, 36th Cong., 2d Sess. 487 (Davis) 489 (Kansas).

43 Thomas Fitnam to James Buchanan, Jan. 25, 1861, Buchanan Papers reel 41; *Chicago Tribune*, Jan. 29, 1861 (report dated Jan. 26); Stephen Douglas to John Barbour, Jan. 25, 1861, endorsed by Crittenden, in Edward McPherson, *The Political History of the United States of America During the Great Rebellion* (Washington, DC: Philp & Solomons, 1865), 39; Nevins and Thomas, eds., *Strong Diary*, 3:94; Johannsen, *Douglas*, 826–28; Crofts, *Reluctant Confederates*, 201–07; McClintock, *Lincoln and the Decision*, 166–68.

44 Henry Adams to C. F. Adams Jr., Jan. 24, 1861, in Levenson, ed., *Letters of Henry Adams*, 1:225; James Ogden to John Crittenden, Jan. 29, 1861, Crittenden Papers, LC; Sowle, *Conciliatory Republicans*, 346–47.

45 Seward to Lincoln, Jan. 27, 1861, Lincoln Papers.

46 Amos Adams Lawrence Diary, Jan. 25, 1861, MHS; Robert Winthrop Journal, Jan. 25, 1861, MHS; Frederick Seward to Frances Seward, Jan. 30, 1861, Seward Papers reel 116; *Boston Daily Advertiser*, Feb. 2, 1861 (Henry Adams); Jane Flaherty, "The Exhausted Condition of the Treasury on the Eve of the Civil War," *Civil War History* 55 (2009): 244–77; Foner, *Business and Slavery*, 250–58.

47 Cong. Globe, 36th Cong., 2d Sess. 657–60.

48 Foreman, *World on Fire*, 7–8; Brian Jenkins, *Britain and the War for Union*, 2 vols. (Montreal: McGill-Queen's University Press, 1974–80), 1:44–45.

49 Lyons to Russell, Feb. 4, 1861, in James Barnes and Patience Barnes, eds., *The American Civil War Through British Eyes*, 3 vols. (Kent, OH: Kent State University Press, 2003–05), 1:28; Lyons to Russell, Feb. 4, 1861, in James Barnes and Patience Barnes, eds., *Private and Confidential: Letters from British Ministers in Washington to the Foreign Secretaries, 1844–67* (Selinsgrove, PA: Susquehanna University Press, 1993), 240.

50 Rudolf Schleiden to Bremen, Jan. & Feb. 1861, quoted in Ralph Lutz, "Rudolf Schleiden and the Visit to Richmond, April 25, 1861," *Annual Report of the*

American Historical Association (Washington, DC, 1915), 211; Lyons to Russell, Feb. 4, 1861, in Barnes and Barnes, eds., *Private and Confidential*, 240.

51 *Alexandria Gazette*, Feb. 4. 1861; George Fogg to Lincoln, Feb. 5, 1861, Lincoln Papers; Seward to Weed, Feb. 5, 1861, Weed Papers; McPherson, *Battle Cry of Freedom*, 256–59; Crofts, *Reluctant Confederates*, 138–44.

52 *New York Evening Post*, Feb. 5 & 11, 1861; W. D. Ross to Seward, Feb. 6, 1861, Seward Papers reel 61; Henry Adams to C. F. Adams Jr., Feb. 8, 1861, in Levenson, ed., *Letters of Henry Adams*, 1:230; James Barbour to Seward, Feb. 8, 1861, Seward Papers reel 61; Crofts, *Reluctant Confederates*, 140.

53 Lincoln to Seward, Feb. 1, 1861, CWL 4:183; C. F. Adams Diary, Feb. 5, 1861; Charles Sumner to John Andrew, Feb. 8 & 10, 1861, in Palmer, ed., *Letters of Charles Sumner*, 2:55–57; McClintock, *Lincoln and the Decision*, 171–75.

54 Lincoln to Seward, Jan. 3, 1861, CWL 4:170; Frederick Seward to Anna Seward, Feb. 14, 1861, Seward Papers reel 116; *New York Times*, Feb. 14, 1861.

55 Seward to Frances Seward, Feb. 15, 1861, Seward 2:505; Rudolf Schleiden to Bremen, Feb. 18, 1861, quoted in Lutz, "Rudolf Schleiden and the Visit to Richmond," 211; Charles Morehead to John Crittenden, Feb. 23, 1862, in Ann Coleman, *Life of John J. Crittenden*, 2 vols. (Philadelphia, 1871), 2:338; Charles Morehead speech, Oct. 9, 1862, in David Barbee and Milledge Bonham, "Fort Sumter Again," *Mississippi Valley Historical Review* (1941): 64 (similar). Morehead did not provide a precise date for the football comment but it seems that it was just before Lincoln arrived in Washington.

56 Lincoln Remarks, CWL 4:195, 211, 237; Holzer, *Lincoln President-Elect*, 308–10, 371–72.

57 C. F. Adams Diary, Feb. 20 & 21, 1861, Adams Papers, MHS; C. F. Adams Jr. to John Andrew, Feb. 22, 1861, Andrew Papers, MHS; McClintock, *Lincoln and the Decision*, 181–83.

58 Memo from Charles Stone, Feb. 21, 1861, Lincoln Papers; Winfield Scott to Seward, Feb. 21, 1861, ibid.; Seward to Lincoln, Feb. 21, 1861, ibid.; Elbridge Spaulding to Elihu Washburne, Feb. 22, 1861, Washburne Papers, LC; Seward 2:508–11 (Frederick); Allen Rice, ed., *Reminiscences of Abraham Lincoln by Distinguished Men of His Time* (Edinburgh: William Blackwood, 1886), 36–37; Holzer, *Lincoln President-Elect*, 377–96; Klein, *Days of Defiance*, 268–71.

59 The principal evidence that Seward met Lincoln at the station is a letter from Seward to his wife, dated February 23, of which we do not have the original, only a copy printed years later by Frederick in his biography of his father. "The president-elect arrived *incognito* at six this morning. I met him at the depot"— Seward to Frances Seward, Feb. 23, 1861, Seward 2:511. Charles Francis Adams recorded in his diary, probably based on a conversation with Seward, that "Mr. Lincoln reached here this morning at six o'clock and was met at the

station by Mr. Seward and Mr. Washburne, who took him to Willard's Hotel"—
C. F. Adams Diary, Feb. 23, 1861, MHS.

The principal evidence that Seward was not at the station is an 1886 account by Washburne in which he recalled that when he arrived at the station, "to my great disappointment Governor Seward did not appear." Lincoln arrived at six, accompanied only by the detective Allan Pinkerton and his own bodyguard, Ward Hill Lamon. Washburne greeted them, they walked out to a waiting carriage, and traveled the short distance to Willard's Hotel. "We had not been in the hotel more than two minutes," Washburne continued, "before Governor Seward hurried up, much out of breath and somewhat chagrined to think he had not been up in season to be at the depot on the arrival of the train"—Rice, ed., *Reminiscences*, 37–39. Washburne's account is supported by Pinkerton and Lamon, in accounts also written years after the fact—Ward Hill Lamon, *The Life of Abraham Lincoln* (Boston: James Osgood, 1872), 526; Allan Pinkerton, *The Spy of the Rebellion* (New York: G. W. Dillingham, 1890), 98. Washburne's version is supported by two news reports: the *Washington Evening Star*, Feb. 23, 1861, quoted in the text, and the *Albany Evening Journal*, Apr. 10, 1861, probably written by Frederick Seward to rebut criticism of Lincoln's passage through Baltimore. Frederick's account states that Washburne met Lincoln at the station, and that Lincoln traveled by carriage from the station to the hotel, "where Senator Seward stood ready to receive him." These two newspaper accounts support Washburne in placing Seward at the Willard Hotel, but they undercut him on Seward's "chagrin," since they suggest that Seward planned to meet Lincoln at the hotel, perhaps to avoid attracting attention at the train station. And the newspapers are not consistent; both the *New York Tribune* and the *New York Herald* reported that Lincoln was met at the depot by Washburne and Seward; the *Daily National Republican* mentioned only Seward as meeting Lincoln at the station—*Daily National Intelligencer*, Feb. 25, 1861; *New York Herald*, Feb. 24, 1861; *New York Tribune*, Feb. 25, 1861. As Van Deusen noted, this is a good example of the "problems that beset the researcher"—Glyndon Van Deusen, "Seward and Lincoln: The Washington Depot Episode," *University of Rochester Library Bulletin* 20 (1965).

60 *Boston Daily Advertiser*, Feb. 27, 1861; *Daily National Intelligencer*, Feb. 25–26, 1861; *New York Herald*, Feb. 26, 1861 (quote); *New York Times*, Feb. 25–27, 1861; *Washington Evening Star*, Feb. 25–26, 1861; Seward to Lincoln, Feb. 25, 1861, Lincoln Papers; Baringer, *House Dividing*, 297–310; Goodwin, *Team of Rivals*, 312–16; Holzer, *Lincoln President-Elect*, 406–22. Some sources state that the two men ate breakfast on February 23 but this is not in the newspapers.

61 Lincoln Draft Inaugural Address, CWL 4:249–62; Holzer, *Lincoln President-Elect*, 437–40.

62 Seward to Lincoln, Feb. 24, 1861, Seward 2:512, or John G. Nicolay and John Hay, *Abraham Lincoln: A History*, 10 vols. (New York: Century, 1890), 3:321. The original of the cover letter does not survive; we have only these two printed versions and a copy in Frederick's handwriting in the Seward Papers.

63 Lincoln's Draft with Seward's Comments, Feb. 1861, Lincoln Papers; Seward Suggestions, Feb. 1861, ibid.; Holzer, *Lincoln President-Elect*, 440–44.

64 Seward Suggestions, Feb. 1861, Lincoln Papers (two documents); Holzer, *Lincoln President-Elect*, 443–44; Ronald White Jr., *The Eloquent President: A Portrait of Lincoln Through His Words* (New York: Random House, 2005), 65–70. Many assume that the "Frederick" draft preceded the "Seward" draft, but there is nothing in the drafts to establish an order.

65 I largely follow McClintock here although, as noted below, there are some indications that Lincoln and Seward conferred on the inaugural before the inauguration—McClintock, *Lincoln and the Decision*, 190–98.

66 Lyons to Russell, Feb. 18, 1861, in Barnes & Barnes, eds., *British Eyes*, 1:33; *Albany Evening Journal*, Feb. 25, 1861; *New York Evening Post*, Feb. 23, 1861; *New York Herald*, Feb. 27, 1861; *New York Tribune*, Feb. 27, 1861; John Bigelow Diary, Mar. 1, 1861, NYPL; Van Deusen, *Thurlow Weed*, 264–65.

67 *Washington Evening Star*, Feb. 27, 1861; *Albany Evening Journal*, Feb. 28, 1861; *Daily National Intelligencer*, Feb. 28, 1861; *New York Evening Post*, Mar. 2, 1861; *New York Herald*, Mar. 1 & 3, 1861; Cong. Globe, 36th Cong., 2d Sess. 1269–70, 1305–06; Robert Gunderson, *Old Gentlemen's Convention: The Washington Peace Convention of 1861* (Madison: University of Wisconsin Press, 1961); Albert Kirwan, *John J. Crittenden: The Struggle for Union* (Lexington: University of Kentucky Press, 1962), 409–15; McClintock, *Lincoln and the Decision*, 184–85.

68 Howard Beale, ed., *The Diary of Edward Bates* (New York: Da Capo Press, 1971) 175; C. F. Adams Diary, Feb. 28, 1861, MHS; C. F. Adams Jr. to R. H. Dana Jr., Feb. 28, 1861, Dana Papers, MHS; *Washington Evening Star*, Mar. 1, 1861; Holzer, *Lincoln President-Elect*, 433.

69 John Austin Journal, Mar. 2, 1861, Harvard University; *Auburn Daily Advertiser*, Mar. 7, 1861.

70 The quote is from a conversation between George Fogg, the New Hampshire editor, and Gideon Welles, recorded by Welles in 1866—Beale, ed., *Welles Diary*, 2:391. Among the many accounts based on Fogg-Welles, see Burlingame, *Abraham Lincoln*, 2:56. For other accounts, see Crofts, *Secession Winter Enigma*, 106–09, 244–46; McClintock, *Lincoln and the Decision*, 193–94.

71 Seward to Lincoln, Mar. 2, 1861, Lincoln Papers. For the traditional view of Seward's letter, see John Nicolay and John Hay, "Abraham Lincoln: A History: The Formation of the Cabinet," *The Century* 35 (1888): 427; Baringer, *House Dividing*, 326–29; Nevins, *Emergence of Lincoln*, 2:454–55. For the newer view,

see Crofts, *Reluctant Confederates*, 254; McClintock, *Lincoln and the Decision*, 190–99; Sowle, *Conciliatory Republicans*, 448–49.

72 *Daily National Republican*, Mar. 4, 1861; John Austin Journal, Mar. 3, 1861, Harvard; C. F. Adams Jr., *Autobiography*, 95–96; Crofts, *Secession Winter Enigma*, 87–88; 251–53; Evan Coleman, "Gwin and Seward: A Secret Chapter in Ante-Bellum History," *Overland Monthly* 18 (1891): 465–71. I have added [not] to the Adams quote because Seward would not have said that Lincoln's address would satisfy the whole country.

73 William Bailhache to wife, Mar. 3, 1861, quoted in Burlingame, *Abraham Lincoln*, 2:49.

74 Cong. Globe, 36th Cong., 2d Sess. 1374–80, 1403 (vote on amendment); Kirwan, *Crittenden*, 415–20; *Cincinnati Commercial*, Mar. 4, 1861 ("Seward-Corwin amendment"); *New York Times*, Mar. 5, 1861 (timing of vote on amendment). For more on Seward and the amendment, see Stegmaier, ed., *Henry Adams* (letter six).

75 John Austin Journal, Mar. 4, 1861, Harvard; *Daily National Republican*, Mar. 5, 1861; *New York Evening Post*, Mar. 5, 1861; *New York Times*, Mar. 5, 1861; *Washington Evening Star*, Mar. 4, 1861.

76 John Austin Journal, Mar. 4, 1861, Harvard; *New York Times*, Mar. 5, 1861; *Washington Evening Star*, Mar. 4, 1861.

77 Lincoln Inaugural, CWL 4:266; Holzer, *Lincoln President-Elect*, 44–45.

78 Lincoln Inaugural, CWL 4:271; John Austin Journal, Mar. 5, 1861, Harvard; White, *Eloquent President*, 74–91. White is especially good on Lincoln's improvements to Seward's draft.

79 Lincoln to Seward, Mar. 4, 1861, CWL 4:273; Seward to Lincoln, Mar. 5, 1861, Lincoln Papers; Seward to Frances Seward, Mar. 8, 1861, Seward 2:518; John Bigelow Diary, Mar. 27, 1861, NYPL; McClintock, *Lincoln and the Decision*, 198.

80 Edward Everett Diary, Jan. 29, 1861, MHS (Seward pressed him to join list of managers); John Austin Journal, Mar. 4, 1861, Harvard; *Washington Evening Star*, Mar. 4, 1861 (lists managers of ball); *New York Herald*, Mar. 6, 1861 (quote).

81 Senate Executive Journal, vol. 11, pp. 289–91; *Washington Evening Star*, Mar. 5–6, 1861; Seward 2:519.

82 Adams, "Secession Winter," 23.

83 Ibid., 28; Crofts, *Reluctant Confederates*, 353–59; Allan Nevins, *The War for the Union*, 4 vols. (New York: Charles Scribner's Sons, 1959–71), 1:39, 72, 74; Potter, *Secession Crisis*, 313–14; Kenneth Stampp, *And the War Came: The North and the Secession Crisis, 1860–61* (Baton Rouge: Louisiana State University Press, 1950), 271–72.

84 On the Baltimore threat, see Holzer, *Lincoln President-Elect*, 390–405 & 583 n. 34; Edward Steers, *Blood on the Moon: The Assassination of Abraham Lincoln* (Lexington: University Press of Kentucky, 2001), 17–21.

NOTES FOR CHAPTER 10

1   William Haley, *Philp's Washington Described: A Complete View of the American Capital* (New York: Rudd & Carlton, 1861), 82–83; Elmer Plischke, *U.S. Department of State: A Reference History* (Westport, CT: Greenwood Press, 1999), 142–43, 150–52; Seward 2:519–20 (house).

2   Seward, *Reminiscences*, 147; Rudolf Schleiden to Bremen, Mar. 4, 1861, quoted in Lutz, "Rudolf Schleiden and the Visit to Richmond," 210; John Lothrop Motley to Mary Motley, June 23, 1861, in George Curtis, ed., *The Correspondence of John Lothrop Motley*, 2 vols. (New York: Harper & Bros., 1889), 1:394.

3   Seward 2:519–20; Peter Bridges, "Some Men Named William Hunter," *Diplomacy and Statecraft* 16 (2005): 251–57.

4   List of State Department Positions, Mar. 1861, Lincoln Papers; Burlingame, *Abraham Lincoln*, 2:90–97; Carman and Luthin, *Patronage*, 79–109; Plischke, *Department of State*, 142–53, 207.

5   *New York Tribune*, Dec. 4, 1857; Cong. Globe, 35th Cong., 2d Sess. 458 ("one grand humbug"); Kenneth Stampp, *America in 1857: A Nation on the Brink* (New York: Oxford University Press), 73.

6   Lincoln to Seward, Mar. 5 & 11, 1861, CWL 4:276 & 281; Seward to Lincoln, Mar. 11, 1861, Lincoln Papers; C. F. Adams Diary, Mar. 10, 1861, MHS; Senate Exec. Journal, 37th Cong., Spec. Sess. 291.

7   Lincoln to Seward, Mar. 18, 1861, Seward Papers; Carl Schurz to wife, Mar. 28, 1861, in Joseph Schafer, ed., *Intimate Letters of Carl Schurz, 1841–1869* (Madison: State Historical Society of Wisconsin, 1928), 252–53; Albert Brown to John Andrew [Mar. 28, 1861], Andrew Papers, MHS; Burlingame, *Abraham Lincoln*, 91–92; Carman and Luthin, *Patronage*, 82–84.

8   Carman and Luthin, *Patronage*, 87–102; Clapp, *Forgotten First Citizen*; Daniel Crofts, "James E. Harvey and the Secession Crisis," *Pennsylvania Magazine of History and Biography* 103 (1979): 177–95; James Crouthamel, *James Watson Webb: A Biography* (Middletown, CT: Wesleyan University Press, 1969); Joseph Fry, *Henry S. Sanford: Diplomacy and Business in Nineteenth-Century America* (Reno: University of Nevada Press, 1982). Another "Seward" appointment was that of one of the Washburn brothers as minister to Paraguay. Kerck Kelsey, *Remarkable Americans: The Washburn Family* (Gardiner, ME: Tilbury House, 2008).

9   Chase to Seward, Mar. 20, 1861, in Niven, ed., *Salmon Chase Papers*, 3:54–55; *Cincinnati Daily Gazette*, Apr. 1, 1861.

10 Chase to Seward, Mar. 27, 1861, Seward Papers reel 62; Seward to Chase, Mar. 27, 1861, Huntington Library; Seward to Chase, Mar. 28, 1861, Chase Papers reel 14; Seward to Lincoln, Mar. 28, 1861, Lincoln Papers; Chase to John

Sherman, Mar. 28, 1861, Chase Papers reel 14; Senate Executive Journal, 37th Cong., Spec. Sess. 364; Carman and Luthin, *Patronage*, 167–68.

11 Augustus Seward to Seward, Nov. 10 & Dec. 10, 1860, & Jan. 11, 1861, Seward Papers reel 116; Seward to Lincoln, Mar. 11, 1861, Lincoln Papers; Simon Cameron to Frances Seward, Mar. 22, 1861, Seward Papers reel 62.

12 Edwin Stanton to Lincoln, Mar. 6, 1861, Lincoln Papers; *Boston Journal*, Mar. 8, 1861 (quote); Seward to Lincoln, Mar. 9, 1861, Lincoln Papers; Edwin Stanton to Buchanan, Mar. 10, 1861, Buchanan Papers reel 41; J. S. Black to Buchanan, Mar. 11, 1861, ibid.; Thomas Hicks to Seward, Mar. 27, 1861, Lincoln Papers; Burlingame, *Abraham Lincoln*, 2:96–97; Carman and Luthin, *Patronage*, 186–227; Crofts, *Reluctant Confederates*, 272–73.

13 Lincoln to Weed, Feb. 4, 1861, CWL 4:185; *Cincinnati Daily Commercial*, Mar. 2, 4, & 11, 1861; *New York Herald*, Jan. 3, 1861; Burlingame, *Abraham Lincoln*, 2:78; Carman and Luthin, *Patronage*, 59–64; Albert Hart, *Salmon Portland Chase* (Boston: Houghton, Mifflin, 1899), 217–18.

14 Seward to Frances Seward, Mar. 16, 1861, Seward 2:530; C. F. Adams Diary, Mar. 28, 1861, MHS; Frederick Seward to Frances Seward, Mar. 12 & 21, 1861, Seward Papers reel 116; Anna Seward to Frances Seward, Mar. 31, 1861, ibid.

15 Beale, ed., *Bates Diary*, 175–77; Goodwin, *Team of Rivals*, 334.

16 Beale, ed., *Bates Diary*, 177; McClintock, *Lincoln and the Decision*, 199–203; Craig Symonds, *Lincoln and His Admirals: Abraham Lincoln, the U.S. Navy, and the Civil War* (New York: Oxford University Press, 2008), 3–8.

17 Sam Ward to Seward, Mar. 4, 1861, in Bancroft, *Life of Seward*, 2:544 (no longer in Seward Papers); Joseph Holt to Lincoln, Mar. 5, 1861, Lincoln Papers; Beale, ed., *Welles Diary*, 1:6.

18 Martin Crawford and John Forsyth to Robert Toombs, Mar. 8, 1861, Toombs Papers, University of South Carolina; Seward to Lincoln, Mar. 9, 1861, Lincoln Papers; Cong. Globe, 37th Cong., Spec. Sess. 1442; McClintock, *Lincoln and the Decision*, 211–12.

19 *Boston Atlas & Bee*, Mar. 11, 1861; *Daily National Intelligencer*, Mar. 12, 1861; *New York Tribune*, Mar. 11–12, 1861; C. F. Adams Diary, Mar. 12, 1861, MHS; Burlingame, *Abraham Lincoln*, 2:100–01.

20 Lincoln to Seward, Mar. 15, 1861, CWL 4:284–85; Seward to Lincoln, Mar. 15, 1861, Lincoln Papers; Burlingame, *Abraham Lincoln*, 2:101–02; Goodwin, *Team of Rivals*, 335–37.

21 Cabinet members to Lincoln, Mar. 15 & 16, CWL 4:285; George Summers to J. C. Welling, Mar. 19, 1861, in McClintock, *Lincoln and the Decision*, 215; ibid., 323 (Lincoln aware of Seward's communications).

22 John Campbell, "Papers of John A. Campbell, 1861–1865," *Southern Historical Society Papers* 4 (1917): 30–33; see John Campbell to Seward, Mar. 15 & 16, 1861, Seward Papers reel 62.

23 Burlingame, *Abraham Lincoln*, 2:104–05; McClintock, *Lincoln and the Decision*, 218–19.

24 *New York Herald*, Mar. 15, 1861; *New York Evening Post*, Mar. 12, 1861; Foner, *Business and Slavery*, 276–84; Flaherty, "The Exhausted Condition of the Treasury on the Eve of the Civil War;" Stampp, *And the War Came*, 223–38.

25 Lincoln to Bates, Chase, and Welles, Mar. 18, 1861, CWL 4:290–93; Lyons to Russell, Mar. 26, 1861, in Barnes and Barnes, eds., *Private and Confidential*, 242–43; Kinley Brauer, "Seward's 'Foreign War Panacea': An Interpretation," *New York History* 55 (1974): 140–42.

26 Lyons to Russell, Mar. 26, 1861, in Barnes and Barnes, eds., *Private and Confidential*, 243–44; Mercier to Thouvenel, Mar. 26, 1861, in Daniel Carroll, *Henri Mercier and the American Civil War* (Princeton: Princeton University Press, 1971), 52; Brauer, "Foreign War Panacea."

27 William Russell, *My Diary North and South*, ed. Eugene Berwanger (Baton Rouge: Louisiana State University Press, 2001), 41–42; Fry, *Henry S. Sanford.*

28 André Roman to Robert Toombs, Mar. 25, 1861, Confederate States Papers, LC; Crawford and Roman to Toombs, Mar. 26, 1861, ibid.

29 Russell, *Diary*, 43–48; A. B. Roman to Toombs, Mar. 25, 1861, Confederate States Papers, LC; C. F. Adams Diary, Mar. 28, 1861, MHS; Adams, *Autobiography*, 112–13; Bancroft, *Life of Seward*, 2:107, 117; Albert Woldman, *Lincoln and the Russians* (Cleveland: World Publishing Co., 1952), 50–51.

30 Seating Chart, Mar. 28, 1861, Nicolay Papers, LC; Russell, *Diary*, 48–51; Burlingame, *Abraham Lincoln*, 2:108–09, 263–64.

31 Scott to Cameron [Mar. 28, 1861], in OR ser. 1, vol. 1, pp. 200–01; Blair to Samuel Crawford, May 6, 1882, Crawford Papers, LC; Burlingame, *Abraham Lincoln*, 2:108–09, 263–64; McClintock, *Lincoln and the Decision*, 226–28.

32 Gustavus Fox Report, in Nicolay and Hay, *Abraham Lincoln*, 3:389; Stephen Hurlbut to Lincoln, Mar. 27, 1861, Lincoln Papers; Cong. Globe, 37th Cong., Spec. Sess. 1519–20; McClintock, *Lincoln and the Decision*, 226–28.

33 Welles to Lincoln, Mar. 29, 1861, Lincoln Papers; Chase to Lincoln, Mar. 29, 1861, ibid.; Seward to Lincoln, Mar. 29, 1861, ibid.; Burlingame, *Abraham Lincoln*, 2:108–11; McClintock, *Lincoln and the Decision*, 228–33.

34 Montgomery Meigs Diary, Mar. 29, 1861, Nicolay Papers, LC. Many books quote from a printed version of the diary, which claims that Seward said he wanted to abandon Sumter because it was "too near the capital." This is not in the manuscript version of the Meigs Diary. "General M. C. Meigs on the Conduct of the Civil War," *American Historical Review* 26 (1921): 285–303; Klein, *Days of Defiance*, 359; Russell Weigley, *Quartermaster General of the Union Army: A Biography of Montgomery C. Meigs* (New York: Columbia University Press 1959), 137–39.

35 Seward 2:534; Klein, *Days of Defiance*, 360.

36 Erasmus Keyes, *Fifty Years' Observation of Men and Events, Civil and Military* (New York: Charles Scribner's Sons, 1884), 381–83; Montgomery Meigs Diary, Mar. 31, 1861, Nicolay Papers, LC; Anna Seward to Frances Seward, Mar. 31, 1861, Seward Papers reel 116.

37 Anna Seward notes the meetings with Lincoln, Scott, and Lyons—Anna Seward to Frances Seward, Mar. 31, 1861, Seward Papers reel 116. Fred Seward recalled the document was drafted on Sunday, April 1, but Sunday was the 31st, not the 1st—Seward, *Reminiscences*, 149.

38 Seward to Lincoln, Apr. 1, 1861, "Some Thoughts for the President's Consideration," Lincoln Papers (in Frederick's handwriting).

39 Seward, *Reminiscences*, 149; Patrick Sowle, "A Reappraisal of Seward's Memorandum of April 1, 1861, to Lincoln," *Journal of Southern History* 33 (1967): 234–39.

40 *New York Times*, Apr. 3, 1861; *Albany Evening Journal*, Apr. 4, 1861; James Swain to John Hay, Feb. 21, 1888, in Sowle, "Reappraisal of Seward's Memorandum."

41 *New York Times*, Mar. 29–30 & Apr. 1, 1861; Brauer, "Foreign War Panacea"; Norman Ferris, "Lincoln and Seward in Civil War Diplomacy: Their Relationship at the Outset Reexamined," *Journal of the Abraham Lincoln Association* 12 (1991): 21–42.

42 Frederick Seward to Frederic Bancroft, June 2, 1894, Bancroft Papers, Columbia University; Woldman, *Lincoln and the Russians*, 50.

43 Lyons to Russell, Apr. 9, 1861, quoted in James Randall and Richard Current, *Lincoln the President: Last Full Measure* (New York: Dodd, Mead & Co., 1945), 81; Richard Current, "Comment," *Journal of the Abraham Lincoln Association* 12 (1991): 43–46; McClintock, *Lincoln and the Decision*, 236–38; Van Deusen, *Seward*, 283.

44 Lincoln to Seward, Apr. 1, 1861, Lincoln Papers.

45 John Nicolay and John Hay, "Abraham Lincoln: A History: Premier or President," *Century Magazine* 35 (1888): 616.

46 Lincoln to David Porter, Apr. 1, 1861, CWL 4:315 (two orders); Montgomery Meigs Diary, Apr. 1–2, 1861, Nicolay Papers, LC; David Porter Diary, Apr. 1, 1861, Porter Papers, Box 22, LC ("smooth the old fellow"); Statement of David Porter, Mar. 25, 1873, Crawford Papers, LC; David Porter, *Incidents and Anecdotes of the Civil War* (New York: D. Appleton & Co., 1885), 15–16. There are slight differences among Porter's accounts.

47 Henry Connor, *John Archibald Campbell: Associate Justice of the Supreme Court* (Boston: Houghton Mifflin, 1920) (quoting Campbell memo); John Campbell to Jefferson Davis, Apr. 3, 1861, in Haskell Monroe, et al., eds., *The Papers of Jefferson Davis*, 11 vols. (Baton Rouge: Louisiana State University Press, 1971–2003), 7:88–89; Klein, *Days of Defiance*, 370.

48 Seward to Tassara, Apr. 2, 1861, NA, M99 reel 86; Lynn Case and Warren Spencer, *The United States and France: Civil War Diplomacy* (Philadelphia: University of Pennsylvania Press, 1970), 35; James Cortada, "Spain and the American Civil War: Relations at Mid-Century, 1855–1868," *Transactions of the American Philosophical Society* 70 (1980): 35–36; Jenkins, *Britain and the War for Union*, 1:36; Charles Tansill, *The United States and Santo Domingo, 1798–1873* (Baltimore: Johns Hopkins University Press, 1938), 213–16.

49 Summers to Seward, Apr. 1, 1861, Seward Papers reel 63; Allan Magruder, "A Piece of Secret History: President Lincoln and the Virginia Convention of 1861," *Atlantic Monthly* 35 (1875): 438–46; Burlingame, *Lincoln*, 2:119–20; Crofts, *Reluctant Confederates*, 301–02; McClintock, *Lincoln and the Decision*, 241–42.

50 John Baldwin, *Interview Between President Lincoln and Col. John B. Baldwin . . . Statements and Evidence* (Staunton, VA: Spectator Job Office, 1866), 10, 22–27; Magruder, "Secret History." For some of the views on the Baldwin-Lincoln conversation, see Burlingame, *Lincoln*, 2:120–22; Crofts, *Reluctant Confederates*, 301–07; Lawrence Denton, *William Henry Seward and the Secession Crisis: The Effort to Prevent Civil War* (Jefferson, NC: McFarland & Co., 2009), 147–49; Klein, *Days of Defiance*, 382–83; McClintock, *Lincoln and the Decision*, 241–44.

51 George Harrington, in his memoir, relates that on April 7, when he informed Seward of a White House meeting at which Lincoln decided to provision Fort Sumter, Seward responded, "Thunder, George! What are you talking about?" Harrington's date cannot be right, however, because by April 7, Gustavus Fox (whom Harrington placed at this White House meeting) was already at sea. Even if one supposes a date of April 4, when Fox was still in Washington, the memoir does not ring true; it seems more likely that Seward was aware through Scott and others of the Sumter expedition—George Harrington, "President Lincoln and His Cabinet: Inside Glimpses" (undated MS at Missouri History Museum), 22; Robert Thompson and Richard Wainwright, eds., *Confidential Correspondence of Gustavus Vasa Fox*, 2 vols. (New York: Naval History Society, 1918), 1:18–30 (orders re Sumter expedition).

52 Meigs to Seward, Apr. 4 & 5, 1861, Seward Papers reel 63; Beale, ed., *Welles Diary*, 1:23–25.

53 Seward to David Porter, Apr. 6, 1861, in *Official Records of the Union and Confederate Navies in the War of the Rebellion* 30 vols. (Washington, DC: Government Printing Office, 1894–1922), ser. 1, vol. 4, p. 112; Porter to Seward, Apr. 6, 1861, ibid.; Porter to Lincoln and Seward, Apr. 6, 1861, Seward Papers reel 63; Montgomery Meigs Diary, Apr. 5–6, 1861, Nicolay Papers, LC; Beale, ed., *Welles Diary*, 1:23–25; Gideon Welles, "Facts in Relation to . . . Fort Sumter," *The Galaxy* 10 (1870): 628–29; Burlingame, *Abraham Lincoln*, 2:115–16; Klein, *Days of Defiance*, 387–89.

54 Montgomery Meigs to Seward, Apr. 1, 1861, Seward Papers reel 63 ("I think that Porter should be ordered to take the *Powhatan* and sail from New York into Pensacola harbor at once"); Statement of David D. Porter, Mar. 25, 1873, Crawford Papers, LC; Burlingame, *Abraham Lincoln*, 2:111–17 (section headed "Seward sabotages the effort to relieve Fort Sumter"); Welles, "Sumter"; Welles, "Fort Pickens: Facts in Relation to the Reinforcement of Fort Pickens, in the Spring of 1861," *The Galaxy* 11 (1871): 92–107.

55 Seward 2:521. The Welles "diary" for 1861 is actually a narrative prepared at some later point.

56 Lincoln to Robert Chew, Apr. 6, 1861, CWL 4:323–24; James Harvey to A. G. Magrath [Apr. 6, 1861], Lincoln Papers; Commissioners to Toombs, Apr. 5–6, 1861, OR ser. 1, vol. 1, pp. 286–87; Burlingame, *Abraham Lincoln*, 2:116 (Seward source); Crofts, "Harvey," 189–90 (does not identify source); John Nicolay and John Hay, *Abraham Lincoln: A History*, 10 vols. (New York: Century Co., 1917), 4:32 (does not identify Harvey's source but suggests Seward).

57 Seward 2:538 ("Faith as to Sumter"); Connor, *Campbell*, 129–32, 137 ("systematic duplicity"); Klein, *Days of Defiance*, 392–94.

58 Russell, *Diary*, 65–66; Seward to Adams, Apr. 10, 1861, NA, M77 reel 76.

59 *Daily National Intelligencer*, Apr. 13 & 15, 1861; *Washington Evening Star*, Apr. 12–15, 1861; Lord Lyons to Earl Russell, Apr. 15, 1861, in Barnes and Barnes, eds., *British Eyes*, 1:50; Klein, *Days of Defiance*, 408–20; Russell, *Diary*, 69–70; Horatio Taft Diary, Apr. 13, 1861, LC.

60 *Chicago Tribune*, Apr. 15, 1861; *Daily National Intelligencer*, Apr. 15, 1861; *New York Times*, Apr. 15, 1861; Russell, *Diary*, 42 ("history tells us"); Seward 2:544–45.

61 *Chicago Tribune*, Apr. 15, 1861; *New York Times*, Apr. 15, 1861; Seward 2:545.

NOTES FOR CHAPTER 11

1 Beriah MacGoffin to Simon Cameron, Apr. 16, 1861, in *New York Times*, Apr. 17, 1861; John Nicolay to Therena Bates, Apr. 26, 1861, in Michael Burlingame, ed., *With Lincoln in the White House: Letters, Memoranda, and Other Writings of John G. Nicolay, 1860–1865* (Carbondale: Southern Illinois University Press, 2000), 39; Seward 2:549; Goodwin, *Team of Rivals*, 347–53; McPherson, *Battle Cry of Freedom*, 274–86.

2 Welles is our only source for the blockade debate, and his accounts were written later—Gideon Welles to Lincoln, Aug. 5, 1861, Lincoln Papers; Proclamation, Apr. 19, 1861, CWL 4:338–39; Welles, *Lincoln and Seward*, 122–24; Stuart Anderson, "1861: Blockade vs. Closing the Confederate Ports," *Military Affairs* 41 (1977): 190–94; John Niven, *Gideon Welles: Lincoln's Secretary of the Navy* (New York: Oxford University Press, 1973), 356–57.

3 Seward to Thomas Hicks, Apr. 22, 1861, in *New York Times*, Apr. 25, 1861; John Hay Diary, Apr. 23, 1861, in Burlingame & Ettlinger, eds., *Inside Lincoln's White House*, 8; Lincoln to Winfield Scott, Apr. 25 & 27, 1861, CWL 4:344 & 347; Francis Carpenter, "A Day with Governor Seward," July 1870, Seward Papers reel 196; Burlingame, *Abraham Lincoln*, 2:138–49; Mark Neely Jr., *The Fate of Liberty: Abraham Lincoln and Civil Liberties* (New York: Oxford University Press, 1991), 4–9. Seward's opposition to the letter of April 25 is inferred from (a) his support of the letter of April 27 and (b) his leading role in the arrest of the Maryland legislators in September 1861.

4 Lutz, "Rudolf Schleiden and the Visit to Richmond," 209–16.

5 Frederick Seward to Frances Seward, Apr. 22 & 24, 1861, Seward Papers reel 116; Anna Seward to Frances Seward, Apr. 28, 1861, ibid.; Beale, ed., *Welles Diary*, 1:549; see Francis Carpenter, *Six Months at the White House with Abraham Lincoln* (New York: Hurd & Houghton, 1866), 73. The quote in the text is from the Welles diary. Carpenter quotes Seward to the same effect; "the meeting which took place when the news came of the attack upon Sumter, when the first measures were organized for the restoration of the national authority, [t]hat was the crisis in the history of this Administration—not the issue of the Emancipation Proclamation."

6 *Alexandria Gazette*, June 4, 1863; *Harrisburg Weekly Patriot & Union*, May 7 & June 4, 1863; John Pruyn Diary, Feb. 6, 1864, NYSL (conversation with Lyons); Dean Sprague, *Freedom Under Lincoln: Federal Power and Personal Liberty Under the Strain of Civil War* (Boston: Houghton Mifflin, 1965), 159 (quote). Some papers claimed in 1863 that the quote was in the *New York Times* of Mar. 7, 1862, and before that in a published dispatch from Lyons to Russell of Nov. 14, 1861. Neither the *Times* nor the published dispatch has this language, however.

7 The best study of this period is Neely, *Fate of Liberty*, chap. 1. A 1,500–page documentary record is in OR ser. 2, vol. 2.

8 OR ser. 2, vol. 2, pp. 212–13, 217–18 (Stewart), 250–51 (list of prisoners), 544–47 (Williams), 561–67 (Greenhow); Ann Blackman, *Wild Rose: Rose O'Neal Greenhow: Civil War Spy* (New York: Random House, 2005); Ruth Kaye, *The History of St. Paul's Episcopal Church, Alexandria, Virginia* (Springfield, VA: Goetz Printing, 1984), 45–52; Ishbel Ross, *Rebel Rose: Life of Rose O'Neal Greenhow, Confederate Spy* (New York: Harper & Row, 1954).

9 Fanny Seward Diary, Sept. 4 & 8, 1861, Seward Papers reel 198; Frederick Seward to Frances Seward, Sept. 21, 1861, ibid. reel 117; George McClellan to Samuel Cox, Feb. 12, 1864, in Stephen Sears, ed., *The Civil War Papers of George B. McClellan* (New York: Ticknor & Fields, 1989), 565; *New York Times*, Sept. 14 & 19, 1861; Burlingame, *Abraham Lincoln*, 2:148–49; George McClellan, *McClellan's Own Story* (New York: Charles Webster & Co., 1887), 146–47; Neely,

Fate of Liberty, 14–18; Seward, *Reminiscences,* 175–78; Janet Seward, *Personal Experiences of the Civil War* (Worcester, MA: F. S. Blanchard, 1899), 4.

10 *Baltimore American,* Sept. 21, 1861, in CWL 4:523; Banks to Seward, Sept. 18, 1861, in OR ser. 2, vol. 2, p. 680; Banks to Seward, Sept. 20, 1861, Seward Papers reel 65; Lyons to Russell, Nov. 4, 1861, in Kenneth Bourne and Cameron Watt, eds., *British Documents on Foreign Affairs. Part I, Series C: North America, 1837–1914,* 15 vols. (Frederick, MD: University Publications of America, 1986), 5:338; Seward, *Reminiscences,* 175–78.

11 William Nelson to Simon Cameron, Oct. 7, 1861, in OR ser. 2, vol. 2, p. 916; Seward to Nelson, Oct. 14, 1861, ibid., 917; Richard Stanton to Seward, Nov. 4, 1861, ibid., 918; Frederick Seward to Martin Burke, Dec. 24, 1861, ibid., 929; Cong. Globe, 37th Cong., 2d Sess. 2114 (Seward's reported comments to the Kentucky delegation).

12 OR ser. 2, vol. 2, pp. 1021–22 (Merrick), 153 (counsel): *New York Times,* Oct. 23, 1861.

13 Seward to Adams, Apr. 10, 1861, FRUS 1861, pp. 71–80; Seward to Fanny Seward, May 1861, Seward 2:584.

14 Seward to Adams, et al., Apr. 24, 1861, FRUS 1861, pp. 34–37; Lyons to Russell, Apr. 27, 1861, in Barnes and Barnes, eds., *Private and Confidential,* 248; Adams to Seward, Aug. 23, 1861, FRUS 1861, pp. 133–34; C. F. Adams, Jr., "The Negotiation of 1861 Relating to the Declaration of Paris of 1856," *Proceedings of the Massachusetts Historical Society* 96 (1912): 23–84; Norman Ferris, *Desperate Diplomacy: William H. Seward's Foreign Policy, 1861* (Knoxville: University of Tennessee Press, 1976), 73–84; Howard Jones, *Blue and Gray Diplomacy: A History of Union and Confederate Foreign Relations* (Chapel Hill: University of North Carolina Press, 2010), 40–44.

15 *New York Times,* Apr. 26, 1861 (Gregory's motion); Faulkner to Seward, Apr. 15, 1861, in *New York Times,* May 5, 1861; Sanford to Seward, Apr. 25, 1861, in Case and Spencer, *United States and France,* 49–50; *New York Times,* May 16–17, 1861; Ferris, *Desperate Diplomacy,* 16–21. Van Deusen errs when he suggests that Seward was aware, on May 19 and 20 when he drafted the Adams instructions, of the British Proclamation of May 13; this news could not have yet crossed the Atlantic—Van Deusen, *Seward,* 296.

16 Seward to Frances Seward, May 17, 1861, Seward 2:575–76; Seward to Henry Sanford, May 20, 1861, Seward Papers reel 64; Fry, *Henry S. Sanford,* 35–65 (on Sanford as Seward's minister to Europe).

17 Seward to Adams, May 21, 1861, Lincoln Papers (draft).

18 Compare ibid. with Seward to Adams, May 21, 1861, NA, M77 reel 76; Seward to Frances Seward, May 17 & June 5, 1861, Seward 2:575, 590; Burlingame, *Abraham Lincoln,* 2:161; Ferris, *Desperate Diplomacy,* 23–26; Allen Rice, "A

Famous Diplomatic Dispatch," *North American Review* 142 (1886): 404 ("saved this nation").

19 *New York Herald*, May 22, 1861; Lyons to Russell, May 23, 1861, in Barnes and Barnes, eds., *British Eyes*, 1:93–94; Mercier to Thouvenel, May 20, 1861, quoted in Ferris, *Desperate Diplomacy*, 218–19; Foreman, *World on Fire*, 100–02.

20 Queen's Proclamation, May 13, 1861, in *New York Times*, May 28, 1861; Seward to Weed, May 23, 1861, Weed Papers.

21 Edward Everett Diary, Aug. 23, 1861, MHS; Charles Sumner to Adam Badeau, July 26, 1869, in Palmer, ed., *Letters of Charles Sumner*, 2:487.

22 Seward to Adams, July 21, 1861, NA, M77 reel 76; Seward to Adams, Feb. 28, 1862, FRUS 1862, p. 41; Lyons to Russell, Feb. 28, 1862, in Barnes and Barnes, *British Eyes*, 1:301; Seward to Pike, Mar. 8, 1862, FRUS 1862, p. 597; Russell to Lyons, Apr. 17, 1862, quoted in Jenkins, *Britain and the War*, 1:258–59.

23 *Ford v. Surget*, 97 US 605, 612 (1878); *Prize Cases*, 67 US 635 (1863); see Ephraim Adams, *Great Britain and the American Civil War*, 2 vols. (New York: Longmans Green & Co., 1925), 1:109; Case and Spencer, *France and the United States*, 122–23, 590–91; Charles Fenwick, *International Law*, 2d ed. (New York: D. Appleton & Co., 1924), 112–13. The quote is from a concurring opinion in *Ford v. Surget* but the *Prize Cases* were decided on the basis that there were two belligerents in the Civil War.

24 Seward, *Reminiscences*, 189–90. Seward's account is accepted by Case and Spencer, *France and the United States*, 70–74, and queried by Carroll, *Mercier*, 75–82. The original documents are: Seward to Dayton, June 17, 1861, FRUS 1861, pp. 224–25; Seward to Adams, June 19, ibid., 106–09; Mercier to Thouvenel, June 18, 1861, in Carroll, *Mercier*, 80–81; Lyons to Russell, June 13 & 17, 1861, in Barnes and Barnes, eds., *British Eyes*, 1:118–21; and Lyons to Russell, June 24, 1861, in Barnes and Barnes, eds., *Private and Confidential*, 250.

25 Adams to Seward, June 14, 1861, quoted in Adams, *Great Britain*, 1:106; Seward to Adams, July 1, 1861, NA, M77 reel 76; D. P. Crook, *The North, the South, and the Powers: 1861–1865* (New York: John Wiley & Sons, 1974), 68; Van Deusen, *Seward*, 299.

26 Sumner to John Andrew, May 24, 1861, in Palmer, ed., *Letters of Charles Sumner*, 2:68; Sumner to the Duchess of Argyll, June 4, 1861, ibid., 69–70; Adams to Seward, June 21, 1861, Adams Papers, MHS reel 165; Seward to Adams, July 9, 1861, ibid. reel 554; David Donald, *Charles Sumner and the Rights of Man* (New York: Alfred A. Knopf, 1970), 18–24.

27 Anna Seward to Frances Seward, May 28, 1861, Seward Papers reel 117; Frederick Seward to Frances Seward, June 18 & 21, 1861, ibid.; Seward to Fanny Seward, June 1861, Seward 2:584 & 586; Seward 2:586–89 (daily routine); Anthony Trollope, *North America*, 2 vols. (New York: Harper & Bros., 1862), 312.

28 Sources cited in note 27; Seward to A. W. Thayer, Aug. 12, 1861, OR ser. 2, vol. 2, p. 41 ("vindication").

29 Anna Seward to Frances Seward, June 18, 1861, Seward Papers reel 117; *New York Times*, May 22, 1861; Seward 2:589 ("his dinner table was rarely without one or more guests").

30 Meigs Diary, May 10 & June 8, 1861, Nicolay Papers, LC; Meigs to Seward, May 14, 1861, Meigs Papers Addition, LC reel 12; Frederick Seward to Frances Seward, June 21, 1861, Seward Papers reel 117; Seward to Fanny Seward, June 1861, Seward 2:586 ("our policy is a Fabian one"); Seward to Weed, June 25, 1861, Weed Papers ("I fear to crowd [the army] too fast"); *New York Tribune*, June 26, 1861; Burlingame, *Abraham Lincoln*, 2:180–81; McPherson, *Battle Cry of Freedom*, 332–36; David Miller, *Second Only to Grant: Quartermaster General Montgomery C. Meigs* (Shippensburg, PA: White Mane Books, 2000), 92–100.

31 B. S. Alexander report, July 21, 1861, OR ser. 1, vol. 2, p. 747; John Nicolay to Therena Bates, July 21, 1861, Nicolay Papers, LC; Burlingame, *Abraham Lincoln*, 2:182–83 (includes Washburne quote); Goodwin, *Team of Rivals*, 370–76; McPherson, *Battle Cry of Freedom*, 339–47.

32 Seward to Frances Seward, July 22, 1861, Seward 2:600; Seward to Edwin Morgan [July 22, 1861], Morgan Papers, NYSL; Seward to Lincoln, July 1861, Seward 2:601 (not in Lincoln Papers); William Sherman, *Memoirs of William T. Sherman*, 2 vols. (New York: D. Appleton & Co., 1875), 1:189–90 (Sherman meets Lincoln and Seward); Burlingame, *Abraham Lincoln*, 2:186–89.

33 Seward to C. F. Adams, July 29, 1861, FRUS 1861, p. 124; Seward to William Dayton, July 30, 1861, ibid., 236. Seward's circular letters are printed in Baker 5:39–185.

34 Seward to Frances Seward, July 31, 1861, Seward 2:604; Frances Seward to Seward, Aug. 4, 1861, Seward Papers reel 117; Fanny Seward Diary, Sept. 1, 1861, ibid. reel 198; Frances Seward to Lazette Worden, Sept. 1861, ibid. reel 119; *New York Times*, Sept. 2, 1861 (speech); McPherson, *Battle Cry of Freedom*, 348.

35 Fanny Seward Diary, Sept. 1, 1861, Seward Papers reel 198; Frances Seward to Lazette Worden, Sept. 1861, ibid. reel 119.

36 Seward to Butler, Mar. 25, 1853, Huntington Library; Fanny Seward Diary, Sept. 2, 1861, Seward Papers reel 198; William Dwight Jr. to William Dwight Sr., Sept. 2, 1861, Dwight Family Papers, MHS (dated Sept. 4 by staff); Adam Goodheart, *1861: The Civil War Awakening* (New York: Alfred A. Knopf, 2011), 299–338.

37 Fanny Seward Diary, Sept. 2–10, 1861, Seward Papers reel 198.

38 Frances Seward to Lazette Worden, Sept. 1861, Seward Papers reel 119 (misdated Aug.); Fanny Seward Diary, Sept. 9, 1861, ibid. reel 198; Elizabeth Keckley, *Behind the Scenes: Or, Thirty Years a Slave, and Four Years in the White House* (Chicago: Lakeside Press, 1988), 131.

39 Frances Seward to Seward, Apr. 28 & Sept. 17, 1861, Seward Papers reel 114; Seward to William Dayton, Apr. 22, 1861, FRUS 1861, pp. 198–99.

40 Frances Seward to Lazette Worden, Aug. 31, 1861, Seward Papers reel 119; Lincoln to Fremont, Sept. 1, 1861, CWL 4:506–07; Burlingame, *Abraham Lincoln*, 2:200–10; McPherson, *Battle Cry of Freedom*, 350–58.

41 *New York Tribune*, Aug. 1, 1861; *Chicago Tribune*, Aug. 2, 1861; Stephen Sears, *George B. McClellan: The Young Napoleon* (New York: Ticknor & Fields, 1988); Goodwin, *Team of Rivals*, 377–79.

42 George McClellan to Mary Ellen McClellan, Aug. 8, Oct. 11, 16, & 31, 1861, in Sears, ed., *Papers of George McClellan*, 81, 106–07, 113–14.

43 John Hay Diary, Nov. 13, 1861, in Burlingame and Ettlinger, eds., *Inside Lincoln's White House*, 32; F. A. Mitchel to John Hay, Jan. 3, 1889, quoted in Burlingame, *Abraham Lincoln*, 2:197.

44 Lyons to Seward, Oct. 14, 1861, NA, M50 reel 42; Seward to Lyons, Oct. 14, 1861, NA, M99 reel 38; *New York Times*, Oct. 21, 1861; *New York Tribune*, Oct. 21, 1861; Lyons to Russell, Oct. 18, 1861, in Barnes and Barnes, *British Eyes*, 1:180–81 (Seward explains publication).

45 Seward to Governors, *New York Times*, Oct. 17, 1861; *New York Times*, Oct. 18, 1861; Burlingame, *Abraham Lincoln*, 2:214 ("proof positive").

46 Benjamin Welch Jr. to George Fogg, Oct. 22, 1861, Fogg Papers, New Hampshire Historical Society.

47 *Baltimore Sun*, Sept. 2, 1861; *Chicago Tribune*, Sept. 16, 1861; *Boston Daily Advertiser*, Sept. 17, 1861; Robert Hunter to James Mason and John Slidell, Sept. 23, 1861, in *Official Records of the Union and Confederate Navies*, ser. 2, vol. 3, pp. 257–73 (instructions); Gideon Welles to S. F. DuPont, Oct. 15, 1861, ibid., ser. 1, vol. 1, p. 113 (order to capture); *New York Times*, Oct. 31, 1861. Although I have not been able to find an October letter from Seward to Welles regarding Mason and Slidell, I have followed Jenkins, *Britain and the War for the Union*, 1:176, and Van Deusen, *Seward*, 308, who both state that Seward suggested the arrest.

48 Winfield Scott to Seward, Nov. 3, 1861, Seward Papers reel 66; Van Deusen, *Seward*, 306–08.

49 *Boston Evening Transcript*, Nov. 16, 1861; *New York Times*, Nov. 18, 1861; *Washington Evening Star*, Nov. 16, 1861; Robert Murray to Seward, Nov. 18, 1861, OR ser. 2, vol. 2, p. 1100 (references and summarizes Seward order of Nov. 16). For accounts of the arrest, see Norman Ferris, *The Trent Affair: A Diplomatic Crisis* (Knoxville: University of Tennessee Press, 1977); Ivan Musicant, *Divided Waters: The Naval History of the Civil War* (New York: HarperCollins, 1995), 108–17; Gordon Warren, *Fountain of Discontent: The Trent Affair and Freedom of the Seas* (Boston: Northeastern University Press, 1981), 1–25.

50 *New York Times*, Nov. 17, 1861; *Boston Evening Transcript*, Nov. 18, 1861; Frederick Seward to Frances Seward, Nov. 17, 1861, Seward Papers reel 117,

Frederick Seward to R. W. Shufeldt, Nov. 22, 1861, NA, Consular Instructions, Havana, Box 240; George Bancroft to Seward, Nov. 25, 1861, Bancroft Papers, MHS; Seward to Bancroft, Nov. 26, 1861, ibid.

51 Welles, *Lincoln and Seward*, 185; Frederick Seward to Frances Seward, Nov. 17, 1861, Seward Papers reel 117; Lyons to Russell, Nov. 19 & Dec. 6, 1861, in Barnes and Barnes, *British Eyes*, 1:228 & 242; Mercier to Thouvenel, Nov. 25, 1861, in Case and Spencer, *United States and France*, 215; Seward to Adams, Nov. 27, 1861, NA, M77 reel 77.

52 Frederick Seward to Frances Seward, Nov. 23, 1861, Seward Papers reel 117; W. F. Weld & Co. to Seward, Dec. 19, 1861, ibid. reel 67; Warren, *Fountain of Discontent*, 38–43, 168–75.

53 Cong. Globe, 37th Cong., 2d. Sess. 5 (Dec. 2, 1861); *New York Tribune*, Dec. 17, 1861; *Chicago Tribune*, Dec. 17, 1861; *Morning Herald*, Nov. 1861, copy in Seward Papers reel 67 (Canadian paper); *New York Times*, Dec. 18, 1861.

54 *Daily National Intelligencer*, Dec. 9 & 14, 1861; *New York Times*, Dec. 17, 1861; *Philadelphia Press*, Dec. 19, 1861. John Forney claimed in an 1884 memoir that he wrote this letter at Lincoln's request, but it seems far more likely that Seward was the instigator, given that Seward was at this point in favor of release, while Lincoln was in favor of arbitration. Burlingame, *Abraham Lincoln*, 2:224–25 (memoir); Crook, *The North, the South, and the Powers: 1861–1865*, 151 ("on the eve of the cabinet's first grappling with the crisis, most of the north's major newspapers were foreshadowing the ultimate settlement").

55 Lincoln Message, Dec. 3, 1861, CWL 5:35; Lyons to Russell, Dec. 6, 1861, in Barnes and Barnes, *British Eyes*, 1:242.

56 Cameron Report, Dec. 1, 1861, quoted in Nicolay and Hay, *Abraham Lincoln*, 5:125–26; Burlingame, *Abraham Lincoln*, 2:238–40; McPherson, *Battle Cry of Freedom*, 357–58.

57 *New York Times*, Dec. 11, 1861; C. F. Adams to Edward Everett, Dec. 26, 1862, Everett Papers, MHS; Everett to Adams, Jan. 20, 1863, ibid.; Plischke, *Department of State*, 207, 609–12.

58 Frank Troxell to Seward, Dec. 8, 1861, Seward Papers reel 67; Seward to Seward Club of Philadelphia, Dec. 16, 1861, in *New York Times*, Mar. 1, 1862; *New York Times*, Feb. 5, 1862 (editorial); Goodwin, *Team of Rivals*, 563–66.

59 *New York Times*, Dec. 13–16, 1861; *Washington Evening Star*, Dec. 16, 1861; Theodore Pease and James Randall, eds., *The Diary of Orville Hickman Browning*, 2 vols. (Springfield: Illinois State Historical Society, 1925), 1:515.

60 DuPont & Co. to Seward, Dec. 13, 1861, NA, M179 reel 186; *New York Times*, Dec. 16–20, 1861; Kenneth Bourne, "British Preparations for War with the North, 1861–1862," *English Historical Review* 76 (1961): 600–632; Alfred Chandler Jr., "Du Pont, Dahlgren, and the Civil War Nitre Shortage," *Military Affairs* 13 (1949): 142–49.

61 George Bancroft to Elizabeth Bancroft, Dec. 16, 1861, MHS; Russell, *My Diary North and South*, 331–32; William Russell to John Delane, Dec. 20, 1861, in Martin Crawford, ed., *William Howard Russell's Civil War: Private Diary and Letters, 1861–1862* (Athens: University of Georgia Press, 1992), 205; Mercier to Thouvenel, Dec. 19, 1861, quoted in Case and Spencer, *United States and France*, 216.

62 *Daily National Intelligencer*, Dec. 18, 1861; *New York Times*, Dec. 18, 1861; Lyons to Russell, Dec. 19, 1861, in Barnes and Barnes, eds., *British Eyes*, 1:250; Lyons to Russell, Dec. 19, 1861, in Barnes and Barnes, *Private and Confidential*, 271–72.

63 Russell to Lyons, Nov. 30, 1861, in *New York Times* Dec. 27, 1861; Russell to Lyons, Nov. 30, 1861 (seven-day limit), in Bigelow, *Retrospections*, 1:427; Lyons to Russell, Dec. 19, 1861, in Barnes and Barnes, *Private and Confidential*, 271–72.

64 *New York Times*, Dec. 16, 1861; Lyons to Russell, Dec. 23, 1861, in Barnes and Barnes, eds., *British Eyes*, 1:255–26; Mercier to Thouvenel, Dec. 23, 1861, in Case and Spencer, *France and the United States*, 218.

65 Lincoln, Memo on Trent, Dec. 1861, Lincoln Papers; Pease and Randall, eds. *Browning Diary*, 1:516; *New York Times*, Dec. 16, 1861 (French mediation); Case and Spencer, *France and the United States*, 224–26. Lincoln's determination to hold the prisoners is confirmed by letters written by Hay, claiming that the president would not "yield one jot" on the prisoners—Michael Burlingame, ed., *Lincoln's Journalist: John Hay's Anonymous Writings for the Press, 1860–1864* (Carbondale: Southern Illinois University Press, 1998), 166, 172–74.

66 Russell to Lyons, Dec. 7, 1861, in T. W. L. Newton, *Lord Lyons: A Record of British Diplomacy*, 2 vols (London, 1913), 1:64; Lyons to Russell, Dec. 23, 1861, in ibid., 69; Nicolay and Hay, *Abraham Lincoln*, 5:34–35 ("I shall then be ready").

67 Weed to Seward, Dec. 2, 5, & 7, 1861, Seward Papers reel 67 (Dec. 2 received Dec. 24; Dec. 7 received Dec. 25); Winfield Scott to "a friend," Dec. 1861, in *New York Times*, Dec. 19, 1861; John Bigelow to Seward, Dec. 5, 1861, Seward Papers reel 67 (received Dec. 25); Richard Cobden to Sumner, Dec. 5 & 6, 1861, Sumner Papers reel 23; John Bright to Sumner, Dec. 7, 1861, ibid.; Sumner to Seward, Dec. 24, 1861, in Palmer, ed., *Letters of Charles Sumner*, 2:91.

68 *New York Times*, Oct. 17, 1860; Duke of Newcastle to Sir Edmund Head, June 5, 1861, quoted in Foreman, *World on Fire*, 58–59; Weed to Seward, Dec. 6 & 7, 1861, Seward Papers reel 67; *New York Times*, Dec. 25, 1861; Seward to Weed, Dec. 27, 1861, Seward 3:34; Foreman, *World on Fire*, 184–85; Van Deusen, *Seward*, 260.

69 Pease and Randall, eds., *Browning Diary*, 1:518; Beale, ed., *Bates Diary*, 213; Seward to Lyons, Dec. 26, 1861, in *New York Times*, Dec. 29, 1861; *New York Tribune*, Dec. 31, 1861 (four or five hours). We do not have Seward's draft, but since Bates tells us that it was adopted with only "verbal and formal

amendments," it seems reasonable to assume that the draft Seward read was nearly the same as the final document—Beale, ed., *Bates Diary*, 216.

70 C. F. Adams to Seward, Dec. 6, 1861, quoted in Bigelow, *Retrospections*, 1:397–99; William Dayton to Seward, Dec. 6, 1861, quoted Case and Spencer, *France and the United States*, 221; Beale, ed., *Bates Diary*, 216; Niven, ed., *Salmon Chase Papers*, 1:318–20; Sumner to Francis Lieber, Dec. 24, 1861, in Palmer, ed., *Letters of Charles Sumner*, 1:88–89.

71 Thouvenel to Mercier, Nov. 30, 1861, quoted in Case and Spencer, *France and the United States*, 202–04; see ibid., 221–23 (delivery during cabinet meeting); Pease and Randall, eds., *Browning Diary*, 518–19 (ditto).

72 Beale, ed., *Bates Diary*, 216; Seward 3:25.

73 Lammot DuPont to Seward, Dec. 26, 1861, NA, M179 reel 186; John Dahlgren to Seward, Dec. 26, 1861, Lincoln Papers; Seward to Weed, Jan. 22, 1862, Seward 3:42; Lyons to Russell, Feb. 3, 1862, quoted in Case and Spencer, *France and the United States*, 230; Beale, ed., *Bates Diary*, 216; C. F. Adams Diary, May 28, 1870, Adams Papers reel 82.

74 C. F. Adams Diary, May 28, 1870, Adams Papers reel 82; Bigelow, *Retrospections*, 1:439–40; Seward 3:25–26.

75 Russell to Lyons, Nov. 30, 1861, in Bourne and Watt, eds., *British Documents*, 5:349–50; Russell to Admiralty, Nov. 30, 1861, in ibid. 5:351.

76 Lyons to Russell, Dec. 27, 1861, in Barnes and Barnes, eds., *British Eyes*, 1:256–58; Lyons to Russell, Dec. 27, 1861, in Newton, *Lord Lyons*, 1:72 ("fires of Tophet").

77 Seward to Weed, Dec. 27, 1861, Weed Papers; *Daily National Intelligencer*, Dec. 28, 1861; *New York Times*, Dec. 29, 1861. For critical legal analysis of Seward's opinion, see Bancroft, *Life of Seward*, 2:245–53; Warren, *Fountain of Discontent*, 183–99. Bancroft concludes that even if Seward was wrong on the law, his letter was "a political masterpiece."

78 Fanny Seward Diary, Dec. 27, 1861, Seward Papers reel 198; Pease and Randall, eds., *Browning Diary*, 519; Seward 3:26. The *New York Times* reported on Dec. 28 that Lyons and Mercier also attended this dinner, but since none of the others who were there noted their presence, it seems this report was an error.

79 *Daily National Intelligencer*, Dec. 28, 1861; *Chicago Tribune*, Dec. 30, 1861; *New York Times*, Dec. 30, 1861; Seward 3:35 (Hay poem).

80 Alfred Paul to Thouvenel, Jan. 22, 1862, quoted in Case and Spencer, *France and the United States*, 193–94; Foreman, *World on Fire*, 197–98; Warren, *Fountain of Discontent*, 211–14.

81 Beale, ed., *Bates Diary*, 216; Graham Allison and Philip Zelikow, *Essence of Decision: Explaining the Cuban Missile Crisis*, 2d ed. (New York: Longman, 1999). The best evidence I can find that Lincoln said "one war at a time" is the *Norfolk [MA] County Journal*, which reported on December 28, 1861, that "President

Lincoln never spoke a wiser word than when he said 'one war at a time.'" See also the *New York Tribune* of December 31, 1861, reporting that Lincoln told his cabinet that "it was doubtful if the course of Captain Wilkes could be justified by international law, and that at all events, he could not afford to have two wars upon his hands at the same time." The *New York Times* stated on April 29, 1865, that Seward's wartime foreign policy was based "upon the President's famous motto: 'one war at a time.'" One of many books that use the quote (generally without cite) is Dean Mahin, *One War at a Time: The International Dimensions of the American Civil War* (Washington, DC: Brassey's, 1999).

82 Among the discussions which, in my view, give too much credit to Lincoln are Burlingame, *Abraham Lincoln*, 2:221–29, and Donald, *Lincoln*, 320–23.

NOTES FOR CHAPTER 12

1 Fanny Seward Diary, Jan. 1, 1862, Seward Papers reel 198; Frances Seward to Lazette Worden, Jan. 1, 1862, ibid. reel 119.

2 Maunsell Field, *Memories of Many Men and Some Women* (New York: Harper & Bros., 1874), 266–67; Niven, ed., *Salmon Chase Papers*, 1:324–25; Burlingame, *Abraham Lincoln*, 2:240–44.

3 Lincoln to Cameron, Jan. 11, 1862, CWL 5:96–97 (two letters); Niven, ed., *Salmon Chase Papers*, 1:326–27 (diary); Seward to Frances Seward, Jan. 15, 1862, Seward 3:46; *New York Times*, Jan. 25, 1862; Goodwin, *Team of Rivals*, 409–15. Soon Lincoln transferred authority for arrests and detention from Seward to Stanton—Lincoln Order, Feb. 14, 1862, OR ser. 2, vol. 2, pp. 221–23.

4 William Gilman, et al., eds., *The Journals and Miscellaneous Notebooks of Ralph Waldo Emerson*, 16 vols. (Cambridge, MA: Belknap Press, 1960–82), 15:186–97; Gay Allen, *Ralph Waldo Emerson: A Biography* (New York: Viking Press, 1981), 611–14.

5 *New York Times*, Jan. 17 & 18, Feb. 1 & 13, 1862; Lyons to Russell, Feb. 11, 1862, in Barnes and Barnes, eds., *British Eyes*, 283–84; Seward to Dayton, Feb. 19, 1862, NA, M77 reel 56.

6 *New York Times*, Jan. 12, Mar. 5 & 11, Apr. 25, 1862; Mahin, *One War at a Time*, 106–21.

7 Seward to Dayton, Mar. 3, June 21 & Aug. 23, 1862, NA, M77 reel 56; Gerolt to Prussian foreign minister, quoted in Thomas Schoonover, *Dollars over Dominion: The Triumph of Liberalism in Mexican-United States Relations, 1861–1867* (Baton Rouge: Louisiana State University Press, 1978), 157.

8 Horatio Taft Diary, Jan. 15, 1862, Taft Papers, LC; Pease and Randall, eds., *Browning Diary*, 1:528; *New York Times*, Feb. 1, 1862; Fanny Seward Diary, Feb.–Mar. 1862, Seward Papers reel 198; Seward to Lincoln, Feb. 6, 1862, Lincoln Papers.

9 Sam Ward to S. L. M. Barlow, Mar. 27, 1862, Barlow Papers, Huntington Library; Fanny Seward Diary, Mar. 30, 1862, Seward Papers reel 198; Burlingame, *Abraham Lincoln*, 2:308–11, 315; McPherson, *Battle Cry of Freedom*, 424–27.

10 Fanny Seward Diary, Mar. 22, 1862, Seward Papers reel 198; Edward Dicey, *Spectator of America*, ed. Herbert Mitgang (Chicago: Quadrangle Books, 1971), 97–100.

11 Fanny Seward Diary, Mar. 27–30, 1862, Seward Papers reel 198 (quotes 30); Seward to Weed, Apr. 1, 1862, Seward 3:81; Peter Cozzens, *Shenandoah 1862: Stonewall Jackson's Valley Campaign* (Chapel Hill: University of North Carolina Press, 2008), 159–208.

12 Seward to Dayton, Mar. 26, 1862, NA, M77 reel 56; Sam Ward to Samuel Barlow, Mar. 27, 1862, Barlow Papers, Huntington Library (Seward's views); Lyons to Russell, Apr. 14, 1862, in Barnes and Barnes, eds., *British Eyes*, 2:14–15; Carroll, *Mercier*, 146–75; Case and Spencer, *The United States and France*, 275–85.

13 Lyons to Russell, Apr. 28, 1862, in Barnes and Barnes, eds., *British Eyes* 2:26–31; Case and Spencer, *United States and France*, 279–82.

14 Seward to Adams, May 12, 1862, NA, M77 reel 77; *New York Times*, May 13, 1862; Seward to Lincoln, May 14, 1862, Lincoln Papers; Frederick Seward to Frances Seward, May 1862, Seward 3:89; Anna Seward to Frances Seward, May 19, 1862, Seward Papers reel 117; George McClellan to Mary Ellen McClellan, in Sears, ed., *Papers of George McClellan*, 267.

15 Seward to Adams, May 28, 1862, NA, M77 reel 77; Frederick Seward to Frances Seward, May 1862, Seward 3:89–93; Anna Seward to Frances Seward, May 19, 1862, Seward Papers reel 117; Seward to Frances Seward, May 19, 1862, Seward 3:94; Seward to Fanny Seward, May 1862, ibid., 93.

16 Seward to Van Limburg, NA, M77 reel 75; Chester Hearn, *When the Devil Came Down to Dixie: Ben Butler in New Orleans* (Baton Rouge: Louisiana State University Press, 2000), 142–50.

17 Butler Order No. 28, May 15, 1862, OR ser. 1, vol. 15, p. 426; Palmerston to Adams, June 11, 1862, in Adams, *Great Britain and the American Civil War*, 1:302–03; Seward to Adams, July 9, 1862, NA, M77 reel 77; Hearn, *When the Devil Came Down*, 101–09.

18 McClellan to Stanton, June 28, 1862, in OR ser. 1, vol. 11, pt. 1, p. 61; Goodwin, *Team of Rivals*, 426–44; McPherson, *Battle Cry of Freedom*, 462–71; Stephen Sears, *To the Gates of Richmond: The Peninsula Campaign* (New York: Ticknor & Fields, 1992).

19 Lincoln to Seward, June 28, 1862, CWL 5:291–92; Seward to Weed and Morgan, June 28, 1862, OR ser. 3, vol. 2, p. 181; McPherson, *Battle Cry of Freedom*, 436–37, 490–91.

20 John Andrew to Edwin Morgan, June 30, 1862, Seward Papers reel 70; Frederick Holbrook to Edwin Morgan, June 30, 1863, ibid.; see Seward 3:101–10; OR ser. 3, vol. 2, pp. 179–200 (other correspondence).

21 Seward to Stanton and Stanton to Seward, June 30 & July 1, 1862, Seward Papers reel 70; Nevins and Thomas, eds., *Diary of George Templeton Strong*, 3:235 (Seward in town, meeting with governors); *Boston Evening Transcript*, July 2, 1862; *Boston Journal*, July 2, 1862; *New York Tribune*, July 2, 1862.

22 *New York Times*, July 2, 1862; Seward to Stanton, July 2, 1862, Seward Papers reel 70; Seward to Stanton, July 3, 1862, OR ser. 3, vol. 2, p. 200; Fanny Seward Diary, July 3–4, 1862, Seward Papers reel 198; Adam Gurowski, *Diary from March 4, 1861, to November 12, 1862* (Boston: Lee & Shepard, 1862), 235.

23 Seward to Edwin Morgan, July 5, 1862, Seward Papers reel 70; Seward to Frances Seward, July 12, 1862, ibid. reel 115; Seward 3:100–01; *Wisconsin State Register*, July 26, 1862 ("instantly show our strength"); *New York Times*, Aug. 15, 1862 (State Department); *Albany Evening Journal*, Aug. 26, 1862; James Geary, *We Need Men: The Union Draft in the Civil War* (DeKalb: Northern Illinois University Press, 1991), 12–35; Goodwin, *Team of Rivals*, 449–50; McPherson, *Battle Cry of Freedom*, 490–94 ("quasi-draft").

24 Fanny Seward Diary, Aug. 29–Sept. 2, 1862, Seward Papers reel 198; Beale, ed., *Welles Diary*, 1:101–04; Seward 3:125–27; Seward to Frances Seward, Sept. 4, 1862, Seward 3:127; *Cincinnati Daily Gazette*, Sept. 5, 1862; Goodwin, *Team of Rivals*, 479–80; Matthew Pinsker, *Lincoln's Sanctuary: Abraham Lincoln and the Soldiers' Home* (New York: Oxford University Press, 2003).

25 Seward to Adams, Sept. 8, 1862, Seward 3:128; ibid., 129–30 (march); Stephen Sears, *Landscape Turned Red: The Battle of Antietam* (New York: Ticknor & Fields, 1983), 97–101.

26 Edward Pierce, ed., *The Works of Charles Sumner*, 15 vols. (Boston: Lee & Shepard, 1870–83), 5:497–98; Leon Litwack, *North of Slavery: The Negro in the Free States, 1790–1860* (Chicago: University of Chicago Press, 1961), 56–57; Seward to Weed, Apr. 25, 1862, Weed Papers.

27 Lincoln Message, Dec. 3, 1861, CWL 5:39; *New York Times*, Feb. 5, 1862; Cong. Globe, 37th Cong., 2d Sess. 1806; Statutes at Large, 37th Cong., 2d Sess. 421.

28 Lincoln Message, Mar. 6, 1862, CWL 5:144–45; Cong. Globe, 33d Cong., 2d Sess. App. 241; *New York Times*, Mar. 8, 1862; Burlingame, *Abraham Lincoln*, 2:333–43.

29 Seward to Adams, Feb. 17, 1862, NA, M77 reel 77; Lincoln Message, Apr. 16, 1862, CWL 5:192; *New York Times*, Apr. 17, 1862; Burlingame, *Abraham Lincoln*, 2:343–47.

30 Foreman, *World on Fire*, 24, 38; Howard Jones and Donald Rakestraw, *Prologue to Manifest Destiny: Anglo-American Relations in the 1840s* (Wilmington,

DE: SR Books, 1997), 71–96; Taylor Milne, "The Lyons-Seward Treaty of 1862," *American Historical Review* 38 (1933): 511–25 (quote on 512); Hugh Thomas, *The Slave Trade: The Story of the Atlantic Slave Trade* (New York: Simon & Schuster, 1997), 769–75.

31 Lyons to Russell, Mar. 21, 25 & Apr. 7, 1862, in Milne, "Lyons-Seward," 519–23.

32 Sumner to Francis Lieber [Apr. 25, 1862], Sumner Papers reel 64; Seward to Frances Seward, Apr. 28, 1862, Seward 3:85; Milne, "Lyons-Seward," 516.

33 Seward to Weed, Apr. 25, 1862, Weed Papers; Seward to Adams, Feb. 17 & Mar. 10, 1862, NA, M77 reel 77; Burlingame, *Lincoln*, 2:333–56; Goodheart, *1861*, 340–47; Allen Guelzo, *Lincoln's Emancipation Proclamation: The End of Slavery* (New York: Simon & Schuster, 2004), 61–109.

34 Seward to Adams, May 28 & July 5, 1862, NA, M77 reel 77; Seward to Dayton, June 3, 1862, ibid. reel 56; Kinley Brauer, "The Slavery Problem in the Diplomacy of the American Civil War," *Pacific Historical Review* 46 (1977): 439–69.

35 Frances Seward to Seward, Mar. 11, Apr. 26, & July 26 (?), 1862, Seward Papers reel 114 (draft in folder 6639).

36 Seward to Frances Seward, Apr. 7, July 12 & 29, 1862, Seward 3:81, 115–16 & 118; Seward to Weed, Apr. 25, 1862, Weed Papers.

37 Beale, ed., *Welles Diary*, 1:70–71: Gideon Welles, "The History of Emancipation," *The Galaxy* 14 (1872): 843–44.

38 Gideon Welles to Edgar Welles, July 13, 1862, Welles Papers LC; Welles to Mary Jane Welles, July 13, 1862, ibid. Some suggest that a sentence in the letter from Welles to his wife—"I scarcely knew what to make of it"—refers to Lincoln's remarks on emancipation. The context makes it clear what puzzled Welles was Seward's invitation to join him in his carriage. Cf. Eric Foner, *The Fiery Trial: Abraham Lincoln and American Slavery* (New York: W.W. Norton, 2010), 217.

39 Pease and Randall, eds., *Browning Diary*, 1:558–59; *New York Times*, July 15, 1862; Burlingame, *Abraham Lincoln*, 2:357–60.

40 Second Confiscation Act, sec. 12, Stat. at Large, 37th Cong., 2d Sess. 592; Stuart to Russell, Sept. 4, 1862, in Barnes and Barnes, eds., *British Eyes*, 2:169; George Baker to Israel Washburn Jr., June 12, 1865, in Gaillard Hunt, *Israel, Elihu and Cadwallader Washburn: A Chapter in American Biography* (New York: Macmillan Co., 1925), 116; Seward 3:227; Nicolay and Hay, *Abraham Lincoln*, 6:357; Paul Scheips, "Lincoln and the Chiriqui Colonization Project," *Journal of Negro History* 37 (1952): 418–53; Phillip Magness and Sebastian Page, *Colonization After Emancipation: Lincoln and the Movement for Black Resettlement* (Fulton: University of Missouri Press, 2011).

41 Draft Proclamation, July 22, 1862, Lincoln Papers; Guelzo, *Emancipation Proclamation*, 117–21, 253–54.

42 Stanton Note, July 22, 1862, Stanton Papers, reel 3; Nicolay and Hay, *Abraham Lincoln*, 6:128 (printed version). Chase, in his diary, did not record Seward's comments—Niven, ed., *Salmon Chase Papers*, 1:351–52.

43 *New York Times*, Apr. 2, 1864 (from *Cincinnati Daily Gazette*).

44 Carpenter, *Six Months*, 20–22.

45 For attempts to reconcile the two versions, see Goodwin, *Team of Rivals*, 463–68; Guelzo, *Emancipation Proclamation*, 117–23. For accounts which recognize that Seward opposed emancipation, see Brauer, "The Slavery Problem," 452 ("Seward opposed the emancipation proclamation and hoped that circumstances would change Lincoln's mind"), and Van Deusen, *Seward*, 387–89 ("he had a genuine distaste for abolishing [slavery] by executive edict").

46 Seward to Adams, July 5, 1862, FRUS 1862, p. 124; Seward to Frances Seward, July 29, 1862, Seward 3:118; Pease and Randall, eds., *Browning Diary*, 1:619; *Sacamento Daily Union*, Feb. 21, 1863; Henry Bellows to Eliza Bellows, Apr. 23, 1863, Bellows Papers, MHS.

47 Francis Cutting to Edwin Stanton, Feb. 20, 1867, Stanton Papers, LC; Guelzo, *Emancipation Proclamation*, 123.

48 McPherson, *Battle Cry of Freedom*, 524–45; Sears, *Landscape Turned Red*.

49 Adams to Seward, July 17, 1862, NA, M77 reel 77; Seward to Motley, July 24, 1862, ibid. reel 13; Motley to Seward, Aug. 26, 1862, Seward Papers reel 70; Brauer, "The Slavery Problem," 455–56; Van Deusen, *Seward*, 332.

50 *New York Tribune*, Aug. 20, 1862; Lincoln to Greeley, Aug. 22, 1862, CWL 5:388–89; Frances Seward to Seward, Aug. 24, 1862, Seward Papers reel 114; Carpenter, *Six Months*, 72–73.

51 Niven, ed., *Salmon Chase Papers*, 1:393–95; Preliminary Emancipation Proclamation, Sept. 22, 1862, CWL 5:433–36; *New York Times*, Sept. 23, 1862; Burlingame, *Abraham Lincoln*, 2:407–09; Guelzo, *Emancipation Proclamation*, 151–57.

52 Seward to Adams, Sept. 22, 1862, NA, M77 reel 77; Seward to Fanny Seward, Sept. 24, 1862; Seward 3:135; Stoeckl to Gorchakov, Sept. 25, 1862, in Woldman, *Lincoln and the Russians*, 185; Burlingame, *Abraham Lincoln*, 2:409–18 (reactions); Donn Piatt, *Memories of the Men Who Saved the Union* (New York: Belford, Clarke, 1887), 150 (Seward skeptical).

53 Lady Emmeline Stuart-Wortley, *Travels in the United States in 1849 and 1850* (New York: Harper & Bros., 1851), 150; *New York Times*, Sept. 2, 1858; Mary Ann Pellew Smith, *Six Years Travels in Russia, by an English Lady*, 2 vols. (London: Hurst & Blackett, 1859), 1:160–61; Alan Dowty, *The Limits of American Isolation: The United States and the Crimean War* (New York: New York University Press, 1971); Norman Saul, *Distant Friends: The United States and Russia, 1763–1867* (Lawrence: University Press of Kansas, 1991), 166–68.

54 *New York Times*, Oct. 21, 1853; Cong. Globe, 34th Cong., 2d Sess. 49; *Albany Evening Journal*, Sept. 17, 1857; *New York Times*, Oct. 28, 1858; Saul, *Distant Friends*, 199 (quote).

55 Seward to Clay, May 6, 1861, FRUS 1861, p. 293; Stoeckl to Gorchakov, May 23, 1861, in Goldman, *Lincoln and the Russians*, 66; Fanny Seward Diary, Apr. 4, 1862, Seward Papers reel 198.

56 Gorchakov to Stoeckl, July 10, 1861, in Woldman, *Lincoln and the Russians*, 127–29; Seward to Stoeckl, Sept. 7, 1861, in *New York Tribune*, Sept. 9, 1861; Lyons to Russell, Sept. 9, 1861, in Barnes and Barnes, eds., *British Eyes*, 1:162; *New York Times*, Sept. 9 & 10, 1861; *Chicago Tribune*, Sept. 12, 1861.

57 Seward to Bigelow, June 25, 1862, in Bigelow, *Retrospections*, 1:499–500; Seward to Dayton, July 10, 1862, NA, M77 reel 56; Seward to Adams, Aug. 2, 1862, ibid. reel 77.

58 *New York Times*, Oct. 25, 1862; Kinley Brauer, "British Mediation and the American Civil War: A Reconsideration," *Journal of Southern History* 38 (1972): 49–64; Foreman, *World on Fire*, 315–28; Howard Jones, *Union in Peril: The Crisis Over British Intervention in the Civil War* (Chapel Hill: University of North Carolina Press, 1992), 162–223.

59 *New York Times*, Nov. 27, 1862; *Washington Daily Morning Chronicle*, Nov. 28, 1862; Seward to Sanford, Nov. 28, 1862, Sanford Papers, Sanford Museum; Seward to Bigelow, Dec. 2, 1862, in Bigelow, *Retrospections*, 1:578; sources cited in note 58.

60 Burlingame, *Lincoln*, 2:419–23; Stewart Mitchell, *Horatio Seymour of New York* (Cambridge, MA: Harvard University Press, 1938); Jennifer Weber, *Copperheads: The Rise and Fall of Lincoln's Opponents in the North* (New York: Oxford University Press, 2006), 43–71.

61 Nevins and Thomas, eds., *Diary of George Templeton Strong*, 3:272; Seward to Adams, Nov. 10, 1862, NA, M77 reel 77; Guelzo, *Emancipation Proclamation*, 167; White, *Eloquent President*, 172–73.

62 Lincoln Message, Dec. 1, 1862, CWL 5:518–37; Seward Circular, Nov. 30, 1862, Seward 5:84–85; White, *Eloquent President*, 170–89.

63 *Boston Commonwealth*, Dec. 6, 1862; Donald, *Sumner and the Rights of Man*, 87–91.

64 T. J. Barnett to Barlow, Nov. 30, 1862, Samuel Barlow Papers, Huntington Library; *New York Herald*, July 24, 1862; *Daily National Intelligencer*, July 26, 1862; *New York Tribune*, July 28, 1862; *Boston Daily Advertiser*, July 28, 1862; *Cleveland Herald*, July 31, 1862.

65 Zachariah Chandler to Lyman Trumbull, Sept. 10, 1862, in William Harris, *Public Life of Zachariah Chandler, 1851–1875* (Chicago: University of Chicago, 1917), 60; Joseph Medill to Schuyler Colfax [Nov. 1862], in O. J. Hollister, *Life of Schuyler Colfax* (New York: Funk & Wagnalls, 1886), 200; *Boston*

Commonwealth, Nov. 22, 1862; Harry Williams, *Lincoln and the Radicals* (Madison: University of Wisconsin Press, 1941).

66 James Hamilton, *Reminiscences of James A. Hamilton . . . Century* (New York: Charles Scribner & Co., 1869), 529–33; Nevins, ed., *Salmon Chase Papers* 1:378, 389; Nicolay and Hay, *Abraham Lincoln*, 6:253–63; Niven, *Salmon P. Chase*, 308–13.

67 Beale, ed., *Welles Diary*, 1:132–33, 135.

68 Francis Blair to John Bigelow, Oct. 26, 1861, in Bigelow, *Retrospections*, 1:375–77; Elizabeth Lee to Samuel Lee, Dec. 21, 1861, in Virginia Laas, ed., *Wartime Washington: The Civil War Letters of Elizabeth Blair Lee* (Urbana: University of Illinois Press, 1991), 94; Pease and Randall, eds., *Browning Diary*, 1:520; Beale, ed., *Welles Diary*, 1:275.

69 George Lincoln to Welles, Apr. 25, 1874, in "New Light on the Seward-Welles-Lincoln Controversy," *Lincoln Lore* 1718 (April 1981): 2–3; Elizabeth Keckley, *Behind the Scenes* (Chicago: R. R. Donnelly & Sons, 1998), 115; Michael Burlingame, "Mary Todd Lincoln's Unethical Conduct as First Lady," in Burlingame, ed., *At Lincoln's Side: John Hay's Civil War Correspondence and Selected Writings* (Carbondale: Southern Illinois University Press), 185–203.

70 Foreman, *World on Fire*, 343–44 ("every attitude of death"); Burlingame, *Abraham Lincoln*, 2:446 ("worse place than hell"); McPherson, *Battle Cry of Freedom*, 570–74; Roy Morris, *The Better Angel: Walt Whitman in the Civil War* (New York: Oxford University Press, 2000), 48–53 (hospitals).

71 Pease and Randall, eds., *Browning Diary*, 1:596–97; Fessenden Memorandum, Dec. 1862, Fessenden Papers, Bowdoin. A printed copy of the memorandum appears in Francis Fessenden, *Life and Public Services of William Pitt Fessenden*, 2 vols. (Boston: Houghton Mifflin, 1907), 1:231–36.

72 Seward to Lincoln, Dec. 16, 1862, Lincoln Papers; Frederick Seward to Lincoln, Dec. 16, 1862, ibid.; Fanny Seward Diary, Dec. 25, 1862, Seward Papers reel 198; Fessenden Memorandum, Fessenden Papers, Bowdoin; *New York Times*, Dec. 22, 1862 (Raymond report); *Washington Daily Morning Chronicle*, Dec. 23, 1862; Seward 2:146–47. There is conflict among the sources as to when Seward resigned. The letters are dated Dec. 16, and Fanny's diary states that the resignations were made on that day, but the best news accounts state that the letters were delivered on Dec. 17, and Fessenden quotes King as saying he advised Seward to resign after the second Senate meeting, i.e., Dec. 17. Perret believes Seward's resignation letter was originally dated December 12. See Geoffrey Perret, *Lincoln's War: The Untold Story of America's Greatest President as Commander in Chief* (New York: Random House, 2004), 434 n.15.

73 Fessenden Memorandum, Fessenden Papers, Bowdoin; *New York Times*, Dec. 22, 1862.

74 Fessenden to Samuel Fessenden, Dec. 20, 1862, Fessenden Papers, Bowdoin; Fessenden Memorandum, ibid.; Burlingame, *Abraham Lincoln*, 2:452–53; Goodwin, *Team of Rivals*, 491–92.

75 Beale, ed., *Welles Diary*, 1:199–200; Seward 2:147; Goodwin, *Team of Rivals*, 492–93.

76 Beale, ed., *Welles Diary*, 1:201–02; Lincoln to Seward and Chase, Dec. 20, 1862, CWL 6:12; Seward to Lincoln, Dec. 21, 1862, Lincoln Papers; Chase to Lincoln, Dec. 22, 1862, ibid.; Lyons to Russell, Dec. 22, 1862, in Barnes and Barnes, eds., *Private and Confidential*, 312.

77 Seward to Richard Blatchford, Dec. 22, 1862, Lincoln Collection, Yale; Chase to Frederick Seward, Dec. 24, 1862, Seward Papers reel 74; Fanny Seward Diary, Dec. 20–31, 1862, ibid. reel 198; Seward to Sanford, Jan. 24, 1863, Sanford Papers, Sanford Museum.

NOTES FOR CHAPTER 13

1 Fanny Seward Diary, Jan. 1, 1863, Seward Papers reel 198; Burlingame, *Abraham Lincoln*, 422–23, 462–63, 468–69; Guelzo, *Emancipation Proclamation*, 176–82.

2 Fanny Seward Diary, Jan. 1, 1863, Seward Papers reel 198; *Sacramento Daily Union*, Jan. 29, 1863 (Brooks); *Washington Daily Morning Chronicle*, Jan. 2, 1863.

3 Seward 3:151 (Frederick); Guelzo, *Emancipation Proclamation*, 182–83; Thomas and Hyman, *Stanton*, 135–37; Elizabeth Lee to Samuel Lee, Jan. 1, 1863, in Virginia Laas, ed., *Wartime Washington: The Civil War Letters of Elizabeth Blair Lee* (Urbana: University of Illinois Press, 1991), 224–25 (Seward's dinner guests that day).

4 Fanny Seward Diary, Jan. 24 & Feb. 5 & 13, Seward Papers reel 198; Seward, *Personal Recollections*, 9–12.

5 Nevins and Thomas, eds., *Diary of George Templeton Strong*, 3:291–92 (comments of Bellows); Henry Bellows to Eliza Bellows, Apr. 23, 1863, MHS.

6 *New York Times*, Jan. 7, 1863; Cong. Globe, 37th Cong., 3d Sess. App. 52–58; Montgomery Meigs to Ambrose Burnside, Dec. 30, 1862, OR ser. 1, vol. 21, p. 917; Weber, *Copperheads*, ix–xi, 72–94.

7 *New York Tribune*, Jan. 9, 14 & 31, 1863; *New York Times*, Jan. 29, 1863; Case and Spencer, *The United States and France*, 393–95; Warren Spencer, "The Jewett-Greeley Affair: A Private Scheme for French Mediation in the American Civil War," *New York History* 51 (1970): 238–68 (Mercier quoted 266).

8 *New York Tribune*, Feb. 4, 5, 10, 12, & 13, 1863; *New York Herald*, Feb. 12, 1863; *New York Times*, Feb. 12 & 13, 1863; Sam Wilkeson to Sydney Howard Gay, Feb. 9 & 11, 1863, Gay Papers, Columbia University; Donald, *Sumner and the Rights of Man*, 101–07.

9 Seward to Dayton, Feb. 6, 1863, in *New York Times*, Feb. 13, 1863; ibid., Mar. 13, 1863 (London); *Sacramento Daily Union*, Mar. 14 & 16, 1863; Nevins and Thomas, eds., *Diary of George Templeton Strong*, 3:293. Strong was reacting not to the published letter but to a rumor regarding Seward's confrontation with Mercier over this issue.

10 Seward to Dayton, Apr. 8 & May 11, 1863, FRUS 1863, 2:724, 738–39; Clay to Seward, June 7, 1863, ibid., 873; *New York Times*, June 24, 1863; *Sacramento Daily Union*, June 18, 1863; Harold Blinn, "Seward and the Polish Rebellion of 1863," *American Historical Review* 45 (1940): 828–33; John Kutolowski, "The Effect of the Polish Insurrection of 1863 on American Civil War Diplomacy," *Historian* 27 (August 1965): 560–77; Joseph Wieczerzak, "American Reactions to the Polish Insurrection of 1863," *Polish American Studies* 22 (1965): 90–98.

11 *Sacramento Daily Union*, May 27, 1863.

12 Sam Wilkeson to Sydney Gay, Feb. 9 & 11, 1863, Gay Papers, Columbia University; *Sacramento Daily Union*, June 12, 1863; Michael Burlingame, ed., *Lincoln Observed: Civil War Dispatches of Noah Brooks* (Baltimore: Johns Hopkins University Press, 1998), 1–12.

13 Seward 3:197.

14 John Hay Diary, Aug. 13, 1863, in Burlingame and Ettlinger, eds., *Inside Lincoln's White House*, 72–73.

15 Dicey, *Spectator of America*, 93; Fehrenbacher and Fehrenbacher, eds., *Recollected Words*, 126; Noah Brooks, *Washington in Lincoln's Time* (New York: Rinehart, 1958), 54.

16 See David Donald, *We Are Lincoln Men: Abraham Lincoln and His Friends* (New York: Simon & Schuster, 2003), 147–76.

17 John Hay, "The Heroic Age in Washington," 1871 lecture, in Burlingame, ed., *At Lincoln's Side*, 128–29.

18 Frederick Seward to ?, May 1863, Seward 3:161–65; Fanny Seward Diary, Apr. 26–May 1, 1863, Seward Papers reel 198; Seward to Bigelow, May 9, 1863, in Bigelow, *Retrospections*, 1:643; Adams, *Adams Autobiography*, 161; Stephen Sears, *Chancellorsville* (Boston: Houghton Mifflin, 1996).

19 Fanny Seward Diary, May–June 1863, Seward Papers reel 198; Seward Speech, May 1863, Seward 3:167; Fanny Seward to Seward, June 7, 1863, Seward Papers reel 116; Seward to Frances and Fanny Seward, June 11, 1863, Seward 3:169; *New York Tribune*, June 11, 1863 (Lee reviewed troops "preparatory to a contemplated raid into Maryland and Pennsylvania").

20 *New York Times*, June 16–17, 1863; Seward to Frances and Fanny Seward, June 19 & 30, 1863, Seward 3:170–71; Seward to Sanford, June 30, 1863, Sanford Papers, Sanford Museum.

21 *New York Times*, July 3, 1863; George Meade to Henry Halleck, July 3, 1863, OR ser. 1, vol. 27, pt. 1, pp. 74–75; Lincoln Message, July 4, 1863, CWL 6:314;

Seward to Frances Seward, July 4, 1863, Seward 3:172; Stephen Sears, *Gettysburg* (Boston: Houghton Mifflin, 2003).

22 *New York Times*, July 6–9, 1863; *Sacramento Daily Union*, Aug. 1, 1863; Goodwin, *Team of Rivals*, 533–34. A slightly different version of Seward's speech appeared in the *New York Herald*, July 9, 1863.

23 *New York Times*, July 9, 1863.

24 Ibid.

25 Seward to ?, *New York Times*, Aug. 2, 1863; Burlingame, *Abraham Lincoln*, 2:520–25 (compensation issue).

26 Sumner to Lincoln, Aug. 7, 1863, Lincoln Papers; Sumner to Bright, July 21 & Aug. 4, 1863, in Palmer, ed., *Letters of Charles Sumner*, 2:183–85; Donald, *Sumner and the Rights of Man*, 118–19; Paul and Stephen Kendrick, *Douglass and Lincoln: How a Revolutionary Black Leader and a Reluctant Liberator Struggled to End Slavery and Save the Union* (New York: Walker & Co., 2008), 156–58.

27 *New York Times*, Jan. 1, 1863; Crook, *The North, the South*, 257–62; Mahin, *One War at a Time*, 142–60.

28 Cong. Globe, 37th Cong., 3d Sess. 1020–28; Lyons to Russell, Feb. 24, 1863, in Barnes and Barnes, eds., *British Eyes*, 3:10–12; Donald, *Sumner and the Rights of Man*, 108–09.

29 Stat. at Large, 37th Cong., 3d Sess. 758; Lyons to Russell, Mar. 10, 1863, in Barnes and Barnes, eds., *British Eyes*, 3:25–27; Seward to Adams, Mar. 9, 1863, FRUS 1863, 1:163.

30 Beale, ed., *Welles Diary*, 1:266–67; Seward to Delafield Smith, Apr. 12, 1863, quoted in Stuart Bernath, *Squall Across the Atlantic: American Civil War Prize Cases and Diplomacy* (Berkeley: University of California Press, 1970), 71; Niven, *Welles*, 455–56.

31 Sumner to Francis Lieber, May 10, 1863, Sumner Papers reel 64; *Sacramento Daily Union*, May 18, 1863; Beale, ed., *Welles Diary*, 1:269–85; Donald, *Sumner and the Rights of Man*, 108; Niven, *Welles*, 456–58.

32 Lyons to Russell, Apr. 13, 1863, in Barnes and Barnes, eds., *British Eyes*, 3:34–35; Richard Cobden to Bigelow, May 22, 1863, in Bigelow, *Retrospections*, 1:643; Bigelow to Seward, May 29, 1863, Bigelow Papers, NYPL; Chester Barrows, *William M. Evarts: Lawyer, Diplomat, Statesman* (Chapel Hill: University of North Carolina Press, 1941), 113–18; Coy Cross, *Lincoln's Man in Liverpool: Consul Dudley and the Legal Battle to Stop Confederate Warships* (DeKalb: Northern Illinois University Press, 2007); Martin Duberman, *Charles Francis Adams, 1807–1886* (Boston: Houghton Mifflin, 1961), 486.

33 *New York Times*, May 1, 1863. For the *Alabama* claims, see Seward to Adams, Jan. 19 & Feb. 2 & 14, 1863, FRUS 1863, 1:67, 114, 135. For the neutral-belligerent issue, see Crook, *The North, the South*, 279; Cross, *Lincoln's Man in Liverpool*, 79.

34 Adams to Seward, Apr. 7, 1863, FRUS 1863, 1:228; Seward to Adams, Apr. 22, 1863, ibid., 255; *New York Times*, Apr. 22 & July 10, 1863; Seward to Adams, July 11, 1863, FRUS 1863, 1:354–56.

35 Adams to Russell, Sept. 5, 1863, FRUS 1863, 1:417–18; Duberman, *Charles Francis Adams*, 310–14; Foreman, *World on Fire*, 515–25; Mahin, *One War at a Time*, 178–83.

36 Seward to Adams, Sept. 5, 1863, FRUS 1863, 1:416–17.

37 Charles Sumner, *Our Foreign Relations* (New York: Young Men's Republican Union, 1863) (quotes on 16, 27, 65); Donald, *Sumner and the Rights of Man*, 122–31.

38 Beale, ed., *Welles Diary* 1:436–37; C. F. Adams Diary, Sept. 8, 1863, Adams Papers, MHS reel 77; *New York Times*, Sept. 22 & 23, 1863; Seward to Adams, Sept. 28, 1863, FRUS 1863, 1:434.

39 *Chicago Tribune*, Sept. 15, 1863; *New York Times*, Oct. 13, 1863 (Russell speech); Adams to John Palfrey, Nov. 10, 1863, Adams Papers, MHS reel 170; Donald, *Sumner and the Rights of Man*, 132–37.

40 Fanny Seward Diary, Mar. 17, 1863, Seward Papers reel 198; Seward to Sumner, Sept. 12, 1863, Sumner Papers reel 29; Frances Seward to Sumner, Nov. 17, 1863, ibid. David Donald, in *Sumner and the Rights of Man*, has many useful details, but ignores the tie between Frances and Sumner.

41 For Bigelow's resignation, see Bigelow to Seward, May 24, 1863, Seward to Bigelow, June 6 & 15, 1863, in Bigelow, *Retrospections*, 2:3–10. For Bigelow's work on the Confederate cruisers, see John Bigelow, *France and the Confederate Navy, 1862–1868* (London: Sampson Low, 1888); Case and Spencer, *France and the United States*, 427–80.

42 Henry Clews, "England and Russia in Our Civil War, and the War Between Russia and Japan," *North American Review* 178 (1903): 812–19 (quote 816); Saul, *Distant Friends*, 339–54; Woldman, *Lincoln and the Russians*, 140–55.

43 Seward to Frances Seward, July 17, 1863, in Seward 3:176; Lyons to Russell, July 17, 1863, in Barnes and Barnes, eds., *Private and Confidential*; Seward to Bigelow, July 21, 1863, in Bigelow, *Retrospections*, 2:32–32; Iver Bernstein, *New York City Draft Riots: Their Significance for American Society and Politics in the Age of the Civil War* (New York: Oxford University Press, 1990); Goodwin, *Team of Rivals*, 536–38; Barnet Schecter, *The Devil's Own Work: The Civil War Draft Riots and the Fight to Reconstruct America* (New York: Walker & Co., 2005).

44 Frances Seward to Augustus Seward, July 20, 1863, Seward Papers reel 115; Seward to Frances Seward, July 17, 21, & 25, 1863, ibid. reel 112; Seward, *Personal Experiences*, 12 (Jenny); *New York Times*, July 24, 1863.

45 Fanny Seward Diary, Aug. 14–21, 1863, Seward House Auburn (section of diary not at Rochester); Lyons to Russell, Aug. 14, 1863, quoted in Foreman, *World on Fire*, 511; *Auburn Advertiser*, Aug. 20, 1863; Peter Wisbey, "A Party with a

Purpose," *New York Archives* 8 (2009): 6–7. Seward later told Adams that his purpose was to confer with Justice Nelson, at his summer home, about the blockade. This seems unlikely; Seward could have conferred with Nelson in Washington—C. F. Adams Diary, May 29, 1870, Adams Papers, MHS.

46 Lyons to Russell, Sept. 2, 1863, quoted in Foreman, *World on Fire*, 511; Seward 3:185–86.

47 Salmon Chase Journal, Sept. 23, 1863, in Niven, ed., *Salmon Chase Papers*, 1:452–53; Burlingame, *Abraham Lincoln*, 2:556–57 ("most successful"); Goodwin, *Team of Rivals*, 557–59.

48 Lincoln Proclamation, Oct. 3, 1863, CWL 6:496–97; Seward 3:194. Sarah Josepha Hale had been advocating a single Thanksgiving day for many years, and wrote Lincoln on the subject—Hale to Lincoln, Sept. 28, 1863, Lincoln Papers.

49 Fanny Seward Diary, Apr. 29, 1862, Oct. 9, 1863, Seward Papers reel 198; Joseph Leach, *Bright Particular Star: The Life and Times of Charlotte Cushman* (New Haven: Yale University Press, 1970), 242–43, 310–11, 321–25.

50 Fanny Seward Diary, draft Oct. 1863, Seward Papers reel 198; Lisa Merrill, *When Romeo Was a Woman: Charlotte Cushman and Her Circle of Female Spectators* (Ann Arbor: University of Michigan Press, 1999), 227–31; Julia Markus, *Across an Untried Sea: Discovering Lives Hidden in the Shadow of Convention and Time* (New York: Alfred A. Knopf, 2000), 180–85.

51 Fanny Seward Diary, Oct. 9–14, 1863, Seward Papers reel 198; Markus, *Across an Untried Sea*, 180.

52 Fanny Seward Diary, Oct. 10, 1863, Seward Papers reel 198; *Daily National Republican*, Oct. 19 & Nov. 14, 1863; Leach, *Bright Particular Star*, 323–25. Goodwin errs in stating that Cushman visited Washington in early 1864; by that time she was back in Rome—Goodwin, *Team of Rivals*, 610–11.

53 *Sacramento Daily Union*, May 28, 1863; Seward to John Bigelow, July 21, 1863, in Bigelow, *Retrospections*, 2:31–32 (discourages talk of Seward); Seward to Edwin Morgan, Sept. 24 & 25, Morgan Papers, NYSL; *New York Herald*, Dec. 1, 1863; Goodwin, *Team of Rivals*, 573–76.

54 *New York Times*, Nov. 5, 1863 (Nov. 2 speech); Seward to Lincoln, Nov. 3, 1863, Lincoln Papers; John Hay Diary, Nov. 8, 1863, in Burlingame and Ettlinger, eds., *Inside Lincoln's White House*, 109; Goodwin, *Team of Rivals*, 578–79.

55 *Norfolk County Journal*, Nov. 24, 1863; *Liberator*, Nov. 13 & Dec. 4, 1863.

56 Stanton to Governors, Nov. 11, 1863, OR ser. 3, vol. 3, pt. 3, pp. 1022–23; Seward to Adams, Nov. 14, 1863, FRUS 1863, supp. LX–LXI; *New York Times*, Nov. 13, 1863; Robin Winks, *Canada and the United States: The Civil War Years* (Baltimore: Johns Hopkins University Press, 1960), 146–51.

57 Lincoln Remarks, Nov. 18, 1863, CWL 7:17; Gabor Boritt, *The Gettysburg Gospel: The Lincoln Speech That Nobody Knows* (New York: Simon & Schuster, 1996), 66–68, 73–75; Burlingame, *Abraham Lincoln*, 2:570–71; Goodwin, *Team of*

Rivals, 583–84; John Russell Young, *Men and Memories: Personal Reminiscences*, 2 vols. (New York: F. T. Neely, 1901), 1:59 ("bad hat").

58 *New York Times*, Nov. 21, 1863; *New York Tribune*, Nov. 21, 1863.

59 Boritt, *Gettysburg Gospel*, 76–78, 317; John Hay Diary, Nov. 18, 1863, in Burlingame and Ettlinger, eds., *Inside Lincoln's White House*, 112; Young, *Men and Memories*, 1:60. Burlingame claims that the *New York Tribune* denounced the "egotism" of Seward's speech, but I do not find this in the *Tribune*—Burlingame, *Abraham Lincoln*, 2:571.

60 Benjamin French, *Witness to the Young Republic: A Yankee's Journal, 1828–1870*, ed. Donald Cole and John McDonough (Hanover, NH: University Press of New England, 1989), 433–34; Goodwin, *Team of Rivals*, 584; Garry Wills, *Lincoln at Gettysburg: The Words That Remade America* (New York: Simon & Schuster, 1992), 31–32.

61 *Chicago Tribune*, Nov. 20 & 21, 1863; *New York Tribune*, Nov. 21, 1863; *Washington Daily Morning Chronicle*, Nov. 21, 1863; Boritt, *Gettysburg Gospel*, 91–96, 102–03.

62 Boritt, *Gettysburg Gospel*, 110–12 & App. A (Everett address); Lincoln Address, CWL 7:17–23; Burlingame, *Abraham Lincoln*, 2:572–75; Goodwin, *Team of Rivals*, 584–86.

63 *Chicago Tribune*, Nov. 25, 1863; Fehrenbacher and Fehrenbacher, eds., *Recollected Words*, 289; Ward Lamon, *Recollections of Abraham Lincoln, 1847–1865* (Chicago: A.C. McClurg, 1895), 172; John Taylor, *William Henry Seward: Lincoln's Right Hand* (Washington, DC: Brassey's, 1999), 234. Taylor's citation for the 1921 letter is curious, and the author was unable to clarify this in response to my e-mail request.

64 John Brien to Seward, July 23, 1863, Lincoln Papers; Lincoln Proclamation, Dec. 8. 1863, CWL 7:-53–56; Paul Escott, *"What Shall We Do with the Negro?": Lincoln, White Racism, and Civil War America* (Charlottesville: University of Virginia Press, 2009).

65 *New York Times*, Dec. 10, 1863; Wendell Phillips to Benjamin Butler, Dec. 13, 1863, in Benjamin Butler, *Private and Official Correspondence of Gen. Benjamin F. Butler*, 5 vols. (Norwood, MA: Plimpton Press, 1917), 3:206–07; McPherson, *Battle Cry of Freedom*, 698–702; John Waugh, *Reelecting Lincoln: The Battle for the 1864 Presidency* (New York: Crown, 1997), 58–71.

66 *New York Times*, Dec. 10, 16, & 21, 1863; Winks, *Canada and the United States*, 244–55.

67 Seward to Lyons, Dec. 18, 1863, FRUS 1864, 2:405; Lyons to Russell, Dec. 24, 1863, in Barnes and Barnes, eds., *British Eyes*, 3:126–27; Seward to Adams, Jan. 11, 1864, FRUS 1864, 1:77; Winks, *Canada and the United States*, 254–55.

68 *New York Herald*, Dec. 1, 1863; *New York Times*, Jan. 23, 1864; *Sacramento Daily Union*, Mar. 23, 1863 (from *Richmond Enquirer*).

NOTES FOR CHAPTER 14

1 Beale, ed., *Welles Diary*, 1:506; *Daily National Republican*, Jan. 15, 16, & 26, 1864; *New York Times*, Jan. 13 & 26, 1864; Frederick Seward to Frances Seward, Jan. 24, 1864, Seward Papers reel 117.

2 Seward 3:206.

3 Fanny Seward Diary, Feb. 10–14, 1864, Seward Papers reel 198; Fanny Seward to Frances Seward, Feb. 11, 1864, ibid. reel 116; *Daily National Republican*, Feb. 5, 1864.

4 Fanny Seward Diary, Mar. 11, 1864, Seward Papers reel 198; *Daily National Republican*, Apr. 11–26 & Nov. 9–14, 1863, Feb. 12–20 & Mar. 2–11, 1864; *Washington Daily Morning Chronicle*, Apr. 11–18, 1863; Kauffman, *American Brutus*, 122–25; Gene Smith, *American Gothic. The Story of America's Legendary Theatrical Family: Junius, Edwin, and John Wilkes Booth* (New York: Simon & Schuster, 1992), 97; Nora Titone, *My Thoughts Be Bloody: The Bitter Rivalry Between Edwin and John Wilkes Booth That Led to an American Tragedy* (New York: Free Press, 2010), 310–15.

5 John Nicolay Memorandum, Mar. 8, 1864, in Burlingame, ed., *With Lincoln in the White House*, 129; *New York Times*, Mar. 10, 1864 (Lincoln and Grant remarks); Burlingame, *Abraham Lincoln*, 2:629–31.

6 Beale, ed., *Welles Diary*, 1:529, 536; Chase to James Hall, Mar. 5, 1864, in *Daily National Republican*, Mar. 11, 1864; Nicolay Memorandum, Mar. 9, 1864, in Burlingame, ed., *With Lincoln in the White House*, 130–31; Nicolay to Lincoln, Mar. 30, 1864, in ibid., 132–33; Burlingame, *Abraham Lincoln*, 2:609–19; Waugh, *Reelecting Lincoln*, 112–20.

7 Beale, ed., *Welles Diary*, 1:543; *New York Times*, Apr. 18, 1864; Stat. at Large, 38th Cong., 1st Sess. 385–87; Dean Mahin, *The Blessed Place of Freedom: Europeans in Civil War America* (Washington, DC: Brassey's, 2002), 51–58.

8 Seward to Zachariah Chandler, May 14, 1864, in *New York Times*, June 10, 1864; Stat. at Large, 38th Cong., 1st Sess. 340–41; Paolino, *Foundations of the American Empire*, 41–75.

9 *Daily National Republican*, May 31, 1864; *New York Evening Post*, May 25, 1864 ("Arguelles Outrage"); *New York Times*, May 27, June 2 & 29, 1864; Cong. Globe, 38th Cong., 1st Sess. 2484, 2772; Seward to Senate, May 30, 1864, in CWL 7:370; Seward to James Wilson, June 24, 1864, FRUS 1864, 4:35–56; John Moore, *A Treatise on Extradition and Interstate Rendition*, 2 vols. (Boston: Boston Book Co., 1891), 1:33–35.

10 Seward to Dayton, Feb. 1 & Apr. 30, 1864, FRUS 1864, 3:28 & 80; Cong. Globe, 38th Cong., 1st Sess. 1408; John Hay Diary, June 24, 1864, in Burlingame and Ettlinger, eds., *Inside Lincoln's White House*, 211; Thomas Schoonover, *Dollars*

over Dominion: The Triumph of Liberalism in Mexican–United States Relations, 1861–1867 (Baton Rouge: Louisiana State University Press, 1978), 117–22.

11 Seward to Dayton, Apr. 7, 1864, FRUS 1865, 3:529; Lincoln to House, May 24, 1864, CWL 7:359; *New York Times*, May 26, 1864; Cong. Globe, 38th Cong., 2d Sess. 65–67; Schoonover, *Dollars Over Dominion*, 122–25.

12 Roberts to Eckart, Dix to Seward, Seward to Public, Lincoln to Dix, Stanton to Dix, all May 18, 1864, in OR ser. 3, vol. 4, pp. 386–89; Beale, ed., *Welles Diary*, 2:37–38; Burlingame, *Abraham Lincoln*, 2:650–52; Robert Harper, *Lincoln and the Press* (New York: McGraw-Hill, 1951), 289–99.

13 *New York Evening Post*, May 26, 1864; Waugh, *Reelecting Lincoln*, 13, 289–90.

14 It is true that in the summer of 1863, Seward was keen to see the Union flag planted in Texas. But Banks captured Brownsville, Texas, in December 1863, allowing Seward to amend the blockade to open Brownsville for foreign trade. So although Halleck claimed, in January 1864, that there were foreign policy reasons for the Red River campaign, there were none; the real reasons included capturing Shreveport, capturing Confederate cotton, and Halleck's desire (in Foote's phrase) to "keep things tidy in his rear." Halleck to Banks, Aug. 10, 1863, OR ser. 1, vol. 26, pt. 1, p. 673; *New York Times*, Dec. 3, 1863; Halleck to Grant, Jan. 8, 1864, OR ser. 1, vol. 32, pt. 2, p. 41; Lincoln Proclamation, Feb. 18, 1864, CWL 7:192–93; Beale, ed., *Welles Diary*, 1:529; Shelby Foote, *The Civil War: A Narrative. Red River to Appomattox* (New York: Random House, 1974), 25–29, 294; Gary Joiner, *One Damn Blunder from Beginning to End: The Red River Campaign of 1864* (Wilmington, DE: Scholarly Resources, 2003) xix, 3–11; Allan Nevins, *The War for the Union: The Organized War to Victory, 1864–1865* (New York: Charles Scribner's Sons, 1971), 2–5.

15 A. P. Howe to Halleck, May 17, 1864, OR ser. 1, vol. 36, pt. 2, p. 886 ("in point of discipline"); Jackson Crossley to "Sam," June 6, 1864, quoted in Ernest Furgurson, *Not War But Murder: Cold Harbor 1864* (New York: Alfred A. Knopf, 2000), 99 ("these heavy artillery men"); Alfred Roe, *The Ninth New York Heavy Artillery* (Worcester, MA: Alfred Roe, 1899), 61–66, 88–90; Seward, *Personal Recollections*, 13–17.

16 Frances Seward to Augustus Seward, May 15, 1864, Seward Papers reel 115; Frances Seward to William Seward Jr., May 20, 1864, ibid.; Seward to Frances Seward, June 1, 1864, Seward 3:223; Seward to William Seward Jr., June 5, 1864, Seward Papers reel 112.

17 OR ser. 1, vol. 36, pt. 1, pp. 174, 720, 734, & 740; Foote, *Red River to Appomattox*, 290–99; Furgurson, *Not War But Murder*, 100–05, 148–50; Roe, *Ninth New York*, 98–101; Seward, *Personal Recollections*, 18–19 (quotes letters).

18 Seward to Frances Seward, June 6, 1864, Seward 3:223; Dana to Stanton, June 8, 1864, OR ser. 1, vol. 36, pt. 1, p. 93.

19 *Sacramento Daily Union*, July 1, 1864 (Brooks); James Smart, ed., *Radical View: The "Agate" Dispatches of Whitelaw Reid, 1861–1865*, 2 vols. (Memphis, TN: Memphis State University Press, 1976), 2:171; Waugh, *Reelecting Lincoln*, 196–201.

20 *New York Evening Post*, June 9, 1864; *New York Times*, June 8–9, 1864; Seward to Charles Spencer, June 10, 1864, in ibid., June 16, 1864; Charles Flood, *1864: Lincoln at the Gates of History* (New York: Simon & Schuster, 2009), 123–24, 134–41; Michael Vorenberg, *Final Freedom: The Civil War, the Abolition of Slavery, and the Thirteenth Amendment* (Cambridge: Cambridge University Press, 2001), 121–27.

21 Seward to Frances Seward, June 1, 1864, Seward 3:223; Goodwin, *Team of Rivals*, 631–39; Waugh, *Reelecting Lincoln*, 172–81, 213–22.

22 C. F. Adams Diary, Jan. 12, 1864, MHS; Adams to Seward, Jan. 14, 1864, Adams Papers, MHS reel 170; Seward to Adams, Feb. 1, 1864, Adams Papers, MHS reel 568; Escott, "*What Shall We Do with the Negro?*"; Stephen Middleton, *The Black Laws in the Old Northwest: A Documentary History* (Westport, CT: Greenwood Press, 1993).

23 Cong. Globe, 38th Cong., 1st Sess. 3448–49; Harold Hyman and William Wiecek, *Equal Justice Under Law: Constitutional Development, 1835–1875* (New York: Harper & Row, 1982), 271–74; William Harris, *With Charity for All: Lincoln and the Restoration of the Union* (Lexington: University Press of Kentucky, 1997), 186–90.

24 Burlingame and Ettlinger, eds., *Inside Lincoln's White House*, 217–19.

25 Lincoln Proclamation, July 8, 1864, CWL 7:433–34.

26 Franklin Cooling, *Monocacy: The Battle That Saved Washington* (Shippensburg, PA: White Mane Publishing, 2000); Mark Leepson, *Desperate Engagement: How a Little-Known Civil War Battle Saved Washington, D.C., and Changed American History* (New York: Thomas Dunne, 2007); Frederick Phisterer, *New York in the War of the Rebellion: 1861–1865* (Albany: Weed, Parsons & Co., 1890), 237; Roe, *Ninth New York*, 127–35.

27 Seward 3:233; Lew Wallace to Seward, July 10, 1864, Seward House scrapbook; Frederick Seward to Frances Seward, July 10, 1864, OR ser. 1, vol. 37, pt. 2, p. 175; Frances Seward to Seward, July 10, 1864, Seward Papers reel 114; undated clipping, Seward House scrapbook (visit to Ninth).

28 *Daily National Republican*, July 11, 1864; John Hay Diary, July 11–12, 1864, in Burlingame and Ettlinger, eds., *Inside Lincoln's White House*, 221–22; Beale, ed., *Welles Diary*, 2:74; Stoeckl to Gorchakov, July 12, 1864, in Woldman, *Lincoln and the Russians*, 237; *Washington Intelligencer*, July 13, 1864; Seward 3:234; Flood, *1864*, 200–01; Pinsker, *Lincoln's Sanctuary*, 135–45.

29 *New York Times*, July 22 & 24, 1864; Grant to Butler, July 23, 1864, in John Simon, ed., *The Papers of Ulysses S. Grant*, 31 vols. to date (Carbondale:

Southern Illinois University Press, 1967–2009), 11:451; Seward 3:229. Frederick errs in placing this visit in June.

30   Butler to Sarah Butler, July 24, 1864, in Butler, *Correspondence of Butler*, 4:532; Sarah Butler to Butler, July 24, 1864, in ibid., 533; Waugh, *Reelecting Lincoln*, 160–63.

31   *New York Times*, Aug. 19, 1864; Foote, *Red River to Appomattox*, 472–92, 508–45; McPherson, *Battle Cry of Freedom*, 751–73.

32   *New York Tribune*, Aug. 5, 1864; *New York Herald*, Aug. 6, 1864; J. K. Herbert to Butler, in Butler, *Correspondence*, 5:8–9; Waugh, *Reelecting Lincoln*, 259–61.

33   J. K. Herbert to Butler, Aug. 6, 1864, in Butler, *Correspondence*, 5:9–10; John Martindale to Butler, Aug. 16, 1864, ibid., 5:47; Seward to Frances Seward, Aug. 16, 1864, Seward 3:240; Weed to Seward, Aug. 22, 1864, Lincoln Papers.

34   Weed to Seward, Aug. 22, 1864, Lincoln Papers; Raymond to Lincoln, Aug. 22, 1864, CWL 7:517–18; Lincoln Memorandum, Aug. 23, 1864, ibid., 514; John Hay Diary, Nov. 11, 1864, in ibid.

35   Seward to Frances Seward, Aug. 27, 1864, Seward 3:241; Nicolay to Hay, Aug. 28, 1864, in Burlingame, ed., *With Lincoln in the White House*, 154.

36   Seward to Frances Seward, Aug. 27, 1864, Seward 3:241.

37   *Albany Evening Journal*, Aug. 31 & Sept. 1, 1864; *Washington Daily Morning Chronicle*, Sept. 1, 1864; Flood, *1864*, 273–78, 282; Goodwin, *Team of Rivals*, 653–54; Waugh, *Reelecting Lincoln*, 276–94; Weber, *Copperheads*, 166–76.

38   Stanton to Seward, Aug. 30 & 31 & Sept. 2, 1864, Seward Papers reel 85; *New York Times*, Sept. 3–7, 1864.

39   *New York Times*, Sept. 7, 1864.

40   Ibid.; *Washington Daily Morning Chronicle*, Sept. 9, 1864 (praises speech); Burlingame, *Abraham Lincoln*, 2:689.

41   Weed to Seward, Sept. 10, 1864, Lincoln Papers; *New York Times*, Sept. 14, 1864 (speech); Seward to Sanford, Sept. 17, 1864, Sanford Papers, Sanford Museum ("the prospects of the presidential election are regarded as satisfactory"); Flood, *1864*, 279–83.

42   Jones to Raymond, Aug. 2, 1864, Welles Papers, NYPL; Raymond to Seward, Aug. 5, 1864, ibid.; John Hay Diary, Oct. 11–12, 1864, in Burlingame and Ettlinger, eds., *Inside Lincoln's White House*, 238 41; Beale, ed., *Welles Diary*, 2:142 & 176; *Brooklyn Daily Eagle*, Oct. 27 & Nov. 2 & 9, 1864; Burlingame, *Abraham Lincoln*, 2:707; Carman and Luthin, *Patronage*, 298.

43   Beale, ed., *Welles Diary*, 2:154 & 175; Seward to Butler, Oct. 26, 1864, Butler, *Correspondence*, 5:286; Burlingame, *Abraham Lincoln*, 2:704–06; Carman and Luthin, *Patronage*, 288–98.

44   OR ser. 1, vol. 43, pt. 2, pp. 128–29; Beale, ed., *Welles Diary*, 2:151; Seward to Adams, Oct. 24, 1864, FRUS 1864, 2:338–42; Winks, *Canada and the United States*, 288–95.

45 Butler to Sarah Butler, Sept. 26, 1864, in Butler, *Correspondence*, 5:168–70; *New York Times*, Sept. 28 & 30, 1864; Fanny Seward to Seward, Oct. 4, 1864, Seward Papers reel 116.

46 John Hay Diary, Oct. 11, 1864, in Burlingame and Ettlinger, eds., *Inside Lincoln's White House*, 238–41; Beale, ed., *Welles Diary*, 2:176; Waugh, *Reelecting Lincoln*, 332–37.

47 John Dix to Provost, Oct. 19, 1864, OR ser. 1, vol. 43, pt. 2, p. 422; *New York Times*, Oct. 20, 1864; *New York Tribune*, Oct. 20, 1864; Seward to Adams, Oct. 24, 1864, NA, M77 reel 78; Lyons to Seward, Oct. 29, 1864, FRUS 1864, 1:754; Seward to Lyons, Nov. 3, 1864, ibid., 760; Winks, *Canada and the United States*, 298–306.

48 Seward to Mayors, Nov. 2, 1864, in *New York Times*, Nov. 4, 1864; *Brooklyn Daily Eagle*, Nov. 5, 1864; Butler Order, Nov. 5, 1864, in *New York Times*, Nov. 7, 1864; Benjamin Butler, *Butler's Book: Autobiography and Personal Reminiscences of Major-General Benj. F. Butler* (Boston: A. M. Thayer & Co., 1892), 752–71; Edward Longacre, "The Union Army Occupation of New York City, November 1864," *New York History* 65 (1984): 133–58; Waugh, *Reelecting Lincoln*, 348–50.

49 Lincoln to Seward, Nov. 5, 6, & 8, 1864, CWL 8:91, 94, & 97; *New York Times*, Nov. 8 & 9, 1864.

50 *New York Times*, Nov. 9, 1864; *New York Tribune*, Nov. 9, 1864; Frances to Seward, Nov. 10, 1864, Seward Papers reel 114; Waugh, *Reelecting Lincoln*, 353–55.

51 *Daily National Republican*, Nov. 11, 1864; *Washington Daily Morning Chronicle*, Nov. 11, 1864; Baker 5:512–14. I have followed the newspaper versions of this speech rather than the more elaborate version in Baker's book.

52 Lincoln Memorandum, Aug. 23, 1864, CWL 7:514; John Hay Diary, Nov. 11, 1864, in Burlingame and Ettlinger, eds., *Inside Lincoln's White House*, 247–48.

53 Lincoln Message, Dec. 6, 1864, CWL 8:36–53; Flood, *1864*, 391–96.

54 *Boston Commonwealth*, Nov. 12 & 19, 1864; Beale, ed., *Welles Diary*, 2:194–95; Flood, *1864*, 162–67, 283–85; William Harris, *Lincoln's Last Months* (Cambridge, MA: Belknap Press, 2004), 82–87.

55 Beale, ed., *Welles Diary*, 2:84; John Nicolay to Theresa Bates, Dec. 8, 1864, in Burlingame, ed., *With Lincoln in the White House*, 166; Charles Sumner to Rudolf Schleiden, Aug. 8, 1865, Sumner Papers reel 79; Burlingame, *Abraham Lincoln*, 2:731–36; Carman and Luthin, *Patronage*, 315–20; Harris, *Lincoln's Last Months*, 71–79.

56 Seward to Adams, Dec. 14, 1864, FRUS 1865, 1:37; *Chicago Tribune*, Dec. 14–15, 1864; *New York Times*, Dec. 14–15, 1864; Dix Order 97, Dec. 14, 1864, OR ser. 1, vol. 43, pt. 2, p. 789; Stanton to Dix, Dec. 15, 1864, ibid., 790; Lincoln Order 100, Dec. 17, ibid., 800; Burnley to Russell, Dec. 15, 1864, in Barnes and

Barnes, eds., *British Eyes*, 3:234–35; Winks, *Canada and the United States*, 314–21.

57 Sherman to Lincoln, Dec. 22, 1864, in *New York Times*, Dec. 26, 1864; Seward to Bigelow, Dec. 25, 1865, in Bigelow, *Retrospections*, 2:250; Flood, *1864*, 416–17.

NOTES FOR CHAPTER 15

1 Useful secondary accounts include Herman Belz, *Reconstructing the Union: Theory and Policy During the Civil War* (Ithaca, NY: Cornell University Press, 1969); Donald, *Sumner and the Rights of Man*; Harris, *With Charity for All*.

2 *New York Times*, Feb. 9, 1865.

3 LaWanda Cox and John Cox, *Politics, Principle, and Prejudice, 1865–1866: Dilemma of Reconstruction America* (New York: Free Press, 1963), 1–30; Vorenberg, *Final Freedom*, 176–211 & 252 (table of vote).

4 Robert Latham to Seward, Jan. 9, 1865, Seward Papers reel 87; Lincoln to Dix, Jan. 20, 1865, CWL 8:226; William Bilbo to Seward, Jan. 23, 1865, Seward Papers reel 87; Richard Schell to Frederick Seward, Feb. 13, 1865, ibid.; *Cincinnati Daily Gazette*, Feb. 14, 1865; Cox and Cox, *Politics, Principle*, 6–15; Harris, *Lincoln's Last Months*, 129–30.

5 William Bilbo to Seward, Feb. 1, 1865, Seward Papers reel 87; Lincoln to James Bennett, Feb. 20, 1865, CWL 8:307; Anson Herrick to Seward, July 3, Aug. 8 & 29, 1865, Seward Papers reel 90; Homer Nelson to Seward, July 29, 1865, ibid.; Clapp, *Bigelow*, 227–34; Cox and Cox, *Politics, Principle*, 28–29; Harris, *Lincoln's Last Months*, 29; Vorenberg, *Final Freedom*, 198–200.

6 Frances Seward to Seward, Feb. 1865, Seward Papers reel 114; *New York Herald*, Feb. 1, 1865; *New York Times*, Nov. 1, 1868 (Seward on Cox's role in the amendment); Burlingame, *Abraham Lincoln*, 2:745–49; Samuel Cox, *Union—Disunion—Reunion: Three Decades of Federal Legislation, 1855–1885* (Providence, RI: J. A. Reid, 1885), 310–11; Osborne Oldroyd, ed., *The Lincoln Memorial: Album-Immortelles* (New York: G. W. Carleton, 1883), 492 (Rollins).

7 *New York Times*, Jan. 17, 23, & 29, 1865; Ashley to Lincoln, Jan. 31, 1865, CWL 8:248; Lincoln to Ashley, Jan 31, 1865, ibid.

8 Burlingame, *Abraham Lincoln*, 2:749–50; William Harris, "The Hampton Roads Peace Conference: A Final Test of Lincoln's Leadership," *Journal of the Abraham Lincoln Association* 21 (2000): 31–61.

9 John Campbell, *Reminiscences and Documents Relating to the Civil War During the Year 1865* (Baltimore: John Murphy, 1877), 7 (Seward and Chase on the House floor); Goodwin, *Team of Rivals*, 688–89 (Seward in gallery).

10 Lincoln to Seward, Jan. 31, 1865, CWL 8:250–51; Seward to Lincoln, Jan. 31, 1865, Lincoln Papers; *Cincinnati Daily Gazette*, Feb. 4, 1865 (House).

11 Seward to Lincoln, Feb. 1, 1865, CWL 8:280; *Daily National Intelligencer*, Feb. 2, 1865; *New York Herald*, Feb. 2 & 5, 1865; *New York Times*, Feb. 2 & 3, 1865.

12 Grant to Stanton, Feb. 1, 1865, CWL 8:282; Lincoln to Seward, Feb. 2, 1865, ibid.; Beale, ed., *Welles Diary*, 2:236 ("Seward did not meet or have interview with them until the President arrived"); *New York Herald*, Feb. 5, 1865; Lincoln to House of Representatives, Feb. 10, 1865, CWL 8:283.

13 Seward to Adams, Feb. 7, 1865, NA, M77 reel 79; Alexander Stephens, *A Constitutional View of the Late War Between the States*, 2 vols. (Philadelphia: National Publishing, 1870), 2:619. Good secondary accounts include Burlingame, *Abraham Lincoln*, 2:755–59; Paul Escott, *"What Shall We Do with the Negro?"*, 202–14; and Harris, "Hampton Roads Peace Conference."

14 Campbell, *Reminiscences*, 11; Stephens, *Constitutional View*, 599–600.

15 Campbell, *Reminiscences*, 12–13; Stephens, *Constitutional View*, 613.

16 Campbell, *Reminiscences*, 13; Stephens, *Constitutional View*, 610.

17 Seward to Adams, Feb. 8, 1865, OR ser. 1, vol. 46, pt. 2, pp. 471–73; *Augusta Chronicle & Sentinel*, June 7, 1865; Campbell, *Reminiscences*, 14; Stephens, *Constitutional View*, 611.

18 Escott, *"What Shall We Do With the Negro?"*, 206–10; Van Deusen, *Seward*, 385–86.

19 Campbell, *Reminiscences*, 14; Stephens, *Constitutional View*, 615; Harris, "Hampton Roads Peace Conference," 52–53.

20 Stephens, *Constitutional View*, 616–18; R. M. T. Hunter, "The Peace Commission of 1865," *Southern Historical Society Papers* 3 (1877): 174.

21 Lincoln to Stephens, Feb. 10, 1865, CWL 8:287 (nephew); Stephens, *Constitutional View*, 615 (prisoner exchange); Sumner to Bright, Feb. 13, 1865, in Palmer, ed., *Letters of Charles Sumner*, 2:268 (Capitol building); Theodore Blegen, *Abraham Lincoln and His Mailbag: Two Documents by Edward D. Neill* (St. Paul: Minnesota Historical Society, 1964), 27 ("Keep the champagne").

22 Beale, ed., *Welles Diary*, 2:236; *New York Herald*, Feb. 5, 1865; *New York Times*, Feb. 5, 6, & 11, 1865; *Washington Evening Star*, Feb. 4, 1865; Goodwin, *Team of Rivals*, 694–95.

23 *New York Times*, Jan. 19, Feb. 22, & Mar. 3, 1865; Foote, *Red River to Appomattox*, 733–63.

24 Frances Seward to Frederick Seward, July 29, 1862, Seward Papers reel 115; Francis Blair to Lincoln, Feb. 22, 1865, Lincoln Papers; Frances Seward to [Fanny] Seward, Mar. 1865, Seward Papers reel 115.

25 *New York Times*, Mar. 5, 1865; *Washington Evening Star*, Mar. 4, 1865; Burlingame, *Abraham Lincoln*, 2:765; Harris, *With Charity for All*, 253–54.

26 *New York Times*, Mar. 5, 1865; *Sacramento Daily Union*, Apr. 10, 1865 (Brooks); Goodwin, *Team of Rivals*, 697–98; Hans Trefousse, *Andrew Johnson: A Biography* (New York: W. W. Norton & Co., 1989), 189–91.

27 Second Inaugural Address, Mar. 4, 1865, CWL 8:332–33; *Sacramento Daily Union*, Apr. 10, 1865; White, *Eloquent President*, 277–303.

28 *Washington National Intelligencer*, Mar. 6, 1865; C. F. Adams Jr. to C. F. Adams Sr., Mar. 7, 1865, in Worthington C. Ford, ed., *A Cycle of Adams Letters, 1861–1865*, 2 vols. (Boston: Houghton Mifflin, 1920), 2:257–58; Isaac Arnold, *The Life of Abraham Lincoln* (Chicago: Jansen, McClurg & Co., 1885), 404–05; Goodwin, *Team of Rivals*, 701.

29 Hay to Seward, July 26, 1865, Seward Papers reel 90; Seward to Hay, Aug. 11, 1865, ibid.; Goodwin, *Team of Rivals*, 702–06; Helen Nicolay, *Lincoln's Secretary: A Biography of John G. Nicolay* (New York: Longmans, Green & Co., 1949), 224–27; Zimmerman, *First Great Triumph*.

30 Fanny Seward Diary, Apr. 4, 1865, Seward Papers reel 198; *New York Times*, Mar. 31, 1865; *New York Tribune*, Mar. 31, 1865; Lincoln to Grant, Apr. 1, 1865, CWL 8:379 (Seward has started back for D.C.); *Daily National Republican*, Apr. 3, 1865 (Seward back in D.C.); Some state that Mary Lincoln returned with Seward, but it seems she returned separately—Goodwin, *Team of Rivals*, 715.

31 *Daily National Republican*, Apr. 3, 1865; *Sacramento Daily Union*, May 8, 1865; Goodwin, *Team of Rivals*, 716.

32 *Daily National Republican*, Apr. 3, 1865; *Philadelphia Press*, Apr. 4, 1865.

33 Seward to Lincoln, Apr. 5, 1865, CWL 8:387; Lincoln to Seward, Apr. 5, 1865, ibid.; Beale, ed., *Welles Diary*, 2:275.

34 Fanny Seward Diary, Apr. 5, 1865, Seward Papers reel 198; Seward 3:270; *Daily National Republican*, Apr. 6, 1865; *New York Herald*, Apr. 6, 1865; *New York Times*, Apr. 6, 1865; *Philadelphia Press*, Apr. 6, 1865; *Washington Evening Star*, Apr. 6, 1865; Dr. T. S. Verdi, "The Assassination of the Sewards," *The Republic* 1 (1873): 289–90. The press reports differ considerably on details.

35 Frances Seward to Lazette Worden, Apr. 7–8, 1865, in Seward 3:270–71; Verdi, "Assassination," 289–90.

36 Fanny Seward Diary, Apr. 5 & 9, 1865, Seward Papers reel 198; Stanton to Lincoln, Apr. 5 & 6, 1865, Lincoln Papers; *New York Times*, Apr. 8, 1865 (Lee's surrender imminent).

37 Fanny Seward Diary, Apr. 9, 1865, Seward Papers reel 198; Seward 3:271–72; Grant to Stanton, Apr. 9, 1865, in *New York Times*, Apr. 10, 1865.

38 Fanny Seward Diary, Apr. 10, 1865, Seward Papers reel 198.

39 Ibid.; Ernest Furgurson, *Freedom Rising: Washington in the Civil War* (New York: Alfred A. Knopf, 2004), 370.

40 Lincoln Address, Apr. 11, 1865, CWL 8:399–405; Jay Winik, *April 1865: The Month That Saved America* (New York: HarperCollins, 2001), 213–17.

41 For slightly different versions of Booth's remarks see: Goodwin, *Team of Rivals*, 728; William Hanchett, *The Lincoln Murder Conspiracies* (Urbana: University

of Illinois Press, 1983), 37; Kauffman, *American Brutus*, 210; Swanson, *Manhunt*, 6.

42 On Booth's motives for targeting Seward, see David Donald, *Lincoln* (New York: Simon & Schuster, 1995), 596; Kauffman, *American Brutus*, 212–13 ("he was one of the few men capable of filling the power vacuum in the event of Lincoln's death"); Swanson, *Manhunt*, 28; Winik, *April 1865*, 224.

43 Seward to Bigelow, July 15, 1862, in Bigelow, *Retrospections*, 1:505 (original in NYPL); Brooks, *Washington in Lincoln's Time*, 38; James Speed to Joseph Barrett, Sept. 16, 1885, Lincoln Special Collections, University of Chicago; Burlingame, *Abraham Lincoln*, 2:807–08.

44 Fanny Seward Diary, Apr. 12–13, 1865, Seward Papers reel 198.

45 Ibid., Apr. 14, 1865; Donald, *Lincoln*, 590–92; Goodwin, *Team of Rivals*, 731–33; Seward 3:273–76 (Frederick's account of cabinet meeting).

46 Fanny Seward Diary, Apr. 14, 1865, Seward Papers reel 198 ("rat").

47 See sources cited in note 2 to the Introduction; Henry Hilliard, *Politics and Pen Pictures* (New York: G. P. Putnam's Sons, 1892), 350 (blade cold).

48 Fanny Seward Diary, Apr. 14, 1865, Seward Papers reel 198; *Washington Evening Star*, Apr. 18, 1865 (Robinson interview). Fanny wrote out this diary entry several weeks after the event, so it is possible that she copied her father's words from Robinson's newspaper account.

49 Fanny Seward Diary, Apr. 14, 1865, Seward Papers reel 198; *New York Times*, May 18, 1865 (Verdi letter originally dated Apr. 21); Pitman, *Assassination of President Lincoln*, 157 (Verdi testimony); Verdi, "Assassination," 291–92. Verdi's accounts differ slightly.

50 Fanny Seward Diary, Apr. 14–20, 1865, Seward Papers reel 198; Weed to Sanford, Apr. 14 & 28, 1865, Sanford Papers, Sanford Museum; William Hunter to Sanford, June 14, 1865, ibid.; Anna Seward to Sanford, Sept. 25, 1865, ibid.

51 Ibid., Apr. 14, 1865, Seward Papers reel 198; *New York Tribune*, Apr. 17, 1865; *Sacramento Daily Union*, May 19, 1865 (Brooks report dated Apr. 20); Goodwin, *Team of Rivals*, 744–45 (quotes Brooks); Taylor, *Seward*, 246 (disbelieves Brooks).

52 Hunter to Bigelow, Apr. 27 & May 15, 1865, in Bigelow, *Retrospections*, 2:522 & 556; *New York Herald*, May 13, 1865; Frances Seward to Dennis Alward, May 27, 1865, Seward 3:280.

53 *New York Times*, June 22, 1865; *Philadelphia Press*, June 22, 1865; Fanny Seward to Amanda—, Jan. 26, 1866, Seward Papers reel 116. Frederick Seward attributes the *Times* obituary to Weed—Seward 3:286.

54 *New York Times*, June 22, 1865; Sumner to Seward, July 12, 1865, in Seward 3:286–87; George William Curtis, in ibid. 287. I have not been able to find the Curtis obituary in a newspaper.

55 *Albany Evening Journal,* June 26, 1865; *Auburn Advertiser & Union,* June 26, 1865; *New York Times,* June 26, 1865; Seward 3:287.

56 *New York Times,* July 2 & 11, 1865; Seward to Bigelow, July 14, 1865, NYPL; Seward to Charlotte Cushman, Jan. 7, 1867, Cushman Papers, LC. For a different view on Seward's faith, see George Baker, "William Henry Seward: A Religious Man," *Unitarian Review* 23 (1885): 163–70.

57 Good secondary accounts include Charles Blackburn, *Military Opposition to Official State Department Policy Concerning the Mexican Intervention, 1862–1867,* PhD diss. (Ball State University, 1969); James Callahan, *American Foreign Policy in Mexican Relations* (New York: Macmillan Co., 1932), 296–322; Alfred and Kathryn Hanna, *Napoleon III and Mexico* (Chapel Hill: University of North Carolina Press, 1971), 236–47; Mahin, *One War at a Time,* 269–87; Schoonover, *Dollars Over Dominion,* 178–250.

58 Seward to Bigelow, Mar. 6 & June 3, 1865, in Bigelow, *Retrospections,* 2:360 & 3:57–58; Seward to Bigelow, Mar. 17, 1865, in Callahan, *American Foreign Policy,* 302.

59 Wallace to Grant, Mar. 14, 1865, in Simon, ed., *Papers of Ulysses Grant,* 13:288; Romero to Lerdo, Apr. 24, 1865, in Thomas Schoonover, ed., *Mexican Lobby: Matías Romero in Washington, 1861–1867* (Lexington: University Press of Kentucky, 1986), 55–57; *New York Times,* May 7, 1865 (re Wallace-Slaughter); Michael Golay, *A Ruined Land: The End of the Civil War* (New York: John Wiley & Sons, 1999), 195–200.

60 Sumner to Cobden, Mar. 27, 1865, in Palmer, ed., *Letters of Charles Sumner,* 2:278; Romero to Lerdo, Apr. 30 & May 8, in Schoonover, ed., *Mexican Lobby,* 58–59.

61 Grant to Steele, May 21, 1865, Simon, ed., *Papers of Ulysses Grant,* 15:80–81; Grant to Sheridan, July 25, 1865, ibid., 286–87; Sheridan, *Personal Memoirs of General Philip H. Sheridan,* 2:210.

62 Seward to Bigelow, June 13, 1865, Seward 3:290; Beale, ed., *Welles Diary,* 2:317; Grant to Johnson, June 19, 1865, OR ser. 1, vol. 48, pt 2, pp. 923–24; Romero to Lerdo, June 18, 1865, in Schoonover, ed., *Mexican Lobby,* 66–69.

63 Beale, ed., *Welles Diary,* 2:317; Romero to Lerdo, June 18, 1865, in Schoonover, ed., *Mexican Lobby,* 66–69.

64 Sheridan to Grant, June 29, 1865, in Simon, ed., *Papers of Ulysses Grant,* 15:259 (endorsed by Grant on July 12); Grant to Johnson, July 15, 1865, ibid., 264–65; Beale, ed., *Welles Diary,* 2:317; Romero to Lerdo de Tejada, July 22, 1865, in Matías Romero, ed., *Correspondencia de la legación Mexicana en Washington, 1860–1868,* 10 vols. (Mexico: Imprenta del Gobierno, 1870–92), 5:495–97; John Schofield, *Forty-Six Years in the Army* (New York: Century Co., 1897), 379–93 (quote on 385).

65 Schofield to Seward, Aug. 4, 1865, Seward Papers reel 90; John Bigelow Diary, Dec. 9, 1896, NYPL; Donald Connelly, *John M. Schofield and the Politics of Generalship* (Chapel Hill: University of North Carolina Press, 2006), 182–86; Schofield, *Forty-Six Years*, 382–85.

66 Seward to Diplomatic Corps, July 26, 1865, in Hanna and Hanna, *Napoleon III and Mexico*, 243; Romero to Lerdo, Oct. 2, 14, 28, & 31, 1865, in Schoonover, ed., *Mexican Lobby*, 99–103.

67 Seward to Bigelow, Nov. 6, 1865, in FRUS 1865, 3:421–22; *New York Times*, Nov. 17, 1865; Montholon to Drouyn, Nov. 30, 1865, in Hanna and Hanna, *Napoleon III and Mexico*, 265; Beale, ed., *Welles Diary*, 2:401 ("scared out of his wits").

68 Seward to Montholon, Dec. 6, 1865, FRUS 1865–66, 3:450; Bigelow to Seward, Dec. 8, 1865, in Bigelow, *Retrospections*, 3:267; *New York Times*, Dec. 27 & 29, 1865 (Austrian reinforcements).

69 *Philadelphia Press*, June 22, 1865; Seward to comte de Gasparin, July 10, 1865, Seward Papers reel 90.

70 *New York Times*, Apr. 25, 1865; Seward to Webb, July 1865, NA, M77 reel 24; Beale, ed., *Welles Diary*, 3:190; William Barney, "Johnson & Reconstruction: Swinging Around the Circle Again," *Reviews in American History* 8 (1980): 367.

71 Johnson Speech, Oct. 24, 1864, in Ralph Haskins, et al., eds., *The Papers of Andrew Johnson*, 16 vols. (Knoxville: University of Tennessee Press, 1967–2000), 7:251–53; *New York Times*, Apr. 19, 1865 ("treason is a crime"); Seward to Fanny Seward, Nov. 9, 1865, Seward 3:300; Myrta Avary, ed., *Recollections of Alexander H. Stephens* (New York: Doubleday & Co., 1910), 509–20 (Seward correspondence); Albert Castel, *The Presidency of Andrew Johnson* (Lawrence: Regents Press of Kansas, 1979), 17–54; Hilliard, *Politics and Pen Pictures*, 349; Trefousse, *Andrew Johnson*, 214–33.

72 *New York Herald*, Oct. 4, 1865; Cox and Cox, *Politics, Principle*, 68–87; Eric McKitrick, *Andrew Johnson and Reconstruction* (Chicago: University of Chicago Press, 1960), 175–86.

73 *Macon Daily Telegraph*, Nov. 7, 1865; W. R. Brock, *An American Crisis: Congress and Reconstruction, 1865–1867* (New York: St. Martin's Press, 1963), 35–36; Castel, *Presidency of Andrew Johnson*, 48–54; Eric Foner, *Reconstruction: America's Unfinished Revolution* (New York: Harper & Row, 1988), 224–27; Michael Perman, *Reunion Without Compromise: The South and Reconstruction* (London: Cambridge University Press, 1973), 86–109.

74 *Albany Evening Journal*, Oct. 21, 1865; *Daily National Republican*, Oct. 23, 1865; *New York Times*, Oct. 21, 1865; *Springfield Republican*, Oct. 23, 1865.

75 Henry Bellows to Eliza Bellows, Oct. 7, 1865, Bellows Papers, MHS.

76 Seward to Fanny Seward, Nov. 17, 1865, Seward 3:301.

77 *New York World*, Nov. 22, 1865; Seward draft, Dec. 1865, Seward Papers reel 185; Cox and Cox, *Politics, Principle*, 129–39.

78 *New York Evening Post*, Dec. 6, 1865; *New York Tribune*, Dec. 6, 1865; *New York World*, Dec. 6, 1865; Castel, *Presidency of Andrew Johnson*, 55–57.

79 *New York Times*, Dec. 5, 1865; Cox and Cox, *Politics, Principle*, 129–39.

80 *Chicago Tribune*, Dec. 1, 1865; Castel, *Presidency of Andrew Johnson*, 73–74; McKitrick, *Andrew Johnson*, 182–84.

81 Donald, *Sumner and the Rights of Man*, 237–38.

82 *New York Times*, Dec. 19, 1865; Seward 3:302; Bruce Ackerman, *We the People: Transformations* (Cambridge, MA: Harvard University Press, 1998), 101–02 (issue of how to count states).

NOTES FOR CHAPTER 16

1 Seward to Chautauqua Convention, Mar. 31, 1846, Baker 3:409; Seward Speech, Sept. 18, 1860, Baker 4:330–34; Sen. Executive Journal, 33d Cong., 1st Sess. 312; Paul Garber, *The Gadsden Treaty* (Gloucester, MA: Peter Smith, 1959), 131–34; Potter, *Impending Crisis*, 177–98. For Seward as a constant expansionist, see Paolino, *Foundations of the American Empire*.

2 *Charleston Daily Courier*, July 29, 1865; *Chicago Tribune*, Feb. 10, June 8, & Nov. 30, 1865; Beale, ed., *Welles Diary*, 3:125; Donald Dozer, "Anti-Expansionism during the Johnson Administration," *Pacific Historical Review* 12 (1943): 253–55; Paolino, *Foundations of the American Empire*; Seward, *Reminiscences*, 360.

3 Charles Tansill, *The Purchase of the Danish West Indies* (Baltimore: Johns Hopkins University Press, 1932), 9–20 (quoting Seward memo and Raasloff dispatches); Olive Risley Seward, "A Diplomatic Episode," *Scribner's Magazine* 2 (1887): 586 (Seward "convinced of the actual necessity").

4 *New York Times*, Jan. 1 & 4, 1866; Beale, ed., *Welles Diary*, 2:406; Georges Clemenceau, *American Reconstruction: 1865–1870* (New York: Dial Press, 1928), 64; Family photo, Seward House; Seward, *Reminiscences*, 266–71; State Department Historian Web site (first official trip outside the United States).

5 Anna and Frederick Seward Journals, Jan. 1866, Seward Papers Addition; Seward, *Reminiscences*, 297, 301, 304. The "journal" of Frederick at Rochester appears to be notes he prepared later, not an original day-by-day journal.

6 Anna Seward Journal, Jan. 14, 1866, Seward Papers Addition; *New York Times*, Feb. 3 (remarks) & 5 (recognition), 1866; Seward, *Reminiscences*, 306–15; Tansill, *Santo Domingo*, 176–98, 224–30.

7 Anna Seward Journal, Jan. 17, 1866, Seward Papers Addition. Frederick borrows his wife's observation without giving her credit—Seward, *Reminiscences*, 315–24.

8 *Chicago Tribune*, Feb. 2, 1866; James Cortada, "Spain and the American Civil War: Relations at Mid-Century, 1855–1868," *Transactions of the American Philosophical Society* 70 (1980): 85–90 (quote 89); Seward, *Reminiscences*, 328–43.

9 Beale, ed., *Welles Diary*, 2:466–67; Seward to Raasloff, July 17, 1866, in Tansill, *Danish West Indies*, 39–40; see ibid., 23–43.

10 *New York Tribune*, Dec. 7, 1866 (Seward called on Stevens); Cong. Globe, 39th Cong., 2d Sess. 113 (Stevens defends appropriation); Beale, ed., *Welles Diary*, 2:466–67, 643; Seward 3:344 (Frederick's version); Tansill, *Santo Domingo*, 232–37.

11 David Porter, "Secret Missions to San Domingo," *North American Review* 128 (1879): 616–30; Tansill, *Santo Domingo*, 237–41; Beale, ed., *Welles Diary*, 2:466–67.

12 *Chicago Tribune*, Jan. 30 & 31, 1866; Castel, *Presidency of Andrew Johnson*, 64–65; Trefousse, *Andrew Johnson*, 240–43.

13 Cong. Globe, 39th Cong., 1st Sess. 655 (Raymond); Castel, *Presidency of Andrew Johnson*, 64–65; Trefousse, *Andrew Johnson*, 240–43.

14 Seward draft, Feb. 1866, Johnson Papers reel 45; Johnson veto, in *New York Times*, Feb. 20, 1866; John and LaWanda Cox, "Andrew Johnson and His Ghost-Writers: An Analysis of the Freedmen's Bureau and Civil Rights Veto Messages," *Mississippi Valley Historical Review* 47 (1961): 460–73; Castel, *Presidency of Andrew Johnson*, 64–68.

15 Castel, *Presidency of Andrew Johnson*, 68–70; Trefousse, *Andrew Johnson*, 243–44.

16 Johnson speech, *New York Times*, Feb. 23, 1866.

17 Seward speech, *New York Times*, Feb. 23, 1866; *New York Evening Post*, Feb. 23, 1866.

18 *Albany Evening Journal*, Feb. 23, 1866; *Chicago Tribune*, Feb. 24, 1866; *New York Evening Post*, May 23, 1866; Seward to Johnson, Feb. 23, 1866, Johnson Papers, LC reel 41; Weed to Johnson, Feb. 23, 1866, ibid.; Weed to Seward, Feb. 28, 1866, Seward Papers reel 93 (imperative that a Republican be appointed collector); "The Way the Union Was Saved," *The Nation* 2 (Mar. 1, 1866): 263–64; Cox and Cox, *Politics, Principle*, 113–28 (collectorship struggle).

19 Weed to Seward, Mar. 25, 1866, Johnson Papers reel 21; Seward to Johnson, Mar. 27, 1866, ibid.; Castel, *Presidency of Andrew Johnson*, 69–72; Trefousse, *Andrew Johnson*, 245–47.

20 Seward draft, Mar. 1866, Johnson Papers reel 45; Johnson veto, in *New York Times*, Mar. 28, 1866; Cox and Cox, "Andrew Johnson and His Ghost Writers," 473–77.

21 Morgan to Weed, Apr. 8, 1866, Weed Papers; Castel, *Presidency of Andrew Johnson*, 70–71; Van Deusen, *Seward*, 447–48.

22 Brock, *American Crisis*, 119–21; Castel, *Presidency of Andrew Johnson*, 72–73 (quote); Trefousse, *Andrew Johnson*, 246–47; Van Deusen, *Seward*, 447–48.

23 *New York Evening Post*, Mar. 24, 1888; William Armstrong, *E. L. Godkin: A Biography* (Albany: State University Press, 1978); Bancroft, *Life of Seward*, 2:455–57 (reprints *Post* article).

24 Seward to Gasparin, Apr. 7, 1866, Seward Papers reel 94; Robert Horowitz, "Seward and Reconstruction," *The Historian* 47 (1985): 382–401; Van Deusen, *Seward*, 429–31.

25 Seward Speech, in *New York Times*, May 22, 1866; Foner, *Reconstruction*, 261–62 (Memphis).

26 *Albany Evening Journal*, May 21, 23, & 28, 1866; *Chicago Tribune*, May 24, 1866; *New York Evening Post*, May 23, 1866; *New York Independent*, May 26, 1866; *New York Times*, May 24, 1866; *New York Tribune*, May 24, 1866; *Springfield [MA] Republican*, May 24, 1866 (tepid praise); "Mr. Seward on the Need of the Nation," *The Nation* 2 (June 7, 1866): 729–30.

27 For the phrase "critical year," see Howard Beale, *The Critical Year: A Study of Andrew Johnson and Reconstruction* (New York: Harcourt Brace & Co., 1930); Patrick Riddleberger, *1866: The Critical Year Revisited* (Carbondale: Southern Illinois University Press, 1979).

28 *New York Times*, Feb. 6 & Apr. 24, 1866 (prints correspondence); Seward to Bigelow, Feb. 8, 1866, Bigelow Papers, NYPL; Seward to Montholon, Feb. 12, 1866, FRUS 1866, 2:813.

29 Cong. Globe, 39th Cong., 1st Sess. 3217–18.

30 Seward to Campbell, Oct. 25, 1866, in Baker 5:470; Bigelow to Seward, Nov. 8 & Dec. 3, 1866, in Bigelow, *Retrospections*, 3:598–600, 617; Seward to Bigelow, Nov. 9 & 23, 1866, ibid., 601–02, 609–11; Mahin, *One War at a Time*, 277–81.

31 Bancroft, *Life of William Seward*, 2:441–42; Hanna and Hanna, *Napoleon III and Mexico*, 302; Mahin, *One War at a Time*, 284–85; Ralph Roeder, *Juarez and His Mexico: A Biographical History*, 2 vols. (New York: Viking, 1947), 2:662.

32 *New York Times*, July 26, 1865; Bruce to Russell, Aug. 8, 1865, quoted in Brian Jenkins, *Fenians and Anglo-American Relations During Reconstruction* (Ithaca, NY: Cornell University Press, 1969), 53; W. S. Neidhardt, *Fenianism in North America* (University Park: Pennsylvania State University Press, 1975).

33 Bernard Killian to Seward, Nov. 18, 1865, NA, M179 reel 230; Seward to Killian, Nov. 20, 1865, Seward Papers reel 92; *Irish People*, Feb. 15, 1868 ("accomplished facts"); Bruce to Clarendon, Dec. 4, 1865, in Barnes and Barnes, eds., *Private and Confidential*, 367–68; Bruce to Clarendon, Feb. 9, 1866, ibid., 371; William D'Arcy, *The Fenian Movement in the United States* (Washington, DC: Catholic University Press, 1947), 84–85.

34 Bruce to Clarendon, Mar. 20, 1866, in Barnes and Barnes, *Private and Confidential*, 375–76; Seward to Adams, Mar. 22, 1866, NA, M77 reel 79; Jenkins, *Fenians*, 86–105.

35 Beale, ed., *Welles Diary*, 2:518–24 (Seward opposed proclamation); Bruce to Seward, June 5, 1866, quoted in D'Arcy, *Fenian Movement*, 163; *New York Tribune*, June 6, 1866 (Seward favored proclamation); Johnson Proclamation, in

New York Times, June 7, 1866; Neidhardt, *Fenianism*, 59–75; Mabel Walker, *The Fenian Movement* (Colorado Springs, CO: R. Myles, 1969), 90–106.

36 *Chicago Tribune*, June 16 & Aug. 16, 1866; *National Intelligencer*, July 25, 1866; *New York Times*, June 9, 1866; Seward to Bruce, June 11, 1866, in *New York Times*, July 27, 1866; Seward to Bruce, Oct. 27, 1866, in *New York Times*, Oct. 29, 1866; *New York Tribune*, Nov. 1, 1866; Neidhardt, *Fenianism*, 93–108; Walker, *Fenian Movement*, 107–21.

37 Cong. Globe, 39th Cong., 1st Sess. 3042, 3148–49; Seward to Governors, June 16, 1866, NA, M40 reel 61; Johnson Message, June 22, 1866, in Haskins, ed., *Papers of Andrew Johnson*, 10:614–15; McKitrick, *Andrew Johnson and Reconstruction*, 326–65; Riddleberger, *1866*, 105–61. For Seward's messages transmitting the two Thirteenth amendments, see Seward to Governors, Mar. 16, 1861, & Feb. 2, 1865, NA, M40 reels 51 & 61.

38 "Extracts from the Journal of Henry J. Raymond," *Scribner's Monthly Magazine* 20 (June 1888): 275–77; Beale, ed., *Welles Diary*, 2:529–31; Riddleberger, *1866*, 202–07; Trefousse, *Andrew Johnson*, 255–58.

39 *New York Times*, July 17, 1866; Paul Bergeron, *Andrew Johnson's Civil War and Reconstruction* (Knoxville: University of Tennessee Press, 2011), 120–23; Castel, *Presidency of Andrew Johnson*, 78–81.

40 *New York Tribune*, July 17, 1866; *Albany Evening Journal*, July 16, 1866; *Chicago Tribune*, July 17, 1866; *New York Times*, July 17, 1866.

41 Seward to Fanny Seward, July 17, 18, 25, & 27, 1866, Seward 3:330–33; Trefousse, *Andrew Johnson*, 253–54.

42 Seward to Fanny Seward, July 29 & Aug. 4, 1866, Seward 3:333–34; *New York Tribune*, Aug. 1, 1866; *New York Times*, Aug. 2, 1866; Foner, *Reconstruction*, 262–64; James Hollandsworth, *An Absolute Massacre: The New Orleans Race Riot of July 30, 1866* (Baton Rouge: Louisiana State University Press, 2001).

43 Seward to Fanny Seward, Aug. 1–24 1866, Seward 3:334–39; *New York Times*, Aug. 17, 1866; Foner, *Reconstruction*, 264–67; Riddleberger, *1866*, 208–14.

44 Seward Papers, Aug. 1866 (letters and telegrams re tour); *New York Tribune*, Aug. 28, 1866 ("Seward has done all the inviting"); *New York Times*, Aug. 30, 1866; Foner, *Reconstruction*, 264–67; Riddleberger, *1866*, 214–23.

45 *Auburn Advertiser & Union*, Sept. 1, 1866; *New York Evening Post*, Sept. 1, 1866; *New York Times*, Sept. 1–2, 1866.

46 Johnson speech, Sept. 3, 1866, in Haskins, ed., *Papers of Andrew Johnson*, 11:175–76; *New York Evening Post*, Sept. 11, 1866; Beale, ed., *Welles Diary*, 2:594; Foner, *Reconstruction*, 264–65; Riddleberger, *1866*, 218–19.

47 Johnson speech, Sept. 8, 1866, in Haskins, ed., *Papers of Andrew Johnson*, 11:194.

48 *New York Herald*, Sept. 13 & 26, 1866; *New York Times*, Sept. 7, 1866; *Albany Evening Journal*, Sept. 8, 11, & 15, 1866; *Chicago Tribune*, Sept. 13, 1866; *New York Evening Post*, Sept. 11, 1866; *New York Tribune*, Sept. 13 & 15, 1866; "A

Leader Without a Party," *The Nation* 3 (Sept. 20, 1866): 233–34; McKitrick, *Andrew Johnson and Reconstruction*, 428–38.

49 *New York Times*, Sept. 15–17, 1866; Beale, ed., *Welles Diary*, 2:594–95.

50 William Seward to Jenny Seward, Sept. 1866, Seward Papers reel 118; Fanny Seward Diary, Sept. 14–24, 1866, ibid. reel 198; *Chicago Tribune*, Sept. 20–21, 1866; *New York Times*, Sept. 18–26, 1866; *New York Tribune*, Sept. 20–26, 1866.

51 *Chicago Tribune*, Sept. 21 & Oct. 2, 1866; Seward to Sumner Stebbins, Oct. 8, 1866, Seward 3:341; *New York Times*, Oct. 27, 1866 (Stebbins letter and Seward reply).

52 Martha Coffin Wright to Marianna Pelham Mott, May 25, 1866, Garrison Family Papers, Smith College ("her lungs are affected now and she coughs a great deal"); Fanny Seward to William Seward Jr., Oct. 11, 1866, Seward Papers reel 116 ("very much stronger"); *New York Times*, Oct. 30, 1866; Pease and Randall, eds., *Browning Diary*, 2:104 (died of "bilious fever"). For more on Fanny, see Patricia Johnson, *Sensitivity and Civil War*, and Deirdre Stam, "Growing Up with Books." I cannot find the Powell quote in print before Fanny's death, making it somewhat suspect—Betty Ownsbey, *Alias "Paine": Lewis Thornton Powell: The Mystery Man of the Lincoln Conspiracy* (Jefferson, NC: McFarland, 1993), 81.

53 *Auburn Advertiser & Union*, Nov. 2, 1866; *Boston Daily Advertiser*, Nov. 1, 1866; *Daily National Republican*, Nov. 1, 1866; *Daily National Intelligencer*, Nov. 1 & 7, 1866; Seward to Stanton, Nov. 3, 1866, Johnson Papers reel 41.

54 Seward to Sanford, Dec. 10, 1866, Sanford Papers; Seward to John Bigelow, Dec. 8, 1866, Bigelow Papers, NYPL; Seward to Charlotte Cushman, Jan. 7, 1867, Cushman Papers, LC.

55 *New York Times*, Sept. 13, Oct. 16 & Nov. 7, 1866; Seward to Sanford, Nov. 6, 1866, Seward Papers reel 97; Seward to William Schouler, Nov. 13, 1866, Schouler Papers, MHS; Castel, *Presidency of Andrew Johnson*, 97–98; Trefousse, *Andrew Johnson*, 269–71.

56 *New York Times*, Nov. 16 & 20, 1866; Seward Draft Message, Dec. 1866, Johnson Papers reel 45; Castel, *Presidency of Andrew Johnson*, 99–100.

57 Castel, *Presidency of Andrew Johnson*, 100–05; Van Deusen, *Seward*, 469–70.

NOTES FOR CHAPTER 17

1 *National Republican*, Jan. 2, 1867; *New York Times*, Jan. 8, 1867; Beale, ed., *Welles Diary*, 3:4–8; Johnson Veto Message, Jan. 5, 1867, in Haskins, ed., *Papers of Andrew Johnson*, 11:577–88.

2 First Reconstruction Act, Stat. at Large, 39th Cong., 2d Sess. 428–29; Ackerman, *We the People: Transformations*, 189–209; Castel, *Presidency of Andrew Johnson*, 106–10.

3 "Prospects of a Third Party," *The Nation* (May, 1, 1866): 553; Trefousse, *Andrew Johnson*, 267–68, 276–77.

4 Tenure of Office Act, Stat. at Large, 39th Cong., 2d Sess. 430–32; Castel, *Presidency of Andrew Johnson*, 111–13; David Stewart, *Impeached: The Trial of Andrew Johnson and the Fight for Lincoln's Legacy* (New York: Simon & Schuster, 2009), 75–77; Trefousse, *Andrew Johnson*, 276–77.

5 Beale, ed., *Welles Diary*, 3:50–52; Johnson Veto Message, Mar. 2, 1867, in Haskins, ed., *Papers of Andrew Johnson*, 12:95–101; Trefousse, *Andrew Johnson*, 277–81.

6 House Report No. 7, 40th Cong., 1st Sess. 369–84 (1867); Beale, ed., *Welles Diary*, 3:90; Stewart, *Impeached*, 74–83; Trefousse, *Andrew Johnson*, 281–85.

7 Beale, ed., *Welles Diary*, 3:77–78; *Charleston Mercury*, Apr. 3, 1867; Castel, *Presidency of Andrew Johnson*, 124–25.

8 Cong. Globe, 39th Cong., 2d Sess. 597–98; *New York Times*, Jan. 22, 1867.

9 George McCracken to Johnson, Oct. 23, 1866, in Haskins, ed., *Papers of Andrew Johnson*, 12:378–80; Seward to Motley, Nov. 21, 1866; Motley to Seward, Dec. 11, 1866, both in *New York Times*, Jan. 30, 1867; Seward to Motley, Jan. 5, 1867, NA, M77 reel 13 (not delivered); *Chicago Tribune*, Feb. 1 & 10, 1867; Cong. Globe, 39th Cong., 2d Sess. 904; John Bigelow, "Mr. Seward and Mr. Motley," *International Review* 5 (1878): 544–56; Donald, *Sumner and the Rights of Man*, 279; Claire Lynch, *The Diplomatic Mission of John Lothrop Motley to Austria, 1861–1867* (Washington, DC: Catholic University Press, 1944), 140–48; C. H. Tuckermann, "Personal Recollections of William H. Seward," *Magazine of American History* 19 (1888): 499–503 (Seward quote).

10 Cong. Globe, 40th Cong., 1st Sess. 207; *Harper's Weekly*, Mar. 30, 1867.

11 John Hay to John Nicolay, Feb. 14, 1867, Tyler Dennett, ed., *Lincoln and the Civil War in the Diaries and Letters of John Hay* (New York: Dodd, Mead & Co., 1939), 276; John Bigelow Diary, Feb. 19 & 28, 1867, NYPL.

12 *New York Times*, July 31, 1852; Seward speech, Sept. 18, 1860, Baker 4:333; Clay to Seward, Nov. 14, 1864, NA, M35 reel 20; Seward to Clay, Dec. 26, 1864, NA, M77 reel 136; Ronald Jensen, *The Alaska Purchase and Russian-American Relations* (Seattle: University of Washington Press, 1975).

13 Washington Petition, Jan. 1866, quoted in Victor Farrar, *The Annexation of Russian America to the United States* (New York: Russell & Russell, 1966), 33–34; House Exec. Doc. 177, 40th Cong., 2d Sess. (Feb. 19, 1868), 4–5; Jensen, *Alaska Purchase*, 44–47; Anatole Mazour, "The Prelude to Russia's Departure from America," *Pacific Historical Review* 10 (1941): 311–19; Saul, *Distant Friends*, 389–90.

14 Stoeckl to Gorchakov, Apr. 19, 1867, Annex 30, Alaska Cession Papers, NA; Jensen, *Alaska Purchase*, 69–70; David Miller, *The Alaska Treaty* (Kingston, Ontario: Limestone Press, 1981), 66–67 (best account of the negotiation).

15 Stoeckl to Gorchakov, Mar. 18, 1867, Annex 21, Alaska Cession Papers, NA; Jensen, *Alaska Purchase*, 70–71; Miller, *Alaska Treaty*, 71–75.

16 Stoeckl to Gorchakov, Mar. 18, 1867, Annex 22 (Denmark); Stoeckl to Gorchakov, Mar. 18, 1867, Annex 21 ("might even go to $5,500,000"); Stoeckl to Gorchakov, Apr. 19, 1867, Annex 28 ("I asked seven"), all in Alaska Cession Papers, NA; Jensen, *Alaska Purchase*, 71–73; Miller, *Alaska Treaty*, 72–90.

17 Pease and Randall, eds., *Browning Diary*, 2:137; Beale, ed., *Welles Diary*, 3:66; Miller, *Alaska Treaty*, 68–80.

18 Pease and Randall, eds., *Browning Diary*, 2:137; Beale, ed., *Welles Diary*, 3:68; Jensen, *Alaska Purchase*, 74–75; Miller, *Alaska Treaty*, 75–80.

19 Stoeckl to Gorchakov, Mar. 25, 1867, Annex 23, Alaska Cession Papers, NA; Miller, *Alaska Treaty*, 97–100.

20 Seward 3:348. Frederick's account was written years later, so the wording may not be right, but the chronology is supported by Bigelow's diary, which states that the telegram arrived around ten, and Sumner's first biography, which states that Seward had already left when Sumner arrived around eleven—John Bigelow Diary, Mar. 30, 1867, NYPL; Miller, *Alaska Treaty*, 84–85; Edward Pierce, ed., *The Works of Charles Sumner*, 15 vols. (Boston: Lee & Shepard, 1875), 11:183.

21 Seward to Sumner, Mar. 29, 1867, Sumner Papers reel 38; Donald, *Sumner and the Rights of Man*, 303–04; Jensen, *Alaska Purchase*, 76.

22 Gorchakov to Stoeckl, Mar. 28, 1867, Annex 24, Alaska Cession Papers, NA; Jensen, *Alaska Purchase*, 75–78; Miller, *Alaska Treaty*, 81–87.

23 Beale, ed., *Welles Diary*, 3:75; Senate Executive Journal, 40th Cong., 1st Sess. 588–89; Johnson to Senate, Mar. 30, 1867, in Cong. Globe, 40th Cong., Spec. Sess. 821; Donald, *Sumner and the Rights of Man*, 304–06; Jensen, *Alaska Purchase*, 79–80. Browning, in his diary entry, did not mention the Russian treaty as a reason for the special session; "there are a large number of nominations not yet acted upon," he wrote, "and should the Senate disperse now, these offices, under the tenure of office bill, will have to go unfilled till Congress meets again"—Pease and Randall, eds., *Browning Diary* 2:140–41.

24 John Bigelow Diary, Mar. 30, 1867, NYPL; Beale, ed., *Welles Diary*, 3:75.

25 *New York Tribune*, Apr. 9, 1867; *The Nation* 19 (Dec. 10, 1874): 374; Sheldon Jackson, *Alaska, and Missions on the North Pacific Coast* (New York: Dodd, Mead & Co., 1880), 14; Seward 3:367; George Herring, *From Colony to Superpower: U.S. Foreign Relations Since 1776* (New York: Oxford University Press, 2008), 258.

26 *New York Herald*, Apr. 12, 1867; *Daily Alta California*, Apr. 3, 1867; *National Republican*, Apr. 8, 1867; *Chicago Tribune*, Apr. 9, 1867; Thomas Bailey, "Why the United States Purchased Alaska," *Pacific Historical Review* 3 (1934): 39–49; Richard Welch, "Public Opinion and the Purchase of Russian America," *American Slavic and East European Review* 17 (1958): 481–94.

27 *New York Tribune*, Apr. 1–10, 1867; *New York Herald*, Apr. 12, 1867; Welch, "Public Opinion," 485–88.

28 *Daily National Intelligencer*, Apr. 5, 1867; *New York Commercial Advertiser*, Mar. 30, 1867; *New York Times*, Mar. 31, 1867; *Washington Evening Star*, Mar. 30, 1867.

29 *Chicago Tribune*, Apr. 9, 1867; *Daily National Intelligencer*, Apr. 6, 1867; *New York Times*, Apr. 6 & 9, 1867; *New York Tribune*, Apr. 8, 1867; [State Department], *Purchase of the Russian Possessions in North America by the United States* (1867); Jensen, *Alaska Purchase*, 82–86.

30 *New York Times*, Apr. 9, 1867; Stevens to Seward, Apr. 11, 1867, in Beverly Palmer and Holly Ochoa, eds., *The Selected Papers of Thaddeus Stevens*, 2 vols. (Pittsburgh: University of Pittsburgh Press, 1997), 2:303; Fawn Brodie, *Thaddeus Stevens: Scourge of the South* (New York: W. W. Norton & Co., 1959), 358–59.

31 Harlan to Seward, Apr. 5, 1867, Seward Papers reel 100; *New York Herald*, Apr. 9, 1867; *New York Tribune*, Apr. 8, 1867; *Milwaukee Daily Sentinel*, Apr. 11, 1867 (fourth and fifth dinners).

32 Charles Beaman Memorandum, Apr. 3, 1867, Charles Sumner Papers, MHS; Fessenden to Elizabeth Warriner, Apr. 1, 1867, Fessenden Papers, Bowdoin (Russian treaty "detains all Mr. Sumner's committee"); Donald, *Sumner and the Rights of Man*, 306–07.

33 *Charleston Mercury*, Apr. 5, 1867 (probable postponement); *New York Times*, Apr. 3, 1867 (same); *New York Tribune*, Apr. 8, 1867; Jensen, *Alaska Purchase*, 83.

34 Reverdy Johnson to Seward, Apr. 8, 1867, Seward Papers reel 100; Sumner draft speech, Apr. 8, 1867, Sumner Papers, MHS; *Milwaukee Daily Sentinel*, Apr. 11, 1867; Senate Exec. Journal, 40th Cong., Spec. Sess. 675; Donald, *Sumner and the Rights of Man*, 308–09; Jensen, *Alaska Purchase*, 88–92.

35 Stevens to Seward, Apr. 11, 1867, in Palmer and Ochoa, eds., *Selected Papers of Thaddeus Stevens*, 2:303 (spelling corrected).

36 *Charleston Mercury*, June 8–12, 1867 (quote 12); *New York Times*, June 4–8, 1867; *New York Tribune*, June 7, 1867; *Raleigh Semi-Weekly Sentinel*, June 5, 1867.

37 *Chicago Tribune*, June 25, 1867; *New York Times*, June 27 & 30, 1867; *New York Tribune*, June 29, 1867.

38 C. F. Adams Jr. to C. F. Adams Sr., June 29, 1867, Adams Papers, MHS reel 582; *Daily Alta California*, July 13, 1867; Cole and McDonough, eds., *Witness to the Young Republic*, 539–41 (French).

39 Johnson to Stanton, Aug. 5, 1867; Stanton to Johnson, Aug. 6, 1867; Johnson to Stanton, Aug. 12, 1867, Stanton to Johnson, Aug. 12, 1867, all in Haskins, ed., *Papers of Andrew Johnson*, 12:461 & 476–77; Beale, ed., *Welles Diary*, 3:163; *Chicago Tribune*, Aug. 15, 1867; *Columbia [SC] Phoenix*, Aug. 7, 1867; Castel, *Presidency of Andrew Johnson*, 133–37; Trefousse, *Andrew Johnson*, 293–96.

40 William Moore Diary, Aug. 14, 1867, Johnson Papers reel 50; *Chicago Tribune*, Aug. 15, 1867; Seward to Johnson, Aug. 23, 1867, Johnson Papers reel 28; *Boston Daily Advertiser*, Aug. 26, 1867; Trefousse, *Andrew Johnson*, 305–06.

41 Fanny Seward Diary, Oct. 14, 1863, Seward Papers reel 198 (Cushman quote); Van Deusen, *Seward*, 474–77, 550.

42 *New York Times*, Aug. 11, 1867; Gideon Welles to Congress, July 26, 1868, in Senate Exec. Doc. No. 79, 40th Cong., 2d Sess. (report on Midway Islands); Nugent, *Habits of Empire*, 252–53.

43 *New York Times*, Nov. 5, 1867; Tansill, *Danish West Indies*, 78.

44 William Bigler to Johnson, Oct. 11, 1867, Haskins, ed., *Papers of Andrew Johnson*, 13:151–52; *New York Times*, Nov. 14, 1867 (Johnson remarks); Stewart, *Impeached*, 97–98; Foner, *Reconstruction*, 311–16.

45 Seward to Halleck, Dec. 2, 1867, NA, M40 reel 63 (has report); *Charleston Daily News*, Nov. 16, 1867; *Chicago Tribune*, Nov. 12 & 14, 1867; Jensen, *Alaska Purchase*, 100–01; Miller, *Alaska Treaty*, 120–37 (includes reports).

46 *New York Times*, Nov. 11, 24, & 26 & Dec. 6, 1867; *New York Tribune*, Nov. 22, 1867; Cong. Globe, 40th Cong., 1st Sess. 791–93; Stewart, *Impeached*, 101–03; Tansill, *Danish West Indies*, 89–90.

47 *Hartford Courant*, Apr. 11 & 18, 1867; *New York Tribune*, Sept. 6, 1867; *Sacramento Daily Union*, Nov. 22, 1867; Seward to Yeaman, Sept. 23, 1867, NA, M77 reel 50; Donald Dozer, "Anti-Expansionism During the Johnson Administration," *Pacific Historical Review* 12 (1943): 253–75; Brainerd Dyer, "Robert J. Walker on Acquiring Greenland and Iceland," *Mississippi Valley Historical Review* 27 (1940): 263–66.

48 Draft Message, Dec. 1867, Seward Papers reel 185; Third Message, Dec. 3, 1867, Haskins, ed., *Papers of Andrew Johnson*, 13:280–306 (quote 287).

49 Cong. Globe, 40th Cong., 2d Sess. 66; Stewart, *Impeached*, 108–13.

50 *New York Times*, June 26, 1867. By far the best study is David Shi, "Seward's Attempt to Annex British Columbia, 1865–1869," *Pacific Historical Review* 47 (1978): 217–38; see also Jean Barman, *The West Beyond the West: A History of British Columbia*, 3d. ed. (Toronto: University of Toronto Press, 2007), 95–100.

51 Seward to Adams, Jan. 12, 1867, NA, M77 reel 80; Adrian Cook, *The Alabama Claims: American Politics and Anglo-American Relations, 1865–1872* (Ithaca, NY: Cornell University Press, 1975), 36–42.; Doris Dashew, "The Story of an Illusion: The Plan to Trade the Alabama Claims for Canada," *Civil War History* 15 (1969): 55–66; Shi, "British Columbia," 227–28.

52 *New York Times*, Feb. 1, 1866; John Bigelow Diary, Apr. 3, 1867, NYPL; C. F. Adams Jr. to C. F. Adams Sr., June 29, 1867, Adams Papers, MHS reel 582; Elias Derby, *A Preliminary Report on the Treaty of Reciprocity with Great Britain* (Washington, DC: Treasury Department, 1866), 64; Shi, *British Columbia*, 221–22.

53 *Daily Alta California*, July 13, 1867; *The Times* (London), May 11, 1867; *Montreal Gazette*, May 24, 1867; *Sacramento Daily Union*, May 24, 1867 (quoting *British Colonist)*; Shi, "British Columbia," 226–27.

54 Adams to Seward, Aug. 2, 1867, NA, M30 reel 90; Pease and Randall, eds., *Browning Diary*, 2:177.

55 *Daily Alta California*, Jan. 31 & Feb. 8, 1868; *Sacramento Daily Union*, Jan. 31, 1868.

56 Paolino, *Foundations of the American Empire*, 105–44.

57 *Daily Alta California*, Feb. 20 & Nov. 20, 1867; Seward to Edward McCook, Sept. 12, 1867, NA, M77 reel 99; John Patterson, "The United States and Hawaiian Reciprocity, 1867–1870," *Pacific Historical Review* 7 (1938): 14–26; David Zmijewski, "The Conspiracy That Never Existed: How Hawaii Evaded Annexation in 1868," *Hawaiian Journal of History* 37 (2003): 119–37 (quote 135).

58 Cong. Globe, 34th Cong., 1st Sess. 2130–31; Salgar to Seward, Mar. 16, 1866, FRUS 1866–67, 2:594–95; Seward to Salgar, Mar. 19, 1866, ibid., 595; Seward to Sullivan, Sept. 5, 1867, NA, M77 reel 45; Sullivan to Seward, Dec. 18, 1867, NA, T33 reel 26; Seward to Sullivan, Mar. 2, 1868, NA, M77 reel 45; Taylor Parks, *Colombia and the United States, 1765–1934* (Durham, NC: Duke University Press, 1935), 338–43; Gregory Stahl, *The Establishment of America's Stake in an Isthmian Transit Route*, PhD diss. (Georgetown University, 1981), 287–306.

59 Seward to Hale, Dec. 20, 1866, FRUS 1867–68, 1:517–18; Kilpatrick to Seward, May 1, 1867, ibid., 2:266–67; *New York Tribune*, June 15, 1867; *New York Times*, July 7, 1867; Cortada, "Spain and the American Civil War," 97–102.

60 *New York Times*, May 2, 12, & 29, 1867; Johnson remarks, May 3, 1867, in Haskins, ed., *Papers of Andrew Johnson*, 12:252–53; Beale, ed., *Welles Diary*, 3:87–92, 99; Van Valkenburgh to Seward, Oct. 7, 1867, FRUS 1867–68, 2:64.

61 Berthemy to Moustier, Mar. 3, 1867, in Tyler Dennett, "Seward's Far Eastern Policy," *American Historical Review* 28 (1922): 45–62; John Bigelow Diary, Mar. 3, 1867, NYPL (mentions plan); Draft message, Dec. 1867, Seward Papers reel 185; Paolino, *Foundations of the American Empire*, 167–69, 194–203.

62 Bancroft to Seward, May 17, 1867, Bancroft Papers, MHS; Seward to Bancroft, May 20, 1867, NA, M77 reel 50; Prussian Treaty, Feb. 22, 1868, Stat. at Large, 13:615–18; William Sloane, "George Bancroft—In Society, in Politics, in Letters," *The Century* 33 (1887): 481–83; Theo Thiesing, "Dual Allegiance in the German Law of Nationality and American Citizenship," *Yale Law Journal* 27 (1918): 479–508.

63 *New York Times*, Dec. 16, 1867.

64 Richard Immerman, *Empire for Liberty: A History of American Imperialism from Benjamin Franklin to Paul Wolfowitz* (Princeton: Princeton University Press, 2010), 98–128; Nugent, *Habits of Empire*, xv ("Seward revived the word

'empire' in connection with U.S. expansion as no one had done since Thomas Jefferson."); Paolino, *Foundations of the American Empire*; Walter Sharrow, "William Henry Seward and the Basis for American Empire, 1850–1860," *Pacific Historical Review* 36 (1967): 325–42; Richard Van Alstyne, *The Rising American Empire* (New York: Oxford University Press, 1960) ("central figure").

65 Chester Barrows, *William M. Evarts: Lawyer, Diplomat, Statesman* (Chapel Hill: University of North Carolina Press, 1941); Tyler Dennett, *John Hay: From Poetry to Politics* (New York: Dodd, Mead & Co., 1933); Allan Nevins, *Hamilton Fish: The Inner History of the Grant Administration*, 2 vols. (New York: Dodd, Mead & Co., 1936); Nugent, *Habits of Empire*, 237–75 (argues continuous process of expansion).

NOTES FOR CHAPTER 18

1 Seward to Sumner, Jan. 18, 1868, Sumner Papers reel 81; *Boston Daily Advertiser*, Jan. 11, 1868; *Chicago Tribune*, Mar. 24, 1868; *Montana Post*, Mar. 7, 1868 ("appropriation to pay for Alaska cannot possibly get through"); *New York Tribune*, Feb. 6, 1868 ("most powerful friend"); Paul Holbo, *Tarnished Expansion: The Alaska Scandal, the Press, and Congress, 1867–1871* (Knoxville: University of Tennessee Press, 1983), 14–20.

2 Stoeckl to Seward, Sept. 11, 1867, and Seward to Stoeckl, Sept. 11, 1867, both in Miller, *Alaska Treaty*, 167; Stoeckl to Gorchakov, in Frank Golder, "The Purchase of Alaska," *American Historical Review* 25 (1920): 422–23; Holbo, *Tarnished Expansion*, 15–18.

3 Castel, *Presidency of Andrew Johnson*, 153–55; Stewart, *Impeached*, 38–39.

4 Beale, ed., *Welles Diary*, 3:262; Welles to Joseph Fowler, Nov. 9, 1875, in *North American Review* 145 (1887): 76–79; Stewart, *Impeached*, 118–22; Trefousse, *Andrew Johnson*, 311.

5 Senate Executive Journal, 40th Cong., 2d Sess. 170–72; Cong. Globe, 40th Cong., 2d Sess. 1382–1400; *New York Times*, Feb. 22, 1868; Bergeron, *Andrew Johnson's Civil War*, 187–89; Clemenceau, *American Reconstruction*, 151–53; Stewart, *Impeached*, 133–50.

6 Barrows, *William M. Evarts*, 141–42; William Moore Diary, Mar. 24, 1868, Johnson Papers reel 50; Stewart, *Impeached*, 151–80; Tansill, *Santo Domingo*, 287–337 (Black's resignation over Alta Vela).

7 William Moore Diary, Mar. 8, 1868, Johnson Papers reel 50; Fessenden to Elizabeth Warriner, Feb. 29, 1868, Fessenden Papers, Bowdoin; Seward 3:376.

8 *Cincinnati Daily Gazette*, Dec. 20 & 25, 1869.

9 Ibid.; Stewart, *Impeached*, 190–91.

10 Richard Schell to Seward, Mar. 16, 1868, Seward Papers reel 103; Weed to Seward, Apr. 1, 1868, ibid. reel 104; R. H. Pruyn to Seward, Apr. 8, 1868, ibid.;

Stanberry to Seward, May 15, 1868, ibid.; copy of accounts in Evarts Papers, LC; Stewart, *Impeached*, 294–96.

11 *Chicago Tribune*, Mar. 19, 1868; *New York Times*, Mar. 19, 1868; *New York Tribune*, Mar. 19, 1868; Banks to Seward, Mar. 20, 1868, in Miller, *Alaska Treaty*, 152–53; Seward to Stoeckl, Mar. 23, 1868, in ibid., 153.

12 Stoeckl to Gorchakov, in Golder, "Purchase of Alaska," 423–24; *Chicago Tribune*, Mar. 24, 1868 (claiming a "ring" was working to secure Alaska appropriation for personal purposes); Holbo, *Tarnished Expansion*, 18–21.

13 *New York Times*, Mar. 31, 1868; Stewart, *Impeached*, 193–217.

14 *New York Times*, Apr. 18–19, 1868; *New York Tribune*, April 18, 1868 (Seward on floor); Stewart, *Impeached*, 193–217 (quote 217).

15 William Moore Diary, Apr. 23–24, 1868, Johnson Papers, LC reel 51; Connelly, *Schofield*, 204–07; Stewart, *Impeached*, 223–27.

16 William Moore Diary, May 5, 1868, Johnson Papers, LC, reel 51; Beale, ed., *Welles Diary*, 3:345; Stewart, *Impeached*, 229–49; Mark Summers, *The Era of Good Stealings* (New York: Oxford University Press, 1993), 36–38.

17 Seward to Gertrude Sanford, May 16, 1868, quoted in Van Deusen, *Seward*, 481; Seward to Johnson, May 16, 1868, Johnson Papers, LC, reel 32; William Moore Diary, May 16, 1868, ibid. reel 51; Beale, ed., *Welles Diary*, 3:358; Castel, *Presidency of Andrew Johnson*, 191–92; Trefousse, *Andrew Johnson*, 325–27.

18 Cong. Globe, 40th Cong., 2d Sess. 2528–29; House Report No. 37, 40th Cong., 2d Sess. (May 18, 1868); *New York Times*, May 19, 1868.

19 *New York Times*, May 26, 1868; House Report No. 75, 40th Cong., 2d Sess. (July 3, 1868); Beale, ed., *Welles Diary*, 3:361, 369–71; Stewart, *Impeached*, 277–87; Sumners, *Good Stealings*, 30–45 (Butler investigation).

20 *New York Times*, May 27, 1868; Beale, ed., *Welles Diary*, 3:367–70; Pease and Randall, eds., *Browning Diary*, 2:199; Stewart, *Impeached*, 280–81.

21 Barrows, *Evarts*, 164; Beale, ed., *Welles Diary*, 3:372 & 391; Clemenceau, *American Reconstruction*, 189.

22 Banks to Seward, June 27, 1868, Seward Papers reel 104; Cong. Globe, 40th Cong., 2d Sess. 3620–21 & App. 392–400; Holbo, *Tainted Purchase*, 24–27.

23 Cong. Globe, 40th Cong., 2d Sess. 3620–21 & App. 392–400; Seward to Johnson, July 2, 1868, in Haskins, ed., *Papers of Andrew Johnson*, 14:307; Walker to Seward, July 2, 1868, Johnson Papers reel 33; Holbo, *Tainted Purchase*, 24–27.

24 *New York Sun*, July 15, 1868; *New York Times*, July 8 & 15, 1868; Cong. Globe, 40th Cong., 2d Sess. 3810–11, 4055 & App. 400–02; Holbo, *Tainted Purchase*, 28–30; Miller, *Alaska Treaty*, 159–60.

25 Cong. Globe, 40th Cong., 2d Sess. 4393–94; *Daily National Intelligencer*, July 18, 1868; *New York Sun*, July 18, 1868; *New York Tribune*, July 18, 1868; Miller, *Alaska Treaty*, 160–61; Randolph Keim, *Our Alaskan Wonderland and Klondike Neighbor* (Washington, DC: Harrisburg Publishing Co., 1898), 66 ("the

quibblers for the unconstitutional interference of the House were on their feet yelling for recognition").

26 Johnson Memo, Sept. 6, 1868, in Haskins, ed., *Papers of Andrew Johnson*, 15:25–26.

27 John Bigelow Diary, Sept. 23, 1868, NYPL (punctuation added).

28 House Report No. 35, 40th Cong., 3d Sess. (Feb. 27, 1869), 9–10.

29 Seward wrote to Bancroft that he believed history would approve of his role in the impeachment, because he had acted "as became equally a patriotic citizen and a minister of an honest, loyal and patriotic president"—Seward to Bancroft, June 22, 1868, MHS. See Stewart, *Impeached*, 265–66; Van Deusen, *Seward*, 547–48.

30 Beale, ed., *Welles Diary*, 3:504; see Seward 3:383–84, 395–96 for "more than forty" treaties.

31 *New York Times*, Jan. 4, 1868; *New York Tribune*, Jan. 8, 1868; Seward to Yeaman, Jan. 29, 1868, NA, M77 reel 50; Sumner to Curtis, May 30, 1868, Sumner Papers reel 81; Seward to McCook, July 1868, NA, M77 reel 99; Donald, *Sumner and the Rights of Man*, 354–56; Tansill, *Danish West Indies*, 91–103; Tansill, *Santo Domingo*, 250–65.

32 Seward Draft, Dec. 1868, Seward Papers reel 185; Johnson Message, Dec. 9, 1868, Haskins, ed., *Papers of Andrew Johnson*, 15:281–304; Seward to Banks, Jan. 29, 1869, NA, M40 reel 65; Tansill, *Santo Domingo*, 267–83.

33 Burlingame to Seward, Dec. 14, 1867, FRUS 1868–69, 1:494; *New York Times*, Dec. 16, 1867, & Feb. 18, 1868; *Charleston Daily News*, June 10 & 20, 1868; Frederick Wells, *Anson Burlingame and the First Chinese Mission to the Foreign Powers* (New York: Charles Scribner's Sons, 1912).

34 Roger Daniels, *Coming to America: A History of Immigration and Ethnicity in American Life* (New York: HarperCollins 1990), 239–46; Tyler Dennett, *Americans in Eastern Asia* (New York: Macmillan Co., 1922), 378–86, 539–41; John Schrecker, "For the Equality of Men—For the Equality of Nations: Anson Burlingame and China's First Embassy to the United States, 1868," *Journal of American-East Asian Relations* 17 (2010): 9–34; Wells, *Burlingame*, 144–45 (drafted by Seward).

35 *New York Times*, Aug. 8–9, 1868; Frances Wright to Elizabeth Stanton, Aug. 27, 1868, Garrison Family Papers, Smith College; Stanton speech, June 25, 1883, in Ann Gordon, et al., eds., *The Selected Papers of Elizabeth Cady Stanton and Susan B. Anthony*, 5 vols. to date (New Brunswick, NJ: Rutgers University Press, 1997–2009), 4:249.

36 Seward to Johnson, July 20, 1868, NA, M77 reel 80; Cook, *Alabama Claims*, 43–51.

37 Seward to Johnson, Oct. 25 & 26, 1868, NA, M77 reel 80; Cook, *Alabama Claims*, 51–54.

38 Pease and Randall, eds., *Browning Diary*, 2:227–28; Beale, ed., *Welles Diary*, 3:468–71; Seward to Johnson, Nov. 27, 1868, NA, M77 reel 80; *New York Tribune*, Jan. 22, 1869; *New York Times*, Jan. 19 & Feb. 23, 1869; *New York Herald*, Feb. 5, 1869; Cook, *Alabama Claims*, 58–71; Donald, *Sumner*, 364–67, 374–94.

39 Seward to Cushing, Nov. 25, 1868, Cushing Papers, LC; Cushing to Seward, Jan. 14, 1869, ibid.; *New York Times*, Jan. 16, 1869; Donald, *Sumner and the Rights of Man*, 327, 401; Paolino, *Foundations of the American Empire*, 137–44; Gregory Stahl, *The Establishment of America's Stake in an Isthmian Transit Route*, PhD diss. (Georgetown University, 1981), 306–13.

40 Seward speech, Feb. 23, 1869, Baker 5:590–91; see also Seward to Sullivan, Sept. 17, 1868, NA, M77 reel 45 ("the Darien canal must be an American work").

41 Senate Exec. Journal, Mar. 3 & Apr. 14, 1869; *Daily Alta California*, Apr. 13, 1869; Cushing to Seward, Apr. 15 & 20, 1869, Seward Papers reel 107; Seward to Cushing, Apr. 19, 1869, Cushing Papers, LC; Seward Speech, Aug. 26, 1869, Baker 5:569–71; Seward to Bancroft, Sept. 18, 1871, Bancroft Papers, MHS; David McCullough, *The Path Between the Seas: The Creation of the Panama Canal, 1870–1914* (New York: Simon & Schuster, 1977); Stahl, *Isthmian Transit Route*, 314–27; Zimmerman, *First Great Triumph*, 49–53 (Seward-Hay).

42 Pease and Randall, eds., *Browning Diary*, 2:211; Beale, ed., *Welles Diary*, 3:398–400; Foner, *Reconstruction*, 338–41; Trefousse, *Andrew Johnson*, 336–40.

43 John Bigelow Diary, Sept. 24, 1868, NYPL; *New York Tribune*, Sept. 23, 1868; *Atlanta Constitution*, Aug. 22, 1868; *Bangor Daily Whig*, Sept. 9, 1868; *Charleston Courier*, Aug. 4, 1868; *Lowell Daily Citizen*, Aug. 5, 1868; Samuel and Isabel Barrows, "Personal Reminiscences of William H. Seward," *Atlantic Monthly* 63 (1889) 379–97 (quote on 392–93); Stewart Mitchell, *Horatio Seymour of New York* (Cambridge, MA: Harvard University Press, 1938); Trefousse, *Andrew Johnson*, 336–40.

44 Seward to Gertrude Sanford, Feb. 27, 1868, Sanford Papers; Olive Risley to Seward, July 5 & 12, 1868, Seward Papers reels 104 & 124; Barrows and Barrows, "Personal Reminiscences," 395; Hanson Risley, Memoir, Risley Papers, Duke University. As Treasury agent, Risley attracted unwelcome attention for the way in which he allocated lucrative cotton permits; some of these permits went to Seward friends—David Surdam, "Traders or Traitors: Cotton Trading During the Civil War," *Business and Economic History* 28 (1999).

45 *Cleveland Herald*, Oct. 15, 1868; *Georgia Telegraph*, Oct. 16, 1868; *Newark Ohio Advocate*, Oct. 23, 1868; Beale, ed., *Welles Diary*, 3:449; Seward to W. H. Seward Jr., Nov. 19, 1868, Seward Papers reel 112.

46 Barrows and Barrows, "Personal Reminiscences," 385–87; *Sacramento Daily Record*, Sept. 7, 1872.

47 *New York Times*, Nov. 1, 1868. The newspaper version of the speech, rather than the pamphlet, is quoted.

48 *Chicago Tribune*, Nov. 2, 1868; *San Francisco Evening Bulletin*, Nov. 2, 1868; *Cleveland Herald*, Nov. 2, 1868; *National Intelligencer*, Nov. 2, 1868; *New York Sun*, Nov. 2, 1868.

49 *New York Times*, Nov. 11, 1868; Pease and Randall, eds., *Browning Diary*, 2:226–27; Beale, ed., *Welles Diary*, 3:465.

50 *Baltimore Sun*, Jan. 18, 1869; *New Orleans Picayune*, Jan. 31, 1869; *New York Herald*, Jan. 25, 1869 ("simpleton"); Seward 3:397 ("I shall leave Washington on the 5th of March, and probably shall never see it again."); Beale, ed., *Welles Diary*, 3:508.

51 Beale, ed., *Welles Diary*, 3:498–500, 536–39; John Bigelow Diary, Mar. 27, 1869, NYPL.

52 William Hunter, et al., to Seward, Mar. 3, 1869, Seward Papers reel 107; Seward to Hunter, et al., Mar. 3, 1869, Seward 3:398; Seward to George Peck, in *New York Times*, Mar. 5, 1869.

53 Seward to Frederick Seward, Mar. 7, 1869, Seward 3:400–01; *New York Times*, Mar. 8–9, 1869; Beale, ed., *Welles Diary*, 540–42; Pease and Randall, eds., *Browning Diary*, 243; Bergeron, *Andrew Johnson's Civil War*, 219; Trefousse, *Andrew Johnson*, 350–51.

54 *Lowell Daily Citizen*, Mar. 9, 1869; John Bigelow Diary, Mar. 27, 1869, NYPL. On the rank of presidents, see Wikipedia, "Historical Rankings of Presidents of the United States."

NOTES FOR CHAPTER 19

1 Lazette Worden to Augustus Seward, Mar. 28 & Apr. 12, 1869, Seward Papers reel 124; Seward to Frederick Seward, Mar. 28, 1869, Seward 3:401–02; Seward to Charlotte Cushman, Apr. 24, 1869, Cushman Papers, LC.

2 Seward to Frederick Seward, Mar. 16, 1869, Seward 3:401; Lazette Worden to Augustus Seward, Apr. 20, 1870, Seward Papers reel 124; *Chicago Tribune*, Mar. 8, 1869; *National Intelligencer*, Mar. 29, 1869.

3 Beale, ed., *Welles Diary*, 3:484; *Chicago Tribune*, Mar. 9, 1869; Hanson Risley to Seward, May 8 & 27, 1869, Seward Papers reel 107; Olive Risley to Seward, June 1 & 4, 1869, ibid. reel 124; Seward 3:402.

4 *New York Sun*, June 23, 1869.

5 Leland Stanford to Seward, June 21 & 26, 1869, Seward Papers reel 107; *Daily Alta California*, July 3, 1869; *New York Times*, June 23 & 25, July 25, 1869; *Sacramento Daily Union*, July 1 & 3, 1869; Seward 3:402–14.

6 *New York Sun*, June 16, 1869; *New York Times*, June 17, 1869; *Daily Alta California*, July 9, 1869.

7 *British Colonist*, July 21, 1869; *Olympia Territorial Republican*, July 26, 1869; *New York Sun*, Aug. 14, 1869; *New York Times*, July 25 & 29, Aug. 27, 1869; Seward 3:415–17.

8 *Daily Alta California*, Sept. 5, 1869; Seward 3:421–24; Ted Hinckley, "William H. Seward Visits His Purchase," *Oregon Historical Quarterly* 72 (1971): 135–39.

9 *Daily Alta California*, Sept. 5, 1869; Seward 3:424–30; U.S. Coast Survey, *Report of the Superintendent for 1869* (Washington, DC: Government Printing Office, 1872), 177–80; Morgan Sherwood, "George Davidson and the Acquisition of Alaska," *Pacific Historical Review* 28 (1959): 141–54; Morgan Sherwood, "A Pioneer Scientist in the Far North," *Pacific Northwest Quarterly* 53 (1962): 77–80.

10 *Alaska Times*, Aug. 20, 1869; Baker 5:559–69; Hinckley, "Seward Visits His Purchase," 141–42.

11 *British Colonist*, Aug. 28, 1869; *National Republican*, Sept. 13 & 24, 1869 (quoting Weed); *New York Tribune*, Sept. 21, 1869; Baker 5:569–79; Hinckley, "Seward Visits His Purchase," 143.

12 Lazette Worden to Augustus Seward, June 10, Aug. 26 & Sept. 29, 1869, Seward Papers reel 124; *Daily Alta California*, July 7 & Sept. 22, 1869; *New York Sun*, Oct. 13, 1869; Seward 3:436–39.

13 Olive Risley to Seward, Aug. 4, 1869, Seward Papers reel 124; Seward to Olive Risley, Sept. 22, Oct. 17, Nov. 4 & 19, 1869, Seward Papers, NYPL.

14 Bancroft, *Life of Seward*, 2:519–20; Albert Evans, *Our Sister Republic: A Gala Trip Through Tropical Mexico, 1869–70* (Hartford, CT: Colombian Book Co., 1870); Seward 3:440–61 (quote 446).

15 *New York Times*, Jan. 21, 1870; Seward 3:462–63.

16 Hanson Risley to Seward, Feb. 21, 22, 23, & 25, 1870, Seward Papers reel 124; Lazette Worden to Augustus Seward, Feb. 24 & Mar. 13, 1870, ibid.; Olive Risley to Seward, Mar. 13, 1870, ibid.; *Auburn Daily Advertiser*, Mar. 12, 1870; *Daily National Republican*, Feb. 22 & 28, 1870; *New York Times*, Feb. 25, Mar. 3, 11, & 12, 1870.

17 Lazette Worden to Augustus Seward, Apr. 20, May 9, 24, & 31, 1870, Seward Papers reel 124; Seward to William Campbell, June 9, 1870, ibid. reel 108.

18 *New York Times*, Apr. 22, 1870; Lazette Worden to Augustus Seward, Apr. 20, May 9 & 24, & June 7, 1870, Seward Papers reel 124.

19 Adams to Seward, May 27, 1870, Seward Papers reel 108; Adams Diary, May 27–30, 1870, Adams Papers reel 82.

20 Lazette Worden to Augustus Seward, May 9 & 31, 1870, Seward Papers reel 124; *New York Times*, Aug. 11, 1870.

21 *Daily Alta California*, Aug. 11, 19, & 26, Sept. 2, 1870; Seward to Lazette Worden, Aug. 26, 1870, Seward Papers reel 112; Olive Risley Seward, ed., *William H. Seward's Travels Around the World* (New York: D. Appleton & Co., 1873), 3–28.

22 *Sacramento Daily Union*, Nov. 18, 1870; Seward, ed., *Seward's Travels*, 719–20.

23 Paul Cohen, *China and Christianity: The Missionary Movement and the Growth of Anti-Foreignism* (Cambridge, MA: Harvard University Press, 1963), 229–47; Seward, ed., *Seward's Travels*, 106–209.

24 *Philadelphia Press*, Jan. 9, 1871 (Randall); Seward to William Seward, Oct. 19 & Nov. 3, 1870, Seward Papers reel 112; Olive Seward to Lazette Worden, Dec. 7, 1870, ibid. reel 124; Seward to Frederick Seward, Dec. 7, 1870, ibid. reel 118 folder 4848; Frederick Seward to Seward, Jan. 31, 1871, ibid. reel 117; William Seward to Seward, Feb. 12, 1871, ibid. reel 118; Seward Will, Nov. 5, 1870, Cayuga County Surrogate's Office.

25 Olive Seward to Lazette Worden, Dec. 7, 1870, Seward Papers reel 124; Seward to Lazette Worden, Mar. 21, 1871, ibid.; *Jamestown [NY] Journal*, July 28, 1871 (Hattie's letter); Seward, ed., *Seward's Travels*, 327–577.

26 Frederick Seward to William Seward, Feb. 24, 1871, Seward Papers reel 117; Seward to William Seward, Apr. 10, 1871, ibid. reel 112; Seward to Risley, Apr. 24, 1871, ibid. reel 109; Risley to Seward, July 7 & 24, 1871, ibid.; Seward, ed., *Seward's Travels*, 627–718.

27 Nathan Appleton Jr., Journal, Jan. 18, 1874, Appleton Papers, MHS; Seward, ed., *Seward's Travels*, 594–713.

28 Benjamin Moran Diary, Sept. 18–20, 1871, Moran Papers, LC.

29 Lazette Worden to Augustus Seward, Oct. 4, 1871, Seward Papers reel 124; *Auburn Daily Bulletin*, Oct. 12, 1871; *New York Times*, Oct. 4 & 13, 1871; *New York Sun*, Oct. 19, 1871; Seward, ed., *Seward's Travels*, 719–20.

30 *New York Sun*, Oct. 19 & 24, 1871; Stanton, *Random Recollections*, 241–42.

31 Lazette Worden to Augustus Seward, Nov. 17 & Dec. 3, 1871, Feb. 11, 1872, Seward Papers reel 124; Frederick Seward to Seward, Aug. 30 & Sept. 4, 1872, ibid. reel 117; Derby, *Fifty Years Among Authors*, 83–85.

32 Seward to Charlotte Cushman, Oct. 8, 1871, Cushman Papers, LC; Lazette Worden to Augustus Seward, Jan. 27, Feb. 11 & Mar. 19, 1872, Seward Papers reel 124; John Hay to Seward, Feb. 8, 1872, ibid. reel 110; Seward 3:486 ("work") and 489 ("woman").

33 Edward Dodd to Weed, Aug. 15, 1872, Seward Papers reel 110; Jonathan Amory to Seward, Aug. 16, 1872, ibid. reel 110; *New York Times*, Oct. 5, 1872, Seward 3:505–07; Van Deusen, *Seward*, 563–64.

34 *Auburn Daily Advertiser*, Oct. 11, 1872; *Auburn Daily Bulletin*, Sept. 9 & Oct. 11, 1872; Lazette Worden to Augustus Seward, Sept. 14 & 26, 1872, Seward Papers reel 124; William Seward to Frederick Seward, Oct. 10, 1872, ibid. reel 118; Frederick Seward to William Seward, Oct. 10, 1872, ibid. reel 117; Seward 3:508; Van Deusen, *Seward*, 563–64. Frederick and Van Deusen assert that Seward gradually declined, but that is not supported by the detailed medical history of his last days in the local papers.

35 *Auburn Daily Advertiser*, Oct. 14, 1872; *Auburn Daily Bulletin*, Oct. 14 & 15, 1872; *New York Times*, Oct. 15, 1872.

36 Charles Francis Adams, *An Address on the Life, Character, and Services of William H. Seward* (Albany: Weed, Parsons & Co., 1873); Jeremiah Black, "Mr. Black to Mr. Adams," *Galaxy* 17 (1874): 108; Welles, *Lincoln and Seward*.

37 Adams, "The Great Secession Winter of 1860–61," 23; Adams, *Adams Autobiography*, 89; Adrian Cook, review of *William Henry Seward: Lincoln's Right Hand*, by John M. Taylor, *Journal of American History* 79 (1992): 666–67 (Seward "a distinctly unpleasant person: egotistic, overweeningly ambitious, mendacious, boastful, and unreliable"); Charles A. Dana, *Recollections of the Civil War* (New York: D Appleton & Co., 1908), 169.

38 Cong. Globe, 35th Cong., 1st Sess. 944.

INDEX

ABOUT THE AUTHOR

Walter Stahr is the author of the well-received *John Jay: Founding Father*. A graduate of Stanford University and Harvard Law School, he practiced international law for twenty-five years, including seven years in Hong Kong and five years with the Securities & Exchange Commission in Washington. He and his family now divide their time between Exeter, New Hampshire, and Vienna, Virginia. His website is walterstahr.com.